GW00541306

The Great Toys of Georges Carette

A Trade Catalogue for mechanical, optical and electrical 'teaching material' and toys (lehrmittel und spielwaren) first published by Georges Carette in 1911, with a Supplement for 1905 and 1914.

Edited and annotated by Allen Levy

ISBN 0 904568 02 4

Reprinted 1979
Published by New Cavendish Books
Copyright © 1975 — New Cavendish Books

Design—John Cooper

Printed and bound in England by
Waterlow (Dunstable) Ltd.

Casebound edition first published July 1976

All rights reserved, this book, or parts thereof, may not
be reproduced in any form without permission, in writing,
from the publisher.

New Cavendish Books are distributed by
Eyre Methuen Limited, 11 New Fetter Lane, London
EC4P 4EE.

ISBN 0 904568 02 4

Georges Carette & Co. of Nuremburg together with
Gebr Bing and Marklin, made up the glorious triptych of
German toy and "teaching material" (Spielwaren und
Lehrmittel) manufacturers at the turn of the century. The
production of "teaching material", i.e. mechanical,
optical and electrical educational aids, was a unique
feature of these great toy makers and one which gained
them pre-eminence throughout the world at that time.
The extremely rare trade catalogue reproduced here
(with the additional supplement for 1905 and 1914)
illustrates the amazing diversity and invention of this firm
which coincided with the explosion of scientific and
engineering ideas that occurred in the wake of the
industrial revolution.

The firm of Georges Carette & Co. was founded in
Nuremburg in 1886 by an expatriate Frenchman who
gave the business its name. Like many of its
contemporary rivals, the company concentrated before
1900 upon the production of a range of mass produced
tin and brass toys, which were in the main hand
enamelled before the invention of photolithography in
1895. Relatively little information is available about the
precise range of these toys during the period 1886-1900,
although it is known that it included many examples of
the ubiquitous single driver type locomotive colloquially
termed the "Storchbein-type" (Storklegs). After the turn
of the century Carette expanded rapidly. A significant
part in this expansion was played by the special work
which Carette undertook, from about 1905 onwards, for
Bassett-Lowke Limited in England. (Before this Carette
had limited itself to supplying Bassett-Lowke with
material from its general range.) The association was to
lead both to the production of an exclusive range of
British-outline rolling stock, and to the perfection by
Carette of the photolithographic process for tin plate
models. While all the Carette locomotives—English types
and otherwise—appear in one form or another in the
trade catalogues, it is evident that from this time forward
the British—outline rolling stock was exclusive to
Bassett-Lowke. It was not offered by Carette in that form
in its general range. Carette/Bassett-Lowke coaches
were, however, generally made available in non-standard
liveries, with the exception of the LNWR Clemenson
range which appears in its original form in the general
trade catalogues.

Carette severed his link with the Nuremburg business
shortly after the outbreak of the first world war, but the
firm did not cease trading until 1917. The period 1905-
1914 covers virtually all the important innovations of this
company's production, and for obvious reasons, little
new was added during the final years, 1915 to 1917.
Although Carette's patterns and tools were widely
dispersed after 1917, the firm's work did not disappear
entirely without trace. Former Carette toy cars appeared
later bearing the Karl Bub trade mark, and Bassett-Lowke
in Northampton continued to produce former Carette
locomotives and rolling stock during the post-war
period. (A Carette still appears on the current
shareholders list of Bassett-Lowke Limited.)

What is offered here is the most comprehensive survey of
the products of Carette published to date. It should
prove an invaluable companion to existing publications
which provide an extensive coverage of the work of
Bing and Marklin.

GEORGES CARETTE & C⁰

NUREMBERG

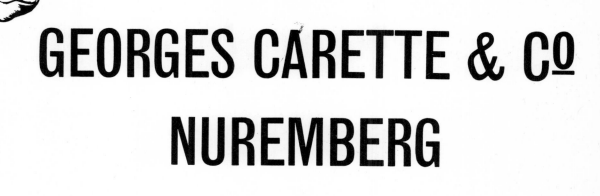

Manufacturers of

Mechanical, Optical, Electrical and Physical

Toys

and

Working Models

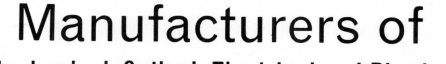

SPACIOUS SHOWROOMS in:

LONDON E.C. Finsbury Square 8
BERLIN S.   Ritterstrasse 93
HAMBURG   Hopfenmarkt 1
PARIS   Rue de Turenne 64
VIENNA VI.   Mariahilferstrasse 19/21

at the LEIPSIC FAIR:
ZEISSIG-HOUSE

Established 1886

Edition 1911

Georges Carette & Co.
NUREMBERG

MANUFACTURERS
of Mechanical, Optical, Electrical and Physical
Toys and Working Models

PRICE LIST
OF MECHANICAL, OPTICAL AND ELECTRICAL :: EDUCATIONAL APPLIANCES AND TOYS ::

EDITION 1911. □□ EDITION 1911.

═══ TERMS. ═══

This **LIST**
> cancels all former terms and prices.

The **PRICES**
> in this list are subject to fluctuations of the market.

ORDERS:
> It will be quite sufficient if the numbers are quoted with the quantities.

DISCOUNT:
> $2^{1}/_{2}$ % for cash received within 40 days from date of invoice or 3 months net.

DELIVERY:
> We keep a large stock of all our goods but it is advisable that seasons orders should be placed with us as early as possible, as all orders are executed in rotation. The dates by which the goods are wanted will be adhered to as far as possible but we cannot be responsible for unforeseen delays.

ELECTROS:
> of every line illustrated in this list can be supplied at cost price. If on loan they must be returned within four weeks. Postage and packing will be charged up to the customer.

NEW ACCOUNTS:
> Are opened only if satisfactory references are given.

PACKING
> is very carefully done and is charged for at cost price.

CLAIMS:
> Our goods are most carefully packed and we must decline all responsibility after the goods have left our premises, even when we deliver "free free".

RETURNS:
> Will not be taken in at our London offices unless previously advised.

TELEGRAPHIC-ADDRESS is "CARETTE NUREMBERG".
> **This list is intended for the trade only.** (A copy of same without our name can be had at cost price on application).
> Orders which have been definitely given cannot be cancelled again.
> We guarantee all our mechanical goods for faultless working, which however is void as soon as any attempt is made to alter or repair them.

NUREMBERG, January 1911.

GEORGES CARETTE & Co.
NUREMBERG.

MODEL STEAM ENGINES
:: AS TOYS AND AS EDUCATIONAL APPLIANCES ::

The principle of the employment of heat as a source of power by means of the evaporation of water cannot be better illustrated to the studious youth than by our Model Steam Engines. The action of the various parts of the large Steam Engines can easily learnt and the different parts recognized from our Models. These Engines on the one hand give stimulus to thought and reflection and on the other hand make the mastering of many problems not easily understood from books, quite simple and easy by watching the Model at work.

All the goods of our manufacture are most substantially made and beautifully finished, and according to the price can be had from simple engines to perfectly complete models resembling the proto-type in every particular. We have always taken care that the various fittings used on our Models should resemble as closely as possible those used on the fullsized engines so that **our Models may be regarded as Educational Appliances.** Every engine before leaving the factory is **tested** and carefully inspected. Further, with each engine full printed instructions are given, these must be closely followed when running the engine. It is indispensable that these instructions be read through by the purchasers for it is only by strictly following these instructions that trouble and complaints can be obviated. We therefore expressly point out to our esteemed customers that we cannot accept the responsibility of putting right any damaged part except at customer's expense.

Repairs sent to us during the months of October, November and December can only be executed in the following year for we are too busy to attend to them during our Haute Saison (busy-time).

This Trade Mark is a guarantee of superior workmanship.

Vertical
Model Steam Engines

Fitted with spirit lamps.

Cheap Class of Steam Engines,

with yellow polished **brass boiler**, brass oscillating cylinder

No. **145/0**	8" high	dozen **15/6**
— **145/2**	the above but with whistle	— **20/-**
— **145/3**	9" high — — —	— **26/6**
— **145/4**	10" — — — —	— **36/-**
— **145/5**	11½" high but with whistle and water gauge	— **48/-**

145/2

145/3, 4, 5

101/1—4

New and extra cheap class of
Steam Engines,

with brass oscillating cylinder, boiler of
blue oxydized finish.

No. **101/1**	-/2	-/3	-/4	
8¼"	10"	11"	12½"	high
dozen **15/6**	**24/-**	**36/-**	**42/-**	
		with whistle		

601/2   601/1

Cheapest Miniature
Steam Engine,

5½" high,
usual quality, boiler of blue
oxydized finish, with
spirit lamp.

No. **601/2**	with brass oscillating cylinder, dozen **7/10**
— **601/1**	as steam turbine . . . . — **6/-**

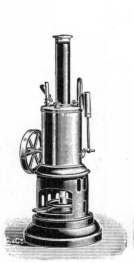

100/1½ and 2   100/3   100/4 and 5

Model Steam Engines

with highly polished **brass boiler, brass cylinder**, mounted on polished **wooden base**, fitted with **steam whistle**, all of **substantial quality**

No. **100/1½**	10" high	each **3/-**
— **100/2**	11½" high	— **3/6**
— **100/3**	13" high with dummy pressure gauge . . .	— **4/6**
— **100/4**	the above but fitted with water gauge, 15" high,	— **6/-**
— **100/5**	the above but 16¾" high,	— **7/-**

Trade Mark.

Handsome **Model Steam Engines**

of very substantial quality, fitted with **fixed double action cylinder**, with **slide valve action** of registered design, **Patent eccentric** so as to allow the engine to be worked either **backwards** or **forwards**, with vertical brass boiler of steel-blue oxydized finish, mounted on a **cast iron stand** complete with **steam whistle** and safety valve, all the fittings are polished and nickelled.

688/1½ and 2

No.				
No. **688/1½**	9″ high	each	**5/-**
— **688/2**	10¼″ —	—	**6/-**
— **688/2½**	ditto fitted with water gauge . . .	—	**7/-**
— **688/3**	11″ high — — — — . . .	—	**8/-**
— **688/4**	12½″ — — — — — and lever		
	safety valve	—	**10/-**
— **688/5**	the above but larger, 14″ high . .	—	**12/-**

Sizes 3, 4, 5 are fitted with pressure gauge screw.

688/4 and 5

Model Steam Engine of same quality as above but fitted with **oscillating brass cylinder** with **reversing motion** and spring safety valve

No. **146/1** 9″ high . . . . each **3/10**

146/1

New, handsome and strongly made, **Steam Engine,** fitted **with fixed double action cylinder, slide valve, eccentric reversing motion** (registered design), with vertical brass boiler with brass fire box steel-blue oxydized finish, nickelled furnace door to open, complete with superior **vapour lamp** (tested of registered design), bell whistle, regulator, spring safety valve, water gauge, all fittings polished and nickelled.

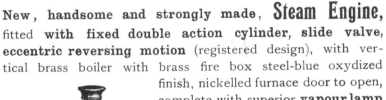

No.			
No. **671/1**	12″ high	each	**13/-**
— **671/1P**	the above, fitted with **feed pump**	—	**16/-**
— **671/2**	14″ high	—	**17/-**
— **671/2P**	fitted with **feed pump** . . .	—	**20/-**
— **671/3**	14½″ high and **drain cock** .	—	**22/-**
— **671/3P**	the above fitted with **feed pump**	—	**25/-**

Sizes 2—3 are provided with pressure gauge screws.

671/2, 2 P, 3, 3 P   671/1 and 1 P

Spirit **Vapour Lamp.**
(Registered)

☞ Our **boiler feed pumps** (after our system) have, since their introduction, always proved themselves to be thoroughly reliable they take up the smallest possible room and with proper management are quite powerful. They can be set in action or out of action while the engine is running.

Trade  Mark.

Best Quality Model Steam Engines

of technically perfect manufacture

with fixed vertical double action cylinder, slide valve of registered design, with patent roller apparatus and ball-pressing arrangement both registered, water gauge with protector, steam whistle,

with vertical brass boiler in steel-blue oxydized finish, nickelled fittings on handsome japanned cast iron stand.

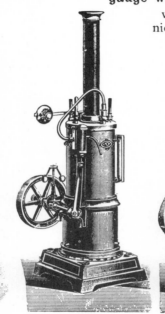

All the engines are provided with a pressure gauge screw so that a pressure gauge as shown on page 32 of the catalogue can be afterwards fitted to the boiler without any trouble, also all the models have reversing gear for forward and backward running. In the case of No. 677/10 this is effected by means of the eccentric.

No. 677/10	11½" high . . each 9/6
— 677/11	12½" — fitted with safety valve . . . each 13/-
— 677/11 P	the same, with feed pump each 16/-
— 677/12	14" high . . . — 17/-
— 677/12 P	the same, with feed pump each 20/-
— 677/12 A	like No. 12 but with lever safety valve, starting cock and governor . each 23/-
— 677/12 AP	the same, with feed pump, each 26/-
— 677/13	15¾" high, like No. 12 A with fire door, each 31/6
— 677/13 P	the same, with feed pump, each 35/-

677/15 P and 14 P 677/12 A 677/12, 11 and 10

No. 677/14 P 17½" high, like No. 13 P but with test cock and water gauge with cocks . . . . — 46/-
— 677/15 P the same but 19½" high . . . . — 59/-

The same engines as above described but with engine mounted on a separate stand. The engine and boiler are screwed on to a handsome polished wooden base.

No. 690/11	12½" high, 9¾" long, 4" wide with safety valve, each 17/-
— 690/11 P	ditto with boiler feed pump, each 20/-
— 690/12	14¼" high, 10¼" long, 4½" wide . . each 23/-
— 690/12 P	ditto with feed pump, each 26/-
— 690/13	14½" high, 11" long, 5¼" wide with lever safety valve, starting cock, governor and fire door . . each 33/8
— 690/13 P	ditto with boiler feed pump, each 36/10
— 690/14 P	17½" high, 12" long, 6" wide like No. 690/13 but with test cock and water gauge, with cocks . each 50/-
— 690/15 P	19½" high, 13" long, 6" wide, same fittings as No. 690/14 P . each 63/-

690/15 P and 14 P 690/12 and 11

Trade  Mark.

4

Latest and most handsome
Model Steam Engines

with **fixed vertical double action "Precision" cylinder,** fitted with lubricating attachment, slide valve, adjustable ball pressing arrangement, strong vertical brass boiler and brass firebox, steel-blue oxydized or yellow finish, excellent tested **spirit vapour lamp** supplied; boiler fitted with **firedoor,** bell whistle, lever safety valve, drain cock, water gauge, water filler screw, pressure gauge, also **feed pump,** the whole of very best quality and most carefully finished. The engine is mounted on a **cast iron stand.**

The most perfect
POWER
SteamEngine
will work **backwards** or **forwards.**

672/5   672/3   672/1

No. **672/1** 12" high . . . . . each **33/-**

— **672/2** 14" — with starting cock, each **42/-**

— **672/3** 15" high, with starting cock and governor . . . . each **50/-**

— **672/4** ditto but larger, 17" high each **60/-**

— **672/5** ditto larger than No. 672/4 and 19" high . . . each **72/-**

Spirit Vapour Lamp.
Legally protected design.

Tra de   Mark.

672/2   672/4

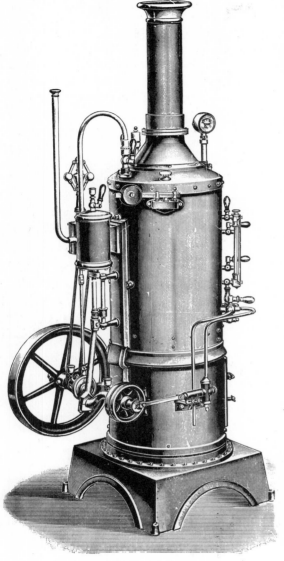

677/8 and 7

Very handsome large

Model Steam Engines

technically perfect model.

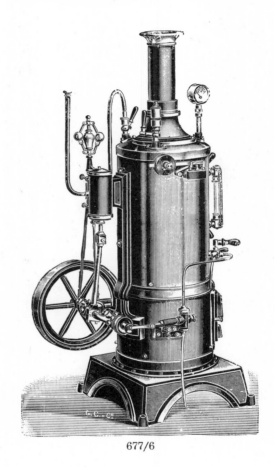

677/6

No. **677/6** 19¹/₂" high with **vertical fixed double action slide valve cylinder,** patent design, very strong brass boiler steel blue oxydized finish. The boiler is brazed and screwed together. Heavy iron fly wheel, pulley, governors, firebox with double doors and large spirit lamp, water gauge with cocks and protector, test cocks, boiler feed pump, steam starting cock, pressure gauge (4 Atm.), filling screw, lever safety valve and lubricator. All the fittings are highly nickelled and the whole mounted on a heavy cast iron stand .   .   .   .   . each **110/-**

— **677/7** 22" high, quality and fittings as No. 677/6 but with **eccentric slide valve to cylinder and guide bar to cross head.** .   .   .   .   — **170/-**

— **677/8** 26" high, same as No. 677/7 but larger .   .   .   .   — **220/-**

Trade Mark.

Horizontal **Model Steam Engines** fitted with spirit lamps.

624/1

No. **624/1** Cheapest **Steam Engine**

with brass oscillating cylinder, brass filling screw, steel-blue finish boiler on japanned tin base, 4¹/₂" long, 5¹/₄" high

dozen **14/-**

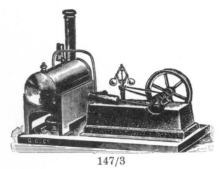

147/3

Low price **Steam Engines**

with polished brass boiler, brass oscillating cylinder, mounted on polished wooden base.

No. **147/1** 7³/₄" long, 6" high . . . . each **2/4**
— **147/2** 8¹/₂" — 7" — with whistle . . . . . — **3/-**
— **147/3** 10" — 7¹/₂" — — — and governors . — **4/-**

149/2 and 3

New cheap **Steam Engines**

with **steel-blue** finish boiler and brass oscillating cylinder, walls of boiler support and chimney enamelled in imitation of masonry, mounted on imitation tiled base,

with **steam whistle**.

No. **149/1** 6¹/₄" long, 6¹/₄" wide, 9" high . . . . . . each **4/-**
— **149/2** 7" — 7" — 10¹/₄" — and governors . — **5/-**
— **149/3** 8" — 8" — 11¹/₂" — with governors
and water gauge . . . . — **6/8**

104/1

New cheap **Semi-Portable Engine**

of good quality with brass oscillating cylinder, spring safety valve, polished brass boiler, mounted on strong metal base.

No. **104/1** 6¹/₄" long, 3¹/₄" wide, 3¹/₂" high . . . . each **3/4**

Trade Mark.

Handsome Model Steam Engines

148/3 and 4

with reversing motion
of most substantial manufacture

fitted with brass oscillating cylinder, brass boiler of steel-blue finish, nickelled fittings, mounted on handsome polished wooden base with ornamental tiled tin-plate face, complete with whistle and safety valve.

No. **148/1** $8^1/_4$" high, 6" long, 6" wide . . . . each **5/10**
—   **148/2**   9" high, 7" long, 7" wide, same fittings as 148/1 . —   **6/6**
—   **148/3**   10" high, $7^1/_2$" long, $7^1/_2$" wide, same as 148/2 but with water gauge with protector . . . . —   **8/6**
—   **148/4** $10^1/_2$" high, $8^1/_4$" long, $8^1/_4$" wide, same as 148/3 —   **11/4**

Sizes 3 and 4 are provided with a pressure gauge screw.

689/3 and 4

The same Engine but fitted with
fixed double action cylinder,

patent valve action and **patent eccentric reversing motion** with **steam whistle** and safety valve.

No. **689/1** $8^1/_4$" high, 6" long, 6". wide . . . . each **6/-**
—   **689/2**   9" high, 7" long, 7" wide, same fittings as 689/1 —   **7/8**
—   **689/3**   10" high, $7^1/_2$" long, $7^1/_2$" wide, same as 689/2 but with water gauge with protector . . . . —   **9/-**
—   **689 4** $10^1/_2$" high, $8^1/_4$" long, $8^1/_4$" wide . . . . —   **12/-**

Sizes 3 and 4 are provided with a pressure gauge screw.

105/3

New and cheap over-type Steam Engine
splendid finish

with fixed cylinder reversing eccentric slide valve motion, steam boiler in steel-blue finish, spring safety valve, steam whistle.

No. **105/2**   single action on strong metal base, $6^1/_4$" long. $3^3/_8$" wide, $8^1/_2$" high. . . . . each **5/4**
—   **105/3**   double action, with governors, mounted on wooden base, 8" long, $4^1/_4$" wide, $9^1/_2$" high . . . . . . —   **7/-**

Trade   Mark.

Twin Cylinder Engines

with horizontal brass boiler of steel-blue finish, high chimney, spring safety valve, whistle, nickelled fittings, and the whole mounted on polished wooden base ornamented with tiled tin-plate face.

No. 174/3

with 2 brass oscillating cylinders and **reversing gear**,

10" high, 7½" long, 7½" wide
each **10/-**

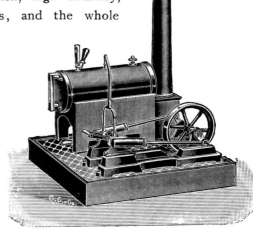

642/1

174/3

New Steam Engines with horizontal brass boiler with steel-blue finish, high chimney, spring safety valve, whistle, central lubricating attachment, also **2 fixed double action patent slide valve cylinders**, with patent eccentric reversing motion, screwed on metal bedplate and the boiler and engine mounted on wooden base with ornamental tiled tin-plate face, all the fittings are highly polished and nickelled.

No. 642/1	7½" long, 7½" wide, 8½" high . . . . each **11/-**
— 642/2	8½" — 8½" — 12" — with water gauge and pressure gauge screw . . . . — **15/6**
— 642/3	10½" long, 9½" wide, 15½" high, lever safety valve, water gauge, starting cock and governors . . . . — **48/-**
— 642/3P	ditto, with feed pump . . . . — **51/6**
— 642/5P	ditto, but larger, 19½" high, 12¾" long, 12¼" wide, handsomely finished . . . . — **80/-**

642/2

642/5 P

Trade Mark.

Very handsome Model Steam Engines

most perfect and complete design,

with fixed double action patent slide valve cylinder, with roller apparatus and ball pressing attachment, both patented, water gauge with protector, steam whistle and safety valve.

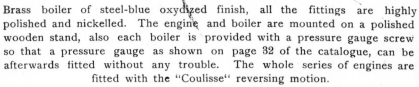

Brass boiler of steel-blue oxydized finish, all the fittings are highly polished and nickelled. The engine and boiler are mounted on a polished wooden stand, also each boiler is provided with a pressure gauge screw so that a pressure gauge as shown on page 32 of the catalogue, can be afterwards fitted without any trouble. The whole series of engines are fitted with the "Coulisse" reversing motion.

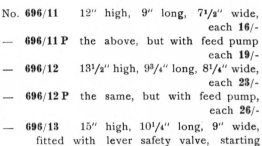

No. **696/11**	12″ high, 9″ long, 7¹/₂″ wide, each **16/-**
— **696/11 P**	the above, but with feed pump each **19/-**
— **696/12**	13¹/₂″ high, 9³/₄″ long, 8¹/₄″ wide, each **23/-**
— **696/12 P**	the same, but with feed pump, each **26/-**
— **696/13**	15″ high, 10¹/₄″ long, 9″ wide, fitted with lever safety valve, starting cock and governors . . . . . each **33/-**

696/15 P and 14 P

696/12 and 11

No. **696/13 P** the same, but with feed pump . . . . each **36/-**
— **696/14 P** 17″ high, 11¹/₂″ long, 10″ wide, with water gauge with cocks and test cock . . . . — **50/-**
— **696/15 P** 19″ — 12¹/₂″ — 11″ — — — — — — — — — — — — — — — — **64/-**

Model Steam Engines — Semi=Portable Over Type.

Technically perfect design, with fixed double action slide valve cylinder with patent valve gear and patent roller apparatus, fitted with water gauge with protector, steam whistle and safety valve. The brass boiler is of steel-blue oxydized finish, all the fittings are highly polished and nickelled, the engine is mounted on a handsomely japanned iron base.

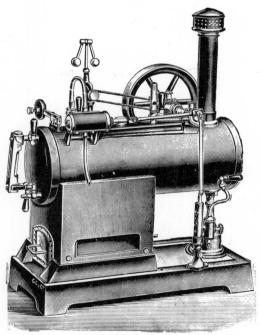

No. **691/1**	8¹/₂″ high, 6¹/₄″ long, 3¹/₈″ wide, each **15/-**
— **691/1 P**	ditto, with feed pump — **18/-**
— **691/2**	9¹/₂″ high, 7″ long, 3¹/₂″ wide, each **21/-**
— **691/2 P**	ditto, with feed pump — **24/-**
— **691/3**	10¹/₂″ high, 8¹/₄″ long, 4″ wide, with lever safety valve, starting cock and governors . . . . . . each **29/6**
— **691/3 P**	ditto, with feed pump — **33/-**
— **691/4 P**	12″ high, 9¹/₂″ long, 4³/₄″ wide, with test cock and water gauge with cocks . . . . each **44/-**
— **691/5 P**	13¹/₂″ high, 10¹/₂″ long, 5¹/₄″ wide, each **56/-**

691/5 P and 4 P

691/2 and 1

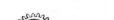

Trade Mark.

2*

New handsome
Semi-Portable Engines

with **fixed double action patent slide valve cylinder**, **patent eccentric reversing motion**, with horizontal brass boiler of steel-blue oxydized finish, fitted with smokebox on cast iron pillar, safety valve, whistle and governors,

all the fittings are highly nickelled. The whole mounted on ornamental tiled wooden base.

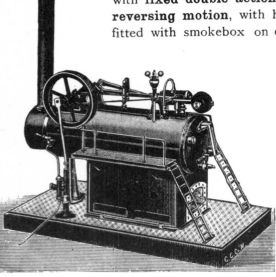

No. **105/4**　9" long, 4½" wide, 12" high　.　.　each **10/6**

— **105/5**　10¼" long, 5" wide, 13½" high, with water gauge, **patent spirit vapour lamp**, 1 gallery with ladder and balustrade　.　.　each **15/6**

— **105/6**　12" long, 6" wide, 15" high, with lever safety valve, blow-off cock, pressure gauge screw, 2 galleries with balustrade and ladder, **patent spirit vapour lamp**　.　.　.　each **23/-**

105/6P

105/4

No. **105/6 P** the same, with **feed pump**　.　.　.　.　.　.　.　.　.　.　.　.　.　— **27/-**

— **105/7**　12½" long, 6½" wide, 16¾" high, with lever safety valve, water gauge with cocks, blow-off cock, pressure gauge, bell whistle, 2 galleries with balustrade and 3 ladders also **spirit vapour lamp**　.　.　.　.　.　.　.　.　.　.　.　.　.　.　.　— **31/-**

— **105/7 P** the same, with **feed pump**　.　.　.　.　.　.　.　.　.　.　.　.　.　— **35/-**

Spirit
Vapour Lamps
Registered

for 105/5, 6, 7.

105/5　　　　105/7

Trade Mark.

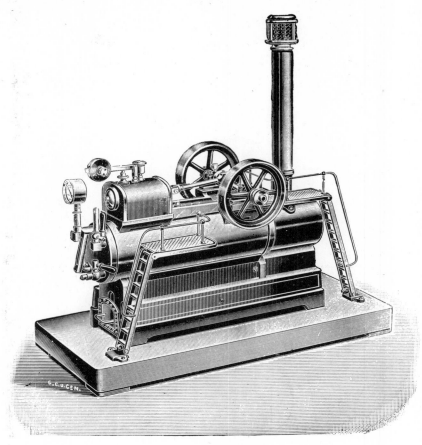

No. **691/21**

High class and heavy design
Over Type Engine.

Facsimile of the most modern engines at work in large industrial centres. Fitted with powerful brass boiler, smoke box fixed on cast iron support, boiler of steel-blue finish and furnished with superior tested **patent spirit vapour lamp**, chimney fitted with spark arrester, the boiler rests on a cast iron support and the whole screwed on a handsomely polished wooden base ornamented with tiled tinplate face. **The cylinder is of the fixed double action "Precision" type** with patent eccentric valve gear, and **ball-pressing attachment,** enclosed in steam jacket, lubricating attachment to cylinder and slide-valve, lever safety valve, 2 massive flywheels, **feed pump,** condenser water tank, water gauge with protector, patent **pressure gauge**, whistle, blow-off cock, **2 well made strong ladders** with 2 massive **galleries** with balustrade, all the fittings are highly polished and nickelled.

$12^1/_2$" long, $6^3/_8$" wide, $7^1/_2$" high to top of flywheels, $12^1/_2$" high to top of chimney. . . . . each **51/-**

For miniature illustration and transparent cover for above, see page 14.

Trade  Mark.

No. **691/23**

High class and heavy design
Over Type Engine.

Facsimile of the most modern engines at work in large industrial centres. Horizontal brass boiler strongly made and of steel-blue finish, smokebox with screwed cast iron support, superior tested **spirit vapour lamp** (registered), chimney with spark arrester; on handsomely japanned **bedplate**, with

fixed double action slide valve "Precision" cylinder

with patent valve gear and **ball pressing attachment**, fitted with steam jacket, lubricating attachment to cylinder and slide valve, lever safety valve, 2 massive flywheels, **feed pump** with condenser water tank (hot well), water gauge with protector, firedoor, starting cock, governors, **patent pressure gauge**, whistle, blow-off cock, **3 handsome ladders, 3** massive **galleries** with balustrade .All the fittings are highly polished and nickelled, the whole is mounted on a handsome wooden base with ornamental tiled face.

15" long, 7¼" wide, 8¾" high to top of flywheels, 15½" to top of chimney. . . . . each **70/-**
For miniature illustration and transparent cover for above, see page 14.

Trade Mark.

No. **691/25**

High class and heavy design

Over Type Engine

Facsimile of the latest compound engines, with horizontal strong brass boiler steel-blue finish, smokebox on screwed cast iron support, with superior tested **patent spirit vapour lamp,** chimney with spark arrester, on handsomely japanned **bedplate,** with **2 fixed double action "Precision" slide valve cylinders, high and low pressure** with guide bars, eccentric valve gear, **ball pressing attachment,** enclosed in steam jacket, lubricating attachment to cylinder and slide valve, lever safety valve, blow-off cock, 2 massive flywheels, **feed pump** with condenser water tank or hot well, water gauge, with 2 cocks, **patent pressure gauge,** whistle, starting cock, 3 handsome strong **ladders,** 3 massive **galleries** with balustrade. All the fittings are highly polished and nickelled, and the whole screwed on a handsome wooden base with ornamental tiled face. $16\frac{1}{2}$" long, $8\frac{1}{4}$" wide, $10\frac{1}{2}$" high to top rim of flywheel, $18\frac{1}{2}$" high to top of chimney . . . each **140/-**

For miniature illustration and transparent cover for above, see page 14.

Trade  Mark.

Illustrations taken from miniature stereo blocks of **Engines** described on pages 11, 12, 13.

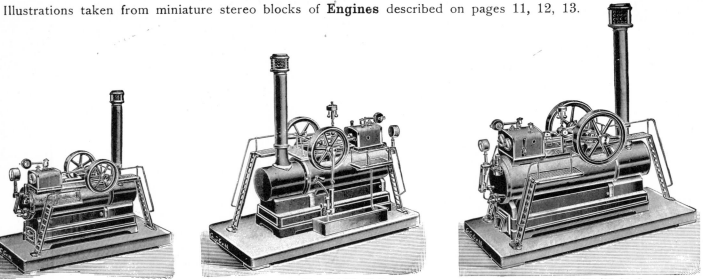

stereo No. 691/21 M C
each **1/-**

stereo No. 691/23 M C.
each **1/6**

stereo No. 691/25 M C.
each **1/10**

Transparent **Covers**

to suit engines described on pages 11, 12, 13.

No. 691/21 S   suitable for model No. **691/21** .   . each **6/-**
— **691/23 S**   —   —   —   **691/23** .   .   —   **7/6**
— **691/25 S**   —   —   —   **691/25** .   .   —   **11/-**

691/21 S -/23 S -/25 S

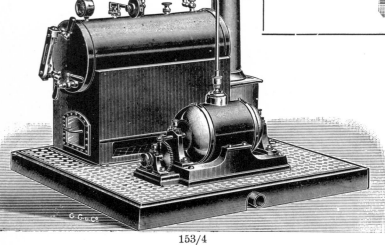

153/4

Steam Turbine of latest design, with strong brass boiler of steel-blue finish, fitted with lever safety valve, filling screw, whistle, starting cock, pressure gauge, water gauge with cocks, blow-off cock, turbine fitted with speed reducing gear wheels, bearings fitted with lubricators, and mounted on handsomely japanned cast iron bed, the boiler and engine is screwed on a wooden base with ornamental tiled tin-plate face.

No. **153/4**   12" long, 12½" wide, 19¾" high
each **50/-**

Trade Mark.

High class
Model Steam Engine
of most complete design

with fixed double action patent slide valve cylinder, heavy iron flywheel, driving pulley, governors, on iron bed, brazed and screwed brass boiler of steel-blue oxydized finish, boiler casing and chimney in imitation relieved brickwork, steam dome, lever safety valve, bell whistle, pressure gauge (4 Atm.), water gauge with cocks and protector, feed pump, starting cock, large furnace with fire door, all the fittings are highly polished and nickelled, boiler and engine mounted on polished wooden stand.

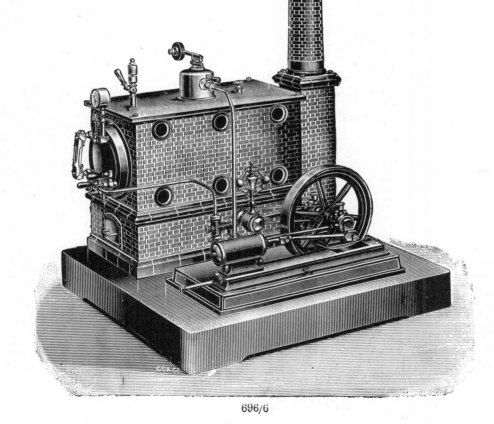

696/6

No. **696/6**   26″ high, 10³/₄″ long, 14″ wide . . . . each **150/-**

Trade Mark.

2 E

Large high class

Model Steam Engine

of most complete design

with fixed double action patent slide valve cylinder, with eccentric valve gear and cross head guide. Heavy iron flywheel, driving pulley, governors on iron bed, brazed and screwed brass boiler of steel-blue oxydized finish, boiler casing and chimney in imitation relieved brickwork, steam dome, bell whistle, pressure gauge (4 Atm. about 60 lbs), water gauge with cocks and protector, test cocks, starting cock, feed pump, large furnace with fire door, all the fittings are highly polished and nickelled, the boiler and engine are mounted on handsomely polished wooden base.

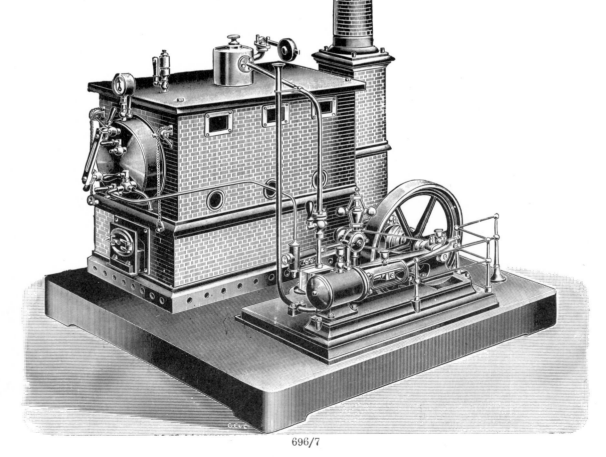

696/7

No. **696/7** 30" high, 19" long, 16½" wide . . . . each **300/-**

Trade Mark.

Large high class
Model Steam Engine

of the most perfect construction and latest design

with two fixed double action slide valve cylinders, eccentric shaft and cross head guide. Heavy iron flywheel, driving pulley, governors on iron bed, brazed and screwed brass boiler of steel-blue oxydized finish, boiler casing and chimney in imitation relieved brickwork, steam dome, bell whistle, lever safety valve, pressure gauge (4 Atm. about 60 lbs), water gauge with cocks and protector, test cocks, starting cock, feed pump, large furnace with fire door, all the fittings are highly polished and nickelled, the boiler and engine are mounted on handsomely polished wooden base.

669/7

No. **669/7**   31" high, 19" long, 17" wide . . . .   each **360/-**

Trade   Mark.

2*

Model Steam Track Engines

692/1

with fixed double action patent slide valve cylinder patent eccentric reversing motion, ball pressing attachment, water gauge with protector, brass boiler of steel-blue oxydized finish. These engines are also constructed for driving models.

All the fittings are highly polished and nickelled.

692/3 P

No. **692/1** 8" high, 7" long, with whistle, safety valve and water gauge . . . . . . each **30/-**

— **692/3P** 12" high, 11½" long, with whistle, lever safety valve, starting cock, governors, water gauge with cocks and feed pump . . . . each **72/-**

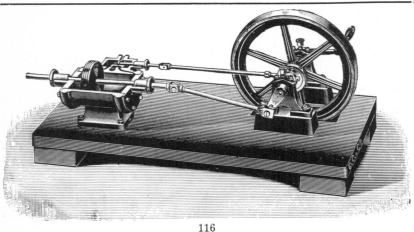

116

Section Model
of slide valve cylinder

for demonstrating the action of steam power with a fixed slide valve cylinder. Made entirely of metal, very nicely finished, on polished wooden base. Worked by turning the wheel.

No. **116** 12½" long, 6" wide . . each **35/-**

Hot Air Engines

heated by spirit lamp.

The component parts are beautifully japanned or nickelled.

The engines work perfectly **without either water or steam.**

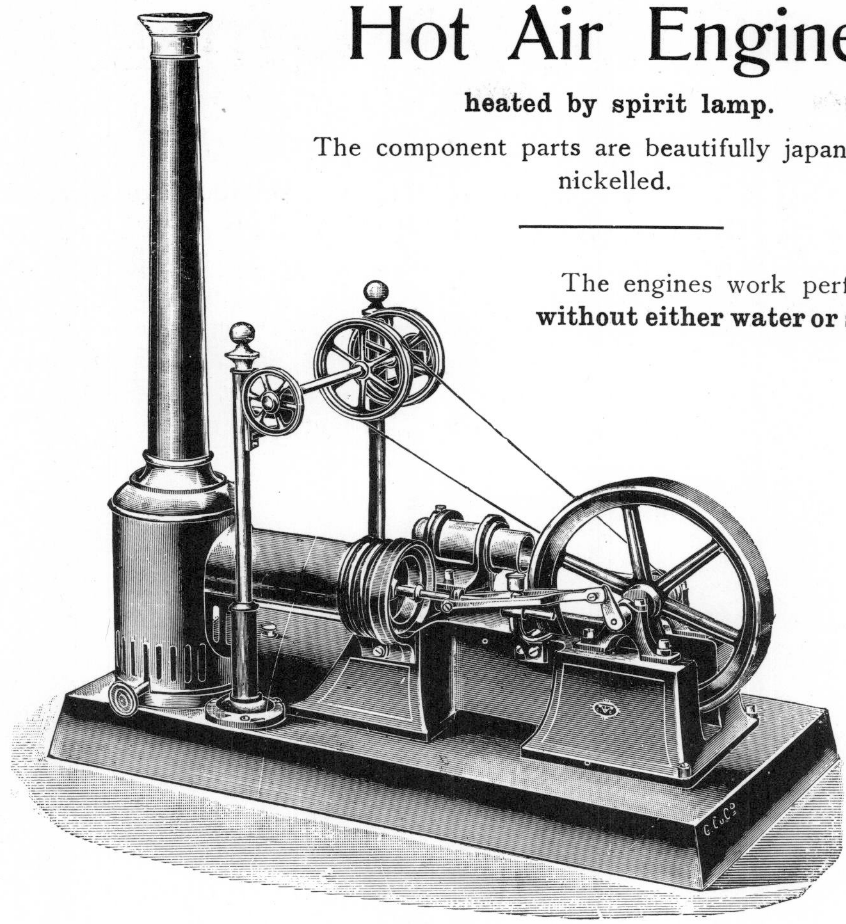

143/1 and 2 mounted on wooden base

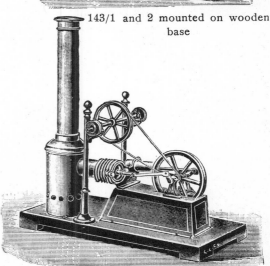

143/3 and 4 mounted on wooden base.

687/1, -/2, -/3

No. **143/1**	8¼" long,	7¼" high	. . . . each	**5/6**
— 143/2	9½" —	8¾" —	. . . . —	**7/6**
— 143/3	9½" —	8¾" —	with shafting . . . . . . —	**9/6**
— 143/4	10½" —	10½" —	— . . . . . —	**13/6**

High class Hot Air Engines

technically complete design, with shafting and nickelled fittings, **horizontal pattern**, mounted on cast iron bed, and screwed on wooden base with ornamental tiled tin plate face.

No. **687/1**	12" high, 10½" long, 6" wide	. each	**20/-**
— 687/2	14½" — 12½" — 7⅛" —	. —	**27/-**
— 687/3	16¼" — 15" — 8" —	. —	**36/-**
— 687 B	suitable **gas burner** for engines 687/1—3 for use when running the engine for a long time . . . . —		**2/10**

687 B

The same in **vertical design**, mounted on handsomely japanned iron base. Very strong and well finished.

No. **686/1**	12" high, 6¼" long, 4" wide, each	**18/-**
— 686/2	14½" — 7½" — 4¾" — —	**24/-**
— 686/3	17½" — 8¾" — 5½" — —	**32/-**
— 686 B/1	suitable gas burner for 686/1 . .	**3/4**
— 686 B/2	— — — 686/2 and 3, —	**3/6**

686 B

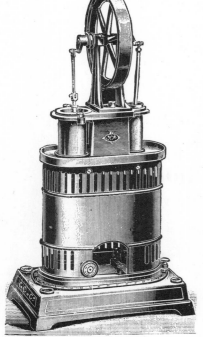

686/1, -/2, -/3

Trade Mark.

Extra powerful Hot Air Engines

of special design, introduced by us in the year 1903. In this design which is protected in Germany **the displacer and the working cylinder are arranged the one inside the other,**

694/1

this improvement results in **much greater** efficiency and developes **a power hitherto unobtainable.**

These engines will work immediately the lamp is lighted and requires neither water nor steam. The cylinder is air cooled by means of the ribs on the outside, rendering a water jacket unnecessary. They are very strong and of elegant appearance, being mounted on a wooden base, adorned with a tiled tin-plate face. By using the specially made gas burner the engine can be run continuously.

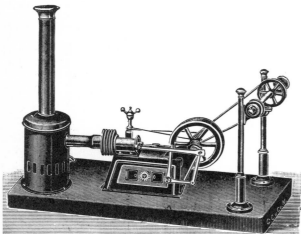

694/1 T

No. **694/1**	$9^1/_2$" long, $3^1/_2$" wide, $9^1/_2$" high on tin-plate bed	each	**5/6**
— **694/1 T**	the same **with shafting**, $12^3/_4$" long, $4^1/_4$" wide, $9^1/_2$" high	—	**7/6**
— **694/2**	with massive iron flywheel, **on cast iron bed**, 12" long, $5^1/_4$" wide, 12" high .	—	**13/-**
— **694/2 T**	the same **with shafting**, $13^3/_4$" long, $5^1/_4$" wide, 12" high	—	**15/6**
— **694/3**	like 694/2, but larger and more powerful, $13^1/_2$" long, $5^1/_4$" wide, $13^1/_2$" high	—	**20/-**
— **694 G/2**	**Gas burner** to suit 694/2 and 2 T . .	—	**2/-**
— **694 G/3**	— — -- — 694/3	—	**2/-**

694/2 T

694 G/2—3

694/3

Trade  Mark.

Twin Cylinder, Hot Air Engines

Quality same as those described on page 20, but fitted with

**2 cylinders with the working and displacer cylinder arranged the one in the other,
double flame spirit lamp**

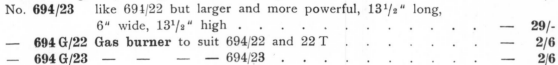

694/21   694 G/22—23   694/21 T

No. **694/21**	9½" long, 4¼" wide, 10" high, on **tin-plate bed**	each	**9/-**
— **694/21 T**	the same, **with shafting**, 12¾" long, 4¾" wide, 10" high	—	**11/-**
— **694/22**	with massive iron flywheel, **on cast iron bed**, 12" long, 5¼" wide, 12" high . . .	—	**19/-**
— **694/22 T**	the same, **with shafting**, 13¾" long, 6" wide, 12" high	—	**21/6**
No. **694/23**	like 694/22 but larger and more powerful, 13½" long, 6" wide, 13½" high	—	**29/-**
— **694 G/22**	**Gas burner** to suit 694/22 and 22 T	—	**2/6**
— **694 G/23**	— — — — 694/23	—	**2/6**

694/23

694/22T

Trade Mark.

New Hot Air Engine

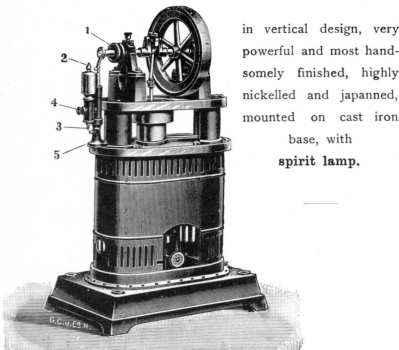

in vertical design, very powerful and most handsomely finished, highly nickelled and japanned, mounted on cast iron base, with **spirit lamp.**

686/2¹/₂

686/2½

The above **engine** can be used either:

1. **Power supply,** by driving from the **driving pulley.**
2. **Pump,** the engine will force water 10—20 yards high and will draw from a depth of about 20" by attaching pump supplied.
3. **For ventilating a room** by employing the **fan** supplied.

The spirit lamp supplied with the engine, will burn about 5 hours according to the quality of the methylated.

No. **686/2¹/₂** 9" lang, 5¹/₂" wide, 19" high, each **40/-**

— **686 B/2 gas burner,** suitable for same enabling engine to be run continuously, each **3/6**

686 B/2

Hot Air Engine with large Fan

686/5

for use solely for ventilation, **most beautifully finished and strongly made.** With patent ball joints which allows a continuous working without smell and with very little wear.

No. **686/5 S** heated by **spirit lamp** giving about 5 hours continuous running without refilling, 10¹/₂" long, 10¹/₂" wide, 22" high, each **77/-**

— **686/5 G** for **gas heating** only, continuous running . . — **77/-**

Trade Mark.

New Power Hot Air Engine,

capable of heavy load,

in handsome and technically complete design, horizontal form with **spirit lamp** giving about a 5 hour's continuous run without refilling.

These hot air engines can be worked by **gas heating** by using the **gas burner** specially made for them.

These new design hot air engines, show a great improvement over the older types, both in the power developed and also in the **odourless continuous running** together with **extremely small wear** on the working parts, due to the patent ball joints.

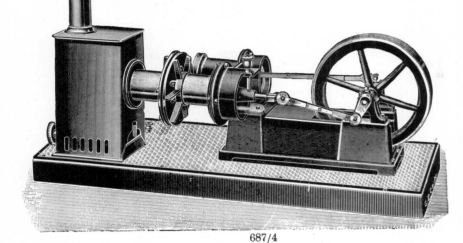

No. **687/4** mounted on highly polished wooden base with ornamental tin-plate tiled face, 18½" long, 8" wide, 18¼" high
each **63/-**

687/4 G

No. **687/4G** suitable **gas burner** for above each **3/4**

687/4

No. **687/5** The same engine but larger and more powerful, with **spirit vapour generator,**

reliable in action and enabling a run of **about 5 hours** to be made without refilling.

Latest design,

mounted on highly polished wooden base ornamented with tiled tin-plate face 2 feet long, 10" wide, 22" high
each **85/-**

687/5 G

No. **687/5 G**
suitable **gas burner**
each **3/8**

687/5

Trade Mark.

152/6

152/3

Water Motors

for coupling direct to watermain,

consisting of massive cast iron casing, fitted with connections for rubber piping (**A**) for water supply and (**B**) for water outlet. The motor casing is water tight and can be fixed in any desired spot. The **motor** is worked on "**Pelton's**" **system** with **double blades** and the axle is fitted with a driving pulley for **power driving.**

No. **152/3** $9^1/_2$ " long, $3^1/_2$ " wide, $6^3/_4$ " high, each **23/6**
— **152/6** special **coupling for direct driving** set **1/6**

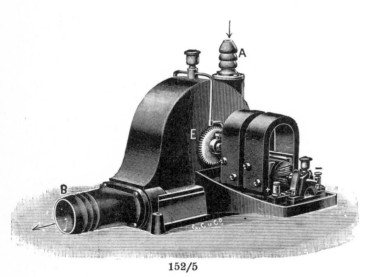

152/5

No. **152/5** The above described

Water Motor

with direct coupled double

Magnet Dynamo

with gearing, lubricators to bearings; for **generating** of **electricity** . . . . each **45/-**

Output with a water pressure

equal to 45 lbs per □ "	2 lamps of	$3^1/_2$ volts each
— —50 —	— —3 —	— $3^1/_2$ —	—
— —65 —	— —4 —	— $3^1/_2$ —	—

can be supplied. As the dynamo generates **continuous current** it can be used to charge small accumulators.

Lamp holders and **lamps** to suit above, see page 193—195, **Accumulators** see page 187.

Trade Mark.

Complete electric Light Plant

consisting of one **Dynamo** and one **Steam Engine,** strongly made and reliable working model, with recent improvements. The engine can be used to drive models if required.

No. **150/10** Horizontal Steam Engine

with brass boiler of steel-blue oxydized finish, spring safety valve; whistle, oscillating cylinder geared direct to

Dynamo

by a pair of gear wheels, also incandescent lamp with miniature screw and holder, 4 Volt, 0,2 Amp. The engine is fitted with pulley for driving models and the whole mounted on a wooden base with tiled tin-plate top, $10^{3}/_{4}$" long, $6^{1}/_{4}$" wide, $9^{3}/_{4}$" high . . . each **13/6**

150/10

No. **150/11** Horizontal Steam Engine

with steel-blue oxydized brass boiler, spring safety valve, whistle, automatic lubricating attachment, oscillating brass cylinder, with **detachable gearing** (for the driving of models without dynamo), with

Dynamo,

switch, handsome **lamp stand** with arc light pattern, incandescent lamp, 4 Volt, 0,2 Amp., with miniature screw, the whole mounted on wooden base with tiled tin-plate face,

$12^{1}/_{2}$" long, 8" wide, $13^{1}/_{2}$" high . . . each **26/-**

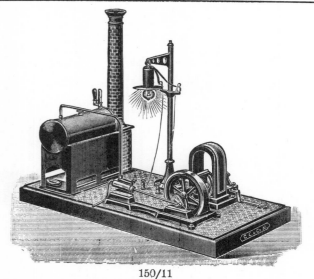
150/11

No. **150/12** Horizontal Steam Engine

with steel-blue oxydized brass boiler, spring safety valve, whistle, water gauge, pressure gauge, starting cock, automatic lubricating attachment, superior double action fixed slide valve cylinder, with patent valve gear and patent ball pressing attachment, with **detachable gear-wheel-coupling** to

Dynamo

(for the driving of models without dynamo), switch, handsome lamp stand, with model arc lamp pattern, incandescent lamp with "Mignon" screw, 4 Volt, 0,25 Amp., mounted on wooden base with tiled tin-plate face,

$13^{1}/_{2}$" long, $9^{1}/_{2}$" wide, 17" high . . . each **34/6**

No. **1045/4**	Incandescent lamps for replacements to suit No. 150/10 and 11 . each **-/10**	
— **1045/21 M**	Incandescent lamps for replacements to suit No. 150/12 . . . . each **1/-**	

150/12

Trade Mark.

Shaftings and Pulleys for driving several models by one engine.

Cheap shafting on tin base.

No. **19/20** with 2 driving pulleys, 3¹/₈" long, 2¹/₂" high, dozen **3/8**

No. **19/21** wit 3 driving pulleys, 4³/₈" long, 2³/₄" high, dozen **6/-**

No. **19/22** with 4 driving pulleys, 5³/₄" long, 2³/₄" high, dozen **8/6**

No. **19/23** wit 5 driving pulleys, 7¹/₂" long, 2³/₄" high, dozen **10/10**

Shafting mounted on wooden base

with removable pulleys and keyfastening. — Strongly made.

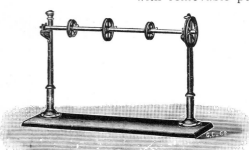 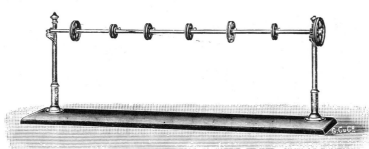

No. **19/0** with 4 pulleys, 10¹/₄" long, 6³/₄" high . . . . dozen **18/-**

No. **19/2** with 7 pulleys, 18¹/₄" long, 6³/₄" high . . . . each **2/6**

 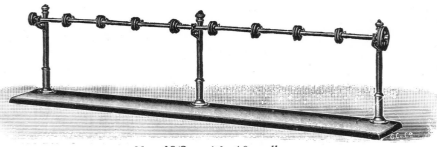

No. **19/1** with 5 pulleys, 12" long, 6³/₄" high . . . . . each **2/-**

No. **19/3** with 10 pulleys, 26¹/₂" long, 6³/₄ high . . . . each **3/8**

Counter Shaft No. **19 V**, strongly made, with cast brackets, each -/**10**

No. **19/3¹/₂** with 12 pulleys, 33¹/₂" long, 7¹/₈" high . . . . each **5/-**

Trade Mark.

Best quality **Shafting** of heavy design.

Handsomely japanned standards, cast iron pulleys, each highly polished and fitted with 2 fixing screws, the whole on a strong highly polished hard wood base.

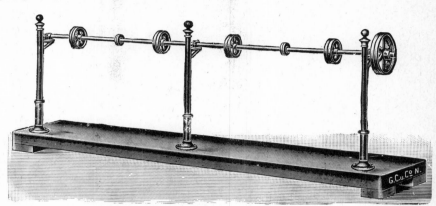

No. **19/6** with 4 pulleys, 15³/₄″ long, 9³/₄″ high . . . . . each **7/8**

No. **19/7** with 7 pulleys, 27¹/₂″ long, 9³/₄″ high, . each **11/8**

Special "Show Model" Shafting, extra well finished

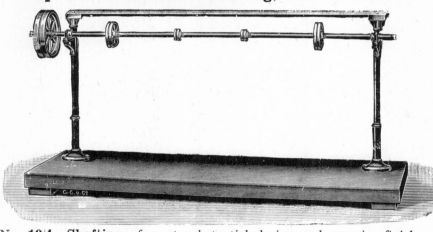

No. **19V/5 Countershaft**
highly nickelled, to suit No. 19/4
each **3/-**

No. **19/4 Shafting** of most substantial design and superior finish, consisting of 2 highly finished pillar standards of cast iron, highly nickelled cross bar, nickelled shaft, 2 small and 2 large grooved driving pulleys, also large engine driven grooved pulley, mounted on highly polished wooden base, 18¹/₂″ long, 9¹/₂″ high . . . . each **10/8**

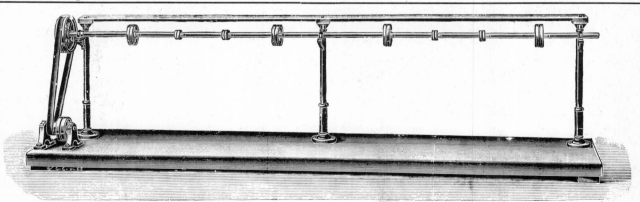

No. **19/5 Shafting** of most substantial design and superior finish consisting of 3 highly finished pillar standards of cast iron, highly nickelled cross bar, nickelled shaft, 4 small and 4 large grooved driving pulleys, also large flat belt-driven pulley with countershaft, and 2 grooved pulleys, mounted on highly polished wooden base, 34¹/₂″ long, 9¹/₂″ high . . . . each **19/-**

Trade Mark.

Separate Parts of Steam Engines
(Fittings).

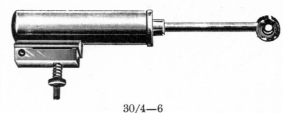

Steam cylinders
oscillating

strongly made in brass, with piston, steam inlet block of solid brass, spring and nut.

30/1—3   30/4—6

No. **30/1**	2	3	4	5	6
diameter	5/16	11/32	13/32	15/32	1/2	19/32″ approx.
length of cyl.	1³/₁₆	1¹/₂	1⁹/₁₆	1⁷/₈	2¹/₈	2³/₈″ —
stroke	19/32	23/32	23/32	13/16	15/16	1¹/₈″ —
each	-/10	1/2	1/4	1/6	1/8	2/-

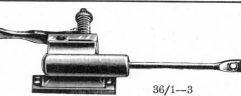

Steam oscillating cylinders

with **reversing motion,** strongly made in brass and **highly nickelled,** with piston and steam inlet block of solid brass, japanned base, spring and nut.

36/4   36/1—3

No. **36/1**	2	3	4
diameter	5/16	11/32	13/32	15/32″ approx.
length of cyl.	1³/₈	1⁵/₈	1⁹/₁₆	1⁷/₈″ —
stroke	3/4	13/16	15/16	15/16″ —
each	1/6	1/10	2/-	2/6

Fixed Steam Cylinders

of brass, highly nickelled and very substantial, double action with patent slide valve and connecting rod.

37/11—15

No. **37/11**	12	13	14	15
diameter	1/2	9/16	5/8	23/32	3/4″ approx.
length of cyl.	1³/₈	1³/₈	1⁵/₈	1⁵/₈	1⁵/₈″ —
stroke	9/16	9/16	19/32	5/8	5/8″ —
each	1/10	2/-	2/4	2/6	2/8 —

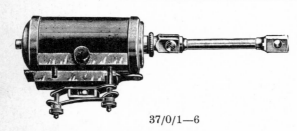

Fixed Steam Cylinders

of brass, highly nickelled and of very superior quality, double action with patent slide valve, with patent ball pressing attachment, **suitable for vertical boilers.**

37/0/1—6

No. **37/0/1**	0/2	0/3	0/4	0/5	0/6
diameter	5/8	11/16	23/32	13/16	29/32	1¹/₈″ approx.
length of cyl.	1¹/₄	1¹/₂	1¹/₂	1³/₄	1³/₄	2³/₈″ —
stroke	11/16	3/4	3/4	7/8	7/8	1″ —
each	4/10	5/4	5/8	6/-	6/6	13/- —

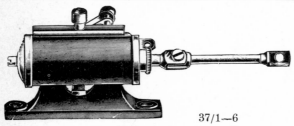

Fixed Steam Cylinders

of brass, highly nickelled and of very superior quality, double action with patent slide valve, with patent rolling and ball pressing attachment, mounted on japanned cast base, suitable for engines with horizontal boilers.

37/1—6

No. **37/1**	2	3	4	5	6
diameter	5/8	11/16	23/32	13/16	29/32	1¹/₈″ approx.
length of cyl.	1¹/₄	1¹/₂	1¹/₂	1³/₄	1³/₄	2³/₈″ —
stroke	11/16	3/4	3/4	7/8	7/8	1″ —
each	4/6	5/6	6/8	7/6	8/6	15/-

Trade Mark.

Large fixed Steam Cylinders

of very best quality and heavy design in massive brass, highly nickelled, double action with slide valve cross head and guide, with cock lubricator to cylinder and oil cup to guide mounted on handsomely japanned cast base.

No. 38/7 1³/₈″ diameter, 9³/₄″ total length, 1³/₁₆″ length of stroke . . . . . each 29/-
No. 38/8 1³/₄″ diamet., 11″ total length, 1⁵/₁₆″ length of stroke. . . . . each 35/-

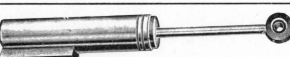

Steam Cylinders for Locomotives.

Brass oscillating cylinder, strongly made, with piston, spring and nut.

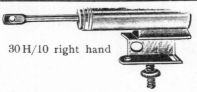

30/10′

No. 30/10	11	12	13	14	15
suitable for	502 and 511/35	502/48	503/35, 504/35	503/48, 504/48	503/54 and 504/54	504/67
diameter	9/32	5/16	9/32	15/32	1/2	19/32″ approx.
length of cyl.	1¹/₂	1¹¹/₃₂	1¹/₂	1³/₄	2	2¹/₂″ —
stroke	23/32	25/32	25/32	29/32	15/16	1³/₁₆″ —
each	-/10	1/-	1/2	1/4	1/6	2/-

Brass oscillating Cylinders,

strongly made, with piston, steam inlet block, spring and nut.

30 H/10 right hand

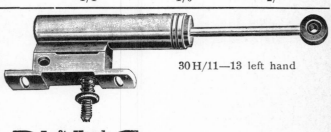

30 H/11—13 left hand

☞ **Right Hand:** ☜

No. 30 HR/10	11	12	13	14	15
diameter	9/32	5/16	9/32	15/32	1/2	19/32″ approx.
length of cyl.	1¹/₂	1¹³/₃₂	1¹/₂	1³/₄	2	2¹/₂″ —
stroke	23/32	25/32	25/32	29/32	15/16	1³/₁₆″ —
each	1/-	1/6	1/8	2/-	2/4	2/8

☞ **Left Hand:** ☜

No. 30 HL/10	11	12	13	14	15
each	1/-	1/6	1/8	2/-	2/4	2/8

Fixed Steam Cylinders

in brass, highly nickelled and of **extra good quality.** Double action with patent slide valve, with patent rolling and ball pressing attachment, with steam inlet and outlet sockets.

No. 37/R and 37 L/20 and 21 are only fitted with slide valve.

☞ **Right Hand:** ☜

No. 37 R/20	21	22	23
diameter	19/32	21/32	21/32	21/32″ approx.
length of cyl.	1¹³/₃₂	1³/₄	1³/₄	1³/₄″ —
stroke	25/32	1	1	1″
each	2/6	4/-	4/6	5/-

☞ **Left Hand:** ☜

No. 37 L/20	21	22	23
each	2/6	4/-	4/6	5/-

Cranks with crank pins

for oscillating cylinders.

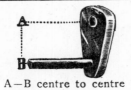

A—B centre to centre = ¹/₂ stroke

In brass						In nickelled brass				
No. 9 K/1	2	3	4	5		No. 10 K/1	2	3	4	5
stroke 19/32	23/32	13/16	1	1³/₃₂″ approx.		stroke 19/32	23/32	13/16	1	1³/₃₂″ approx.
dozen -/8	-/10	1/-	1/-	2/6		dozen 1/-	1/2	1/2	1/4	3/-

Crank Shafts with cranks and pins

suitable for oscillating cylinders

A—B centre to centre = ¹/₂ stroke

in brass							in highly nickelled brass			
No. 9/1	2	3	4	5	6		No. 10/1	2	3	4
length of shaft 3	3¹⁵/₃₂	3²⁵/₃₂	4¹¹/₃₂	4¹¹/₁₆	5²/₁₆″ app.		length of shaft 1³/₄	2	2⁵/₃₂	2³/₈″ app.
stroke 19/32	23/32	23/32	13/16	1	1³/₃₂″		stroke 23/32	13/16	1	1″
dozen 1/4	1/4	1/6	1/8	2/-	3/-		dozen 1/8	2/-	2/2	2/6

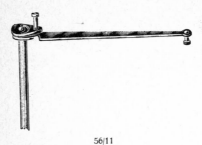

56/11

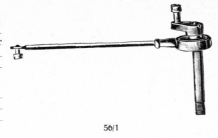

56/1

Shafts with **eccentric, eccentric rod** and **crank**

for horizontal or vertical steam engines, **cut from brass plate** and nickelled

No.	56/11	12	13	14	15
length of shaft	3	$3^3/_{16}$	$3^{19}/_{32}$	$3^7/_8$	$4^3/_{16}''$ appr.
stroke	9/16	9/16	19/32	5/8	5/8'' —
suitable for cyl.	37/11	12	13	14	15
each	-/8	-/8	-/10	-/10	1/-

The same in **heavy brass and highly nickelled.**

No.	56/1	2	3	4	5	6	7	8
length of shaft	$2^{29}/_{32}$	3	3	$3^1/_8$	$3^1/_8$	$2^{29}/_{32}$	4	$5^1/_8''$ appr.
stroke	21/32	3/4	3/4	7/8	7/8	1	$1^1/_8$	$1^5/_{16}''$ —
suitable for cyl. 37 and	37/0/1	37/0/2	37/0/3	37/0/4	37/0/5	37/0/6	38/7	38/8
each	1/8	1/10	2/-	2/4	2/6	3/4	6/-	7/10

44/7—8

Eccentric with rod,

heavy pattern in brass, highly nickelled.

No **44/7** $1^3/_{16}''$ diameter suitable for cylinder No 38/7, $3/_8''$ hole . . . . each 3/6

— **44/8** $1^{17}/_{32}''$ — — — — 38/8, $1^3/_{32}''$— . . . . — 4/6

55/1—6

Connecting rods, highly nickelled.

No.	55/1	2	3	4	5	6
length	$1^{27}/_{32}$	$2^5/_{32}$	$2^{19}/_{32}$	3	$3^7/_{16}$	$4^3/_{16}''$ appr.
distance between centres	$1^9/_{16}$	$1^7/_8$	$2^9/_{32}$	$2^3/_4$	$3^1/_{16}$	$3^3/_4''$ —
dozen	1/-	1/2	2/4	2/10	3/8	3/10

20 F 20 M

No. **20 F M** **Springs** for oscillating cylinders in brass . . . . dozen -/2

— **20 F S** — — — — — steel . . . . — -/3

— **20 M** **Nuts** — — — — brass . . . . — -/4

Through way cocks.

22/0½

22/1

22/3

32

No. **22/0½** brass with wood handle $1^9/_{32}''$ long . . . . each -/5

— **22/1** — — — — $3/_4''$ — . . . . . . — -/6

Union cocks with union,

wood handle and ferrule.

No. 22/3	$1^3/_8''$ long	each -/8
— 22/3 N	$1^3/_8''$ nickelled	— -/10
— 22/5	$1^{15}/_{32}''$ long	1/4
— 22/5 N	$1^{15}/_{32}''$ nickelled	1/6
— 22/6	$1^{25}/_{32}''$ long	2/-
— 22/6 N	$1^{25}/_{32}''$ nickelled	2/2

Union

with nut, lining and ferrule.

No. 32	$1^1/_{16}''$ long	each -/5
— 32 N	$1^1/_{16}''$ nickelled	— -/6
— 32/1	$1^5/_{16}''$ long	— -/5
— 32/1 N	$1^5/_{16}''$ nickelled	— -/6

Steam whistles

in brass with wood handles and ferrules.

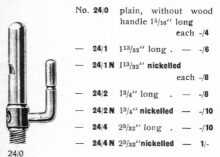

24/0

24/1—4

No. **24/0** plain, without wood handle $1^5/_{16}''$ long each -/4

— **24/1** $1^{13}/_{32}''$ long . — -/6

— **24/1 N** $1^{13}/_{32}''$ nickelled each -/8

— **24/2** $1^3/_4''$ long . — -/8

— **24/2 N** $1^3/_4''$ nickelled — -/10

— **24/4** $2^3/_{32}''$ long . — -/10

— **24/4 N** $2^3/_{32}''$ nickelled — 1/-

Bell whistles

in brass, with wood handle and ferrule.

46/00—1

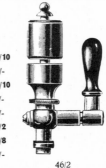

46/2

No. 46/00	$1^3/_8''$ long	each -/10
— 46/00 N	$1^3/_8''$ nickelled	1/-
— 46/0	$1^7/_{16}''$ long	-/10
— 46/0 N	$1^7/_{16}''$ nickelled	1/-
— 46/1	$1^7/_{16}''$ long	1/-
— 46/1 N	$1^7/_{16}''$ nickelled	1/2
— 46/2	$2^1/_8''$ long	1/8
— 46/2 N	$2^1/_8''$ nickelled	2/-

Blow off cocks

in brass, with wood handle and ferrule.

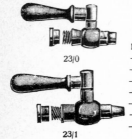

23/0

23/1

No. 23/0	$1^9/_{32}''$ long	each -/5
— 23/0 N	$1^9/_{32}''$ nickelled	— -/6
— 23/1	$1^1/_{32}''$ long	— -/7
— 23/1 N	$1^1/_{32}''$ nickelled	— -/8
— 23/3	$1^1/_{32}''$ long	1/1
— 23/3 N	$1^1/_{32}''$ nickelled	1/2
— 23/4	$1^3/_8''$ long	1/6
— 23/4 N	$1^3/_8''$ nickelled	1/8

Three way cocks.

No. 23/11	$7/_8''$ long	each 1/1
— 23/11 N	$7/_8''$ nickelled	— 1/2
— 23/12	$1^3/_{16}''$ long	1/6
— 23/12 N	$1^3/_{16}''$ nickelled	1/8

23/11

Wood handles

for whistles and cocks.

14/1—4

No.	14/1	2	3	4
	$7/_8$	$1^1/_{16}$	$1^1/_{16}$	$1^5/_{16}$ long
doz.	-/10	1/-	1/2	1/6

Trade ⚙ Mark.

Water gauge

consisting of 1 bent glass tube, ⁵/₃₂″ diameter,
2 brass sockets with cocks and ferrules

No. 50/39	50/54	50/59
1¹⁷/₃₂	2¹/₈	2⁵/₁₆″ length over all
each 1/4	1/4	1/4

50/39—59   No. 50 H **cocks only** for water gauge, brass, each - 8

Water gauge

consisting of 1 bent glass tube, ⁵/₃₂″ diameter,
2 packing nuts and ferrules

No 50 K/39	54	59
1¹⁷/₃₂	2¹/₈	2⁵/₁₆″ total length
each ·/6	-/6	-/6

50 K/39—59   No. 50 KV Packing nuts and ferrules only, each -/2

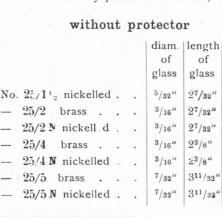

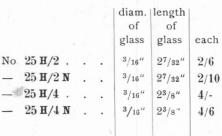
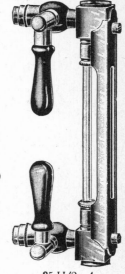

Water gauges

heavy pattern with cocks, ferrules, stuffing boxes and rubber washer.

without protector

	diam. of glass	length of glass	each
No. 25/1½ nickelled . .	⁵/₃₂″	2⁷/₃₂″	2/-
— 25/2 brass . .	³/₁₆″	2⁷/₃₂″	2/6
— 25/2 N nickelled . .	³/₁₆″	2⁷/₃₂″	2/8
— 25/4 brass . . .	³/₁₆″	2³/₈″	3/10
— 25/4 N nickelled . .	³/₁₆″	2³/₈″	4/2
— 25/5 brass . . .	⁷/₃₂″	3¹¹/₃₂″	7/-
— 25/5 N nickelled . .	⁷/₃₂″	3¹¹/₃₂″	7/6

25/1½—5

with protector.

	diam. of glass	length of glass	each
No. 25 H/2 . . .	³/₁₆″	2⁷/₃₂″	2/6
— 25 H/2 N . .	³/₁₆″	2⁷/₃₂″	2/10
— 25 H/4 . . .	³/₁₆″	2³/₈″	4/-
— 25 H/4 N . .	³/₁₆″	2³/₈″	4/6

25 H/2—4

Gauge glass protectors in brass, highly nickelled. -

| No. 25/10 | 2¾″ long (distance from hole to hole 2⁵/₃₂″) . . . . . each -/2 |
| — 25/11 | 3¹/₈″ — (— — — — — 2¾″) . . . . . — -/3 |

for suitable screws No. 6 M/10 see page 33.

Bent glass tubes to suit water gauges
No. 50/39—59 and 50 K/39—59

No. 50 ·/39	54	59
1¹⁷/₃₂	2¹/₈	2⁵/₁₆″ total length
dozen 1/-	1/2	1/2

Straight tubes suitable for water gauges No. 25

No. 25 G/1½	2	3	4
⁵/₃₂	³/₁₆	⁷/₃₂	⁵/₁₆″ diameter
dozen -/5	-/6	-/6	1/-

50 G 25 G

Straight tubes in lengths up to 3 feet,
(also cut to special lengths)

No. 25 G/10	11	12	13
⁵/₃₂	³/₁₆	⁷/₃₂	⁵/₁₆″ diameter
unpacked yard -/4	-/5	-/7	-/10

Lubricators
or
oil cups,

in brass, for steam engines,
without ferrule

63/0—2

63/3—4

No. 63/0	⁵/₃₂″ diameter . . . dozen -/8
— 63/0 N	do., nickelled . . . — -/10
— 63/1	³/₁₆″ diameter . . . — 1/2
— 63/1 N	do., nickelled . . . — 1/6
— 63/2	¼″ diameter . . . — 1/6
— 63/2 N	do., nickelled . . . — 2/-

Capped oil cups with ferrule

No. 63/3	⁹/₃₂″ diameter . . . dozen 3/8
— 63/3 N	do., nickelled . . . — 4/10
— 63/4	¹⁵/₃₂″ diameter . . . each -/6
— 63/4 N	do., nickelled . . . — -/8

63/6—7

63/2 S

63/20 L

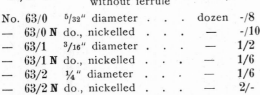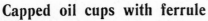

63/9—10

63/21

Lubricators

with **cap, cock** and ferrule, in heavy brass

No. 63/6	brass, ⁹/₃₂″ diameter . . each -/8
— 63/6 N	do., nickelled . . . — -/10
— 63/7	brass, ¹⁵/₃₂″ diameter . . — 1/2
— 63/7 N	do., nickelled . . . — 1/4
— 63/9 N	lubricator with cap, nickelled, ⁹/₃₂″ diameter . . . dozen 1/4
— 63/10 N	lubricator with cap, nickelled, ⁷/₁₆″ diameter . each -/2
— 63/20 S	lubricator, brass, ¹¹/₃₂″ diam. — -/5
— 63/20 SN	— nickelled . . — -/6

Steam-pipe lubricator

to fit on steam supply, with cap

| No. 63/20 L | brass, ¹³/₃₂″ diameter . each -/4 |
| — 63/20 LN | do., nickelled . . . — -/5 |

Larger size steam pipe lubricator

to fit on steam supply pipe, with cap

No. 63/21 N nickelled brass, ²⁵/₃₂″ diam., each -/5

13/1

Finest special model engine oil

in bottle, with oiling rod, indispensible
for steam engines and locomotives etc.

No. 13/1 . . . . dozen 1/6

3 E

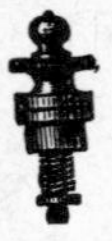

26/0

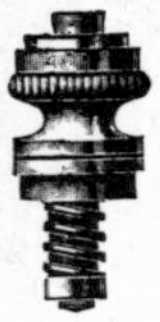

26/1

Spring Safety Valve

in brass, with ferrule.

No. 26/0	$^{13}/_{16}$" long . . .	each	-/3
— 26/0 N	$^{13}/_{16}$" nickelled .	—	-/3
— 26/1	$1^{7}/_{32}$" long . . .	—	-/4
— 26/1 N	$1^{7}/_{32}$" nickelled .	—	-/4

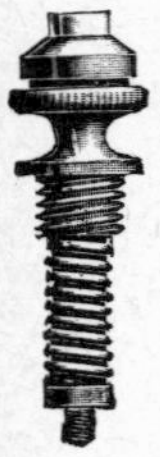

26/2

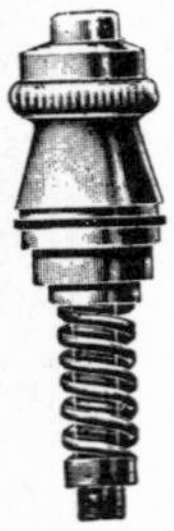

26/3

Stronger and better finish.

No. 26/2	$1^{7}/_{32}$" long . . .	each	-/4
— 26/2 N	$1^{7}/_{32}$" nickelled .	—	-/5
— 26/3	$1^{3}/_{8}$" long . . .	—	-/5
— 26/3 N	$1^{3}/_{8}$" nickelled .	—	-/6

Lever Safety Valve and Weight.

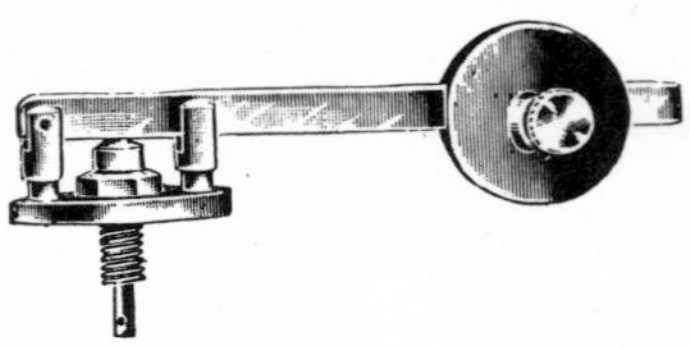

40/3

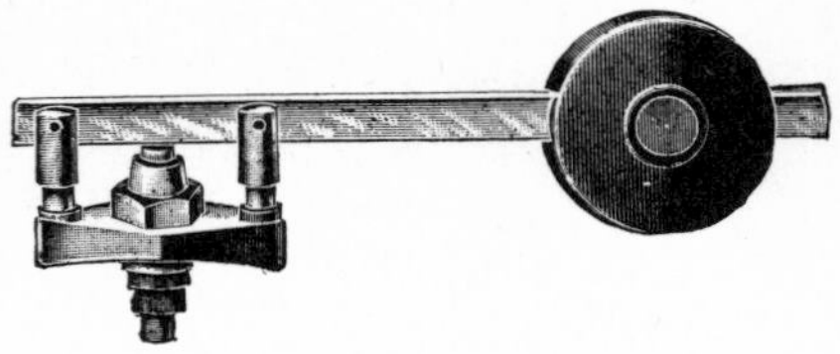

40 L/3

in brass, very strong design, with ferrule.

No. 40/3	for vertical boilers, with flat top	each	1/-
— 40/3 N	do., nickelled	—	1/2
— 40 L/3	for horizontal boilers, with curved top	—	1/6
— 40 L/3 N	do., nickelled	—	1/8

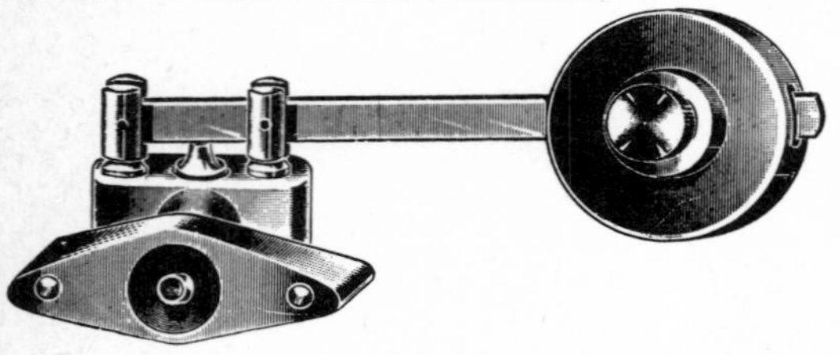

40/4—6

Large Lever Safety Valve with Weight.

Strongly made, in brass, with ferrule.

No. 40/4	brass	each	3/8
— 40/4 N	do., nickelled	—	4/-
— 40/5	brass	—	4/4
— 40/5 N	do., nickelled	—	5/-
— 40/6	brass	—	5/2
— 40/6 N	do., nickelled	—	5/10

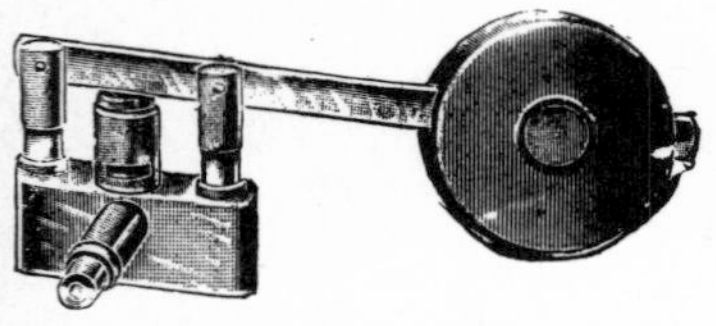

40/7— 8

Best Quality "Precision" Safety Valve and Weight.

Very strong and beautifully finished, in brass, with ferrule.

No. 40/7	brass	each	1/8
— 40/7 N	do., nickelled	—	1/10
— 40/8	brass	—	1/10
— 40/8 N	do., nickelled	—	2/-

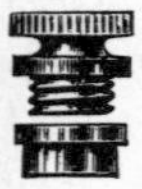

52

Filling Screws

brass, with ferrule.

No. 52/1 M	screwed $^{1}/_{4}$"	doz.	1/8
— 52/1 N	do., nickelled	—	1/10
— 52/2 M	screwed $^{9}/_{32}$"	—	2/10
— 52/2 N	do., nickelled	—	3/2

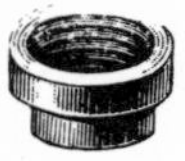

42

Ferrules

in brass, with inside screw.

No. 42/3	screwed $^{3}/_{16}$" . . .	dozen	-/4
— 42/3 N	do., nickelled . . .	—	-/5
— 42/4	screwed $^{1}/_{4}$"	—	-/6
— 42/4 N	do, nickelled . . .	—	-/8
— 42/5	screwed $^{9}/_{32}$"	—	-/9
— 42/5 N	do., nickelled. . . .	—	-/10

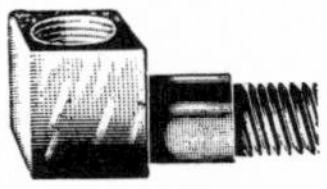

34/10

Angle Adaptors

for fixing fittings, such as pressure gauge, whistles, side ways in boiler, strongly made, with ferrule.

No. 34/10	$^{3}/_{4}$" long . .	each	-/4
— 34/10 N	do., nickelled	—	-/5

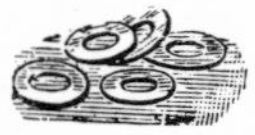

Washers

No. 42 V/1	fibre, $^{3}/_{16}$" inside diam.	Grs.	1/-
— 42 V/2	— $^{1}/_{4}$" — —	—	1/-
— 42 V/3	**rubber,** for straight water gauges, $^{5}/_{32}$" inside and $^{1}/_{4}$" outside diam. .	dozen	-/3
— 42 V/4	**do.,** for bent water gauges, $^{1}/_{8}$" inside and $^{9}/_{32}$" outside diam.	—	-/5
— 42 V/5	**do.,** for spring safety valves 26/1	—	-/4
— 42 V/5½	**do.,** for spring safety valves 26/2 and 26/3, very stiff	—	-/4
— 42 V/6	for filling screws 52/2, $^{9}/_{32}$" inside and $^{7}/_{16}$" outside diam.	—	-/8

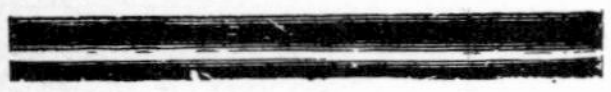

41

Brass Steam Pipe.

No.	41/2	2,5	2,8	3	3,5	4	5	6
diameter	$^{1}/_{16}$	$^{3}/_{32}$	$^{7}/_{64}$	$^{1}/_{8}$	$^{1}/_{8}$	$^{5}/_{32}$	$^{3}/_{16}$	$^{1}/_{4}$"
yard	-/8	-/9	-/10	1/-	1/-	1/2	1/6	1/8

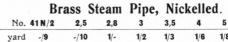

Brass Steam Pipe, Nickelled.

No.	41 N/2	2,5	2,8	3	3,5	4	5	6
yard	-/9	-/10	1/-	1/2	1/3	1/6	1/8	1/10

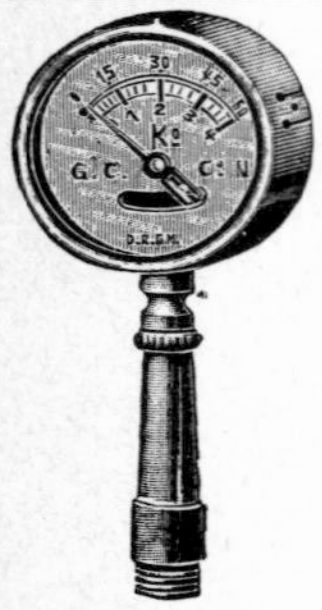

34/23

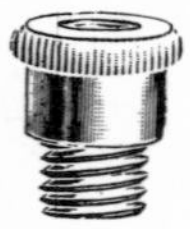

34/1 and 2

Pressure Gauges.

No. 34/23 M	**Pressure gauges** in brass, reliable in action, indicates to 4 kg., about 9 lbs. per □", 1" diameter	each	2/-
— 34/23 N	do., nickelled.	—	2/4

Pressure Gauge Boiler Screw

to fit above gauges.

These can be put in the place of a filling screw on the top of boiler and pressure gauges 34/23 M and 34/23 N can be fitted without trouble. The fitting has a screw of about $^{7}/_{32}$" outside diameter.

No. 34/1 M	in brass	each	-/2
— 34/1 N	the same highly nickelled	—	-/2
— 34/2 M	as above, with $^{5}/_{16}$" screw	—	-/2
— 34/2 N	ditto nickelled.	—	-/3

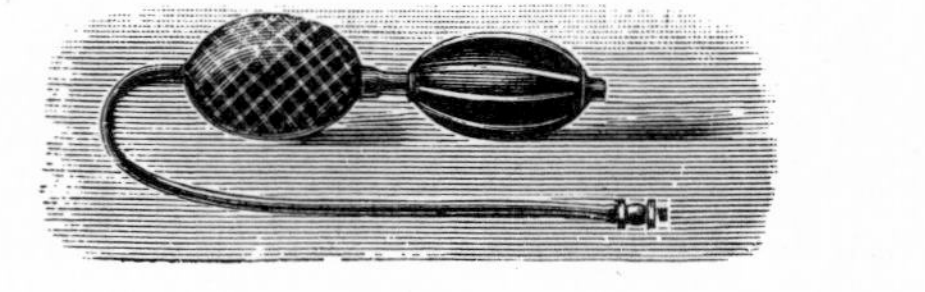

No. 33 C

Rubber Ball

with **metal air compressor**

for testing engines by means of compressed air. The metal compressor has the advantage in holding a pressure of about 1½ Atm. 20 lbs., whereas with a simple air-blower this is not possible without bursting. Supplied with two mouth pieces and will fit all engines, each 8/6

Trade Mark.

Governors.

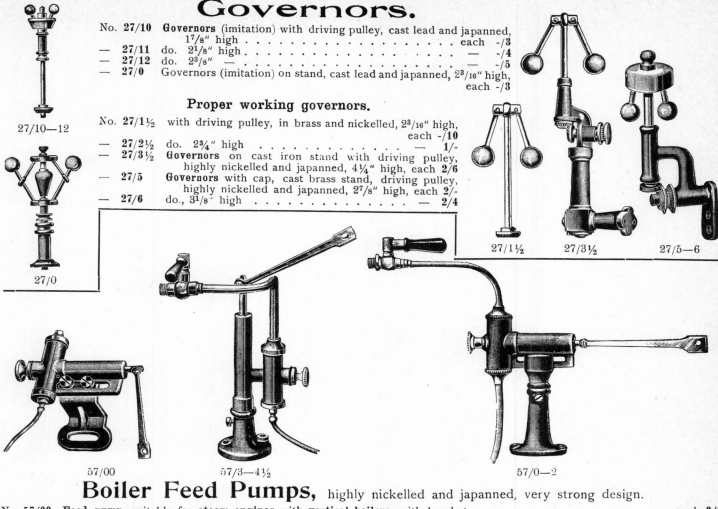

No. **27/10** **Governors** (imitation) with driving pulley, cast lead and japanned,
  1⁷/₈" high . . . . each -/3
— **27/11** do. 2¹/₈" high . . . . — -/4
— **27/12** do. 2³/₈" — . . . . — -/5
— **27/0** **Governors** (imitation) on stand, cast lead and japanned, 2³/₁₆" high,
  each -/3

Proper working governors.

No. **27/1½** with driving pulley, in brass and nickelled, 2³/₁₆" high,
  each -/10
— **27/2½** do. 2¾" high . . . . — 1/-
— **27/3½** **Governors** on cast iron stand with driving pulley,
  highly nickelled and japanned, 4¼" high, each 2/6
— **27/5** **Governors** with cap, cast brass stand, driving pulley,
  highly nickelled and japanned, 2⁷/₈" high, each 2/-
— **27/6** do., 3¹/₈" high . . . . — 2/4

27/10—12

27/0

27/1½   27/3½   27/5—6

57/00   57/3—4½   57/0—2

Boiler Feed Pumps, highly nickelled and japanned, very strong design.

No. **57/00** **Feed pump**, suitable for **steam engines** with **vertical boilers**, with bracket . . . . each **3/2**
— **57/3** ditto, with cast iron stand, delivery pipe with cock and rubber supply pipe, for small boilers . . . . — **4/-**
— **57/4** — larger for medium size boilers . . . . — **4/-**
— **57/4½** — larger than 57/4 for large boilers . . . . : . . . . — **4/-**
— **57/0** **Feed pump** suitable for **steam engines** with **horizontal boilers** with cast iron stand, delivery pipe with cock
  and rubber supply pipe, for small boilers . . . . — **4/-**
— **57/1** ditto, larger for medium size boilers . . . . — **5/-**
— **57/2** — larger than 57/1 for large boilers . . . . — **6/6**

Screws (iron).

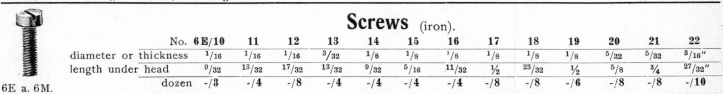

	No. 6E/10	11	12	13	14	15	16	17	18	19	20	21	22
diameter or thickness	¹/₁₆	¹/₁₆	¹/₁₆	³/₃₂	¹/₈	¹/₈	¹/₈	¹/₈	¹/₈	¹/₈	⁵/₃₂	⁵/₃₂	³/₁₆"
length under head	⁹/₃₂	¹³/₃₂	¹⁷/₃₂	¹³/₃₂	⁹/₃₂	⁵/₁₆	¹¹/₃₂	½	²³/₃₂	½	⁵/₈	¾	²⁷/₃₂"
dozen	-/3	-/4	-/8	-/4	-/4	-/4	-/4	-/8	-/8	-/6	-/8	-/8	-/10

6E a. 6M.

Screws (brass).

	No. 6M/10	11	12	13	14	15	16	17	18
diameter	¹/₁₆	¹/₁₆	³/₃₂	³/₃₂	¹/₈	¹/₈	¹/₈	³/₁₆	³/₁₆"
length under head	¼	¹⁷/₃₂	³/₁₆	¹¹/₃₂	½	¹⁷/₃₂	²¹/₃₂	²¹/₃₂	²⁷/₃₂"
dozen	-/3	-/6	-/4	-/4	-/6	-/8	-/6	-/8	1/10

Screws with plain part.

6M/20

	No. 6M/20	21	22	23	24	25	26	27	28
length	¹¹/₃₂	¼	¹¹/₃₂	³/₈	⁷/₁₆	²/₃	¹⁵/₃₂	¹⁹/₃₂	²⁹/₃₂"
length of screwed portion	¹/₁₆	¹/₁₆	¹/₁₆	³/₃₂	³/₃₂	³/₃₂	¹/₈	¹/₁₆	¼"
diameter of screw thread	¹/₁₆	¹/₁₆	³/₃₂	³/₃₂	³/₃₂	³/₃₂	¹/₈	¹/₁₆	⁵/₃₂"
dozen	-/6	-/4	-/4	-/6	-/6	-/6	-/8	1/-	1/8

Nuts (brass).

No. **6/0** hexagon, up to 3/32" diam. of thread . dozen -/3
— **6/1** ditto, up to 1/8" — — — — -/4
— **6/2** — — 1/8" — — — — -/4
— **6/3** — — 5/32" — — — — -/4
— **6/4** round up to 1/16" — — — — -/2
— **6/5** — 3/32" — — — — -,2
— **6/5½** — 1/8" — — — — -/4
— **6/5¾** — 3/16" — — — — -/6
— **6/6** — suitable for oscillating cylinders of No. 688,
  dozen -/4
— **6/7** — suitable for oscillating cylinders of No. 677,
  dozen -/5

Large Fittings for large size Boilers,
made of brass and heavy design, best finish.

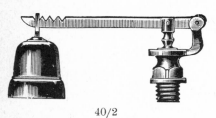

40/2

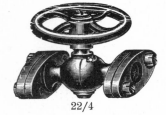

22/4

35/1

23/2

25/3

35/2

35/3

34/20—50

No. **40/2** **Lever safety valve** and **weight**, 4″ long and 2″ high
each **5/8**

— **22/4** **Through way cock** with wheel and flanges, 2″ diameter, 2″ high . . . . each **7/4**

— **23/2** **Blow off cock**, 2″ high, with wood handle — **3/8**

— **25/3** **Water gauge** with removable cap for changing the glass, stuffing box nuts with packing rings, 2 main cocks and one blow through cock, length over all 7¼″ . each **14/6**

— **35/1** **Screwed flanges**, 1⁷⁄₁₆″ high, 1¼″ wide . . — **3/6**

— **35/2** **Filling screw**, 1⅓″ high . . . . — **1/6**

— **35/3** **Pressure gauge screw**, with inside thread, 1³⁄₈″ high
each **1/10**

— **34/50** **"Precision" pressure gauge**, with spring tube, very strong pattern, in iron case with brass cap, 4 Atm. about 60 lbs, screwed dial, 2″ diameter . . . . . each **3/8**

— **34/20** ditto, 1³⁄₁₆″ diameter . . . . — **7/6**

— **24/3** **Steam whistle**, 4″ high, ½″ diameter . . . — **5/8**

— **42/2** **Ferrules** tapped to suit above fittings . . . — -/8

— **27/4** **Large governor** with balls and sliding weight in brass, highly nickelled and japanned, very best finish . . . each **9/6**

Feed pumps.

No. **57** in brass, **nickelled, very best finish**, suitable for all the large engines, with **geared drive** and dri- ving pulley, **mounted on cast iron stand** 5½″ high, 2½″ wide, each **14/-**

24/3

42/2

27/4

57

Trade  Mark,

47 C

47 D

47 A

47 B

47 F

47 E/8

47 E/6—7

Wall Brackets

No. 47 C   cast in lead, with holes for shaft
and fixing screws, 1³/₄" high, dozen 2/6

Bearings

No. 47 D   cast lead, with holes for shaft
and fixing screws, ¹³/₁₆" high, dozen 1/2
— 47 A/1 ditto, ²⁵/₃₂" high . . . . — -/10
— 47 A/2 — ¹⁵/₁₆" — . . . . — 1/-
— 47 A/3 — 1¹/₁₆" — . . . . — 1/2
— 47 B/1 — in iron, ¹³/₁₆" high . each -/2
— 47 B/2 — — — ¹⁵/₁₆" — . — -/2

Bearings

in cast iron.

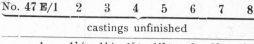
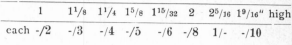

No. 47 E/1	2	3	4	5	6	7	8
castings unfinished							
1	1¹/₈	1¹/₄	1⁵/₈	1¹⁵/₃₂	2	2⁵/₁₆	1⁹/₁₆" high
each -/2	-/3	-/4	-/5	-/6	-/8	1/-	-/10

No. 47 F/1	2	3	4	5	6	7	8
holes for shaft and fixing screws bored							
1	1¹/₈	1¹/₄	1⁵/₈	1¹⁵/₃₂	2	2⁵/₁₆	1⁹/₁₆" high
each -/4	-/6	-/7	-/8	1/-	1/6	2/4	2/8

Feet for Engine Bases

in cast iron.

47/10

No. 47/10   ⁹/₁₆" high, with fixing screw-holes
dozen 1/-

Shafting Supports.

47 N/4—5

47/1—3

47/11 — 12   47 N/6

No. 47/1   cast lead with shaft- and screw-holes, 3" high . . each -/4
— 47/2   ditto, 4" high, light pattern . . . . — -/2
— 47/3   — 6" — — — . . . . . — -/5
— 47/11   cast iron, not bored, 1³/₄" high . . . . . . — -/2
— 47/12   — — — — 2⁵/₃₂" — . . . . . — -/3
— 47 N/4   cast lead, with holes for shaft and fixing screws,
6⁹/₁₆" high . . . . — -/6
— 47 N/5   cast iron, with holes for shaft and fixing screws,
8½" high . . . . — 1/4
— 47 N/6   cast iron, with holes for shaft and fixing screws,
8¼" high . . . . — 1/10

29 W

Shafting

No. 29 W   iron, with keyway, ³/₁₆" thick . . . . . yard 1/-
— 29 W/1 the same, without keyway, ¼" thick . . . — -/4

---

29 K   29 F

No. 29 K Couplings to
connect shafting with
keys, cast lead with
hole for shaft and key-
way, ¹³/₁₆" diameter
dozen -/10

— 29 F Keys for same
diameter gross . 1/10

Driving pulleys

with groove in **cast
lead**, with hole.

29/0—7

No. 29/0	0½	1	1¼
diam. ⁷/₁₆"	¹⁹/₃₂"	²⁵/₃₂"	1⁷/₃₂"
dozen -/4	-/6	-/8	1/-
No. 29/1½	2	3	7
diam. 1¹³/₃₂"	1²⁷/₃₂"	2³/₈"	3¹¹/₁₆"
dozen 1/4	1/6	2/-	3/8

Driving pulleys

with groove in cast
lead, with hole
and **keyway**.

29 E

No. 29 E/1	1½	3
diam. ²⁵/₃₂"	1¹³/₃₂"	2³/₈"
dozen 1/-	1/2	2/6

Lighter pattern.

No. 29 E/1½	1¼	2
diam. ¹⁵/₁₆"	1¼"	1⁵/₈"
dozen -/8	-/10	1/-

29 D   29 R/4

No. 29 D/1½   Driving pulley,
with double groove, in cast
lead, with hole, 1³/₈" diam.
dozen 1/2

— 29 R/4 Pulley in cast lead,
with hole, 2⁹/₁₆" diam, doz. 3/4

Grooved Brass Pulleys

well turned,
with hole

29 M

No. 29 M/0	1	1½	2
diameter ⁷/₁₆"	¹⁹/₃₂"	²⁹/₃₂"	1¹³/₁₆"
dozen -/8	1/8	7/4	9/8

Cast Iron Pulleys

castings unfinished,

29 G

No. 29 G/1	2	3	4
diam. ²⁵/₃₂"	1⁷/₁₆"	1½"	2⁷/₁₆"
dozen 2/-	3/-	3/-	4/10

Ditto **turned** and with fixing screw.

No. 29 A/1	2	3	4
diam. ²⁵/₃₂"	1⁷/₁₆"	1½"	2⁷/₁₆"
each -/8	-/10	1/-	1/2

Driving Band

(coiled brass)

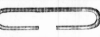

No. 29 S/0	diameter ¹/₃₂", 100 gards 17/-, ñ. 15/-
— 29 S/1	— ¹/₁₆", yard -/4, — 11/-
— 29 S/2	— ³/₃₂", — -/8, — 11/-

Driving Band

No. 29 (**corded yarn**) green   ball 1/4

Flywheels, in **cast lead**, **light** pattern, not turned.

No. 28 L/0	1	2	3	4	5	6
diameter 1¹¹/₃₂	1½	1¾	2	2⁷/₁₆	2¹⁵/₁₆	3¼"
dozen 1/2	1/6	2/8	1/8	2/6	3/-	3/2

28 L/3—6

Flywheels, in **cast lead**, with hole, **heavier** pattern.

	Size 0	1	2	3	4	5
	diameter 2	2⁵/₃₂	2³/₈	2¾	3	3¹¹/₃₂"
No. 28 U not turned or japanned . . . . . dozen 2/-	2/8	3/-	4/2	4/10	6/-
— 28 T turned, japanned and nickelled with groove, — 3/10	4/6	5/6	6/8	7/10	9/8

28 U

Flywheels, in **cast lead**, with hole, **very heavy** pattern.

	Size 1	2
	diameter 2⁵/₈	2¾"
No. 28 M not turned or japanned . . . . each -/8	-/8
— 28 V turned, japanned and nickelled with groove . . . — 1/-	1/-

Massive flywheels in cast iron

castings only, not bored

No. 28 D/0	1	2	3	4	5	6	7	8	9
diameter 2⁹/₁₆	3	3¹/₈	3⁹/₁₆	4	4⁵/₁₆	4¾	5¹/₈	6	7¹/₈"
each -/5	-/6	-/8	-/10	1/-	1/2	1/4	1/10	3/-	4/8

28 D—F

turned and bored

No. 28 E/0	1	2	3	4	5	6	7	8	9
each 1/-	1/2	1/4	1/8	1/10	2/4	2/8	3/-	4/6	6/8

turned, bored, nickelled and japanned, without groove

No. 28 G/0	1	2	3	4	5	6	7	8	9
each 1/6	2/-	2/4	2/8	3/2	3/10	4/6	5/2	7/-	10/-

Heavier pattern flywheels in cast iron, castings only, unbored

No. 28 F/3	5	7	9	10
diameter 3⁹/₁₆	4⁵/₁₆	5¹/₈	7¹/₈	13¹/₈"
weight about ³/₄	1	1½	5	7 ℔
each 1/2	2/-	3/-	7/-	8/8

Massive cast iron flywheels with **extension piece for pulley**

castings only, not bored		turned and bored, with groove		turned, bored, nickelled and japanned with groove	
No. 28 S/1	2	No. 28 SE/1	2	No. 28 SG/1	2
diameter 3⁹/₁₆	4⁵/₁₆"	diameter 3⁹/₁₆	4⁵/₁₆"	diameter 3⁹/₁₆	4⁵/₁₆"
each -/8	1/2	each 1/8	2/-	each 2/10	3/8

the same, **but very much heavier pattern**

No. 28 S/3	4	No. 28 SE/3	4	No. 28 SG/3	4
diameter 3⁹/₁₆	4⁵/₁₆"	diameter 3⁹/₁₆	4⁵/₁₆"	diameter 3⁹/₁₆	4⁵/₁₆"
each 1/4	1/8	each 2/4	2/10	each 3/-	4/-

28 S

Massive cast iron flywheels with **double grooves**

castings only, not bored		turned and bored with double groove		turned, bored, nickelled and japanned, with double groove	
No. 28 Z/1	2	No. 28 ZE/1	2	No. 28 ZG/1	2
diameter 2³/₈	2¾ "	diameter 2³/₈	2¾ "	diameter 2³/₈	2¾ "
each -/8	-/9	each 1/8	1/10	each 2/4	2/6

28 Z

Loose pulley in hook

No. **29/10** lead pulley on holder, 1⁹/₁₆" long, dozen -/9
— **29/11** massive pattern, specially made for exercising in schools, it is fitted with swivelling handle, easily turned and strengthened at corners, 3¹/₁₆" long . . . . each -/8
(Suitable clamps No. 48/5).

29/10 29/11

48/9 48/5

Table clamps

for fixing engines etc. to the table

No. **48/9** japanned metal, will open 2" . . . each -/2
— **48/5** wood, will open 2" . . . . . . — 1/-

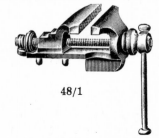

48/1

Vices

No. **48/1** cast lead, japanned, 2" long . . . . each -/4

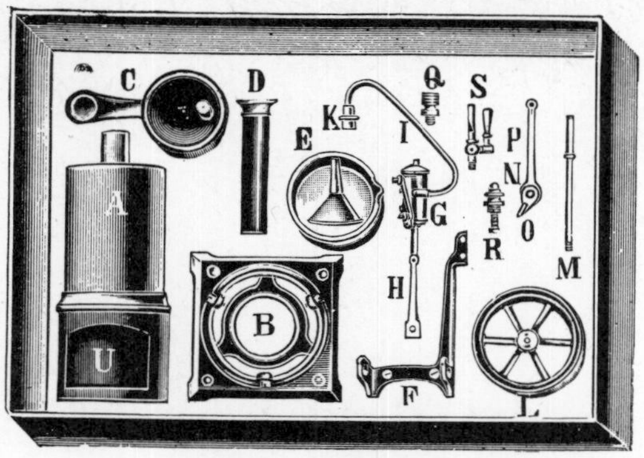

18/8

18/10

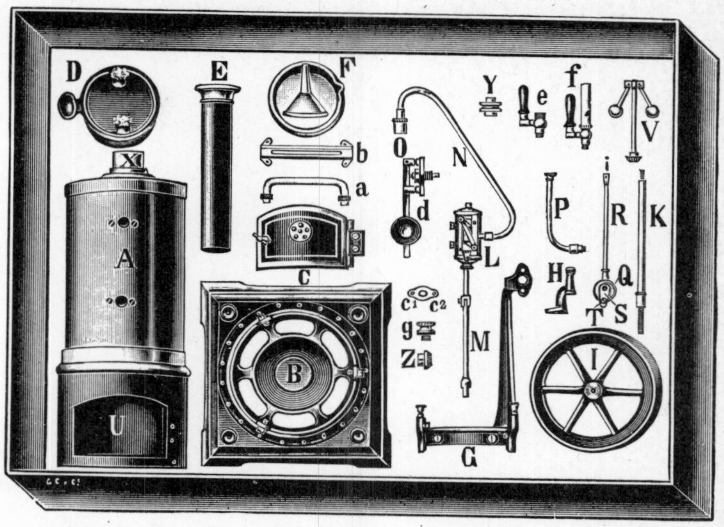

Steam Engines in parts.

Ready for assembling. Very instructive and amusing.

No. **18/8** **"The little mechanic"** contains all the parts of a steam engine and boiler. Every part ready for screwing together. **No soldering required.** Sewn on card, in handsome cardboard box, with full instructions for putting together . . . . each **11/-**

— **18/10** **"The big mechanic"** contains all the parts of a handsome large steam engine and boiler. Every part ready for screwing together. **No soldering required.** Sewn on card, in handsome cardboard box, with full instructions for putting together . . . . each **36/-**

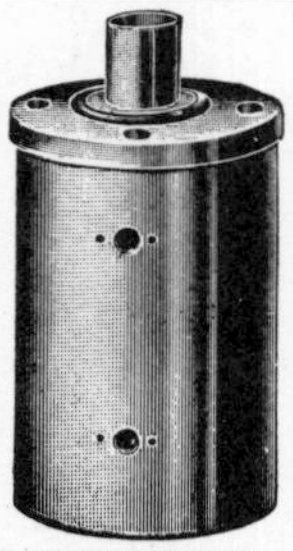

Boilers for Steam Engines,

Very strong quality, made of steel-blue oxydized brass, with holes for fittings.

Vertical type

(with centre flue and socket for chimney).

No. **21/1**	$2^5/_8$" high without chimney socket,	$1^{15}/_{16}$" diam.,	each	**1/-**
— **21/2**	3" — — — —	$2^5/_{32}$"	— —	**1/4**
— **21/3**	$3^5/_{16}$" — — — —	$2^7/_{16}$"	— —	**1/8**
— **21/4**	4" — — — —	$2^7/_{16}$"	— —	**3/-**
— **21/5**	$4^5/_{16}$" — — — —	$2^3/_4$"	— —	**4/-**
— **21/6**	5" — — — —	$3^1/_8$"	— —	**5/-**

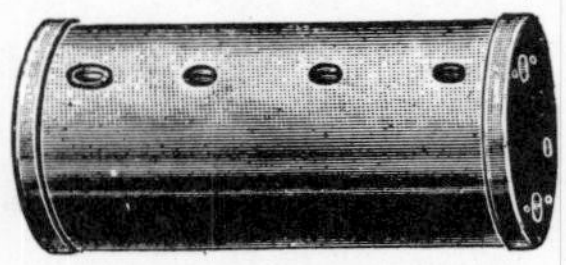

21/13—17, 10—12

Horizontal type.

No. **21/13**	$3^1/_2$" long,	$1^{17}/_{32}$" diamet,	each	**1/2**
— **21/14**	4" —	$1^3/_4$"	— —	**1/6**
— **21/15**	$4^7/_{16}$" —	$1^{15}/_{16}$"	— —	**1/8**
— **21/16**	$7^7/_8$" —	$1^{13}/_{16}$"	— —	**2/8**
— **21/17**	$9^1/_2$" —	$3^{15}/_{32}$"	— —	**11/-**

The same but of simple design and plain brass

No. **21/10**	$3^1/_2$" long,	$1^{17}/_{32}$" diamet.,	each	**-/6**
— **21/11**	4" —	$1^3/_4$"	— —	**-/10**
— **21/12**	$4^7/_{16}$ —	$1^{15}/_{16}$"	— —	**1/-**

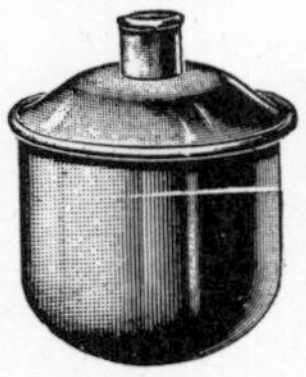

No. 48/15 **Copper boilers**

made of pure copper, for laboratory use . . . . each **3/-**

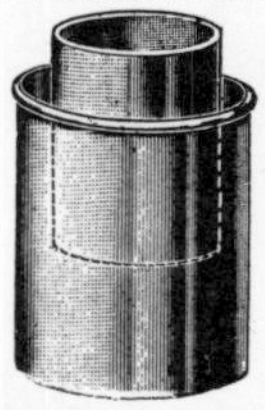

No. **48/20** **Calorimeters**

consisting of two thin brass containers, nickelled on the outsides, for determination of specific heat (calories).

each **1/6**

Lamps for Steam Engines.

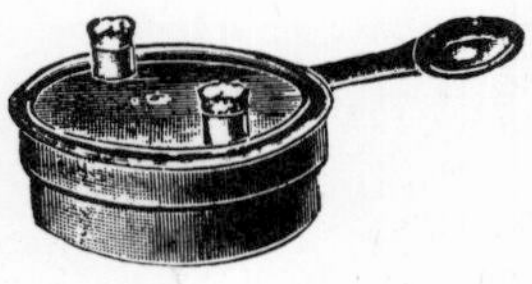

12 D

Spirit lamps

of plain tin-plate, round,

for 1 flame

No. **12 N/1**	$1^1/_2$" diameter	each	**-/2**
— **12 N/2**	$1^7/_8$" —	—	**-/3**
— **12 N/3**	$2^5/_8$" —	—	**-/4**

for 2 flames

No. **12 D/1**	$1^7/_8$" diameter	—	**-/2**
— **12 D/2**	$2^1/_4$" —	—	**-/4**
— **12 D/3**	$2^5/_8$" —	—	**-/5**

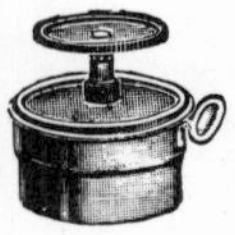

12 V

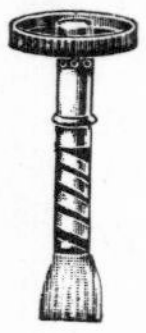

12 V B

Spirit vapour lamps

D. R.-G.-M.

of plain tin-plate, round for **vertical boilers.**

No.	**12 V/1**	**2**	**3**	**4**	**5**
diameter of reservoir	$1^7/_8$	$2^9/_{32}$	$2^9/_{32}$	$2^5/_8$	$2^5/_8$"
— of burner cap	$^5/_8$	$^{13}/_{16}$	1	$1^1/_8$	$1^3/_{16}$"
each	**-/6**	**-/8**	**-/10**	**-/10**	**1/-**

Vaporizer only, for above lamps, with wickholder and wick

No.	**12 V B/1**	**2**	**3**	**4**	**5**
each	**-/3**	**-/4**	**-/5**	**-/6**	**-/6**

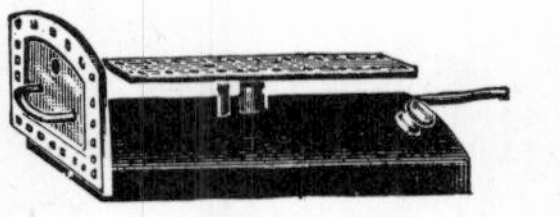

12 V/10

Spirit vapour lamps,

D. R.-G.-M.,

of plain tin-plate with handsomely nickelled fire door, also filling screw, for **horizontal boilers.**

No. **12 V/10**	$4^1/_2$" long,	$1^7/_8$" wide,	$1^3/_8$" high,	each	**2/8**
— **12 V/11**	$4^{13}/_{16}$" —	$1^7/_8$" —	$1^1/_2$" —	—	**3/-**
— **12 V/12**	$5^3/_8$" —	$1^7/_8$" —	$1^5/_8$" —	—	**3/2**

Locomotive lamps of plain tin-plate (locos see page 58).

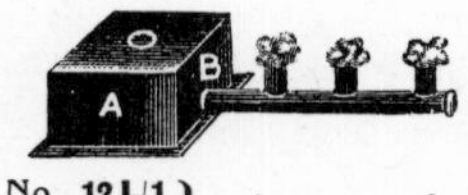

Spirit lamps with wick.

No.	for gauge	length	height	reservoir	flame	each
No. **12 L/1**	for gauge 0	$5^3/_8$"	$^{25}/_{32}$"	$1^1/_2 \times 1^3/_8$"	2	**-/5**
— **12 L/2**	for gauge 0	$5^1/_2$"	$^{25}/_{32}$"	$1^1/_2 \times 1^3/_8$"	4	**-/6**
— **12 L/3**	— — 1	$5^{11}/_{16}$"	$1^1/_{16}$"	$1^{13}/_{16} \times 1^5/_8$"	3	**-/8**
— **12 L/4**	— — 1	$5^{11}/_{16}$"	$1^1/_{16}$"	$1^{13}/_{16} \times 1^5/_8$"	4	**-/10**

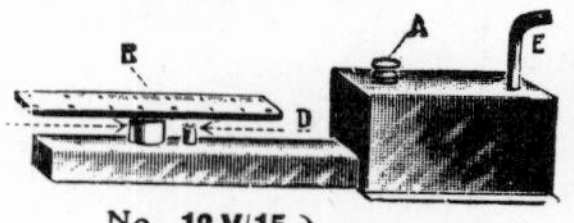

Spirit vapour lamps, D. R.-G.-M., of plain tin-plate, strongly made, with filling screw.

No.	for gauge	length	height	reservoir	No. of holes	each
No. **12 V/15**	for gauge 0	$5^{11}/_{16}$"	$^{29}/_{32}$"	$1^3/_{16} \times 2^3/_{16}$"	12	**2/-**
— **12 V/16**	for gauge 0	$6^7/_8$"	$1^3/_{16}$"	$1^1/_4 \times 2^5/_8$"	16	**2/6**
— **12 V/17**	— — 1	$5^5/_{16}$"	$1^5/_{16}$"	$^3/_4 \times 2$"	12	**2/-**
— **12 V/18**	— — 1	$6^7/_8$"	$1^{13}/_{32}$"	$1^1/_8 \times 2^3/_8$	16	**3/-**

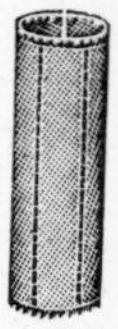

7 F

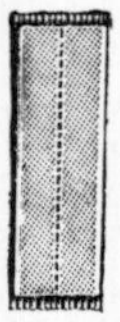

7 A

Wicks for lamps.

For **spirit lamps**

No.	**7 F/3'''**	**4'''**	**5'''**	**6'''**
diameter	$^3/_{16}$	$^9/_{32}$	$^5/_{16}$	$^3/_8$"
yard	**-/4**	**-/5**	**-/6**	**-/8**

Spirit wick f vapour lamps

No.	**7 V/1**	**2**	**3**
to suit	12 V/1	2	3
yard	**-/1**	**-/2**	**-/2**

Astral wick for hot air engines.

No.	**7 A/8'''**	**10'''**
width	$^5/_8$	$^7/_8$"
yard	**-/4**	**-/5**

Wick string for vapour lamps.

No. **7 V/0** $^1/_8$" diameter, each **-/1**

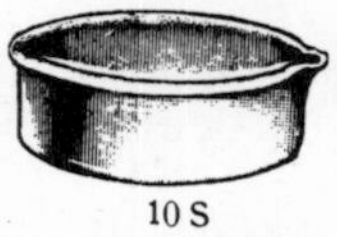

10 S

No. **10 S/1½** **Tin measures,** $1^7/_8$" diameter, dozen **-/8**

No. **10 S/2** same, $2^5/_{32}$" diameter, dozen **1/-**

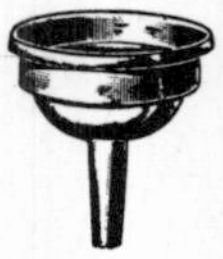

11

No. **11/1** **Small funnels,** $1^{15}/_{32}$" diameter, dozen **-/8**

— **11/2** **Larger funnels,** $2^1/_8$" diameter . . . dozen **1/6**

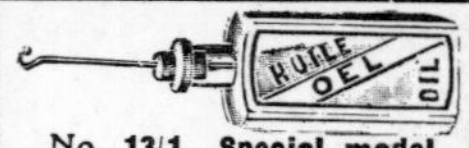

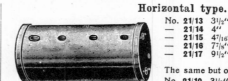

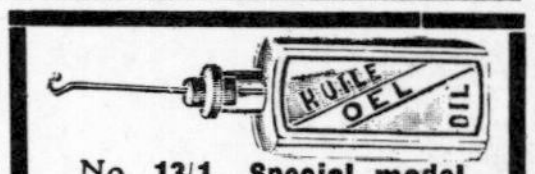

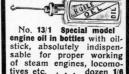

No. **13/1** **Special model engine oil in bottles** with oilstick, absolutely indispensable for proper working of steam engines, locomotives etc. . . . dozen **1/6**

Working Models for attaching to engines.

Cheap class in japanned tin.

No. 111/00 Circular saw	No. 173/00 Grindstone	No. 196/00	No. 615/00 Lathe
3¼" high,	3¼" high,	Drilling machine	3¼" high,
dozen **3/-**	dozen **3/6**	4⅛" high, dozen **4/-**	dozen **4/10**

Better quality made from castings, highly japanned.

No. 615/1	No. 615/2	No. 630/0	No. 636/0
Small lathe	**Large lathe**	**Band saw**	**Press**
mounted on walnut,	mounted on walnut,	5" high	with dies,
4¼" long, 3¼" high,	6" long, 4⅛" high	each **1/8**	5¼" high,
each **1/8**	each **2/6**		each **1/8**

High quality design and finish.

No. 173/0	No. 196/0	No. 651/00	No. 649/0
Grindstone	**Drilling machine**	**Helve or tilt hammer**	**Drop hammer**
4" high	5¼" high	mounted on walnut,	6¾" high
each **2/6**	each **2/6**	6¾" long, 3" high, each **1/10**	each **1/8**

Trade Mark.

Working Models (figures)

with original movements and novel coloured plastic figures.

No. 195/6
Circular saw and man
dozen **9/-**

No. 195/7
Man drilling
dozen **8/6**

No. 195/8
Grinder
dozen **9/-**

No. 195/9
Lock-Smith filing
dozen **9/6**

No. 195/10
Black-Smith
dozen **9/-**

No. 195/2
Miner
dozen **9/-**

No. 195/3
Cooper
dozen **8/6**

No. 195/5
Man planing
dozen **8/6**

No. 195/14
Man sawing wood
dozen **8/-**

No. 195/15
Man chopping wood
dozen **8/6**

No. 195/16
Butcher
dozen **11/-**

No. 195/17
Turner
dozen **9/6**

No. 195/11
Smiths
dozen **14/6**

No. 195/12
Carpenters
dozen **13/-**

No. 195/4
Cooper, runs round barrel when
working, very novel
dozen **18/-**

No. 195/13
Firemen, with working fire engine
dozen **30/-**

No. 195/20
Organ grinder,
with organ of 8 notes
dozen **15/-**

Cheap mechanical Workshops

consisting of:

1 shafting, simple working models mounted on tiled face floor, with grooved pulley for driving by engine. In the sets with figures, the latter are the coloured and plastic type, with novel movements; the sets of models **all run easily** and require a **minimum** of power to drive.

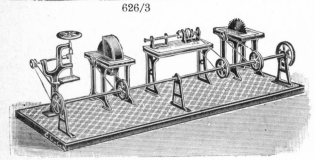

626/3

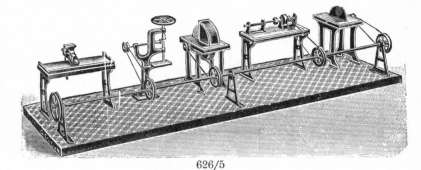

626/5

626/4

626/15

626/14

No. **626/3** with circular saw, lathe, grindstone, 10" long . . each **1/10**
— **626/4** ditto with 1 drilling machine, 13" long . . . . . — **2/4**
— **626/5** — also work bench and vice, 17½" long . . . — **3/-**

Above **workshops** with **moving figures:**

No. **626/13**	**626/14**	**626/15**	
with 3	4	5	models
each **3/-**	**4/-**	**5/-**	

626/13

Complete Factories

No. **626/20** **Locksmith's shop** with 1 smith at the fire, 1 smith at the anvil, 1 fitter, 1 machine hand, 1 grinder, shafting and arc lamp, 16½" long, 6¼" wide, 8¾" high, **strong quality** each **7/-**

No. **626/21** the above, **larger**, also 1 turner and 1 arc lamp extra, 21½" long, 6½" wide, 8¾" high . . . . each **8/6**

626/20 and 626/21

Trade Mark.

Working Models (Hand-workers).

698/16

No. **698/16 Fitter,** filing, with vice and drilling machine, handsomely japanned, 5¼" long, 5¼" high dozen **15/6**

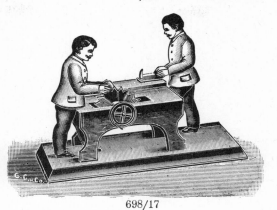

698/17

No. **698/17 Joiner's shop,** consisting of planer and circular sawyer, highly japanned, 6½" long, 4½" high, dozen **15/6**

108/00

No. **108/00 Smith** handsomely japanned, 5" high, 5¼" wide dozen **14/6**

108/1

108/2

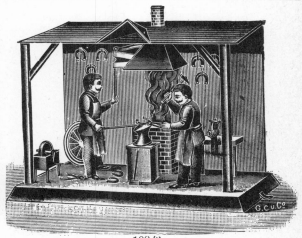

108/3

651/12

Smithies

in quite original design,
with moving figures, handsomely japanned.

No.								
651/12	8¼" long,	4¾" high			with 1 figure,	dozen	**15/6**
— **108/1**	6¾" —	7" —	4½" wide	—	1	—	—	**24/-**
— **108/2**	8¼" —	8¾" —	5½" —	—	2 figures,	—	**36/-**
— **108/3**	13" —	10" —	6" —	—	2	—	each	**5/8**

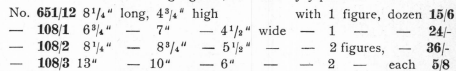

626/22

Complete factories

No. **626/22 Joinery** with 1 hand sawyer, 1 planer, 1 hand sawyer, 1 grinder, shafting and 1 arc lamp, 17" long, 6½" wide, 8¾" high, strong design . . . each **7/6**

Trade Mark.

Working Models (continued)

698/31

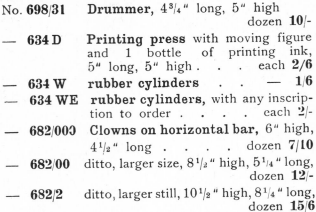

634 D

No. **698/31**   **Drummer**, 4³/₄" long, 5" high
dozen **10/-**

— **634 D**   **Printing press** with moving figure and 1 bottle of printing ink, 5" long, 5" high . . . each **2/6**

— **634 W**   rubber cylinders . . — **1/6**

— **634 WE**   rubber cylinders, with any inscription to order . . . . each **2/-**

— **682/000**   **Clowns on horizontal bar**, 6" high, 4¹/₂" long . . . . dozen **7/10**

— **682/00**   ditto, larger size, 8¹/₂" high, 5¹/₄" long, dozen **12/-**

— **682/2**   ditto, larger still, 10¹/₂" high, 8¹/₄" long, dozen **15/6**

— **698/32**   **"Looping, the loop"**, quite original, 8¹/₂" long, 5¹/₄" high, dozen **21/-**

682/000

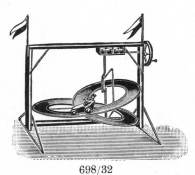
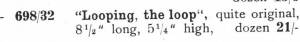

698/32

682/2

Zoeotropes

of russian iron, fitted with grooved pulley for driving by a model engine, for giving an exhibition of living pictures, with 12 pictures.

773/2¹/₂

773/4¹/₂

No. **773/2¹/₂**	**3¹/₂**	**4¹/₂**	**5¹/₂**
5"	6¹/₄"	7"	9¹/₂" diameter
each **1/8**	**2/6**	**3/6**	**4/8**

Extra Pictures, 2 further sets

No. **773/2 B**	**3 B**	**4 B**	**5 B**
suitable for 773/2¹/₂	3¹/₂	4¹/₂	5¹/₂
set of 12 pictures -/6	-/8	1/-	1/4

Musical Boxes

657/3/0

195/21 and 22

as working models, in many coloured organ case, 5" high, 4¹/₄" long.

No. **657/3/0** with 8 notes . . . . dozen **9/6**

— **657/18** best quality swiss mechanism 18 notes, . each **3/-**

— **657/36** — — — — 36 — . — **5/-**

—— Organ Grinder ——

No. **195/21** with musical box No. 657/18 plastic fig., each **3/4**

— **195/22** — — — — 657/36 — — — **5/4**

Trade Mark.

633/1

633/2

633/4 and 633/5

Cranes.

No. **633/1** simple design, without swivelling motion, rising and falling, well japanned, 8" high . . . . dozen **15/6**

— **633/2** ditto better design and finish, 8¼" high . . each **3/-**

No. **633/4** Derrick Crane, very strong and well finished with shelter (tin) **windlass** for raising and lowering of load and **mechanical swivelling attachment**, 12" high, 12" long each **2/10**

— **633/5** ditto larger and stronger, 16" high, 15½" long . . . . each **4/-**

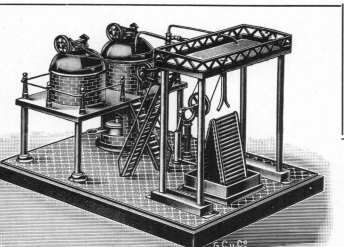

122/1

No. **122/1 Brewery as working model**, strongly made and best quality finish, consisting of: 1 brewing pan with lamp, mash vat, pumping installation with circulating apparatus, cocks, cooler, irrigation apparatus with reservoir, pulleys, belting etc. all the implements for beer brewing, mounted on tiled top wooden base, 13½" long, 10" wide, 8½" high each **14/8**

No. **122/2 Complete brewery works**, consisting of the above described brewery with a high class **Model Steam Engine** with horizontal boiler, fitted with safety valve, whistle, water gauge, fixed double action steam cylinder and eccentric valve gear (patented), 25½" long, 10" wide, 8½" high each **27/6**

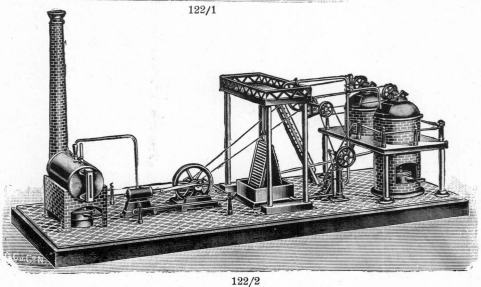

122/2

Trade Mark.

Working Models (Dredgers etc.)

631/10—13

631/21

631/15—17

Dredgers well finished.

No. **631/10**	4³/₄" long,	6" high,	dozen	**7/10**	No. **631/21**	No. **631/15**	5¹/₈" long,	4¹/₄" high,	dozen	**9/6**
— **631/11**	6"	— 7"	—	— **14/6**	4³/₄" long,	— **631/16**	6³/₄"	— 5¹/₂"	—	— **19/-**
— **631/12**	6³/₄"	— 8"	—	— **19/-**	4¹/₄" high	— **631/17**	8¹/₄"	— 6"	—	— **24/-**
— **631/13**	8"	— 8³/₄"	—	— **24/-**	dozen **7/10**					

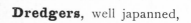

631/25—26

697/16

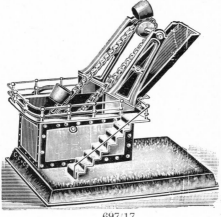

697/17

Dredgers, well japanned,

No. **631/25**   6¹/₄" long, 4³/₄" high
each **1/10**

— **631/26**   7" long, 5¹/₈" high
each **2/6**

Dredger

superior quality,
No. **697/16**   6³/₄" long, 5³/₄" high
dozen **15/6**

Dredger

very strong design and high
class finish
No. **697/17**   6³/₄" long, 6" high
each **2/6**

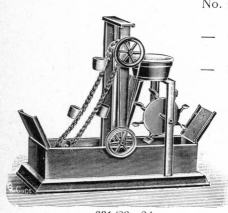

631/23—24

No. **631/23** **Dredger** with **water mill,** well japanned,
8" long, 8" high . . . . dozen **24/-**
— **631/24** ditto, smaller, 6¹/₄" long, 5¹/₂"
high . . . . — **13/-**
— **189/000** **Elevator** with dredger, well japanned, 8¹/₄" long, 7¹/₂" high   dozen **24/-**
No. **189/00** ditto larger, 9¹/₄"
long, 9" high   dozen **36/-**
— **189/1** very handsomely
finished **elevator** and
dredger with **spiral
conveyor,** 12¹/₄" long,
9" high . . . . each **4/-**

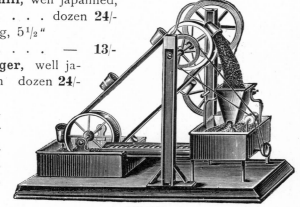

189/000—1

Trade   Mark

Working Models (continued).

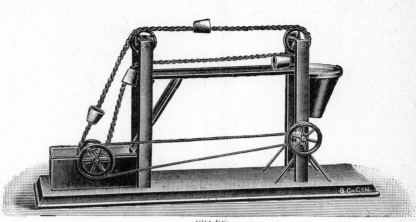

631/31

Sand dredger with removing waggon,
well japanned

No. 631/31	10¼" long,	9¾" high	. . . . each	2/10
— 631/32	10¾" —	11" —	. . . . —	3/8
— 631/33	12¼" —	12" —	. . . . —	4/8

631/27

Horizontal dredger
beautiful enamelling

No. 631/27	9¼" long,	6⅛" high	. . . . each	2/-
— 631/28	13¼" —	6¾" —	. . . . —	3/-

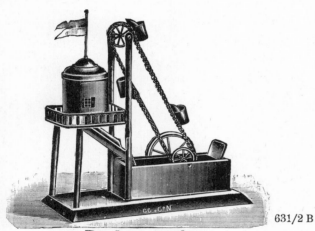

631/2 B

Dredger works

No. 631/2B	well japanned, 6¾" long, 7" high	. . dozen	15/6
— 631/2A	ditto, larger, 7½" — 8" —	. . each	2/-

697/14

Windmill with wheel dredger

No. 697/14	6¾" long,	7½" high	. . . . dozen	15/6
— 697/14½	8¾" —	8¾" —	. . . . each	2/-
— 697/15	10" —	10¾" —	. . . . —	2/10

697/19

Windmill with **chain dredger**

No. 697/19	6¾" long,	7½" high	. . dozen	15/6
— 697/20	8¾" —	8¾" —	. . each	2/-
— 697/21	0" —	10¾" —	. . —	2/10

697/25

699/4

**Revolving
grinding mill**

No. 699/4 7½" high,
dozen 14/6

Mortar mixing machine,
with shovels, well finished,
No. 697/25 8¾" long, 8" high . . each 2/10

Trade Mark.

Working Models
(continued).

Windmills etc.
in best finish.

697/34

697/32 and 33

697/35—36

697/40

697/41—42

697/43

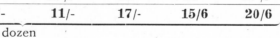

No. **697/32**	**33**	**34**	**35**	**36**	**40**	**41**	**42**	**43**
6¾″	8″	8″	10¼″	13″	10″	12¾″	15½″	20½″ high
4/-	6/6	6/-	11/-	17/-	15/6	20/6	2/10	5/6
		dozen					each	

697/37

697/38

697/27

No. **697/37 Windmill, with tilt hammer**, well japanned, 9″ long, 4″ wide, 10¼″ high, each **2/-**

No. **697/38 Windmill** with spiral drive, quite original design, 9″ long, 8″ high . . each **2/-**

No. **697/27 Water mill** with tilt hammer, 6½″ long, 6¼″ wide, 6¼″ high, each **3/-**

Trade Mark.

Working Models (continued). Windmills etc. in best finish, well japanned.

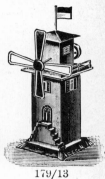

179/8/0   179/7/0   179/9/0   179/11   179/12   179/13

No	179/8/0	179/7/0	179/9/0	179/11	179/12	179/13
	5½"	6½"	7½"	5¼"	7½"	8¼" high
dozen	4/-	6,6	7/-	6/-	7/10	11/-

697/30 A   699/1—3   179/4/0   179/3/0   179/2/0

No. 697/30 A **Windmill,** well japanned, 9" high, dozen 12/-
— 697/1½ same, 9½" high . . . . . . — 14/6
— 699/1 **Sand mill,** well japanned, 8½" high, — 15/6
— 699/2 ditto, larger, 10" high . . . . — 24/-
— 699/3 larger than 699/2, 11½" high . . — 34/-
— 179/4/0 **Windmill,** well japanned, 12" high, — 20/6
— 179/3/0 **Windmill,** with 2 figures, which move round the mill, well japanned, 10¼" high . . . . — 24/-
— 179/2/0 **Windmill with grain elevator,** mill does not swivel, well japanned, 13¼" high — 36/-
— 179/14 **Windmill with water wheel** and stairway, well japanned, 12½" high, each 2/10
— 179/15 ditto, larger size, 13½" high . . — 4/-
No. 631/18½ **Windmill with dredger** and water wheel, well japanned, 10" high, 6" wide . . — 3/-
— 631/18 same, larger and well finished, 12" high, 8" wide, — 4/10

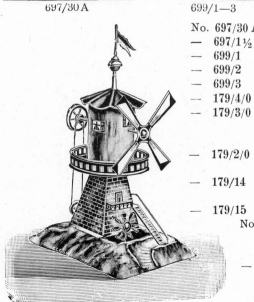

179/14—15

631/18½ and 631/18

Trade Mark.

4 E

Working Models (continued).

631/35

No.631/35 **Water wheel, with hammer,** well japanned, 6½" long each **1/-**

697/11

No. 697/11 **Water wheel, with hammer,** with plastic, well japanned background, 6" long, 5¼" high . . . . dozen **9/6**

No. 697/26 **Water mill, with hammer,** well japanned, 6½" long, 6¼" high dozen **22/-**

697/28 A and 28 B

No. 697/28 A **Water mill,** with sawing machine, with pathway, quite novel, well japanned, 7" long, 6" wide, 8" high . . . dozen **22/-**
— 697/28 B ditto larger, 8¾" long, 7¼" wide, 6" high . . . . dozen **34/-**

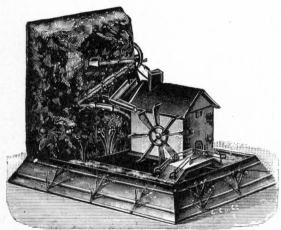

No. 697/28 C **Water** mill, with water basin, pump etc. in original colouring, a very well got up back ground, representing mountain scenery, 9½" long, 7¼" wide, 7½" high, each **6/6**
— 697/28 D ditto somewhat smaller, 8½" long, 5½" wide, 7½" high . . . . each **4/-**

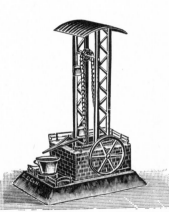

Sand- and Water Dredger
best quality finish.

No. 631/36   No. 631/37 ditto larger, with fine
6½" long, 10½" high   japanned galleries, 8½" long,
each **2/10**   11¼" high . . . . each **3/6**

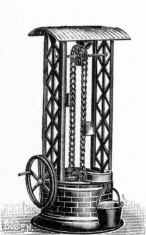

No. 631/34 **Draw well** with water bucket, well japanned
9½" high . . . . cach **2/4**

No. 179/1/0 **Windmill** well japanned, in imitation brickwork,
12" high . . . . each **2/10**

No. 631/38 **Sand and water dredger,** best quality finish, with stairway and galleries, handsome japanned superstructure, with 2 supports, 12¾" long, 14" high . . . . each **6/6**

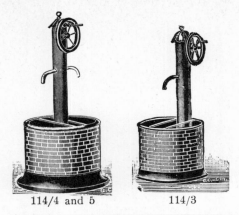

114/4 and 5   114/3

Wells

as **Working models,** also arranged for hand driving, **very good pumping mechanism** and well japanned.

No. **114/3**	5½" high	. . . . .	dozen	**7/10**
— **114/4**	7¼"	—	—	**13/-**
— **114/5**	8¼"	—	—	**18/-**

No. **697/4**   cheap small **fountain,** plainly japanned, 8" high, 6¼" diameter . . each **2/4**

697/4

No. **197/00**

Wells,

strongly made, well japanned, with double outlet and 2 water tubs, 6½" long, 3½" wide, 7½" high, each **3/-**

No. **675/3/0**

Windmill,

with flowing fountain

of improved design, with brass pump cylinder, handsomely japanned, 14¼" high, 12" wide each **6/-**

675/3/0

197/00

No. **115/3**

Fountain

working by compressed air (with motor or hand drive). The air compressor A consists of an oscillating brass cylinder with 3 grooved pulleys. The cylinder is connected to the fountain by rubber tubing (about 1 yard supplied with the model) pushed on to tube B. The water is admitted through C, handsome and strong design, 10¼" diameter, 10¼" high each **6/4**

Draw wells,

high class finish,

No. **631/22 A**	5½" high	. .	dozen	**7/-**
— **631/22 B**	6½"	— . .	—	**12/-**
— **631/22 C**	7½"	— . .	—	**15/6**

115/3

631/22 A, 22 B, 22 C

Trade Mark.

4*

Working Models (continued).
Fountains
well japanned and very beautifully designed and finished, with brass cylinder.

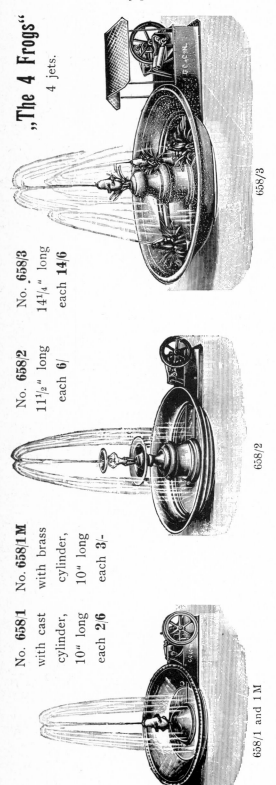

„The 4 Frogs"
4 jets.

No. 658/3
14¼" long
each 14/6

658/3

No. 658/2
11½" long
each 6/

658/2

No. 658/1
with cast
cylinder,
10" long
each 2/6

No. 658/1 M
with brass
cylinder,
10" long
each 3/-

658/1 and 1M

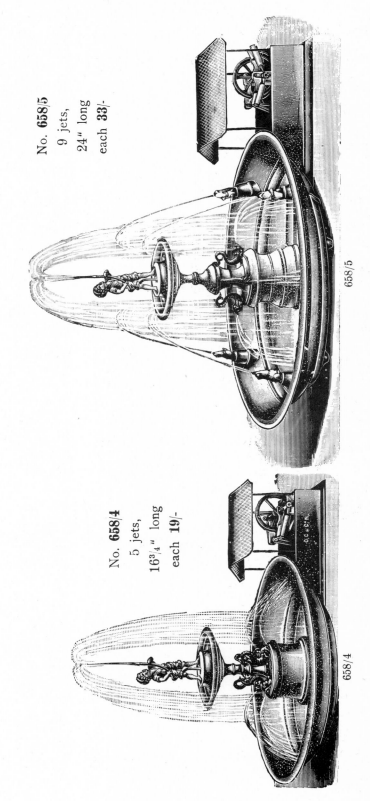

No. 658/5
9 jets,
24" long
each 33/-

658/5

No. 658/4
5 jets,
16¾" long
each 19/-

658/4

Trade  Mark.

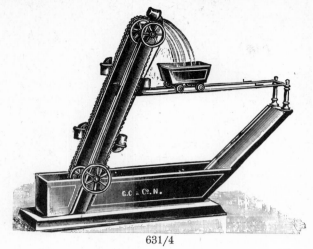

631/4

Better Quality Working Models.

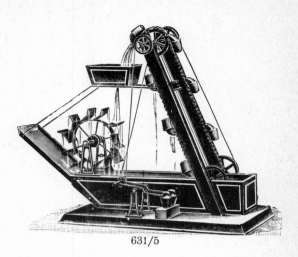

631/5

631/6

No. **631/4** **Dredger with rolling and tipping wagon**,
superfine japanning and very strongly made,
9½" long, 12¾" high . . . . each **7/-**

— **631/5** **Dredger with water wheel and hammer**,
superbly japanned and of very strong design,
16" long, 12¼" high . . . . each **9/6**

— **631/6** **Large water elevator** wheel with 14 buckets
and mill wheel, beautifully japanned and
very strong design, 16¾" long, 9½" wide,
10" high . . . . each **12/-**

No. **634/1** **Platten printing press**, very solid and well finished model,
works well and is of latest and improved design, will
print 3⅛" × 1½", with self-acting inking arrangement,
with removable type holder and 120 rubber types. Prints
while working — very entertaining and absorbing pastime
printing with this model, 5½" high, 4½" wide . . . each **11/-**

— **634 T** Set of supplementary types with 120 rubber typess, in box
with tweezers . . . . set **1/10**

634/1

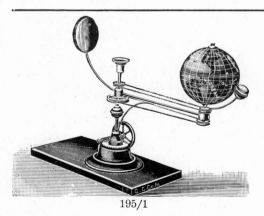

195/1

No. **195/1** **Cheap tellurium** as working model, also with hand
drive, illustrating the revolution of the earth
around the sun and of the moon around the
earth; also the eclipses of the sun and moon.

Consisting of globe, moon and candle-stick
with screen.

10¼" long, 9" high . . . . each **5/-**

Trade Mark.

Working Models (continued).

Swing Boats.

119/13

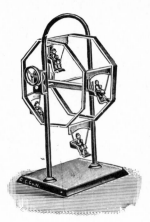

119/15 and 16

No. **119/12** plain quality, with 2 seats, 8" high . . . . dozen **7/10**

— **119/13** ditto, larger, with 4 seats, 8" high . . . . — **12/-**

— **119/15** well japanned and novel design, with 3 seats, 9½" high, — **18/-**

— **119/16** ditto, larger, with 4 seats, 11½" high . . . . — **24/-**

— **119/17** ditto, larger, with 4 seats, 13¼" high . . . . — **34/-**

— **119/18** ditto, larger, with 6 seats, 15" high . . . . — **42/-**

No. 119/15—18 are fitted with gear wheels, by which a slow even motion is obtained.

119/18

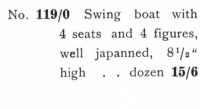

119/0

Swing Boats.

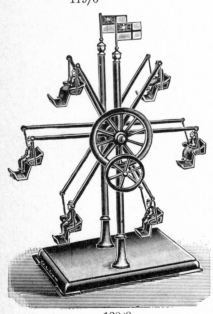

120/0

No. **119/0** Swing boat with 4 seats and 4 figures, well japanned, 8½" high . . dozen **15/6**

— **120/0** Swing boat with 6 seats and 6 figures, well japanned, 12" high, each **2/-**

— **120/1** ditto, with **musical box of 8 notes,** 12" long, 4" wide, 12" high, each **3/-**

120/1

Trade Mark.

Working Models (continued).
Roundabouts well finished and handsomely enamelled.

138/31　　　　　138/33　　　　　　138/38

138/40

High class air **roundabout** with **Zeppelin type Air-ships,** well japanned and quite **original design**
No. **138/40** with 4 air-ships and 4 figures, 14″ high . . . . each 2/-
— **138/41** ditto, larger, with 4 figures, 16″ high . . . . each 4/-
— **138/42** ditto, larger than 138/41, with staircase, best quality japanning, 20″ high. . . each 6/-

No. 138/31	32	33	34	35	36	37	38	
with 3	3	3	3	3	3	3	4	figures
8¼″	9″	10¼″	11″	12¼″	13″	14¼″	15½″	high
dozen 7/10	12/-	15/6	24/-	30/-	36/-	42/-	48/-	

Better quality
Working Models
Dairy implements
proper working design, well japanned and strongly made.

No. 614/1 Cream separator
7″ high . . . . each 3/8

No. 614/3 Kneading machine
4″ high . . . . each 1/8

No. 614/2 Churn
6¾″ high . . . . . each 2/10

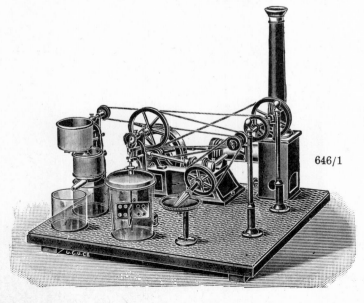

646/1

No. 646/1
Complete **Butter Manufactory**
consisting of:
cream separator No. 614/1, churn No. 614/2, kneading machine No. 614/3, shafting and a **hot air engine**, size 1 on cast iron bed, superfine finish, the whole mounted on a tiled face, wood base
each **33/-**

No. 646/2
ditto, but with size 2 **hot air engine**
each **40/-**

Trade　Mark.

Agricultural Machines

as **working models**, highly japanned.

614/7

614/8

614/12

614/9

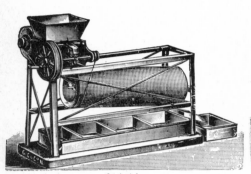

614/14

614/11

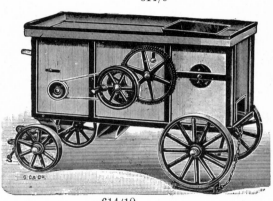

614/10

No. **614/7 Chaff cutter,** 4³/₄" long . . . . . each **1/10**
— **614/8** ditto, 6" long . . . . — **3/6**
— **614/9 Threshing machine,** 10" long, 6" high — **6/10**
— **614/12 Drum sieve** 5¹/₂" long,
4³/₄" high . . — **3/-**

No. **614/14 Drum sieve,** 9" long, 7¹/₂" high each **7/-**
— **614/11 Grain dresser,** 6³/₄" — 4³/₄" — — **4/10**
— **614/10 Portable threshing machine,** for attaching
to locomotives etc., 10¹/₄" long, 6¹/₄" high,
4³/₄" wide . . . . each **14/8**

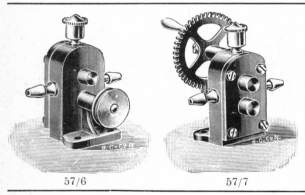

Model Rotary Pumps

Very strong, mechanical piece of work, best efficiency.

No. **57/6** for **driving by an engine,** can be driven by any of
the better class engines from size 3 upwards or by a powerful hot air engine, **suction,** will draw up to 2", **delivery,**
will force up to 3 meters (10 feet) according to speed of
drive . . . . each **4/-**
— **57/7** ditto, with gear wheels for **hand driving** . . — **4/6**

57/6   57/7

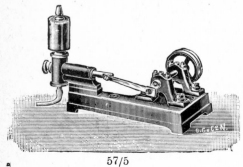

No. 57/5 Force Pump

horizontal type, very strong design, surprising efficiency, **suction,** will draw
up to 20", **delivery,** will force according to no. of turns, up to 20 meters
(65 feet), mounted on cast iron bed . . . . each **5/6**

57/5

Trade  Mark.

High Class Working Models arranged for power driving.

Scale model design.

These models are near as possible exact facsimiles of the large machines they must therefore be looked upon, not merely as toys, but as **Educational models**. They are constructed from massive iron castings, the various parts being either highly nickelled or handsomely japanned. The execution of the work is all that can be desired, both elegant and strong.

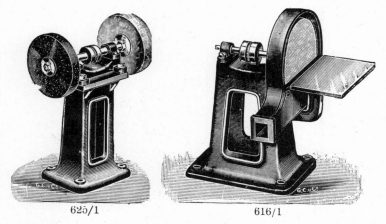

625/1   616/1

No. 625/1 Grinding and polishing machine

with polishing bob and emery wheel, 4" high

each **4/6**

No. 616/1 Wood polishing machine,

with highly polished table, 4³/₄" high

each **4/10**

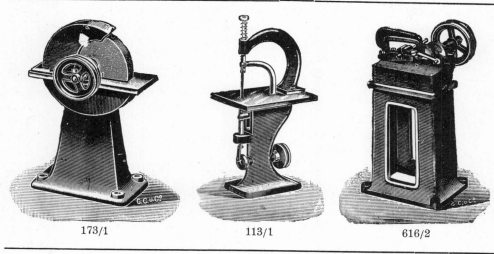

173/1   113/1   616/2

No. 173/1 Grindstone,

with regular emery stone, 4¹/₂" high

each **4/4**

No. 113/1 Power fret saw

with steel saw, 5³/₄" high

each **6/6**

No. 616/2 Cold saw

with steel saw, 4¹/₄" high

each **4/-**

111/1   616/3

No. 111/1 Circular saw

with table, also adjustable and removable gauge block,

4" high, 3¹/₂" wide,

each **5/10**

No. 616/3 Engineer's planing machine

with 3 speed driving pulley, steel planing tool, highly finished slides, adjustable by means of screwed spindles in all directions,

7¹/₄" long, 5" high

each **37/-**

Trade   Mark.

High Class Working Models

(continued).

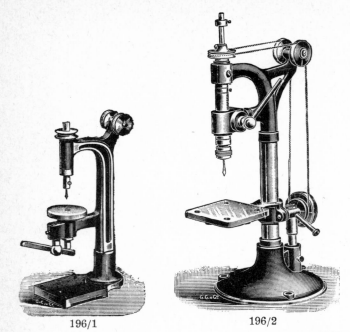

196/1   196/2

No. 196/1 Small sensitive drilling machine

with lever rising table and steel drill, 4½" high

each 4/10

No. 196/2 Large high speed drilling machine

with table adjustable in all directions, drill spindle has lever feed, chuck and steel, 9¼" high

each 22/-

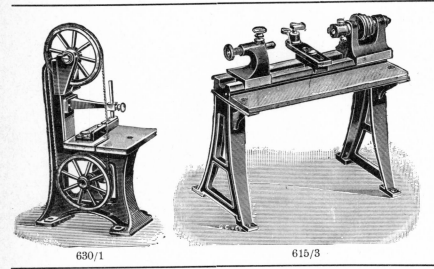

630/1   615/3

No. 630/1 Band sawing machine

fitted with band saw and adjustable gauge block. The upper wheel is provided with attachment for setting and arranging tension of the saw, 6¾" high

each 12/-

No. 630/1 B Band saw, extra for 630/1

each -/8

No. 615/3 Lathe

with fixed head, and sliding poppet head and hand rest also wood table,

5" long, 4¾" high . . . . . . each 6/6

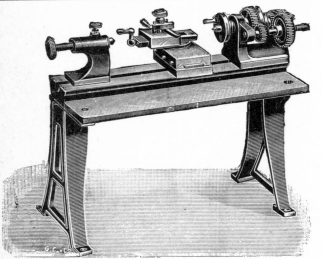

615/4

No. 615/4 Large lathe

headstock with back gear, can be put in and out of motion; compound slide rest, poppet head or backcentre as well as wood table

6" long, 5¼" high . . . . each 26/6

Trade  Mark.

STEAM LOCOMOTIVES
heated by methylated spirit.

Every locomotive is tested by **steam** in our factory, and before being packed undergoes a further rigorous trial. We guarantee therefore the perfect working of our engines, provided that the full instructions supplied with each model are carefully followed, and that **our make rails** are used. Our rails, not only hold their own against all other make rails but are finding favour with an ever increasing number of customers, on account of their simple laying and at the same time, their strong and durable qualities. — Up to the present, the packing washer of the safety valves, caused some inconvenience. The frequent screwing and unscrewing, as well as the heat of the boiler, caused it to be spoilt or worn away, till the boiler would not hold the pressure without leakage, and the engine in consequence worked imperfectly. This trouble is now removed by our **new Safety valve** which is covered by several patents. By means of this safety valve the pressure is held while running. — Sometimes the necessary pressure of steam is not obtained because the wick is allowed to burn away, or to become too short to reach the bottom of the lamp, consequently the flame is too small and insufficient steam is generated. The locomotive then fails to pull its load. It should be noticed that the wick always reaches the correct height (for prices of fresh wicks see page 37).

In the case of the new locomotives No. 515, 525 etc. (page 62) we have overcome the difficulty with the wicks by introducing, covered by patent, a vertical **spirit vapour lamp**. The flame in this lamp burns evenly, from the time the lamp is ignited to the time it is extinguished, and the worry with the wicks is entirely absent. Moreover this lamp is a safety lamp, for should the engine happen to turn over, the spirit is prevented from running out of the reservoir.

On locomotives No. 515/48, 525/35 and 48 etc. an **automatic lubricator** is fitted, and on all the rest, a lubricating attachment is arranged. We wish to emphasize the need of using good oil in these cylinder lubricators (we advise the use of our **Specialoil** No. 13/1 page 37). — It is advisable, before using a locomotive, to examine the rails. By following the **instructions** given with all the complete trains, No. 81/10 for 35 mm (1³/₈") No. 81/11 for 48 mm (1⁷/₈") gauge, any defect or distortion caused in laying the rail can be easily detected and remedied. If this is not seen to the defect would impede the wheels of the locomotive and also those of the tender and coaches and might stop the train.

Our method of connecting the rails is acknowledged to be simple, yet at the same time to be so strong that it renders any accidental detachament impossible. Our system of rail formation does not necessitate the stocking of a large number of special rails. — Avoid taking to pieces the various parts of the engine, more especially the eccentric and cylinder components, or twistings the cranks, as a slight error in replacing will result in the locomotive refusing to run again.

CLOCKWORK LOCOMOTIVES.

Our clockwork locomotives likewise undergo a rigorous testing. For these locomotives only our rails must be used They are all fitted with the very best, hardened and tempered springs. If a spring should happen to break they are easily replaced by a new one in the following manner: Loosen the ratchet which is shown in the accompanying illustration by lifting the spring of the ratchet, then turn the spindle backwards with the winding key. The spring will then become disengaged and can be easily drawn off, provided the end hanging on the bolt has been previously pulled off with a pair of pliers or other tool. Before putting in the new winding spring, oil both the spring and the winding spindle with good oil, then replace the ratchet and ratchet spring in their usual position, as shown in illustration, the end of the spring with the hole must be fixed on the hook on the winding spindle, this hook must be twisted with a pair of pliers so that it does not stand up. The other end of the spring with the loop is hung on the bolt or pin where the former spring was fastened. The clockwork is then wound up in the usual way, but carefully and slowly to avoid damaging the spring. **Springs for replacement in various locomotives are listed on page 118.**

500/35

501/35

Steam Locomotives

heated by methylated spirit.

Cheap locomotives in strong simple design with 1 brass oscillating cylinder and gear drive, with brass boiler, spring safety valve, flanged wheels.

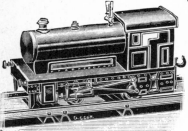

501/48

Gauge	35	48	54	67 mm
equal to	$1^3/_8$	$1^7/_8$	$2^1/_8$	$2^5/_8$ "

Tank Locomotives.

No. **500/35**   **35 mm gauge,** 8" long . . . .   each **3/-**
—   **501/35**   ditto, **with whistle** . . . .   —   **4/-**
—   **501/48**   **48 mm gauge,** 10" long, with whistle . . . .   —   **6/10**

511/35

No. **511/35**

Tank Locomotive

with 2 brass oscillating cylinders, brass boiler, with dome and safety valve, whistle, $8^3/_4$" long, for **35 mm gauge** . . . .   each **8/-**

502/35 and 502/48

Better class Locomotives
with tender,

brass boiler of blue finish, dome with safety valve, whistle, 2 brass oscillating cylinders.

No. **502/35**   **35 mm gauge,** $12^1/_4$" long, ...   each **9/6**
—   **502/48**   48   —   —   16"   — . . . .   —   **11/8**

503/35 and 503/48

Handsome Steam Locomotives

of very strong design and beautifully finished, superfine japanning. Strong brass boiler blue finish, massive flanged wheels, nickelled fittings, 2 oscillating cylinders, dome and safety valve, whistle, nickelled buffers.

No. **503/35**   **Locomotive with tender,** 35 mm gauge, $12^1/_4$" long . . . .   each **13/**
—   **503/48**   ditto, for **48 mm gauge,** $16^1/_4$" long   —   **17/-**

Locomotives 503 can be had in the colours of the
1) **Great Northern Railway,** 2) **London and North Western Railway,** 3) **Midland Railway.**
When ordering these please write 1) **G N** for **G N R.** **M** for **M R.** 2) **L** for **L & N W R**
after the number of the locomotive; for example **503/35 L** signifies locomotive 503/35 in **L & N W R** coulours.

For coaches and rails, see pages 94—102 of this list.

Trade Mark.

Handsome Steam Locomotives

of very strong design, beautifully finished and exquisitly japanned. **With reversing attachment.** Strong brass boiler blue finish, massive flanged wheels, nickelled fittings, 2 oscillating cylinders, dome, safety valve, nickelled brass buffers.

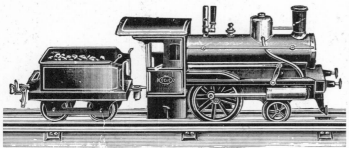

504/35 and 504/48

> All locomotives can be had in the colours of:
> **Great Northern Railway**
> **London and North Western Railway**
> **Midland Railway**
> When ordering please write:
> **GN** for Great Northern Railway, **L** for London and North Western Railway, **M** for Midland Railway, after the number of the locomotive.

No. 504/35 **Locomotive** and **tender**, 12$\frac{1}{4}$" long, reversing gear, steam exhausts through chimney, for **gauge 35 mm** . . . . each **15/-**
-- 504/48 ditto, for **48 mm gauge**, 16$\frac{1}{4}$" long . . — **19/-**

505/35 and 505/48 MR

Steam Locomotives, with **fixed double action patent slide valve cylinders,** with **roll apparatus** and **ball pressing attachment** patented, **locomotive runs either way,** simply by being pushed a little way in the direction it is to run.

No. 505/35 **Locomotive** and **tender**, 12$\frac{1}{4}$" long, for **gauge 35 mm** . . each **18/-**
— 505/48 ditto, for **48 mm gauge**, 16$\frac{1}{4}$" long . . . . each **23/-**

506/48

With self-acting Reversing Gear.

These locomotives are fitted with a **patent "Coulisse" reverse,** by which an **automatic forward or backward running** of the locomotive is obtained. The locomotives are also arranged so as to be reversed from the cab by hand.

No. 506/48 **Locomotive** and **tender** with fixed double acting patent slide valve cylinders, with **reversing gear,** also **automatic reversal,** patented; fittings as above, also starting cock, exhausts through chimney, for **48 mm gauge,** 16$\frac{1}{4}$" long . . . . each **31/6**

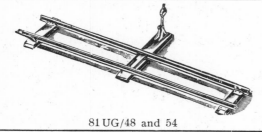

81 UG/48 and 54

Reversing Rails for Locomotives 506

straight 81 UG/48	round 81 UR/48
for 48 mm	for 48 mm gauge
each 1/-	each 1/-

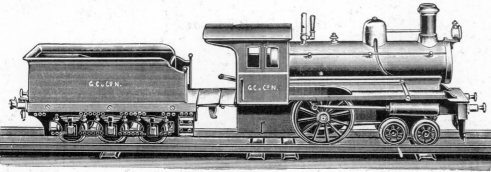

504/67

With Reversing Gear.

No. 504/67 **Locomotive** and **tender,** **67 mm gauge,** 23" long, with massive flanged wheels, strong brass boiler blue finish, nickelled fittings, 2 oscillating cylinders, dome, safety valve, nickelled brass buffers, water gauge, steam exhausts through chimney . . . . each **46/-**

For coaches and rails for above locos see pages 94—102 of this list.

Handsomely finished locomotives

of strong and elegant construction, and best quality enamelling.

Express locomotive

with reversing gear, latest design,

bogie with 4 small wheels, 4 massive flanged wheels, brass boiler blue finish, with 2 double action patent slide valve cylinders, nickelled brass buffers, safety valve, dome, whistle, 8 wheeled tender.

No. **509/35** for **35 mm gauge**, 18″ long incl. tender, each 33/-

☞ Only large radius rails (No. 80 page 97) may be used with this locomotive. ☜

509/35

508/48

Beautifully japanned **"Lady of the Lake"** locomotive and tender with massive flanged wheels, handsomely japanned brass boiler, dome, whistle, safety valve, 2 nickelled oscillating cylinders, **reversing gear**, nickelled brass buffers, exhausts through chimney
No. **508/48** for **48 mm gauge**, 20″ long including tender . . . . each 37/6
— **508/54** — **54 mm gauge** — 20″ long . . . . — 41/-

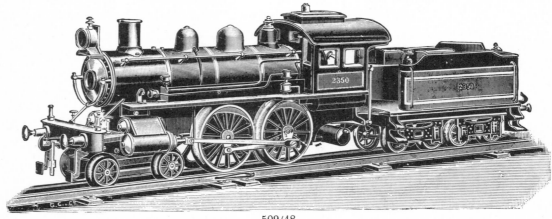

509/48

Express locomotive

latest design (an original scale model), bogie with 4 small wheels, 4 massive flanged driving wheels, beautifully japanned strong brass boiler, with **2 fixed double action patent slide valve cylinders, with patent "Coulisse" reversing**, dome, safety valve, bell whistle, water gauge, starting cock, nickelled brass buffers, well japanned head-light, exhausts through chimney
No. **509/48** for **48 mm gauge**, 24″ long with tender . . . . each 100/-

☞ Only rails of large radius can be used with loco **509/48** (No. 80 on page **97**).

For coaches and rails for above locos, see pages **94—102** of this list.

Trade Mark.

Best Quality Locomotives

very strong design and fine workmanship as well as superfine enamelling with reversing gear for for-or backward running.

Only rails of large radius No. 80 (page 97) can be used with these locos.

No. 507/67 **Great Northern Railway Locomotive, 67 mm gauge,** with massive flanged wheels, well japanned brass boiler with 2 fixed double action patent slide valve cylinders, with reversing gear, nickelled brass spring buffers, water gauge, whistle, safety valve, starting cock, exhausts through funnel, 27½" long including tender . . . . . . each 170/-

510/48—67

No. 510/48 **Great Eastern Railway Locomotive, 48 mm gauge,** strongly made, with massive flanged wheels, with 2 fixed double action patent slide valve cylinders, "coulisse", reversing gear, handsomely japanned brass boiler, nickelled brass spring buffers, safety valve, bell whistle, water gauge, starting cock, 24" long, incl. tender . . . . each 150/-
— 510/67 **Great Eastern Railway Locomotive** same as above but 67 **mm gauge,** 30" long incl. tender . . . — 200/-

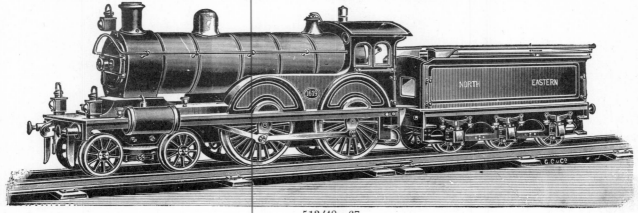

513/48—67

No. 513/48 **North Eastern Railway Locomotive, 48 mm gauge,** strongly made with massive flanged wheels with 2 fixed double action patent slide valve cylinders, "coulisse", reversing gear, handsomely japanned brass boiler, nickelled brass spring buffers, safety valve, bell whistle, water gauge, starting cock, 24" long incl. tender . . . . each 150/-
— 513/67 **North Eastern Railway Locomotive** same as above but 67 mm gauge, 30" long incl. tender . . . — 200/-

Only rails of large radius No. 80 (page 97) can be used with above locomotives.

Trade Mark.

Latest design Goods Steam Locomotives.

Best Quality.

Fitted with **safety spirit vapour lamp,** 2 superior, fixed, double action patent slide valve "Precision" cylinders, with patent eccentric **reversing gear.** Strong brass boiler, steel-blue finish, steam dome, new patent steam safety valve, bell whistle. The **spirit vapour lamp** supplied has an excellent flame and burns evenly from start to finish, besides the additional advantage of preventing the spirit running out in case of an accidental overturn of the loco. Affixed to the boiler are our well known and thoroughly reliable flame protecting plates.

515/35 and 48

2 wheel coupled Locomotives with Tender.

New design.

No. **515/35** for **35 mm gauge,** 14" long, each **21/-**
— 515/48 — 48 — — 16½" — with central lubricating attachment . . . . each **31/6**

516/35 and 48

The same locomotive with

cow-catcher
American Type.

No. **516/35** for **35 mm gauge,** 15¼" long, each **22/-**
— 516/48 — 48 — — 18¼" — with central lubricating attachment each **33/6**

525/35 and 48

4 wheel coupled Locomotives
with Tender, with bogie and central lubricating attachment.

New design.   New design.

No. **525/35** for **35 mm gauge,** 16" long . . . . . . each **36/-**
— **525/48** for **48 mm gauge,** 20½" long . . . . . each **50/-**

526/35 and 48

The same locomotives with

cow-catcher
American Type.

No. **526/35** for **35 mm gauge,** 17¼" long . . . each **37/-**
— **526/48** for **48 mm gauge,** 22¼" long . . . each **52/-**

The above locomotives will run on both small and large radius rails.
☞ For rails, coaches and wagons see pages 94—102 of this list. ☜

═══ Scale Models. ═══
English Railway Locomotives
constructed from the original English Models. — Best quality.

Fitted with **safety spirit vapour lamp,** 2 superior, fixed, double action patent slide valve "precision" cylinders, with patent eccentric **reversing gear.** Strong brass boiler, steel-blue finish, steam dome, new patent steam safety valve, bell whistle. The **spirit vapour lamp** supplied has an excellent flame and burns evenly from start to finish, besides the additional advantage of preventing the spirit running out in case of an accidental overturn of the loco. Affixed to the boiler are our well known and thoroughly reliable flame protecting plates.

2 wheel coupled locomotives with tender

517/35—48

Great Northern Railway Company

No. **517/35** for **35 mm gauge,** 14" long . . . . each **29/—**
— **517/48** — **48** — — with central lubricating attachment, 16½" long . . . . — **37/—**

518/35—48

London and North Western Railway Company

No. **518/35** for **35 mm gauge,** 14" long . . . . each **29/—**
— **518/48** — **48** — — with central lubricating attachment, 16½" long . . . . — **37/—**

519/35—48

Midland Railway Company

No. **519/35** for **35 mm gauge,** 14" long . . . . each **29/—**
— **519/48** — **48** — — with central lubricating attachment, 16½" long . . . . — **37/—**

The above locomotives will run on both small and large radius rails.

 For rails, coaches and wagons see pages **94—102** of this list.

Trade ✠ Mark

═══ **Scale Models.** ═══
English Railway Locomotives

Best quality.

constructed from the original English Models.

☞ Same fittings as described on page 63. ☜

4 wheel coupled locomotives with tender, with bogie and central lubricating attachment.

Best quality.

527/35—48

Great Northern Railway Company.

No. 527/35 for **35 mm gauge,** 16″ long . . . . each **40/-**
— 527/48 — 48 — — 20½″ — . . . . — **60/-**

528/35—48

London and North Western Railway Company.

No. 528/35 for **35 mm gauge,** 16″ long . . . . each **40/-**
— 528/48 — 48 — — 20½″ — . . . . — **60/-**

529/35—48

Midland Railway Company.

No. 529/35 for **35 mm gauge,** 16″ long . . . . each **40/-**
— 529/48 — 48 — — 20½″ — . . . . — **60/-**

The above locomotives will run on both small and large radius rails.

☞ For rails, coaches and wagons see pages 94—102 of this list. ☜

Trade Mark.

Cheap quality sets of Steam Trains.

(The sign against the number indicate the shape of track formed by the rails supplied with the train.)

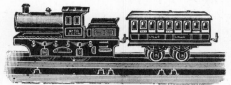

540/35 AE

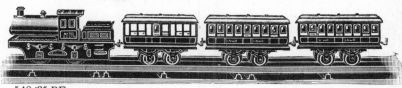

540/35 BE

No. 540/35 AE consisting of **tank loco 500/35 = 35 mm gauge** (page 58), 1 coach, length of train 14", 4 round rails, total length of rails 5 ft. 2", packed in handsome cardboard box . . . . each 4/8

— 540/35 BE consisting of **tank loco 500/35 = 35 mm gauge** (page 58), 2 coaches, 1 brake van, 4 round and 2 straight rails, length of train 2 ft. 4", total length of rails 7 ft. 6", packed in handsome cardboard box
each 6/4

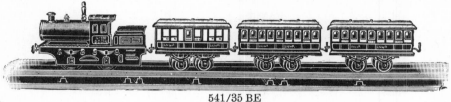

541/35 BE

No 541/35 BE consisting of **tank loco 501/35 with whistle = 35 mm gauge** (page 58), 2 coaches, 1 brake van, 4 round and 2 straight rails, length of train 2 feet 4", total length of rails 7 feet 6", packed in handsome cardboard box . . . . each 7/6

No. 571/35 BE consisting of **tank loco 501/35 with whistle — 35 mm gauge** (page 58), 2 coaches, 1 brake van with sliding doors, 4 round and 2 straight rails, length of train 2 feet 6½", total length of rails 7 feet 6", packed in handsome cardboard box. . . . . each 8/-

571/35 BE

No. 561/35 BE consisting of **tank loco 501/35 with whistle = 35 mm gauge** (page 58), 2 large coaches, 1 large brake van, 6 round rails, length of train 2 feet 4½", length of rails 6 feet 2", packed in handsome cardboard box
each 10/-

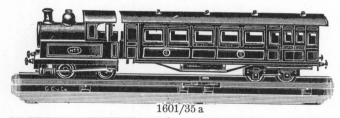

1601/35 a

New Design Motor Train.

No. 1601/35 A consisting of 1 loco direct coupled to large coach, 35 mm gauge, finest japanning, locomotive fitted with brass oscillating cylinder, length of train 15", with 6 round rails, packed in elegant cardboard box
each 11/-
— 1601/48 A ditto, **48 mm gauge**, length of train 24", 8 curved rails . . . . . each 14/6

Steam Railway Trains
48 mm gauge.

561/48 BE

No. 561/48 BE consisting of **tank loco 501/48 with whistle, = 48 mm gauge** (page 58), 2 large coaches and 1 large brake van, 8 round and 2 straight rails, length of train 3 ft. 5", total length of rails 11 ft. 6", packed in handsome cardboard box . . . . each 16/-

 For separate rails, wagons and coaches for above railways see pages 94—102 of this list.

5*

High class Steam Railway Trains packed in elegant cardboard boxes.

1511/35 B

No. 1511/35 B — consisting of **tank loco 511/35 = 35 mm gauge** (page 58), 2 coaches, 1 brake van, 6 round and 2 straight rails, length of train 2 feet 4", total length of rails 8 feet . . . . each **13/-**

— 1511/35 C — consisting of **tank loco 511/35 = 35 mm gauge** (page 58), 2 coaches, 1 brake van, 10 round and 4 straight rails also 1 crossing, length of train 2 feet 4", total length of rails 16 feet, each **17/-**

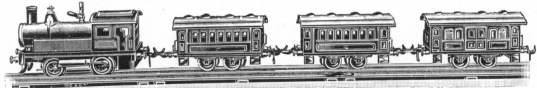

1511/2/35

No. 1511/2/35 — consisting of **tank loco 511/35 = 35 mm gauge** (page 58), 2 large coaches, 1 large brake van, 6 round and 2 straight rails, length of train 2 feet 6", total length of rails 8 feet, each **15/-**

572/48 AE

No. 572/35 AE — consisting of **loco with brass boiler blue finish 502/35 with tender = 35 mm gauge** (page 58), 1 large coach, 6 round rails, length of train 2 feet 8", total length of rails 6 feet, each **13/6**

— 572/35 BE — consisting of **loco with blue finish brass boiler 502/35 with tender = 35 mm gauge** (page 58), 2 large coaches and 1 large brake van, 6 round and 4 straight rails, length of train 2 feet 10", total length of rails 9 feet 9" . . . . each **17/-**

— 572/48 AE — consisting of **loco with blue finish brass boiler 502/48 with tender = 48 mm gauge** (page 58), 2 large coaches and 1 large brake van, 8 round rails, length of train 3 feet 6", total length of rails 9 feet 3" . . . . each **20/-**

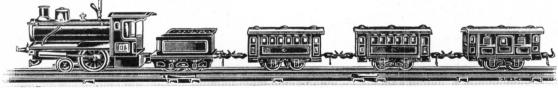

563/35 B

No. 563/35 B — consisting of **loco with strong brass boiler steel-blue finish, 503/35 with tender, all fittings nickelled, 35 mm gauge** (page 58), 2 coaches and 1 brake van, 6 round and 4 straight rails, length of train 2 feet 8", total length of rails 9 feet 9" . . . . each **18/6**

— 563/35 C — the same set as 563/35 B but with 10 round and 4 straight rails also **1 crossing,** total length of rails 16 feet . . . . each **21/-**

— 563/48 B — consisting of **loco, steel-blue finish brass boiler, 503/48 with nickelled fittings and tender, 48 mm gauge** (page 58), 2 coaches and 1 brake van, 8 round and 4 straight rails, length of train 3 feet 6", total length of rails 13 feet 9" . . . . each **25/4**

— 563/48 C — the same set as 563/48 B but with 14 round and 4 straight rails also **1 crossing,** total length of rails 20 feet . . . . each **29/-**

Separate rails, wagons and coaches are listed on pages 94—102.

High class Steam Railway Trains,

packed in elegant cardboard boxes.

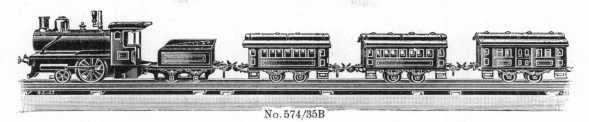

No. 574/35 B

No. 554/35 B		consisting of: **Locomotive with strong brass boiler of steel-blue finish and nickelled fittings** — 504/35 with **reversing gear** — **35 mm gauge** with tender, 2 coaches, 1 brake van, 6 round and 4 straight rails. Length of train 32", total length of rails 9 feet 9" . . . . each complete **20/8**
— 554/48 B		consisting of: **Locomotive with strong brass boiler of steel-blue finish and nickelled fittings** — 504/48 with **reversing gear** — **48 mm gauge** with tender, 2 coaches, 1 brake van, 8 round and 4 straight rails. Length of train 32", total length of rails 13 feet 8" . . . . each complete **27/6**
— 573/35 B		consisting of: **Locomotive with strong brass boiler of steel-blue finish and nickelled fittings** — 503/35 **35 mm gauge**, with tender, 2 **large** coaches, 1 **large** brake van, 6 round and 4 straight rails. Length of train 3 feet 6", total length of rails 9 feet 9" . . . . each complete **20/6**
— 573/48 B		consisting of: **Locomotive with strong brass boiler of steel-blue finish and nickelled fittings** — 503/48 **48 mm gauge**, with tender, 2 **large** coaches, 1 **large** brake van, 8 round and 4 straight rails. Length of train 3 feet 8", total length of rails 13 feet 8" . . . . each complete **28/6**
— 574/35 B		consisting of: **Locomotive with strong brass boiler of steel-blue finish and nickelled fittings** — 504/35 with **reversing gear** — **35 mm gauge**, with tender, 2 large coaches and 1 large brake van, 6 round and 4 straight rails. Length of train 34", total length of rails 13 feet 8", each complete **22/8**
— 574/48 B		consisting of **Locomotive with strong brass boiler of steel-blue finish and nickelled fittings** — 504/48 with **reversing gear** — **48 mm gauge**, with tender, 2 **large** coaches and 1 large brake van, 8 round and 4 straight rails. Length of train 3 feet 8", total length of rails 13 feet 8", each complete **30/8**
— 555/35 B		consisting of: Same locomotive as with 574/35 B, but with **fixed double action cylinders** — 505/35 with **reversing gear** — **35 mm gauge**, with tender, 2 large coaches and 1 large brake van, 6 round and 4 straight rails. Length of train 34", total length of rails 9 feet 9". . . . each complete **25/6**
— 555/48 B		consisting of: Same locomotive as with 574/48 B, but with **fixed double action cylinders** — 505/48 with **reversing gear** — **48 mm gauge**, with tender, 2 large coaches and 1 large brake van, 6 round and 4 straight rails. Length of train 3 feet 8", total length of rails 13 feet 8", each complete **34/6**
— 556/48 B		consisting of: Same locomotive as with 555/48 B but with **patent automatic reversing** — 506/48 with **reversing gear** — **48 mm gauge** with tender, 2 large coaches and 1 large brake van, 8 round and 3 straight rails, also reversing rail. Length of train 3 feet 8", total length of rails 13 feet 8" each complete **43/8**
— 556/48 C		the same set, but with 14 round, 3 straight rails, and 1 straight reversing rail, also 1 crossing, total length of rails 23 feet. . . . . each complete **47/-**
— 556/48 D		the same set as 556/48 B but with 10 round rails, 1 straight reversing rail, **1 pair of switches**. Total length of rails 20 feet. . . . . each complete **50/-**
— 556/48 E		the same set as 556/48 B but with 18 round and 7 straight rails, 2 half round rails and 1 reversing rail, **1 crossing** and **1 pair of switches**. Total length of rails 36 feet. . . . . . each complete **56/-**

Separate rails, coaches and wagons for above railways are listed on pages 94—102.

Trade  Mark,

High class Steam Railway Trains,

packed in elegant cardboard boxes.

1505/3/35 B

No. 1505/3/35 B		consisting of: **Locomotive with strong brass boiler of steel-blue finish and nickelled fittings — 505/35 with fixed double action cylinders,** also **reversing gear** — with tender, **35 mm gauge** — 2 D-express coaches (1 passenger coach and 1 brake van), 6 round and 4 straight rails. Length of train 29", total length of rails 9 feet 9" . . . . each complete **27/6**
— 1505/3/48 B		ditto — **48 mm gauge** — with 8 round and 4 straight rails, length of train 3 feet 1", total length of rails 13 feet 8" . . . . each complete **36/8**
— 1506/3/48 B		consisting of: **Locomotive with strong brass boiler of steel-blue finish and nickelled fittings — 506/48 with patent automatic reversing,** also **reversing gear** — **48 mm gauge** — with tender, 2 D-express coaches (1 passenger coach and 1 brake van), 8 round and 3 straight rails, also 1 reversing rail. Length of train 3 feet 1", total length of rails 13 feet 8", each complete **46/-**

565/35 B

No. 565/35 B		consisting of: **Locomotive with strong brass boiler of steel-blue finish and nickelled fittings — 505/35 with fixed double acting cylinders,** also **reversing gear** — **35 mm gauge** — with tender, 2 large 8 wheel express coaches (1 passenger coach and 1 brake van), 6 round and 4 straight rails. Length of train 33", total length of rails 9 feet 9" . . . . each complete **34/-**
— 565/48 B		ditto — **48 mm gauge,** with 8 round and 4 straight rails. Length of train 3 feet 4", total length of rails 13 feet 8" . . . . each complete **43/-**
— 566/48 B		consisting of: **Locomotive with strong brass boiler and nickelled fittings — 506/48 with patent automatic reversing,** also **reversing gear** — **48 mm gauge** — with tender, 2 large 8 wheel L-express coaches (1 passenger coach and 1 brake van), 8 round and 3 straight rails, also 1 reversing rail. Length of train 3 feet 4", total length of rails 13 feet 8", each complete **52/-**

☛ Separate rails, coaches and wagons for above railways are listed on pages 94—102. ☚

Trade Mark.

English Railway Trains

constructed from the **original models** of the different **Railway Companies**.
High class finish. Packed in elegant cardboard boxes.

583/35 B

Consisting of:

Locomotive, tender, 2 coaches, 1 guard's van, 6 curved and 4 straight rails, **35 mm gauge**

No. 583/35 B . . . . each 21/-	No. 584/35 B . . . . each 23/-	No. 585/35 B . . . . each 26/-
with locomotive 503/35	with locomotive 504/35	with locomotive 505/35
	with reversing gear	with fixed double action cylinders
length of train . . . . . 34″		and reversing gear
— — rails . . 9 ft. 9″	length of train . . . . . 34″	length of train . . . . . 34″
	— — rails . . . 9 ft. 9″	— — rails . . . 9 ft. 9″

These trains can be delivered in the colours of: Great Northern Railway / London and North Western Railway / Midland Railway

when ordering please write after the number of the train either **G. N. R.** or **L. & N. W. R.** or **M. R.**

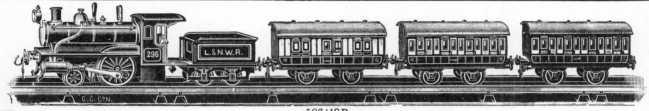

586/48 B

Consisting of:

Locomotive, tender, 2 coaches, 1 guard's van, 8 curved and 4 straight rails, **48 mm gauge**

No. 583/48 B . . . . each 28/-	No. 584/48 B . . . . each 30/-	No. 585/48 B . . . . each 34/-	No. 586/48 B . . . . each 42/6
with locomotive 503/48	with locomotive 504/48	with locomotive 505/48	with locomotive 506/48
	with reversing gear	with fixed double action cylinders	with patent automatic reversing
length of train . . . . . . 42″		and reversing gear	also reversing gear
— — rails . . . . 13 ft. 8″	length of train . . . . . . 42″	length of train . . . . . . 42″	length of train . . . . . . 42″
	— — rails . . . . 13 ft. 8″	— — rails . . . 13 ft. 8″	— — rails . . . 13 ft. 8″

These trains can be delivered in the colours of: Great Northern Railway / London and North Western Railway / Midland Railway

when ordering please write after the number of the train either **G. N. R.** or **L. & N. W. R.** or **M. R.**

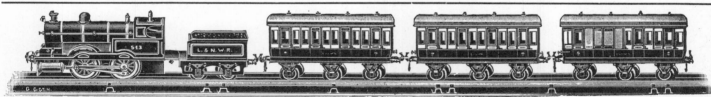

1518/35 B

Best Quality Steam Railway Trains.

35 mm gauge:	**48 mm gauge**
consisting of: Locomotive with spirit vapour lamp, fixed double action "Precision" cylinders with patent reversing gear, tender, 2 superfine 3 wheel coupled coaches, 1 ditto guard's van, 6 curved and 4 straight rails, length of train 39″, length of rails 9 ft. 9″ packed in elegant cardboard box.	consisting of: Same locomotive as in train 35 mm gauge but with central lubricating attachment, tender, 2 superfine 3 wheel coupled coaches, 1 ditto guard's van, 8 curved and 4 straight rails, length of train 50″, length of rails 13 feet 8″, packed in elegant cardboard box.
No. 1517/35 B Great Northern Railway . . . each 45/-	No. 1517/48 B Great Northern Railway . . . each 56/-
— 1518/35 B London and North Western Railway — 45/-	— 1518/48 B London and North Western Railway — 56/-
— 1519/35 B Midland Railway . . . . . . — 45/-	— 1519/48 B Midland Railway . . . . . . — 56/-

The same trains but with high class powerful locomotive, **4 driving wheels and bogie**, with central lubricating attachment, length of train 41″	The same trains but with high class powerful locomotive, **4 driving wheels and bogie**, with central lubricating attachment, length of train 54″
No. 1527/35 B Great Northern Railway . . . each 56/-	No. 1527/48 B Great Northern Railway . . . . each 83/-
— 1528/35 B London and North Western Railway — 56/-	— 1528/48 B London and North Western Railway — 83/-
— 1529/35 B Midland Railway . . . . . . — 56/-	— 1529/48 B Midland Railway . . . . . . — 83/-

For separate rails, coaches and wagons for above railways see pages 94—102 of this list.

Best quality and most up-to-date design Steam Railway Trains
packed in elegant cardboard boxes.

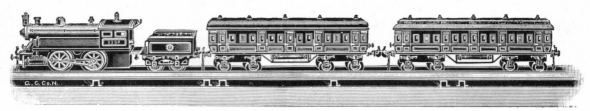

1515/35 B

No. 1515/35 B		consisting of: **powerful locomotive with safety spirit vapour lamp,** fixed double action "precision" cylinders with patent **reversing gear,** with strong brass boiler of steel blue finish, with highly nickelled fittings 515/35 — 35 mm gauge — with tender, 2 large superfine 8 wheel **express coaches** with doors to open, 12 round rails (large radius), 4 straight rails. Length of train 3 feet 5", total length of rails 16 feet . . . . each complete **40/-**
— 1516/35 B		same train but locomotive with cow catcher, **American type** . . . . each **41/-**
— 1515/48 B		the same train, but with locomotive 515/48 **with central lubricating attachment, 48 mm gauge,** 16 round (large radius) and 4 straight rails. Length of train 4 feet 5", total length of rails 30 feet . . . . each complete **58/-**
— 1516/48 B		same train but locomotive with cow catcher, **American type** . . . . each **60/-**

1509/35 B

No. 1509/35 B		consisting of: **high class 8 wheel locomotive** with bogie, 2 patent fixed double action "precision" cylinders, with **reversing gear,** with strong brass boiler of steel blue finish and highly nickelled fittings 509/35 — **35 mm gauge** — with 8 wheel tender, 2 large superfine **8 wheel express coaches** with doors to open, 12 round and 4 straight rails (large radius). Length of train 3 feet 9", total length of rails 16 feet . . . . each complete **52/-**
— 1509/48 B		consisting of: **best quality express locomotive,** 4 driving wheels and bogie (scale model) with 2 patent fixed double action "precision" cylinders with "coulisse" **reversing gear,** strong, well japanned brass boiler, highly nickelled fittings 509/48 — **48 mm gauge** — with 8 wheel tender, 2 large best quality **express coaches with 8 wheels** and doors to open, 16 round and 4 straight rails (large radius). Length of train 5 feet, total length of rails 30 feet . . . each complete **130/-**
— 1525/35 B		consisting of: **high class powerful locomotive, 4 driving wheels** and bogie, **safety spirit vapour lamp,** fixed double action patent slide valve "precision" cylinders with **reversing gear,** with strong brass boiler of steel-blue finish, with highly nickelled fittings and central lubricating attachment 525/35 — **35 mm gauge** — with 8 wheel tender, 2 large, superfine **express coaches** with doors to open, 12 round and 4 straight rails (large radius). Length of train 3 feet 7", total length of rails 16 feet . . . . each complete **55/-**
— 1526/35 B		same train but locomotive with cow catcher, **American type** . . . . each **56/-**
— 1525/48 B		consisting of: **high class powerful locomotive, with 4 driving wheels** and bogie, safety spirit vapour lamp, patent fixed double action slide valve "precision" cylinders, with **reversing gear,** fitted with strong brass boiler of steel-blue finish, with highly nickelled fittings and central lubricating attachment 525/48 — **48 mm gauge** — with tender, 2 large, high class **express coaches** with doors to open, 16 round and 4 straight rails (large radius). Length of train 4 feet 9", total length of rails 30 feet . . . . each complete **76/-**
— 1526/48 B		same train but locomotive with cow catcher, **American type** . . . . each **78/-**

☞ For separate rails, coaches and wagons for above railways see pages 94—102 of this list. ☜

Trade ⚙ Mark.

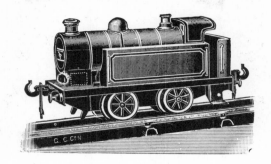

CLOCKWORK RAILWAYS

Separate Accessories for the Formation of Railways.

RAILS ▢ CROSSINGS ▢ SWITCHES

RAILS WITH ORNAMENTAL PARAPET
RAILS FOR ELEVATED RAILWAYS

▢ ▢ ▢

RAILWAY STATIONS ▢ RAILWAY
WAITING ROOMS ▢ TUNNELS
BRIDGES ▢ SIGNALS
ARC LAMPS etc.

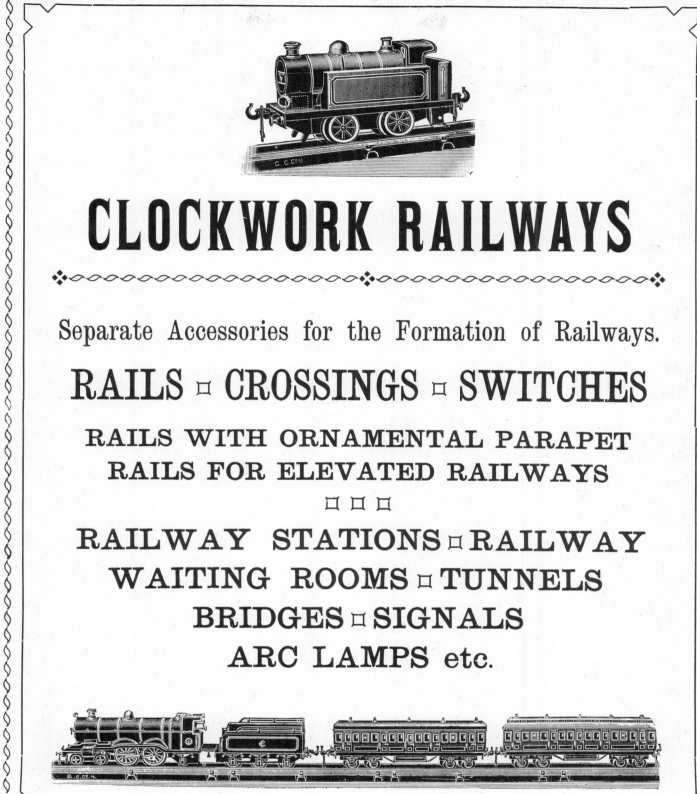

Trade Mark.

Clockwork Railways
Cheap clockwork-railways with controlled spring motors
exact english models

28 mm gauge

No. 871/3 Great Northern Railway Company. — No. 872/3 London and North Western Railway Company.
No. 873/3 Midland Railway Company

Each railway consisting of: **Locomotive, tender** also 2 coaches, 4 round rails (circle) length of train 16″ . . . . dozen 15/6

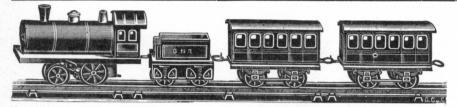

Railways
with powerful spring motors and brake.
exceptionally good value!
35 mm gauge

No. 1701 **Great Northern Railway Company**
— 1702 **London and North Western Railway**
[Comp.
— 1703 **Midland Railway Company.**

No. 1701 or 1702 or 1703/2 consisting of: **locomotive** and **tender, 2 coaches,** 4 round rails (circle), length of train 18″, dozen 24/-
— 1701 — 1702 — 1703/3 — — — — — 3 — 4 — — — — — — 22″, — 30/-

Railways with powerful spring motors and brake
35 mm gauge

881/5

Great Northern Railway Company
consisting of: Locomotive with brake, tender and:

No. 881/0 1 **coach**, 4 curved rails, length of train 13½″ . . . . each 2/6
— 881/2 1 — and **guard's van**, 4 curved rails, length of train 20″ . . . . — 3/4
— 881/5 2 **coaches** and **guard's van**, 6 curved and 2 straight rails, length of train 26″ . . . . . — 4/8
— 881/6 1 **coach**, 6 curved, 4 half straight rails and crossing, length of train 13½″ . . . . — 4/6
— 881/8 1 — and **guard's van**, 10 curved rails and crossing, length of train 20″ . . . . — 5/10
— 881/10 1 — — — — 7 — — — 1 pair of switches, length of train 20″ . . . . — 7/-

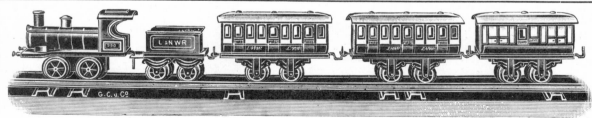

882/5

London and North Western Railway Company
consisting of: Locomotive with brake, tender and:

No. 882/0 1 **coach**, 4 curved rails, length of train 13½″ . . . . each 2/6
— 882/2 1 — and **guard's van**, 4 curved rails, length of train 20″ . . . . — 3/4
— 882/5 2 **coaches** and **guard's van**, 6 curved and 2 straight rails, length of train 26″ . . . . . — 4/8
— 882/6 1 **coach**, 6 curved, 4 half straight rails and crossing, length of train 13½″ . . . . — 4/6
— 882/8 1 — and **guard's van**, 10 curved rails and crossing, length of train 20″ . . . . — 5/10
— 882/10 1 — — — — 7 — — — 1 pair of switches, length of train 20″ . . . . — 7/-

For separate rails, coaches and wagons for above railways see pages 81—83 of this list.

Trade **[Trade Mark logo]** Mark.

Clockwork Railways with powerful spring motors and brake.

35 mm gauge.

883/5

Midland Railway Company

consisting of: Locomotive with brake, tender and.

No. 883/0	1 coach, 4 curved rails, length of train 13½"	. . . . each 2/6
— 883/2	1 — and guard's van, 4 curved rails, length of train 20"	. . . . — 3/4
— 883/5	2 coaches — — — 6 — and 2 straight rails, length of train 26"	. . . . — 4/8
— 883/6	1 coach, 6 curved, 4 half straight rails and crossing, length of train 13½"	. . . . — 4/6
— 883/8	1 — and guard's van, 10 curved rails and crossing, length of train 20"	. . . . . . — 5/10
- 883/10	1 — — — — 7 — — 1 pair of switches, length of train 20"	. . . . . — 7/-

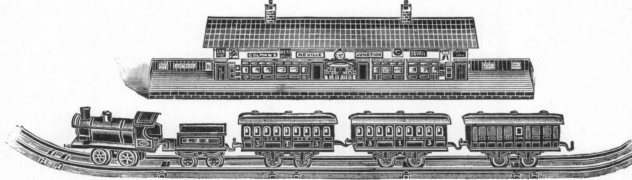

918/10

Clockwork Railway with Station

35 mm gauge.

No. 918/10   consisting of: Locomotive with brake, tender, station 918, 2 coaches and 1 guard's van, 6 curved and 4 straight rails, length of train 26" . . . . each 8/-

☞ **These trains can be had in the colours of:** Great Northern Railway Company. — G. N. R.
London and North Western Railway Company. — L. & N. W. R.
Midland Railway Company — M. R.

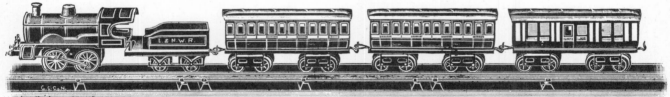

898/3

Railways with very powerful spring motors and strong make.

Great Northern Railway Company.
in the colours of: **London and North Western Railway Company.**
Midland Railway Company.

consisting of: Locomotive, tender, 4 wheel coupled coaches with bogies and:

No. 898/1	1 coach, 6 curved rails (circle), length of train 19"	. . . . each 4/8
— 898/2	2 coaches, 6 curved and 2 straight rails, length of train 27"	. . . . — 5/8
— 898/3	2 — and 1 guard's van, 6 curved and 4 straight rails, length of train 35"	. . . . . — 7/-

When ordering please write to the number of the train.

G. N. R.   for Great Northern Railway.
L. & N. W. R. — London and North Western Railway.
M. R.   — Midland Railway.

For separate rails, coaches and wagons for above railways, see pages 81—83 of this list.

Trade Mark.

RAILWAYS with very powerful spring motors and brake.

Exact english models. — 35 mm gauge.

1711/3

Great Northern Railway Company

consisting of: **locomotive with brake** and **reversing gear, tender** and:

No. 1711/1	**1 coach**, circle of 8 rails, length of trains 18″ . . . . each **7/-**
— 1711/2	**1 —** and **1 guard's van**, track of 8 curved and 2 straight rails, length of train 25″ . . . . — **8/6**
— 1711/3	**2 coaches** and **1 guard's van**, 8 curved and 2 straight rails, length of train 32″ . . . . — **10/-**

The above trains can also be delivered in the colours of:

London and North Western Railway or } When ordering please state the number
Midland Railway. } 1712 for **London and North Western Railway.**
1713 — **Midland Railway.**

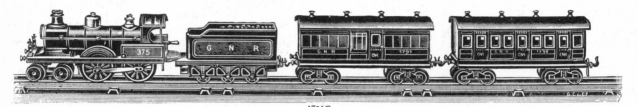

1721/2

Great Northern Railway Company

consisting of: **high class finished locomotive** with **brake** and **reversing gear**, tender and **4 wheel coupled coaches with bogies** and:

No. 1721/1	**1 coach**, circle of 8 rails, length of train 22″ . . . . each **14/-**
— 1721/2	**1 —** and **1 guard's van**, track of 8 curved and 2 straight rails, length of train 30″ . . . . — **16/-**
— 1721/3	**2 coaches** and **1 guard's van**, 8 curved and 2 straight rails, length of train 38″ . . . . — **20/-**

The above trains can also be delivered in the colours of:

London and North Western Railway or } When ordering please state the number
Midland Railway. } 1722 for **London and North Western Railway.**
1723 — **Midland Railway.**

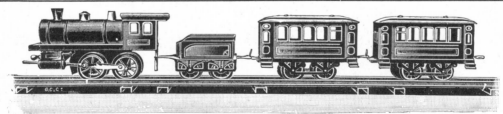

831/2

Railways with powerful spring motors and brake.

Superior quality; 35 mm gauge.

Consisting of: **Locomotive with brake, tender** also:

No. 831/0	**1 coach**, 4 round rails (circle), length of train 15″ . . . . . . each **2/10**	No. 831/6 **1 coach** 6 round rails 2 round half rails and crossing, length of train 15″ each **4/6**
— 831/2	**2 coaches**, 4 — — 20″ . . . . . . — **3/8**	— 831/8 **2 coaches**, 6 — — 2 — 20″ — **5/4**
— 831/4	**3** — 4 — — 25″ . . . . . . — **4/6**	— 831/9 **1 coach**, 5 round rails and 1 pair of switches, length of train 15″ — **5/4**
		— 831/10 **2 coaches**, 7 — — 1 — — 20″ — **7/-**

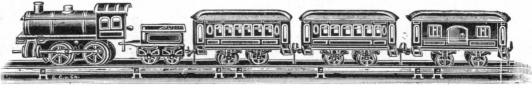

830/3

Railways with very powerful spring motors and brake.

Substantial and well finished quality; 35 mm gauge.

Consisting of: **Locomotive with brake, tender** also:

No. 830/1	**1 D-coach,** 6 round rails (circle), length of train 18″ . . . . each **4/-**
— 830/2	**2 D-coaches,** 6 — — 25″ . . . . — **4/8**
— 830/3	**2** — and **1 D-brake van** with sliding door, 6 round and 2 straight rails (oval formation), length of train 32″ . . . . — **6/-**
— 830/4	**2** — 6 round and 4 straight half rails also crossing, length of train 25″ . . . . — **6/6**
— 830/5	**2** — 7 — rails, 1 pair of switches, length of train 25″ . . . . — **7/6**

For separate rails, coaches and wagons for above railways see pages 81 to 83 of this list.

Clockwork Railways.

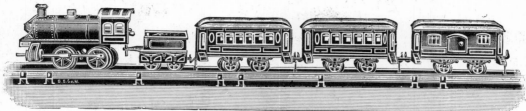

833/3

Railways with very powerful spring motors and brake, also reversing gear, very strong and well finished quality; 35 mm gauge.

Consisting of: **Locomotive with brake and reversing gear, tender** also:

No. 833/1	**1 D-coach,**	6 round rails (circle), length of train 18″	each	**5/-**
— 833/2	**2 D-coaches,**	6 — — — — 25″	—	**6/-**
— 833/3	**2 D- —**	and **1 D-brake van** with sliding doors, 6 round and 2 straight rails (oval formation), length of train 32″	—	**7/-**
— 833/4	**2 D- —**	6 round rails, 4 straight half rails and crossing, length of train 25″	—	**8/-**
— 833/5	**2 D- —**	7 — — and 1 pair of switches, length of train 25″	—	**9/-**

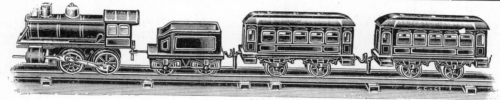

806/2

Railways with powerful spring motors and brake, 48 mm gauge.

Exceptionally good value!

Consisting of: **Locomotive with brake, tender** also:

No. 806/1	**1 express coach,**	6 round rails (circle), length of train 22″	each	**5/6**
— 806/2	**2 — coaches,**	6 — — — — — — 30″	—	**7/-**

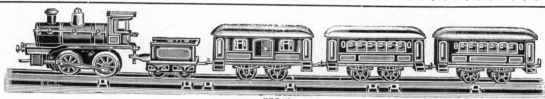

822/3

Railways with very powerful spring motors, brake and reversing gear very strong and most superior quality; 35 mm gauge.

Consisting of: **Locomotive with brake and reversing gear, tender** also:

No. 822/1	**1 D-coach,**	6 round rails (circle), length of train 17½″	each	**8/-**
— 822/2	**2 D-coaches,**	6 — — and 2 straight rails (oval formation), length of train 25″	—	**9/-**
— 822/3	**2 D- —**	and **1 D-brake van** with sliding doors, 6 round and 2 straight rails (oval formation), length of train 32½″	—	**10/-**
— 822/4	**2 D- —**	10 round rails and crossing, length of train 25″	—	**9/8**
— 822/5	**2 D- —**	7 — — 2 straight rails and 1 pair of switches, length of train 25″	—	**11/-**

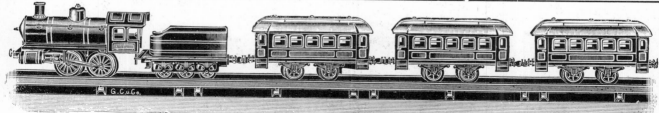

807/3

Railways with very powerful spring motors and brake, very strong and most superior quality; 35 mm gauge.

Consisting of: **Locomotive with brake, tender** also:

No. 807/1	**1 express coach,**	8 round rails (circle), length of train 22″	each	**11/-**
— 807/2	**2 express coaches,**	8 — — and 2 straight rails (oval formation), length of train 31″	—	**12/-**
— 807/3	**3 — —**	8 — — 4 — — — — — — — — 40″	—	**14/-**
— 807/4	**2 — —**	14 — — — crossing, length of train 31″	—	**15/6**
— 807/5	**2 — —**	14 — — — 2 straight rails and 2 straight half rails also 1 pair of switches, length of train 31″	—	**18/-**

For separate rails, coaches and wagons for above railways, see pages 81—83 of this list.

Clockwork Railways.

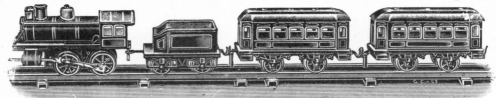

829/3

Railways with powerful spring motors, with brake and reversing gear, strong and superior quality, 48 mm gauge, consisting of: locomotive with brake and reversing gear, tender also:

No. 829/1 1 express coach, 8 round rails (circle,) length of train 22" . . . . each 8/-
— 829/2 2 —   coaches, 8 — — — — — — 30" . . . . — 9/6
— 829/3 3 —   8 — and 2 straight rails (oval formation), length of train 38". . . . . — 12/6

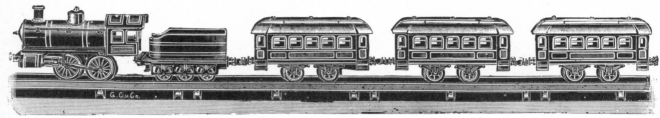

808/3

Railways with very powerful spring motors, with brake and reversing gear, very strong and most superior quality, 35 mm gauge, consisting of: locomotive with brake and reversing gear, tender also:

No. 808/1 1 express coach, 8 round rails (circle), length of train 22" . . . . each 13/-
— 808/2 2 —   coaches, 8 — and 2 straight rails (oval formation), length of train 31" . . . . — 14/6
— 808/3 3 —   — 8 — 4 — — — — — — 40" . . . . — 16/-
— 808/4 2 —   — 14 — — crossing, length of train 31" . . . . — 18/-
— 808/5 2 —   -- 14 — — 2 straight and 2 straight half rails also 1 pair of switches, length of train 31" — 20/-

Clockwork railways with extra strongly built locomotives, 35 mm gauge.
Excellent spring motor of great power.

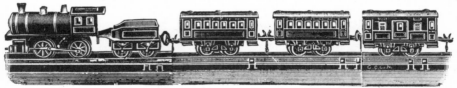

1819/1/35 B

No. 1819/1/35 B consisting of: **locomotive with extra strong and powerful motor, tender, 2 coaches and 1 brake van,** 6 round rails (circle), length of train 31" . . . . each 7/4

1819/2/35 B

No. 1819/2/35 B consisting of: **locomotive with extra strong and powerful motor, tender, 2 D-coaches and 1 D-brake van,** 6 round rails (circle), length of train 35" . . . . each 10/8

For separate rails, coaches and wagons, see pages 81 to 83 of this list.

Trade  Mark,

Clockwork Railways.

1107/62

Clockwork Tramway.
28 mm gauge.

No. **1107/61** consisting of: **Motorwagon** with spring motor, 4 round rails (circle), length of car 8" . . . each **2/-**

— **1107/62** consisting of: **Motorwagon** with spring motor and trailing car, 4 round and 2 straight rails (oval formation), total length of cars 16" . . . each **3/-**

— **1107/3** Trailing car . . . . — **—/10**

Tramway with automatic switching attachment, 30 mm gauge.

No. **805/3** consisting of: **Motorwagon with spring motor**, oval formation with double set of lines, length of rails 10 feet 4" each **4/6**

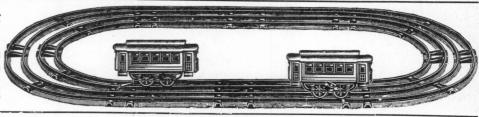

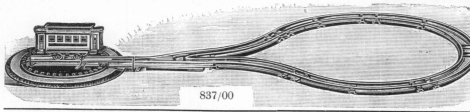

837/00

Tramway with mechanical turntable.
Quite original design.   Quite original design.
30 mm gauge.

No. **837/00** consisting of: 1 Motorwagon, 4 round and 2 round half rails, 1 switch and 1 mechanical turntable, length of rails 5 feet 9" . . . . each **5/6**

Quite original design.   **Railway with mechanical turntable.**   Quite original design.

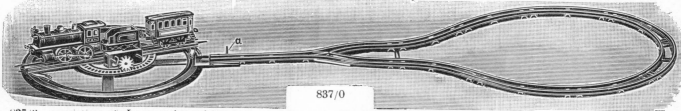

837/0

No. **837/0** consisting of: Locomotive with tender and 1 coach, 35 mm gauge, 7 round and 1 straight rail, switch and 1 mechanical turntable, length of rail formation 8 feet, length of train 15" . . . . each complete **10/6**

This railway with turntable is a most charming toy for a boy. The action is as follows. The train on reaching the turntable stops automatically, then the turntable begins to turn after the clockwork has been wound up, and continues to turn, till the rails on the turntable are again in a line with the track: then the motion stops and the train travels off again automatically. The cycle of operations continues until the clockwork of either the train or turntable has run down.

Elevated Railway quite original.
Quite original.   **35 mm gauge.**   Quite original.

No. **805/4** consisting of: Motorwagon and trailing car, 4 round and 2 straight rails. 8 supports also a flight of stairs, length of rails, 5 feet 7", each **4/-**

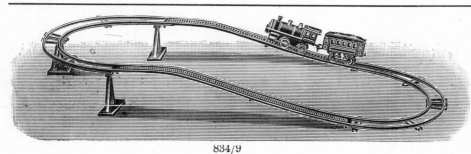

805/4

834/9

Rack Railway, 35 mm gauge.

No. 834/9

consisting of: Locomotive, 1 coach, 4 round rails, 2 straight rail parts, 3 supports.

Length of train 11", total length of rail formation 40" . . . . each **5/-**

Clockwork Railways.

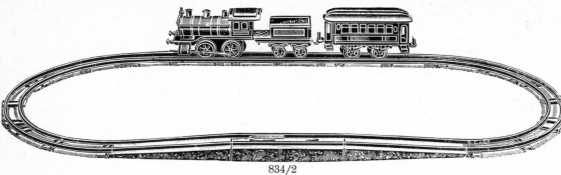

834/2

Railways with mechanical stop-ping, and automatic ringing attachment

strong quality,
35 mm gauge.

Immediately the train has reached the embankment, it is stopped by an automatic contrivance. As long as the train remains stationary, a clockwork bell fitted under the slope will ring. After an automatic shifting of a lever the train starts off again.

No. **834/2** consisting of: **Locomotive**, with clockwork bell, 2 sloping tender, **1 coach**, 6 round and 3 straight rails, 1 straight embankment approaches, length of train 16" . . . . each 8/-

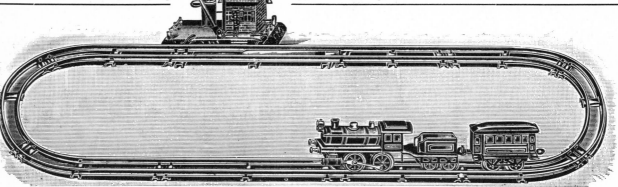

834/4

Clockwork railway and automatic stopping arrangement, 35 mm gauge.

No. **834/4** As soon as the train reaches the waiting-room, it stops and a signal bell at the waiting room starts ringing, then the train starts off again automatically, and repeats the performance.

This set consists of: Locomotive, tender and 1 coach, 6 round and 4 straight rails, also 1 mechanical railway waiting room. Length of train 15" . . . . each 11/-

Railway

with covered railway station and automatic stop.
35 mm gauge.

=== **Quite original!** ===

As soon as the train has entered the station, it stops automatically and the bell attached to the station begins to ring. By pulling a knob fitted to the station, the train is re-started and the bell ceases to ring. This cycle of operations can be continued till the clockwork requires re-winding.

No. **834/6** consisting of: **Locomotive, tender, 2 coaches,** 6 round, 2 straight and 2 straight half-rails, also **railway station with clockwork bell,** length of train 21" total length of rails 9 feet 8" . . . . each 13/-

No. **834/7** the same railway but station without bell and only 1 coach length of train 16" . . . . — 10/6

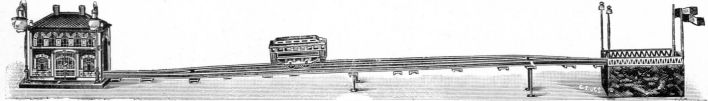

Striking novelty!   837/3   Striking novelty!

Mountain railway with automatic stopping and reversing gear also bell.

The train automatically leaves the station, runs up the embankment by one branch line, reverses, runs back by the other branch and reaches the station again by means of a switch. The bell in the station rings and the train remains stationary till one of the knobs on the station is pressed then the bell ceases and the train departs on its journey once more.

This railway ranks as one of the most interesting among model railway sets.

No. **837/3** consisting of: **Motor wagon,** very strong design fitted with powerful spring motor, 2 switches, 3 sets of straight double pairs of rails, 2 rail supports, 1 reversing station with 2 flags and 2 telegraph poles, 1 well japanned railway station with 2 large arc lamps and mechanical bell, every part very strongly made, length of motor wagon 8", length of the whole railway 6 feet 9" . . . . each complete 22/-

For separate rails, coaches and wagons for above railways, see pages 81 to 83 of this list.

Clockwork Railways.

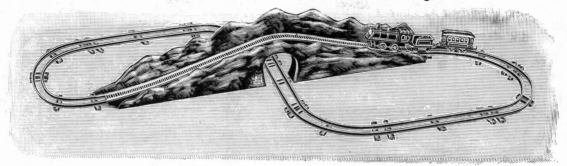

Quite original!

Quite original!

834/8

Mountain rack railway with handsome moulded landscape artistically japanned,

35 mm gauge

No. 834/8 consisting of: **Locomotive with extra powerful spring motor, tender, 1 coach,** 6 round rails, 2 straight long and 1 straight rail, also a straight half-rail, very fine mountain landscape with tunnel, length of rail formation 5 feet 4" . . each 16/-

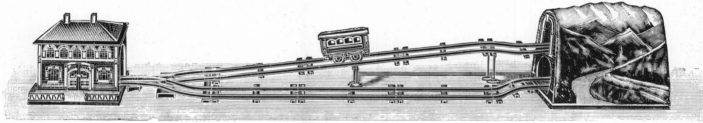

837/4

Very interesting!   **Quite original!**

Mountain Railway with automatic reverse at both stations and automatic bell.

The motor wagon, which is fitted with an extra powerful spring motor, runs first up the sloping embankment and enters the tunnel at the top. In this upper tunnel is a set of rails and as soon as the motor wagon runs on to them, they are automatically lowered into the bottom tunnel. When the rails register with the lower branch line, the train goes back on the lower set of rails till it reaches the station, here it reverses itself and repeats the above described cycle of operations. A special feature of the railway is the ringing of a bell while the train is being lowered and a second ringing when the rails are lifted up after the train has left the lower tunnel. The whole apparatus is very strongly made and consists of a well japanned railway station, 2 tunnels situated one over the other, enamelled to resemble a mountain road, with bell ringing appliance, very best finish, 1 motor wagon with powerful spring motor, 6 straight rails, 2 of same with supports, 1 switch, 2 curved rails. Length of the route 6 feet 2", length of the motor wagon 5".

No. 837/4 . . . . each complete 20/-

918

No. 918

English Railway Station

handsomely made and nicely japanned, 23" long, 5" wide each 3/-

Separate Locomotives fitted with spring motors.

Suitable for railways listed on pages 72—79.   Coaches, Wagons and rails for same are listed on pages 81—83.

1701/35 T

831/35 T

819/35 T

No. 1701/35 Locomotive with brake, 35 mm gauge, simple design, 5" long, each 1/-

No. 1701 T Tender for above 3½" long, each -/4

Locomotives and tenders 1701 can be delivered in the colours of **Great Northern Railway,** **London** and **North Western Railway,** **Midland Railway.**
When ordering please state the number No. **1701** for **G. N. R.**
No. **1702** for **L. & N. W. R.**
— **1703** — **M. R.**

No. 831/35   Locomotive better quality, with brake, 35 mm gauge, 6¼" long . . . . dozen 15/6

No. 831 T Tender for above 4¼" long, each -/6

No. 819/35 Locomotive with extra strong mechanism and powerful spring 35 mm gauge, well made, 6" long, each 3/6

No. 819 T Tender for above 4½" long each -/6

No. 830/35 Locomotive with strong motor and brake, 35 mm gauge, strong design, 6¾" long . . each 2/-

No. 830 T
Tender for above 4¼" long, each -/6

No. 833/35
Locomotive, with strong motor and brake, also reversing, 35 mm gauge strong and handsome design, 6¾" long, each 3/4

No. 833 T
Tender for above 4½" long, each -/8

830/35 with tender

833/35 with tender

829/48 with tender

No. 829/48 Locomotive with strong motor and brake, also reversing gear 48 mm gauge, 8" long   each 4/-
— **829 T Tender** for above, 6" long . . . . . — 1/-

822/35 with tender

No. 822/35 Locomotive with very strong motor and brake, also reversing gear 35 mm gauge, 6¼" long each 5/-
— **822 T Tender** for above, 4" long . . . . . — -/8

No. 807/808/35 with tender

No. 807/35 Locomotive with very powerful motor and brake, 35 mm gauge, very strong and elegant design, 8" long. . . . . each 7/-
No. 808/35 above loco. **with reversing gear** . . — 9/-
— **808 T Tender** for above locos, 6¾" long . . — 1/8

821/48 with tender

No. 821/48 Locomotive with most powerful motor and brake, also reversing gear, 48 mm gauge, very strong and superior design with 2 highly nickelled domes and connecting rods, 10" long . . . each 11/-
— **821 T Tender** for above, 6" long . . . . — 1/-

For separate rails, coaches and wagons for above locomotives see pages 81 to 83 of this list.

Trade   Mark.

Separate Clockwork Locomotives and Coaches

35 mm gauge,

suiting trains on pages 72—74.

881/35 T

898/35 T. L. & N. W. R.

Exact English Models.

No. 881/35 Great Northern Railway Locomotive, 5" long, with brake . . dozen 17/-
— 882/35 London and North Western Railway, 5" — — — . — 17/-
— 883/35 Midland Railway, 5" — — — . — 17/-
— 881 T
— 882 T } Tenders for same, 3¾" long . . . . — 4/-
— 883 T

No. 898/35 **Locomotive**, better quality, with brake, 6¼" long . . . . dozen 24/-
— 898 T **Tender** for same, 5" long . . . . — 4/-
When ordering please write after the number
G. N. R. for Great Northern Railway
L. & N. W. R. — London and North Western Railway
M. R. — Midland Railway.

1711/35 T

1722/35 T

High class Clockwork-Locomotives with **powerful spring motors,** brake and reversing gear, 4 wheel coupled locomotives with bogies.

No. 1711/35 Great Northern Railway Locomotive, 7" long . . . . . each 4/6
— 1712/35 London and North Western Railway, 7" — . . . . . . — 4/6
— 1713/35 Midland Railway, 7" — . . . . . . — 4/6

Tenders for same

No. 1711 T suitable for 1711/35, 5¼" long . . . . each 1/2
— 1712 T — 1712/35, 5¼" — . . . . . . — 1/2
— 1713 T — 1713/35, 5¼" — . . . . . . — 1/2

High class execution.

No. 1721/35 Great Northern Railway, 8" long . . . . each 9/-
— 1722/35 London and North Western Railway, 8" long . . . . . . — 9/-
— 1723/35 Midland Railway, 8" long . . . . — 9/-

Tenders for same

No. 1721 T suitable for 1721/35, 7" long . . . . each 1/4
— 1722 T — 1722/35, 7" — . . . . — 1/4
— 1723 T — 1723/35, 7" — . . . . — 1/4

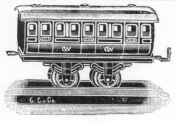

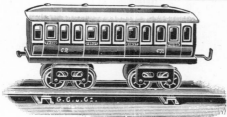

COACHES.

Passenger Cars

No. 881 P Great Northern Railway, 5¼" long, dozen 6/-
— 882 P London and North Western Railway,
5¼" long . . . . — 6/-
— 883 P Midland Railway, 5¼" long . . . . — 6/-

Guard's Van

No. 881 V Great Northern Railway, 5¼" long, dozen 6/-
— 882 V London and North Western Railway,
5¼" long . . . . . — 6/-
— 883 V Midland Railway, 5¼" long . . . — 6/-

Passenger Cars with bogies

No. 898 P/1 Great Northern Railway, 8" long, dozen 9/-
— 898 P/2 London and North Western Railway,
8" long . . . . — 9/-
— 898 P/3 Midland Railway, 8" long . . . — 9/-

Guard's Van with bogies

No. 898 V/1 Great Northern Railway, 8" long, dozen 9/-
— 898 V/2 London and North Western Railway,
8" long . . . . — 9/-
— 898 V/3 Midland Railway, 8" long . . . . — 9/-

Strongly made Passenger Cars

No. 126/1/35 Great Northern Railway, 6¾" long,
dozen 14/6
— 126/2/35 London and North Western Railway,
6¾" long . . . . dozen 14/6
— 126/3/35 Midland Railway, 6¾" long . — 14/6

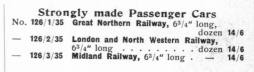

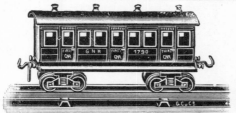

Strongly made Guard's Van.

No. 124/1/35 Great Northern Railway, 6¾" long,
dozen 14/6
— 124/2/35 London and North Western Railway,
6¾" long . . . . dozen 14/6
— 124/3/35 Midland Railway, 6¾" long . — 14/6

Beautifully made coaches, with bogies, compartment doors to open.

Passenger Cars

No. 127/1/35 Great Northern Railway, 8¼" long,
each 2/8
— 127/2/35 London and North Western Railway,
8¼" long . . . . each 2/8
— 127/3/35 Midland Railway, 8¼" long . . — 2/8

Guard's Van

No. 125/1/35 Great Northern Railway, 8¼" long,
each 2/8
— 125/2/35 London and North Western Railway,
8¼" long . . . . each 2/8
— 125/3/35 Midland Railway, 8¼" long . . — 2/8

For rails for above locomotives and coaches see pages 83 of this list.

Separate Coaches and Wagons for Railways.

Suitable for railways and locomotives listed on pages 72—81.

Cheap Quality
35 mm gauge.

Passenger coaches	Coal wagons	Oil wagons	Tipping wagons	Timber trucks
No. 130/30/35 5" long, dozen **4/-**	No. 130/34/35 5" long, dozen **3/-**	No. 130/35/35 5" long, dozen **3/8**	No. 130/36/35 5" long, dozen **4/-**	No. 130/37/35 5" long, dozen **2/8**

Strong quality.

No. 130/1/35 Passenger coach
5¹/₂" long, 3¹/₂" high,
each **-/6**

No. 130/2/35 D-Passenger coach
6¹/₄" long, 3¹/₂" high
each **-/8**

No. 130/7/35 D-Brake Van
with movable sliding doors,
6¹/₄" long, 3¹/₂" high
each **1/-**

No. 130/12/35 D-Passenger coach,
8" long, 4" high, each **1/8**
No. 130/3/35 D-Passenger coach,
better quality with doors to open,
8" long, 4" high,
each **2/6**

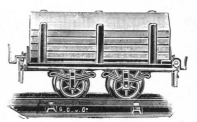

No. 130/11/35 Long timber wagon,
4³/₄" long, 2¹/₄" high,
each **-/8**

No. 130/9/35 Coal wagon,
with brake shelter, 5¹/₂" long, 3¹/₂" high,
each **1/-**

No. 130/18/35 Timber truck,
with side stays, 6" long, 2³/₄" high,
each **1/2**

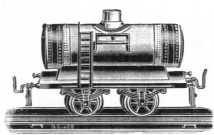
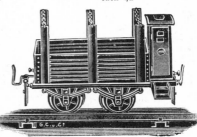

No. 130/14/35 Lime wagon,
with lifting lid, 4¹/₂" long, 3" high,
each **1/2**

No. 130/13/35 Oil wagon,
5¹/₂" long, 3¹/₂" high,
each **1/4**

No. 130/19/35 Luggage wagon,
with brake shelter, 5¹/₂" long, 3¹/₂" high,
each **1/-**

No. 130/15/35 Cattle wagon,
4³/₄" long, 2³/₄" high,
each **1/-**

No. 130/16/35 Crane wagon,
5³/₄" long, 5¹/₄" high
each **1/-**

No. 130/10/35 Covered wagon,
5¹/₂" long, 4¹/₄" high,
each **1/2**

 Trade Mark.

Separate Rails for Railways.

☛ To suit all railways and locomotives, from page 72 to 82 of this list. ☚

4 round rail parts of rails No. 938/4/35 R will make a circle of 20" diameter
6 — — — — — 939/6/35 R — — — — 22½" —
8 — — — — — 939/8/35 R — — — — 30½" —
6 — — — — — 939/6/48 R — — — — 29½" —
8 — — — — — 939/8/48 R — — — — 36"

Round Rails.

No. 938/4/35 **R**	35 mm gauge . . . . dozen	2/-
— 939/6/35 **R**	35 — — —	— 2/-
— 939/8/35 **R**	35 — — —	— 2/-
— 939/6/48 **R**	48 — — —	— 3/8
— 939/8/48 **R**	48 — — —	— 3/8

Straight Rails.

No. 939/35 **G**	35 mm gauge . . . . dozen	2/-
— 939/48 **G**	48 — — —	— 3/8

939/HR

Half and Quarter curved Rails.

No. 939 **HR**/35	Half 35 mm gauge . . . . dozen	1/6
— 939 **HR**/48	— 48 — — —	— 2/-
— 939 **VR**/35	Quarter 35 mm gauge	— 1/4
— 939 **VR**/48	48 — — —	— 1/10

939/HG

Half and Quarter straight Rails.

No. 939 **HG**/35	Half 35 mm gauge . . . . dozen	1/6
— 939 **HG**/48	— 48 — — —	— 2/-
— 939 **VG**/35	Quarter 35 mm gauge	— 1/4
— 939 **VG**/48	— 48 — — —	— 1/10

Brake Rail, straight
35 mm gauge.

No. 939/35 **BG** . . . . dozen 4/6

939/BG

Brake Rail, straight
48 mm gauge

No. 939/48 **BG** . . . . dozen 7/2

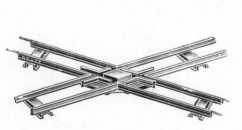

Crossings.

No. 939/6/35 **K**	35 mm gauge, each	1/4
— 939/8/35 **K**	35 — —	— 1/4
— 939/6/48 **K**	48 — —	— 1/10
— 939/8/48 **K**	48 — —	— 1/10

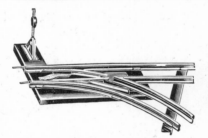

Switches, left and right hand.

No. 939/6/35 **W**	35 mm gauge, pair	2/6
— 939/8/35 **W**	35 — —	— 4/-
— 939/6/48 **W**	48 — —	— 5/-
— 939/8/48 **W**	48 — —	— 5/-

Turntables.
Simple design.

No. 647/1/35 for 35 mm gauge, 10" diam.
each 2/-
— 647/1/48 — 48 — — 10" diam.
each 2/-

937 R/28

937 G/28

No. 937 **R**/28 **Round Rails, 28 mm gauge** suitable for clockwork tramways No. 1107/61, 1107/62 (for circle formation of 18"
4 pieces are necessary) . . . . dozen 1/8
— 937 **G**/28 **Straight Rails, 28 mm gauge** for above . . . . — 1/8

Trade Mark.

957/1
and 2/35

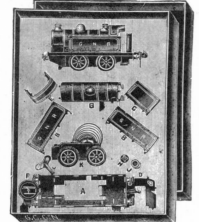

957 P/1
and 957 P/2

966/35, 967/35

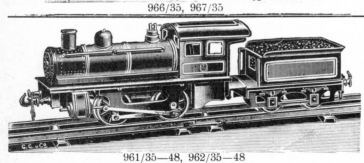

961/35—48, 962/35—48

968/35—48

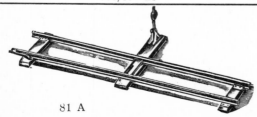

81 A

Handsome Locomotives
with Spring Motors
very strong quality.

New Suburban tank locomotive
well japanned,

No. 957/1/35 **35 mm gauge**, with **brake**, 7¹/₂" long, each 3/8
— 957/2/35 the same loco but with **reversing gear**, — 4/-

These locomotives can be delivered in the colours of:

||| **Great Northern Railway Company.** |||
London and **North Western Railway Company.**
Midland Railway Company.

When ordering please write after the number
G. N. R. or L. and N.W.R. or M. R.

Suburban tank locomotives in parts.

This elegant cardboard box contains all the necessary parts
to build the above locomotives.

Very instructive!

No. 957 P/1 **Locomotive in parts**, for **35 mm gauge**,
clockwork with **brake** . . . . each 3/10
— 957 P/2 **Locomotive in parts**, for **35 mm gauge**,
clockwork with **brake and reversing gear**,
each 4/6

These locomotives can be delivered in the colours of:

||| **Great Northern Railway Company.** |||
London and **North Western Railway Company.**
Midland Railway Company (see above).

No. 966/35 **Tank locomotive**, strong motor,
with **brake 35 mm gauge**, 9" long . each 8/-
— 967/35 the same loco with **brake and
reversing gear**, 9" long . . . . — 9/8

Handsome locomotives with spring motors
of high class finish, with **very strong motors** and massive
turned flanged wheels.

No. 961/35 **Locomotive and tender, 35 mm gauge**,
very strong clockwork, with **brake**,
13" long incl. tender, locomotive only, each 9/-
tender extra . . . . — -/10
— 961/48 the same loco, but **48 mm gauge**,
17" long incl. tender, locomotive only, — 12/-
tender extra . . . . — 1/6

No. 962/35 **Locomotive and tender, 35 mm gauge**,
fitted with very powerful motor and
brake, also **reversing gear**, 13" long
incl. tender, locomotive only . . . each 10/6
tender extra . . . . — -/10
— 962/48 the same loco but, **48 mm gauge**,
17" long incl. tender, locomotive only, — 16/-
tender extra . . . . — 1/6

Handsome locomotives with spring motors and
patent automatic reversing gear

The patent automatic reversing gear fitted to these
locomotives allows the locomotives to be reversed either by
hand from the cab, or automatically by means of a reversing rail.

No. 968/35 **35 mm gauge with brake and reversing
gear either automatic or by hand**,
13" long incl. tender, locomotive only, each 17/-
tender extra . . . . — -/10

— 968/48 the same loco, **48 mm gauge**, 17" long
incl. tender, locomotive only . . . — 22/-
tender extra . . . . — 1/6

Reversing rails for above

No. 81 **A**/35 for 968/35 . . . . each -/10
— 81 **A**/48 for 968/48 . . . . — 1/-

For separate rails coaches and wagons for
above locomotives see pages 94—102 of this list.

High class Locomotives with Spring Motors

superfine finish and best quality japanning.
Constructed from the original models of the different English Railway Companies.

Scale Models.
═══ Peckett tank locomotive. ═══

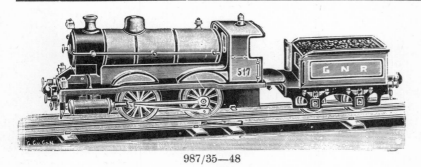

939/35—48

No. 969/35 for 35 mm gauge, with **brake** and reversing gear, 9¼" long . each **16/-**
— 969/48 ditto for 48 mm gauge, 12" long . . . . — **30/-**
These locomotive No. 969 can be de delivered in the colours of:

Great Northern Railway
London and North Western Railway
Midland Railway.

When ordering please write after the number either G. N. R., L. & N. W. R. or M. R.

Scale Models.
High class Locomotives
with very powerful motors,

massive turned flanged wheels, **brake** and **reversing** gear. The new reversing gear fitted to these locomotives allows the locomotives to be reversed either by hand from the cab or by means of a reversing rail.

Best quality japanning.

987/35—48

No. 987/35 **Great Northern Railway** Locomotive with tender, for **35 mm gauge**, 14" long . . . . each **18/-**
— 987/48 ditto for **48 mm gauge**, 16½" long . . . . — **24/-**

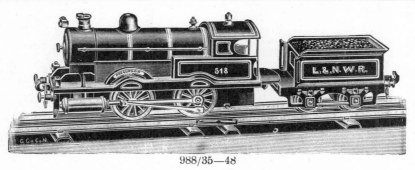

988/35—48

No. 988/35 **London and North Western Railway** Locomotive with tender, for **35 mm gauge**, 14" long . . . . each **18/-**
— 988/48 ditto, for **48 mm gauge**, 16½" long . . . . — **24/-**

989/35—48

No. 989/35 **Midland Railway** Locomotive with tender, for **35 mm gauge**, 14" long . . . . each **18/-**
— 989/48 ditto, for **48 mm gauge**, 16½" long . . . . — **24/-**

☞ For rails, coaches and wagons see pages 94—102 of this list. ☜

Trade Mark

High class Locomotives with Spring Motors.

Superfine finish and best quality japanning.

997/35—48

Scale Models.

4 wheel coupled locomotives with **most powerful** motors, massive turned flanged wheels, **brake** and **reversing gear**. The new reversing gear fitted to these locomotives allows the locomotives to be reversed either by hand from the cab or by means of a reversing rail.
— **Best quality japanning.** —

No. 997/35 **Great Northern Railway Locomotive** with tender with bogie, **for 35 mm gauge**, 16" long each **28/-**
— 997/48 ditto, for **48 mm gauge**, 20½" long . . . . — **36/-**

998/35—48

No. 998/35 **London and North Western Railway Locomotive** with tender with bogie, for **35 mm gauge**, 16" long . . . . each **28/-**
— 998/48 ditto, for **48 mm gauge**, 20½" long . . . . — **36/-**

999/35—48

No. 999/35 **Midland Railway Locomotive** with tender with bogie, for **35 mm gauge**, 16" long, each **28/-**
— 999/48 ditto, for **48 mm gauge**, 20½" long . . . . — **36/-**

For rails, coaches and wagons see pages 94—102 of this list.

Trade Mark.

Superfine Locomotives with Spring Motors

963/35—48

Express Locomotives.

Highly japanned and with complete detail, fitted with very powerful spring motor.

No. **963/35** **35 mm gauge**, 14″ long incl. tender, with **brake** and **reversing gear** . . . . locomotive only each **16/-**
tender extra — **2/6**

— **963/48** the same locomotive, **48 mm gauge**, 18¼″ long incl. tender . . . . locomotive only — **20/-**
tender extra — **3/4**

These locomotives can be had in the colours of: **London** and **North Western, Great Northern** or **Midland Railway.**
When ordering these please write **L & NWR, GNR,** or **MR,** after the number of the locomotive.

965/35—54

Modern 4 wheel coupled Express Locomotives with bogie and double bogie type tender.
Scale model.
Fitted with the most complete detail and beautifully japanned, **brake and reversing gear.**

No. **965/35** 35 mm gauge, 17½″ long (incl. tender) . . . . each complete **44/-**
— **965/48** 48 — — 22½″ — — — — . . . . — — **55/-**
— **965/54** 54 — — 26″ — — — — . . . . — — **68/-**

☞ Only large radius curves No. 80 (page 97) are suitable for these locomotives.

1513/6, 1514/6

Latest type Express Locomotive with bogie, 4 driving wheels, 2 trailing wheels and 6 wheel tender.
Most perfect scale model, superfine japanning. **Very strong and powerful spring motor, brake and reversing gear,**
fitted with brass handrail, imitation starting valve, massive well turned flanged wheels, highly nickelled **spring buffers.**

Great Northern Railway Model

No. **1513/6** 35 mm gauge, 19½″ long, (incl. tender) . . . . each complete **40/-**
— **1514/6** 48 — — 25″ — — — — . . . . — — **70/-**

☞ Only large radius curves No. 80 (page 97) are suitable for locomotives 1513 and 1514.
Suitable express coaches for locomotives No. 965 and 1514 are listed on pages 101 No. 132 DB and 132 DR.

Railways fitted with very powerful Spring Motors packed in handsome cardboard boxes.
Trains with new Suburban Tank Locomotive, 35 mm gauge.

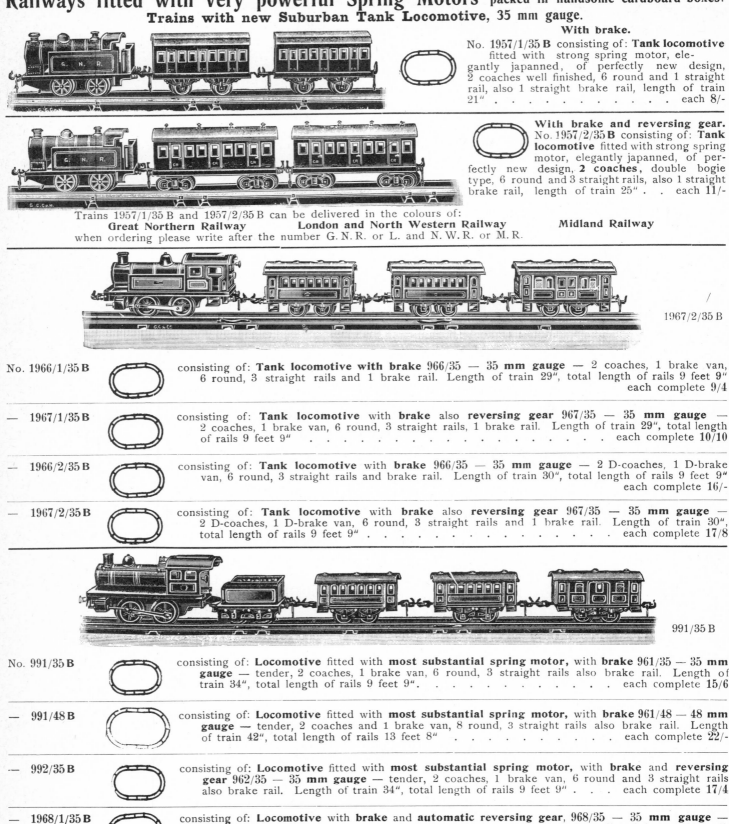

With brake.

No. 1957/1/35 B consisting of: **Tank locomotive** fitted with strong spring motor, elegantly japanned, of perfectly new design, 2 coaches well finished, 6 round and 1 straight rail, also 1 straight brake rail, length of train 21" . . . . each 8/-

With brake and reversing gear.

No. 1957/2/35 B consisting of: **Tank locomotive** fitted with strong spring motor, elegantly japanned, of perfectly new design, **2 coaches**, double bogie type, 6 round and 3 straight rails, also 1 straight brake rail, length of train 25" . . each 11/-

Trains 1957/1/35 B and 1957/2/35 B can be delivered in the colours of:
Great Northern Railway   London and North Western Railway   Midland Railway
when ordering please write after the number G. N. R. or L. and N. W. R. or M. R.

1967/2/35 B

No. 1966/1/35 B	consisting of: **Tank locomotive with brake** 966/35 — 35 mm gauge — 2 coaches, 1 brake van, 6 round, 3 straight rails and 1 brake rail. Length of train 29", total length of rails 9 feet 9" each complete 9/4
— 1967/1/35 B	consisting of: **Tank locomotive** with **brake** also **reversing gear** 967/35 — 35 mm gauge — 2 coaches, 1 brake van, 6 round, 3 straight rails, 1 brake rail. Length of train 29", total length of rails 9 feet 9" . . . . each complete 10/10
— 1966/2/35 B	consisting of: **Tank locomotive** with **brake** 966/35 — 35 mm gauge — 2 D-coaches, 1 D-brake van, 6 round, 3 straight rails and brake rail. Length of train 30", total length of rails 9 feet 9" each complete 16/-
— 1967/2/35 B	consisting of: **Tank locomotive** with **brake** also **reversing gear** 967/35 — 35 mm gauge — 2 D-coaches, 1 D-brake van, 6 round, 3 straight rails and 1 brake rail. Length of train 30", total length of rails 9 feet 9" . . . . each complete 17/8

991/35 B

No. 991/35 B	consisting of: **Locomotive** fitted with **most substantial spring motor, with brake** 961/35 — 35 mm gauge — tender, 2 coaches, 1 brake van, 6 round, 3 straight rails also brake rail. Length of train 34", total length of rails 9 feet 9". . . . . each complete 15/6
— 991/48 B	consisting of: **Locomotive** fitted with **most substantial spring motor, with brake** 961/48 — 48 mm gauge — tender, 2 coaches and 1 brake van, 8 round, 3 straight rails also brake rail. Length of train 42", total length of rails 13 feet 8" . . . . each complete 22/-
— 992/35 B	consisting of: **Locomotive** fitted with **most substantial spring motor, with brake** and **reversing gear** 962/35 — 35 mm gauge — tender, 2 coaches, 1 brake van, 6 round and 3 straight rails also brake rail. Length of train 34", total length of rails 9 feet 9" . . . each complete 17/4
— 1968/1/35 B	consisting of: **Locomotive** with **brake** and **automatic reversing gear**, 968/35 — 35 mm gauge — tender, 2 coaches, 1 brake van, 6 round, 2 straight rails, 1 brake rail and 1 reversing rail. Length of train 33", total length of rails 9 feet 9" . . . . each complete 26/-
— 1968/1/48 B	the same set as 1968/1/35 B for 48 mm gauge, with 8 round, 2 straight rails, 1 brake rail, 1 reversing rail. Length of train 42", total length of rails 13 feet 8" . . . . each complete 34/-

For separate rails, coaches and wagons to suit above railways see pages 94 to 102 of this list.

Railway Trains fitted with very powerful Spring Motors.

Packed in handsome cardboard boxes.

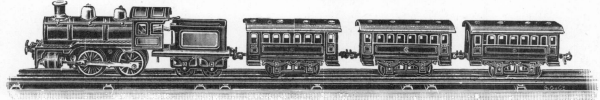

1821/1/48 B

No. 1821/1/48 B		consisting of: **Locomotive with brake and reversing gear** strong and handsome quality, 821/48 — **48 mm gauge** — tender, 2 coaches and 1 brake van, 8 round, 3 straight rails, also brake rail, length of train 40″, total length of rails 13 ft. 8″. . each complete **20/-**
— 1821/1/48 C		the same set as 1821/1/48 B, but with 14 round, 3 straight rails, brake rail, also **crossing**. Total length of rails 30 feet . . . . each complete **25/-**
— 1821/1/48 D		the same set as 1821/1/48 B, but with 10 round, 3 straight rails, brake rail and **1 pair of switches.** Total length of rails 19 feet 8″ . . . . each complete **28/-**
— 1821/1/48 E		the same set as 1821/1/48 B, but with 18 round, 7 straight and 2 curved half rails, brake rail, **crossing** and **1 pair of switches**. Total length of rails 36 ft. . . . each complete **34/-**

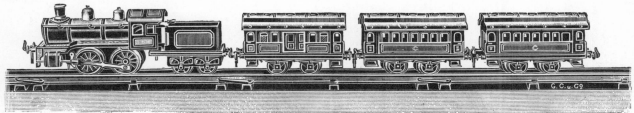

1821/2/48 B

The same railway trains as above described, but with 2 D-coaches and 1 D-brake van, length of train 42″.

No. 1821/2/48 B	Same set of rails as in 1821/1/48 B	each complete		**23/4**
— 1821/2/48 C	— — — — — — 1821/1/48 C	—	—	**28/-**
— 1821/2/48 D	— — — — — — 1821/1/48 D	—	—	**31/4**
— 1821/2/48 E	— — — — — — 1821/1/48 E	—	—	**37/4**

Railway Trains fitted with very powerful Spring Motors (continued).

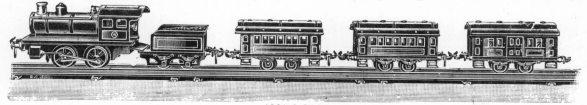

1961/2/35 B

No. 1961/2/35 B		consisting of: Locomotive with **brake** 961/35 — **35 mm gauge**, tender, 2 D-coaches and 1 D-brake van, 6 round and 3 straight rails also brake rail, length of train 34″, total length of rails 9 ft. 9″ . . . . each complete **17/6**
— 1961/2/48 B		consisting of: Locomotive with **brake** 961/48 — **48 mm gauge**, tender, 2 D-coaches, 1 D-brake van, 8 round and 3 straight rails, also brake rail. Length of train 44″ total length of rails 13 ft. 8″ . . . . each complete **25/-**
— 1961/2/54 B		consisting of: **Locomotive** with **brake** 961/54 — **54 mm gauge**, tender, 2 D-coaches, 1 D-brake van, 12 round, 3 straight rails, also brake rail. Length of train 48″, total length of rails 18 feet 4″. . . . . each complete **34/8**

For separate rails, coaches and wagons to suit above railways, see pages 94 to 102 of this list.

Railway Trains fitted with very strong Spring Motors, packed in handsome cardboard boxes.

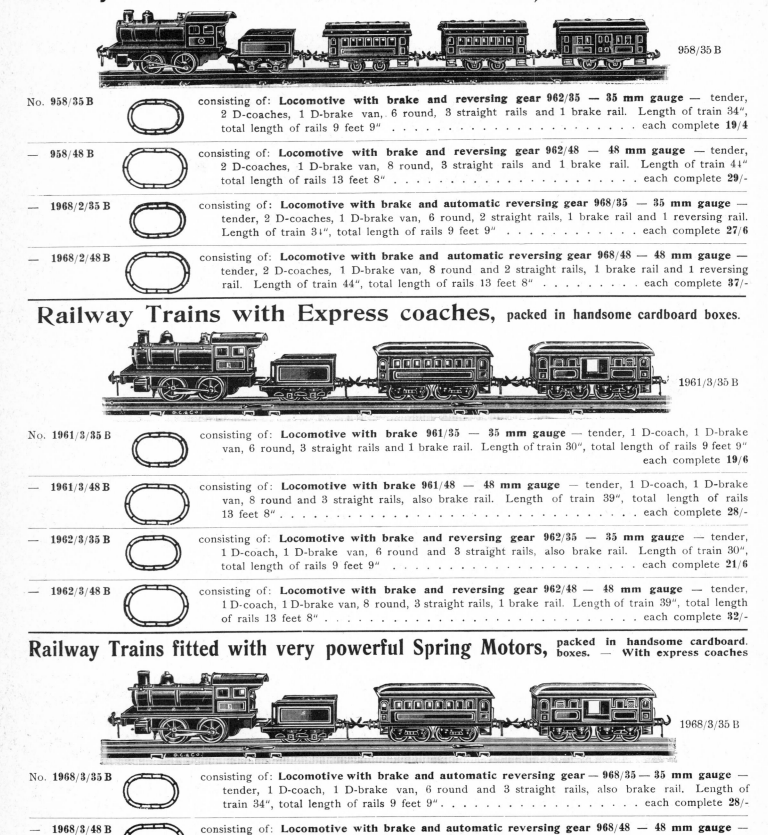

958/35 B

No. 958/35 B		consisting of: **Locomotive with brake and reversing gear 962/35 — 35 mm gauge** — tender, 2 D-coaches, 1 D-brake van, 6 round, 3 straight rails and 1 brake rail. Length of train 34″, total length of rails 9 feet 9″ . . . . each complete **19/4**
— 958/48 B		consisting of: **Locomotive with brake and reversing gear 962/48 — 48 mm gauge** — tender, 2 D-coaches, 1 D-brake van, 8 round, 3 straight rails and 1 brake rail. Length of train 44″, total length of rails 13 feet 8″ . . . . each complete **29/-**
— 1968/2/35 B		consisting of: **Locomotive with brake and automatic reversing gear 968/35 — 35 mm gauge** — tender, 2 D-coaches, 1 D-brake van, 6 round, 2 straight rails, 1 brake rail and 1 reversing rail. Length of train 34″, total length of rails 9 feet 9″ . . . . each complete **27/6**
— 1968/2/48 B		consisting of: **Locomotive with brake and automatic reversing gear 968/48 — 48 mm gauge** — tender, 2 D-coaches, 1 D-brake van, 8 round and 2 straight rails, 1 brake rail and 1 reversing rail. Length of train 44″, total length of rails 13 feet 8″ . . . . each complete **37/-**

Railway Trains with Express coaches, packed in handsome cardboard boxes.

1961/3/35 B

No. 1961/3/35 B		consisting of: **Locomotive with brake 961/35 — 35 mm gauge** — tender, 1 D-coach, 1 D-brake van, 6 round, 3 straight rails and 1 brake rail. Length of train 30″, total length of rails 9 feet 9″ each complete **19/6**
— 1961/3/48 B		consisting of: **Locomotive with brake 961/48 — 48 mm gauge** — tender, 1 D-coach, 1 D-brake van, 8 round and 3 straight rails, also brake rail. Length of train 39″, total length of rails 13 feet 8″ . . . . each complete **28/-**
— 1962/3/35 B		consisting of: **Locomotive with brake and reversing gear 962/35 — 35 mm gauge** — tender, 1 D-coach, 1 D-brake van, 6 round and 3 straight rails, also brake rail. Length of train 30″, total length of rails 9 feet 9″ . . . . each complete **21/6**
— 1962/3/48 B		consisting of: **Locomotive with brake and reversing gear 962/48 — 48 mm gauge** — tender, 1 D-coach, 1 D-brake van, 8 round, 3 straight rails, 1 brake rail. Length of train 39″, total length of rails 13 feet 8″ . . . . each complete **32/-**

Railway Trains fitted with very powerful Spring Motors, packed in handsome cardboard boxes. — With express coaches

1968/3/35 B

No. 1968/3/35 B		consisting of: **Locomotive with brake and automatic reversing gear — 968/35 — 35 mm gauge** — tender, 1 D-coach, 1 D-brake van, 6 round and 3 straight rails, also brake rail. Length of train 34″, total length of rails 9 feet 9″ . . . . each complete **28/-**
— 1968/3/48 B		consisting of: **Locomotive with brake and automatic reversing gear 968/48 — 48 mm gauge** — tender, 1 D-coach, 1 D-brake van, 8 round and 3 straight rails, also brake rail. Length of train 42″, total length of rails 13 feet 8″ . . . . each complete **38/-**

For separate rails, coaches and wagons to suit above railways, see pages 94 to 102 of this list.

High class Railway Trains

with powerful spring motors, superfine finish and best quality japanning.

Exact English Models constructed from the original models of the

different English Railway Companies.

Scale Models.

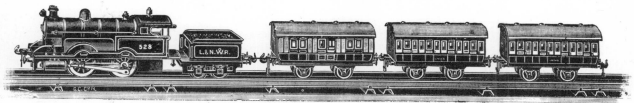

1988/35 B

No. **1987/35 B** — **Great Northern Railway.** Consisting of high class finished locomotive with very powerful motor, **brake** and **reversing gear,** best quality japanning, **35 mm gauge,** tender, 2 coaches, 1 guard's van, 6 curved, 3 straight rails and 1 brake rail, length of train 34¹/₄", length of rails 9 ft. 9" . . . . each **27/-**

— **1987/48 B** — ditto, for **48 mm gauge,** 8 curved, 3 straight rails and 1 brake rail, length of train 43¹/₂", length of rails 13 ft. 8" . . . . each **36/-**

— **1988/35 B** **London and North Western Railway,** for **35mm gauge,** same as 1987/35 B . each **27/-**
— **1988/48 B** ditto, for **48 mm gauge,** same as 1987/48 B . . . . — **36/-**
— **1989/35 B** **Midland Railway** for **35 mm gauge,** same as 1987/35 B. . . . . . . — **27/-**
— **1989/48 B** ditto for **48 mm gauge,** same as 1987/48 B . . . . — **36/-**

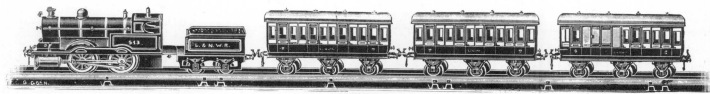

1998/48 B

No. **1997/35 B** — **Great Northern Railway** consisting of high class finished **4 wheel coupled locomotive** with most powerful motor, **brake** and **reversing gear,** best quality japanning, **35 mm gauge,** tender with bogie, 2 superfine, 3 wheel coupled coaches, 1 ditto guard's van, 6 curved, 3 straight rails and 1 brake rail, length of train 36¹/₄", length of rails 9 ft. 9". . . . . each **45/-**

— **1997/48 B** — ditto for **48 mm gauge,** 8 curved, 3 straight rails and 1 brake rail, length of train 47¹/₂", length of rails 13 ft. 8" . . . . each **60/-**

— **1998/35 B** **London and North Western Railway** for **35 mm gauge,** same as 1997/35 B . — **45/-**
— **1998/48 B** ditto for **48 mm gauge,** same as 1997/48 B . . . . — **60/-**
— **1999/35 B** **Midland Railway** for **35 mm gauge,** same as 1997/35 B . . . . — **45/-**
— **1999/48 B** ditto for **48 mm gauge,** same as 1997/48 B . . . . — **60/-**

For separate rails, coaches and wagons to suit above railways, see pages **94** to **102** of this list.

Trade Mark.

Spring Motor driven Railways, packed in handsome cardboard boxes.

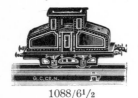

Electric Railways

48 mm gauge with simple motor strongly made and well japanned.

1088/6½

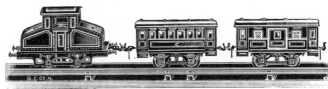

1088/60

No. **1088/6½** Electric Locomotive only, 8½" long . . . . each **3/6**

No. **1088/60** Electric Locomotive with 1 coach, 1 brake van, 8 round and 2 straight rails, length of train 26½" . . . . each **9/-**

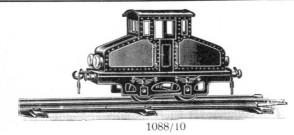

1088/10

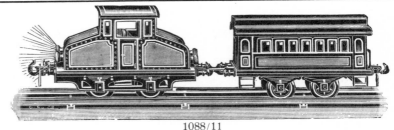

1088/11

Electric Railways, 48 mm gauge. Fitted with very strong motor, brake and reversing gear.

No. **1088/10** Electric Locomotive with 8 round, 3 straight rails, also 1 brake rail, 8½" long, packed in handsome box . . . each **7/6**
— **1088/11** — — with 1 handsome D-coach, 8 round and 1 straight, also 1 straight brake rail. Length of train 18" — **13/-**

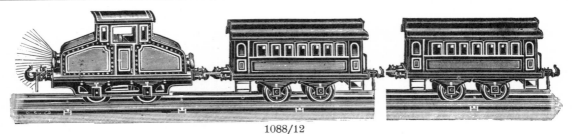

1088/12

No. **1088/12** Electric Locomotive with **2 handsome D-coaches**, 8 round and 3 straight rails also brake rail. Length of train 27", each **16/6**

Under Ground Railway, 48 mm gauge.

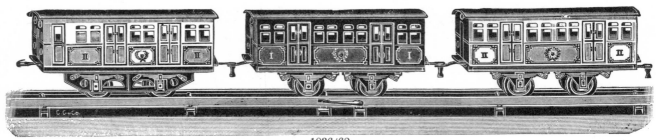

1036/62

No. **1036/64** Under Ground Railway consisting of 1 locomotive with strong motor, 1 coach, 8 round and 2 straight rails. Length of train 18" . . . . each **9/8**
— **1036/62** **ditto with stronger and more powerful spring motor,** with brake, 2 coaches, 8 round and 3 straight rails, also 1 brake rail — **17/-**
— **1036/6** Electric Locomotive only, for above railway, with very strong motor . . . . — **7/-**
— **1036/3** Coaches, brown . . . . — **1/8**
— **1036/4** — yellow . . . . — **1/8**
— **1036/5** — red . . . . — **1/8**

Elevated railway rails, covered stations etc. to suit, are listed pages 98—99.

Trade  Mark.

New Electric Street Tramways driven by spring motors

packed in handsome cardboard boxes.

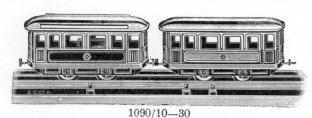

1090/10—30

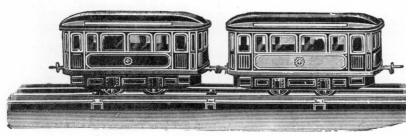

1091/10—20

Centre rail system, well finished and japanned

No. **1090/10** **Motor wagon, 35 mm gauge** with strong spring motor, 8″ long, with 6 round rails . . each **5/6**

— **1090/20** **Motor wagon** and **1 trailing car, 35 mm gauge** with 6 round and 2 straight rails . . . each **8/6**

No. **1090/30** **Motor wagon** and **2 trailing cars, 35 mm gauge** with 6 round and 2 straight rails, length of train 24″ . . . . each **11/-**

— **1091/10** **Motor wagon, 48 mm gauge** with strong spring motor, 10″ long with 8 round rails . . each **7/-**

No. **1091/20** **Motor wagon** and **1 trailing car, 48 mm gauge** with 8 round and 4 straight rails, length of train 20″ . . . . each **11/-**

— **1090/3** **Trailing car, 35 mm gauge**, to suit 1090/10—30, 8″ long . . . . — **1/10**

— **1091/3¼** — — **48** — — — — 1091/10—20, 10″ — . . . . — **2/6**

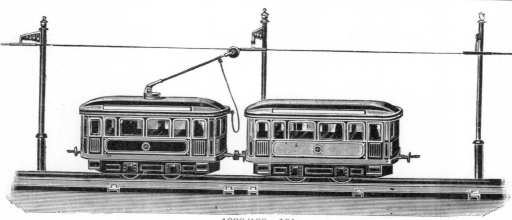

1090/100—101

Overhead system well finished and japanned.

No. **1090/100** **Motor wagon, 35 mm gauge,** with strong spring motor, 8″ long, with 6 round and 2 straight rails, with wire and supports . . . . each **7/6**

— **1090/101** **Motor wagon** and **1 trailing car, 35 mm gauge,** with 6 round and 2 straight rails, with wire and supports, length of train 16″ . . . . each **11/-**

— **1091/100** **Motor wagon, 48 mm gauge,** with strong spring motor, 10″ long, with 8 round rails with wire and supports . . . . each **9/6**

— **1091/101** **Motor wagon with 1 trailing car, 48 mm gauge,** with 8 round and 4 straight rails with wire and supports . . . . each **14/10**

For separate rails, centre rail system see **pages 94—97** of this list.

For separate rails for overhead system see page **184** of this list.

Trade ✦ Mark.

Separate Rails

for locomotives, wagons and railways, worked by steam or spring motors.

Rail parts, for laying railways of any gauge.

Rails with chairs

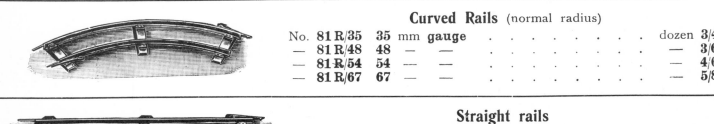

1100 S/8½   (patented)   81 S/9

No. **1100 S/8½**   for **small** section with 1 spike, 15" long . . . . gross **10/-**
—   **81 S/9**   — **large** —   — 1 — 15" — . . . . — **16/-**

Cheap complete rails

on sleepers, with rails of **small** section

No. **938 R/28**   Curved rails, **28** mm gauge (4 pieces form a circle of 18" diam.) . . . . . . dozen **2/-**
—   **938 G/28**   Straight — **28** — — . . . . — **2/-**
—   **938 R/35**   Curved — **35** — — (4 pieces form a circle of 20" diam.) . . . . . — **2/-**
—   **938 G/35**   Straight — **35** — — . . . . — **2/-**

The last 2 sizes suitable for locomotives 500, 501/35.

Complete strong rails

with our protected **automatic** acting connecting clasps and the spike on the opposite ends, simplified system, making the stocking of numberless special rails, quite unnecessary, **large** section, suitable for all remaining steam and spring motor driven railways.

gauge	35	48	54	67	mm
gauge No.	0	1	2	3	
No. of rails in circle	6	8	12	12	
diam. of circle	24	32	53	57"	

Curved Rails (normal radius)

No. **81 R/35**   **35** mm **gauge** . . . . dozen **3/4**
—   **81 R/48**   48 — — . . . . — **3/6**
—   **81 R/54**   54 — — . . . . — **4/6**
—   **81 R/67**   67 — — . . . . — **5/8**

Straight rails

No. **81 G/35**   **35** mm **gauge** . . . . dozen **3/4**
—   **81 G/48**   48 — — . . . . — **3/6**
—   **81 G/54**   54 — — . . . . — **4/6**
—   **81 G/67**   67 — — . . . . — **5/8**

Curved half rails (normal radius)

No. **81 HR/35**   **35** mm **gauge** . . . . dozen **2/6**
—   **81 HR/48**   48 — — . . . . — **3/-**
—   **81 HR/54**   54 — — . . . . — **3/6**
—   **81 HR/67**   67 — — . . . . — **4/-**

Straight half rails

No. **81 HG/35**   **35** mm **gauge** . . . . dozen **2/6**
—   **81 HG/48**   48 — — . . . . — **3/-**
—   **81 HG/54**   54 — — . . . . — **3/6**
—   **81 HG/67**   67 — — . . . . — **4/-**

Trade   Mark.

Separate Rail Parts (continued).

To suit all Wagons, Coaches, Locomotives, Railways listed on pages 58—70, 84—102.

Straight Brake Rails

for spring motor locos 966, 967, 961, 962, 963, 965, 987—989, 997—999, 1036, 1088, 1091.

No. 81 B/35	35 mm gauge	. .	each -/10
— 81 B/48	48 — —	. —	1/-

Reversing Rails.

to suit steam locomotives 506.

curved No.	81 UR/48	48 mm gauge	. . . . each	1/-
—	81 UR/67	67 — —	. . . . —	1/6
straight —	81 UG/48	48 — —	. . . . —	1/-
—	81 UG/67	67 — —	. . . . —	1/6

Straight Reversing Rails

for spring motor loco 968.

No. 81 A/35	35 mm gauge	. . . . each	-/10
— 81 A/48	48 — —	. . . . —	1/-

Acute angle Crossings.

No. 81 K/35	35 mm gauge	. . . . each	1/4
— 81 K/48	48 — —	. . . . —	1/6
— 81 K/54	54 — —	. . . . —	2/-
— 81 K/67	67 — —	. . . . —	3/-

Right angle Crossings.

No. 81 KR/35	35 mm gauge	. . . . each	1/8
— 81 KR/48	48 — —	. . . . —	1/10
— 81 KR/54	54 — —	. . . . —	2/-
— 81 KR/67	67 — —	. . . . —	3/-

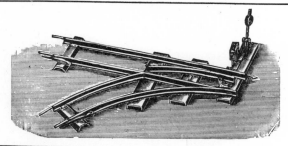

Switches or Points, right and left hand.

No. 81 W/35	35 mm gauge	. . . . pair	4/8
— 81 W/48	48 — —	. . . . —	5/10
— 81 W/54	54 — —	. . . . —	6/6
— 81 W/67	67 — —	. . . . —	7/8

Curved Switches.

No. 81 WS/35	35 mm gauge	. . . . pair	4/8
— 81 WS/48	48 — —	. . . —	5/10
— 81 WS/54	54 — —	. . . —	6/6
— 81 WS/67	67 — —	. . . —	7/8

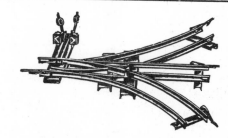

Three way Switches.

No. 81 WT/35	35 mm gauge	. . . . pair	5/-
— 81 WT/48	48 — —	. . . —	6/-
— 81 WT/54	54 — —	. . . —	8/-
— 81 WT/67	67 — —	. . . —	9/-

Trade Mark.

Separate Rail Parts (continued).

To suit all locomotives, wagons, coaches and railways listed on pages 58—70, 84—102.

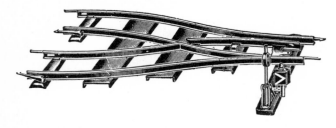

Fork Switches

No. 81 WA/35	35 mm gauge	. . . . .	each	3/-
— 81 WA/48	48 — —	. . . . .	—	3/4
— 81 WA/54	54 — —	. . . . .	—	4/-
— 81 WA/67	67 — —	. . . . .	—	4/6

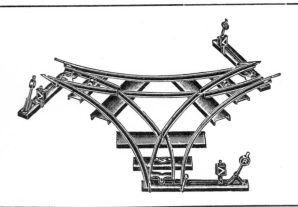

Three curve Switches (3 points)

No. 81 WC/35	35 mm gauge	. . . . .	each	5/10
— 81 WC/48	48 — —	. . . . .	—	7/-
— 81 WC/54	54 — —	. . . . .	—	8/-
— 81 WC/67	67 — —	. . . . .	—	9/-

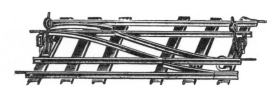

Parallel Switches (2 points)

No. 81 WD/35	35 mm gauge	. . . . .	each	5/-
— 81 WD/48	48 — —	. . . . .	—	5/8
— 81 WD/54	54 — —	. . . . .	—	7/-
— 81 WD/67	67 — —	. . . . .	—	8/-

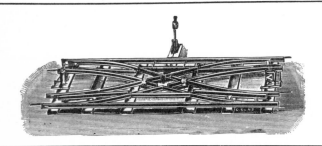

Parallel crossing Switches (2 Points)

No. 81 WK/35	35 mm gauge	. . . . .	each	9/-
— 81 WK/48	48 — —	. . . . .	—	10/-
— 81 WK/54	54 — —	. . . . .	—	12/-
— 81 WK/67	67 — —	. . . . .	—	14/-

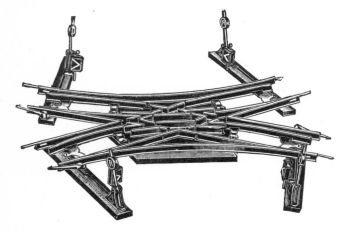

Curve crossing Switches (4 points)

No. 81 WB/35	35 mm gauge	. . . . .	each	9/4
— 81 WB/48	48 — —	. . . . .	—	11/4
— 81 WB/54	54 — —	. . . . .	—	12/-
— 81 WB/67	67 — —	. . . . .	—	14/-

Trade Mark.

Separate large radius Rail Parts

to suit all locomotives, wagons and coaches. **These rails however must be used with the large locomotives pages 60, 61 and 87 also with the large coaches and wagons page 101.**

The following rails offer a considerable advantage, by reason of the diminished friction of the wheels of the locomotives and coaches in negotiating the **larger curves** and naturally the power of the locomotives is increased in proportion.

Gauge	35	48	54	67	mm
No. of rails necessary to form a circle	12	16	20	24	
Diam. of the circle	4 ft.	6 ft.	7 ft. 2"	9 ft. 4"	

Curved Rails

No. 80 R/35	35 mm gauge	. . . . .	dozen	4/4
— 80 R/48	48 —	—	—	4/10
— 80 R/54	54 —	—	—	6/-
— 80 R/67	67 —	—	—	7/4

Curved Half Rails.

No. 80 HR/35	35 mm gauge	. . . .	dozen	3/2
— 80 HR/48	48 —	—	—	3/6
— 80 HR/54	54 —	—	—	3/8
— 80 HR/67	67 —	—	—	4/4

Switches, right and left hand.

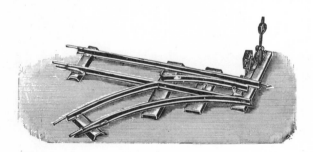

No. 80 W/35	35 mm gauge	. . . . .	pair	5/8
— 80 W/48	48 —	—	—	7/-
— 80 W/54	54 —	—	—	8/-
— 80 W/67	67 —	—	—	9/8

Curve Switches (2 points).

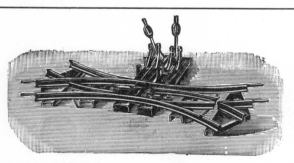

No. 80 WS/35	35 mm gauge	. . . . .	pair	5/8
— 80 WS/48	48 —	—	—	7/-
— 80 WS/54	54 —	—	—	8/-
— 80 WS/67	67 —	—	—	9/8

Acute angle Crossings.

No. 80 K/35	35 mm gauge	. . . . .	each	2/-
— 80 K/48	48 —	—	—	2/8
— 80 K/54	54 —	—	—	3/10
— 80 K/67	67 —	—	—	4/6

Trade Mark.

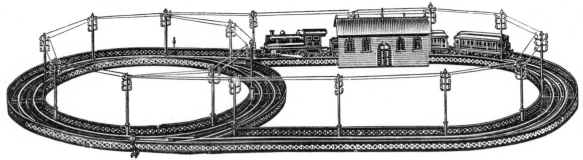

Fig. 1

Illustration of a Railway consisting of the following rails with side parapets :
10 round No. 78R/48, 3 straight No. 78G/48, 1 straight with station No. 647/62, 1 pair of switches No. 78W/48, 16 telegraph poles No. 1051/12.

Rails with side parapets or railing

New! *New!*

for steam or spring motor driven Locomotives and Railways

(Locomotives pages 58, 59, 63, 84, 85, 87 (only for loco No. 963), Railways pages 65—68, 88—90)

have the advantage that any spirit, oil or water falling from the engine while running will not smear or soil the floor or carpet etc. since all such is caught by the rail bottom plate; further, should the train from some cause or other run off the track, it cannot mount the parapet and cause a trail of burning spirit to be left behind. Every parapet rail is fitted with sockets in which telegraph poles specially made for this purpose, can be arranged, or imitation arc lamps, or arc lamps fitted with miniature screw. Incandescent lamps 3½ volts, also signals with insulated standards can be put. Beside these advantages, the parapets improve the appearance of the whole railway. The station, introduced in station formations is very strong, being built from japanned tin plate. The whole railway is connected together in an unsurpassed manner by means of our favourite connecting clasps which always fit but never let go. All sorts of rail formation can be fitted together by means of these rails without any trouble whatever. If required the railway can always be converted into an **"elevated"** railway by the use of standards.

78 R

Round Parapet Rails

No. 78R/35	35 mm gauge . . . . . . each	-/10
— 78R/48	48 — — . . . . . . —	1/-

6 rails of 78R/35 form a circle
8 — — 78R/48 — — —

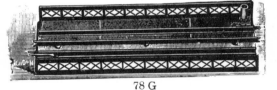

78 G

Straight Parapet Rails

No. 78G/35	35 mm gauge . . . . . . each	-/10
— 78G/48	48 — — . . . . . . —	1/-

78 T

Standards

for converting the parapet rails, if desired, into an "Elevated Railway" with 2 wing nut bolts. (1 standard per rail is required) (2 standards for crossing or switch)

No. **78 T/35**
35 mm gauge, dozen **5/4**

No. **78 T/48**
48 mm gauge dozen **6/-**

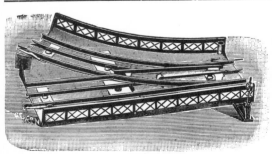

78 W

Switches with Parapet

No. 78W/35	35 mm gauge . . . . . pair	7/8
— 78W/48	48 — — . . . . . —	8/-

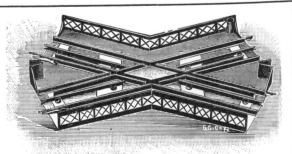

78 K

Crossings with Parapet

No. 78K/35	35 mm gauge . . . . . . each	4/-
— 78K/48	48 — — . . . . . —	4/6

Trade Mark.

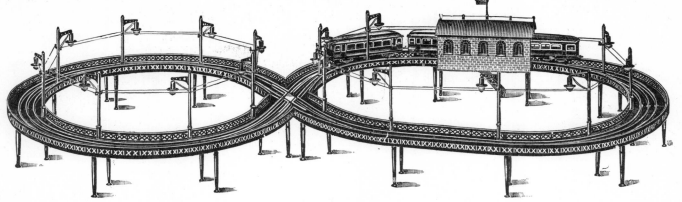

Fig. 2.

Fig. 2 illustrates an "**Elevated Railway**" consisting of the following parapet·rails: 13 round No. 78 R/48, 1 straight parapet rail 78/G 48, 1 crossing No. 78/K 48, 1 covered, elevated, Railway station, with standards and stairway, and a rail, No. 647/65, 16 standards, 16 arc lamps No. 647/47 EO or No. 1051/11.

Supplementary accessories for parapet Railways
Covered Railway Stations

No. **1051/12**

Telegraph poles

dozen **3/8**

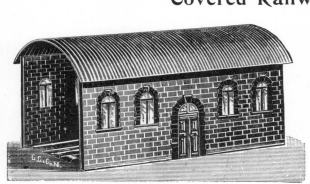

No. 647/58 and 59

No. 647/61 and 647/62
with 1 straight rail. — Best quality.

No. **647/58**	for **35**	**mm gauge**	**without** rail	each	**1/6**
— 647/59	— 48	—	— —	—	2/6
— 647/61	— 35	—	with 1 rail	—	7/-
— 647/62	— 48	—	— 1	—	9/8
— 647/63	— 35	—	— 1 —	—	8/-
— 647/65	— 48	—	— 1 —	—	11/-

No. **647/47 E 0**

Arc lamps

for putting in the sockets of the parapet rails

dozen **3/4**

No. 647/47 E 0

No. **1051/11**
with 1 miniature screw incandescent lamp can be lighted by dry batteries or accumulators, or if placed in series to the corresponding voltage, they can be connected to town current . each **1/6**

No. 1051/11

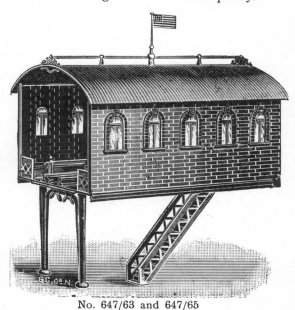

No. 647/63 and 647/65

Elevated Railway Station. Best quality.

Trade Mark.

Separate Coaches for Steam, or Spring Motor driven Locomotives

to suit locomotives on pages 58—64, 84—87, **very strong, handsomely finished and japanned.**

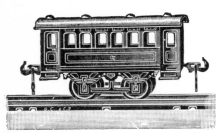

135/21/35—48

Passenger coaches

No. 135/21/35 — **35 mm gauge,** 6¼" long, 2¾" high . . . . . dozen 7/4

— 135/21/48 — **48 mm gauge,** 8" long, 3¾" high dozen 12/-

Brake, or luggage vans

No. 135/26/35 — **35 mm gauge,** 6¼" long, 2¾" high . . . . . dozen 7/4

— 135/26/48 — **48 mm gauge,** 8" long, 3¾" high dozen 12/-

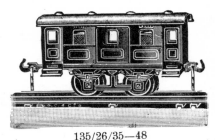

135/26/35—48

135/22/35—48

D=passenger coaches

No. 135/22/35 — **35 mm gauge,** 6½" long, 3¼" high, dozen 14/6

No. 135/22/48 — **48 mm gauge,** 9" long, 4¼" high . dozen 24/-

D=brake, or luggage vans

No. 135/27/35 — **35 mm gauge,** 6½" long, 3¼" high, dozen 15/6

No. 135/27/48 — **48 mm gauge,** 9" long, 4¼" high . dozen 26/6

135/27/35—48

135/22/54—67

D=passenger coaches

No. 135/22/54 — **54 mm gauge,** 10" long, 4¼" high . . . each 3/10

— 135/22/67 -- **67 mm gauge,** 12" long, 6¼" high . . . each 8/-

D=brake, or luggage vans

No. 135/27/54 — **54 mm gauge,** 10" long, 4½" high . . . each 3/10

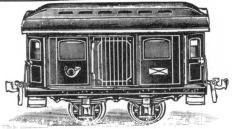

135/27/54

135/23/35—54

D-express passenger coaches, 8 wheels

No. 135/23/35 — **35 mm gauge,** 8" long, 3¼" high . each 2/6

— 135/23/48 — **48** — — 10½" — 4½" — . — 4/-

— 135/23/54 — **54** — — 11½" — 4¾" — . — 7/2

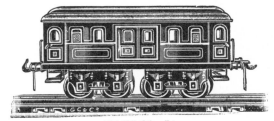

135/28/35—54

D-express brake van, 8 wheels

No. 135/28/35 — **35 mm gauge,** 8" long, 3¼" high . each 2/10

— 135/28/48 — **48** — — 10½" — 4½" — . — 4/6

— 135/28/54 — **54** — — 11½" — 4¾" — . — 7/8

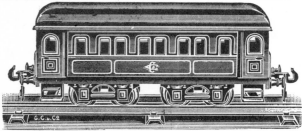

135/24/35—48

L-express passenger coaches, 8 wheels

No. 135/24/35 — **35 mm gauge,** 10" long, 4" high . each 5/8

— 135/24/48 — **48** — — 11½" — 4½" — . — 8/6

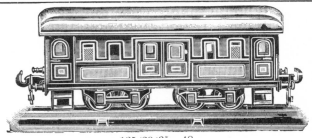

135/29/35—48

L-express brake van

No. 135/29/35 — **35 mm gauge,** 10" long, 4" high . each 6/-

— 135/29/48 — **48** — — 11½" — 4½" — . — 9/-

Trade Mark

128/2/35—48

129/2/35—48

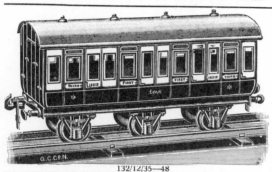

132/12/35—48

133/12/35—48

132DB/35—48

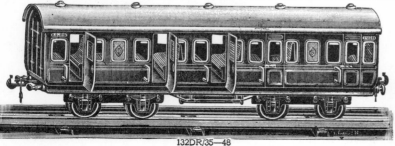

132DR/35—48

Handsomely finished Coaches

Constructed from the original models of the different **English Railway Companies**.
Suitable for all locomotives and trains pages 58—70, 84—93 of this list.

Passenger coaches.

35 mm gauge, 6¾" long.

No	128/1/35	Great Northern Railway Company	dozen 15/6
—	128/2/35	London and North Western Railway Company	— 15/6
—	128/3/35	Midland Railway Company	— 15/6

48 mm gauge, 9" long.

No	128/1/48	Great Northern Railway Company	dozen 20/-
—	128/2/48	London and North Western Railway Company	— 20/-
—	128/3/48	Midland Railway Company	— 20/-

Luggage vans.

35 mm gauge, 6¾" long.

No.	129/1/35	Great Northern Railway Company	dozen 15/6
—	129/2/35	London and North Western Railway Company	— 15/6
—	129/3/35	Midland Railway Company	— 15/6

48 mm gauge, 9" long.

No.	129/1/48	Great Northern Railway Company	dozen 20/-
—	129/2/48	London and North Western Railway Company	— 20/-
—	129/3/48	Midland Railway Company	— 20/-

High class 3 wheel coupled Passenger coaches.

35 mm gauge, 8¼" long.

No.	132/11/35	Great Northern Railway Company	each 4/-
—	132/12/35	London and North Western Railway Company	— 4/-
—	132/13/35	Midland Railway Company	— 4/-

48 mm gauge, 11½" long.

No.	132/11/48	Great Northern Railway Company	each 5/6
—	132/12/48	London and North Western Railway Company	— 5/6
—	132/13/48	Midland Railway Company	— 5/6

Luggage vans.

35 mm gauge, 8¼" long.

No.	133/11/35	Great Northern Railway Company	each 4/-
—	133/12/35	London and North Western Railway Company	— 4/-
—	133/13/35	Midland Railway Company	— 4/-

48 mm gauge, 11½" long.

No.	133/11/48	Great Northern Railway Company	each 5/6
—	133/12/48	London and North Western Railway Company	— 5/6
—	133/13/48	Midland Railway Company	— 5/6

Very handsomely finished Express coaches.

To suit all the large size locomotives (may be used only with Nr. 80 rails of large radius).

Modern design; compartment doors to open.

No.	132DB/35	35 mm gauge, 13½" long, 4¼" high, each 5/6
—	132DB/48	48 — — 17½" — 5½" — — 7/6

No.	132DR/35	35 mm gauge, 13½" long, 4" high, each 5/6
—	132DR/48	48 — — 17½" — 5¼" — — 7/6

Bellows trough connections

to fit all corridor coaches (Express-coaches)
made of cloth with metal frames.

No.	17/70	for 35 and 48 mm gauge, each -/8
—	17/71	— 54 mm gauge . . . — -/10
—	17/72	— 67 — — . . . — 1/-

Well japanned Goods Wagons

135/8/35—48

Coal or Open Wagon

No. 135/8/35   **35 mm gauge, 5¹/₂" long, 2" high** . . dozen 12/-

— 135/8/48   **48 mm gauge, 7¹/₂" long, 2³/₄" high** . dozen 16/-

135/9/35—48

Coal or Open Wagon

No. 135/9/35   **35 mm gauge, 5¹/₂" long, 3¹/₄" high** . dozen 16/-

— 135/9/48   **48 mm gauge, 7¹/₂" long, 4¹/₄" high** . . dozen 20/-

135/10/35—48

Covered Wagon

No. 135/10/35   **35 mm gauge, 5¹/₂" long, 3¹/₄" high**. dozen 16/-

— 135/10/48   **48 mm gauge, 7¹/₂" long, 4³/₄" high**. dozen 20/-

135/11/35—54

Long Timber Wagons

No. 135/11/35   **35 mm gauge, 5¹/₂" long, 3¹/₂" high**. dozen 12/-

— 135/11/48   **48 mm gauge, 7¹/₂" long, 4" high** . dozen 16/-

— 135/11/54   **54 mm gauge, 8¹/₄" long, 4¹/₄" high**. dozen 20/-

135/12/35—54

Tipping Wagons

No. 135/12/35   **35 mm gauge, 5¹/₂" long, 3¹/₂" high** . . dozen 18/-

— 135/12/48   **48 mm gauge, 7¹/₂" long, 4" high** . . dozen 26/-

— 135/12/54   **54 mm gauge, 8¹/₄" long, 4" high** . . . dozen 34/-

135/13/35—48

Oil Tank Wagons

No. 135/13/35   **35 mm gauge, 5¹/₂" long, 3" high** . dozen 18/-

— 135/13/48   **48 mm gauge, 7¹/₂" long, 3¹/₂" high**. dozen 28/-

135/14/35—54

Lime Wagons

No. 135/14/35   **35 mm gauge, 5¹/₂" long, 2³/₄" high**. dozen 16/-

— 135/14/48   **48 mm gauge, 7¹/₂" long, 3³/₄" high**. dozen 22/-

— 135/14/54   **54 mm gauge, 8¹/₄" long, 4" high** . dozen 28/-

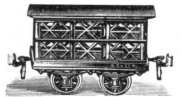

135/15/35—54

Poultry Wagons

No. 135/15/35   **35 mm gauge, 5¹/₂" long, 2³/₄" high** . . dozen 16/-

— 135/15/48   **48 mm gauge, 7¹/₂" long, 3³/₄" high** . . dozen 28/-

— 135/15/54   **54 mm gauge, 8¹/₄" long, 4" high** . . dozen 38/-

135/16/35—54

Crane Wagons

No. 135/16/35   **35 mm gauge, 5¹/₂" long, 4" high** . dozen 32/-

— 135/16/48   **48 mm gauge, 7¹/₂" long, 5¹/₄" high**. dozen 40/-

— 135/16/54   **54 mm gauge, 8¹/₄" long, 5¹/₂" high**. dozen 52/-

135/17/35—54

Railway Horse Boxes

No. 135/17/35 **35 mm gauge, 5¹/₂" lg., 2³/₄" high, dozen 16/-**
— 135/17/48 48 —   —   7¹/₂" — 4"   —   22/-
— 135/17/54 54 —   —   8¹/₄" — 4¹/₂" —   28/-

Gas Wagons

No. 130/20/35 **35 mm gauge, 5¹/₂" lg., 2³/₄" high, dozen 16/-**
— 130/20/48 48 —   —   8" — 4"   —   22/-

130/20/35—48

Trade Mark.

Railway Accessories.

No. 647/3/35 with 1 door and 1 straight brake rail for **35 mm gauge**, suitable for cheap railways. Shed japanned in imitation brickwork, 19¹/₂" long, 6¹/₂" wide, 5³/₄" high . . . . each **5/-**

970/3/35—48

Locomotive Sheds, handsomely japanned and well finished.

No. 970/4/35 **35 mm gauge**, with double doors, and 1 automatic switch, with brake attachment, in order to prevent the loco entering too rapidly. In imitation brickwork, 26" long, 8¹/₂" wide . . . . each **6/10**

No. **970/4/48** ditto
for **48 mm gauge**, 33" long, 12" wide
each **9/8**

No. **970/3/35** same design as **970/4/35**, **35 mm gauge**, but much more handsome, brickwork, and superbly japanned, with 4 side windows, 2 chimneys, 26" long, 8¹/₂" wide, each **13/4**

— **970/3/48** the same but **48 mm gauge** and with 6 side windows and 4 chimneys, 33¹/₂" long, 12" wide . . . . . each **24/-**

Locomotive sheds, best japanning, very strongly made, with **removable turntable** and 4 ways for locomotives

No. **970/35** for locos. of **35 mm gauge**, 18" long, 21" wide, 8¹/₂" high . . . . each **21/6**

— **970/48** for locos. of **48 mm gauge**, 29" long, 28" wide, 10¹/₄" high . . . . each **30/6**

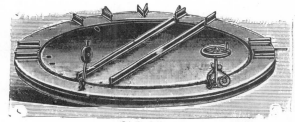

970/35—48

81 D/35—48

Turntables, with mechanical turning attachment and sockets for rails. Best finish

No. **81 D/35**	**35 mm gauge**, 11" diam.	each **5/6**	
— **81 D/48**	48 — — 14" —	— **9/4**	

Railway Stations.

Covered stations.

647/58 and 59

No. **647/58** for **35 mm gauge**, without rails, 11" long, 7" wide each **1/6**

— **647/59** — 48 — — — 14" long, 8¹/₂" wide each **2/6**

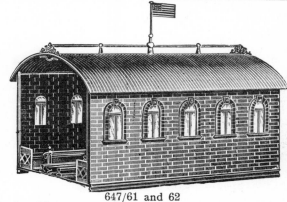

647/61 and 62

No. **647/61** for **35 mm gauge**, with rails, high class finish; 12¹/₂" long, 7" wide . . . . each **7/-**

— **647/62** for **48 mm gauge**, with rails, 14¹/₂" long, 8" wide each **9/8**

English Railway Station

No. **918** handsomely finished,
23" long, 5" wide
each **3/-**

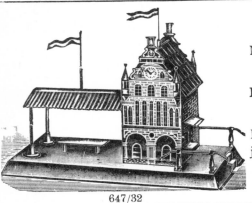

Railway station with porch.

No. **647/32** plain quality, 12" long,
5¹⁄₂" wide, 8" high, each **2/10**

Railway station with porch and thoroughfare.

No. **647/131** strong quality, and well
japanned, 9" long, 9¹⁄₂" wide, 7¹⁄₂" high,
each **5/6**

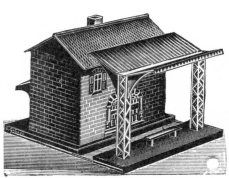

647/32

647/131

Well made Railway Station

No. **647/126** well japanned,
candles can be arranged inside,
giving good effect through the
red gelatine windows,
9¹⁄₂" long, 6¹⁄₂" wide, 8" high,
each **4/8**

Covered Railway station
very strong quality

No. **647/21** with through rails,
for **35 mm gauge,**
11" long, 8" wide, 10" high,
each **5/-**

647/126

647/21

Lugagge Examination Depots

No. **647/135** well japanned,
9¹⁄₂" long, 6¹⁄₂" wide, 7¹⁄₄" high
each **4/-**

No. **647/136** larger,
9¹⁄₂" long, 9" wide, 9³⁄₄" high,
each **6/8**

647/135

647/136

Railway stations.

No. **647/130** strongly made, with imitation brickwork well, japanned, with red gelatine windows for internal illumination efect by candles, 9" long, 6" wide, 7" high. . . . . each **3/6**

No. **647/34** handsome design and finest japanning, arranged for candle illumination, 14" long, 8" wide, 12" high, each **8/-**

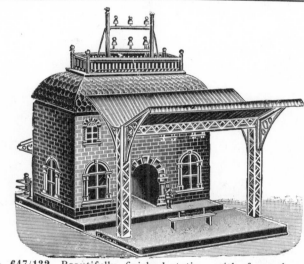

No. **647/127** handsome design, with 2 side porches and telegraph post, with gelatine windows (candle illumination), 14" long, 6" wide, 10" high . . . . . each **8/-**

No. **647/132** Beautifully finished station with front thorough-fare, telegraph, finest japanning, with red gelatine windows (candle illumination), 10" long, 14" wide, 12¹⁄₂" high . . . . each **13/6**

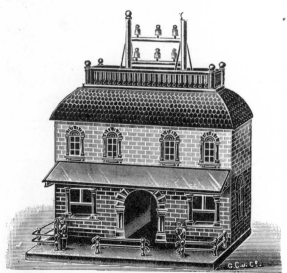

No. **647/128** **Larger railway station**, well japanned, telegraph, with red gelatine windows (candle illumination). 9¹/₂" long, 9" wide, 12¹/₂" high . . . . each **9/8**

No. **647/129** the same with 2 large side porches, mechanical signal bell, 2 platform boxes with ticket offices, telegraph, best quality finish and japanning, 20" long, 9" wide, 12¹/₂" high . . . . . each **16/-**

Trade  Mark.

Best quality Railway Stations.

647/56

647/57

No. **647/56** with removable cover to platform, **for the use of gauge 35 and 48 mm locos**, 13¼″ long, 11″ wide, 12″ high . . . . each **17/-**

No. **647/57** Large station building, superbly japanned and of richly ornamented design, arranged for candle illumination, with 2 arc lamps and clock, 17″ long, 11″ wide, 14″ high . . . . each **25/-**

Ticket office

647/81 A

No. **647/81 A** Automatic ticket office. By pulling a knob a ticket drops out. Fitted with 2 arc lamps, 7″ long, 7″ wide, 7¼″ high . . . . . . each **4/-**

No. **647/54** Ticket case, well japanned, with 12 pigeon holes and 120 tickets for various destinations, 6″ long, 7″ high . . . . each **4/10**

Ticket punches

No. **647/55** 5″ long . . . . each **-/6**

647/55

For tickets see page 117.

Ticket case

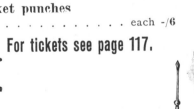

647/54

Goods sheds

No. **971/000 Small goods shed**, simple design with sliding doors and loading platform, 7″ long, 4½″ high each **2/-**

No. **971/00** the same, larger, well japanned, with sliding door, goods platform and loading crane, 10″ long, 5½″ high . . . . . . each **3/-**

No. **971/0 Small goods shed**, best japanning with 2 sliding doors, removable roof and goods platform, 8½″ long, 9½″ high . . . . each **6/-**

971/0

971/1

No. **971/1 Large goods shed**, best quality finish, with removable roof, 4 sliding doors, loading platform crane and delivery office, suitable for the larger model railways, 16″ long, 7½″ wide, 10½″ high . . . . each **20/-**

Signal Boxes and Level Crossings.

647/123

No. **647/122** plain quality, with movable signal and figure, 4¼" long, 6¼" high, dozen **7/10**

— **647/123** larger with barrier and movable signal, 6" long, 7½" high, dozen **13/-**

647/125

No. **647/124** with larger box with movable signal and figure, 6" long, 7½" high, dozen **15/6**

— **647/125** with barrier and movable signal, also figure, 6" long, 7½" high, dozen **22/-**

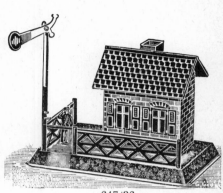

647/36

No. **647/36** with fine imitation brick-work, barrier and movable signal, 7¼" long, 4¼" wide, 6½" high, each **2/-**

No. **647/29 A** Signal box and level crossing, well japanned and of superior finish, can be fitted to any gauge rail, signal box in imitation brickwork, with closing bars and signal with lifting arm, 9½" long, 6¼" high . . . . each **2/10**

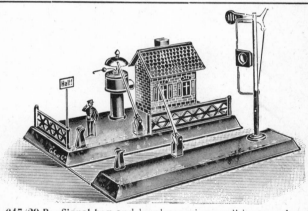

No. **647/29 B** Signal box and level crossing, well japanned and of superior finish, raised imitation brickwork signal box, to suit any gauge rail, with closing bars, signal bell telegraph pole and signal with movable arms, 12¼" long, 9½" high, each **5/8**

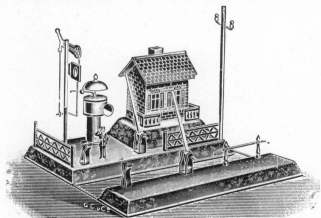

No. **647/29 C** Signal box and level crossing, well japanned and of superior finish, imitation brickwork box, with closing bars, signal bell and signal with movable arms, 12¼" long, 8½" high, each **4/6**

No. **647/31** Mechanical signal box and crossing, well japanned and of superior finish; when the train runs on the rails supplied in model, the bell rings, strong mechanism. With rails, mechanical bell and telegraph pole, **rails for 35 mm gauge, as well as 48 mm gauge**, 15" long, 7½" high, each **4/6**

Trade Mark.

108

Signal Boxes with level crossing.

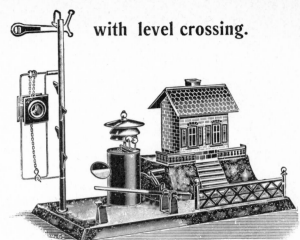

No. 647/30 C **Mechanical signal box** and level crossing well japanned and of superior finish, box in imitation brickwork, with strong mechanism. By pulling a lever the crossing is closed, the signal is "off" and the signal bell rings, 10¼" long, 6½" wide, 8" high . . . each 5/-

No. 647/30 A **Mechanical signal box** and level crossing well japanned and of superior finish, signal box in imitation brickwork, with strong work. By pulling a lever the crossing is closed, the signal is "off" and the signal bell rings, 13" long, 6" wide, 11½" high . . . each 8/6

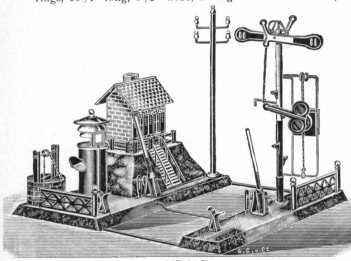

647/30 B

No. **647/30 B** **Mechanical signal box and crossing,** well japanned and of superior finish with strong mechanism. By pulling a lever the crossing becomes closed, the signal shows "Line clear" and the signal bell rings; can be adjusted to any desired gauge, 13" long, 14" wide, 12" high, each **13/-**

Level crossings, only.

974/10—11

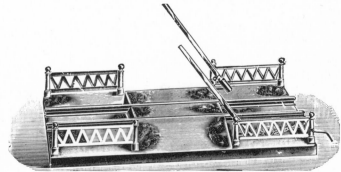

973/35—48

No. **974/10** well japanned, to suit **35 mm gauge,** each -/10

— **974/11** to suit **48 and 54 mm gauges,** — 2/-

No. **973/35** with arrangement to open and close; with rail, well japanned, to suit **35 mm gauge,** each 4/-

— **973/48** to suit **48 mm gauge** . . . — 5/8

Trade Mark.

Railway Bridges

well japanned and of handsome design, can be taken to pieces, with rails,

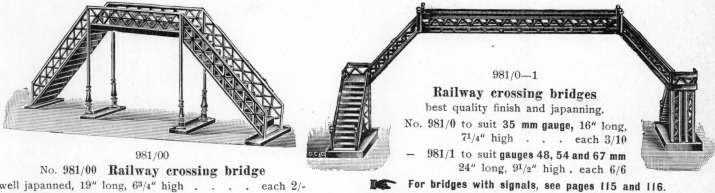

981/00

No. 981/00 **Railway crossing bridge**

well japanned, 19" long, 6¾" high . . . . each 2/-

981/0—1

Railway crossing bridges

best quality finish and japanning.

No. 981/0 to suit **35 mm gauge**, 16" long, 7¼" high . . . each 3/10

— 981/1 to suit **gauges 48, 54 and 67 mm** 24" long, 9½" high . each 6/6

☞ **For bridges with signals, see pages 115 and 116.**

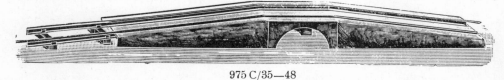

975 C/35—48

Railway bridges

No. 975 C/35 simple design, with rail connections, suitable for cheap spring motor driven railways, **35 mm gauge**, 28" long, 1¼" high . . . each 2/-

No. 975 C/48 the same but for **48 mm gauge**, 30" long, 1½" high, each 2/-

975 B/35—48

Railway bridges

with imitation girders.

No. 975 B/35 well japanned, for **35 mm gauge**, 32" long . each 4/-

— 975 B/48 for **48 mm gauge**, 32" long each 4/6

975/5—8

To suit either steam or spring motor driven railways

No. 975/5 for **35 mm gauge**, 34" long . each 4/-

No. 975/8 for **48 mm gauge**, 42" long . each 6/10

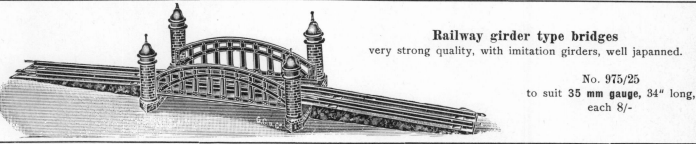

Railway girder type bridges

very strong quality, with imitation girders, well japanned.

No. 975/25

to suit **35 mm gauge**, 34" long, each 8/-

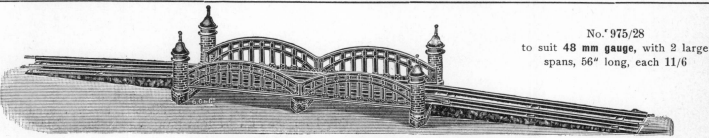

No. 975/28

to suit **48 mm gauge**, with 2 large spans, 56" long, each 11/6

For bridges to suit electric railways see page 181 of this list.

Trade Mark.

Tunnels.

Well japanned, for cheap spring motor driven railways.

979/2—3

No. **979/2** for **35 mm gauge**, 6" long, 5" wide, 6" high, dozen **12/-**

— **979/3** 8" long, 6" wide, 5½" high . . . dozen **15/6**

— **979/00** original design showing mountain scenery true to nature, 8" long, 6¼" wide, 5½" high . . . dozen **20/-**

979/00

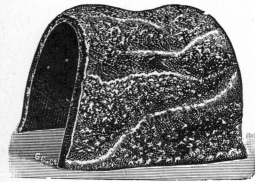

979/4—5

No. **979/4** for **48 mm gauge**, 10¼" long, 10" wide, 8" high, each **2/10**

— **979/5** larger size to suit any gauge, 14" long, 10" wide, 10" high, each **5/-**

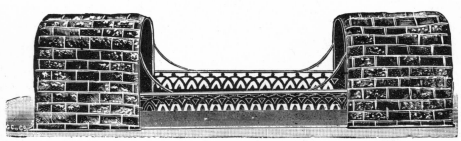

979/6

Double Tunnel with Parapet Bridge.

No. **979/6** for **35 mm gauge**, 21½" long, 5½" wide, 6" high, each **2/10**

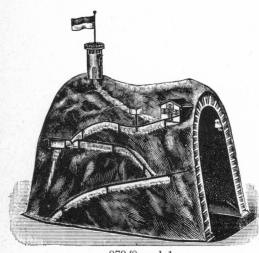

979/0 and 1

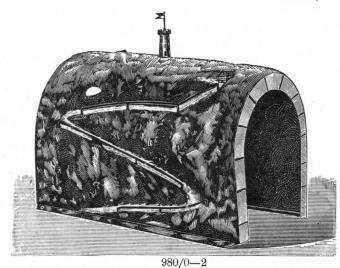

980/0—2

Tunnels of high class finish and japanning.

No. **979/0** for **35 mm gauge**, 10½" long, 8" wide, 11¼" high . . . . each **4/-**

— **979/1** for **48 mm gauge**, 14½" long, 10¼" wide, 12½" high . . each **7/6**

No. **980/0** superbly japanned and **very handsome** design, for **35 mm gauge**, 12" long, 6½" wide, 8½" high, each **6/6**

— **980/1** for **48 mm gauge**, 14" long, 8" wide, 10½" high . . . . each **9/-**

— **980/2** for **54 and 67 mm gauges**, 19" long, 10" wide, 14" high . . . . each **14/6**

Trade Mark.

Tunnels.

Modelled in plastic, perfectly new and unequalled design and finish. The tunnels faithfully represent mountain districts showing ice and snow above and rich verdure below.

Quite Original

No. **980/5** to suit railways of **35 mm gauge**, 9¹/₂″ long, 4³/₄″ wide, 7¹/₄″ high, each **2/-**

No. **980/6** for railways **48 mm gauge**, 14¹/₄″ long, 6¹/₄″ wide, 9″ high, each **4/-**

980/5

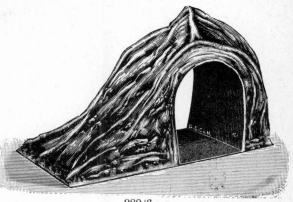

980/6

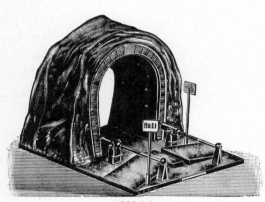

980/10

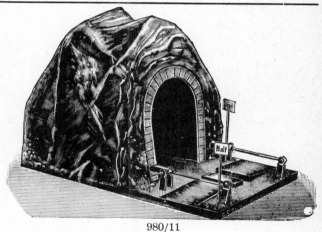

980/11

The above tunnels with mountain crossing, 2 closing bars and 2 notices "Beware of the trains". Finest japanning and very superior finish.

No. **980/10** for railways of **35 mm gauge**, 10″ long, 9¹/₂″ wide, 8″ high . . . . each **5/8**
— **980/11** — — — **48** — — 14¹/₄″ — 9¹/₂″ — 10¹/₄″ — . . . . — **7/6**

No. **980/7 Larger tunnel**, best japanning, for railways of **35 and 48 mm gauge**, 20″ long, 7¹/₄″ wide, 12″ high . . . each **5/8**

No. **980/15 Larger tunnel**, best japanning, with 2 tunnel entrances in imitation masonry and retaining wall, for railways of **35 and 48 mm gauge**, 20″ long, 10″ wide, 11″ high, each **10/6**

Signal Bells.

647/10 A

647/10 C

647/10 D

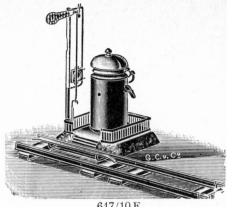

647/10 F

Signal bell, well japanned.

No. **647/10 A** 4¹/₂" high . . . . . dozen **7/10**
— **647/10 C** with double ring, 6" high — **15/6**

Mechanical signal bell, well japanned, with strong mechanism.
When the train reaches the track fitted to the model, the bell starts ringing,
in sets 647/10 F the signal moves. When the train has passed, the bell
stops automatically.

No. **647/10 D** for **gauges 35** and **48 mm,** 4¹/₂" high . . . . each **1/10**
— **647/10 F** with signal, for **gauges 35** and **48 mm,** 8¹/₂" high — **2/10**

647/26

No. **647/26 Sloping gangway** for cattle, well
japanned, with rollers, 8" long,
4" high . . . . each **2/6**

Buffer Stops.

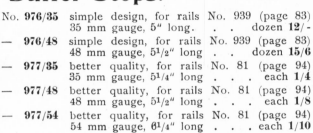

976/35—48
977/35—54

No. **976/35** simple design, for rails No. 939 (page 83)
35 mm gauge, 5" long. . . dozen **12/-**
— **976/48** simple design, for rails No. 939 (page 83)
48 mm gauge, 5¹/₂" long . . dozen **15/6**
— **977/35** better quality, for rails No. 81 (page 94)
35 mm gauge, 5¹/₄" long . . . each **1/4**
— **977/48** better quality, for rails No. 81 (page 94)
48 mm gauge, 5¹/₂" long . . . each **1/8**
— **977/54** better quality, for rails No. 81 (page 94)
54 mm gauge, 6¹/₄" long . . . each **1/10**

Train Indicators

well japanned

647/74

647/16 E

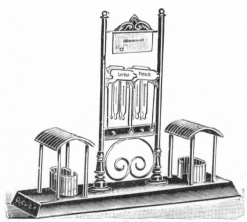

647/42

647/20 E

647/15 E

No. **647/74** with different station arms, 7" high . . . . dozen **7/10**
— **647/16 E** with 4 movable printed finger indicators, 6¹/₂" high, 4¹/₂" long . . . . . . — **11/-**
— **647/15 E** larger size, with 6 movable printed indicators, also board showing the No. of
minutes overdue of the coming train, 8¹/₄" high, 7¹/₄" long . . . . — **15/6**
— **647/42** very strong construction, with movable printed indicators, 8¹/₄" high, 4¹/₄" long each **2/6**
— **647/20 E** with movable printed indicators also 2 attendant boxes, 12¹/₄" long, 3" wide,
10" high . . . . — **3/-**

Trade  Mark.

Cranes.

647/70

647/72

617/83—84

647/73

No. **647/70**	**Loading Crane** for raising and lowering, 4¾" high	dozen **7/10**
— **647/83**	the same but **larger**, well japanned, 7¼" high	dozen **15/6**
— **647/84**	larger than 647/83, 8¼" high —	**24/-**
— **647/72**	Very strong construction, well japanned, raising and lowering also side motions, 10" high	each **3/-**
— **647/73**	with raising, lowering and side motions, well japanned and strongly made, 9" high	each **4/-**
— **633/4**	**Swivelling Cranes,** well and strongly made, with covered winding gear for raising or lowering the load with mechanical turning attachment, 12" high, 12" long	each **2/10**
— **633/5**	the same but larger and stronger, 16" high, 15½" long	each **4/-**

647/50

Travelling and Swivelling Harbour Cranes.

New!   **To work by hand**   **New!**

mounted on massive flanged wheels to run on rails (No. 81 page 94).

No. **647/50** with gear drive, for the raising and lowering of loads. The motor house, together with the crane arm will twist round. Very strong and steady design, well japanned girder frame, 10" long, 6¼" wide, 10¼" high, will unload to 6", **suitable for lifting locos 35 mm gauge** . . . . each **7/6**

— **647/51** the same larger, motor house turned by hand crank and worm gearing, well japanned. Very strong design, 13½" long, 6¼" wide, 13½" high, will take up to 8" under crane. **Suitable for lifting locos 48 mm gauge,** each **11/-**

These cranes with **Electric Motors** are listed on page 177.

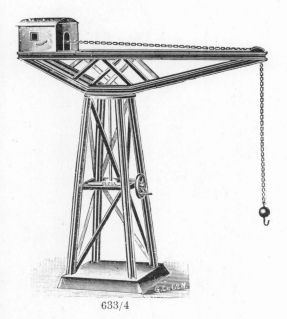

633/4

647/51

Trade Mark.

Arc Lamps

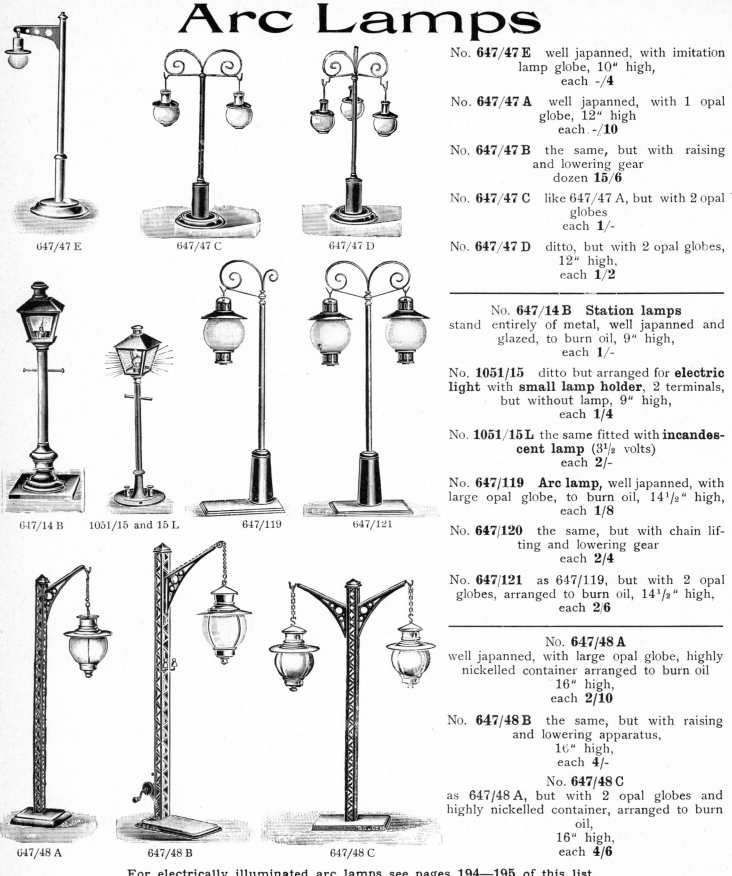

No. **647/47 E** well japanned, with imitation lamp globe, 10" high,
each -/4

No. **647/47 A** well japanned, with 1 opal globe, 12" high
each -/10

No. **647/47 B** the same, but with raising and lowering gear
dozen **15/6**

No. **647/47 C** like 647/47 A, but with 2 opal globes
each **1/-**

No. **647/47 D** ditto, but with 2 opal globes, 12" high,
each **1/2**

No. **647/14 B** Station lamps stand entirely of metal, well japanned and glazed, to burn oil, 9" high,
each **1/-**

No. **1051/15** ditto but arranged for **electric light** with **small lamp holder**, 2 terminals, but without lamp, 9" high,
each **1/4**

No. **1051/15 L** the same fitted with **incandescent lamp** ($3\frac{1}{2}$ volts)
each **2/-**

No. **647/119** **Arc lamp,** well japanned, with large opal globe, to burn oil, $14\frac{1}{2}$" high,
each **1/8**

No. **647/120** the same, but with chain lifting and lowering gear
each **2/4**

No. **647/121** as 647/119, but with 2 opal globes, arranged to burn oil, $14\frac{1}{2}$" high,
each **2/6**

No. **647/48 A** well japanned, with large opal globe, highly nickelled container arranged to burn oil
16" high,
each **2/10**

No. **647/48 B** the same, but with raising and lowering apparatus,
16" high,
each **4/-**

No. **647/48 C** as 647/48 A, but with 2 opal globes and highly nickelled container, arranged to burn oil,
16" high,
each **4/6**

647/47 E   647/47 C   647/47 D

647/14 B   1051/15 and 15 L   647/119   647/121

647/48 A   647/48 B   647/48 C

For electrically illuminated arc lamps see pages 194—195 of this list.

Trade Mark.

Signals.

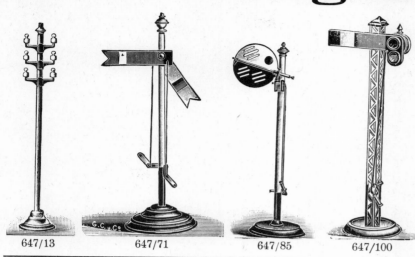

647/13   647/71   647/85   647/100

No. **647/13** **Telegraph poles**, well japanned, with 6 insulators, 10″ high . . . . . dozen **4/4**

No. **647/71** plain design, well japanned, with 2 movable arms, 10″ high . . . dozen **7/10**

No. **647/85** well japanned, with rattling signal disc, 11″ high . . . . dozen **12/-**

No. **647/100** well japanned, post in imitation iron girderwork, with movable arm, lantern, and shifting coloured signal glasses, 11½″ high dozen **15/6**

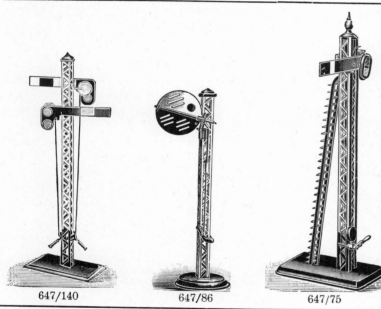

647/140   647/86   647/75

No. **647/140** well japanned, imitation iron post, with 2 movable arms, and shifting coloured signal-glasses, 13″ high . . . . dozen **15/6**

No. **647/86** well japanned, imitation iron post, with rattling signal disc, 11″ high . . . dozen **15/6**

No. **647/75** handsomely japanned, imitation iron post, with movable arm and lantern, also ladder, 12″ high . . . . each **2/10**

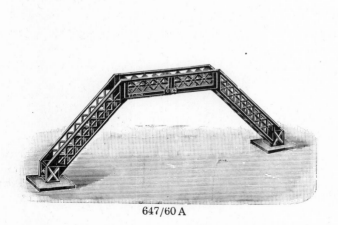

647/60 A

647/60

Railway Bridges.

No. **647/60 A** well japanned, 16½″ long, 6½″ high, dozen **7/10**

No. **647/60** well japanned, with 2 signals with movable arms, 16½″ long, 11½″ high, dozen **15/6**

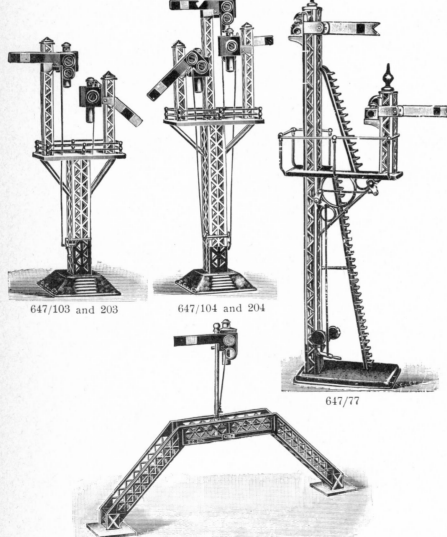

647/200

647/101 and 201

647/102 and 202

647/103 and 203

647/104 and 204

647/77

647/60 B

Signals
for oil or electrical illumination.
With lanterns to burn oil.

No. **647/101** with 2 movable arms and 2 lanterns, well finished and strong, 11 1/2 " high, each **2/-**

No. **647/102** with 2 movable arms and 2 lanterns, 18 1/2 " high, each **2/10**

— **647/103** with 2 movable arms and 2 lanterns, 18 1/2 " high, each **4/6**

— **647/104** with 3 movable arms and 3 lanterns, 22" high, each **5/8**

The above signals with lanterns adapted for electricity without incandescent lamps (for lamps to suit, see page 193 of this list),

No. **647/200** with 1 movable signal arm and 1 lantern, 11 1/2 " high, each **1/10**

— **647/201** with 2 movable arms and 2 lanterns, 11 1/2 " high, each **2/4**

— **647/202** with 2 movable arms and 2 lanterns, 18 1/2 " high, each **3/2**

— **647/203** with 2 movable arms and 2 lanterns, 18 1/2 " high, each **5/2**

— **647/204** with 3 movable arms and 3 lanterns, 22" high, each **6/6**

No. 647/77
Large signal
handsomely japanned and of elegant design, with 2 movable arms and lantern with coloured signal glasses, with 2 ladders and gallery, 18 1/2 " high, each **6/6**

No. 647/60 B
Railway bridge
well japanned, with 1 movable arm and 1 lantern to burn, 16 1/2 " long, 11 1/2 " high, dozen **15/6**

Trade  Mark.

Ticket blocks.

No. 982/20 E   Block of 36 tickets for **various journeys**, english . . . . dozen blocks **4/10**

— 982/21 E   loose tickets for **various journeys** . . . . gross **1/4**

983/8 and 9

Passenger figures,
in **well japanned pewter.**

Seated figures in assortments of 3 different figures, made to fit our coaches.

No. 983/8   to suit **gauge 35 mm** railways, 24 figures in cardboard box . . . . each **1/8**

— 983/9   to suit **gauge 48 mm** railways, 24 figures in cardboard box . . . . each **2/-**

983/7

Railway Employees.

No. **983/6**   in half massive design, 3 kinds assorted, 2″ high . . . . dozen **1/-**

No. **983/7**   solid design, 3 kinds assorted, 2″ high, dozen **2/6**

983/20 and 21

Railway figures

High class design, artistically painted, to suit our coaches, box containing 4 men, 4 ladies, 2 boys, 2 girls.

No. **983/20**   to suit **gauge 35 mm** railways, price per box of 12 figures **2/4**

No. **983/21** — — — 48 — — — — — — 12 — **2/8**

983/2

Railway Figures

pewter well japanned, in prettily covered box.

No. **983/1**   with 12 original design figures and mail coach driver, in semi massive quality . . . . box **1/-**

— **983/2**   with 14 original design figures and 1 mail coach driver, semi massive quality . . . . box **1/10**

— **983/3**   with 12 original design figures and 1 mail coach driver, massive quality . . . . box **3/-**

— **983/4**   with 14 original design figures and mail coach driver, massive quality . . . . box **5/-**

Trade  Mark.

Separate Accessories for Railways.

Flanged wheels for coaches etc. of stamped iron plate.

plain No. 31 A/00	0	1	2	spoked No 31 B/1	2	3
diam. of tread 5/8	7/8	1	1 1/8"	diam. of tread 13/16	1 1/8	1 1/4"
— over flange 13/16	1 1/16	1 1/8	1 7/16"	— over flange 1 1/8	1 7/16	1 1/2"
dozen -/4	-/10	1/-	1/4	dozen -/10	1/-	1/2

31 A · **31 B**

Flanged wheels for coaches etc. of cast lead castings only, with axle hole.

No. 31 E S/1	1 1/2	2	2 1/2	3	3 1/2	4	5
diam. of tread 13/16	13/16	1	1 1/8	1 1/4	15/16	1 7/16	1"
— over flange 1 1/16	1 1/16	1 1/4	1 7/16	1 1/2	1 1/2	1 9/16	1 1/4"
without crank, doz. 1/-	-/10	1/-	1/6	1/8	1/8	2/-	1/2

with crank.

Heavy wheels not spoked.

No. 31 BL/35	48	54
13/16	1 1/8	2 1/8"
1 1/16	1 3/8	1 1/2"
dozen 1/8	2/6	3/-

31 B S · **31 B L**

Heavier flanged wheels, cast iron.

	size	26	29	32	38	52	58
diameter of tread		13/16	7/8	1	1 1/4	1 3/4	2"
— over flange		1	1 1/8	1 1/4	1 3/4	2 1/16	2 1/4"
No. 31 F casting only, not bored	dozen	1/6	1/8	2/6	2/8	3/2	3/8
— 31 H — — — with crank		—	—	—	2/8	3/2	3/8
— 31 E turned with hole		—	4/10	5/-	5/6	6/8	7/2	8/-
— 31 T turned, with holes for axle and crank pin,	—	—	—	—	7/2	8/-	8/4

Massive cast iron wheels, not spoked

	size	48	54	67
diameter of tread		1 1/8	1 1/2	1 5/8"
— over flange		1 7/16	1 5/8	1 13/16"
No. 31 EL casting only, unbored	each	-/2	-/3	-/4
— 31 EL/0 turned and bored	—	-/8	-/8	-/10

31 F · **31 EL**

Heavier flanged wheels in brass

	size	27	34	36	53	64	70	79	110
					with crank				
diameter of tread		7/8	1 1/8	1 1/4	1 13/16	2 1/4	2 1/2	2 3/4	4"
— over flange		1 1/16	1 5/16	1 3/8	2 1/8	2 1/2	2 3/4	3 1/8	4 5/16"
No. 31 P casting only, unbored	each	-/2	-/4	-/5	-/6	1/-	1/4	1/6	2/6
— 31 M turned and bored	—	-/6	-/8	-/10	1/-	1/6	1/8	2/-	3/6
— 31 N turned, japanned and nickelled	—	-/8	-/10	1/-	1/-	1/8	2/-	2/4	4/-

31 P

Couplings draw hooks etc.

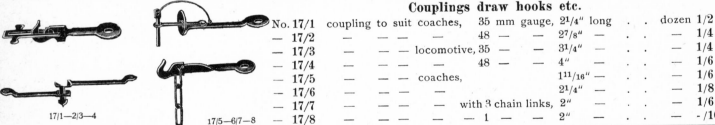
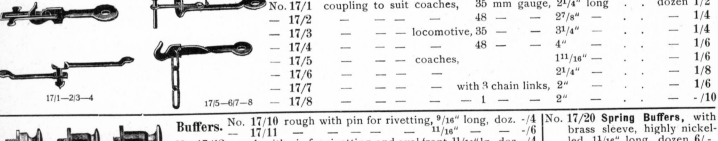

No. 17/1	coupling to suit coaches,	35 mm gauge,	2 1/4" long	dozen 1/2
— 17/2	— — —	48 —	2 7/8" —	— 1/4
— 17/3	— — locomotive, 35	—	3 1/4" —	— 1/4
— 17/4	— — —	48 —	4" —	— 1/6
— 17/5	— — coaches,		1 11/16" —	— 1/6
— 17/6	— — —		2 1/4" —	— 1/8
— 17/7	— — —	with 3 chain links, 2" —	— 1/6
17/5—6/7—8 — 17/8	— — —	— 1	— 2" —	— -/10

17/1—2/3—4

Buffers.

No. 17/10 rough with pin for rivetting, 9/16" long, doz.	-/4
— 17/11 — — 11/16" —	-/6
No. 17/12 rough with pin for rivetting and oval front, 11/16" lg., doz.	-/4
— 17/13 — — 13/16" —	-/6
— 17/14 — — 1" —	1/-
— 17/15 — screw for screwing into frame, 11/16" lg, doz.	-/10
— 17/16 — — 13/16" —	-/10
— 17/17 Brass front and lead sleeve, japanned and nickelled, 5/8" long	dozen 3/-
— 17/18 — — 11/16"	— 3/4
— 17/19 — — 7/8"	— 3/10

No. 17/20 Spring Buffers, with brass sleeve, highly nickelled, 1 1/16" long, dozen	6/-
— 17/21 do., 1 1/4" lg., —	6/10
— 17/22 Brass, highly nickelled 5/8" long, with screw to fix to frame, dozen	3/4

17/10—11 17/12—14 17/15—16
17/17—19 17/20—21 17/22

Locomotive lanterns
to push on, japanned.

No. 17/30 7/16" high, each -/1
— 17/31 1/2" high, each -/2

Locomotive lanterns
to screw, with nickel reflector, japanned.

No. 17/32 1" high, each -/4
— 17/33 1 1/8" — — -/4

No. 17/75 Elec. inc. lamp, without lamp, each -/4
No. 17/75/0 do., without bracket, — -/3
(Lamps to fit, see page 193).

No. 17/74 Electr. inc. lamp, without lamp, each -/2

Lanterns for switches,
well japanned.

No. 17/36 1 3/4" high, each -/4

Trade Mark.

Spring Motor Accessories

Motor Springs of good steel,
for railways and locos, pages 71—80

No.						
16/20	for railways	1701/2	. . . .	dozen	1/6
— 16/21	— —	831/0	. . . .	—	1/8
— 16/22	— —	805/2—4	. . .	—	2/2
— 16/23	— —	831/9	. . . .	—	2/2
— 16/24	— —	1701/3	. . . .	—	2/6
— 16/25	— —	831/2—6, 830/1—5,	—	3/2
— 16/26	— —	806/1	. . . .	—	3/8
— 16/27	— —	831/10	. . . .	—	4/2
— 16/28	— —	806/2	. . . .	—	4/6
— 16/29	— —	830/3, 834/4, 837/0,	—	5/-
— 16/30	— —	834/9	. . . .	—	5/6
— 16/31	— —	833/1—3, 1819	. .	—	6/6
— 16/32	— —	829	. . . .	—	7/-
— 16/33	— —	822/1—5	. . .	—	7/-
— 16/34	— —	834/8	. . . .	—	8/-
— 16/35	— —	807/808, 827	. .	—	12/-
— 16/36	— —	821, 1821	. . .	—	20/-

16

Motor Springs
of best hardened steel

No.					
16/0	for loco	961/35	. . . . .	each	1/10
— 16/1	— —	962/35	. . . . .	—	2/-
— 16/2	— —	963 and 968/35	. .	—	2/-
— 16/3	— —	965/35	. . . . .	—	2/-
— 16/4	— —	966/35	. . . . .	—	1/6
— 16/5	— —	967/35	. . . . .	—	1/6
— 16/6	— —	969/35 and 1513/6	. .	—	2/-
— 16/7	— —	961/48	. . . . .	—	3/4
— 16/8	— —	962/48	. . . . .	—	3/8
— 16/9	— —	963, 968 and 969/48	.	—	4/-
— 16/10	— —	965/48 and 1514/6	. .	—	5/6
— 16/11	— —	961/54	. . . . .	—	4/8
— 16/12	— —	965/54	. . . . .	—	7/-

Winding Keys, cast iron, strong quality

No.					
15/00	to suit cheap spring motors	. . . .	dozen	1/6
— 15/0	— — Morse Telegraphs No. 1026/3 and 4	. . .	—	1/8
— 15/1	— — better class locos 35 mm gauge	. .	—	2/8
— 15/2	— — — — 48 —	. .	—	4/-
— 15/3	— — — — 54 —	. .	—	5/4

Brass spur or cog wheels, with centre hole

Strong pattern

No.	58/28	30	40	45	50	60
No. of teeth	40	40	48	66	60	68
diam.	1 1/8	1 3/16	1 9/16	1 3/4	2	2 3/8"
thickness	1/16	3/32	3/32	3/32	3/32	3/32"
dozen	1/6	2/-	3/-	4/10	5/4	6/-

58

Light pattern

No.	58 L/13	16	18	20	23	24	26	27
teeth	20	30	40	40	42	48	40	48
diam.	1/2	5/8	11/16	3/4	7/8	15/16	1	1 1/16"
thickness	1/32	1/32	1/32	1/32	1/32	1/32	1/32	1/32"
gross	3/-	4/4	5/4	6/-	7/-	7/-	8/-	9/4

Brass crown spur wheels

with centre hole and 30 teeth
No. 58/17 K
11/16" diam., 1/32" thickness
dozen -/8

58/17 K

Brass driving pinion with hole and 10 teeth

59/3-6

No.						
59/3	1/8" long,	1/4" diam.,	. . .	to suit 58 L in all sizes	gross	4/-
— 59/4	5/32" —	1/4" —		—	4/6
— 59/4 a	5/32" —	1/4" —	extended	—	4/1
— 59/6 L	1/4" —	1/4" —	. . . .	—	6/-
— 59/6	1/4" —	1/4" —	to suit 58/28, 58/45,	—	7/40

Steel driving pinion, with hole

59/10-11

No.					
59/10	with 12 teeth, 1/4" long, 3/8" diam.	. . .	dozen	1/8
— 59/11	— 14 — 1/4" — 7/16" —		—	2/-

Bevel gear wheels

5/1-2

No.				
5/1	1/2" diam. as drawing, set	-/4
— 5/2	5/8" — — —	-/8

Complete winding gear with winding

spindle, ratchet wheel and ratchet in brass

No.	58 A/1	2	3	4
for	35	35	48	54 mm gauge
diam.	1 11/16	1 11/16	2 1/4	2 7/16"
thickness	1/16	1/16	1/16	1/16"
No. of teeth	60	60	80	88
each	-/10	-/10	1/-	1/-

58 A

Brass intermediate wheels

with steel driving axle

No.	58 S/1	2	3
for	35	35 48 and 54 mm gauge	
diam.	1 7/16	1 7/16	1 3/4"
thickness	1/16	1/16	1/16"
No. of teeth	55	54	60
each	-/4	-/4	-/6

58 S

17/40—43

Bells, Gongs

No.				
17/43	brass bell, 5/8" diam.,	dozen	1/2
— 17/40	steel gong highly nickelled, 7/8" diam.	. .	dozen	1/-
No. 17/41	ditto but 1 3/4" diam.	. . . .	—	2/-
— 17/42	— — 2 3/8" —	. . . .	—	2/4

Fancy chains

17/60—66

No.			
17/60	light curb chain, brass, 1" thick	. . .	yard	-/4
— 17/61	strong curb chain, iron, 1 3/16" thick	. .	yard	-/1
— 17/62	clock chain, iron, 1 9/16" thick	. . .	yard	-/2
No. 17/63	narrow band chain, 9/32" wide brass	.	yard	-/8
— 17/64	wide — 3/8" —	. . .	—	-/10
— 17/65	"Kremple" chain, 9/16" wide iron	. .	—	2/-

(No. 17/65 specially for revolving stereoscopes).

No. 81/10 **Rail Coach and Wagon Gauge**, for rails and coaches
of 35 mm gauge. This gauge enables one to accurately gauge
coaches and rails, as shown in adjoining sketches, dozen -/10
No. 81/11 the same but for rails and coaches of 48 mm gauge,
dozen 1/2

Trade Mark.

Steam Ships. Strong quality, well japanned.

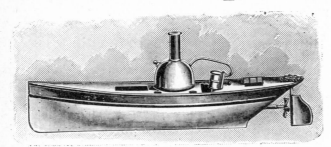

141/00

141/11

Cheap steam ships with brass boiler and oscillating cylinder.

No. 141/000	10″ long	dozen 15/6		No. 141/0½	19″ long	each 4/-
— 141/00	11½″ —	— 24/-		— 141/10	20″ —	— 5/8
— 141/0	13″ —	— 34/-		— 141/11	21½″ —	— 7/-
— 141/0¼	16″ —	— 42/-		— 141/12	23″ —	— 8/6

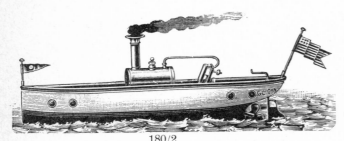

180/2

River steamers, well japanned with brass boiler and brass cylinder

No. 180/2	18″ long	each 8/6

the same but with **high hull** and **deck**

— 180/3	14″ long	— 8/6
— 180/4	18″ —	— 10/10

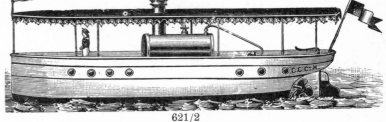

621/2

High class **River steamers** with **long covered deck,** well japanned

No. 621/2	18″ long	each 15/-
— 621/3	**better finish,** 22″ long	— 30/-

162

Handsome Saloon Yacht
(Screw steamer)

well japanned, with strong brass boiler and brass cylinder.

No. 162 22″ long . . . . each **20/6**

622/3

Handsome large
Ocean going Steam Ship
(Screw steamer)

very handsomely finished and japanned, full equipment, such as bridge, lifeboats, anchor and chain etc.

No. 622/3	22″ long	each 33/-
— 622/4	26″ —	— 44/-
— 622/5	30″ —	— 59/-

Trade  Mark.

New Screw Steamers

with strong **spring motors**

well finished and handsomely japanned.

731/10

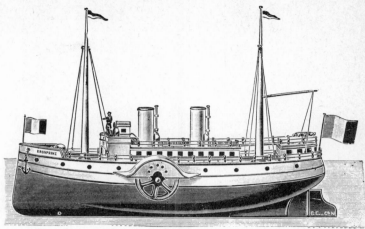

731/15

Paddle Steamers

of handsome finish, with bridge, mid-saloon and stern-saloon and handsome gilded upper deck.

No. 731/10	8" long			
— 731/11	8¾" —	. . . .	each	2/-
— 731/12	9½" —	. . . .	—	2/10
— 731/13	11¼" —	. . . .	—	4/-
— 731/14	13½" — with bridge	. . . .	—	5/8
— 731/15	16¾" —	. . . .	—	8/6
— 731/16	18" —	. . . .	—	11/6
— 731/17	20¼" — with 2 masts, anchor and capstan, promenade deck	. . .	—	14/-
			—	17/-

Ships from 731/14 are supplied with the names of the most well known steam ships of the present day.

Pleasure Steamers

713/21

with very strong spring motors

handsomely japanned with double decks and saloon, with crow's nest, scale tackle and fittings, large funnels, lifeboats, well made anchor and capstan bridge, steering gear.

713/24

Our Models are of the latest type and scale design.

No. 713/20	in plain finish, 7¼" long	. . . .	dozen	15/6
— 713/21	— — — 8" —	. . . .	each	2/-
— 713/22	— — — 9" —	. . . .	—	2/10
— 713/23	— — — with 3 funnels, 11¼" long	. . . . .	—	4/-

713/27

No. 713/24 with 4 funnels and masts also double deck 12¼" long . . . . . . each 5/8

— 713/25 ditto 13½" long . . . . . — 8/6
— 713/26 — 15¼" — . . . . . — 10/-
— 713/27 — 16¾" — . . . . . — 11/6
— 713/28 double deck with gallery, 17¼" long — 14/-
— 713/29 — — — — 18¼" — — 17/-
— 713/30 — — — also anchor with
capstan, 2 lifeboats, 19" long each 21/-
— 713/31 ditto, 20¼" long . . . . . — 25/4
— 713/32 double deck with gallery, also anchor with
capstan, 4 lifeboats, masts with crow's nest,
22" long . . . . . . each 28/-
— 713/33 ditto, 23¼" long . . . . . — 32/-

From size 713/25 down, our ships are delivered with the names of most well known ocean steam ships.

Illustration No. 713/31 see next page.

Trade Mark.

Large Pleasure Steamers

with very strong spring motors and superfinely japanned.

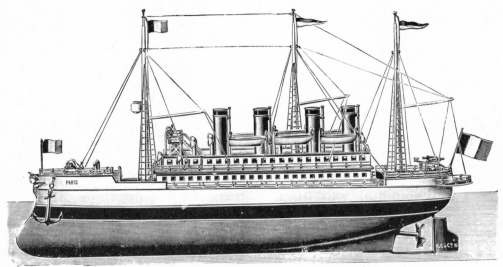

713/31

With names of the best known ocean steamers of the present time.

No. **713/34** Double deck and saloon, masts with look-out station, scale design tackle, large funnels, lifeboats, beautifully made anchor capstan, steering wheel, etc., 25" long . . . . each **36/-**
— **713/35** do. do. 26¼" long . . . . — **46/-**
— **713/36** — — 28" — . . . . — **52/-**
— **713/37** — — 29" — . . . . — **64/-**
— **713/38** — — 30" — . . . . — **76/-**

Battle Ships (Armour plated)

Most modern 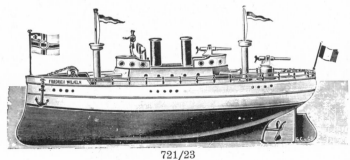 construction!

721/23

With very strong spring motors, armoured gun room, quick firing guns, funnels and signalling masts, armoured turrets, life boats, anchors with capstan, rudder etc. full detailed model and best japanning, from size **721/25** the ships are named after the best known battle ships of the present time.

No. **721/20** with 3 guns, 7¼" long, ... dozen **15/6**
— **721/21** — 3 — 8" — . . . . each **2/-**
— **721/22** — 3 — 9½" — . . . . — **2/10**
— **721/23** — 4 —, deck, with gilt rails, 10½" long. . . . . — **4/-**
— **721/24** — 5 — — — — — 12" — . . . . — **5/8**
— **721/25** — 5 — — — — — 13¼" — . . . . — **8/6**

Trade Mark.

Large Battle ships (Armour plated).

721/36

Best make and finest japanning, **strong substantial spring motor**, protected gun chamber, quick-firing guns, chimneys and signalling masts, swivelling crane, armoured turrets, lifeboats, anchors with capstan, rudder etc. Very full detailed model, named after the best known battle ships of the present day.

No. 721/26	with 5 guns, 14³/₄" long	. . . .	each 10/-
— 721/27	— 5 — 16¹/₂" —	. . . .	each 10/-
— 721/28	— 9 — 18" —	. . . .	— 11/6
— 721/29	— 2 masts and 10 guns, heavily armoured, anchor with capstan, 18¹/₂" long,		— 17/-
— 721/30	— — — — — — — —		— 21/-
— 721/31	— — — — — — —	2 lifeboats, 20" long .	— 24/-
— 721/32	— — — — — — —	21" long	— 27/-
— 721/33	— — — — 11 — — — —	and crane, 22" long .	— 30/-
— 721/34	— — — — — — —	— — 24" — .	— 36/-
— 721/35	— — — — — — —	— — 26" — .	— 46/-
— 721/36	— — — — — — —	— — 28" — .	— 60/-

with 4 lifeboats and swivelling crane, 30" long, each **76/-**

737/11

New Coasting Cruisers

with **very strong spring motor**, well made and japanned, with protected quick-firing guns, masts with look-out stations, search light and lifeboats.

No. 737/10	plain quality, 7¹/₄" long with 3 guns	. . . .	dozen 15/6
— 737/10³/₄	— — 8" —	. . . .	each 2/-
— 737/11	— — 9" —	. . . .	— 2/10
— 737/11¹/₂	— — 10¹/₄" —	. . . .	— 4/-
— 737/12	— — 12" —	. . . .	— 5/8
— 737/13 A	— — 13¹/₄" —	. . . .	— 7/-

Trade 🗲 Mark.

Large Coasting Cruisers.

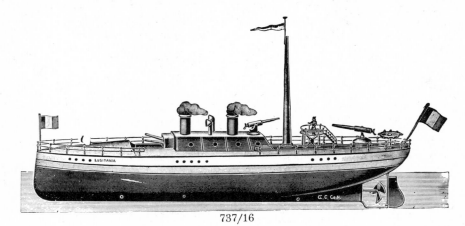

737/16

With very strong spring motor. Finest finish and japanning, armour protected quick-firing guns, masts with look-out, search light and lifeboats.

No. **737/13**	with 3 guns and plain mast, 14" long	. . . .	each	**8/6**
— **737/14**	— 3 — — — — 15" —	. . . .	—	**11/6**
— **737/15**	— 3 — — — — 20" —	. . . .	—	**14/-**
— **737/16**	— 4 — — — — 22" —	. . . .	—	**17/-**
— **737/17**	— 4 — — — — 22" —	. . . .	—	**21/-**
— **737/18**	— 4 — — double mast with look-out, search light, lifeboats, bridge etc., **very full detailed model**, 24" long	. . . .	each	**28/-**

From 737/13 the above ships are named after the best known battle ships.

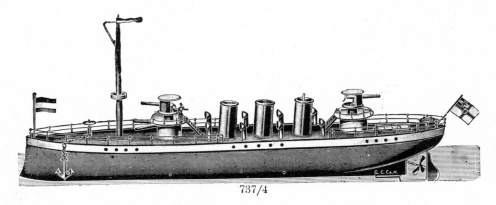

737/4

Torpedo Boat, latest type

with very strong spring motor, superbly japanned, with signalling apparatus, armoured turret with quick-firing guns, torpedo tubes, anchor, capstan etc.

No. **737/0**	6½" long	. . . .	dozen	**15/6**
— **737/0³/4**	8¼" —	. . . .	each	**2/-**
— **737/1**	10 " —	. . . .	—	**2/10**
— **737/1½**	11¼" —	. . . .	—	**4/-**
— **737/2**	14½" —	. . . .	—	**5/8**
— **737/2½**	16½" —	. . . .	—	**7/-**
— **737/3**	18¼" —	. . . .	—	**8/-**
— **737/4**	20¼" —	. . . .	—	**11/-**
— **737/5**	22 " —	. . . .	—	**14/-**

Trade Mark.

Despatch Boat "Sleipner".
(Scale model.)

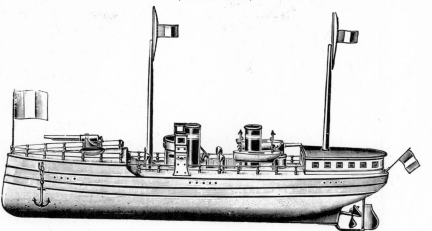

**Ship in attendance
on His Majesty
the
German Emperor.**

Very fine japanning
and handsomely made,
with bridge with look
out station, 2 masts,
lifeboats, quick-firing
guns, anchor.
No. **737/5¹/₂**
20" long
each **14/-**

737/5¹/₂

724/1

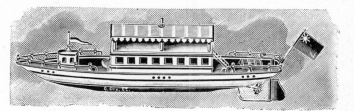

724/4

Pleasure Yachts
With very strong spring motors, well japanned, with promenade deck.

No.				
No. **724/1**	7¹/₂" long	. . . .	dozen	**15/6**
— **724/2**	8¹/₄" —	. . . .	each	**2/-**
— **724/3**	9¹/₂" —	. . . .	—	**2/10**
— **724/4**	11¹/₄" —	. . . .	—	**4/-**
— **724/5**	12¹/₂" —	. . . .	—	**5/8**

718/00—3

Submarines
with very strong spring motors, well japanned,
**swims under water up to the
air chamber.
Quite original design.**

No.				
No. **718/00**	8" long	. . .	dozen	**15/6**
— **718/0**	9¹/₄" —	. . .	each	**2/-**
— **718/1**	10" —	. . .	—	**3/-**
— **718/2**	11¹/₂" —	. . .	—	**4/6**
— **718/3**	13¹/₄" —	. . .	—	**6/-**

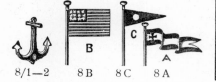

8/1—2 8B 8C 8A

Ships anchors.
No. **8/1** Cast, 1" high
dozen **-/4**
— **8/2** Cast, 2" high
dozen **-/8**

Flags
of different nations, finely executed

No.				
No. **8A**	Flag, 3¹/₂" long,	.	dozen	**2/-**
— **8B**	Flag, 2³/₄" —	.	—	**1/10**
— **8C**	Pennon, 2¹/₂" long	.	—	**-/6**

Trade ⚙ Mark.

Fire Extinguishing Appliances.

118/1

118/3

Steam fire engines

No. 118/1

with bright polished brass boiler heated by spirit lamp, safety valve, oscillating cylinder, which works a force pump, the whole on a well japanned wheel carriage with 2 figures and alarm bell, $8^1/_4$" long . . . . . . each **7/-**

No. **118/2 ditto,** but driven by **clockwork (or spring motor)** . . each **8/-**

No. **118/3 Model motor fire engine** with strong bright brass boiler, with spirit lamp, safety valve, steam whistle, oscillating cylinder, force pump with 4 feet of rubber tubing on hose reel, the whole fitted on a handsomely japanned carriage with 5 figures and 2 head-lights. A special gear is fitted so that either the pump is worked or the carriage propelled. Very strong and well made, 12" long, each **11/-**

Fire escapes

No. **118/5** with strong spring motor (clockwork) and **removable** ladder, 5 figures and alarm bell, $12^3/_4$" long . . . . . . each **5/6**

— **118/5 A Model motor fire escape** same design as 118/5 but fitted with **swivelling platform** so that fire escape is movable in all directions with 2 head lights, $12^3/_4$" long, each **9/4**

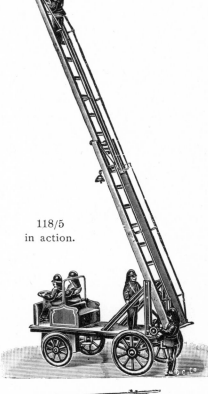

118/5
in action.

118/5

118/5 A

Hose cart

(and firemen wagon)

No. 118/7

driven by strong spring motor, with 2 ladders, hose on reel, with 9 figures and alarm bell, 9" long . . each **5/6**

No. 118/7 A

Model motor wagon same as 118/7, but with 2 head lights, $11^1/_2$" long . each **7/2**

No. 118 F/10

Figures only, seating dozen **2/6**

No. 118 F/11

Figures only, standing dozen **2/6**

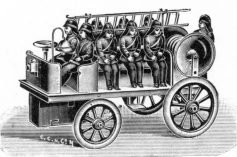

118/7

118/7 A

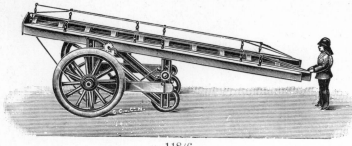

118/6

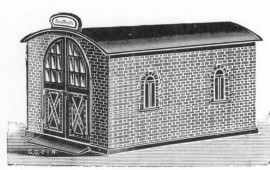

645/4 F

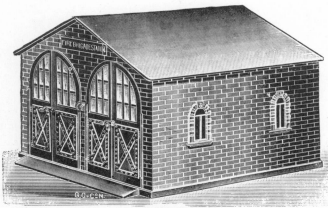

118/8 F

Sliding Fire Escapes

No. **118/6** Escape is adjustable for length, 12¼" long, each **2/6**

Motor Bus

No. **741/2** Model motor omnibus, driven by steam, bright polished brass boiler with oscillating cylinder and 1 chauffeur, 12" long . . . . . . each **6/6**

741/2

Central fire stations

No. **645/4 F** Building in imitation brickwork, with 1 large double door and 4 windows, well japanned, 14½" long, 9½" wide, 8½" high . . . . each **4/-**

— **118/8 F** the same, but with 2 large double doors, 14½" long, 13½" wide, 10" high . . . . each **5/10**

— **118/9 F** the same, but with 3 large double doors, 18½" long, 14¼" wide, 12" high . . . each **15/10**

Central fire brigade station

with most perfect fire extinguishing appliances which start off automatically with opening the doors.

Quite original!

Building in imitation brickwork well japanned and imitation tiled roof.

No. **118/13 F** Consisting of building 118/9 F, steam fire engine 118/2, fire escape 118/5 and hose cart 118/7, all driven by strong spring motors (clockwork). By touching a lever at the side, all the 3 doors open and the vehicles start off automatically, 18½" long, 14¼" wide, 12" high, complete **35/-**

Very entertaining game.

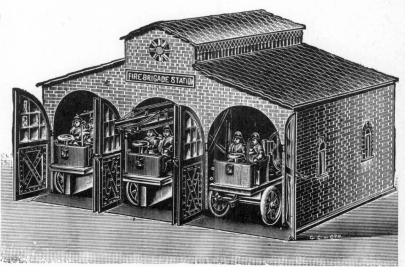

118/13 F

Trade Mark.

9 E

Magic Lanterns.

Cheap Magic Lanterns.

Plain quality, of russian iron.

Fitted with 3 lenses, paraffin lamp with glass chimney also glass slides.

No. **215/00** and **0**

are packed in plain pasteboard boxes.

No. **215/1** to **6**

are packed in covered pasteboard boxes with partition for pictures.

No. 215/00 has objective with 2 lenses.

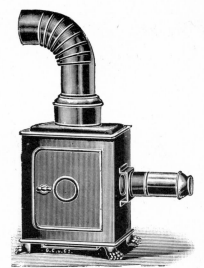

215/00—1

215/2—6

No. **215/00**	**0**	**1**	**2**	**3**	**4**	**5**	**6**
with 3	6	12	12	12	12	12	12 slides
$1^3/_{16}$	$1^3/_{16}$	$1^3/_{16}$	$1^3/_8$	$1^5/_8$	$1^3/_4$	2	$2^3/_8$ " wide
Objective 1	1	1	$1^3/_{16}$	$1^3/_{16}$	$1^3/_8$	$1^5/_8$	$1^3/_4$ " diameter
dozen **15/6**	**24/-**	**36/-**	**54/-**	**72/-**	**90/-**	**108/-**	**126/-**

Good Magic Lanterns

Strong quality.

of polished russian iron, objective with 3 lenses, paraffin lamp with glass chimney, slides; packed in pretty pasteboard box.

No. 244/2½ with 2 lenses only.

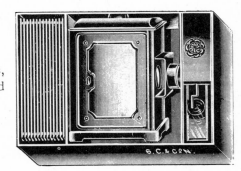

244

244 B

No. **244/2**½	**3**	**3**½	**4**	**4**½	**5**	**6**
with 6	12	12	12	12	12	12 slides
1	$1^3/_{16}$	$1^3/_8$	$1^5/_8$	$1^3/_4$	2	$2^3/_8$ " wide
Objective 1	1	$1^3/_{16}$	$1^3/_8$	$1^5/_8$	$1^3/_4$	2 " diameter
each **1/8**	**2/6**	**3/4**	**4/10**	**5/8**	**7/-**	**8/-**

The same lanterns with 1 chromotrope, 1 moving landscape and 1 transformation slide.

No. **244 B/3**		**3**½	**4**	**4**½	**5**	**6**
with 12 slides and 3 moving slides	$1^3/_{16}$	$1^3/_8$	$1^5/_8$	$1^3/_4$	2	$2^3/_8$ " wide
Objective	1	$1^3/_{16}$	$1^3/_8$	$1^5/_8$	$1^3/_4$	2 " diameter
each	**3/6**	**4/6**	**6/-**	**7/-**	**8/8**	**10/-**

Trade Mark.

High class Magic Lanterns

of polished russian iron,

with **brass fittings, brass objective with 3 lenses,** 12 slides, packed in prettily covered pasteboard box with separate partition for slides.

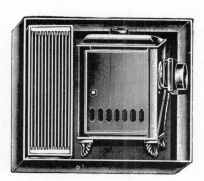

No.	**245 C/4**	**4¹/₂**	**5**	**6**	**7**	**8**	
slides	1⁵/₈	1³/₄	2	2³/₈	2³/₄	3¹/₈ "	wide
Objective	1³/₈	1⁵/₈	1³/₄	2	2³/₁₆	2³/₈ "	diam.
each	**6/-**	**7/-**	**9/8**	**10/8**	**13/8**	**15/-**	

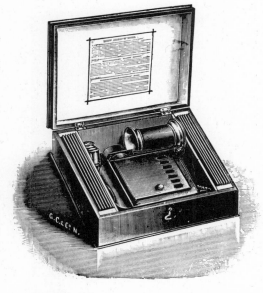

The same lanterns in well covered wood case with partition for slides.

No.	**245/4**	**4¹/₂**	**5**	
slides	1⁵/₈	1³/₄	2 "	wide
Objective	1³/₈	1⁵/₈	1³/₄ "	diam.
each	**7/-**	**8/-**	**10/6**	

No.	**245/6**	**7**	**8**	
slides	2³/₈	2³/₄	3¹/₈ "	wide
Objective	2	2³/₁₆	2³/₈ "	diam.
each	**11/6**	**15/-**	**16/-**	

The same lanterns but with **1 chromotrope, 1 moving landscape and 1 comic transformation** slide.

No.	**245 A/4**	**4¹/₂**	**5**	**6**	**7**	**8**	
moving slide	1⁵/₈	1³/₄	2	2³/₈	2³/₄	3¹/₈ "	wide
each	**8/-**	**9/6**	**12/-**	**13/-**	**17/-**	**18/6**	

Acetylene Gas illumination can be used in lanterns 245/5, 6, 7, 8; burners for same are listed on page 130 (see illustration 387 A on page 130).

For electric illumination see page 130.

Trade Mark.

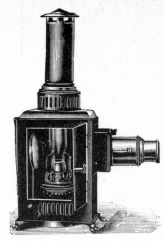

No. 387

High class Magic Lanterns

body of polished russian iron, with fine brass objective, double condenser, paraffin lamp with round wick, automatic slide holder, holding either thick or thin slides always in focus.

Each lantern has:

12 fine long glass slides,	1 transformation scene,
1 chromotrope,	1 moving landscape slide,

in handsome and prettily covered wood box with separate sliding case for slides.

No.	**387/1**	**2**	**3**	
Slides	2	$2^3/_8$	$2^3/_4$ "	wide
Objective	$1^3/_4$	2	$2^3/_{16}$ "	diam.
each	**15/-**	**17/6**	**20/-**	
No.	**387/4**	**5**	**6**	
Slides	$3^1/_8$	$3^1/_2$	4 "	wide
Objective	$2^3/_8$	$2^3/_4$	$3^1/_8$ "	diam.
each	**24/6**	**29/-**	**33/-**	

For above lanterns we also supply an attachment, by which **electric lighting** can be used (see illustration 307 E) for connecting to town current.

Universal Lamp

for electric illumination

for incandescent lamps (carbon or mettalic or Nernst) to fit all the lanterns from $1^5/_8$" width of slide, with adjustment for height, 2 yards of duplex wire and with the following type of adaptor, but without lamp.

307 E

No. 307 E/5	with Edison standard screw connection, each	4/-
— 307 E/6	— plug connection	— 3/10
— 307 E/7	— combined adaptor for either connection	— 5/-
— 307 E/8	— bayonet plug and swan bayonet lamp holder	— 5/-
— 307 E/9	with plug adaptor and swan bayonet lamp holder	— 4/-

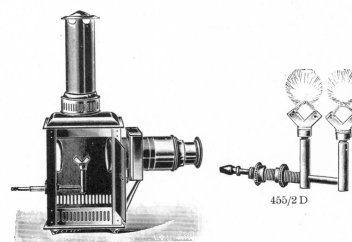

387 with 455/2

455/2 D

Further the Lantern No. 387 can be lighted by **Acetylene Gas** (see above illustration) **by using the Acetylene Burner** No. 455/2 or the **Acetylene Double Burner** No. 455/2 D, in conjunction with the **Gas Generator** No. 455/4 and 455/5 respectively for double burner.

No. 455/2	Acetylene Burner	each 4/6
— 455/2 D	Acetylene Double Burner	— 6/10
— 455/4	Acetylene Gas Generator to supply gas for 3 hours	— 8/6
— 455/5	Acetylene Gas Generator to supply gas for 6 hours	— 14/6

(For fuller description and illustrations of Acetylene Burner and Generator see page 141 of this list).

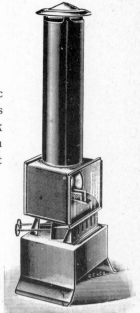

Best Quality
Magic Lanterns
Excellent definition.

Body of polished, blue steel plate, with automatic slide holder to keep either thick or thin slides properly in focus, fine **brass objective with rack and pinion movement**, with superior, new design 2 flame paraffin lamp, giving a brilliant light without smoking.

Each lantern has
- 12 handsome covered glass slides
- 1 chromotrope
- 1 transformation scene
- 1 moving landscape scene

in handsome, elegantly covered wood case with 2 separate removable case for the slides.

No. **388/1**	**2**	**3**	**4**	**5**	**6**
slides 2	$2^3/_8$	$2^3/_4$	$3^1/_8$	$3^1/_2$	4 " wide
lenses $1^3/_4$	2	$2^3/_{16}$	$2^3/_8$	$2^3/_4$	$3^1/_8$ " diam.
each **23/-**	**26/6**	**34/-**	**40/6**	**50/6**	**55/-**

These lanterns can also be supplied with an attachment **permitting the use of electric lighting.**

Universal Lamp
for electric illumination

for incandescent lamps to fit all the lanterns from $1^5/_8$ " width of slide, with adjustment for height, 2 yards of duplex wire and with the following type of adaptor, but without lamp.

No. **307 E/5** with Edison standard screw connection, each **4/-**

— **307 E/6** with plug connection, each **3/10**

— **307 E/7** with combined adaptor for either connection, each **5/-**

— **307 E/8** with bayonet plug and swan bayonet lamp holder . . . each **5/-**

307. E

No. **307 E/9** with plug adaptor and swan bayonet lamp holder . . . . . each **4/-**

Further with lantern 388 **acetylene gas** can be used, (see illustration 388 A) by employing the **acetylene lamp** No. 388 A in conjunction with the **acetylene generators** No. 455/4 or 455/5.

No. **388 A** acetylene lamp with **burner** for lanterns 388/1—6, each **8/-**

— **455/4** acetylene generator for 3 hour's light, each **8/6**

— **455/5** acetylene generator for 6 hour's light, each **14/6**

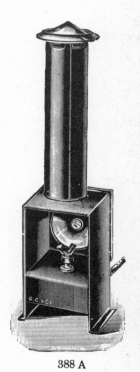

388 A

(For further description and illustrations see page 141 of this list.)

Trade Mark.

Handsome Magic Lantern

red or black japanned, in covered wood case, with fine objective fitted with 3 lenses, paraffin lamp with glass chimney and 12 slides.

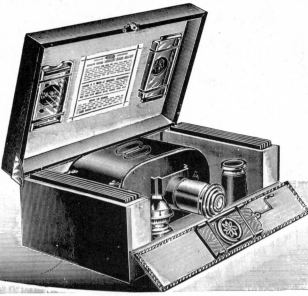

290—295

300 B—305 B

No. 290	slides 1¾" wide, objective	1⁵⁄₈" diam.	. . . . each	7/-
— 291	— 2" —	— 1¾" —	. . . . —	9/-
— 292	— 2³⁄₈" —	— 2" —	. . . . —	11/-
— 293	— 2¾" —	— 2³⁄₁₆" —	. . . . —	12/8
— 294	— 3¹⁄₈" —	— 2½" —	. . . . —	16/-
— 295	— 3½" —	— 2¾" —	. . . . —	20/-

The same lanternes, but in **very best wood case partitioned for slides,** with **1 chromotrope, 1 moving landscape slide,** and **1 transformation scene.**

No.	300 B	301 B	302 B	303 B	304 B	305 B
slides	1¾	2	2³⁄₈	2¾	3¹⁄₈	3½" wide
each	8/6	11/4	13/6	14/6	19/-	24/-

Universal-Lamp

for Electric-Illumination

307 E

For connecting to town current, for Incandescent lamps (carbon or metallic or Nernst), to fit **all the lanterns** from 1⁵⁄₈" width of slide, with adjustment for height, 2 yards of duplex wire, and with the following type of adaptor but without lamp.

No. 307 E/5	with Edison standard screw connection each	4/-
— 307 E/6	plug connection . . . . —	3/10
— 307 E/7	combined adaptor for either connection —	5/-
— 307 E/8	bayonet plug and swan bayonet lamp holder —	5/-
— 307 E/9	plug adaptor — — — — — — —	4/-

478/0

High class Projection-Lantern

very strong quality.

Body of russian iron, **achromatic objective with rack and pinion movement,** double condenser 4" diam. Will take all slides up to 4¼" wide. These lanterns are especially adapted for photographic lantern slides. All kinds of illumination described on pages 141 to 143 are suitable.

No. **478/0** without lamp or slides . . . . each 54/-

— **479/0** body and fitting as described and illustrated under No. **319** (page 138), but without cinematograph attachment, strong quality, with removable slide case . . . . . . each 84/-

— **453** **Slide holder** for glass slides 3¼"×4" and 3¼"×3¼" or 3⁵⁄₁₆" x 3⁵⁄₁₆" . . . . each 2/10

— **452** **Covering curtain** of opaque cloth for covering rear of lantern when using large projection lamp (also for cinematographs 318, 319, 322) 27¹⁄₂"×19³⁄₄", with 2 rings . . . each 1/6

For suitable slides for above projection lantern see pages 151 to 153.
For suitable lamps for above projection lantern see pages 141 to 143.

Trade Mark.

CINEMATOGRAPHS

HIGH CLASS PROJECTION CINEMATOGRAPHS

FOR ALL KINDS OF ILLUMINATION.

Artistically
executed

SETS OF FILMS

Artistically
executed

LANTERN SLIDES

Several patents.

CINEMATOGRAPHS.

Several patents.

With superior mechanism and of **unsurpassed definition and effect** when used as cinematograph or ordinary magic lantern. Our cinematographs can be rightly classed „**Precision Apparatus**" since they are built up with reasonable and superior arrangements. Our mechanism, striking in its simplicity, causes a precise presentation of the pictures with practically no noise and moreover possesses the advantage of being able to exhibit the pictures as easily in the reverse order. Regarding the **optical** part and the **illumination** we have done the **best possible** according to the size lantern. From size 321/4 upwards the paraffin lamp can be superseded by **Acetylene Gas**, or **Incandescent Gas** illumination; or even **Electrical** and **Nernst lamp illumination** can be fitted. The films supplied are **artistically executed** and are in fact taken from original photographs (all copyright) and are varied to suit all tastes.

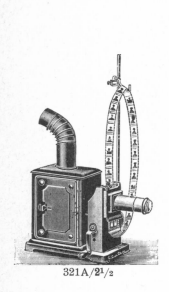

321A/2¹/₂

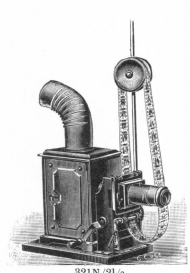

321N/2¹/₂

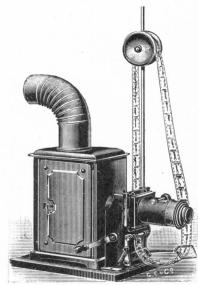

321/4

Cinematographs.

Body of fine blue plate mounted on metal base, objective with good lenses, film carrier, guide rod with film roller adjustable for height, automatic film presser, excellent paraffin lamp with glass chimney, artistically executed films with Edison perforation, can be used as an ordinary magic lantern without alteration. Full instructions are sent with each lantern. Each packed in a smart box.

No. **321 A/2¹/₂ Cinematograph** simple design, with 2 black films and 3 coloured lantern slides, 1" wide each **4/-**
— **321 N/2¹/₂** do. with patent shutter and 3 black films — 3 — — — 1" — — **4/10**
— **321 N/3** the same with 6 black films and 12 coloured slides 1³/₁₆" wide . . . . — **6/4**
— **321 N/3¹/₂** — — — 8 — — — 12 — 1³/₈" — . . . . . . — **8/4**

The same lanterns but with high class coloured films.

No. **321 M/2¹/₂** with **3 coloured** films and 6 lantern slides 1" wide. . . . . . each **6/-**
— **321 /2¹/₂** — 6 — — — 6 — 1" — . . . . . . — **6/10**
— **321 /3** — 6 — — — 12 — 1³/₁₆" — in covered boxes — **8/-**
— **321 /3¹/₂** — 8 — — — 12 — 1³/₈" — — — **10/-**

Cinematographs with fine **brass objectives** with **rack and pinion movement**, in handsome cardboard boxes with **partition for slides**.

No. **321/4** with **6 coloured** films and 12 lanterns slides 1⁵/₈" wide each **11/8**
— **321/4¹/₂** — 8 — — — 12 — 1³/₄" — — **14/6**

Acetylene, incandescent gas, or electric illumination for above see pages 141 and 142 of this list.

 **For extra films** see page 144 of this list.

Trade ⬡ Mark.

Cinematographs

Body of fine blue plate, on a highly polished mahogany base, with handsome brass objective fitted with rack and pinion focussing motion, film carrier, shutter D. R. G. M., guide rods, with film guide roller adjustable for any height, automatic film presser; excellent paraffin lamp with circular wick, fitted with glass chimney, artistically coloured films with Edison perforation; with attachment enabling the cinematograph lantern to be changed into an ordinary magic lantern without further trouble, full instructions are supplied with each lantern.

—— **In elegant, handsomely covered cases with partition for the slides.** ——

No. **321/5** with **8 long coloured films and 12 slides of 2" wide** each 20/-

— **321/6** with **8 long coloured films and 12 slides of 2³/₈" wide** each 23/-

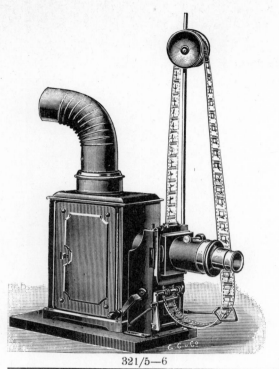

321/5—6

The apparatus produced till now, we also supply in a **large strong**, and most **handsome case** with partitions for parts, and with
=== **5 mechanical slides** for the **magic lantern**, ===
namely 1 transformation scene, 1 landscape scene, 1 rotating slide and 1 chromotrope.

	No. of coloured films	No. of plain slides	No. of moving slides	width of pictures	Price
No. 321 B/3	6	12	5	1³/₁₆"	each 10/-
— 321 B/3¹/₂	8	12	5	1³/₈"	— 12/4
— 321 B/4	6	12	5	1⁵/₈"	— 14/4
— 321 B/4¹/₂	8	12	5	1³/₄"	— 17/4
— 321 B/5	8	12	5	2"	— 23/6
— 321 B/6	8	12	5	2³/₈"	— 27/-

321 B

Cinematograph Attachments
for fitting to any of the stock magic lanterns taking suitable width of slide.

For normal films with Edison perforation, with attachment so as to be used without alteration, for showing ordinary slides. Fitted with film carrier, shutter (patented) guide rods with roller adjustable for height, automatic film presser.

No. 321/3 S	for 1³/₁₆" width of slide	each 3/8
— 321/3¹/₂ S	— 1³/₈" — —	— 4/4
— 321/4 S	— 1⁵/₈" — — objective with rack and pinion focussing	— 4/10
— 321/4¹/₂ S	— 1³/₄" — —	— 5/6
— 321/5 S	— 2" — —	— 6/8
— 321/6 S	— 2³/₈" — —	— 7/4

321 S

321 KS

Lengthening Rods
for cinematographs and cinematograph attachments when using very long films.

No. 321 ST/1	Lengthening rod only, 14½" long	each -/2
— 321 KS/1	— — — with clamp	— -/3
— 321 ST/2	— — — 20" long, for No. 325/5 and 6, page 136	— -/4
— 321 KS/2	— — — with clamp — — —	— -/6

Trade ⚙ Mark.

New Cinematographs
very strong quality

with **achromatic brass objective** with **rack focussing**, special presser to avoid dancing and glittering of the films. Very strong lantern body of fine blue plate with **brass fittings, strong guide rod** fitted with lengthening rod and film roller adjustable for any height, with paraffin lamp round wick, the whole mounted on a highly polished wood base.

Cased in very strong and handsome box.

No. **325/5** with attachment so that it can be used without further alteration as an **ordinary lantern,** with 8 long endless films, artistically coloured, 3 yards **genuine photo-films**, 12 slides, 3 mechanical slides in frames, 2″ wide, with full instructions . . . . each **34/-**

No. **325/6** the same but **larger**, with 8 long artistically coloured films, 6 yards **genuine photo-films,** 12 slides 2³/₈″ wide and 3 mechanical slides in frames, 2³/₈″ wide, with full instructions . . . . each **40/-**

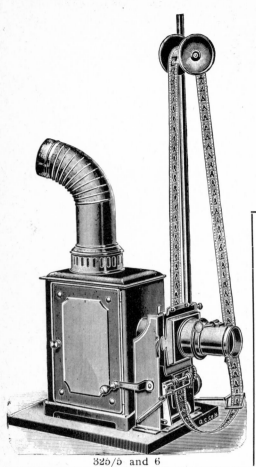
325/5 and 6

Cinematographs supplied with more powerful light.

For cinematographs **321/5** and **6** and **325/5** and **6** we supply an excellent and economical

Incandescent gas lamp

of 75—80 candle power namely

No. **321 G** complete, mantel, strong cast stand, gas pipe, burner and glass chimney each **3/8**

— **321 GS** replacement mantels . . . . — -/10
— **321 GC** — glass chimneys . . . . — -/6

Attachment for electric lighting.

For above lanterns we also supply an attachment, by which **electric lighting** can be used (see illustration 307 E) for connecting to town current. Incandescent lamp (carbon or metallic or Nernst) to fit all the lanterns from 1⁵/₈″ width of slide, with adjustment for height, 2 yards of duplex wire and with the following type of adaptor, but without lamp.

No. **307 E/5** with Edison standard screw connection . . each **4/-**
— **307 E/6** with plug connection each **3/10**
— **307 E/7** with combined adaptor for either connection each **5/-**
— **307 E/8** with bayonet plug and swan bayonet lamp holder each **5/-**
— **307 E/9** with plug adaptor and swan bayonet lamp holder each **4/-**

321/6 with 321 G

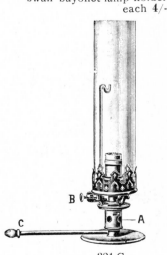
321 G

321/6 with 307 E

For extra sets of films see page 144 of this list.

Trade  Mark.

High class
Projection Cinematographs

for either photographic or endless coloured films.

322/6

Body of strong blue plate on highly polished mahogany base fitted with india rubber feet, with fine **achromatic objective, rack focussing,** with attachment allowing positives up to 2³/₈" wide to be projected. With film carrier, special film presser to stop the film dancing and dazzling. 2 large film spools to take photo films to 100 feet in length also a small roller for endless films with guide rod. Everything packed in a handsome wood case **without** films or glass slides; with full instructions.

Without lamp

No. 322/6 OB . . . . each 53/-

With paraffin duplex lamp

No. 322/6   with steady burning, and non smoking duplex lamp . . . . each 58/-

With incandescent gas lamp

No. 322/6 G with incandescent gas lamp ready for fixing to gas supply, gives an excellent and very powerful light of 75—80 candle power, using very little gas, the lamp is similar to illustration 321 G (page 136) but with stronger base and of different height . . each 57/-

With acetylene gas lamp

No. 322/6 A/1	with single burner, without generator, gives a light of about 125 candle power	each 57/6
— 322/6 A/2	— double — — — — — — 250 —	— 60/-
— 322/6 A/4	— quadruple — — — — — — 500 —	— 64/-

suitable Generators :
No. **455/4** lasting 3 hours with single burner . . . .
— 1½ — — double — . . . . } each **8/6**
— ¾ — —quadruple— . . . .

No. **455/5** lasting 6 hours with single burner . . . .
— 3 — — double — . . . . . . } each **14/6**
— 1½ — —quadruple— . . . . . .
For illustration and fuller description see page 141.

☞ When ordering these Cinematographs it is important to state the kind of current available, whether continuous or alternating, and if the Voltage is 110 or 220, ☜

With electric lamp (Nernst hanging lamp)

No. 322/6 HN* with 100 candle power Nernst hanging lamp with 2 yards of insulated duplex wire and combination adaptor ready for fixing to current. . . . . each 75/-

With Nernst automatic lighting projection lamp

No. 322/6 P/13	with Nernst lamp ot 400 cp. 220 volts 200 cp. 110 volts	each 93/-
— 322/6 P/10	— — — — 1400 — 220 — 700 — 110	— 133/-

With electric arc lamps

No. 322/66 BG*	with 800 cp. continuous current lamp, 6 Amps.	each 165/-
— 322/610 BG*	— 1300 — — — 10 —	— 180/-
— 322/66 BW*	— 800 — alternating — 6 —	— 185/-
— 322/610 BW*	— 1300 — — — 10 —	— 200/-

with regulating resistance, switches, cable, adaptor ready for immediate use.

These cinematographs can also be delivered with **Swan bayonet type** of connection when specially ordered.

The above Cinematographs are also supplied with **8 finely executed coloured films** and **12 handsome slides of 2³/₈" width as follows**

	No. 322/6	322/6 G	322/6 A/2	322/6 HN
and are then called	No. 322/16	322/16 G	322/16 A/2	322/16 HN
	each 71/-	70/6	72/6	88/6

☞ **For photographic films see page 144.** ☜

Trade  Mark.

Cinematograph
arranged for working and lighting by electricity.

With automatic carrier for photographic films, fine **achromatic objective** with **rack and pinion focussing**, ready for connecting to nearest current supply, with lamp resistance, 3 yards of duplex insulated wire with hanging lamp holder 307 E, 2 yards cable (both with Edison adaptors or adaptors for bayonet type), switches, packed in very strong travelling case.

No. **326 NE** with 100 c. p. **Nernst hanging lamp** with 2 yards of duplex cable and combined adaptor, ready for immediate connection . . . . each **102/-**
— **326 P/13** with 400 c. p. **Nernst projection lamp** with automatic lighting . . . . each **120/-**
— **326 P/10** with 1400 c. p. **Nernst projection lamp** with automatic lighting . . . . each **160/-**
— **326 B G/6** with **arc lamp** of 800 c. p. (6 amps) for continuous current . . . . each **192/-**
— **326 B G/10** with **arc lamp** of 1300 c. p. (10 amps) for continuous current . . . . each **208/-**
— **326 B W/6** with **arc lamp** of 800 c. p. (6 amps) for alternating current . . . . each **212/-**
— **326 B W/10** with **arc lamp** of 1300 c. p. (10 amps) for alternating current . . . . each **228/-**

> It must always be stated when ordering for what current (continuous or alternating) and for what voltage the lanterns are required. Further it must always be stated when ordering which adaptors are required, if adaptors for Edison screw or adaptors for bayonet type.

The above apparatus can be used as an

Advertising Cinematograph

by means of a specially constructed camera shown in the accompaning illustration.

The price is increased as under

No. **327 R** . . . . each **18/-**

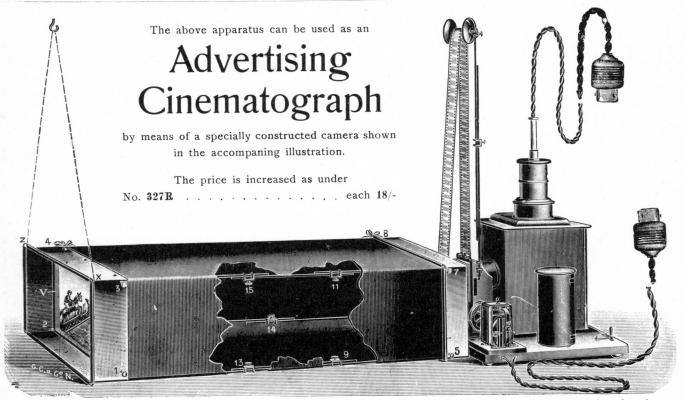

The camera is partly of white plate and partly of opaque cloth and is arranged for a transparent screen to be placed one end. It is easily put together and easily taken apart. The screen is of paper stretched in a frame but a ground glass slide can be used and fitted where the lantern is to be used. When fully extended the apparatus (**Cinematograph and camera**) occupies a length of about 5 feet, but if necessary the distance can be reduced to 3 feet. By this arrangement cinematograph pictures can be exhibited in a lighted place at any time. When fully extended the pictures measure 14" × 10" when least extended only 6" × 4½".

☞ For photographic films for above see page 144. ☜

Trade Mark.

High class Cinematographs

315

to take all Edison gauge perforations also can be used at the same time as a **Projecting lantern** for slides of $2^3/4$" wide. The body is of the finest strong blue plate, with double condenser, $2^3/8$" diam. can be fitted with any kind of lamp. The **driving mechanism** is fitted with a **maltese cross** and works **continuously** with **certainty and accuracy**, and causes by reason of its strong and precise mechanism, scarcely any noise. The objective is provided with rack and pinion focussing, and if the cinematograph holder is turned a 1/4 of a turn the lantern is ready for use for simple projection. The whole is mounted on a handsome base and packed in a strong wood case.

No. **315/0** without lamp . . . . each **96/-**
— **315 P** with duplex paraffin lamp . . . . . . — **100/-**
— **315 G** with 80 c. p. incandescent gas lamp . . . — **100/-**
— **315 AD** with 250 c. p. double burner acetylene lamp — **104/-**
— **315 HN***with 100 c. p. Nernst lamp and attachment No. 307 E each **116/-**
— **315 L*** with 400 or 200 c. p. Nernst projection lamp No. 313 L each **136/-**

|| ☞ Extra for above apparatus if supplied with 1 dozen slides and about **65 yards of genuine photographic film** . . . . each viz. **20/-** ||

	315/0	315 P	315 G	315 AD	315 HN*	315 L
No. is then	**315/0/7**	**315 P/7**	**315 G/7**	**315 AD/7**	**315 HN/7***	**315 L/7** the proper
	116/-	**120/-**	**120/-**	**124/-**	**136/-**	**156/-**

319

> ***** When ordering it must always be stated for which current (continuous or alternating) the lanterns are required, also for what voltage. Further it must always be stated when ordering which adaptors are required if adaptors for Edison screw or adaptors for bayonet type.

Cinematographs

with **Projection apparatus** of superior quality for all Edison gauge films and for slides up to $4^1/4$" wide, with **2 first class achromatic objectives**, 1 for the cinematograph and 1 for the projection lantern, double condenser 4" diam., driving mechanism as above, but with **automatic winding and unwinding gear**, the very best and strongest quality, without lamp.

No. **319/0** . . . . each **200/-**
— **318/0** the same, but driving mechanism No. 315 with 2 achromatic objectives, double condenser, 4" diam, in strong but simple design each **120/-**

Suitable lamps pages 141, 142 and 143.

For projection slides see page 145—155. For photographic films see page 144.

Trade Mark.

Cinematograph Attachment

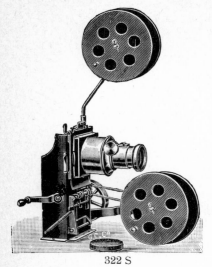

322 S

For attaching to any stock magic lantern of suitable width of slide

for standard films with Edison gauge perforations, can be fitted to lanterns without further alteration

fine achromatic brass objective with rack and pinion,

specially for photographic films with film carrier, with automatic presser to stop dancing and shimmering of the pictures, 2 large film spools, for receiving photographic films and 1 small roller for use with coloured endless films with guide rod.

No. **322 S** for 2³/₈" width of slide . . . . each **42/-**

	No. **322 T/1 Empty spools**	
to take photographic films up to 100 feet, for 322/6	each	**1/2**
	No. **322 T/2 Empty spools**	
to take photographic films up to 200 feet, for 322/6	—	**1/6**
	No. **322 T/3 Empty spools**	
322 T/1, 2, 3 to take photographic films up to 650 feet, for 315, 318 and 319	—	**2/-**

New ≡ Advertising Magic Lantern

Advertising lantern for shop windows, with very strong spring motor which will run for half an hour.

With the above magic lantern a long felt need has been met, since it is not only adapted for a **paraffin lamp** but also for **incandescent gas or electric lighting**. To install this lantern only about a length of 4 feet is required. The pictures reach a **diam. of** 18" and are sharply focussed by means of the rack and pinion fitted to the objective. The extra strong spring motor runs about **half an hour continuously**. The screen is of paper stretched in a frame, but a ground glass screen can be fitted when the apparatus is in position. The funnel can be taken to pieces, it is made of opaque cloth so that the lantern can be used in **lighted places**. The important innovation we have effected consists in the rotating metal disc fitted with 10 pictures each of which **remain before the objective** about **6—8 seconds** so that the public can conveniently examine the pictures.

With this lantern we supply 48 slides and can supply further sets to order, picture discs inscribed with **suitable advertisements** we supply also.

No. **466/5**	with paraffin lamp	each	**78/-**
— **466/5 G**	— incandescent gas lamp	—	**80/-**
— **466/5 A/1**	— single burner acetylene gas lamp	—	**80/-**
— **466/5 A/2**	— double —	—	**82/4**
— **466/5 A/4**	— quadruple burner acetylene gas lamp	—	**86/4**
	For suitable generator see page 141.		
— **466/5 HN***	— 100 c. p. Nernst hanging lamp		**98/-**
— **466/5 P/13***	— 400 — — projection lamp	—	**116/-**
— **466/5 P/10***	— 1400 — —	—	**156/-**
— **466 S**	empty picture discs	—	**3/4**

---

* When ordering it must always be stated for which current (continuous or alternating) and for what voltage the lanterns are intended. Further it must always be stated when ordering which adaptors are required, if adaptors for Edison screw or adaptors for bayonet type.

Cinematograph with more powerful lighting

321/6 with double burner 455/2 D

Besides the gas light and electric light we provide our apparatus with **Acetylene Lighting.**

Although we supply with all our lanterns suitable lamps according to their sizes and price, we provide a more powerful light by which means the lantern can be removed much farther from the screen and a very much larger picture produced.

For this purpose we have made a slot in all our lanterns in the back plate from size 321/4 in which a specially made acetylene single burner No. 455/2 can be fitted, in conjunction with a specially made safety and odourless gas generator can be used supplying gas for about 3 hours or 455/5 for 6 hours without refilling. With the larger lanterns 321/5 and 6, 325/5 and 6 the double burner No. 455/2 D is recommended together with the larger generator No. 455/5. Full instructions are supplied with these lamps, which give a perfectly reliable lighting. When employing simple or double acetylene burners a cinematograph picture can be obtained with 321/6 or 325/6 of 6 feet by 5 feet or a lantern picture of about 13 feet diameter, with a distance from the screen of about 16 feet; when the lantern is 32 feet distant the cinematograph picture measures 10 feet by 8 feet and the lantern picture 16 to 20 feet in diameter.

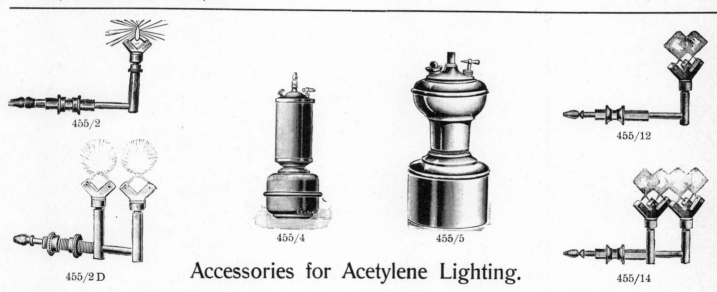

455/2

455/2 D

455/4

455/5

455/12

455/14

Accessories for Acetylene Lighting.

No.			
455/2	**Acetylene Gas Burner** with 2 fixing screws to fix and adjust for height, to suit all lanterns from size 321/4	each	**4/6**
— **455/2 D**	**Acetylene Double Gas Burner** to suit all lanterns from 321/4	—	**6/10**
— **455/12**	**Acetylene Gas Burner with double flame,** otherwise as 455/2	—	**6/4**
— **455/14**	**Acetylene Gas Burner with 2 double flames,** otherwise as 455/2 D	—	**10/10**
— **455/4**	**Acetylene Gas Generator** very strong quality in brass with carbide and water holder, with regulating screw, very reliable working design, giving gas supply for about **3 hours** .	—	**8/6**
— **455/5**	**Acetylene Gas Generator,** larger, making sufficient gas for about **6 hours**	—	**14/6**
— **455/3**	**Rubber tubing** for connecting generator to burner	yard	**2/-**
— **455/6**	**Separate Steatite burner jets**	each	**2/-**
— **455/7**	**Separate Steatite double flame burner jets**	—	**4/-**

Trade ⊕ Mark.

Nernst Projection Lamps.

By reason of their white intense light and the perfect steady illumination the Nernst lamps are practically unequalled for projection purposes. The working of the Nernst is the simplest conceivable, so that all that is required is to connect the adaptor to the nearest wall plug or lamp holder (Edison or bayonet type). Any strong current may be used whether it be continuous or alternating current. We supply the lamps all fixed and ready so that the lantern can be set up without further arranging. The enlargement obtained by using the projection lamp is most excellent in both for cinematograph and ordinary lantern purposes, on account of the intensely brilliant light.

The lamps consist of, beside the stand, 2 important parts, the burner and the normal resistance. The latter serves to protect the light body from fluctuations in voltage and to keep the light constant. The resistances absorb 20 volts so that the voltage of the burner is 20 volts lower than the working voltage, that is, the burner voltage plus the resistance voltage most be the voltage used.

When ordering burners it must be stated whether the current obtainable is alternating or continuous, the voltage must also be given.

In order to use the projection lamp with our cinematographs 321/5 and 6, 325/5 and 6, a hanging attachment, adjustable for height is necessary.

Electric Hanging Attachments for Projection Lamps

to **use for projection lamps, intended for lanterns 321/5 and 6, 325/5 and 6,** adjustable for height, with Edison or bayonet connections, without lamp, with 2 yards of insulated cables and combination adaptor.

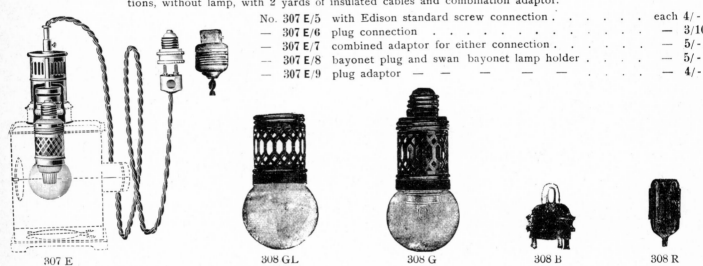

No. 307 E/5   with Edison standard screw connection . . . . . . each 4/-
— 307 E/6   plug connection . . . . — 3/10
— 307 E/7   combined adaptor for either connection . . . . . — 5/-
— 307 E/8   bayonet plug and swan bayonet lamp holder . . . . — 5/-
— 307 E/9   plug adaptor — — — — — — — . . . . — 4/-

307 E   308 GL   308 G   308 B   308 R

Nernst Projection Lamps to fit above attachment fitted with Edison standard holder.

These Nernst projection lamps give a light of 50 to 100 c. p. with 110 and 220 volts respectively and are supplied as follows. —
(If other voltage than 110 or 220 is required customers are requested to state the voltage when ordering).

	for continuous current		for alternating current		
110—160 Volts	**161—320 Volts**	**110—160 Volts**	**161—320 Volts**	**Hanging lamp**	
0,5 Amp. 50 c. p.	0,25 Amp. 50 c. p.	0,5 Amp. 50 c. p.	0,25 Amp. 50 c p.		
No. 308 G/110 Volts	No. 308 G/220	No. 308 W/110	No. 308 W/220	complete lamp.	each 11/-
— 308 BG/110	— 308 BG/220	— 308 BW/110	— 308 BW/220	burner	— 7/-
— 308 RG/15	— 308 RG/20	— 308 RW/15	— 308 RW/20	resistance	— -/10
— 308 GL	— 308 GL	— 308 GL	— 308 GL	globe.	— -/10
1,0 Amp. 100 c. p.	0,5 Amp. 100 c. p.	1,0 Amp. 100 c. p.	0,5 Amp. 100 c. p.		
No. 309 G/110	No. 309 G/220	No. 309 W/110	No. 309 W/220	complete lamp.	each 16/-
— 309 BG/110	— 309 BG/220	— 309 BW/110	— 309 BW/220	burner	— 9/-
— 309 RG/15	— 309 RG/20	— 309 RW/15	— 309 RW/20	resistance	— 1/-
— 309 GL	— 309 GL	— 309 GL	— 309 GL	globe	— 1/4

Nernst Projection Lamps for **standing** with screwed base, adaptor and 2 yards of duplex insulated wire, to suit projection lanterns No. 478/0 and 479/0 (page 132). (Quality, candle power as 308 and 309). (Separate burners etc. see under 308 and 309).

No. 306 **G**/110   or 220 volts continuous current }
— 306 **W**/110 — 220 — alternating — } each 19/-

Trade   Mark.

Nernst Projection Lamps

to suit our lanterns 322/6, 315, 318 and 319, 478/0 and 479/0.

The adjoining illustrated Nernst lamp can be fitted without trouble in the lanterns. They are especially suitable for projecting photographic films in a large room on account of their brilliant white light. The cinematograph pictures projected by the Nernst projection lamp are strikingly large, sharp and clear. The method of using them is the simplest conceivable, and while working, require not the least attention.

Nernst Projection Lamps

with self ignition for continuous or alternating current of 100 to 300 volts.

The light obtained with 1,3 Amps. at 110 Volts is about **200 candle power,** at 220 Volts **400 candle power.**

No. 313 L	Lamp complete*	each 40/-
— 313 B	Burner only*	— 12/-
— 313 R	Resistance only*	— 3/-

Nernst Projection Lamps

with self ignition, for continuous or alternating current of 65 to 300 volts.

The light obtained with 4 Amps. at 110 volts is about **700 candle power,** at 220 Volts **1400 candle power.**

No. 310 L	Lamp complete*	each 80/-
— 310 B	Burner only*	— 30/-
— 310 R	Resistance only*	— 3/-

Electric Arc Lamps

Self regulating, giving a brilliant steady light, requires no attention while working. Complete with resistance, switch, adaptor for Edison connections or bayonet type ready for connecting to nearest supply, 800 candle power with 6 Amps and 1300 candle power at 10 Amps.

No. 311/6 G/110	for **continuous current*** of 110 Volts, 6 Amp.	each	**112/-**
— 311/6 G/220	—	—	— *	— 220	— 6 —	— **132/-**
— 311/10 G/110	—	—	— *	— 110	— 10 —	— **128/-**
— 311/10 G/220	—	—	— *	— 220	— 10 —	— **148/-**
No. 311/6 W/110	for **alternating current*** of 110 Volts, 6 Amp.	each	**112/-**
— 311/6 W/220	—	—	— *	— 220	— 6 —	— **132/-**
— 311/10 W/110	—	—	— *	— 110	— 10 —	— **128/-**
— 311/10 W/220	—	—	— *	— 220	— 10 —	— **148/-**

Carbons of best selected brands
No. 311 K $1/2''$ or $3/8''$ diam., $2 3/4''$ long . . . . pair -/2

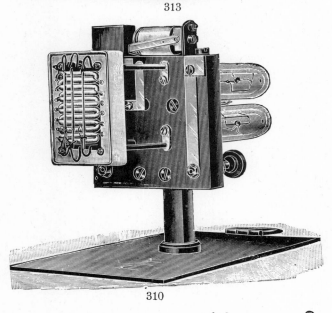

313

310

311

> * When ordering lamps or parts 313, 310 and 311 the current, whether continuous or alternating, must be stated, also the voltage whether 110 or 220.
>
> Further it must always be stated when ordering, which adaptors are required, if adaptors for Edison screw or adaptors for bayonet type.

Trade  Mark.

10 E

Extra-Sets of coloured Films of excellent cinematographic effect

with Edison-standard-perforations **fitting all cinematographs,** artistically coloured and from our own copyright photographs.

Number / Price	Statement of subjects contained in each set, the number of pictures in each film and the length of each film				total / total length
No. 329/20 A	Exercise, Tobogganing, Leap frog				
3 films	30	30	29		89
set 1/-	22½"	22½"	22"		5 feet 7"
No. 329/21 A	Skipping, Jumping horse, Motoring				
3 films	35	35	35		105
set 1/4	26²/₃"	26²/₃"	26²/₃"		6 feet 8"
No. 329/21 B	Acrobats, Tigh-rope performers, Horizontal bars				
3 films	35	35	35		105
set 1/4	26²/₃"	26²/₃"	26²/₃"		6 feet 8"
No. 329/21 C	Recreation ground, Stag, Head over heels				
3 films	35	35	35		105
set 1/4	26²/₃"	26²/₃"	26²/₃"		6 feet 8"
No. 329/21 D	Tasting sweets, Handkerchief, Pursuit				
3 films	35	35	35		105
set 1/4	26²/₃"	26²/₃"	26²/₃"		6 feet 8"
No. 329/22 A	Looping the loop, The performing poodle, Skittles				
3 films	42	42	46		130
set 1/8	32"	32"	34"		8 feet 2"
No. 329/23 A	Gymnastic, Ducks in pond, Children on stairs				
3 films	46	47	48		141
set 1/10	34"	35"	36"		8 feet 9"
No. 329/24 A	Caravan, Practise on horizontal bars, Coopers				
3 films	51	52	53		156
set 2/-	38"	39"	40"		9 feet 9"
No. 329/25 A	An uncomfortable seat, Leap frog, Riding School				
3 films	54	55	55		164
set 2/-	41"	42"	42"		10 feet 5"
No. 329/26 A	Ring a ring of roses, The mischevious shoeblack, A sweet tooth				
3 films	58	62	62		182
set 2/4	44"	47"	47"		11 feet 6"
No. 329/27 A	Climbing ladder, Acrobat, Sledge party				
3 films	66	70	70		206
set 2/6	50"	53"	53"		13 feet
No. 329/28 A	the clumsy servant, The cow crossing the road, Stags				
3 films	70	70	70		210
set 2/8	53"	53"	53"		13 feet 3"
No. 329/29 A	Fond of snuff, Canoe and swimming party, American sausage machine				
3 films	73	76	78		227
set 2/10	56"	58"	59"		14 feet 5"
No. 329/30 A	Pyramid, Acrobats, Elephants				
3 films	79	80	90		249
set 3/-	60"	61"	68"		15 feet 9"
No. 329/31 A	Carriage party, Gymnastics, Children with mailcart				
3 films	94	105	105		304
set 3/8	71"	80"	80"		19 feet 3"
No. 329/15 C	Disappearing lady, Garden hose				
2 films	155	132			287
set 3/6	118"	100"			18 feet 2"

☞ The films 329/20 A to 329/15 C adjoining are not supplied in any of our lantern sets but the following coloured films are supplied, in part, in our sets.

Number / Price	Statement of subjects contained in each set, the number of pictures in each film and the length of each film				total / total length
No. 329/11 CA	Builder,	Tosser,	Smithy,	See-saw	
4 films	24	24	27	28	103
set 1/8	18"	18"	20½"	21½"	6½ feet
No. 329/11 CB	A good drop,	Wrestler,	Serpentine,	Magician	
4 films	46	54	57	61	218
set 3/6	35"	40½"	43"	46"	13½ feet

Extra sets of Black (Lithographic) Films.

No. 329/12 SA	Gymnastics,	Acrobats,		Skipping	
3 films	30	35		35	100
set 1/-	22½"	26½"		26½"	6¼ feet
No. 329/12 SB	Horseman,	Mounting a ladder,		Sweetness	
3 films	35	36		38	109
set 1/-	26½"	27"		29"	6¾ feet

☞ The above black films are not supplied in our lantern sets but the following are now partly supplied in our lantern sets.

No. 329/11 SA	A good drop,	Builder,	Tosser,	Wrestler	
4 films	23	24	24	25	96
set 1/-	17½"	18"	18"	19"	6 feet
No. 329/11 SB	Smithy, See-saw, Serpentine, Magician				
4 films	27	28	29	30	114
set 1/4	20½"	21½"	22"	22½"	7¹/₅ feet

☞ **Genuine Photographic films** with Edison perforations, specially for our lanterns No. 322, 315, 318, 319 in lengths of 2, 4, 5, 8, 10, 20, 30 up to some 100 yards are stocked in large quantities and varied selections. A list is sent on request of the subjects and length of films. Per yard varies from -/10 to 1/6 and above.

No. 329/50 **Light printed films** from original negatives about 44" long, with Edison perforation, packed in sets of 3 films (8 sets A, B, C, D, E, F, G, H), are in stock and can be had . . . per set of 3 films **2/10**

===== **Films cannot be returned nor exchanged.** =====

Trade Mark.

List of Extra Lantern Slides for magic lanterns and cinematographs.

☞ When ordering extra lantern slides for any lantern or cinematograph the **width** of slide used in the lantern must always be stated. The slides are offered only in sets and cannot be supplied singly, not even when a slide has been broken and it is desired to replace same.

Long lantern slides (To draw through lantern)

These superbly executed slides are remarkable on account of their **magnificent colouring**. Sets II, III, IV, V, VI, VII, VIII etc., are all different and consist of every day scenes, caricatures, landscapes, animal pictures, portraits, children, sea pieces etc., partly with black, and partly with blue back ground. The **drawings** of the slides are **perfectly new** and satisfy all fancies.

Set 1 is included in the lantern sets.

Stocked in the most varied, new and finest sets

No. 400 Without cover glass

No. 400/2½	1″	wide,	3½″	long.	.	gross	7/-
— 400/3	1³/₁₆″	—	4³/₈″	—	.	—	7/10
— 400/3½	1³/₈″	—	5¼″	—	.	—	12/-
— 400/4	1⁵/₈″	—	6″	—	.	—	16/-
— 400/4½	1³/₄″	—	6³/₄″	—	.	—	22/-
— 400/5	2″	—	7¹/₈″	—	.	—	27/6
— 400/6	2³/₈″	—	8″	—	.	—	38/-
— 400/7	2³/₄″	—	8³/₄″	—	.	—	48/-
— 400/8	3¹/₈″	—	9½″	—	.	—	66/-
— 400/9	3½″	—	11″	—	.	—	84/-
— 400/10	4″	—	12″	—	.	—	120/-
— 400/11	4¼″	—	12″	—	.	—	132/-

No. 402 With cover glass

No. 402/4	1⁵/₈″	wide,	6″	long	.	dozen	2/-
— 402/4½	1³/₄″	—	6³/₄″	—	.	—	3/-
— 402/5	2″	—	7¹/₈″	—	.	—	3/8
— 402/6	2³/₈″	—	8″	—	.	—	4/6
— 402/7	2³/₄″	—	8³/₄″	—	.	—	5/8
— 402/8	3¹/₈″	—	9½″	—	.	—	7/-
— 402/9	3½″	—	11″	—	.	—	9/8
— 402/10	4″	—	12″	—	.	—	13/8
— 402/11	4¼″	—	12″	—	.	—	15/4

Magic lantern films

specially intended for countries where the weight tariff is high.

In exactly the same dimensions as sets of slides in set 400 but instead of being on glass the pictures are finely executed on transparent and unbreakable films.

For showing these slides we supply so-called **draw through glasses,** so as to draw these through the slide frames of the lantern. In each doz. slides is supplied a corresponding draw glass.

No. 401/3	3½	4	4½	5	6	7	8	9	10	
-/10	1/-	1/4	1/8	2/4	3/4	4/-	5/8	10/-	11/-	per doz. films.

Trade Mark.

Fairy tales and story slides with text.

Assortments of 12 long slides (4 on each) consisting of:

Dwarf nose, caliph stork, the little noise, the phantom ship.

$1^3/_{16}$	$1^3/_8$	$1^5/_8$	$1^3/_4$	2	$2^3/_8$	$2^3/_4$	$3^1/_8$	$3^1/_2$" wide
$4^3/_8$	$5^1/_4$	6	$6^3/_4$	$7^1/_8$	8	$8^3/_4$	$9^1/_2$	11" long

No. **449 A** without cover glass		No. **449B** with cover glass	
No. **449A/3** $1^3/_{16}$" wide . . . . . dozen **-/10**		No. **449B/4** $1^5/_8$" wide . . . . . dozen **2/4**	
— **449A/3$^1/_2$** $1^3/_8$" — . . . . . . — **1/4**		— **449B/4$^1/_2$** $1^3/_4$" — . . . . . . — **3/4**	
— **449A/4** $1^5/_8$" — . . . . . . — **1/8**		— **449B/5** 2" — . . . . . . — **3/8**	
— **449A/4$^1/_2$** $1^3/_4$" — . . . . . — **2/-**		— **449B/6** $2^3/_8$" — . . . . . . — **5/-**	
— **449A/5** 2" — . . . . . . — **2/10**		— **449B/7** $2^3/_4$" — . . . . . . — **6/-**	
— **449A/6** $2^3/_8$" — . . . . . . — **3/8**		— **449B/8** $3^1/_8$" — . . . . . . — **7/8**	
— **449A/7** $2^3/_4$" — . . . . . . — **4/6**		— **449B/9** $3^1/_2$" — . . . . . . — **10/-**	
— **449A/8** $3^1/_8$" — . . . . . . — **6/-**			
— **449A/9** $3^1/_2$" — . . . . . . — **8/-**			

Well executed story slides with text.

in the following sizes

$1^5/_8$	$1^3/_4$	2	$2^3/_8$" wide
6	$6^3/_4$	$7^1/_8$	8" long

the set consists of 12 long slides (4 pictures on each) namely:

Little Red Riding Hood, Cinderella, little Snow White, sleeping beauty, Robinson Crusoe, the magic table, Utopia, Jack and Jill, hop-o' my Thumb or Tom Thumb.

No. **429A** without cover glass		No. **429B** with cover glass	
No. **429A/4** $1^5/_8$" wide . . . . . dozen **1/8**		No. **429B/4** $1^5/_8$" wide . . . . . dozen **2/4**	
— **429A/4$^1/_2$** $1^3/_4$" — . . . . . . — **2/-**		— **429B/4$^1/_2$** $1^3/_4$" — . . . . . . — **3/4**	
— **429A/5** 2" — . . . . . . — **2/10**		— **429B/5** 2" — . . . . . . — **3/8**	
— **429A/6** $2^3/_8$" — . . . . . . — **3/8**		— **429B/6** $2^3/_8$" — . . . . . . — **5/-**	

	$2^3/_4$	$3^1/_8$	$3^1/_2$	4" wide
	$8^3/_4$	$9^1/_2$	11	12" long

The following assortments can be had in the sizes below:

No. **429** I. assortment of 6 slides. Containing the following tales **Robinson Crusoe**, 2 slides, **little Red Riding Hood**, 1 slide, **sleeping beauty**, 1 slide, **little Snow-White**, 1 slide, Utopia, 1 slide.

— **430** II. assortment of 6 slides consisting of: **God over all, the 7 Swans, Tom Thumb, hares guard, Jack and Jill, the enchanted princess**, 1 on each slide.

No. **429A** and **430A** without cover glass		No. **429B** and **430B** with cover glass	
No. **429A** or **430A/7** $2^3/_4$" wide . . . set **2/6**		No. **429B** or **430B/7** $2^3/_4$" wide . . . . set **3/4**	
— **429A** — **430A/8** $3^1/_8$" — . . . . — **3/2**		— **429B** — **430B/8** $3^1/_8$" — . . . . — **4/-**	
— **429A** — **430A/9** $3^1/_2$" — . . . . — **4/4**		— **429B** — **430B/9** $3^1/_2$" — . . . . — **5/6**	
— **429A** — **430A/10** 4" — . . . . — **5/8**		— **429B** — **430B/10** 4" — . . . . — **6/8**	

The discovery of America

by Christopher Columbus

quite an artistic set and not at all to be compared to the cheap coloured slides; consisting of 16 pictures on 4 long slides, **with text**, in the following sizes:

$1^5/_8$	$1^3/_4$	2	$2^3/_8$	$2^3/_4$	$3^1/_8$	$3^1/_2$	4" wide
6	$6^3/_4$	$7^1/_8$	8	$8^3/_4$	$9^1/_2$	11	12" long

No. **447CA** without cover glass		No. **447CB** with cover glass	
No. **447CA/4** $1^5/_8$" wide . . . . . set **-/8**		No. **447CB/4** $1^5/_8$" wide . . . . . set **1/-**	
— **447CA/4$^1/_2$** $1^3/_4$" — . . . . . — **-/10**		— **447CB/4$^1/_2$** $1^3/_4$" — . . . . . — **1/4**	
— **447CA/5** 2" — . . . . . — **1/2**		— **447CB/5** 2" — . . . . . — **1/8**	
— **447CA/6** $2^3/_8$" — . . . . . — **1/6**		— **447CB/6** $2^3/_8$" — . . . . . — **1/10**	
— **447CA/7** $2^3/_4$" — . . . . . — **1/8**		— **447CB/7** $2^3/_4$" — . . . . . — **2/4**	
— **447CA/8** $3^1/_8$" — . . . . . — **3/8**		— **447CB/8** $3^1/_8$" — . . . . . — **4/4**	
— **447CA/9** $3^1/_2$" — . . . . . — **4/-**		— **447CB/9** $3^1/_2$" — . . . . . — **5/-**	
— **447CA/10** 4" — . . . . . — **4/6**		— **447CB/10** 4" — . . . . . — **5/6**	

For further information about slides see page 153 under 447CS.

Military slides.

These pictures represent the most important branches of the army of the following countries. Germany, Austria, Italy, France, Spain, England, Russia, Turkey. Greece, Japan, North America.

The 12 long slides are supplied **with text** and in the following sizes.

$1^5/_8$	$1^3/_4$	2	$2^3/_8$	$2^3/_4$	$3^1/_8$" wide
6	$6^3/_4$	$7^1/_8$	8	$8^3/_4$	$9^1/_2$" long

No. **451A without cover glass**		No. **451B with cover glass**	
No. **451A/4** $1^5/_8$" wide . . . . . dozen **1/8**		No. **451B/4** $1^5/_8$" wide . . . . . . dozen **2/4**
— **451A/4$^1/_2$** $1^3/_4$" — . . . . . — **2/-**		— **451B/4$^1/_2$** $1^3/_4$" — . . . . . . — **3/4**
— **451A/5** 2" — . . . . . — **2/10**		— **451B/5** 2" — . . . . . . — **3/8**
— **451A/6** $2^3/_8$" — . . . . . — **3/8**		— **451B/6** $2^3/_8$" — . . . . . . — **5/-**
— **451A/7** $2^3/_4$" — . . . . . — **4/6**		— **451B/7** $2^3/_4$" — . . . . . . — **6/-**
— **451A/8** $3^1/_8$" — . . . . . — **6/-**		— **451B/8** $3^1/_8$" — . . . . . . — **7/8**

Best quality Slides of Scrad Sacred Subjects.

The old Testament

No. **447 The old and the new Testament** in 32 pictures on 8 long slides. An artistically got up serie and must not be confussed with the cheap coloured slides extant.

The new Testament

$1^5/_8$	$1^3/_4$	2	$2^3/_8$	$2^3/_4$	$3^1/_8$	$3^1/_2$	4" wide
6	$6^3/_4$	$7^1/_8$	8	$8^3/_4$	$9^1/_2$	11	12" long

No. **447A without cover glass**		No. **447B with cover glass**	
No. **447A/4** $1^5/_8$" wide . . . . . set **1/6**		No. **447B/4** $1^5/_8$" wide . . . . . set **1/8**
— **447A/4$^1/_2$** $1^3/_4$" — . . . . . — **1/8**		— **447B/4$^1/_2$** $1^3/_4$" — . . . . . — **2/4**
— **447A/5** 2" — . . . . . — **2/4**		— **447B/5** 2" — . . . . . — **3/-**
— **447A/6** $2^3/_8$" — . . . . . — **2/10**		— **447B/6** $2^3/_8$" — . . . . . — **3/8**
— **447A/7** $2^3/_4$" — . . . . . — **3/6**		— **447B/7** $2^3/_4$" — . . . . . — **4/6**
— **447A/8** $3^1/_8$" — . . . . . — **7/8**		— **447B/8** $3^1/_8$" — . . . . . — **8/10**
— **447A/9** $3^1/_2$" — . . . . . — **8/-**		— **447B/9** $3^1/_2$" — . . . . . — **9/8**
— **447A/10** 4 " — . . . . . — **9/-**		— **447B/10** 4 " — . . . . . —**10/10**

Fuller picture lists see page 153 under No. 447 S.

Life and business in the United States of America.

Assortment consisting of 12 long slides (4 pictures each) **with text** and in the following sizes.

$1^5/_8$	$1^3/_4$	2	$2^3/_8$	$2^3/_4$	$3^1/_8$	$3^1/_2$	4"' wide
6	$6^3/_4$	$7^1/_8$	8	$8^3/_4$	$9^1/_2$	11	12" long

No. **438A without cover glass**		No. **438B with cover glass**	
No. **438A/4** $1^5/_8$" wide . . . . dozen **1/8**		No. **438B/4** $1^5/_8$" wide . . . . . dozen **2/4**
— **438A/4$^1/_2$** $1^3/_4$" — . . . . . — **2/-**		— **438B/4$^1/_2$** $1^3/_4$" — . . . . . — **3/4**
— **438A/5** 2" — . . . . . — **2/10**		— **438B/5** 2" — . . . . . — **3/8**
— **438A/6** $2^3/_8$" — **3/8**		— **438B/6** $2^3/_8$" — . . . . . — **5/-**
— **438A/7** $2^3/_4$" — **4/6**		— **438B/7** $2^3/_4$" — . . . . . — **6/-**
— **438A/8** $3^1/_8$" — **6/-**		— **438B/8** $3^1/_8$" — . . . . . — **7/8**
— **438A/9** $3^1/_2$" — **8/-**		— **438B/9** $3^1/_2$" — . . . . . — **10/-**
— **438A/10** 4" — . . . . . — **11/-**		— **438B/10** 4" — . . . . . — **14/-**

Fuller particulars are given on page 151 under No. 438 S.

This set, taken from American life is most interesting.

148

New!

Slides of Air Ship
and
Aeroplane Voyages

New!

This set consists of 12 high class slides (4 pictures, on each) with the well known views of Zeppelins voyages. The air ship shed at Manzell, the rising, the catastrophe near Echterdingen. Besides the Zeppelin pictures this interesting set contains a number of views of other air appliances such as Aeroplanes, Ballons, Monoplanes etc. In this set, moreover, is the history of aviation from Montgoltier to the present time; we therefore specially recommend these pictures as === **interesting and instructive.** ===

1	1³/₁₆	1³/₈	1⁵/₈	1³/₄	2	2³/₈	2³/₄	3¹/₈	3¹/₂" wide
3¹/₂	4³/₈	5¹/₄	6	6³/₄	7¹/₈	8	8³/₄	9¹/₂	11" long

No. 405 A without cover glass			**No. 405 B with cover glass**		
No. 405 A/2¹/₂	1" wide . . . . . dozen	-/8	No. 405 B/4	1⁵/₈" wide . . . . . dozen	2/4
— 405 A/3	1³/₁₆" — . . . . . —	-/10	— 405 B/4¹/₂	1³/₄" — . . . . . —	3/4
— 405 A/3¹/₂	1³/₈" — . . . . . —	1/4	— 405 B/5	2" — . . . . . —	3/8
— 405 A/4	1⁵/₈" — . . . . . —	1/8	— 405 B/6	2³/₈" — . . . . . —	5/-
— 405 A/4¹/₂	1³/₄" — . . . . . —	2/-	— 405 B/7	2³/₄" — . . . . . —	6/-
— 405 A/5	2" — . . . . . —	2/10	— 405 B/8	3¹/₈" — . . . . . —	7/8
— 405 A/6	2³/₈" — . . . . . —	3/8	— 405 B/9	3¹/₂" — . . . . . —	10/-
— 405 A/7	2³/₄" — . . . . . —	4/6			
— 405 A/8	3¹/₈" — . . . . . —	6/-			
— 405 A/9	3¹/₂" — . . . . . —	8/-			

Views of Switzerland, Munich, and Vienna, Bavarian Royal Palaces and Castles, and Celebrated Churches.

The set consists of 12 long slides magnificently executed (4 pictures on each) in the following sizes, with text.

1³/₁₆	1³/₈	1⁵/₈	1³/₄	2	2³/₈	2³/₄	3¹/₈	3¹/₂" wide
4³/₈	5¹/₄	6	6³/₄	7¹/₈	8	8³/₄	9¹/₂	11" long

No. 456 A without cover glass			**No. 456 B with cover glass**		
No. 456 A/3	1³/₁₆" wide . . . . dozen	-/10	No. 456 B/4	1⁵/₈" wide . . . . . dozen	2/4
— 456 A/3¹/₂	1³/₈" — . . . . . —	1/4	— 456 B/4¹/₂	1³/₄" — . . . . . —	3/4
— 456 A/4	1⁵/₈" — . . . . . —	1/8	— 456 B/5	2" — . . . . . —	3/8
— 456 A/4¹/₂	1³/₄" — . . . . . —	2/-	— 456 B/6	2³/₈" — . . . . . —	5/-
— 456 A/5	2" — . . . . . —	2/10	— 456 B/7	2³/₄" — . . . . . —	6/-
— 456 A/6	2³/₈" — . . . . . —	3/8	— 456 B/8	3¹/₈" — . . . . . —	7/8
— 456 A/7	2³/₄" — . . . . . —	4/6	— 456 B/9	3¹/₂" — . . . . . —	10/-
— 456 A/8	3¹/₈" — . . . . . —	6/-			
— 456 A/9	3¹/₂" — . . . . . —	8/-			

Travel round the world.

Representing a journey with Bremen as starting point, to Gibralter, through the Suez Canal, to India, China, Japan, Australia, Cape Town and England by 48 artistical illustrations with description. Land and Peoples wonderfully described.

Assortments consisting of 12 long slides (4 pictures each) in the following sizes:

1⁵/₈	1³/₄	2	2³/₈	2³/₄	3¹/₈	3¹/₂	4" wide
6	6³/₄	7¹/₈	8	8³/₄	9¹/₂	11	12" long

No. 439 A without cover glass			**No. 439 B with cover glass**		
No. 439 A/4	1⁵/₈" wide . . . . dozen	1/8	No. 439 B/4	1⁵/₈" wide . . . . . dozen	2/4
— 439 A/4¹/₂	1³/₄" — . . . . . —	2/-	— 439 B/4¹/₂	1³/₄" — . . . . . —	3/4
— 439 A/5	2" — . . . . . —	2/10	— 439 B/5	2" — . . . . . —	3/8
— 439 A/6	2³/₈" — . . . . . —	3/8	— 439 B/6	2³/₈" — . . . . . —	5/-
— 439 A/7	2³/₄" — . . . . . —	4/6	— 439 B/7	2³/₄" — . . . . . —	6/-
— 439 A/8	3¹/₈" — . . . . . —	6/-	— 439 B/8	3¹/₈" — . . . . . —	7/8
— 439 A/9	3¹/₂" — . . . . . —	8/-	— 439 B/9	3¹/₂" — . . . . . —	10/-
— 439 A/10	4" — . . . . . —	11/-	— 439 B/10	4" — . . . . . —	14/-

For further information about slides see page 152 under No. 439 S.

Pictures of the Nile, Tropical Scenery, Polar Regions, Natural Phenomena.

A magnificently executed set consisting of 12 long slides (4 pictures each) **with explanatory text**, in the following sizes:

1 3/16	1 3/8	1 5/8	1 3/4	2	2 3/8	2 3/4	3 1/8	3 1/2 " wide
4 3/8	5 1/4	6	6 3/4	7 1/8	8	8 3/4	9 1/2	11 " long

No. 450 A without cover glass		No. 450 B with cover glass	
No. 450 A/3 1 3/16" wide . . . . dozen	-/10	No. 450 B/4 1 5/8" wide . . . . dozen	2/4
— 450 A/3½ 1 3/8" — . . . . —	1/4	— 450 B/4½ 1 3/4" — . . . . —	3/4
— 450 A/4 1 5/8" — . . . . —	1 8	— 450 B/5 2" — . . . . —	3/8
— 450 A/4½ 1 3/4" — . . . . —	2/-	— 450 B/6 2 3/8" — . . . . —	5/-
— 450 A/5 2" — . . . . —	2/10	— 450 B/7 2 3/4" — . . . . —	6/-
— 450 A/6 2 3/8" — . . . . —	3/8	— 450 B/8 3 1/8" — . . . . —	7/8
— 450 A/7 2 3/4" — . . . . —	4/6	— 450 B/9 3 1/2" — . . . . —	10/-
— 450 A/8 3 1/8" — . . . . —	6/-		
— 450 A/9 3 1/2" — . . . . —	8/-		

Sights worth seeing in different lands

A collection of illustrations of interesting spots in various parts of the world: **Holland, Belgium, France, Spain, Turkey, Germany, Scandinavia, Greece, Italy, Russia, Japan, India, Egypt, Australia, America** etc. The set consists of 12 long slides (4 pictures each) **with text**, in the following sizes:

1 5/8	1 3/4	2	2 3/8	2 3/4	3 1/8	3 1/2	4 " wide
6	6 3/4	7 1/8	8	8 3/4	9 1/2	11	12 " long

No. 425 A without cover glass		No. 425 B with cover glass	
No. 425 A/4 1 5/8" wide . . . . dozen	1/8	No. 425 B/4 1 5/8" wide . . . . dozen	2/4
— 425 A/4½ 1 3/4" — . . . . —	2/-	— 425 B/4½ 1 3/4" — . . . . —	3/4
— 425 A/5 2" — . . . . —	2/10	— 425 B/5 2" — . . . . —	3/8
— 425 A/6 2 3/8" — . . . . —	3/8	— 425 B/6 2 3/8" — . . . . —	5/-
— 425 A/7 2 3/4" — . . . . —	4/6	— 425 B/7 2 3/4 — . . . . —	6/-
— 425 A/8 3 1/8" — . . . . —	6/-	— 425 B/8 3 1/8" — . . . . —	7/8
— 425 A/9 3 1/2" — . . . . —	8/-	— 425 B/9 3 1/2" — . . . . —	10/-
— 425 A/10 4" — . . . . —	11/-	— 425 B/10 4" — . . . . —	14/-

Sights worth seeing in different lands

A collection of illustrations of interesting spots in various parts of the world: **America, Egypt, Greece, Asia Minor, Italy, Austria, Germany, Holland, Sweden, England, Russia** etc. The serie consists of 12 long slides (each 4 pictures) **with text** in the following sizes:

2 3/8	2 3/4	3 1/8	3 1/2	4 " wide
8	8 3/4	9 1/2	11	12 " long

No. 424 A without cover glass		No. 424 B with cover glass	
No. 424 A/6 2 3/8" wide . . . . dozen	3/8	No. 424 B/6 2 3/8" wide . . . . dozen	5/-
— 424 A/7 2 3/4" — . . . . —	4/6	— 424 B/7 2 3/4" — . . . . —	6/-
— 424 A/8 3 1/8" — . . . . —	6/-	— 424 B/8 3 1/8" — . . . . —	7/8
— 424 A/9 3 1/2" — . . . . —	8/-	— 424 B/9 3 1/2" — . . . . —	10/-
— 424 A/10 4" — . . . . —	11/-	— 424 B/10 4" — . . . . —	14/-

Further information about slides on page 152 under No. 424 S.

Trade Mark.

Journey through Switzerland and on the Rhine.

A very high class set, consisting of 12 long slides (4 pictures on each
with text, in the following size:

2	2³/₈	2³/₄	3¹/₈	3¹/₂	4" wide
7¹/₈	8	8³/₄	9¹/₂	11	12" long

No. **440 A** without cover glass

No. **440 A/5**	2" wide	. . . .	dozen **2/10**
— 440 A/6	2³/₈" —	. . . .	— **3/8**
— 440 A/7	2³/₄" —	. . . .	— **4/6**
— 440 A/8	3¹/₈" —	. . . .	— **6/-**
— 440 A/9	3¹/₂" —	. . . .	— **8/-**
— 440 A/10	4" —	. . . .	— **11/-**

No. **440 B** with cover glass

No. **440 B/5**	2" wide	. . . .	dozen **3/8**
— 440 B/6	2³/₈" —	. . . .	— **5/-**
— 440 B/7	3³/₄" —	. . . .	— **6/-**
— 440 B/8	3¹/₈" —	. . . .	— **7/8**
— 440 B/9	3¹/₂" —	. . . .	— **10/-**
— 440 B/10	4" —	. . . .	— **14/-**

Further information about slides on page 152 under No. 440S.

No. **460** The life of Dr. Martin Luther, in 12 pictures also the
following **fairy tales, the man without a heart, Robert the
Lazybones, the little flying mother, Bucur,** the true frontier guard,
Shalga Mihu the hero (4 pictures each) and **Neaga** (8 pictures),
together 12 long slides, 12" long, 4" or 4¹/₄" wide with **explanatory text**

without cover glass

No. **460 A/10**	4" wide	. . . .	dozen **7/-**
— 460 A/11	4¹/₄" —	. . . .	— **9/-**

with cover glass

No. **460 B/10**	4" wide	. . . .	dozen **9/-**
— 460 B/11	4¹/₄" —	. . . .	— **11/-**

High class Lantern slides
Original Photographs!

Taken on first class plates, quite sharp
and clear, suitable for even weak
illumination. — **Most interesting for
young or grown up.** Each set consists
of 6 slides with 4 pictures = 24 pictures and packed in durable cases. In the following sets:

Set I **Berlin**	Set IV **London**	
— II **Rhine**	— V **North Italy**	When ordering please
— III **Paris**	— VI **South Italy**	state **exact** set wanted.

In the following sizes

No. **444/4**	1⁵/₈" wide, 5¹/₄" long, per set of 6 slides each with 4 pictures	set **3/8**
— 444/5	2" — 6³/₄" — — — 6 — — — 4 —	— **5/8**
— 444/6	2³/₈" — 8¹/₄" — — — 6 — — — 4 —	— **6/4**

Each set is accompanied with an explanatory lecture.

No. **443** Coloured slides.

Very fine quality with cover glasses.
The set consists of **48 views** of
remarkable monuments, buildings, landscapes as very fine general pictures.

No. **443/5**	6	8	9	
2	2³/₈	3¹/₈	3¹/₂" wide	
3¹/₄	3¹/₂	4	4³/₄" long	
set **5/8**	**7/8**	**10/-**	**12/-**	

1. The Colossus at Rhodes.
2. Light-house near Alexandria.
3. The pyramids of Egypt (Gizeh).
4. Mosque in Cairo.
5. Temple of Kom Ombu.
6. Temple of Isis on Philoe.
7. Rock temple Abu Simpel.
8. Temple of Diana, Ephesus.

9. Heidelberg Castle.
10. Rock bastion (Switz.).
11. Isle of Ischia nr Naples.
12. Tower of Anguillara.
13. Garden of Villa Doria ⎱ Pamphilia.
14. — — — — ⎰
15. Railway Viaduct over the Laguna
16. Wartburg. [to Venice.

17. Berchtesgaden.
18. Cathedral at Milan.
19. Sonneck on the Rhine.
20. Hellbrunn near Salzburg.
21. Porta Settimana in Travestere Italy.
22. Via Mala (Switz.).
23. Caub on the Rhine.
24. Cemetary Garden (Switz.).

Subjects No. 25—48 every day scenes, comic scenes, hunting adventures etc.

Trade Mark.

Projection Lantern slides of best quality.

Photographs with cover glasses.

**Sets of 12 long slides
4 pictures each, total 48.**

I. Slide : 1. King Edward †, 2. Queen Alexandra, 3. Prince of Wales, 4. Princess of Wales (England).
II. —   5. Prince Regent Luitpold, 6. Prince Ludwig, 7. Prince Rupprecht, 8. Prince Leopold (Bavaria).
III. —   9. Kaiser Wilhelm II., 10. Kaiserin Victoria, 11. Crown Prince Friedrich Wilhelm, 12. Prince Eitel Friedrich (Prussia).
IV. — 13. King Victor Imanuel, 14. Queen Helene, 15. Princess Yolantha, 16. King Humbert † (Italy).
V. — 17. King Wilhelm of Wurttemberg, 18. Queen Charlotte, 19. Grand Duke of Baden †, 20. King George of Greece.
VI. — 21. Emperor Franz Josef I., 22. Franz Ferdinand and 23. Duchess Sophie Chotek, 24. Kossuth (Austria Hungary).
VII. — 25. Tsar Nicholas II. of Russia, 26. Empress Alexandra, 27. Nicholas I., Prince of Montenegro, 28. Muzzaffer Shah of Persia.
VIII. — 29. King George †, 30. King Friedrich August, 31. Ex Crown Princess Louise and child (Saxony).
     32. King Carlos of Portugal †.
IX. — 33. King Leopold II. †, 34. King Albert (Belgium), 35. Prince Heinrich of the Netherlands, 36. Queen Wilhelmine (Netherlands).
X. — 37. President Loubet (France), 38. King Christian IX. (Denmark), 39. King Oskar II. (Sweden), 40. Crown Prince Gustav Adolf (Sweden).
XI. — 41. Pope Leo XIII. †, 42. King Alfonso XIII. (Spain), 43. King Alexander I. †, 44. Queen Draga † (Servia).
XII. — 45. Prince Ferdinand (Bulgaria), 46. King Charles I. (Roumania), 47. Grand Sultan Abdul Hamid Khan (Turkey), 48. President Roosevelt (America).

The separate slides are stocked in the following sizes

Slide	$1^{3}/_{16}$	$1^{3}/_{8}$	$1^{5}/_{8}$	$1^{3}/_{4}$	2	$2^{3}/_{8}$	$2^{3}/_{4}$	$3^{1}/_{8}$	$3^{1}/_{2}$	4″ wide
	I	I	I	I	I	VII	I	I	I—V	I—II
—	VII	III	II	II	II	VIII	III—IV	II	VII—XII	IV—V
—	VIII	IV—XII	IV—XII	IV—XII	IV	X	VI—VII	IV—X		VII—XI
—	IX				V		IX—XII			
—	XII			VII—XII						

When stating width of slide the exact No. of slide must be given

No. 408/3

	$1^{3}/_{16}$	$3^{1}/_{2}$	4	$4^{1}/_{2}$	5	6	7	8	9	10
	$1^{3}/_{16}$	$1^{3}/_{8}$	$1^{7}/_{8}$	$1^{3}/_{4}$	2	$2^{3}/_{8}$	$2^{3}/_{4}$	$3^{1}/_{8}$	$3^{1}/_{2}$	4″ wide
Slides with 4 pictures	-/8	-/10	1/-	1/2	1/6	1/8	2/8	2/10	4/-	4/8

Projection Slides of best quality

for larger size lanterns.

Original Photographs! On first class plates of excellent definition and transparancy, even suitable for weak illumination. Each set consists of **24 pictures** $3^{1}/_{4} \times 3^{1}/_{4}$″ and is supplied in a durable protecting case. **Most interesting for young people as well as grown up.**

With each set is supplied an excellent lecture on the pictures:

Set I Berlin.
 — II Rhine.
 — III Dresden etc.
 — IV Hartz and Thuringia.
 — V Paris.
 — VI London.
 — VII Across Holland

Set VIII North Italy (from Lago Maggiore to Venice.
 — IX South Italy (Rome to Palermo).
 — X Upper Bavaria and the royal Palaces.
 — XI Through the Tyrol.
 — XII Upper Austria, Steiermark and Salzkammergut.

Set XIII The Wonderworld of Dolomites.
 — XIV The struggle for the pole.
 — XV The conquest of the air.
 — XVI Stellar wonders.
 — XVII The Holy Land and the places of the Bible.

No. 444 S/$8^{1}/_{2}$ **Price per set of 24 pictures 9/8.**

(When ordering please state exact set.)

Coloured slide sets for larger size magic lanterns.

No. 438 S Life and Work in America.

A complete set **with text** consisting of 48 pictures, $3^{1}/_{4}$″ wide, 4″ long **set 15/-.**

1. An Indian Medizine man.
2. An Opium Den in San Francisco.
3. A Hotel at the Goldfields.
4. In a Negro Church.
5. Mu-koon-ju-weap. Canon Colorado.
6. Yosemite Valley.
7. Shulykill Stream. Falls Bridge.
8. Mountain Formations in South Utah.
9. Mammoth Caves in Kentucky.
10. Niagara Falls.
11. Niagara Falls General View.
12. River St. Lawrence.
13. A Pair of Negros.
14. Indian in Winter Dress.
15. Pimo Indians, Arizona.
16. A Comanchen Warrier.
17. On the War-Path.
18. Scalping the enemy.
19. Prairie Dogs.
20. The Pacific Railway.
21. A Mile stone on the Prairie.
22. An Indian Burial Place.
23. Hot springs in California.
24. The Geyser.
25. Montgomery St. San Francisco.
26. Street in Florida.
27. Canal Street New York.
28. Broadway New York.
29. The oyster Port of New York.
30. A Nigger village in Louisiana.
31. Cincinatti, Negro Quarter.
32. The white House Washington.
33. St. Louis.
34. The Light-house of Atlantic City.
35. On the banks of the Hudson.
36. Lincoln's Monument.
37. Trinidad, In the Mexican district.
38. Gold washing.
39. An Indian Village.
40. Cotton Gathering.
41. City Park, New York.
42. Brooklyn Bridge.
43. Sacramento Street, San Francisco.
44. Union Square, New York.
45. The Mosquito plague.
46. A travelling Exchange.
47. Interior of a Hudson River Steamer.
48. The Elevated Railway of New York.

Trade  Mark.

Coloured sets of slides
for the larger size magic lanterns.
No. 439 S

439 S

A Tour round the World.

A complete set **with text** consisting of 48 pictures

3¼" wide, 4" long . . . . each **15/-**

1. Departure from Bremen
2. Lisbon
3. Gibraltar
4. Bedouin
5. Messina
6. Malta
7. Cairo
8. Street in Cairo
9. Caliphs' Tombs near Cairo
10. Suez
11. Temple at Philae
12. The Nile by Assouan
13. Hunting Hippotomi
14. Egyptian Women
15. Gulf of Aden
16. Bombay

17. Palace at Lahore (India)
18. Temple at Delhi (India)
19. Benares (India)
20. Source of the Ganges
21. Body Guard of an Indian Prince
22. Palace in Vellore
23. Vehicles of Madras
24. Indian Dancer
25. A Tartar Chief
26. Indian Soldiers
27. Calcutta
28. Cremation in Calcutta
29. A part of the Chinese Wall
30. Hong Kong
31. A Japanese Carriage
32. The Golden Island

33. Japanese Girls
34. Street in Yokohama
35. Japanese Lute Player
36. Gate of Pekin
37. New Zealander
38. Siamese Village
39. Japanese temple in Kamakura
40. Singapore
41. Sydney
42. Blue Mountains, Australia
43. Native of Samoa
44. Village of the Sandwich Islands
45. Capetown
46. St. Helena
47. Peak of Teneriffe
48. Greenwich

No. 424 S

424 S

Objects of interest in various lands

complete set **with text** consisting of 48 pictures

3¼" wide, 4" long . . . . set **15/-**

1. Market Place, Rotterdam
2. At the Voompies, Rotterdam
3. Crystalgade with round tower, Copenhagen
4. Iron ore, Svatberg Sweden
5. Sackville Street with Nelson's column Dublin
6. Old Market Place, Edinburg
7. Goethe's House, Weimar
8. Room in Goethe's House
9. Pontoon Bridge, Cologne
10. Triumphal Arch, Munich
11. Market Place and Fountain Schiltach
12. Farm in Kinzigtal
13. Maas Bridge Rotterdam
14. Raft on the Kinzig
15. Girls in bridal ornaments (Kinzigtal)
16. Farewell of the Dairymaid, Tirol
17. Coast of Amalfi (Italy)

18. The Parthenon, Greece
19. Dionysos Theatre, Greece
20. Byzantine Church
21. Bedouins, Arabia
22. Business House, Teheran, Persia
23. Beggar on Horseback, Persia
24. Courier in Anam, India
25. Temple and Burial Place, Arabia
26. Palace at Teheran, Persia
27. Pilgrims at Grave of a saint, Persia
28. Old Treasure House of Pharaoh, Arabia
29. French Captive Balloon
30. Winter Sports in Russia
31. Greek Brigands
32. Greek Bishop
33. Market in Tunis
34. Giant Tree in Usugara

35. Natural Bridge in Africa
35. Diamond Mines, Kimberley, Africa
37. Dancer of Tunis
38. Hunting the Eagle, Africa
39. On a Dhowa, Africa
40. Spring Bucks, Africa
41. Indian Farm, New Mexiko
42. Oil Well, Pennsylvania
43. Grand Avenue in Milwaukee
44. Corn Steamer, Milwaukee
45. Indian Torture, New Mexico
46. Indians on the War Path, New Mexico
47. Indian Idolater, New Mexico
48. Mara's Rodents of Patagonia

No. 440 S

440 S

Tour through Switzerland and on the Rhine.

A complet set **with text** consisting of 48 pictures

3¼" wide, 4" long . . . . set **15/-**

1. Appenzell
2. Shaffhausen
3. Zurich
4. Einsiedeln
5. Lucerne
6. Tell's Chapel
7. Fluelen
8. Rigi Railway
9. Basle
10. Berne
11. Thun
12. Interlaken

13. The Staubach nr. Lauterbrunnen
14. Grindelwald Glacier
15. Reichenbach Falls
16. Genf, Rousseau-Island
17. Chillon
18. Zermatt
19. Simplon Pass
20. Devil's Bridge, Gotthard
21. Locarno
22. Bellinzona
23. Bernina Falls
24. Valley of Tamina nr. Ragaz

25. Source of the Rhine
26. Via Mala
27. Thusis
28. Ragaz
29. Stein
30. Laufenburg
31. Falls of the Rhine nr. Shaffhausen
32. Basle
33. Speier
34. Worms
35. Mayence
36. Bingen

37. Rheinstein
38. Sonneck
39. Bacharach
40. Pfalz, Kaub and Gutenfels
41. Oberwesel
42. St. Goar
43. Loreley
44. Rheinfels
45. Stolzenfels
46. Coblenz
47. Drachenfels
48 Cologne

Trade  Mark.

425 S

No. 425 S
Objects of interest in different lands.

A complete set **with text** consisting of 48 pictures,

3¹/₄" wide, 4" long . . . . set **15/-**

1. Water Tower in Haarlem.
2. Harbour Party, Ostend.
3. Trocadero, Paris.
4. Eiffel tower Paris.
5. Heidelberg Castle.
6. Wartburg.
7. Hamburg, old Jungfernstieg and
8. Falls of the Rhine.   [Alster-basin.
9. Constantinople.
10. Athens, Acropolis.
11. Alhambra nr. Grenada.
12. Spanish Bull Fight.
13. Seal-hunting in the Artic Seas.
14. Exquimaux-camp.
15. Russian Trojka.
16. Kremlin at Moscow.

17. Tower of London.
18. Crystal Palace, London.
19. Church in Bergen Norway.
20. Trollhatta Falls in Sweden.
21. Colosseum at Rome.
22. Bay of Naples.
23. Venice with Palace of the Doges.
24. Leaning Tower of Pisa.
25. Brooklyn Bridge.
26. Niagra Falls.
27. Statue of Liberty, New York Harbour.
28. Buffalo-hunting.
29. Hoangko Harbour.
30. Opium-den.
31. Temple of Kioto (Japan).
32. Japanese singer.

33. Indian Tiger Hunt.
34. Palace at Delhi.
35. Indian Snake Charmer.
36. Indian Dancer (Odaliske).
37. Australian Gold Diggings.
38. Street in Melbourne.
39. Kangeroo Hunt.
40. View of Melbourne.
41. Market in Cairo.
42. Pyramids and Sphinx near Gizeh.
43. Casis in the Libyan desert.
44. Lion Hunt.
45. African Ostrich Rider.
46. Young Nyam-Nyam Warrier.
47. Ashantee Women.
48. Sacrificing Hottentots.

No. 447 CS
The discovery of America
by Christopher Columbus.
16 very finely executed, short slides with cover glass.

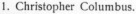

1. Christopher Columbus.
2. Genoa.
3. Council of the University of Salamanca.
4. Columbus at the court of Isabella.
5. The Ship of Columbus.
6. "Land" "Land".
7. San Salvator.
8. Deputation of Red Skins at the Spanish Court.

9. Citadel of Santo-Domingo.
10. Burial place in Valladolid.
11. Punta Isabella.
12. Columbus Memorial, Genoa.
13. Administration's Buildings.
14. Machinery Hall.
15. Government Buildings.
16. Art and Industrial Buildings.

International Exhibition Chicago 1893.

No. **447 CS**/6	7	8	8¹/₂	9	10
2³/₈	2³/₄	3¹/₈	3¹/₄	3¹/₂	4" wide
set **2/8**	**3/-**	**5/8**	**6/6**	**7/-**	**7/8**

Sacred subjects.
No. 447 S Very finely executed set of short slides with cover glass for larger size lanterns, consisting of 32 pictures.

The old Testament:
1. The Fall of Man.
2. Driven from Paradise.
3. Cain kills Abel.
4. The Flood.
5. Noah's Thank-offering.
6. Jacob's Ladder.
7. Joseph is sold.
8. Moses in the Rushes.
9. Moses breaks the tables of Stone.
10. The Spies.
11. Dividing the land by Lot.
13. Simon kills a Lion.
14. David and Goliath.
12. The Judgment of Salomon.
15. The Babalonian Captivity.
16. How Jerusalem's walls were built.

The new Testament:
17. The Holy Night (Birth of Jesus).
18. Flight into Egypt.
19. Baptism of Jesus.
20. Jesus in the temple.
21. The good Samaritan.
22. The Prodigal Son.
23. Suffer little Children to come on to Me.
24. Jesus Entry into Jerusalem.
25. Washing the Disciples Feet.
26. The last Supper.
27. The Betrayal.
28. Jesus bearing the cross.
29. Jesus derided.
30. The Crucifixion of Jesus.
31. The Resurrection of Jesus.
32. The Ascension of Jesus.

No. **447 S**/5	6	7	8	8¹/₂*	9	10
2	2³/₈	2³/₄	3¹/₈	3¹/₄	3¹/₂	4" wide
Price each set **4/-**	**5/-**	**6/-**	**8/10**	**12/6**	**13/8**	**14/8**

Only complete sets offered. — 8¹/₂* (3¹/₄") is sciopticon size.

No. 448
Dozen Assortments of
well executed
Coloured Slides

for larger size lanterns, **new subjects**, magnificently coloured, $3^5/_{16}'' \times 3^5/_{16}''$ with cover glass, dozen **4/-**

3. Paul and Virginia.
4. African life.
5. Views of the Arctic Regions.
6. Hunting and Animal Pictures.
7. Wild Animal Hunter.
8. Natural Phenomena.
9. The little Noise (Hauff).
10. Caliph Storck (Hauff).
11. Dwarf Nose (Hauff).
12. The Phantom Ship (Hauff).
14. Reynard Fox (Part 1).

15. Reynard Fox (Part II).
16. The last of the Mohicans.
17. Red Riding Hood and Sleeping Beauty.
19. Robinson Crusoe.
20. Don Quixote.
21. The Passion.
22. Tomb Thumb, little brother, little sister.
23. The wonderful Table, the brave little Tailor.
24. The Wolf and the 7 kids, the Race between the Hare and the Tortoise.

25. Jack and Jill and Snow-white.
26. Puss in Boots and Cinderella.
27. 2 bad boys and Boxer.
28. Nile pictures and Views of Egypt.
29. Palestine and the Sacred places.
30. Pictures of Italy.
31. General pictures.
32. Pictures of Switzerland.
33. Pictures of Upper Bavaria.
34. Famous Water Falls.
Children's Entertainment at strand.

☞ **Very interesting and instructive assortments.**

Prepared Microscopic Slides for the Lantern.

Prepared with great care, to meet all departments of science as:

blood, bones, zoological slides, tintions and injections from man, dogs, cats, rabbits etc., sections of wood, yarn, fibres, starch, meals, vegetables, insects artificial and adulterated food stuffs (100 different slides).

No. 760/21	for cheap magic lanterns . . . . Assortments of 12 slides	**2/-**
— 760/22	— better . . . . — — — —	**4/-**
— 760/23	— projection lanterns . . . . — — — —	**4/-**

Moving Slides in tin frames
for magic lanterns and cinematographs.

No. **426** (coloured) comic transformation slides. In 36 various pretty subjects.

No. 426/3	$3^1/_2$	4	$4^1/_2$	5	6	7	8
$1^3/_{16}$	$1^3/_8$	$1^5/_8$	$1^3/_4$	2	$2^3/_8$	$2^3/_4$	$3^1/_8''$ wide
dozen 1/8	2/-	2/4	3/-	3/4	4/4	5/4	7/4

Comic transformation slides with cover
in finely executed chromo lithographs.

No. 411N/3	$3^1/_2$	4	$4^1/_2$	5	6	7	8	9	10
$1^3/_{16}$	$1^3/_8$	$1^5/_8$	$1^3/_4$	2	$2^3/_8$	$2^3/_4$	$3^1/_8$	$3^1/_2$	$4''$ wide
dozen 2/8	3/2	3/10	4/4	6/-	6/10	7/4	8/6	9/8	10/10

In the following subjects:

1. The Spiritualist.
2. Schinderhannes.
3. The bottle Artist.
4. The shocked pater.

5. The first kiss.
6. Baker's and Cobbler's apprentices.
7. The great Drum.
8. The man without head.

9. The laughing and crying face.
10. The Changing Noses.
11. The butcher.
12. The charming Rope dancer.

Only original pictures offered (copyright design).

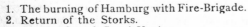

413 N

Landscapes with sliding figures in well executed chromo-lithographs.

No. 413N/3	$3^1/_2$	4	$4^1/_2$	5	6	7	8	9	10
$1^3/_{16}$	$1^3/_8$	$1^5/_8$	$1^3/_4$	2	$2^3/_8$	$2^3/_4$	$3^1/_8$	$3^1/_2$	$4''$ wide
dozen 2/8	3/2	3/10	4/4	6/-	6/10	7/4	8/6	9/8	10/10

Drawings are registered copyright.

In the following subjects:

1. The burning of Hamburg with Fire-Brigade.
2. Return of the Storks.
3. On the Grand Canal Venice.
4. Moschee near Cairo with Caravan.

5. Light-house (ship).
6. Bridge (Railway).
7. Flood.
8. Gossensass with Balloon.

9. Berchtesgaden (Herd of Cattle).
10. Chapel with Procession.
11. Castle (Skating party).
12. Park (Aeroplanes).

Trade Mark.

Moving Slides in tin frames

for magic lanterns and cinematographs

Mechanically rotating slides

fine chromolitographs

No. **415 N/3**	**3½**	**4**	**4½**	**5**	**6**	**7**	**8**	**9**	
	1³/₁₆	1³/₈	1⁵/₈	1³/₄	2	2³/₈	2³/₄	3¹/₈	3¹/₂ " wide
dozen **3/8**	**4/2**	**4/8**	**4/10**	**5/4**	**7/8**	**9/8**	**12/-**	**14/6**	

in the following 6 subjects: Watermill, Windmill, Soap, Bubble-blowing, Gymnast, Conjurer, Clown with 8 heads.

Lever moving slides in tin frames.

No. **416 N/3**	**3½**	**4**	**4½**	**5**	**6**	**7**	**8**	**9**	**10**	
	1³/₁₆	1³/₈	1⁵/₈	1³/₄	2	2³/₈	2³/₄	3¹/₈	3¹/₂	4 " wide
dozen **3/8**	**4/2**	**4/8**	**4/10**	**5/4**	**7/8**	**9/8**	**12/-**	**14/6**	**16/10**	

in the following subjects:

1. The Butcher.
2. The clumsy Rider.
3. Grimaces.
4. The Cello Player.
5. The Frog Conductor.
6. Cobbler's boy as nurse.
7. Old Times.
8. The Swing.
9. The Stonebreaker.
10. Give me a light.
11. A dangerous road.
12. The industrious Artist.
13. How Teacher punishes.
14. The Crocodile Doctor.
15 The House wife.

From size 6 upwards only available in 12 subjects.

Chromotropes

in tin frames

with rack and pinion, assorted in 12 patterns

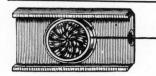

No. **428/3**	**3½**	**4**	**4½**	**5**	**6**	**7**	**8**	**9**	**10**	
	1³/₁₆	1³/₈	1⁵/₈	1³/₄	2	2³/₈	2³/₄	3¹/₈	3¹/₂	4 " wide
dozen **3/8**	**4/2**	**4/8**	**4/10**	**5/4**	**7/8**	**9/8**	**12/-**	**14/6**	**16/10**	

High class slides in frames

Specially suitable for projection lanterns and the better class lanterns.

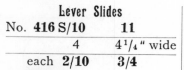

All the pictures are protected designs.

In widths of 4" and 4¼"

Lever Slides		Slipping Slides		Comic Transformations		Rotating Slides	
No. **416 S/10**	**11**	No. **413 S/10**	**11**	No. **411 S/10**	**11**	No. **415 S/10**	**11**
4	4¼ " wide	**4**	4¼ " wide	**4**	4¼ " wide	**4**	4¼ " wide
each **2/10**	**3/4**	each **2/10**	**3/4**	each **2/-**	**2/6**	each **3/4**	**4/-**

Lever Slides
1, Grimaces.
2. The Trumpeter.
3. The Shepherd's Sunday Song.
4. A Ship coming to port.
5. Welcome (Beginning the show)
Good Night (End of the show).

Slipping Slides
1. Swiss View with Alpine Glow.
2. The beautiful Galathea (a bust becomes alive).
3. The North Pole Expedition.
4. The Young Man's Dream.
5. Garden Party with Kalospinthechromokrene.
6. Railway Viaduct.

Comic Transformations
1. Baby laughing and crying.
2. The Bandit.
3. A Clown's Trick.
4. Jack and the Fly.

Rotating Slides
1. Watermill.
2. Windmill.
3. Moon rising.
4. Necromancer.
5. The Persian Smoker.
6. Clown with 12 different heads.

Best quality Chromotropes

in 5 patterns.

No. **410 S/10**	4 " wide	. . . .	each	**3/8**
— **410 S/11**	4¼ " —	. . . .	—	**4/6**

The same, finely painted, 24 patterns.

No. **410 SM/10**	4 " wide	. . . .	each	**5/-**
— **410 SM/11**	4¼ " —	. . . .	—	**5/6**

Trade  Mark.

Separate Accessories and Replacements for Magic Lanterns and Cinematographs.

☞ Paraffin lamps for magic lanterns and cinematographs.

No. 60/10	with glass container and flat burner to take,	2''' wick,	to suit No.	215/00	each -/6
— 60/11	—	3''' —	— —	215/0-2	— -/8
— 60/12	large —	3''' —	— —	215/3	— -/10
— 60/13	—	5''' —	— —	215/4—5	— 1/-
— 60/14	—	8''' —	— —	215/6	— 1/-
— 60/1	tin —	2''' —	— —	244/2½	— -/6
— 60/2	—	3''' —	— —	244/3—3½, 245/4—4½, 290	— -/7
— 60/3	large —	3''' —	— —	244/4—4½	— -/8
— 60/4	—	5''' —	— —	245/5—6, 291, 292, 293	— -/9
— 60/5	—	5''' —	— —	244/5—6	— -/10
— 60/6	—	8''' —	— —	245/7—8	— 1/-
— 60/7	—	11''' —	— —	294. 295	— 1/4
— 62/1	Round burner to take	10''' wick, to suit		387/1—2	2/4
— 62/2	—	12''' — —		387/3—4	2/6
— 62/3	—	14''' — —		387/5—6	3/-
— 62/4	**Duplex lamp** with 2 wicks (glass chimney not required) for 388/1—6				7/-
— 61/1	with flat burner to take	2''' oder chimney wick to suit No.		321 A/2½	— -/6
— 60/2	—	3''' —	— —	321 N/2½—3, 321 M/2½, 321/2½—3	— -/7
— 61/2	—	5''' —	— —	321 N/3½, 321/3½	— -/8
— 61/3	—	8''' —	— —	321/4—4½	— -/8
— 61/4	round —	10''' —	— —	321/5, 325/5	1/10
— 61/5	—	12''' —	— —	321/6, 325/6	2/6
— 61/6	**Duplex Lamp** with 2 wicks (glass chimney not required) to suit 322/6 and 466/5 etc.				6/10

60/1—7
61/1—3
61/4—5
62/1—3

☞ Paraffin wicks for above lamps. ☜

8 F | 8 R

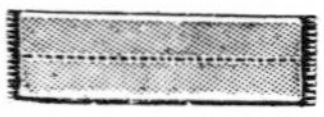

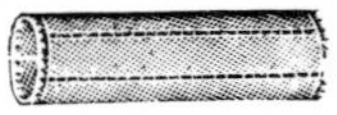

Flat burner wicks

No. 8 F/2''	3'''	5'''	8'''	11''
to suit 2	3	5	8	11''' lamps
width 1/4	3/8	7/16	9/16	1''
yard -/1	-/2	-/2	-/4	-/6

Round burner wicks.

No. 8 R/10''	12'''	14'''
to suit 10	12	14''' lamps
width 1¾	2⅛	2½''
yard -/10	1/-	1/-

☛ Flat wicks for duplex lamps. ☜

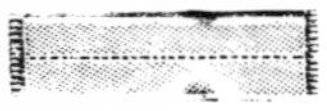

No. 8 D 1 1/16'' wide .... yard -/8

☞ Glass chimneys for above lamps. ☜
Bulge chimneys for flat burners.

No. 65/2	65/3 K	65/3 L	65/5 K	65/5 L	65/8 K	65/8 L	65/11
for 2	3	3	5	5	8	8	11''' burners
1	1¼	1¼	1 7/16	1 7/16	1 5/8	1 5/8	1 7/8'' outer diameter
dozen 1/-	1/2	1/4	1/4	1/6	1/6	1/8	2/-
to suit 215/00	to suit 215/0, 1	to suit 244/4, 4½	to suit 215/4, 5	to suit 244/5—6	to suit 215/6	to suit 245/7, 8	to suit 294
244/2½	'15/2, 3	245/4—/4½	245/5, 6	291, 292	321/4	—	295
321 A 2½	244/3, 3½	290	321/N 3½	293	321/4½	—	—
—	321 N/2½—3	—	321/3½	—	—	—	—
—	321 M/2½	—	—	—	—	—	—
—	321/2½	—	—	—	—	—	—
—	321/3	—	—	—	—	—	—

65   67

Straight chimneys for round burners.

No. 67/10''' to suit 387/1—2, 321/5 and 325/5 .... dozen	1/6
— 67/12''' — — 387/3—4, 321/6 — 325/6	1/8
— 67/14''' — — 387/5—6	2/-

High class objectives.

For lanterns or for photographic enlargers in solid brass with rackwork focussing movement. Achromatic lenses including scewed ring to fasten to apparatus.

68/3

No. 68/1 without cap. lenses 1 11/16'' and 2'' diameter	each 16/-
— 68/2 with leather cap, lenses 1 11/16'' and 2'' diameter	— 19/-
— 68/3 — revolving metal cap, lenses 1 11/16'' and 2'' diameter	— 20/-
— 68/6 Achromatic objective for cinematographs	— 18/-

68/2

Double convex and plano-convex lenses
see page 227.

72 SA

Condensers
with 2 plano convex lenses in massive brass screw cell

No. 72 SA/103	115	130	150	72C
4	4½	5 1/8	5 7/8'' diameter	
each 9/-	13/-	20/-	30/-	

——— Spare lenses. ———

No. 72 C/103	115	130	150 (diameter as above)
each 3/-	3/8	6/8	9/-

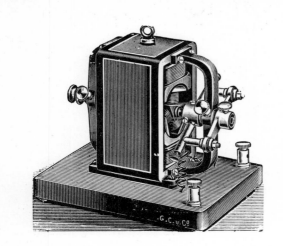

Electrical Toys and Educational Apparatus.

Trade Mark.

Electric Motors
for feeble or strong current,
Electric Railways,

Electric Tramways,
Cells, Batteries,
Accumulators,

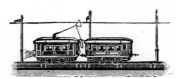

Dynamos for Lighting and Electric Power Supply, Electric Arc Lamps
and Incandescent Lamps, Steam Engines with Dynamos,
Apparatus for Demonstration with Galvanic Electricity,
Apparatus for Wireless Telegraphy, Ruhmkorff's Induction Coils,
Cases of Experimental Apparatus.

ELECTRICAL TOYS AND EDUCATIONAL APPLIANCES

The growing acquisition of knowledge in the department of Electricity for which we are indebted to the acumen, in conjunction with information derived from experiments, of eminent men, induces the rising generation to work, study, and experiment with great eagerness in the department of Electricity. The interesting experiments described in the text books, only inspire the moment the electrical effects are observed by means of simple apparatus.

To experiment is the best way of exciting interest.

By means of our very simple — though faultless in action to the slightest detail — apparatus, every opportunity can be siezed to carry on various researches.

Every apparatus is tested before leaving the factory so that the question of anything not acting is excluded. Above all the unpacking of the goods must be made with the greatest care and attention, as the slightest damage may dislocate or in some way prevent the working of the article. Further, before using the apparatus, the instructions supplied must be very carefully read through and followed out.

General Remarks

concerning the handling of the various electrical articles.

═══ ELECTRIC MOTORS. ═══

Electric motors we divide into 2 groups:

1. Weak Current Motors.   2. Strong Current Motors.

Weak Current Motors are such electric motors by which the current generated by **cells, batteries, or accumulators** is changed into mechanical power in driving the motor. The current is carried by means of insulated lead wires (copper) of not less than about $1/32''$ thick, these at one end are connected to the two poles of the current generator (cell or battery) and at the other, to the two poles of the motor respectively. From these, the current passes by the wires on the motor to the brushes (tongues of thin metal pressing on the commutator). We specially point out that these brushes which close the circuit & which show electric sparks when the motor is running, must not be bent, or else the motor will not work.

Before the motor is started, see that both bearings and all bearing surfaces are lubricated with a few drops of good machine or neats foot oil, as this will considerably ease the working. Of course too much oil must not be used or else the motor will hardly work.

The best adapted for **driving the electric motor,** as already mentioned, are chromic acid cells, batteries or accumulators with a tension of 2—4 volts.

The **chromic acid cells** are filled in the following manner:

To a quart of lukewarm water, ¼ lb. of bichromate of potash and ¼ lb. of sulphuric acid is added, and the mixture allowed to stand till all is perfectly dissolved. As soon as this chromic acid solution is ready the zinc and carbon plates are immersed & the current is started. To stop the current one has simply to lift out the zinc and carbon plates from the solution and to fix the screw. When using the motor continuously the battery will last about ¼—½ an hour. If however the working of the cell or battery is occasionally stopped it will last much longer. If it is required to work the motor after the solution is exhausted it is simply necessary to make up a fresh solution. Zinc and carbon plates when requiring renewal are always obtainable from us.

For a battery of several cells the above also applies.

For continuous working **accumulators** are strongly recommended.

The capacity (output of power) also working duration of the accumulators is given exactly with each. (Fuller information given under accumulators page 187).

Electric motors for strong current: By strong current motors we understand those electric motors which take current of higher tension, from the electric light wires or mains.

The electric motors for strong current (continuous or alternating) are so wound that when connecting with a lampholder etc. it is always necessary to insert a lamp resistance. The lamp resistances, supplied by us, are provided with an adaptor to fit any lamp holder either with Edison standard screw or with bayonet holder.

Our resistances are so constructed that all danger in handling is prevented, and consequently the greatest conceivable safety is offered. Toys-electric motors, electric railways and tramways are run with facility, by attaching to the aforementioned strong current (Light holder).

With the **electric railways, electric locomotives and tramways** the current is taken by the rails. In order not to break the circuit, the separate rails must be connected in unbroken contact.

As we supply to all our railways all possible rail accessories to suit electric power, it is just as easy to build up the various rail-formations, as it is in the case of the steam and spring motor (or clockwork) railways, also our simplified system renders the stocking of innumerable kinds of rails unnecessary.

As a specially interesting model for illustrating the large machines in use at the present day we recommend our

DYNAMOS
for LIGHTING or POWER GENERATION.

These Dynamos are capable, as soon as a minimum no. of 2500 revs. is reached, of supplying current for incandescent lamps, induction apparatus, spark coils and electric motors, besides working model workshops. The dynamos are, by reason of their wide range of application, the best demonstration model for electrical engineering, schools, students etc. Not last to be mentioned are our

DYNAMOS coupled to a STEAM ENGINE PLANT.

In these sets the dynamo is driven by a strong and reliable steam engine to the necessary no. of revolutions in order to light a miniature arc lamp.

These engines can be justly designated **ideal playthings for the older youths.** They are also suitable for driving working models & mechanical toys etc. by disengaging the dynamo gearing.

INDUCTION APPARATUS.

Induction apparatus, especially the Ruhmkorff type coils convert the current supplied to them from weak or low tension, into high tension current. The curative effect of the electric current is recognized by all and there are in consequence induction apparatus adapted (Faradic current) for the **physiological electrification of persons.** The **Ruhmkorff coils** are chiefly employed for illuminating Vacuum or Geissler tubes, they are also used in „**wireless telegraphy**" which department of electricity is arousing general interest on account of its great importance. We list in a special section all apparatus necessary for experimenting with **wireless telegraphy.**

In addition to the electrical apparatus already mentioned, we manufacture a large number of so called **minor apparatus** which are very important aids to the experimenter.

Our manufacturing extends to the most **varied accessories for weak or strong current articles** such as incandescent lamp stands, arc lamps etc.

Trade  Mark.

Electric Motors for Weak Current.

Driven by means of bichromate batteries or accumulators.

For suitable working models in wide variety see pages 38—56 of this list.

With revolving armatures, **very strong quality**, all cast parts well japanned.

1001/1

No. **1001/1** Electric motor

with permanent magnet and tripolar armature D. R.-G.-M., on polished wood base
3½" long, 2½" wide, 3" high
each **1/10**

1011

No. **1011** Electric motor

with tripolar armature on highly polished round wood base
2¾" high, 4¼" diameter
each **3/8**

1077/0

No. **1077/0** Electric motor

with tripolar armature, strong design on highly polished wood base,
3½" long, 3¼" wide, 3" high
each **4/6**

1078/0

No. **1078/0** Electric motor

vertical type, on highly polished wood base with H pattern armature
4" long, 3½" wide, 3½" high
each **5/6**

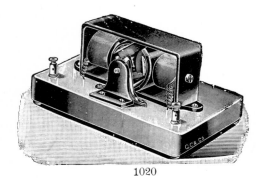

1020

No. **1020** Electric motor

horizontal type, with tripolar armature, on highly polished wood base,
5" long, 3¼" wide, 2" high
each **4/6**

1079/0 and 1079 F

No. **1079/0** Electric motor

with tripolar armature, on highly polished wood base, 3½" long, 2¾" wide, 3½" high, without fan, each **5/4**

No. **1079 F** Fan

to use above motor as ventilator, highly nickelled, 5" diameter, each **-/6**

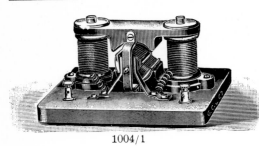

1004/1

No. **1004/1** **Electric motor** very strong and serviceable quality, with tripolar armature, on highly polished wood base, 5" long, 4" wide, 2½" high . . . . . each **7/-**

— **1004/2** the same but larger, 5½" long, 4½" wide, 3½" high . . . . — **11/-**

— **1004/3** the same but larger, 7¼" long, 5" wide, 4½" high — **16/-**

For suitable batteries and accumulators see pages 185—187 of this list.

Trade Mark.

Electric Motors for Weak Current.

For suitable working models, in wide variety see pages 38—56 of this list.
For suitale batteries or accumulators see pages 185—187 of this list.

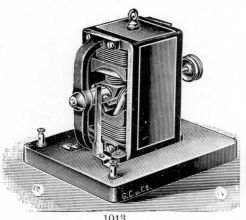 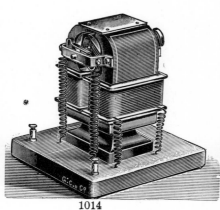 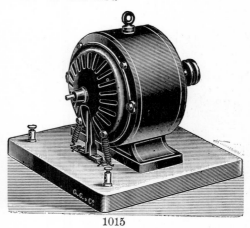

1013   1014   1015

Very strong and handsome quality, very powerful design, with tripolar armature, highly nickelled fittings, on highly polished wood base, the power corresponds to the number of battery cells or accumulators used.

No. **1013/1**	3½" long, 2¾" wide, 4" high . each **9/8**	No. **1014/1**	3½" long, 3" wide, 3½" high . each **9/-**	No. **1015/1**	4" long, 3½" wide, 4" high . each **12/-**
— **1013/2**	4" long, 3½" wide, 4¼" high , each **15/-**	— **1014/3**	4¾" long, 4½" wide, 5" high . each **18/-**	— **1015/2**	4½" long, 4¼" wide, 5" high . each **18/-**
— **1013/3**	6" long, 4¼" wide, 4¾" high, each **20/6**			— **1015/3**	6" long, 5¾" wide, 5½" high, each **23/-**

Fan Motor for weak current

on highly japanned cast iron stand, with electric motor 1015/1 with tripolar armature, highly nickelled fan (5" diam.), very handsome and strong quality, on highly polished wood base.
No. **1010/1**   7¼" high . . . . each **13/8**
If the motor is driven by an accumulator it is very useful for a cooling appliance.

1010/1

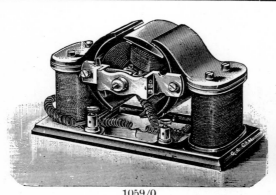 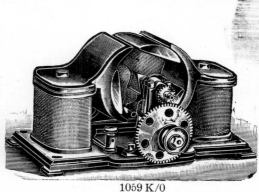

1059/0   1059 K/0

Very powerful Electric Motor

No. **1059/0** with tripolar armature, very strong and handsome design. This electric motor is adapted, owing to its excellent efficiency, for driving show models. On well japanned iron base.
7½" long, 5¼" wide, 4¼" high . . . each **27/-**

Electric Motor with speed reduction gearing

No. **1059 K/0** Quality same as 1059/0 but with speed reduction gearing, in order to change the rapid rotation into a slower motion, consequently gaining more power.
7½" long, 5¼" wide, 4¼" high . . . each **29/-**

 For suitable batteries and accumulators see pages 185—187.

Trade Mark.

Electric Toys for Weak Current.

1002

1025

No. **1002 Electric motor** with **Chromotrope Disc**, by a slow lifting of the disc and by different retarding by the fingers very surprising and magnificent **moving** figures are obtained which continually change shape, with 6 double discs, 4″ long, 3½″ wide, 5½″ high . . . . each **5/4**

No. **1025 Electric Swing** works by one battery for over an hour (suitable for shop window attraction) with dressed doll of porcelain, (D. R.-G.-M.), 4½″ long, 4½″ wide, 10″ high, each **5 8**

No. **1025 P** Doll only . . . . . — -/8

New! Electric Harbour Cranes. New!

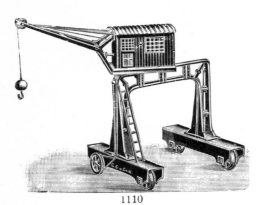

1110

No. **1110** to suit all steam, spring motor and electric locomotives of **35 mm gauge**. This crane is fitted with an electric motor, which, by means of a switch, will raise or lower the load. Moreover this crane is provided with an arrangement by which the crane will bring the load to a certain height and move the crane backwards or forwards. The motor house can be turned by hand. A small dry battery (No. 1 P, page 186) which can be put on the crane itself, suffices to work it. The crane is fitted with flanged wheels for moving on rails (for suitable rails see below). Very strong and well made, handsome japanning, 10¼″ high, 10″ long, 6″ high under crane, 6½″ wide . . . . each **17/-**

No. **1111 the same** but **larger,** to suit all steam, spring motor and electric locomotives of **48 mm gauge**. With arrangement for fitting a pocket-lamp-battery in the motor house. The motor house can be turned by means of a crank and spiral drive. Very strong and well finished, handsomely japanned,

13½″ high, 13¾″ long, will take 8″ under crane, 6½″ wide . . . . each **20/-**

1111

Rails with chairs

(patented.)

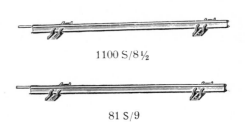

1100 S/8½

81 S/9

No. **1100 S/8½** for **small** section with 1 spike, 15″ long . . . gross **10/-**

No. **81 S/9** for **large** section with 1 spike, 15″ long . . . . . gross **16/-**

 **For suitable batteries and accumulators see pages 185—187.**

Trade Mark.

Electric Motors for Strong Current

Continuous or alternating.

Our electric motors are wound for high tension, namely, from 65 to 250 volts, no matter whether **continuous or alternating current.** The insertion in the circuit of a lamp resistance (page 164) is indispensable and has the advantage that one does not come into direct touch with the strong current thus avoiding all danger. With each motor full instructions are given. In the lamp resistance, incandescent lamps corresponding to the voltage of the current must be used. We would emphasize the fact that only carbon filament lamps, never metal filament lamps must be used in these resistances. The motors are all fitted with tripolar armatures and will start off at once when in any position; very strong and highly finished quality, handsome japanning, mounted on a highly polished wood base. The bearings are fitted with lubricators to prevent them heating.

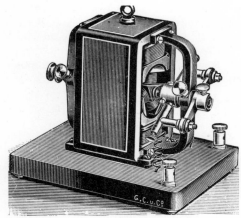

1013 H

1014 H

1015 H

No. **1013 H/2** Electric motor for strong current, with adjustable carbon brushes and lubricating attachment, 4" long, 3½" wide, 4¼" high . . each **20/-**

No. **1013 H/3** the same but larger, 6" long, 4½" wide, 4¾" high each **28/-**

No. **1014 H/3** Electric motor for strong current

with lubricating attachment, 4¼" long, 4½" wide, 5" high each **24/-**

No. **1015 H/2** Electric motor for strong current, in well japanned case, 4¾" long, 4" wide, 5" high, each **25/-**

No. **1015 H/3** the same but larger, 6" long, 5¾" wide, 5½" high, each **28/-**

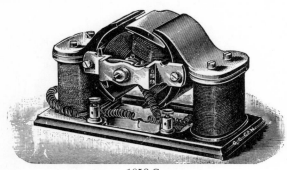

1059 G

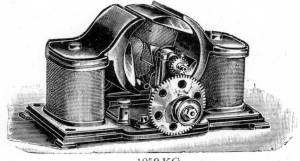

1059 KG

No. **1059 G** Very powerful electric motor for strong current, with copper brushes in very strong and high class finish, specially adapted for working the larger mechanical show models, mounted on well japanned iron base, 7½" long, 5¼" wide, 4¼" high, each **66/-**

No. **1059 KG** Power motor, quality as 1059G but with speed reduction gearing, to convert the rapid rotation into a slower motion and increasing the power in proportion, 7½" long, 5¼" wide, 4¼" high each **68/-**

 For suitable lamp resistances for above strong current motors see page 164.

Trade Mark.

Lamp Resistances

for strong current electric motors and for strong current electric railways,
either continuous or alternating current.

In order to sufficiently reduce the available high tension standard current, as the motors are worked with only 2, 4, 6 or 8 volts according to the kind of motor, and the available tension of 65, 110 or 220 would be too strong and would burn through the motor. When inserting a lamp resistance its 2 terminals must be connected respectively to the 2 terminals of the motor, or of the conducting rails as the case may be, as soon as the connections are made, notice that nothing metallic is touching or lying across the terminals or over the rails, or a short circuit will be formed and the motor or railway will not work. We supply resistances fitted with either plug adaptors if such connection is available, it being only necessary to insert the plug and to put in the corresponding lamp; or if plug adaptors are not suitable for connecting, adaptors fitted with Edison standard screw which will fit a lamp holder if the lamp is removed, or we can supply both types of adaptor combined No. 1074/7, 1075/7 and 1076/7. We also can supply these resistances with bayonet lamp holder as per illustration below. In using these adaptors no risk of short circuiting is run, consequently these offer the greatest possible safety in use. In the lamp sockets on the resistance, incandescent lamps are fitted but only **carbon filament** lamps of the corresponding available voltage, (metal filament lamps on no account to be used). The resistances are provided with 2 yards of good insulated duplex wire. As a rule a resistance with 1 lamp is sufficient (No. 1074). If more power is required of the motor then lamp resistance No. 1075 is used, by which one lamp is inserted or two lamps for more power, just as desired. Full instructions are furnished with each. The resistance 1076 is specially adapted for 220 volts when 110 volt lamps are fitted as are used on the three wire system.

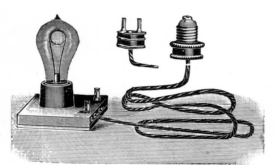  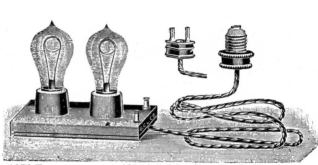

1074/5, 6   to 1074/7, to 1075/7, to 1076/7.   1075/1076/5, 6

For 1 Lamp.			For 2 Lamps in parallel.		
No. 1074/5	with Edison screw adaptor	each 3/-	No. 1075/5	with Edison screw adaptor	each 3/6
— 1074/6	with plug adaptor	— 2/8	— 1075/6	with plug adaptor	— 3/2
— 1074/7	with combination adaptor	— 4/4	— 1075/7	with combination adaptor	— 4/10

For 2 Lamps in series.

No. 1076/5	with Edison screw adaptor	— 3/6
— 1076/6	with plug adaptor	— 3/2
— 1076/7	with combination adaptor	— 4/10

1074/8 and 9   1075/8 and 9, 1076/8 and 9

For 1 Lamp.			For 2 Lamps in parallel.		
No. 1074/8	with bayonet holder	each 4/-	No. 1075/8	with bayonet holder	each 4/6
— 1074/9	— — — and adaptor	— 3/4	— 1075/9	— — — and adaptor	— 4/-

For 2 Lamps in series.

No. 1076/8	with bayonet holder	each 4/6
— 1076/9	— — — and adaptor	— 4/-

 The above resistances are also admirably suited **for use when charging accumulators**

No. 1074 for single cell accumulators
— 1075 — multiple cell accumulators

The method of charging accumulators is explained in the instructions.

Trade   Mark.

Electric Railways for Weak Current

Fitted with superior quality permanent magnet (D. R.-G.-M.), can be **reversed** viz. **run backwards** or **forwards,** by inserting a **commutator** (a current reverser). A bichromate battery or pocket lamp dry battery or accumulator of 2 to 4 volts will work these railways (for illustrations and prices of batteries etc. see pages 185—187.

1100

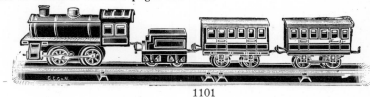

1101

 No. 1100 — **Electric railway** consisting of: locomotive and tender, 2 coaches, 4 round rails (circle), **28 mm gauge,** length of train 15½", total length of rails 4 feet 8", in pretty box . . . . each 4/-

— 1100 B — **the same,** with two extra straight rails (oval formation) . . . . each 4/8

 — 1101 — **Electric railway** consisting of: locomotive and tender, 2 coaches, 4 round rails (circle), **35 mm gauge,** length of train 20", total length of rails 5 feet 2" in pretty box . . . . each 6/-

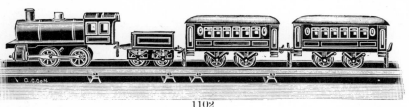

1102

No. 1102 — **Electric railway** consisting of: locomotive and tender, **2 coaches,** 4 round and 2 straight rails, **35 mm gauge,** length of train 2 feet 1", in smart box

total length of rails 7 feet 8", each 8/-

1157/35

New Suburban Tank Locomotive

well japanned and high class finish.

35 mm gauge

No. 1157/35 — **Electric Locomotive** for **weak current** (2 Volt), with superior permanent magnet motor, 7½" long . . . . each 3/10

These locomotives and trains can be delivered in the colours of:
Great Northern Railway Company.
London and **North Western Railway Company.**
Midland Railway Company.
When ordering please write after the number
G. N. R. or L. and N.W.R. or M. R.

1157/11

═ Complete electric Railways ═

for **weak current** (2—4 Volt),

35 mm gauge

 No. 1157/11 — consisting of: **Tank locomotive** 1157/35, 2 coaches well finished, 4 round and 2 straight rails, length of train 22½", total length of rails 7 feet 8" . . . . each 9/-

 — 1157/12 — consisting of: **Tank locomotive** 1157/35, 2 coaches and 1 guard's van but with **8 piece oval track,** 6 round and 2 straight rails, length of train 28", total length of rails 8 feet 1" . . . each 12/-

 ## Commutator

(Current reverser) in order to work above trains either **forwards or backwards** as desired or to break the circuit. The terminals marked 1 and 2 are to be connected to the terminals of the rails, those marked — and + are to be connected to the battery.

No. 1051/70 2¼" long, 1½" wide . . . . each -/10

By inserting a lamp resistance No. 1075 (page 164) fitted with 2 carbon filament incandescent lamps of 32 c. p. and voltage corresponding to the available supply, the above railways can be worked without any other alteration, from a **strong current lamp holder (high tension)** but only with **continuous current.**

For extra rails for above railways, see page 176.

Electric Locomotives and Railways.

For **weak** or **strong** current; strong design and handsome finish, with powerful motor with speed reduction gearing. When worked by means of weak current, can be **reversed** by using a **commutator** (current reverser) No. 1051/71. When using strong current from a standard lamp holder, a lamp resistance (page 164) must be inserted between the connection and the railway. In the case of the locomotives with headlights the **ordinary** carbon filament incandescent lamps with miniature screws (No. 1045/1) are used, they are suitable for the railway when using either weak **or strong current**.

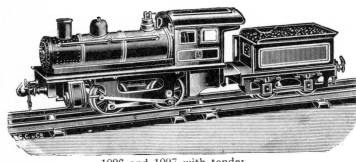

1096 and 1097 with tender

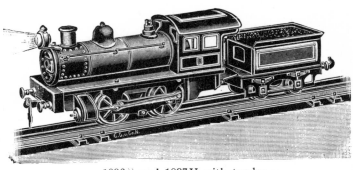

1096 V and 1097 V with tender

No.	1096	Electric **locomotive** for **weak** current of 3—4 volts, with superior permanent magnet motor, with massive flanged wheels, 12¹/₂" long, **with tender**, 35 mm gauge . . . . each	15/-
—	1096 V	**the same** with **1 head light**	— 16/4
—	1096 H	— — for **strong current** (continuous or alternating) with electro magnet, only runs forwards	— 16/10
—	1096 HV	as 1096 H but **with 1 headlight**	— 19/6

No.	1097	Electric **locomotive** for **weak** current of 4—6 volts, with superior permanent magnet motor, with massive flanged wheels 16¹/₂" long, **with tender**, 48 mm gauge . . . . each	22/-
—	1097 V	**the same** with **1 head light**	— 23/4
—	1097 H	— — electro magnet for **strong current** (continuous or alternating) runs only one way	— 28/-
—	1097 HV	as 1097H but **with 1 head light**	— 30/8

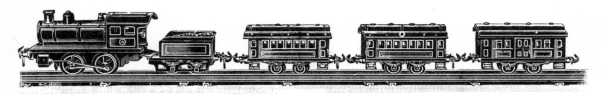

1096/2

No. 1051/71
Switch and commutator,
(current reverser) for working trains backwards or forwards, each **1/4**

Complete **Electric railways,** handsomely packed.

No. 1096/2	consisting of: Locomotive 1096 for **weak current**, with tender, 2 D-coaches and 1 D-brake van, 5 round rails and 1 round terminal rail, 2 straight rails, **with commutator, 35 mm gauge**, length of train 34", total length of rails 8 feet 1" . . . . each	25/6
1096 V/2	**the same train with 1 head light** on the locomotive . . . . each	26/6
1096 H/2	**the same train** as 1096/2, but for **strong current** (continuous or alternating), runs only one way, without commutator each	26/-
1096 HV/2	like 1096 H/2 **but with 1 head light**	— 28/6

No. 1097/2	consisting of: Locomotive 1097 for **weak current**, with tender, 2 D-coaches and 1 D-brake van, 7 round rails and 1 round terminal rail, 2 straight rails, **with commutator, 48 mm gauge**, length of train 3 feet 8", total length of rails 11 feet 8" . . . . each	36/6
1097 V/2	**the same train** with 1 head light on the locomotive . . . . each	38/-
1097 H/2	train as 1097/2, but for **strong current** (continuous or alternating), runs only one way, without commutator	— 41/6
1097 HV/2	as 1097H/2 **but with 1 head light**	— 44/-

The locomotives 1096, as well as 1097 can also be worked by strong current (though only continuous current may be used), by inserting between the connection and the railway a lamp resistance No. 1075, page 164 with 2 carbon filament incandescent lamps of 32 c. p. of voltage corresponding to the supply and if a commutator be used the trains will run in both directions.

☞ **For extra rails, switches, crossings, bridges, railway stations** to suit above railways, see pages 176 to 179.

☞ **For batteries and accumulators for weak current railways see pages 185—187.**

Trade ✹ Mark.

Electric Railways.

For **weak** or **strong cu.rent,** strong design and handsome finish, powerful motor with speed reduction gearing. When used with weak current can be **reversed** so as to **run either way** by means of the commutator (current reverser).

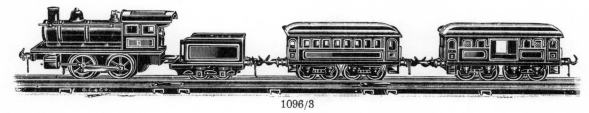

1096/3

Complete **Electric Railways, handsomely packed**.

No. **1096/3**   consisting of: Locomotive 1096 for **weak current** (3—4 volts) with tender, 1 each large D-coach and D-brake van, 5 round and 4 straight rails, also 1 round terminal rail, **with commutator, 35 mm gauge,** length of train 30″, total length of rails 9 ft. 9″ . . . . each **29/-**
—   **1096 V/3**   the same train with 1 head light on the locomotive . . . . — **30/-**
—   **1096 H/3**   — — — as 1096/3 but for **strong current** (continuous or alternating), train only runs one way, without commutator . . . . — **30/8**
—   **1096 HV/3** as 1096H/3 but with 1 head light . . . . — **33/4**

No. **1097/3**   consisting of: Locomotive 1097 for **weak current** (4—6 volts) with tender, 1 large D-coach and D-brake van, 7 round and 4 straight rails, also 1 round terminal rail, with **commutator, 48 mm gauge,** length of train 39″, total length of rails 13 ft. 8″ . . . . each **40/-**
—   **1097 V/3**   the same train, with 1 head light on the locomotive . . . . — **41/4**
—   **1097 H/3**   train as 1097/3 but for **strong current** (continuous or alternating) only runs one way, without commutator — **46/-**
—   **1097 HV/3** as 1097H/3, but with 1 head light . . . . — **48/8**

The strong current railways for continuous or alternating current marked "H" can be connected at once to a lamp holder, but a lamp resistance page 164 must be inserted in the circuit between the railway and the source of electrical supply.

For **extra rails, switches, crossings, bridges** and **stations** to suit above railways see pages **176—179.**

No. 1603/4

South Eastern and Chatham Railway Coach

48 mm gauge.

strong and well finished with powerful motor with friction drive, for **weak current** 4½—6 volts (3 bichromate batteries) will run only on rails of **large radius** No. 1040 page 176.

No. **1603/4** consisting of: **motor coach with commutator** for forward or backward running, 7 round rails and 1 round terminal rail, packed in handsome box, length of train 17½″, total length of rails 19 ft. . each **35/-**

For **Batteries** and **Accumulators for working weak current electric railways** see pages 185—187.

Trade   Mark

Electric Locomotives and Railways.

for **weak** or **strong** current, very strong and most handsomely finished, also finest japanning, with most powerful motor with geared drive.

1513/4 and 1514/4

No. **1513/4**   Locomotive for **weak current**, $4\tfrac{1}{2}$—6 volts (3 bichromate batteries), with **reversing motion, 35 mm gauge**, with tender, 20" long, with commutator . . . . each **54/-**

— **1513/4 H*** the same for **strong current** (continuous or alternating) only runs one way . . . . — **52/-**

— **1514/4**   Locomotive for **weak current**, 6—8 volts (4—5 bichromate batteries) with **reversing motion, 48 mm gauge** with tender, 25" long, with commutator . . . . — **90/-**

— **1514/4 H*** the same for **strong current** (continuous current), with **reversing** by commutator supplied — **90/-**

— **1514/4 HW*** the same for **strong current** (alternating), runs only one way . . . . — **96/-**

The above electric locomotiveswill run only on electric rails of large radius No. 1040 R page 176.

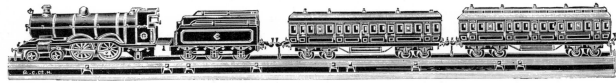

1513/4 B

Electric Railway Trains.

No. **1513/4 B**   consisting of: locomotive 1513/4 for **weak current**, with tender, 2 large, 8 wheel express coaches, 11 round rails and 1 terminal rail also 4 straight rails, **with commutator, 35 mm gauge**, in handsome box, length of train 4 ft., total length of rails 16 ft. . . . each **77/-**

— **1513/4 HB*** the same train for **strong current** (continuous or alternating) runs forwards only . — **75/-**

— **1514/4 B**   consisting of: locomotive 1514/4 for **weak current**, with tender, 2 large, 8 wheel express coaches, 15 round rails and 1 terminal rail also 4 straight rails, **with commutator, 48 mm gauge**, in handsome box, length of train 5 ft., total length of rails 13 ft. . — **122/-**

— **1514/4 HB*** the same train for **strong current** (continuous), runs forwards and backwards, **with commutator** . . . . -- **122/-**

— **1514/4 HWB*** the same train for **strong current** (alternating) runs forwards only . . . . . — **128/-**

For electric rail accessories as crossings and switches, see pages 176—179.

☞ *** All the strong current railways for continuous or alternating current marked "H" can be connected at once to the high tension current supply but must have lamp resistance, see page 164, inserted between connection and railway.**

**For batteries, accumulators etc. for the driving of weak current models
see pages 185—187.**

Trade ⚙ Mark.

Electric Railways

for **weak** or **strong current**

in strong and handsome quality, **48 mm gauge**
powerful motor with speed reduction gearing.

1088/22 V

No. 1088/21		**Motor wagon** for weak current, 3—4 volts, 7 round rails, 1 round terminal rail, 9" long, total length of rails 9 feet 3" . . . . each **13/-**
— 1088/22		the same with 1 **D-coach**, 7 round and 4 straight rails also 1 round terminal rail, length of train 19", total length of rails 13 feet 8" . . . . each **17/4**
— 1088/21 V		the same set as 1088/21, but with **2 electric head lights** (for working by 3 bichromate batteries) without batteries each **15/4**
— 1088/22 V		the same with 1 D-coach . . . . — **19/6**
— 1088/21 H		**Motor wagon** for **strong current** (continuous or alternating), 7 round and 1 round terminal rail, 9" long, total length of rails 9 feet 3" . . . . each **14/6**
— 1088/22 H		the same with 1 D-coach, 7 round and 4 straight rails, also 1 round terminal rail, length of train 19", total length of rails 13 feet 8" . . . . each **18/8**
— 1088/21 HV		the same set as 1088/21 H, but with 2 electric head lights . . . . — **19/-**
— 1088/22 HV		the same, but with 1 D-coach . . . . — **23/4**

Electric Railways with automatic reversing.

The reversing is effected by means of a reversing rail. This is not like the ordinary reversing because by means of these rails placed in a certain part of the track the reversing is done automatically. If for example a reversing rail is placed each end of a straight track, the train will reverse at each end automatically.

1088/32 V

1042 UG

No. 1042 **UG**/48 straight reversing rail . . . . . each **1/2**
— 1042 **UR**/48 round — — . . . . . — **1/2**

No. 1088/31		**Motor wagon** for **weak current,** 3—4 volts, 6 round rails, 1 round terminal rail and 1 reversing rail, 9" long, total length of rails 9 feet 3" . . . . each **16/8**
— 1088/32		the same with **1 D-coach**, 6 round rails and 1 each terminal and reversing rail, length of train 19", total length of rails 13 feet 8" . . . . each **19/6**
— 1088/31 V		the same set as 1088/31 but with 2 electric head lights (to work by 3 bichromate batteries) without batteries, each **18/10**
— 1088/32 V		the same but with 1 D-coach . . . . — **22/-**
— 1088/31 H		**Motor wagon** for **strong current** (continuous or alternating), 6 round rails and 1 each terminal and reversing rail, 9" long, total length of rails 9 feet 3" . . . . each **18/-**
— 1088/32 H		the same with 1 D-coach, 6 round and 4 straight rails and 1 each terminal and reversing rail, 19" long, total length of rails 13 feet 8" . . . . each **21/-**
— 1088/31 HV		the same set as 1088/31 H, but with 2 electric head lights . . . . — **22/8**
— 1088/32 HV		— — — but with 1 D coach. . . . . — **25/6**

☞ **All the sets marked „H" for continuous or alternating current can be connected at once to the power supply (high tension) but a lamp resistance, page 164, must be inserted between connection and the railway.**

For extra rails, switches, crossings, bridges, railway stations etc. to suit above railways see pages 176—179.

For batteries and accumulators for running weak current railways see pages 185—187.

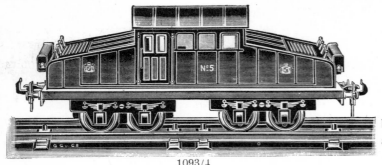

1093/4

New London Metropolitain Locomotive

With reversing for forward or backward running by means of the accompanying commutator. Very strong and well finished, most powerful motor with geared drive, **48 mm gauge**.

No. 1093/4 Locomotive for **weak current** $4^1/2$—6 volts (3 bichromate batteries) with commutator for reversing, 14″ long, without batteries . . . . each 33/-

☞ These locomotives can be worked with **strong current** (but only continuous) from electric mains, a lamp resistance No. 1075, page 164 fitted with 2 carbon filament incandescent lamps of 32 c. p. and of voltage to suit supply, must be inserted between connection and railway. When using continuous current from lamp holder the train will run in one direction only.

Complete London Metropolitain Trains, 48 mm gauge

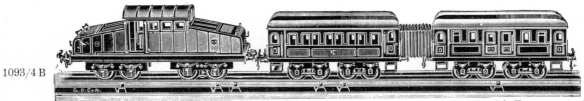

1093/4 B

No. 1093/4 B consisting of: Locomotive 1093/4 for **weak current** ($4^1/2$—6 volts) also 1 each 8 wheel L-Express coach and brake van, 7 round and 4 straight rails also 1 round terminal rail, with **commutator for reversing**, packed in handsome box, length of train 38″, total length of rails 13 ft. 8″ . . . . each 56/-

☞ This railway is also for **strong current** (but only continuous) and then a lamp resistance No. 1075, page 164 with 2 carbon filament incandescent lamps of 32 c. p. and voltage to suit supply, must be inserted between the connection and the railway. When connected to continuous current the railway runs in one direction only.

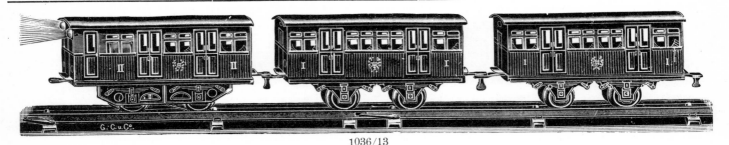

1036/13

Electric Underground Railway, 48 mm gauge.

For **weak** or **strong current**, strong quality and well finished, fitted with powerful motor.

No. 1036/11 **Motor wagon** for **weak current**, 3—4 volts, 7 round rails and 1 terminal rail, 9″ long, total length of rails 9 ft. 3″ . . . . each 15/-

— 1036/12 the same railway, but with **trailing coach**, and 4 straight rails extra, length of train 18″, total length of rails 13 ft. 8″ . . . . each 18/-

— 1036/13 the same railway but with **2 trailing coaches**, length of train 27″ . . . . — 22/-

The above railways with motor wagon with **2 electric head lights** (runs on $4^1/2$—6 volts).

	1036/11 V	1036/12 V	1036/13 V
	each 17/6	18/4	24/4

No. 1036/11 H **Motor wagon** for **strong current**, same set as No. 1036/11 . . . . each 16/4
— 1036/12 H — — — — — — — 1036/12 (1 trailer) . . . . — 19/6
— 1036/13 H — — — — — — — 1036/12 (2 trailers) . . . . — 23/6

The **strong current railways** marked „H" **for continuous** or **alternating current** must have a lamp resistance page 164 between connection and railway, they can then be run without further attention.

For **extra Rails, Switches, Crossings, Bridges, Railway Stations** for above railways, see pages 176—179.

For Batteries and Accumulators for running **weak current** railways see pages 185—187.

Trade Mark.

New large Underground Railway

for **weak** or **strong current,** strong design and handsomely finished, with **powerful motor**, with geared drive, well packed in strong box. 3 bichromate batteries $4\,{}^1\!/_2$—6 volts will drive weak current railways, in the case of strong current railways, they can be connected to the nearest lamp holder, whether continuous or alternating current, with a lamp resistance page 164 between railway and connection. The coaches fitted with head lights take the ordinary carbon filament incandescent lamps with miniature screws $3\,{}^1\!/_2$ volts (No. 1045/1 page 193). Each coach is fitted with 2 bogies **48 mm gauge** and will run on curves of small radius.

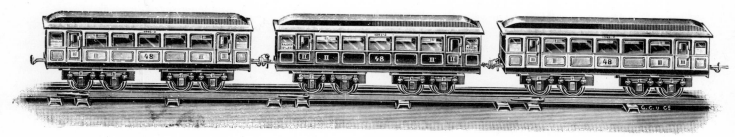

1092

Complete Underground Railways

consisting of: 1 driving coach, long oval track, 7 round rails, 1 round terminal rail, 4 straight rails, all packed in partitioned, handsome cardboard box.

48 mm gauge	For weak current (4 ${}^1\!/_2$—6 volts)		For strong current continuous or alternating	
	no head light	with head light	no head light	with head light
with 1 **driving** coach only . each	No. **1092/10** 31/6	No. **1092 V/10** 34/6	No. **1092 H/10** 36/6	No. **1092 HV/10** 44/-
with 1 driving coach and 1 trailer each	No. **1092/11** 38/-	No. **1092 V/11** 42/6	No. **1092 H/11** 43/6	No. **1092 HV/11** 53/-
with 1 driving coach and 2 trailers each	No. **1092/12** 45/-	No. **1092 V/12** 51/-	No. **1092 H/12** 50/-	No. **1092 HV/12** 62/-

No. **1092/1**	**Driving coach** for weak current, 14" long, 4³/₄" high	each	**22/-**
— 1092/1 V	— — with head light	—	**25/6**
— 1092/1 H	— — for strong current	—	**27/6**
— 1092/1 HV	— — — — and with 1 head light	—	**34/6**

Trailing coaches, 14" long, 4³/₄" high, if **yellow** No. 1092/2,   if **red** No. 1092/3 . . . . . each **6/6**
the same with 1 head light for weak current . . — 1092/2 V, — — — 1092/3 V . . . . . — **8/-**
— — — 1 — — strong — . . — 1092/2 HV, — — — 1092/3 HV . . . . . — **8/8**

☞ Our **parapet rails** which can easily be arranged as an **elevated railway** are admirably adapted for the above underground railways and if equipped with arc lamps, telegraph poles, stations, as well as switches and crossings, form a most interesting model and as true a likeness to the real railways as possibly could be. Further particulars are given on pages 178—179.

Trade   Mark.

Electric Tramways or Street Railways for Weak Current

1107/11

1107/12

With superior permanent magnet motors (D. R.-G.-M.) can be **reversed,** viz. **run in both directions,** by inserting a commutator in the circuit. Bichromate batteries, pocket lamp re-fils or accumulators can be used to run these trams.

No. 1107/11   **Electric tramway,** consisting of: **1 motor wagon,** 3 round rails, 1 round terminal rail, **28 mm gauge,** 7½" long, total length of rails 4 feet 8" . . . . each 3/8

— 1107/12   **Electric tramway,** consisting of: 1 motor wagon with 1 trailing car, 3 round and 2 straight rails also 1 round terminal rail, **28 mm gauge,** length of train 15", total length of rails 6 feet 9", each 5/-

— 1107/3 **Trailing car** only, to suit above railway, 7½" long. . . . . each -/10

For extra rails No. 1100 R/28 and 1100 G/28 see page 176.

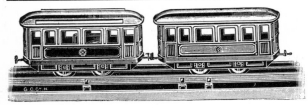

1090/1 A and 1 B

Better Electric Tramways

35 mm gauge, for weak current (2—4 volts)

with superior permanent magnet motor (D. R.-G.-M.)

No. 1090/1 A   **Electric tramway,** consisting of: motor wagon, 3 round rails and 1 round terminal rail, **35 mm gauge,** packed in handsome box, 7½" long, total length of rails 5 feet 2" . . . . . . each 6/-

— 1090/1 B   the same, with **1 trailing car** and 2 straight rails extra, length of train 15½", total length of rails 7 feet 7" . . . . each 8/8

No. 1090/3 **Trailing car** for above tramway, 7½" long . . . . each 1/10

1090/3

Commutator (Current reverser) for **reversing** the above tramways so that cars **run in either direction,** or to stop them where required. The terminals marked 1 and 2 are to connect to rails, those marked — and + to the battery.

No. 1051/70   2½" long, 1½" wide . . . . each -/10

1051/70

👉   By inserting a resistance No. 1075 (page 164), the **above tramways** can be run by **high tension current,** but only **continuous current** should be used. (By using 2 carbon filament incandescent lamps of 32 c. p. of the voltage of the supply).

For extra rails No. 1101 R and 1101 G to suit above tramways, see pages 176.

For bichromate batteries or accumulators for driving above tramways,
see pages 185—187.

Trade ⚙ Mark.

High class Electric Tramways.

Electric tramways for weak current

(2—4 volts)

with superior permanent magnet motors with geared drive.

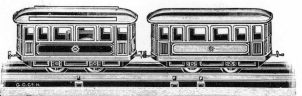

35 mm gauge

1090/12

 No. 1090/11 — consisting of: **motor wagon**, 5 round rails and 1 round terminal rail, **35 mm gauge**, 7½″ long, total length of rails 6 ft. 2″, packed in handsome box . . . . each **8/-**

 — 1090/12 — the same railway, but with **1 trailing car** and 2 straight rails extra, length of train 15½″, total length of rails 8 ft. . . . . — **11/-**

Commutator (current reverser) for running above cars **in either direction**, or to stop them, when and where desired.

No. **1051/70** . . . . each **-/10**

By inserting a lamp resistance No. 1075 (page 164) between connection and railway the above railways may be worked from high voltage, **continuous** current mains, by using 2 carbon filament incandescent lamps of 32 c. p. of same voltage as supply.

High class Electric Tramways

of very strong design, for **weak** or **strong current**, with powerful electric motor, fitted with geared drive (by using commutator 1051/71 for weak current the cars will **run either way**). For weak current railways 2 bichromate batteries (3—4 volts), for those with head lights, 3 batteries are required (4½—6 volts). The head light lamps are 3½ volts and have miniature screws.

48 mm gauge.

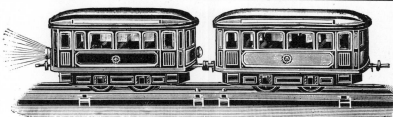

1091/12 V

 No. 1091/11 — consisting of: **motor wagon** for weak current, 7 round rails and 1 terminal rail, 9½″ long, total length of rails 9 ft. 3″ . . . . each **15/8**

 — 1091/12 — **motor wagon** with **trailing car**, 7 round rails, 1 round terminal rail and 4 straight rails, length of train 19″, total length of rails 13 ft. 8″ . . . . — **21/-**

— 1091/11 V the same railway as 1091/11 but with **2 electric head ligths** . . . . — **18/-**

— 1091/12 V — — — — 1091/12 — — 2 — — — and **lighted trailing car** . . . . . . — **25/-**

 No. 1091/11 H — consisting of: **motor wagon** for **strong current**, 7 round rails and 1 round terminal rail, 9½″ long, length of rails 9 ft. 3″ . . . . each **17/-**

 — 1091/12 H — **motor wagon** with **trailing car**, 7 round rails, 1 round terminal rail, 4 straight rails, length of train 19″, total length of rails 13 ft. 8″ . . . . — **22/6**

— 1091/11 HV the same railway as 1091/11 H but with **2 electric head ligths** . . . . — **22/-**

— 1091/12 HV — — — — 1091/12 H — — 2 — — — and **lighted trailing car** . . . . . . — **29/-**

 **Commutator** (current reverser) in order to run cars of above railways, for **weak current**, in **either direction**, or to stop the current.

No. **1051/71** . . . . each **1/4**

For **extra rails, switches crossings etc.** for forming all shapes of track for above railways, see pages 176—179.

For bichromate batteries and accumulators for driving above railways for **weak current**, see pages 185—187.

The **strong current** (continuous or alternating) railways marked "H" are ready for connecting to nearest electrical supply, but must have a lamp resistance page 164, between connection and railway.

Trade Mark.

Electric Tramways 48 mm gauge

with **automatic reversing attachment,** for **weak** or **strong** current. The reversing is effected by means of a reversing rail. This method of reversing must not be compared with the ordinary reversing by commutator, as the reversing by a reversing rail is quite automatic. If, for instance, a reversing rail is placed each end of a straight track the tram reverses itself **automatically** when it reaches the end.

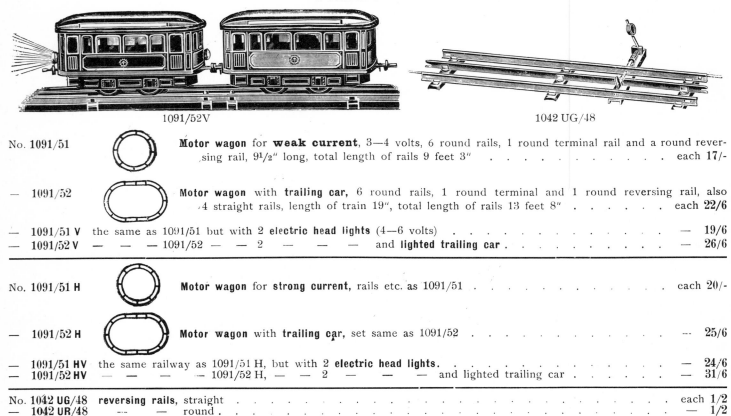

1091/52V   1042 UG/48

No. 1091/51		**Motor wagon** for **weak current**, 3—4 volts, 6 round rails, 1 round terminal rail and a round reversing rail, 9½" long, total length of rails 9 feet 3"	each 17/-
— 1091/52		**Motor wagon** with **trailing car,** 6 round rails, 1 round terminal and 1 round reversing rail, also 4 straight rails, length of train 19", total length of rails 13 feet 8"	each 22/6
— 1091/51 V	the same as 1091/51 but with 2 **electric head lights** (4—6 volts)	— 19/6
— 1091/52 V	— — — 1091/52 — — 2 — — — and **lighted trailing car**	— 26/6
No. 1091/51 H		**Motor wagon** for **strong current**, rails etc. as 1091/51	each 20/-
— 1091/52 H		**Motor wagon** with **trailing car,** set same as 1091/52	— 25/6
— 1091/51 HV	the same railway as 1091/51 H, but with 2 **electric head lights**.	— 24/6
— 1091/52 HV	— — — — 1091/52 H, — — 2 — — — and lighted trailing car	— 31/6
No. 1042 UG/48	**reversing rails,** straight	each 1/2
— 1042 UR/48	— — round	— 1/2

Electric Railway with Branch Line for weak-or strong current
48 mm gauge.

Very novel

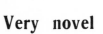

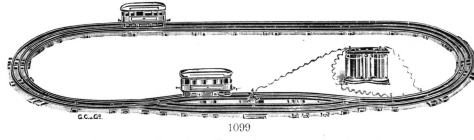

and fascinating model!
D. R.-P. and D. R.-G.-M.

1099

After the batteries have been properly connected to the rails, both cars are placed on the branch lines or sidings. One car will then start off and after running round the track enters the other branch line, here it actuates a commutator which causes the other car to start off while the first remains stationary on the siding, when the 2nd car returns the 1st starts off again and so on as long as the current lasts.

No. 1099 consisting of: 2 Motor wagons for **weak current** (3½—4 volts) 7 round rails, 1 round terminal rail, 3 straight rails and 1 special branch of 3 pieces with **automatic commutator,** length of rails 15 ft. 9" length of each car 9½", without batteries, packed in handsome box. . . . . each 42/-

No. 1099 H the same railway for **strong current** (continuous or alternating) . . . . — 45/-

For **extra rails, crossings, switches** for building all kinds of rail formation to suit above railways, see pages 176—179.

For batteries and accumulators for **weak current** railways, see pages 185—187.

The **strong current** railways marked "H" are ready for connecting to the nearest power supply, continuous or alternating, but a lamp resistance page 164 must be inserted between the connection and the railway.

Trade Mark.

Separate Motor Wagons and Electric Locomotives
for electric railways, 48 mm gauge.

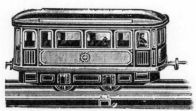

1088

No. 1088/2	for **weak** current		each	8/-
— 1088/2 V	— — — with lighting		—	10/6
— 1088/2 H*	— **strong** current		—	9/8
— 1088/2 HV*	— — with lighting		—	14/-
— 1088/3	(automatic reversing) for **weak** current		—	11/-
— 1088/3 V	— — — with lighting . . .		—	13/4
— 1088/3 H*	— — — **strong** current		—	12/6
— 1088/3 HV*	— — — with ligthing		—	17/-
No. 1036/1	for **weak** current		each	9/-
— 1036/1 V	— — — with lighting		—	11/6
— 1036/1 H*	— **strong** current		—	10/6
— 1036/1 HV*	— — with lighting		—	15/-

(Fuller information page 169. / Fuller information page 170.)

1091

1090

Trailing cars or coaches to suit:

— 1036/3 brown	—	1/8
— 1036/4 yellow	—	1/8
— 1036/5 red	—	1/8

No. 1090/1 for **weak** current, 35 mm gauge . . . . each 4/10

Fuller information on page 172.

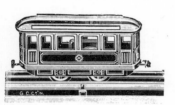

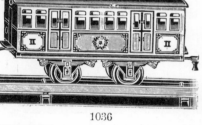

1036

No. 1091/1	for **weak** current	each	10/6
— 1091/1 V	— — — with lighting . . .	—	12/10
— 1091/1 H*	— **strong** current	—	12/-
— 1091/1 HV*	— — with lighting . . .	—	16/8
— 1091/5	— (automatic reversing) for **weak** current .	—	10/10
— 1091/5 V	— — — with lighting .	—	13/6
— 1091/5 H*	— — — **strong** current .	—	13/8
— 1091/5 HV*	— — with lighting . .	—	18/4

(Fuller information page 173.)

1090/3

Separate Trailing Cars or Coaches
for electric railways.

No. **1090/3** for tramway, 35 mm gauge, 7½" long each 1/10

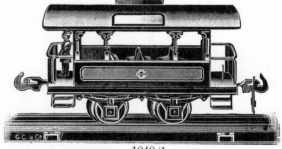

1040/1

For 48 mm gauge.
Summer trailing cars.

No. 1040/1 8½" long . . . . each 4/-

1091/3

Winter trailing cars for 48 mm gauge.

No. 1091/3	9½" long	each 3/4
— 1091/3 V	for weak current motors with lighting	— 4/10
— 1091/3 HV	— strong current motors — —	— 5/8

For rails to suit above motor wagons see page 176.

For batteries and accumulators for driving **weak current** motor wagons see pages 185—187.

* For lamp resistances for connecting **strong current** motor wagons to mains see page 164.

For **commutators** for forward or backward running of cars see page 177.

983/20

Passenger Figures and Conductors

to suit our electric railways. Well finished and artistically painted. Each box contains 4 gentlemen and 4 ladies, also 2 boys and 2 girls.

No. 983/20	Passengers to suit 35 mm gauge coach . .	box of 12 fig. 2/4
— 983/21	— — — 48 mm — —	— 2/8
— 983/10	Conductor for 35 and 48 mm gauge pretty enamelling doz.	-/8

Trade Mark.

Separate Rail Accessories for Electric Railways

with central rail conductor for **weak** or **strong current**, the rails are fixed and insulated.

1100 G

Straight rails with 3 spikes on one end.

No. 1100G/28 28 mm gauge for railways 1100 and 1107 . . . . dozen **3/-**
— 1101G/35 35 — — — 1101, 1102, 1157 . . . — **3/6**
1090/1a and 1b.

1100 R

Round rails with 3 spikes on one end.

No. 1100R/28 28 mm gauge for railways 1100 and 1107 . . . . dozen **3/6**
— 1101R/35 35 — — — 1101, 1102, 1157 . . . — **3/8**
1090/1a and 1b.

No. of pieces to form circle:
of rails 28 mm gauge . . 4 pieces. | of rails 35 mm gauge . . 4 pieces.

Rail Parts for forming all kinds of shape track, **strong pattern** with our patent **automatic spring connecting clasps**, with spike opposite (**simplified system**) rendering the stocking of a large no. of special rails unnecessary. To form a circle 6 pieces of 35 mm gauge, and 8 pieces of 48 mm gauge are required.

1042 G

Straight rails

No. 1042G/35 35 mm gauge . . . . dozen **4/10**
— 1042G/48 48 — — . . . . — **6/-**

1042 R and 1040 R

Round rails

No. 1042R/35 35 mm gauge . . . . dozen **4/10**
— 1042R/48 48 — — . . . . — **6/-**

Round rails with terminals

No. 1042RP/35 35 mm gauge . . . . . . dozen **7/4**
— 1042RP/48 48 — — . . . . — **8/6**

Round rails of large radius (to form a circle 12 pieces of 35 mm gauge and 16 pieces of 48 mm gauge are required) for the large locomotives 1513, 1514 (page 168) and 1603/4 (page 167). These rails can be used likewise with **all the electric railways** if a larger circle is wanted.

No. 1040R/35 35 mm gauge . . . . . dozen **6/-** | No. 1040R/48 48 mm gauge . . . . . dozen **7/4**

the same with **terminals**

No. 1040RP/35 35 mm gauge . . . . . dozen **8/6**
— 1040RP/48 48 — — . . . . . — **9/8**

Straight reversing rails

No. 1042UG/48 48 mm gauge . . . . . each **1/2**

Round reversing rails

— 1042UR/48 48 mm gauge . . . . . each **1/2**

1042 UG

Crossings

No. 1042K/35 35 mm gauge . . . . each **3/-**
— 1042K/48 48 — — . . . . — **3/6**

Crossings in large radius to suit 1040R rails

No. 1040K/35 35 mm gauge . . . . each **3/-**
— 1040K/48 48 — — . . . . — **3/6**

1042 K and 1040 K

Switches
☞ **Right and left hand** ☜

No. 1042W/35 35 mm gauge . . . . pair **7/4**
— 1042W/48 48 — — . . . . — **8/6**

Switches of large radius to suit rails 1040R

No. 1040W/35 35 mm gauge . . . . pair **7/4**
— 1040W/48 48 — — . . . . — **8/6**

1042 W and 1040 W

1051/70—72   1051/55B   1051/55   1051/54

Commutators

(current reverser) for all electric railways with permanent magnets, **weak or strong (continuous) current.**

The terminals marked 1 and 2 are for connecting to rail terminals, those marked — and + are for connecting to battery.

No. **1051/70**	plain quality on polished base, $2^1/_2'' \times 1^1/_2''$	each -/10
— **1051/71**	the same, but larger and better quality, $3^1/_2'' \times 2''$	— 1/4
— **1051/72**	larger still and superfine quality with fuse, $4'' \times 2^3/_4''$	— 2/8

1051/52

Regulating resistances

of 3—4 Ohms, for **weak** current, for controlling the speed of model when using freshly filled batteries, which give a slightly higher voltage.

No. **1051/55 B** plain quality
each -/10

No. **1051/55** better quality, on round base
each 1/-

Safety fuse holders

with 3 fuses for **weak** and **strong current**, to protect lamps or motors from injury in case of an accidental short circuit or too much current.

No. **1051/54 A** with 2 terminals
each -/10

No. **1051/54 B** on porcelain, with cover, no terminals and no fuses, each -/4

No. **1051/54 L** fuses for above, 10 pieces -/1

Multiple battery switch

for use with new dry batteries or wet Leclanche batteries with salammoniac, when using 6, 8, or 10 for driving weak current railways.

No. **1051/52** strong quality on round polished base, each 2/8

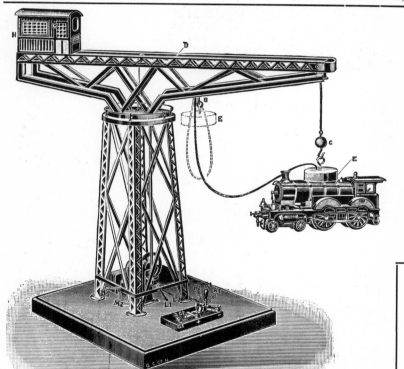

Electric Crane.

This is one of the latest type, scale model, harbour cranes, it combines the following features:

1. **Automatic raising** and **lowering gear,**
2. **Electric winch for lifting loads,**
3. **Automatic stopping device for 1. and 2.**
4. **Automatic turning motion** while other motions are in progress or stationary,
5. **The electric motor** can be disconnected and used for other purposes.

Will lift about $4^1/_2$ lbs., also locomotives, wagons etc.

If a similar weight is put in the engine house, the crane can be used to lift much heavier loads.

High class design and finish, mounted on tiled top wood base.

No. **1112** 19" long, $10^1/_4''$ wide, $19^1/_2''$ high
each 21/6

(For suitable batteries or accumulators see page 185—187.)

Railway Bridges for electric railways,

finest japanning and handsome design.

No. **1975/5**	to suit electric railways, **35 mm gauge,** 34" long	each 6/-
— **1975/8**	to suit electric railways, **48 mm gauge,** 42" long	each 7/-
— **1975/28**	finest quality, with 2 large spans, **48 mm gauge,** 56" long	each 12/-

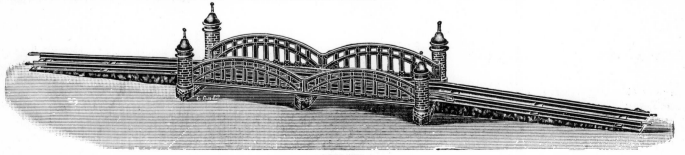

1975/28

Parapet Rails for Electric Railways

Railways, Tramways, Elevated Railways, with central rail conductor for weak or strong current, each end fitted with a connecting spike and one of our patent connecting clasps.

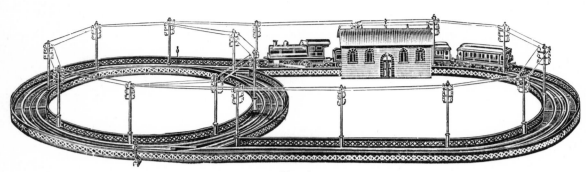

Fig. 1

Illustration of a rail formation, consisting of:
9 round rails **1092 R/48**
1 round rail with terminals **1092 RP/48**
3 straight rails **1092 G/48**
1 straight rail with railway station **1092/5 A**
1 pair of switches **1092 W/48**
16 telegraph poles **1051/12**

Each length of parapet rail is fitted with a socket in which specially made telegraph poles, imitation arc lamps, or arc lamps fitted with miniature screw electric lamps, can be placed; or signals can be arranged all with insulated supports. These fit into the sockets firmly and do not slip about. The rails will form all shapes of track without alteration. Besides these advantages a railway formed of parapet rails looks very realistic. A railway station strongly made of japanned tin improves the appearance of the model. By procuring arched supports the track can be converted into an **"Elevated Railway"**.

1092 R

Round Parapet Rails

No. **1092 R/35**   for **35 mm gauge** . . . . each 1/-
— **1092 RP/35**   the same with terminals — 1/2
— **1092 R/48**   for **48 mm gauge** . . . . — 1/2
— **1092 RP/48**   the same with terminals — 1/6
6 pieces of round rail are required to form a circle with No. **1092 R/35**
8 pieces of round rail are required to form a circle with No. **1092 R/48**

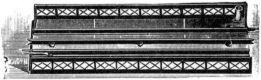

1092 G

Straight Parapet Rails

No. **1092 G/35**   for **35 mm gauge** . . . . each 1/-
— **1092 G/48**   — 48 — — . . . . — 1/2

78 T

Supports

for converting the adjoining parapet railway into an

"Elevated Railway";

with 2 wing nuts, rails require 1 support each, switches and crossings require 2 supports each.

No. **78 T/35**
35 mm gauge, dozen 5/4

No. **78 T/48**
48 mm gauge, dozen 6/-

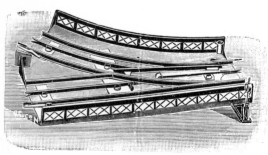

1092 W

Switches with Parapet

right and left hand (2 sockets),

No. **1092 W/35**   for **35 mm gauge** . . . . pair 8/8
— **1092 W/48**   — 48 — — . . . . — 11/-

1092 K

Crossings with Parapet

(2 sockets)

No. **1092 K/35**   for **35 mm gauge** . . . . each 4/6
— **1092 K/48**   — 48 — — . . . . — 5/8

Trade Mark.

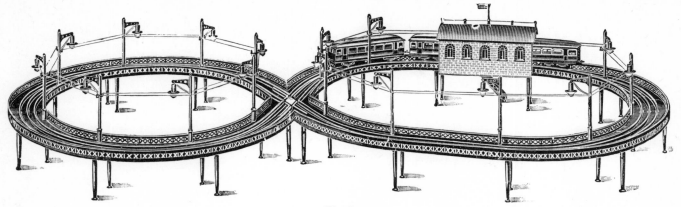

Fig. 2.

Fig. 2 represents an "**Elevated Railway**" with parapet consisting of the following parts: 13 round rails No. 1092 R/48, 1 round rail with terminals No. 1092 RP/48, 1 straight rail No. 1092 G/48, 1 crossing No. 1092 K/48, 1 railway station with 1 length of rail No. 1092/5, 18 supports No. 78 T/48, 16 arc lamps No. 647/47 EO or No. 1051/11.

Supplementary parts for parapet railways

No. 1051/12   1051/13

1094/5 A, 5 AV, 1092/5 A, 5 AV.

1094/5, 5 V, 1092/5, 5 V.

Covered Railway Stations

with 1 length of track,

with central rail conductor for weak or strong current.

No.				
1094/5 A	for 35 mm gauge	each	**7/2**
— 1094/5 AV	the same with provision for 1 incandescent lamp with miniature screw	—	**8/10**
— 1092/5 A	for 48 mm gauge	—	**10/-**
— 1092/5 AV	the same with provision for miniature screw lamp	—	**11/8**
— 1094/5	for **Elevated Railway**, 35 mm gauge	—	**8/-**
— 1094/5 V	the same with provision for miniature screw lamp	—	**9/8**
— 1092/5	for **Elevated Railway**, 48 mm gauge	—	**11/4**
— 1092/5 V	the same with provision for miniature screw lamp	—	**12/10**
— 1051/12	**Telegraph poles** for parapet rails	dozen	**3/8**
— 1051/13	the same insulated with tin stand, 10" high	—	**4/6**
— 647/47 EO	**Arc lamps** (imitation) for parapet rails	—	**3/4**
— 1051/11	— — with 1 miniature screw lamp holder for lighting by accumulator, dry or bichromate batteries, or if placed in series to the corresponding voltage can be lighted by strong current	each	**1/6**

For **incandescent lamps** see page 193, for **telegraph** wire see page 186.

No. 647/47 EO

No. 1051/11

Trade Mark.

Electric Tramways (overhead system).

Several patents.

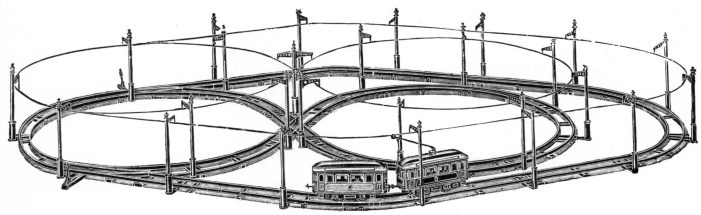

Fig. 1

The above illustration shows how track can be laid in all possible shapes and forms by using the rail parts, switches and crossings listed on page 184. We supply with each railway a book containing diagrams of a large number of different rail formations. The insulated columns with the conducting wires are placed in the rails, one of the columns is fitted with 2 terminals. The railway can be worked by weak current of 3½—4 volts (2 bichromate batteries), those with lamps by 3 bichromate batteries. When using strong current, the lamp resistance on page 164 must be inserted between the connection and the railway. The ordinary carbon filament incandescent lamps 3½ volts with miniature screw page 193 are used in the lighted cars. Each motor wagon with lighting has an incandescent lamp at each end. The lighted trailing cars are fitted with a lamp inside.

For resistances for speed control see page 177.

Several patents.

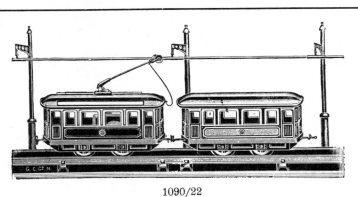

1090/22

Several patents.

Complete Electric Tramway on overhead system

(with trolley) for **weak current.**

With a superior and efficient permanent magnet with geared drive, packed in handsome box.

For **35 mm gauge,** consisting of:

No. 1090/21 **Motor wagon,** 6 round rails, 6 standards incl. 1 with terminals, with wires, 7½" long, total length of rails 6 feet 2" . . . . each 9/-

— 1090/22 **Motor wagon and trailing car,** 6 round and 2 straight rails, 8 standards incl. 1 with terminals, with wires, length of train 15½", total length of rails 8 feet . . . . each 12/6

☞ By inserting a lamp resistance No. 1075, page 164 between connection and railway, the above railways can be worked by strong current though only **continuous current** may be used, the resistance must be fitted with 2 carbon filament lamps of 32 c. p. each and of same voltage as supply.

For extra rails, crossings and switches see page 184.

Trade  Mark.

Electric Tramways on Overhead System
for weak or strong current

1091/22

Trolley contact

with an excellently working permanent magnet with geared drive, packed in handsome box.

For **weak current, 48 mm gauge,** consisting of:

No. 1091/21   **Motor wagon,** 8 round rails, 8 standards (including 1 standard with terminals) 8 wires, 9½" long, total length of rails 9 feet 3" . . . . each **17/6**

— 1091/22   **Motor wagon and trailing car,** 8 round and 4 straight rails, 12 standards (incl. 1 terminal standard), with 12 wires, length of train 19", total length of rails 13 feet 8" . . . . each **23/-**

— 1091/21 **V**   the same tramway as No. 1091/21 but with **2 electric head lights** . . . . each **20/-**
— 1091/22 **V**   — — — — 1091/22 — — 2 — — — and lighted trailing car . . . . . — **27/-**

For **strong current,** consisting of:
No. 1091/21 **H**   **Motor wagon** etc. as No. 1091/21 . . . . each **19/-**
— 1091/22 **H**   — — **and trailing car** etc. as No. 1091/22 . . . . — **24/8**
— 1091/21 **HV**   as No. 1091/21 H but with **2 electric head lights** . . . . — **23/8**
— 1091/22 **HV**   — — 1091/22 H — — 2 — — — and lighted trailing car . . . . — **30/8**

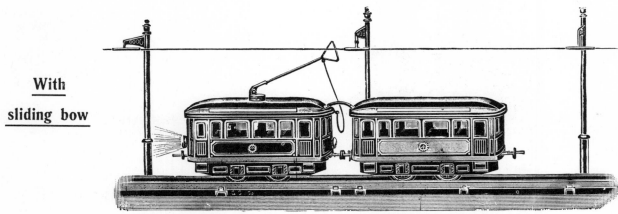

With sliding bow

With sliding bow

1091/82 V

Exactly the same as above described, but **with sliding bow** instead of trolley contact.

For **weak current, 48 mm gauge,** consisting of:
No. 1091/81   **Motor wagon,** 8 round rails, 8 standards (incl. 1 terminal standard) with 8 wires, 9½" long, total length of rails 9 feet 3", each **17/6**
— 1091/82   — — **and trailing car,** 8 round and 4 straight rails, 12 standards (incl. 1 terminal standard), with 12 wires, length of train 19", total length of rails 13 feet 8" . . . . each **23/-**
— 1091/81 **V**   the same tramway as No. 1091/81, but with **2 electric head lights** . . . . — **20/-**
— 1091/82 **V**   — — — — 1091/82, — — 2 — — — and lighted trailing car . . . . . — **27/-**

For **strong current,** consisting of:
No. 1091/81 **H**   **Motor wagon,** etc. as No. 1091/81 . . . . each **19/-**
— 1091/82 **H**   — — **and trailing car,** etc. as 1091/82 . . . . — **24/8**
— 1091/81 **HV**   as No. 1091/81 H, but with **2 electric head lights** . . . . — **23/8**
— 1091/82 **HV**   — — 1091/82 H, — — 2 — — — and lighted trailing car . . . . — **30/8**

☞ The **strong current** tramways for continuous or alternating current are ready for connecting to lamp holder etc. after a lamp resistance page 164 has been inserted between connection and the tramway. ☜

For bichromate batteries and accumulators for working weak current railways see pages 185—187.

For extra rails, crossings and switches see page 184.

Trade  Mark.

Special Electric Tramways on Overhead System
with commutator for reversing (patented).

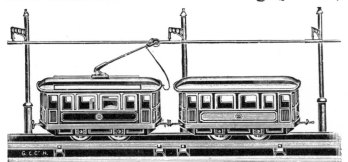

Trolley contact   Trolley contact

1090/72

The reversing is effected by simply turning the trolley pole in the proper position for the car to run, just the same as the actual cars are reversed at the end of the journey. This method considerably adds to the interest of the model.

Weak current, 35 mm gauge
with an excellently working permanent magnet, with geared drive, packed in handsome boxes.

No. 1090/71   **Motor wagon** with **reversing attachment**, 6 round rails, 6 standards (including one with terminals), with wires, 7½" long, total length of rails 6 ft 2" . . . . each **10/8**

— 1090/72   **Motor wagon** and **trailing car**, 6 round and 2 straight rails, 8 standards (including one with terminals) with wires, length of train 15½", total length of rails 8 ft . . . . each **14/-**

☞ The above tramways can be worked with **strong current** (only continuous current) by inserting in the circuit a lamp resistance (page 164) fitted with 2 carbon filament lamps of 32 c. p. each and of voltage to suit supply.

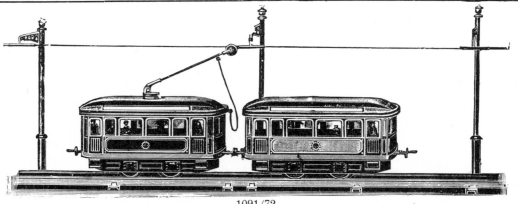

Trolley

System   Trolley

System

1091/72

The same tramway as described above, but for

weak current, 48 mm gauge: consisting of:

No. 1091/71   **Motor wagon** with **reversing attachment**, 8 round rails, 8 standards (including one with terminals), with wires, 9½" long, total length of rails 9 ft. 3" . . . . each **19/-**

— 1091/72   **Motor wagon** and **trailing car**, 8 round and 4 straight rails, 12 standards (including one with terminals), 12 wires, length of train 19", total length of rails 13 ft. 8" . . . . . each **24/8**

— 1091/71 V   The same railway as 1091/71, but with **2 electric head lamps** . . . . each **21/6**
— 1091/72 V   — — — — 1091/72, — 2 — — — and lighted trailing car . . . . — **28/8**
With the motor wagons with head lights, only the lamp in the direction the car is running lights up.

Strong current:
— 1091/71 H   **Motor wagon** etc. as 1091/71 . . . . — **20/6**
— 1091/72 H   **Motor wagon** and trailing car etc. as 1091/72 . . . . — **26/-**
— 1091/71 HV   as 1091/71 H, but with **2 electric head ligths** . . . . — **24/6**
— 1091/72 HV   — 1091/72 H, — 2 — — — and lighted trailing car . . . . . . — **31/8**

☞ The **strong current** railways marked "H" for continuous or alternating current can be connected at once to the supply, but must have inserted between connection and railway, a lamp resistance (page 164).

For extra rails, crossings, and switches see page 184.

For **bichromate batteries** and accumulators for working **weak current** railways see pages 185—187.

Trade 🜸 Mark.

Electric Tramways **overhead system**
with **special reversing arrangement.**

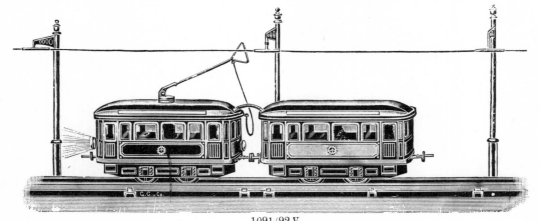

Sliding bow contact.

Sliding bow contact.

1091/92 V

These cars are reversed by simply turning the pole round in the position opposite to the direction of the motion of the car. As this method of reversing is used in actual practice, it adds considerably to the interest of the model.

Weak current, 48 mm gauge:
consisting of:

No. **1091/91**   **Motor wagon** with **reversing attachment**, 8 round rails and 8 standards (including one with terminals), with wires, 9$^{1}/_{2}$" long, total length of rails 9 feet 3" . . . . each **19/-**

— **1091/92**   **Motor wagon** and **trailing çar**, 8 round and 4 straight rails, 12 standards (including one with terminals), with wires, length of train 19", total length of rails 13 feet 8" . . . . each **24/8**

No. **1091/91 V**   the same tramway as 1091/91, but with **2 electric head lights** . . . . each **21/6**
— **1091/92 V**   —   —   —   — 1091/92,   —   **2**   —   —   —   and **lighted trailing car** . . . . — **28/8**

The head lights only light up in the direction the car runs.

_____

Strong current:
No. **1091/91 H**   Motor wagon etc., as 1091/91 . . . . each **20/6**
— **1091/92 H**   —   —   and **trailing car** etc., as 1091/92 . . . . — **26/-**
— **1091/91 HV**   as 1091/91 H, but with 2 electric head lights . . . . — **24/6**
— **1091/92 HV**   — 1091/92 H,   —   **2**   —   —   —   and lighted trailing car . . . . — **31/8**

1080/2

Barmen-Elberfeld Hanging Railway
for **weak** or **strong current.** Very strong, handsomely finished and japanned.

For **weak current,** 6 volts (4 bichromate batteries) are required to work the railway. For strong current, either continuous or alternating, a lamp resistance page 164 must be inserted between the connection and railway.

No. **1080/2**   **Weak çurrent** ⎱   without station and without lengthening piece, only oval track, 6 feet long, 16" wide, ⎱ . each **40/-**
— **1080/2 H**   **Strong**   —   ⎰   13" high, with full instructions   ⎰   — **53/-**
— **1081**   **Middle piece** with **supports** to lengthen the formation, 30" long . . . . — **13/-**

_____

The strong **current railways** marked "H" for continuous or alternating current are ready for connecting to lamp holder etc. after ☞ a lamp resistance (page 164) has been inserted between the connection and the railway.

For extra rails, crossings and switches, see page 184.
For **bichromate batteries and accumulators** for working **weak current** railways, see pages 185—187.

Separate **Rail Accessories** for electric tramways etc.
for **overhead system.**

The standards are insulated and are fitted to the rails after the wire has been fastened (patented).

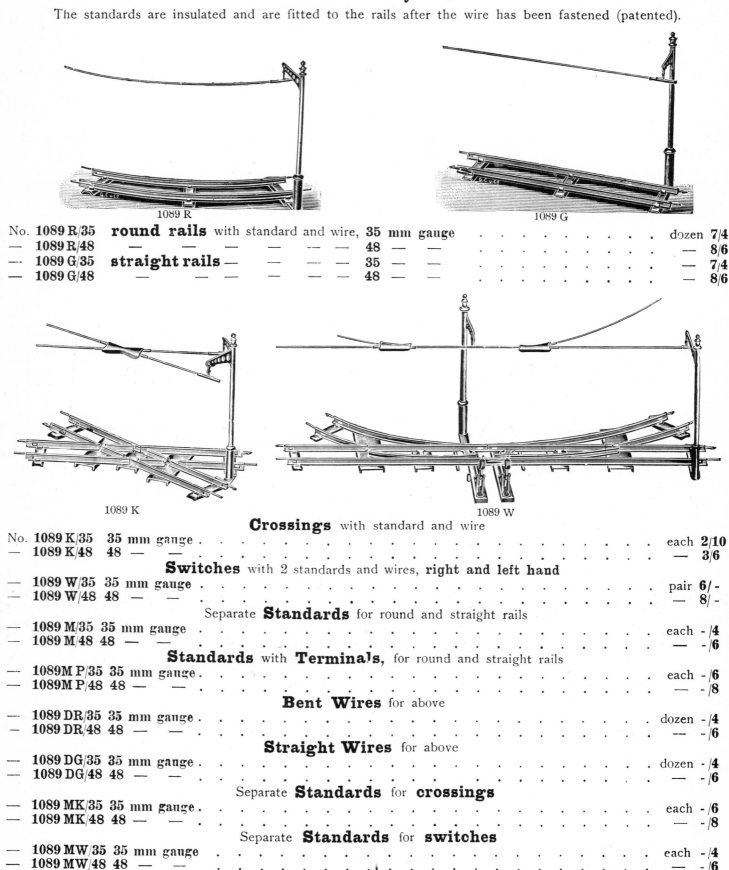

No. 1089 R/35	**round rails** with standard and wire, **35 mm gauge**	dozen	7/4
— 1089 R/48	— — — — — 48 — —	—	8/6
— 1089 G/35	**straight rails** — — — 35 — —	—	7/4
— 1089 G/48	— — — — — 48 — —	—	8/6

Crossings with standard and wire

| No. 1089 K/35 | 35 mm gauge | each | 2/10 |
| — 1089 K/48 | 48 — — | — | 3/6 |

Switches with 2 standards and wires, **right and left hand**

| — 1089 W/35 | 35 mm gauge | pair | 6/- |
| — 1089 W/48 | 48 — | — | 8/- |

Separate **Standards** for round and straight rails

| — 1089 M/35 | 35 mm gauge | each | -/4 |
| — 1089 M/48 | 48 — | — | -/6 |

Standards with **Terminals**, for round and straight rails

| — 1089 M P/35 | 35 mm gauge | each | -/6 |
| — 1089 M P/48 | 48 — | — | -/8 |

Bent Wires for above

| — 1089 DR/35 | 35 mm gauge | dozen | -/4 |
| — 1089 DR/48 | 48 — | — | -/6 |

Straight Wires for above

| — 1089 DG/35 | 35 mm gauge | dozen | -/4 |
| — 1089 DG/48 | 48 — | — | -/6 |

Separate **Standards** for **crossings**

| — 1089 MK/35 | 35 mm gauge | each | -/6 |
| — 1089 MK/48 | 48 — | — | -/8 |

Separate **Standards** for **switches**

| — 1089 MW/35 | 35 mm gauge | each | -/4 |
| — 1089 MW/48 | 48 — | — | -/6 |

Batteries and Accumulators

for all the previously described electric motors and railways

Bichromate batteries

with carbon and zinc.

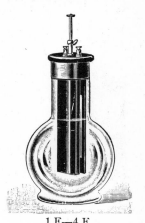

| 1 A | 1 B | 0 C | 0 F | 1 F—4 F |

No. **1 A** round glass cell, 2″ diam., 4″ high, with wood cover . . . . each 1/6
— **1 B** rectangular glass cell, 2³/4″ long, 2″ wide, 5″ high, with wood cover . . . — 2/-
— **0 C** carbon container, 3¹/2″ diam., 4″ high, with porcelain cover . . . . . — 3/-
— **0 F** glass cell with 2 carbons and **lifting** zinc, 2³/4″ diam. 4³/4″ high . . . — 3/2

Bottle form batteries, well finished with 2 carbons and lifting zinc.

No. **1 F** 1/2 pint size . . . . each 3/6 | No. **3 F** 2 pint size . . . . each 6/6
— **2 F** 1 — — . . . . — 4/8 | — **4 F** 4 — — . . . . — 11/-

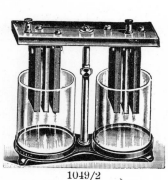

| 1047/2 | 1049/2 | 1049/3 | 1049/4 |

No. **1047/2 Double cell battery** with adjustable lifting elements, with glass cells, each with 1 carbon and zinc . . . . each 9/8

Batteries with lifting elements, high class finish on japanned cast iron stands.

Wood cover with **strong lifting mechanism,** adjustable for height, 2 carbon plates and 1 zinc per cell, with full printed instructions for working in series or parallels as well as for grouping in the case of 1049/4 — very strongly made.

No. **1049/2** with 2 Cells . . . . each 9/8
— **1049/3** — 3 — . . . . — 14/6
— **1049/4** — 4 — . . . . — 19/6

To suit battery	**Glass jars, zincs and carbons for batteries.**										**Zinc plates and carbon jars 0 c**
	0 F	**1 A**	**1 B**	**1047**	**1049**	**1F**	**2F**	**3F**	**4F**		
length ⎱ of carbon	3¹/4″		3¹/2″		4″	5″	6″	7¹/2″	8³/4″		
width ⎰	1³/4″		1¹/2″		2″	1″	1¹/4″	1¹/2″	2″		Diam. . . . . 3¹/4″
length ⎱ of zinc	1¹/4″		3¹/2″		4″	2″	2¹/2″	3¹/2″	4″		Height . . . . 4″
width ⎰	1³/4″		1¹/2″		2″	1″	1¹/4″	1¹/2″	2″		Carbon . . . . -/10 each
price of carbon	-/8		-/6		-/10	-/4	-/6	-/10	1/2 each		Zinc 2¹/2″ long, 1³/4″ wide
— — zinc	-/6		-/10		1/-	-/4	-/6	-/10	1/2 —		each -/4
— — glass jar	-/6	-/2	-/6		-/8	-/6	-/10	1/4	2/- —		

No. **1035/1** **Prepared chemicals for bichromate batteries,** only requires dissolving in warm water, 2 oz. bottle . . . . each -/8
— **1035/2** the same in 7 oz. bottles . . . . — 1/10
— **1035 P/50** finely powdered bichromate of potash in 2 oz. boxes . . . . — -/4
— **1035 P/100** — — — in 1/4 lb. boxes . . . . — -/6
— **1035 P** — — — in quantities of 2 lbs. . . . . — 2/8

Trade ⚙ Mark.

Batteries

for induction apparatus, bell sets, Morse apparatus, wireless telegraphy etc.

☞ **Improved type, more efficiency, greater regularity and longer life.**

Filling batteries can be stocked for any time without deterioration, they only need to be filled with water and are then ready for use.

Single Cell Dry Battery 1,5 to 1,6 Volt.

No. **1 L** filling battery, 3½"×1¼"×1¼" . each 1/10

— **1 T** the same, as **dry battery** each 1/10

— **3 L** filling battery, 5"×2¼"×2¼" . . each 4/-

Wet Batteries for constant use 1,5 to 1,6 Volts

excellent efficiency, chemicals supplied.

No **00 D** rectangular, 6"×2½"×2½" each 2/4

— **0 D** round, 5½"×2¾" each 2/-

00 D   0 D

Triple Cell Dry Batteries, 3,5—4 Volts

for small electric motors, small electric railways, pocket lamps, cranes No. 1110—1112, arc lamps No. 1051/17 etc.

No. **1 P** can be stocked 3 months . . each -/8

— **1 PG** for 6—9 months each -/10

— **1 PA** the same but **for filling** . . . . each 1/-

1 P and 1 PG   1 PA

Double Cell Dry Batteries, 3 Volts

1½"×2½"×2¾"

No. **1 K** as dry battery ready for use . . . . each 1/6

— **1 KA** the same but **for filling** . . . . each 1/8

1 K   1 KA

Separate Accessories for Electrical Apparatus.

Silk and cotton covered wires.

1031

Double cotton covered.

No. **1031 B/3**	0,3 mm thick,	coil of 10 yards . .	-/6
— **1031 B/4**	0,4 — —	— 10 — . .	-/6
— **1031 B/5**	0,5 — —	— 10 — . .	-/8
— **1031 B/6**	0,6 — —	— 10 — . .	-/10
— **1031 B/8**	0,8 — —	— 10 — .	1/-
— **1031 B/10**	1 — —	— 10 — . .	1/4

Double silk covered (green).

No. **1031 S/1**	0,1 mm thick,	coil of 25 yards . .	-/8
— **1031 S/2**	0,2 — —	— 25 — . .	-/10
— **1031 S/3**	0,3 — —	— 10 — . .	-/6
— **1031 S/4**	0,4 — —	— 10 — . .	-/8
— **1031 S/5**	0,5 — —	— 10 — . .	-/10
— **1031 S/8**	0,8 — —	— 10 — . .	1/6

When ordering in 2 lb. lots, the prices are as follows:

	No. **1031 B/5**	6	8	10	**1031 S/5**	8
2 ℔	10/-	9/8	9/-	7/8	19/6	16/10

Duplex wire, well covered, No. **1031 DL** 3/4"×1/32" thick . . . . yard -/10
Induction coil cords (green) — **1031 J** . . . . — -/4

Brass terminals.

     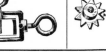

58/0-1½   58/2   58/3   58/4   58/5   58/6   59/1 and 2

No. **58/0** ½" long, with fixing screw . . . . doz. 1/4
— **58/1** 9/16" — the same — . . . . — 1/6

No. **58/1½**	11/16" long, the same	doz. 2/6
— **58/2**	13/16" — —	— 2/6
— **58/3**	13/16" — with rough conical screw for wood	— 2/6
— **58/4**	13/16" — — slit	— 1/8
— **58/5**	1⅛" — — 2 terminal screws —	— 3/-
— **58/6**	Clamps for large galvanic batteries, 1½" long	— 4/10
— **59/1**	**Star contacts**, 3/8" diam.	— -/10
— **59/2**	— — 9/16" —	— 1/4

Armature commutators for electric motors, railways etc.

1037

No. **1037/000**	00	0	1	2	3	3½	3½H	4	4½	4½H	5
of	3	1	2	2	3	2	3	3	2	3	3 parts
diam.	9/32	9/32	9/32	3/8	3/8	9/16	9/16	9/16	5/8	5/8	5/8	1 "
each	-/2	-/4	-/8	-/6	-/8	-/10	-/10	1/4	1/-	1/-	1/4	1/6

The commutators marked „H" are for motors **wound for strong current**.

1037/9

1037/11   1037/12

1037/6—7   1037/8 and 10

No. **1037/6** Brass brush springs for **weak current** motors 1½" long . . . . . . doz. -/3
— **1037/6½** the same, 1¾" long . . . . — -/4
— **1037/7** German silver for **strong current** . . . . — -/6
— **1037/8** **Copper brushes** for **strong current** motors, 2" long, 5/16" wide, 1/8" thick, each 3/-
— **1037/10** **Carbon brushes** for **strong current** motors, 2/3" long, 3/16" diam. . . . . — -/10
— **1037/9** **Sliding springs** for electric railways with centre rail (only work one way) 3" long . . . . doz. 1/4
— **1037/11** the same but for running in both directions, 3¼" long . . . . — 2/6
— **1037/12** the same but for cheap quality reversing railway with centre rail . . . . — -/4

Accumulators.

Specially adapted for working **weak current electric motors, electric railways, small lighting sets, miniature arc lamps** etc. Very specially adapted for working shop window attractions, when long continuous running is required. The accumulators are fitted **with terminals,** and are consigned without solution, they must be filled immediately upon receipt with chemically pure sulpuric acid diluted to 24° (viz. 1,2 specific gravity) by means of a glass or porcelain funnel and then charged. After 3 or better 4 chargings after first using, the cell is ready for work and reaches the capacity given separately with each cell. Full printed instructions are supplied with each cell. Each cell when loaded has a tension of 2,1—2,2 volts and must not be discharged below 1,75 volts, 2 cells in series have therefore about 4 volts, 3 cells, 6 volts etc.

By **capacity** of an accumulator is meant the amount of the current flowing from the discharging accumulator, multiplied by the length of time in hours till the voltage per cell drops to 1,8 volts. This is expressed in ampere-hours. Suppose an accumulator discharges 1 ampere for 10 hours, this would be $1 \times 10 = 10$ ampere-hours capacity. Now it must be taken into consideration that an accumulator which is charged or discharged slowly has a much greater capacity than one soon charged or discharged. The capacity and the time of discharge of an accumulator must not be confused. The duration of light in the case of a lamp is proportional to the amount of current used by the lamp. Take for example No. 1038/6 by which 1 ampere is discharged for 36 hours, capacity 36 ampere-hours. If 1 ampere is used by a lamp the light lasts 36 hours, but with 2 lamps each using 1 ampere the duration is not only half but even less owing to the overload of 2 amps., so about 13 hours light is obtained. If a lamp using about $1/2$ an ampere is connected, this would give a light for more than 72 hours.

The strength of the charging, as well as the discharging current exercises a considerable influence on the capacity. The weaker the charging current the more the accumulator is able to take up the current; the weaker the discharging current the more energy it is able to give out.

| 1038/2¹/₂ | 1038/3 | 1038/6 | 1038/20—26 | 1038/30—33 |

Accumulators, 1 cell (2 volts) can be exported uncharged, ribbed glass case with terminals.

No.	1038/1	1038/2	1038/2¹/₂	1038/3	1038/4¹/₂	1038/6	1038/7	1038/9
Capacity in ampere-hours . .	4	6	8	14	28	36	54	72 amp.
Maximum charging current .	0,6	0,8	1,2	1,8	3,6	5	7,5	10 —
— discharging current	0,8	1,2	1,8	2,7	5,4	7,5	10,5	15
Length	2″	2¼″	3½″	4″	4″	4¾″	5″	5″
Width	1¾″	1¾″	1½″	2″	2¾″	3″	4½″	7¼″
Height	5½″	6½″	5¼″	7″	7½″	7½″	8″	8″
each	4/-	5/6	6/6	8/6	12/10	20/-	30/-	42/-

Accumulators: encased in double ribbed glass, **2 cells in one glass (4 volts).**

No.	1038/20	1038/21	1038/23	1038/26
Capacity in ampere-hours	2,1	4	8	18
Current in amperes . . .	0,3	0,4	0,8	1,8
Length	1½″	3½″	4″	4½″
Width	2¼″	2″	3½″	5″
Heigth	4″	5½″	5¼″	8″
each	6/10	10/10	16/-	32/-

Accumulators: **double cell in wood cases (4 volts), very light portable type.**

No.	1038/30	1038/31	1038/33
Capacity in ampere-hours . . .	2,2	4	7,8
Maximum charging current. . .	0,3	0,4	0,8
— discharging current .	0,5	0,6	1,2
Length	3½″	4½″	4″
Width	2″	2¾″	4½″
Height	4½″	6½″	6½″
each	9/8	14/-	19/-

☞ **The resistance No. 1074 and 1075, page 164 are suitable for use in charging the above accumulators. For current testing appliances and pole finders see page 188.**

Trade Mark.

Electrical Measuring Instruments

very accurate and reliable, in handsome nickelled brass watch cases, will indicate in any position, scarcely warm when in action.

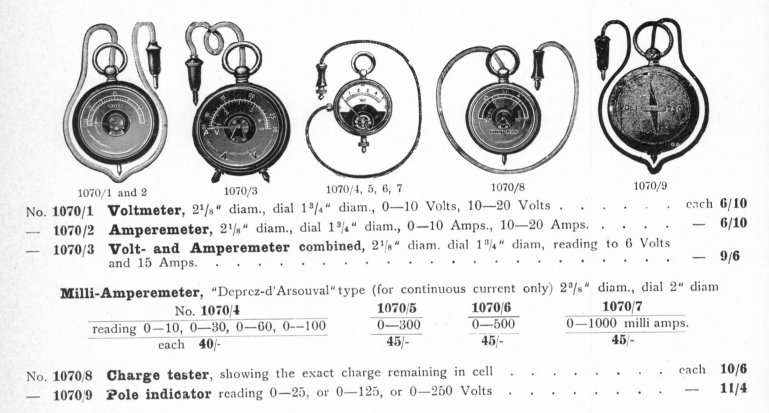

| 1070/1 and 2 | 1070/3 | 1070/4, 5, 6, 7 | 1070/8 | 1070/9 |

No. 1070/1 **Voltmeter**, 2¹/₈" diam., dial 1³/₄" diam., 0—10 Volts, 10—20 Volts . . . . . each **6/10**

— 1070/2 **Amperemeter**, 2¹/₈" diam., dial 1³/₄" diam., 0—10 Amps., 10—20 Amps. . . . . — **6/10**

— 1070/3 **Volt- and Amperemeter combined**, 2¹/₈" diam. dial 1³/₄" diam, reading to 6 Volts and 15 Amps. — **9/6**

Milli-Amperemeter, "Deprez-d'Arsouval" type (for continuous current only) 2³/₈" diam., dial 2" diam

No. **1070/4**	**1070/5**	**1070/6**	**1070/7**
reading 0—10, 0—30, 0—60, 0—100	0—300	0—500	0—1000 milli amps.
each **40/-**	**45/-**	**45/-**	**45/-**

No. 1070/8 **Charge tester**, showing the exact charge remaining in cell . . . . each **10/6**

— 1070/9 **Pole indicator** reading 0—25, or 0—125, or 0—250 Volts . . . . — **11/4**

1070/10   1070/11

Miniature Measuring Instruments,

accurate reading, patented, in brass case with 2 terminals, for fixing to switch board, 1¹/₄" outside diam.

No. 1070/10 **Voltmeter** reading between 2—8 Volts . . . each **1/8**

— 1070/11 **Milli-Amperemeter** between 0—500 milli amps. — **1/8**

Accessories for strong current connections.

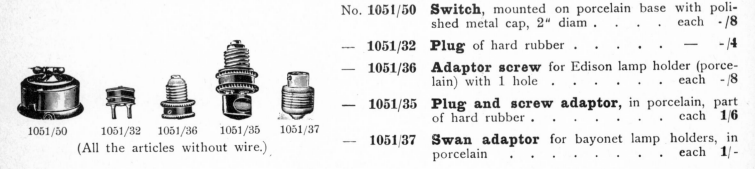

1051/50   1051/32   1051/36   1051/35   1051/37

(All the articles without wire.)

No. 1051/50 **Switch**, mounted on porcelain base with polished metal cap, 2" diam . . . . each **-/8**

— 1051/32 **Plug** of hard rubber . . . . . — **-/4**

— 1051/36 **Adaptor screw** for Edison lamp holder (porcelain) with 1 hole . . . . . . each **-/8**

— 1051/35 **Plug and screw adaptor**, in porcelain, part of hard rubber . . . . each **1/6**

— 1051/37 **Swan adaptor** for bayonet lamp holders, in porcelain . . . . each **1/-**

Dynamos
for lighting or power.

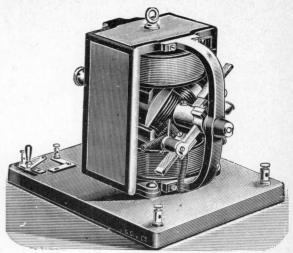

For practical work, suitable for electrical engineering students, schools, experimental purposes etc., specially adapted for illustrating the principles of the large machines now so extensively used. They are mounted on strong base with terminals, with double-T-armature fitted with grooved driving pulley. The dynamos give from 1 to 1½ amps. according to no. of revolutions they are shunt wound. When run at 3000 to 4000 rev. per minute are not only capable of lighting incandescent lamps, but of suppling current for induction apparatus, spark coils, small electric motors plating outfits, also for charging accumulators if a suitable lamp is inserted in the circuit.

1067/6 and 10

1066/25

Very strong and of high class finish

No.										each	
1067/6	for	6 volts.	4¾" long,	4¼" wide,	4" high	. . . .	each	**23/-**
—	**1067/10**	— 10 —	6¾" —	5" —	4¾" —	. . . .	—	**33/-**
—	**1066/25**	— 25 —	8" —	6¾" —	7½" —	. . . .	—	**65/-**

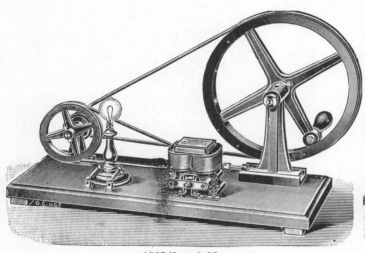

1068/6 and 25

1068/10

The above dynamos arranged for hand driving, with adjustable tension to driving cord, flywheel and stand, with lamp stand to take miniature screw lamp and incandescent lamp,
mounted on highly polished board.

No.				each	
1068/6	with dynamo 1067/6	. . . .	each	**56/-**
—	**1068/10**	— — 1067/10 driving wheel with adjustable tension lamp stand with lamp	. . . .	—	**70/-**
—	**1068/25**	with dynamo 1066/25	. . . .	—	**98/-**

1041/11

No.	**1041/10**	**Driving attachment** with adjustable tension, with holes for fixing, to suit above dynamos 1067 and 1066, of well japanned cast iron wheel, 10¼" diam. each **19/-**
—	**1041/12**	the same with wheel, 13½" diam. . — **30/-**
—	**1041/11**	**Intermediate pulley stand** to suit above, well japanned cast iron, 4½" high . each **5/-**
—	**1041/13**	**Round belting** for above . . . yard **1/6**

1041/10

Trade ⚙ Mark.

Hand driven Lighting Dynamos.

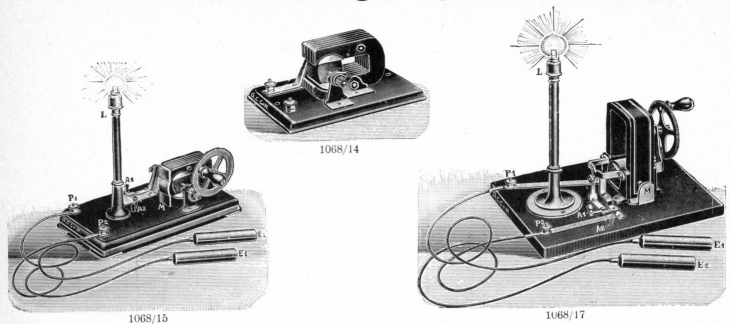

1068/14

1068/15   1068/17

With superior permanent magnets, fitted with double-T-armature, generating **alternating current**. Very suitable for medical purposes. Complete with lamp stand and incandescent lamp.

No. **1068/15** Lighting dynamo with geared drive, easy to turn, output about 3½ volts, 0,2 amps., alternating current, lamp stand fitted with miniature screw lamp of 3½ volts. This dynamo is provided with a switch by which the current is cut off from the lamp and used as a medical machine, 2 handles with flexible cords are supplied with each set. Strongly made and mounted on metal base, 6½" long, 4½" wide, 5½" high . . . . each **8/-**

— **1068/17** Lighting dynamo as above but larger, output about 4 volts, 0,25 amps, with handles for use as medical machine, also regulator. Very strong quality, mounted on highly polished wood board, 7¼" long, 4¾" wide, 7" high . . . . each **14/-**

— **1068/14** Dynamo of No. 1068/15 without other apparatus for driving by power . . . . — **4/-**

Hand driven Lighting Dynamos.

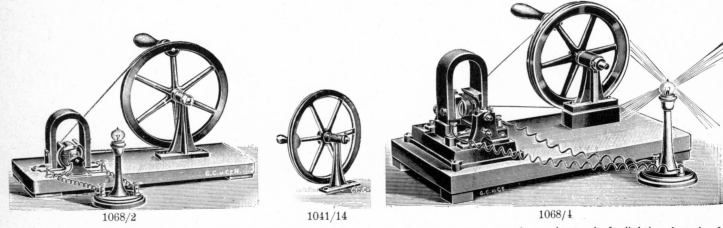

1068/2   1041/14   1068/4

With excellent permanent magnets fitted with double-T-armature, generating **continuous current** can be used not only for lighting, but also for working **small motors** not requiring much current, for **plating**, and further, for **charging accumulators** (by inserting in the circuit a suitable lamp).

No. **1068/2** Lighting dynamo, complete, driving attachment, lamp stand with lamp 3½—4 volts, 0,2 amps. (lamp with miniature screw), mounted on highly polished wood board, 9" long, 4" wide, 4½" high . . . . each **11/-**

— **1068/4** Lighting dynamo, complete, larger, giving 5 volts, 0,25 amps., most substantial construction, 12" long, 5½" wide, 7½" high — **22/-**

— **1068/11** Dynamo only of No. 1068/2 . . . . — **8/-**

— **1068/12** — — — 1068/4 . . . . — **12/6**

— **1041/14** Driving attachment only of No. 1068/2 well japanned cast iron . . . . — **2/4**

— **1041/15** — — — — 1068/4 — . . . . — **3/8**

For incandescent lamps to suit above dynamos see page 193.
For additional apparatus to suit above dynamos see page 191.
For apparatus for decomposition of water see page 191.

Trade  Mark.

Separate Additional Demonstration Apparatus.

Apparatus for giving ocular demonstration of the effects of electricity. Current can be supplied, to amount stated, by dynamos, batteries or accumulators.

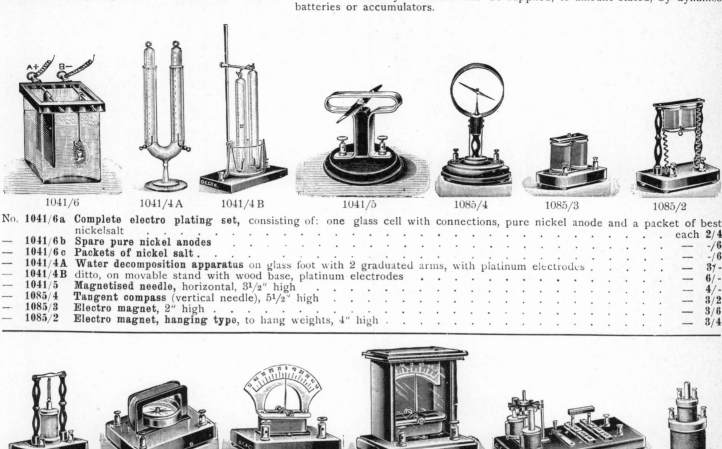

1041/6	1041/4 A	1041/4 B	1041/5	1085/4	1085/3	1085/2

No. 1041/6a **Complete electro plating set,** consisting of: one glass cell with connections, pure nickel anode and a packet of best nickelsalt . . . . each **2/4**
— 1041/6b **Spare pure nickel anodes** . . . . — **-/6**
— 1041/6c **Packets of nickel salt** . . . . — **-/6**
— 1041/4A **Water decomposition apparatus** on glass foot with 2 graduated arms, with platinum electrodes . . . . — **3/-**
— 1041/4B **ditto,** on movable stand with wood base, platinum electrodes . . . . — **6/-**
— 1041/5 **Magnetised needle,** horizontal, 3½" high . . . . — **4/-**
— 1085/4 **Tangent compass** (vertical needle), 5½" high . . . . — **3/2**
— 1085/3 **Electro magnet,** 2" high . . . . — **3/6**
— 1085/2 **Electro magnet, hanging type,** to hang weights, 4" high . . . . — **3/4**

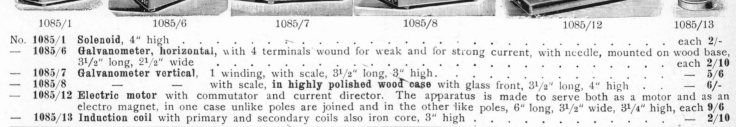

1085/1	1085/6	1085/7	1085/8	1085/12	1085/13

No. 1085/1 **Solenoid,** 4" high . . . . each **2/-**
— 1085/6 **Galvanometer, horizontal,** with 4 terminals wound for weak and for strong current, with needle, mounted on wood base, 3½" long, 2½" wide . . . . each **2/10**
— 1085/7 **Galvanometer vertical,** 1 winding, with scale, 3½" long, 3" high . . . . — **5/6**
— 1085/8 — — with scale, **in highly polished wood case** with glass front, 3½" long, 4" high . — **6/-**
— 1085/12 **Electric motor** with commutator and current director. The apparatus is made to serve both as a motor and as an electro magnet, in one case unlike poles are joined and in the other like poles, 6" long, 3½" wide, 3¼" high, each **9/6**
— 1085/13 **Induction coil** with primary and secondary coils also iron core, 3" high . . . . — **2/10**

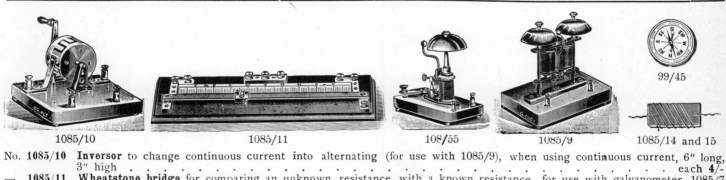

1085/10	1085/11	108/55	1085/9	99/45 1085/14 and 15

No. 1085/10 **Inversor** to change continuous current into alternating (for use with 1085/9), when using continuous current, 6" long, 3" high . . . . each **4/-**
— 1085/11 **Wheatstone bridge** for comparing an unknown resistance with a known resistance, for use with galvanometer 1085/7 or 1085/8 with sliding contact and scale of 100 divisions to the wire, 10" long, 3" wide . . . . . . each **3/6**
— 1085/5 **Bell on stand** with key, 4" high, 3½" long . . . . — **3/4**
— 1085/9 **Alternating current electric bells,** 4" high, 3¾" long . . . . — **6/-**

Resistances on flat wood	No. 1085/14/1	1 ohm			dozen **1/4**	the same, double wound	No. 1085/15/1	1 ohm		dozen **7/4**
	— 1085/14/2	2	—		— **1/6**	with 2 terminals	— 1085/15/2	2 —		**8/6**
	— 1085/14/5	5	—		— **2/2**	on polished wood bobbin	— 1085/15/5	5 —		**9/8**

No. **99/45** **Compass** in brass case, 1¾" diameter, each **1/-**

For batteries, see pages 185—186. — For accumulators, see page 187.

Complete electric Light Plant

consisting of one **Dynamo** and one **Steam Engine**, strongly made and reliable working model, with recent improvements. The engine can be used to drive models if required.

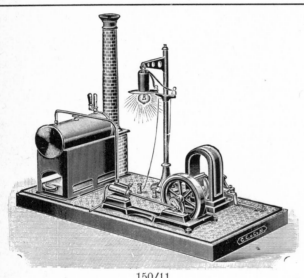

150/10

No. **150/10** Horizontal Steam Engine

with brass boiler of steel-blue oxydized finish, spring safety valve; whistle, oscillating cylinder geared direct to

Dynamo

by a pair of gear wheels, also incandescent lamp with miniature screw and holder, 4 Volt, 0,2 Amp. The engine is fitted with pulley for driving models and the whole mounted on a wooden base with tiled tin-plate top, 10¾" long, 6¼" wide, 9¾" high . . . each **13/6**

No. **150/11** Horizontal Steam Engine

with steel-blue oxydized brass boiler, spring safety valve, whistle, automatic lubricating attachment, oscillating brass cylinder, with **detachable gearing** (for the driving of models without dynamo), with

Dynamo,

switch, handsome **lamp stand** with arc light pattern, incandescent lamp, 4 Volt, 0,2 Amp., with miniature screw, the whole mounted on wooden base with tiled tin-plate face,

12½" long, 8" wide, 13½" high . . . each **26/-**

150/11

No. **150/12** Horizontal Steam Engine

with steel-blue oxydized brass boiler, spring safety valve, whistle, water gauge, pressure gauge, starting cock, automatic lubricating attachment, superior double action fixed slide valve cylinder, with patent valve gear and patent ball pressing attachment, with **detachable gear-wheel-coupling** to

Dynamo

(for the driving of models without dynamo), switch, handsome lamp stand, with model arc lamp pattern, incandescent lamp with "Mignon" screw, 4 Volt, 0,25 Amp., mounted on wooden base with tiled tin-plate face,

13½" long, 9½" wide, 17" high . . . each **34/6**

| No. **1045/4** | Incandescent lamps for replacements to suit No. 150/10 and 11 . each -/**10** |
| — **1045/21 M** | Incandescent lamps for replacements to suit No. 150/12 . . . . each **1/-** |

150/12

Trade  Mark.

Miniature Incandescent Lamps.

With miniature screw.

1045/1—3

No. **1045/1** **Flat bulb**, ½″ diameter, without reflector, with **ordinary carbon filament**, 0,2½—0,3½ amp., 2—4 volts. . . . . each -/8
— **1045/2** The same but only for 3½ volts, 0,2 amp., ½″ diameter, with **loop carbon** . . . . — -/10
— **1045/3** — — with **metal filament** . . . . — 1/-
— **1045/4** **Round bulb**, about ¾″ diameter, with **loop carbon**, 3½ volts, 0,2 amp. . . . . — -/10
— **1045/5** The same with **metal filament** . . . . — 1/4
— **1045/6** 1½, 2, 2½, 3 volts, with **loop carbon** . . . . — -/10
— **1045/7** 10—22 volts, with **loop carbon** filament . . . . — -/10

1045/4—7

With Mignon (small Edison) screw, round bulb, 1—1³/₁₆″ diameter.

No. **1045/21** 3½ volts, 0,2 amp., with **loop carbon** . . . . each -/10
— **1045/21M** The same, frosted . . . . — 1/-
— **1045/22** Up to 10 volts, with **loop carbon** filament . . . . — -/10
— **1045/23** The same with **metal filament** . . . . — 1/4
— **1045/24** From 11—25 volts, with **loop filament** . . . . — 1/-

The above incandescent lamps can be supplied coloured (for special illumination), when ordering coloured lamps add "C" to the no. of lamp. In this case the price is -/2 each lamp extra.

1045/21—24

Lamps with loop carbons last longer than ordinary, lamps with **metal filament** use less current but are more delicate than carbon lamps.

Lamps can neither be returned nor exchanged. We also decline all responsibility for breakages.

Incandescent lamp holders and accessories for lighting.

1045/50

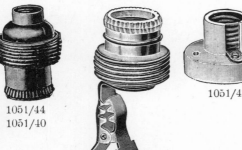

1051/44
1051/40

1051/43

1051/59
1051/60—62

1051/80—81

a) with miniature Edison screw.

No. **1045/50** **Lamp holder**, brass . . . . 100 pieces **3/8**
— **1051/44** **Complete holder** with porcelain ring and screwed socket . . . . each -/6
— **1051/59** **Reflector** to fit this holder, nickelled, 2″ diameter . . . . dozen -/6
— **1051/80** **Christmas tree lamp holder** with porcelain ring and screwed socket (reflector for same No. 1051/59) . . . . each -/6
— **1051/43** **Illumination lamp holder**, on porcelain base — -/4

b) With Mignon (small Edison) screw.

No. **1051/40** **Complete lamp holder**, with porcelain ring and brass screwed socket . . . . each -/6
— **1051/40 H** **The same with switch in holder** . . . — 1/2
— **1051/81** **Christmas tree lamp holder** complete with porcelain ring and screwed socket . . — -/8
— **1051/60** **Reflectors** for No. 1051/40, 40 H, 81, 2½″ diameter . . . . — -/2
— **1051/61** The same, but 3⅛″ diameter . . . . . — -/4
— **1051/62** — — — 3½″ — . . . . — -/6
— **1051/41** **Illumination lamp holder**, on porcelain base — -/4

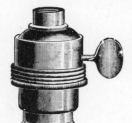

1051/41

1051/40 H   1051/67

c) With Edison standard screw.

No. **1051/67** **Complete holder**, without switch, with porcelain ring and brass socket . . . . each -/6
— **1051/68** **The same with switch** . . . . — 1/2
— **1051/63** **Illumination holder** on porcelain base . — -/4

d) Swan or bayonet lamp holders.

No. **1051/45** **Mignon swan bayonet lamp holder** . . . each -/8
— **1051/65** **Standard** — — — — heavy pattern . . . . — -/6
— **1051/66** **Illumination swan standard lamp holder**, bayonet connection, heavy pattern . . — 1/6

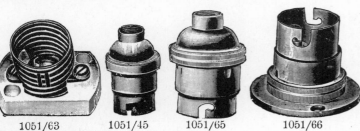

1051/63   1051/45   1051/65   1051/66

13*

Electric Arc Lamps.

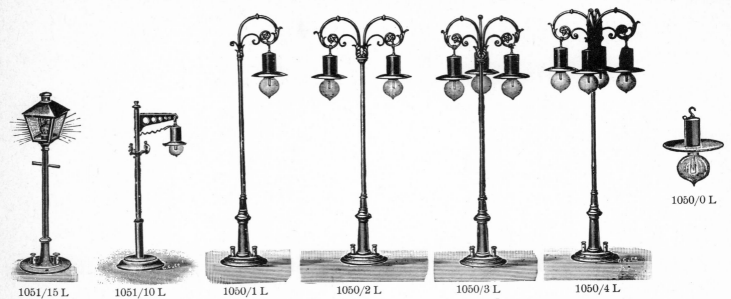

1051/15 L   1051/10 L   1050/1 L   1050/2 L   1050/3 L   1050/4 L

1050/0 L

Without incandescent lamps.

No. 1051/15   **electric street lamp,** entirely of metal, fitted with **miniature screw lamp holder,** 2 terminals, 8¾" high, each 1/4

—   1051/10   **electric arc lamp,** entirely of metal, with insulated **miniature lamp holder,** 10" high . . . . . each 1/-

—   1050/1   the same entirely of metal, with 2 terminals, finest japanning, **Mignon screw holder,** 13½" high . each 2/4

—   1050/2   the same with 2 lamp holders . . . — 3/2

—   1050/3   —   —   — 3   —   — . . . — 4/-

—   1050/4   —   —   — 4   —   — . . . — 5/-

—   1050/0   **arc lamp holder,** only with **Mignon screw,** with shade, each -/8

With incandescent lamps.

No. 1051/15 L   the same with **incandescent miniature screw lamp,** each 2/-

—   1051/10 L   the same with **incandescent miniature screw lamp,** each 1/10

—   1050/1 L   the same with **incandescent Mignon screw lamp,** each 3/4

—   1050/2 L   the same with 2 **incandescent lamps,**   — 5/2

—   1050/3 L   —   —   — 3   —   —   — 7/-

—   1050/4 L   —   —   — 4   —   —   — 9/-

—   1050/0 L   —   —   — **incandescent lamp,**   — 1/6

NB. The arc lamp standards No. 1050/2, 3 and 4 with 2, 3 and 4 lamps are supplied by us ready connected in parallel and can be lighted by a double cell accumulator (page 187) of **4 volts** or any other source of current supply of 4 volts, all the lamps will light together. Therefore the lamps must each be of same voltage as supply.

For separate incandescent lamps for above arc lamps, see page 193.

1060/1   1060/2

Demonstration Arc Lamps

with **pencil carbons,** strong design and high class workmanship.
Very massive construction.

For use in conjunction with batteries No. 1049/4 (page 185) or a four cell accumulator (8 volts) or of any other current supply of 8 volts. Faultless action, with self regulating solenoïd attachment. Nickelled parabolic reflector. Current required 1 amp. at 8 volts. Each lamp is supplied with 10 pencil carbons. (1/32" diameter).

No. 1060/1   **Arc lamp** vertical pattern, 9½" high . . . . each 8/-

—   1060/2   —   —   with guide rollers, 11½" high . . . . — 11/6

—   1060/3   —   —   horizontal, hand regulated only, 7¼" long, 2½" wide,   — 6/-

1061/1

Spare Carbons
for above lamps.

No. 1061/1   1/32" diam. . . . . 10 pieces -/6

1060/3

Trade   Mark.

Electric Lamp Stands and Brackets.

(The articles marked "L" are supplied with 3½ **Volt** incandescent lamps.)

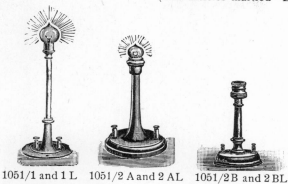

1051/1 and 1 L   1051/2 A and 2 AL   1051/2 B and 2 BL

Stands for lamps with miniature screws

No. 1051/1	**Table stand,** entirely of metal, well japanned, 6" high, each	-/10
— 1051/1 L	the same with **lamp**. . . . . —	1/6
— 1051/2 A	**Table stand** of polished mahogany, with simple holder, 3½" high . . . . each	1/4
— 1051/2 AL	the same with **lamp** . . . . —	2/-
— 1051/2 B	**Table stand,** as 1051/2 A, but with complete massive metal lamp holder, 5" high . . . . each	1/6
— 1051/2 BL	the same with **lamp** . . . . —	2/4

1051/4 and 4 L   1051/5 and 5 L

Wall brackets for miniature screw lamps.

No. 1051/4	**Wall bracket,** one arm, without lamp, 2" long. . . doz.	3/8
— 1051/4 L	the same with **lamp** . . . . each	1/-
— 1051/5	**Wall bracket,** 2 arms, without lamp, 3" long. . . doz.	6/-
— 1051/5 L	the same with **lamp** . . . . each	2/-

1051/3 A and 3 AL   1051/3 B and 3 BL   1051/17 and 17 L

Stands for lamps with Mignon (small Edison) screw.

No. 1051/3 A	**Table stand** of polished mahogany with complete massive metal lamp holder, 6" high. . . . . each	2/-
— 1051/3 AL	the same with **lamp,** . . . . —	2/6
— 1051/3 B	**Lamp stand** as 1051/3 A but with switch. . . . —	2/6
— 1051/3 BL	the same with **lamp** . . . . —	3/2
— 1051/8	**Table stand** as No. 1051/3 A, buth with **Mignon swan (bayonet)** lamp holder . . . . each	2/-
— 1051/8 L	the same with **lamp** . . . . —	2/10
— 1051/17	**Lamp stand** with base for a dry battery (no further wire connection necessary) of polished mahogany, very strong design, with switch, 8" high. . . . . each	3/4
— 1051/17 L	the same with **lamp** . . . . —	4/-

(No. 1 P page 186 is a suitable dry battery for above.)

1051/6 and 6 L   1051/7 and 7 L   1051/7 H and 7 HL

Wall brackets for incandescent lamps with Mignon (small Edison) screw.

No. 1051/6	**Wall bracket** with complete massive lamp holder and porcelain ring for hanging without terminals, 5" long, each	1/2
— 1051/6 L	the same with **lamp**. . . . . —	2/⁻
— 1051/7	**Wall bracket** mounted on wood base with terminals and shade 3¼" diam. **very effective design,** 6" long .	2/4
— 1051/7 L	the same with **lamp**. . . . . —	3/-
— 1051/7 H	**Wall bracket** as 1051/7 but with **switch** in holder . . . . —	3/-
— 1051/7 HL	the same **with lamp**. . . . . —	3/8

For separate incandescent lamps for above table stands and wall brackets see page 193.

Trade   Mark.

Medical Coils

fitted with slide tube regulator to adjust the current to any strength, can be worked by bichromate, or several Leclanche batteries, or by a good dry battery (2 volts). The terminals marked + and — must be connected to battery, but those marked P and S are connected to the cords of the handles. P denotes primary current, continuous current of weak action, S denotes secondary current, alterna ing current of strong action.

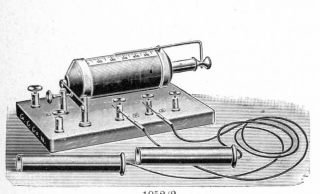

1052/2

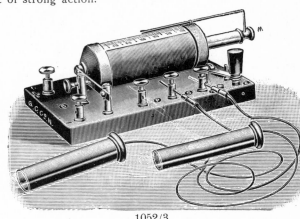

1052/3

No.	1052/00	mounted on polished wood base, 5″×3″, only secondary current, no terminals	each 2/6
—	1052/0	the same, but of better quality, with terminals and scale	— 3/6
—	1052/1	the same, with 5 terminals, for primary and secondary current.	— 4/6
—	1052/2	the same, **with larger coil,** fine quality	— 5/4
—	1052/3	the same, but **with still larger coil,** mounted on highly polished base, 5″×3″ and with switch	— 7/8

1083/3

1083/1

1062 E

1062

Magneto Machines

(no battery etc. required) with superior permanent magnet with crank and geared drive, with 2 handles and cords, always ready for use.

No.	1083/3	**Magneto machine,** 4½″ long, 3½″ wide	each 3/6
—	1083/1	do. very strong quality, powerful action, 4″ high, 4″ wide	— 10/6
—	1083/2	the same with **current regulator** (patent), to generate strong or weak current as desired.	— 11/4
—	1062	**High class magneto machine** in highly polished mahogany case, 4½″ long, 3½″ high, 3½″ wide .	— 13/-
—	1062 E	**Electrodes,** flat of covered carbon, to suit above apparatus	pair 3/8

For medical coils for use at same time for vacuum tube lighting see page 190.

Regulating resistances for above apparatus, specially when using freshly filled batteries see page 177 under 1051/55 and 55 B.

1083/2

Ruhmkorff Induction-Coils

for lighting **Vacuum Tubes**, or for use in *"**Wireless Telegraphy**"* etc., to be worked by bichromate batteries or accumulators.

Best quality, on highly polished genuine mahogany base.

☞ Length of spark guaranteed. ☜

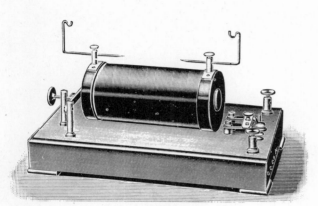

1022A/3

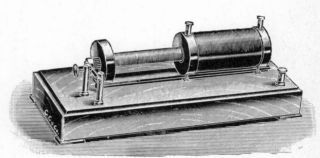

1022D/1

No. **1022/00**	**0**	**1**	**2**	**3**	**3½**	**4**	**5**	**5½**	
Length of spark ⅛	5/32	¼	5/16	⅜	7/16	⅝	¾	1"	
each **6/8**	**7/4**	**8/8**	**12/-**	**18/-**	**22/-**	**27/-**	**36/-**	**48/-**	without commutator
No. **1022 A** **8/10**	**9/6**	**10/10**	**14/6**	**21/4**	**25/4**	**30/4**	**39/4**	**52/-**	with commutator

No. **1022/6**	**7**	**8**	**9**	**10**	**11**	**12**	**13**	**14**	**16** with Ebonite cover
Length of spark 1 3/16	1½	2	2½	2¾	3¼	4	5	6	8"
each **57/-**	**79/-**	**102/-**	**120/-**	**156/-**	**172/-**	**196/-**	**250/-**	**320/-**	**430/-** without commut.
No. **1022 A** **63/6**	**90/-**	**113/-**	**131/-**	**167/-**	**183/-**	**207/-**	**262/-**	**332/-**	**442/-** with commutator

Sectional-Induction-Coils after Prof. Dubois-Reymond, on highly polished mahogany base with removable secondary coil

No. **1022 D/1** length of spark ¼" **without** commutator . . . . each **12/-**

— **1022 DA/3** — — — ⅜" **with** — . . . . — **23/-**

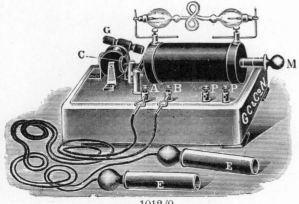

1012/0

Induction-Coil

No. **1012/0** **Induction-Coil** can be used at the same time as induction coil for lighting **Geissler (Vacuum) Tubes**, as well as a medical coil. With slide tube regulator, handles and cords, very strong quality, mounted on real mahogany base, 6½" long, 3½" wide   each **23/-**

Trade ⚙ Mark.

Geissler or Vacuum Tubes.

Of uranium and white glass with metal caps, eyes and points, assorted in various shapes. They can be lighted by Ruhmkorff coils or influence machines.

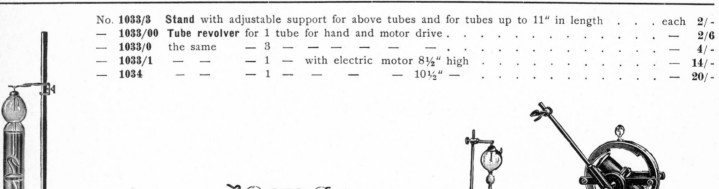

No.		8	10	12	16	20
Length about		3"	4"	5"	6½"	8"
No. 1019A	dozen	7/4	8/6	10/10	13/4	16/10
— 1019C with fluorescent liquid	—	8/6	9/8	13/4	15/8	18/-
— 1019D uranium glass figures in cylinder .	each	..	..	1/-	1/4	1/6
— 1019G filled with gases	—	..	..	-/10	1/4	1/6
— 1019H with layers of light	—	..	..	1/-	1/4	1/8
— 1019I with iodide of mercury, when warmed the colours change	—	..	..	1/-	1/4	1/8
— 1019L with mercury, becomes lustrous when shaken	—	..	..	1/8	2/4	2/10
— 1019M with phosphorescent powder . . .	—	..	..	1/8	2/4	2/10

1019A

1019A

1019D and 1019C

G H J L M

Collections

consisting of: **6 different tubes** in cardboard boxes.

No. **1019K/1** containing one each A, B, D, G, H, I, 5" long . . . . set **6/-**
— **1019K/2** the same, with tubes 6½" long . . . . — **7/8**
— **1019K/3** — — — — 8" . . . . — **8/10**
— **1019K/5** containing one each A, G, H, I, L, M, 6½" long . . . . — **9/6**
— **1019K/9** — — — C, G, H, I, L, M, 8" — . . . . — **11/8**

No. **1033/3** **Stand** with adjustable support for above tubes and for tubes up to 11" in length . . . each **2/-**
— **1033/00** **Tube revolver** for 1 tube for hand and motor drive . . . . — **2/6**
— **1033/0** the same — 3 — — — — . . . . — **4/-**
— **1033/1** — — — 1 — with electric motor 8½" high . . . . — **14/-**
— **1034** — — — 1 — — — 10½" — . . . . — **20/-**

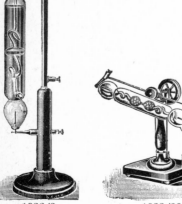

1033/3   1033/00   1033/0   1033/1   1034

Trade  Mark.

Very effective Stand-Vacuum-Tubes
can be lighted by means of Ruhmkorff coils or influence machines.

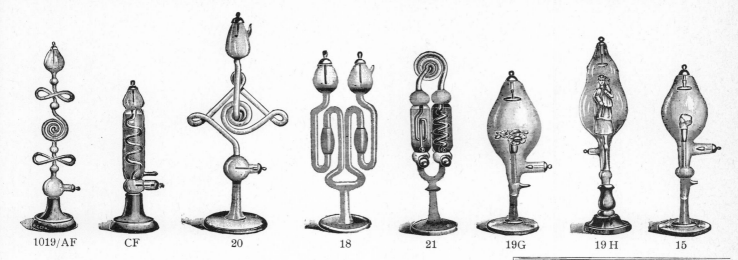

1019/AF   CF   20   18   21   19G   19 H   15

		Height in inches	12	16	20	23
	on wood stand:		5	6½	8	9
No. **1019/AF**	of uranium and white glass . . . . each		1/6	2/-	2/6	—
— **1019/CF**	with fluorescent fluid . . . . —		2/-	2/-	3/6	—
	on glass stand:					
— **1019/20**	in 4 designs . . . . —		—	—	2/10	—
— **1019/18**	with 2 glass tubes . . . . —		—	2/8	—	—
— **1019/21**	— 2 — — and 2 fluorescent fluids . . . . . —		—	—	—	3/6
— **1019/19 G**	— flowers or butterflies, or birds, or figures **on glass** foot, 6½" high . . . . —		—	—	2/10	—
— **1019/19 H**	the same, on wood base, 8" high . . . . —		—	—	4/-	—
— **1019/15**	with luminous stone (chalk or lime) . . . . —		3/6	—	—	—

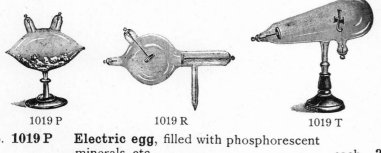

1019 P   1019 R   1019 T

No. **1019 P**   **Electric egg**, filled with phosphorescent minerals etc.. . . . . each   **3/-**

— **1019 R/4**   **X ray tubes** for coils of ½" to 1¼" spark length . . . . —   **10/6**

— **1019 T**   **Crooke's tubes** showing after-glow of cross shadow . . . . —   **4/-**

— **1019/1**   **Radiometers** with 2 discs, 4" high . —   **2/-**

— **1019/2**   do.   — 4 — 6" — . —   **2/8**

— **1019/3**   do.   — 4 — 10" — . —   **3/4**

— **1019/4**   do.   — 8 — 10" — . —   **7/6**

— **1019/10**   do.   — 4 — 6" — for electric energy . . . . —   **4/-**

Radiometers (Crooke's)

with discs which turn under the influence of bright light, heat, and in the case of No. 1019/10, electric energy.

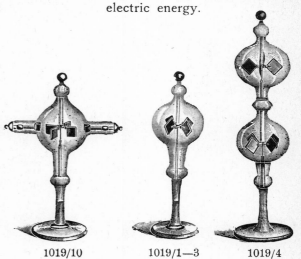

1019/10   1019/1—3   1019/4

Trade ⬡ Mark.

1053

Self exciting Influence-Machines

Wimshurst form

well made and highly finished
with 2 opposite turning **ebonite** plates,
which will work reliably without reversal, even in damp weather.
Every machine is accompanied
with full detailed description and instructions.

No. **1053/1**	with plates 7¼" diam, length of spark 2½—2¾"	each	**26/6**
— **1053/2**	— — 8" — — — — 3½—4"	—	**35/-**
— **1053/3**	— — 10" — — — — 4½—5"	—	**52/-**
— **1053/4**	— — 12" — — — — 5—6"	—	**90/-**
— **1053/5**	— — 14" — — — — 7—8"	—	**140/-**
— **1053/6**	— — 16" — — — — 8—9"	—	**190/-**
— **1053/7**	— — 18" — — — — 9—11"	—	**270/-**

Cases of Experimental Apparatus

for use with above influence machines,
with full detailed and illustrated description of 85 experiments,

1044/9 A

No. **1044/9 A** containing:

1. Universal stand with insulated foot
2. Paper tassel
3. Bell set
4. Flying wheel
5. Geissler vacuum tubes
6. Holder for above
7. Luminous plate and pendulum
8. 1 pair of handles with chains
9. 1 glass plate and tin foil
10. Pith balls and figures

complete each **15/-**

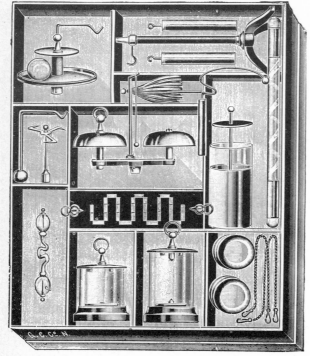

1044/9 B

No. **1044/9 B** containing:

1. Universal stand with insulated foot
2. Paper tassel
3. Bell set with 2 bells
4. Flying wheel
5. Luminous plate and pendulum
6. Geissler vacuum tubes
7. Holder for above
8. Dancing balls
9. Luminous tube
10. Racing balls
11. Smoke apparatus
12. 1 pair of Leyden jars
14. Discharger for above
15. 1 pair of chains
16. Illustrated instructions

Packed in handsome partitioned case

complete each **28/-**

Trade Mark.

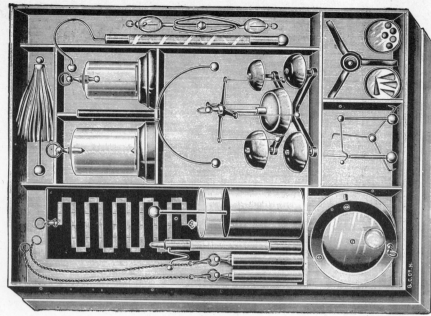

1044/9D

Large
Cases of Experimental Apparatus

for use with influence machines,
of superior quality.

No. **1044/9D** containing:

1. Universal Stand
2. Paper tassel
3. Bell set, with 5 musical bells
4. Flying wheel
5. Luminous plate
6. Geissler vacuum tubes
7. Holder for above
8. 1 pair of electrodes for shocks
9. 1 pair of connecting chains
10. Illustrated instructions for the experiments
11. Dancing balls
12. Luminous tube
13. Racing balls with balls
14. Smoke apparatus
15. Leyden jars
16. Discharger for above

in most handsome partitioned case

complete each **54/-**

No. **1044/9C Case of experimental apparatus**, consisting of No. 1—10 of above collection, in handsome partitioned case

complete each **29/-**

Supplementary Cases of Apparatus

to use with influence machines and the other
sets 1044/9A, 9B, 9C, 9D.

No. **1044/9E** containing:

1. Motor for static electricity
2. Breath pictures apparatus
3. Sand apparatus
4. Quadrant electric motor
5. Electric mortar
6. Apparatus for surface sparking
7. Wind apparatus
8. Rotating discs.
9. Radiating apparatus
10. Spark deviating apparatus
11. Igniting apparatus
12. Handsome partitioned case with illustrated book of instructions each **64/-**

No. **1044/9ES** the same case, buth with 1 universal stand
complete each **69/-**

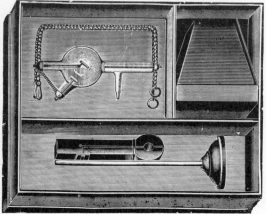

1044/9E

Cases of X Ray
Experimental Apparatus

for use with influence machine.

No. **1044/10A** containing: X ray tube, stand, florescope with barium cyanide screen 3" × 4", chain and instructions, in handsome case
complete each **41/-**

No. **1044/10B** containing the same but considerably larger apparatus for machines 1053/3 and 1053/4 . . . . complete each **64/-**

1044/10A and 10B

Trade  Mark.

Various Requisites for use with Influence Machines.

Specially adapted for static electricity.

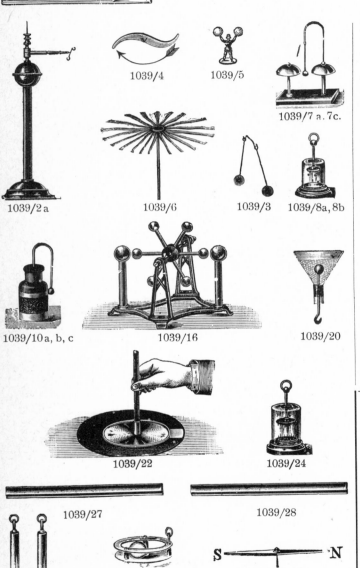

1039/4   1039/5

1039/7 a. 7 c.

1039/2 a   1039/6   1039/3   1039/8a, 8b

1039/10 a, b, c   1039/16   1039/20

1039/22   1039/24

1039/27   1039/28

1039/29   1039/30   1039/34

No. 1039/2 a	**Stand** with removable support and removable wire hook, of insulated ebonite, on solid base . each 3/8
— 1039/3	**Double pendulum** with pith balls to suit No. 1039/2a, each -/2
— 1039/3 H	**Pith ball** in different colours . . . dozen -/4
— 1039/4	**Flying wheel** of brass for affixing to stand No. 1039/2a, each -/2
— 1039/34	**Magnetic needle** for stand No 1039/2a with small case . . . . dozen 4/-
— 1039/5	**Athlete** . . . . each -/6
— 1039/6	**Paper tassel** for stand No. 1039/2a . . — -/6
— 1039/7	**Bell set** . . . . — 2/6
— 1039/7c	the same, but smaller size . . . — 1/6
— 1039/8 a	**Dancing balls** . . . . — 3/-
— 1039/8 b	the same with removable plate . . — 7/-
— 1039/10a	**Leyden jars**, small size . . . . . — 1/10
— 1039/10b	— — middle . . . . . — 3/4
— 1039/10c	— — large . . . . . — 5/4
— 1039/16	**Electric motor** . . . . —10/10
— 1039/20	**Glass funnel** for igniting ether or alcohol — 2/-
— 1039/24	**Smoke condensing apparatus**; the smoke from a candle or a tobacco pipe is caused to disappear by electricity each 7/-
— 1039/22	**Electrophorus** with round plate and tinfoil — 9/-
— 1039/27	**Glass rods**, 8" long . . . . . . — -/6
— 1039/28	**Ebonite rods**, 8" long . . . . . . — -/10
— 1039/29	**Handles** for shocks . . . . . — 3/-
— 1039/30	**Ball race** . . . . — 6/-

Sundries for Magnetism:

1039/33

N ———— S

1039/35 a. 32   1039/42   1039/34

Horse-shoe Magnets.

No. 1039/35 a	35 b	35 c	35 d
1½	2	2½	3¼" high
gross 8/-	9/8	14/6	19/4

Best quality No. 1039/32 a	32 b	32 c	32 d
2	2¾	3½	4½" high
dozen 2/-	3/-	4/4	6/8

Most powerful quality to suit dynamos or strong coils each provided with hole on either side for fixing.

No. 1039/42   3" high, ¼" thickness of sides . . . . each 2/6

No. 1039/33 a   **Best quality bar magnets**, highly nickelled and red japanned, 3½" long, ½" wide, ⅛" diameter . . dozen 4/10
— 1039/33 b   — — — — 6¾" — ½" — ⅛" . . . — 8/-

No. 1039/34   **Magnetic needle** with case, 2" long . . . . dozen 4/-

Trade Mark.

Cases of Apparatus for galvanic electrical experiments

Packed in handsome partitioned cases.

No. 1044/11
for the study of
Galvanic Electricity.

1044/11

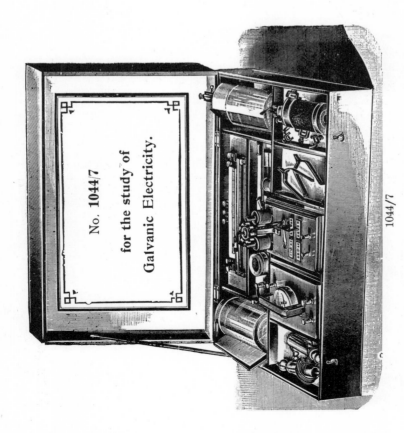

No. 1044/7
for the study of
Galvanic Electricity.

1044/7

No. **1044/7** containing: Wheatstone bridge with sliding contact and 100 division scale to wire, electric motor with commutator and current regulator. The apparatus is so constructed that it can be used as a) motor, as b) electro-magnet, in the first case with unlike poles connected and in the second with like poles connected. Galvanometer with 2 different windings with compass, primary coil, secondary coil, solid iron core, 1 ohm unit resistance, core of separate iron wires, permanent magnet, 2 thermo-batteries (iron and german silver), 2 glass battery jars for same, 2 porous cells, 2 copper plates, 2 zinc plates, 2 carbon plates, 4 brass hoops, 2 connecting terminals, sieve with iron fillings, coil of copper wire .   .   .   .   each **42/-**

No. **1044/11** containing bell with key, solenoïd, electro- magnet, galvanometer, vertical compass needle, electric motor, batteries with lifting elements, primary coil, secondary coil, lead wires, bichromate chemicals, medical induction coil with handles, lamp stand with incandescent lamp, illustrated book of instructions .   .   .   .   each **57/-**

Trade Mark.

Cases of Experimental Apparatus

for the experimental study of heat.

No. 1044/8 Collection of physical apparatus for the experimental study of heat.
Packed in a handsomely arranged partitioned case, containing the following articles:

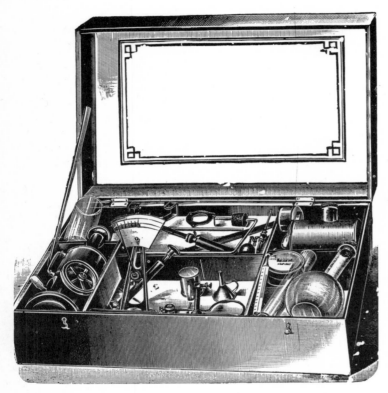

1. Lever pyrometer with 5 metal rods (copper, brass, iron, hard and soft steel).
2. Stand with iron ring.
3. Brass ball with chain and hook.
4. A ring with foot.
5. Two compensating strips of brass and steel riveted together.
6. Reamur thermometer.
7. Reagent glass.
8. Boiling flask with cork.
9. Double wick spirit lamp.
10. Single — — —
11. Brass dish for Leidenfrost drops.
12. Round tin can with cork.
13. Apparatus for determining the different conductivity of metals.
14. Fire syringe with 1 piece of tinder.
15. Glass tube, twice bent at right angles, with cork.
16. Pipette.
17. Funnel and 1 beaker.
18. High pressure steam engine with oscillating cylinder, water gauge, safety valve, also arranged for use as steam fountain.
19. Round glass.
20. Illustrated book instructions.

complete each **35/-**

The Little Electro-plater

No. **1055**

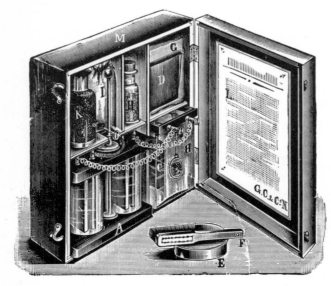

A complete set, enabling nickel plating to be easily and properly done.

In a strong wood box containing:

Double battery with lifting elements.
Plating box.
Pure nickel anode.
A packet of prepared nickel salt.
Bath.
Brush to remove grease.
Polishing cloth.
A bottle of slaked lime.
A bag of saw dust.
Large bottle of prepared bichromate chemicals.
Full detailed instructions.

complete each **21/-**

Trade Mark.

Morse Printing Telegraph.

Our instruments, with paper roll moved by clockwork on which the message is received, being printed by a coloured pen actuated by an electro magnet, differ somewhat by reason of their simplicity from the instruments in use in the post-offices, but are exactly the same in principle. Their strong design and excellent working render them most essential to those who wish to study telegraphy after the Morse systems. The instrument 1026/3 requires a dry battery ($1\frac{1}{2}$ volts). To work the complete set (2 instruments) 3 volts will be needed. The instruments are accompanied with full printed instructions, besides a complete Morse alphabet for learning the Morse code.

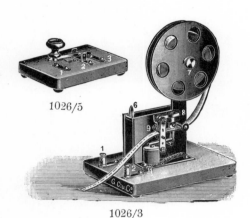

1026/5

1026/3

No. 1026/3 Morse telegraph of strong quality with powerful clockwork, with stopping lever, ink roller and strong electro magnet, mounted on highly polished wood base, $5\frac{1}{2}$" long, 4" wide, $7\frac{1}{2}$" high, each **10/-**

1026/4

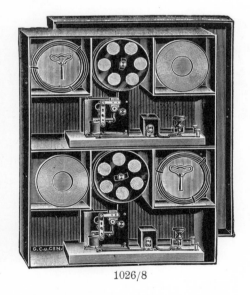

1026/8

No. **1026/5 Transmitter** or **key** for above, strong quality (absolutely necessary for working the telegraph), 4" long, each **1/6**

— **1026/4 Complete telegraph set** consisting of Morse telegraph 1026/3 with excellent battery, ready for immediate use, 3 rolls of paper, 10 yards of suitable insulated wire, Morse alphabet and full instructions, $8\frac{1}{4}$" long, $4\frac{3}{4}$" wide, 7" high . . . . each **19/6**

— **1026/8 Double station;** complete double set of instruments for sending and receiving messages. By means of the wire and batteries supplied in this set, telegraphic communication can be set up between two stations about 10 yards distant from each other using the Morse code supplied. If stronger batteries be employed, for example, bichromate batteries (page 185) the instruments can be separated by a much greater distance than above.

The complete double set consists of:

 2 Telegraph sets 1026/4 with 2 excellent batteries, each with 10 yards of suitable insulated wire, 6 rolls of paper, Morse alphabet and full printed instructions, packed in handsome covered case
each complete **39/-**

No. **1026 P Extra paper rolls** . . . . doz. **2/-**

— **1026 D Wire, waxed** . . . . 10 yards **-/10**

— **1 L Dry battery** for above (requires water before using) . . . . each **1/10**

Trade Mark.

Morse Printing Telegraph

best quality and very strong design.

No. 1026/2 Morse printing instruments

with strong and regular working clockwork and Morse alphabet.
Each instrument is supplied with full instructions.
Specially suited for **"wireless telegraphy"**.
Fine polish and nickelling, mounted on highly finished wood base
8" long, 4" wide, 7 1/8" high each **50/-**

No. 1086/8 Transmitter

to insert in circuit between Rhumkorff coil and
batteries, can be used also with Morse
instrument each **3/4**

Exactly same design as instruments used in the post offices.

Electric bells

for fixing to wall with 2 coils (the child's electric bell set) can be rung with current from a dynamo,
battery or accumulator. Very good demonstration model for showing before the eyes the effects
of electricity.

No. **1084/3 1/2** Wall electric bell, 3 1/8" high, gong 1 1/2" diam. . . . . each **1/6**
— 1084/4 1/2 — — — 4 1/2" — — 2" — . . . . . . — **2/-**

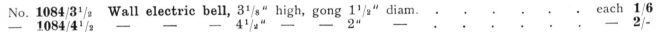

No. 1084/7

Electric bell sets

ready for fixing.

Consisting of electric bell with 2 bobbins, push, filling battery and
connecting wire, packed in cardboard box, each **4/-**

Trade ⊕ Mark.

Apparatus for "Wireless Telegraphy"

of very strong and high class quality.

1086/1

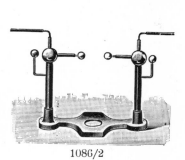

1086/2

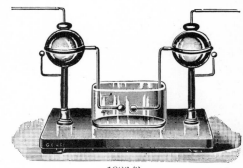

1086/3

No. **1086/1 Coherer,** for receiving the electric waves, with hand de-coherer, receiving wires adjustable for length, mounted on polished wood base. The performance of the instrument is excellent, 4½" long, 4½" high each **7/4**

No. **1086/2 Small spark transmitter** with aerial wires adjustable for length for use with Rhumkorff coils to ⁹/₈" length of spark, 6½" long, 5½" high, each **6/-**

No. **1086/3 Large spark transmitter** with aerial wires, adjustable for length, with oil bath, for use with Rhumkorff coils up to ³/₈–1½" length of spark, also for use with influence machine, 11" long, 7¾" high each **14/6**

1086/4

1086/5

1086/6

1086/7

No. **1086/4 Wireless bell,** very useful for experimenting with above apparatus. For use with 1086/1 and 2, influence machine 1053/1 (page 200) and battery No. 0 F (page 185). The bell will ring without wire over a distance of several yards, even through walls or closed doors, 4¾" long, 5½" high, each **8/-**

— **1086/5 Relay,** very sensitive, by which message can be received over long distances, 4" long, 4" wide . . each **11/6**

No. **1086/6 Relay** more sensitive than No. 10 6/5, suitable for more distant working, 5¼" long, 4" high, 3¹/₈" wide each **12/6**

— **1086/7 Resistance coil** for above relays wound on wood bobbin with terminals. The resistance is required if the coherer and relay be used as single instrument, 1¾" diam. each **2/4**

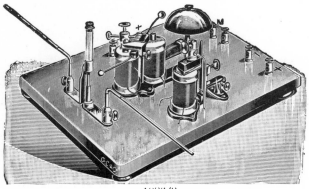

1086/9

1086/12 and 13

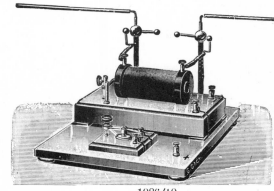

1086/10

No. **1086/9 Receiving station** complete with coherer, aerial wires, relay, automatic de-coherer, which rings the bell, resistance, 3 pair of terminals, 10½" long, 8" wide . . . each **40/-**

— **1086/12 Separate coherer tube** to suit 1086/1 and 1086/9 with filling . . . . each **2/6**

— **1086/13 Spare metal filings** in glass . . . . . — **1/-**

No. **1086/10 Transmitting station** consisting of one Rhumkorff coil ³/₈" spark length, tapping key, transmitter and aerial wires, 12¾" long, 8" wide, 7½" high . . . . each **34/-**

— **1086/11 Guide to wireless telepraphy** also containing instructions for using above apparatus, **with illustrations** copy **-/2**

Complete Wireless Installations.

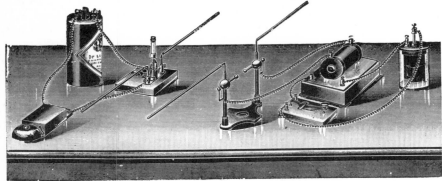
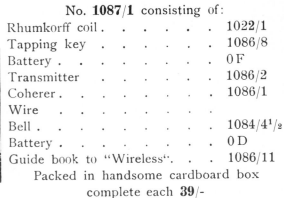

No. **1087/1** consisting of:

Rhumkorff coil	1022/1
Tapping key	1086/8
Battery	0 F
Transmitter	1086/2
Coherer	1086/1
Wire	
Bell	1084/4$^{1}/_{2}$
Battery	0 D
Guide book to "Wireless". . .	1086/11

Packed in handsome cardboard box
complete each **39/-**

1087/1

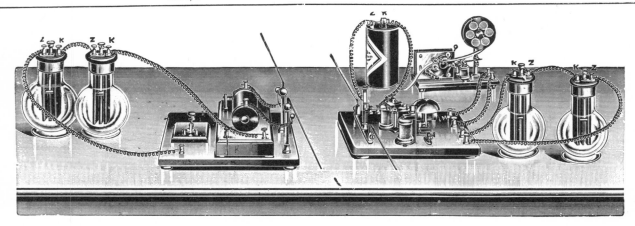

1087/2

No. **1087/2** consisting of:

Sending station	1086/10	Battery	0 D
Receiving station	1086/9	Wire	
Morse apparatus	1026/2	Book of instructions etc.	1086/11
4 Bottle-form batteries	2 F		
Packed in handsome box		. . . . complete each **152/-**	

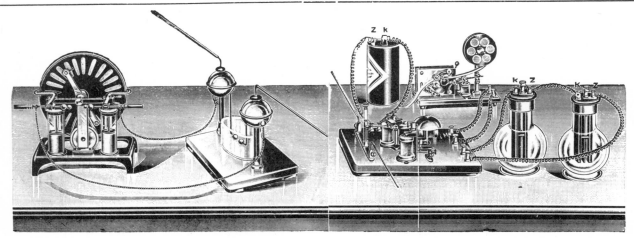

1087/3

No. **1087/3** consisting of:

Sending station	1086/3	2 Bottle-form batteries	2 F
Receiving station	1086/9	Wire	
Influence machine	1053/1	Connecting chains	
Morse apparatus	1026/2	Book of instructions	1086/11
Packed in handsome box		. . . . complete each **148/-**	

MOTOR CARS
Motor omnibuses.

MOTOR GARAGES
etc.

RAILWAYS

Cheap quality

with or without **Spring motors.**

LOCOMOTIVES with **Roller** Mechanism.
FIRE ENGINES — — — —
STEAM BOATS — — — etc.

ZEPPELIN AIR SHIPS

PARSEVAL

AEROPLANES
A large selection of all the principle types.

Motor Cars propelled by Spring Motor

strong quality and high class japanning.

3358/10

Very original

3358/28 and 29

No. 3358/10 Motor car
with 1 plastic figure and glass screen
runs in circles
6½ " long . . . . dozen 7/10

No. 3358/28 Motor car
with 1 plastic figure, **runs automatically forward and backward**
6½ " long . . . . dozen 13/-

No. 3358/29 The same **motor car**
with 1 dressed **self moving** figure
6¾ " long . . . . dozen 15/6

Motor landaulette.

3358/11

3358/12

No. 3358/11 Motor cabs with chauffeur, 6½" long . dozen 9/-

— **3358/12 Landaulette** with wind screen, with chauffeur,
6½" long . . . . dozen 12/-

No. **3358/31 Motor cab (taxi-cab)** adjustable, can be made to run in circle or straight, with chauffeur, 8¾" long, 5⅛" high . . . . dozen **15/6**

No. **3358/33 Motor landaulette** can be made to run in circle or straight with chauffeur, doors to open; large and strongly built car, 8¾" long, 5½" high, dozen **21/-**

3358/34 and 35

No. **3358/34 Landaulette motor**
high class quality, japanned white, **adjustable** for **circular** or **straight running**, as well as **reversing gear for forward** or **backward** motion, with chauffeur, doors to open, 8¾" long, 5¾" high . . . . dozen **34/-**

No. **3358/35**
the same, but with genuine rubber **tyres** . . . . . dozen **42/-**

3358/36

No. **3358/36 Large motor cab, taximeter,**
with fare indicator and "Disengaged" tablet, strong and solid design with good spring motor, adjustable for circular or straight running, with chauffeur.

13" long, 7⅛" high . . . . dozen **48/-**

Trade Mark.

High class Motor Cars propelled by Spring Motors of most substantial manufacture and
magnificent japanning. Can be adjusted to run in circular or straight direction.

3358/37

3358/39

No. 3358/37 **Landaulette body** with 2 head lights and chauffeur, strong mechanism, adjustable for circular or straight runs, 13" long, 7½" high . . each 5/-

— 3358/38 **The same car,** but **with reversing gear** for **forward or backward running**, with brake and chauffeur, 13" long, 7½" high . . . . each 5/8

No. 3358/39 **Landaulette body** with **polished glass windows,** 2 nickelled head lights and chauffeur, adjustable for going in straight or circular direction, 13" long, 7½" high . . . . each 7/-

— 3358/40 **the same car,** but with thick tyres of genuine rubber, each 9/-

3358/23

Open Touring Cars.

3358/21

No. 3358/23 **High class motor car,** finest hand japanning, very strong mechanism, steering wheel, bonnet, 2 fine head lights, adjustable for running straight or circular, with chauffeur and hollow rubber tyres, 8¼" long . . . . each 4/10

No. 3358/21 **High class motor car,** finest hand japanning, very strong mechanism, steering wheel, bonnet, 2 fine head lights, glass screen adjustable for straight or circular running, with chauffeur and 1 finely painted figure, hollow tyres of rubber, 8¼" long, each 6/-

3358/42

3358/43

No. 3358/42 **High class motor car,** very best quality and finest hand enamelling, with extra strong mechanism, bonnet 4 fine head lights, glass screen, adjustable for straight or circular running, also reversing gear for running in both directions, with brake, 1 finely painted chauffeur on upholstered seat, 10½" long, each 13/-

No. 3358/43 **High class motor car,** finest quality finish and japanning, very strong mechanism, bonnet, 4 highly nickelled head lights, glass screen, adjustable for running straight or circular, with brake, 1 well painted chauffeur and 1 finely painted figure on upholstered seats, 13" long . . . . each 18/-

Trade Mark.

Best quality Motor Cars with spring motor mechanism.

Strongest quality and best japanning,
adjustable for running in straight or circular direction.

3358/41

3358/44

Motor car of handsome and prettily got up style, doors to open, fine rubber tyres, well designed figures, nickelled head lights, with reversing gear for running in either direction, with brake, adjustable for straight or circular running, handsomely painted chauffeur

| No. **3358/41** Motor landaulette to seat 4 with 1 figure, 9½" long, 6" high, each 7/4 | No. **3358/44** Motor landaulette with 4 upholstered seats and 1 figure, 4 highly nickelled head lights, 13" long, 7½" high each 20/- |

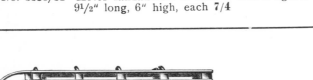

741/3 R

741/3 A

Motor Omnibus, strong quality and fine japanning

No. **741/3 R** Motor Omnibus with strong mechanism, adjustable for straight or circular runs, with brake and strong rubber tyres, 12" long, 6½" high, each 4/10

No. **741/3 A** Motor Bus with various lettering
Exact model of the London Motor Bus,
adjustable for running in circle or straight, with brake, also strong rubber tyres, 12" long, 6½" high, each 4/10

741/3 RC

No. **741/3 RC Motor Bus with passengers,** same quality as 741/3 R but with 24 handsomely painted figures, namely 11 ladies, 11 gentlemen, 1 conductor and 1 chauffeur, fitted with 2 head lights, packed in handsome covered cardboard box, each 10/-

No. **741/3 AC Motor Bus with passengers,** same quality as 741/3 A, but with 24 handsomely painted figures, as above described, also with 2 head lights, packed in handsome covered cardboard box, each 10/-

739/7

739/4

No. 739/7

707/1

Motor Wagons
well japanned, with strong circular, 10½" long . . . . mechanism and brake, with chauffeur adjustable for running straight or . . . . . each 2/4

739/8

No. 739/4 **Goods delivery motors** well japanned, strong mechanism and brake, adjustable for running straight or circular with chauffeur, 10½" long, 5" high, each 2/6

No. 707/1 **Royal mail van** well japanned, strong mechanism, with chauffeur, 7½" long . . . . dozen 15/6

No. 739/8 **Motor road-water-wagon** best japanning, with strong mechanism, sprinkling attachment with stop cock, brake, adjustable for straight or circular running with chauffeur, wheels with rubber tyres, 11" long, 5½" high each 5/4

Motor Garages
strong quality and well japanned.

645/1

645/4

No. 645/1 with 2 windows, work bench with vice, 11" long, 7½" wide, 6¾" high, each 2/6

— 645/2 the same, but larger, with 4 windows, 14¼" long, 10" wide, 9" high, each 3/4

— 645/4 with large closing double doors, 4 windows, 14¼" long, 9" wide, 8¾" high, each 4/-

741 F

Separate Figures for motor cars.

No. 741 F

1 Box of figures to suit motor bus 741/3 R and 3 A, containing 24 figures sewn on card, namely 11 ladies, 11 gentlemen, 1 conductor and 1 motor driver

box 4/6

Chauffeurs for motor cars.
(Papier maché figures) of fine quality

741 F/2   740 F/6

No. 741 F/1 3" high . . . . doz. 2/4
— 741 F/2 4" high — — 3/4
— 741 F/3 High class design, with goggles, 4½" high (specially for cars No. 3358/42—44, page 211—212) . . . . . each -/10

Passengers (ladies and gentlemen) for motors
(Papier maché)

No. 740 F/4 Gentlemen, fine quality, 3½" high . . . . . doz. 2/4
— 740 F/5 Ladies — — 3⅛" high — — 3/4
— 740 F/6 Ladies, best quality with motor veils, 4½" high (specially for cars 3358/42—44 page 211—212) . . . . . each -/10

Motor head lights
No. 741 L
with bull's eye front
(specially for motor bus 741)
each -/3

Railways **without** Spring Motors

and without rails.

No. **905** each piece packed in cardboard box, No. 3 and 4 packed in dozen sets, length of each coach or wagon 2¹/₂"

No. 905/3	**4**	**5**	**6**	**7**	**8**	**11**	**18**	
consisting of loco. and tender and 1	2	3	4	5	6	9	16	coaches etc.
6¹/₂	8¹/₂	11	13¹/₂	16	18	25	42"	long
dozen 4/-	4/6	5/6	6/8	8/6	9/8	13/-	20/-	

No. **906** each piece packed in pretty box, length of coaches etc. 3¹/₈"

No. 906/3	**4**	**5**	**6**	**7**	**9**	**10**	**12**	
consisting of loco. and tender and 1	2	3	4	5	7	8	10	coaches and wagons
9¹/₂	12³/₄	16	19	23	30	33	40"	long
dozen 6/-	7/4	9/8	12/-	14/-	18/-	20/-	24/-	

No. **909** each piece in box, length of coach and wagon 3³/₄"

No. 909/2	**3**	**4**	**5**	**6**	**7**	**8**	**9**	**10**	
consisting of loco. and tender and 1	2	3	4	5	6	7	8		coaches and wagons
6	8¹/₂	14	18	22	26	29	33	38"	long
dozen 3/8	5/8	7/10	9/-	11/-	13/-	15/-	17/-	19/-	

No. **910** The same trains as 909 but painted in the colours of
Great Northern Railway
London and **North Western Railway**
Midland Railway (assorted)

No. 910/2	**3**	**4**	**5**	**6**	**7**	**8**	**9**	**10**
dozen 3/8	5/8	7/10	9/-	11/-	13/-	15/-	17/-	19/-

Railways **with** Spring Motors

without rails.

No. **915** each piece in box, length of coaches and wagons etc. 3³/₄"

No. 915/2	**3**	**4**	**5**	**6**	**7**	**8**	**9**	**10**	
consisting of loco. and tender and 1	2	3	4	5	6	7	8		coaches and wagons
6¹/₂	10¹/₂	14	18	22	26	30	33	38"	long
dozen 8/8	12/-	13/8	15/8	19/4	21/8	24/-	27/-	30/-	

Motor Cars, Locomotives, Ships and Fire Brigade Appliances
worked by **Spring motor** or **Revolving Flywheel.**

Motor car with chauffeur.

No. 704/1 R   with flywheel or roller drive, 5½" long   dozen 6/-
—   704/1 U   —   spring motor . . . .   —   7/6

Motor delivery van with driver.

—   705/1 R   with roller drive, 5½" long. . . . . .   —   5/4
—   705/1 U   —   spring motor, 5½" long . . . .   —   6/10

704/1

705/1

Tank locomotives.

No. 702/10   with roller drive, 5½" long. . . . .   dozen 6/-

Locomotive and tender.

—   702/11 R   with roller drive, 6" long . . . . . .   —   5/8
—   702/11 U   —   spring motor, 6" long . . . .   —   7/2

702/10

702/11

Saloon steam ship with deck.

No. 717/1 R   with roller drive, 6¾" long . . . . .   dozen 6/-
—   717/1 U   —   spring motor, 6¾" long. . . .   —   7/6

Torpedo boat.

—   717 A   with roller drive, 9½" long . . . . .   —   6/-

717/1

717 A

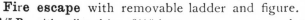

=== **Fire brigade appliances.** ===

Fire engine with figure.

No. 706/1 R   with roller drive, 5½" long . . . .   dozen 5/8
—   706/1 U   —   spring motor, 5½" long . . . .   —   7/2

Fire engine with proper working jet and hose.

No. 706/2 R   with roller drive, 5½" long . . . .   dozen 8/4
—   706/2 U   —   spring motor, 5½" long. . . . .   —   10/-

Fire escape with removable ladder and figure.

No. 706/5 R   with roller drive, 6¼" long . . . .   dozen 6/4
—   706/5 U   —   spring motor, 6¼" long . . . .   —   8/-

Hose carts with 3 figures.

No. 706/7 R   with roller drive, 5½" long . . . .   —   6/-
—   706/7 U   —   spring motor, 5½" long . . . .   —   7/4

706/1

706/5

706/2

706/7

These fire brigade appliances in complete sets
in smart boxes.

No. 706/11 R   consisting of: fire engine, fire escape and hose cart with roller drive. . . . . . .   each 1/8
—   706/11 U   the same with spring motor drive   —   2/-
—   706/12 R   consisting of proper working water jet engine (No. 706/2), fire escape and hose cart with roller drive. . . . . . .   —   1/10
—   706/12 U   the same with spring motor . .   —   2/2

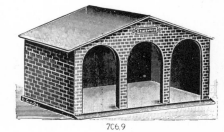

706/9

Fire stations.

No. 706/9   to accommodate 3 vehicles, 11" long, 8" wide, 6¼" high . . . .   each 1/4

Fire stations with fire brigade.

No. 706/13 R   consisting of fire engine with working water jet (706/2), fire escape and hose cart with **fire station** all driven by rollers, packed in smart box   each 3/4
—   706/13 U   the same driven by spring motors   —   3/8

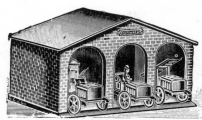

706/13

706/11

Zeppelin Air Ships

strong quality and durable japanning.

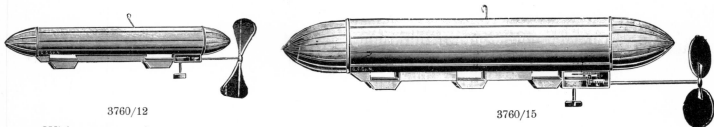

3760/12   3760/15

With strong spring motor
and very durable hard propellers of unparalleled duration of flight describes a large circle.

No.											
No. 3760/10½	with	2	cars and long gangway,		9½″	long (measured **without** propeller)	.	.	dozen		**11/-**
— 3760/10	—	2	— —	—	11⅛″	—	—	—	—	.	**13/-**
— 3760/11	—	2	— —	—	14½″	—	—	—	—	.	**14/-**
— 3760/12	—	2	— —	—	15″	—	—	—	—	.	**15/6**
— 3760/13	—	2	— —	—	16½″	—	—	—	—	.	**21/-**
— 3760/14	—	3	— —	2 gangways	20″	—	—	—	—	.	**24/-**
— 3760/15	—	3	— —	2	22″	—	—	—	—	.	**33/-**
— 3760/16	—	3	— —	2	25½″	—	—	—	—	.	**42/-**

Zeppelin Air Ships strongest and best quality,

fine durable japanning, with strong propeller and unparalleled duration of flight only possible by reason of the excellent mechanism.

   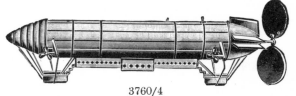

3760/1   3760/4

No. 3760/1	finest japanning, with 2 cars, long gangway, and **2 side propellers which work as the ship is flying**, 10″ long (measured without the propeller)	dozen **26/-**
— 3760/2	the same with **4 side propellers which work during the flight**, 11″ long . .	— **36/-**
— 3760/3	— — — 4 — — — — — — 13″ — . .	— **48/-**
— 3760/4	— — — 4 — — — — — — 14¼″ — . .	— **62/-**
— 3760/5	— — — 4 — — — — — — 16½″ — . .	— **84/-**

Parseval Air Ships

substantial quality and well japanned, with excellent mechanism and strong propeller.

  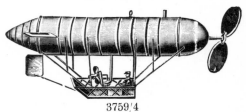

3759   3759/2   3759/4

No. 3759	with car,	plain quality,	5½″ long (measured without propeller)	dozen **5/6**
— 3759/1	— —	fine —	7½″ — . . .	— **7/10**
— 3759/2	— — and figure — —		8″ — . . .	— **14/-**
— 3759/3	— — — — — —	with 2 propellers which work during the flight, 9½″ long	— **26/-**
— 3759/4	the same as 3759/3, but 11″ long	— **42/-**
— 3759/5	— — — 3759/3, — 13″ —	— **62/-**

Trade ⚙ Mark.

Aeroplanes of various types, substantial quality with strong mechanism and well japanned.

3776

3777/1

3777/3

3777/4

"Wright" type Model Aeroplane.

No.						dozen	
No. **3776**	plain quality,	$5^{1}/_2$" long,	$3^{1}/_2$" wide	. . . .		dozen	**6/-**
— **3777/1**	fine —	$6^{3}/_4$" —	$6^{1}/_4$" —	. . . .		—	**14/-**
— **3777/2**	— —	8" —	$7^{1}/_8$" —	. . . .		—	**15/6**
— **3777/3**	— —	$10^{3}/_4$" —	$7^{1}/_8$" —	. . . .		—	**24/-**
— **3777/4**	very strong	$10^{3}/_4$" —	$8^{3}/_4$" —	. . . .		—	**36/-**
— **3777/5**	— —	$12^{3}/_4$" —	$8^{3}/_4$" —	. . . .		—	**48/-**

"Blériot" type Model Monoplane.

Strong quality, powerful mechanism and fine japanning.

3776/1

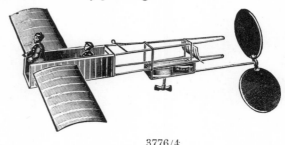
3776/4

No.						dozen	
No. **3776/1**	with 1 figure,	$5^{3}/_4$" long,	$5^{1}/_2$" wide	. . . .		dozen	**7/10**
— **3776/2**	— 1 —	$7^{1}/_2$" —	$7^{1}/_2$" —	. . . .		—	**14/-**
— **3776/3**	— 1 —	9" —	9" —	. . . .		—	**21/-**
— **3776/4**	— 1 —	10" —	9" —	. . . .		—	**15/6**
— **3776/5**	— 2 figures,	$12^{1}/_2$" long,	12" wide	. . . .		—	**24/-**
— **3776/6**	— 2 —	with field glasses,	$14^{1}/_2$" long, $13^{1}/_2$" wide	. . . . . .		—	**33/-**

773/2—5

Wheels of Life or Zoeotropes

of fine **polished steel blue plate**, with 12 very striking pictures, mounted on wood base.

No. **773/1**	**2**	**3**	**4**	**5**	
$4^{1}/_4$	$5^{1}/_8$	$6^{1}/_4$	$7^{1}/_8$	$9^{1}/_2$" diam.	
dozen **7/10**	**14/-**	**24/-**	**32/-**	**48/-**	

Extra pictures for above (1 black and 1 coloured set)

No. **773/1B**	**2B**	**3B**	**4B**	**5B**
set **-/2**	**-/6**	**-/8**	**1/-**	**1/4**

773/1

Trade  Mark.

Stereoscopes
with sliding view holder and folding handle.

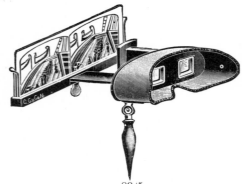

89/1—4   89/5   89/6

No.		Prisms					
89/1	Prisms	1×1"	with fixed handle, plain wood, for stereo pictures, size	3½×7"	dozen	**14/8**
— 89/1½	—		with round lenses, 1 5/16" diam, folding handle, walnut	3½×7"	—	**19/-**
— 89/1¾	—	1 3/16×1 3/16"	folding handle, mahogany, ... size	3½×7"	—	**23/-**
— 89/2	—	1¼×1 3/8"	— — — . . . . . —	3½×7"	—	**26/6**
— 89/2P	—	1¼×1 3/8"	— — — with plush edge . . —	3½×7"	—	**30/-**
— 89/3	—	1 9/16×1 9/16"	— — walnut — . . —	3½×7"	—	**28/6**
— 89/3P	—	1 9/16×1 9/16"	— — with plush edge . . —	3½×7"	—	**32/-**
— 89/4	—	1 9/16×1 9/16"	— mahogany, polished all over —	3½×7"	—	**41/6**
— 89/4P	—	1 9/16×1 9/16"	— — — — with plush edge	3½×7"	—	**45/-**
— 89/4NP	—	1 9/16×1 9/16"	— walnut — — — size	3½×7"	—	**45/-**
— 89/4S	—	1 9/16×1 9/16"	— black polished all over —	3½×7"	—	**50/-**
— 89/4SP	—	1 9/16×1 9/16"	— — — with plush edge	3½×7"	—	**54/-**
— 89/5P	—	1 9/16×1 9/16"	with **aluminium holder and hood**, folding handle in plain wood, mahogany or walnut		—	**30/-**
— 89/5PF	—	1 9/16×1 9/16"	with **aluminium holder and hood**, folding handle of fine quality, of green or black wood		—	**32/6**
— 89/10	—	1 3/16×1 3/16"	folding handle, mahogany, to take stereo pictures	2½×5"	. .	**26/-**
— 89/10P	—	1 3/16×1 3/16"	— with plush edge —	2½×5"	. .	**30/-**
— 89/6	—		with **round lenses**, 1 5/8" diam., folding handle, black polished oculars, walnut, fine instrument		—	**48/-**

New!
Hand and table-

89/15 **as hand stereoscope**

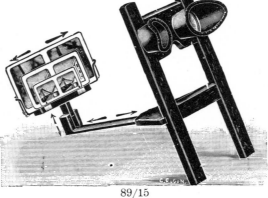

89/15

New!
Stereoscope

89/15 **as table stereoscope**

Universal stereoscope (several D. R.-G.M.)

of handsomely finished indian hard wood, with a pair of oculars of 1¼" diam., with a sliding **view holder** so arranged that it will allow views of 1¾×4¼" to 3½×7" to be shown in stereoscope relief. Beside this it is adjustable for height to the line of sight. The oculars are bordered with plush. The entire instrument can be folded flat, packed in flat box   dozen **36/-**

For stereoscopic views see page 222.

Trade Mark.

Stereoscope

latest design.

(D. R.-G.-M.)

The **oculars** are adjustable to the distance between the eyes. The sliding view holder has the advantage of holding a number of views so that the observer need not move the eyes in order to look at another view. The instrument is also arranged to take glass slides. A further advantage lies in the patent stand allowing the instrument to be placed on any table and need be no longer held by hand.

No. 89/8 Walnut, fine quality, strongly made, with round lenses 1½″ diam., to take stereoscopic views on card or glass size 3½″×7″ . . . . each 7/6

Cabinets for stereoscope and views

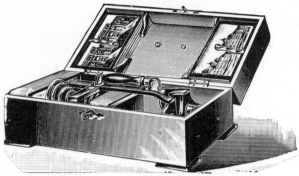

to hold about 200 views together with stereoscope, conveniently aranged, of massive walnut polished with matt surface, fitted with strong lock and highly nickelled handle, clamp attachment for holding a number of views,

16″ long, 8½″ wide, 6″ high

No. 88/1 Walnut, matt surface . . . . each 9/6
— 88/1 **G** the same with lettering „Stereoscopy" . . . . — 12/6
— 88/1 **GM** — — — — and with monogram . . . . — 14/-

Stereoscope Stands.

No. 89 **S/0** to suit stereoscopes 89/1—2
doz. 9/8
— 89 **S/1 M** of dull mahogany to suit 89/1—3
doz. 17/-
— 89 **S/1 N** the same in walnut
doz. 17/-
— 89 **S/2 M** polished mahogany to suit 89/4
doz. 22/-
— 89 **S/2 N** the same, walnut
doz. 22/-
— 89 **S/2 S** the same, fine black polish, to suit 89/4 S
doz. 22/-
— 82 **S** polished mahogany with folding plate to suit No. 82—87
doz. 25/-

89 S

82 S

Small Pocket Stereoscopes

of handsome and strong quality, prettily japanned tin plate, good stereoscopic effect

No. 353/1 with magazine view holder and 6 views . . . . doz. 6/-
— 353/1½ — — — — —12 — — 7/10
— 353/2 — plain — — 6 — . . . — 4/8
— 353/2½ — — — — —12 — — 6/6

No. 353 B Stereoscopic views

to suit above pocket stereoscopes, a **large selection** (General views and landscapes) in sets of 20 views . . . . 100 pieces 2/6

353 B

353 B

New! Cartoscopes (several patents) Novel!

for viewing picture post-cards and photographs of all kinds. Magnificent relief effect, very low price, of fine bronzed indian hard wood, with finely ground magnifying lens, can be folded flat, shows the pictures correctly and not distorted as is the case when using looking glasses.

94/1

No: **94/1** with 3" diam. lens, each **2/-**

— **94/2** — 4" — —
with adjustable card holder, — **4/-**

— **94/3** with 4¹/₄" diam. lens,
with adjustable card holder, — **5/-**

— **94/4** with 5¹/₂" diam. lens,
with adjustable card holder, — **8/-**

The front lens holder can be removed without trouble and used as a reading glass or magnifying glass.

94/2

94/3 and 94/4

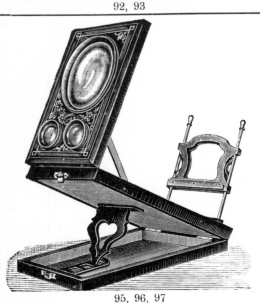

92, 93

95, 96, 97

Microphore with foot and stand

(Instrument for magnifying photographs.)

Extremely strong and handsome design.

with 4¹/₄" diam. lens

No. 92 M	Mahogany	each	**11/-**
— 92 N	Walnut	—	**12/-**
— 92 S	Black polished, rich gold ornamentation .	—	**15/6**

with 5¹/₂" diam. lens

No. 93 M	Mahogany	each	**20/-**
— 93 N	Walnut	—	**22/-**
— 93 S	Polished black, gold ornamentation . .	—	**28/-**

Pantoscopes

with foot and base, for cabinet photographs and stereoscopic views

with 4¹/₄" diam. lens

No. 95 M	Mahogany	each	**13/6**
— 95 N	Walnut	—	**14/6**
— 95 S	Black polished, rich gold ornamentation .	—	**17/6**

with 5¹/₂" diam. lens

No. 96 M	Mahogany	each	**24/-**
— 96 N	Walnut	—	**26/-**
— 96 S	Black polished, rich gold ornamentation .	—	**30/-**

with 6¹/₈" diam. lens

No. 97 M	Mahogany	—	**36/-**
— 97 N	Walnut	—	**38/-**
— 97 S	Black polished, rich gold ornamentation .	—	**42/-**

Pantoscopes fitted with **achromatic stereoscope lenses**

cost No. 95 M—S	. . . .	each extra	**2/8**
— 96 M—S	. . . .	—	**3/8**
— 97 M—S	. . . .	—	**4/4**

For stereoscopic views, see page 222.

Stereoscopes, best quality and strongest design.

82

No. 82/4 M Curved form, mahogany, with hinged cover, prisms. 1⅜"×1¼", glass reflector and ground glass each 3/6
— 82/4 N the same in walnut each 3/6
— 82/5 M the same in mahogany, 1½"×1½" prisms each 4/-
— 82/5 N the same in walnut each 4/-
— 82/5 S the same, black polished . . . . each 6/-

83

No. 83 M
Curved form

with 2 screwed, round oculars with 1¼" diameter lenses, mahogany, highly polished, with flap, reflector and ground glass, each 5/6

No. 83 N the same in walnut . . . . each 5/6

83/4

No. 83/4 M
Stereoscope

high class quality, with 2 screwed oculars, mahogany, only suitable for views on card or glass size 3½"×7" . . . each 8/10

83

No. 88 M
Stereoscope

high class quality, with 2 oculars, with 1¼" lenses, with central focussing screw, reflector and ground glass, mahogany, each 11/6

No. 88 N the same in walnut each 11/6

86

No. 86 M
Stereoscope

high class quality, with 2 oculars fitted with 1¼" diameter lenses, rack and pinion focussing screw at side, reflector with ground glass, mahogany, each 14/8

No. 86 N the same in walnut . . . . each 14/8

87

No. 87 M
Stereoscope

finest quality

2 oculars 1¼" diameter lenses with rack and pinion. Side screw for fixing focus, glass reflector with ground glass with cheek, in mahogany . . . . each 17/-

No. 87N the same in walnut . . . . each 17/-
— 87S — — extra fine black polish . . . . . — 19/6
— 87SG — — — — — — and lettered — 20/-

Stereoscope Helmholtz form

with micrometer screw and objective adjustable sideways, a remarkable improvement in stereoscopy.

Handsome design accurate workmanship.

83/3

No. 83/3 Polished mahogany or walnut, objectives adjustable, right and left hand at same time by means of screw at side. Lenses 1¼" diameter, each 12/-

— 85 Polished mahogany, walnut or rosewood. The oculars are connected to 2 side screws,
1. for side adjustment,
2. for focussing adjustment.
They can also be unscrewed and have 1½" diameter lenses. each 24/-

— 85 G the same with fine lettering . . . . . each 28/-

85

— 84 Polished mahogany, walnut or rosewood. The oculars can be moved at the same time by a side screw. (1) left and right (2) focussed. They can also be unscrewed and are fitted with light shades. Lenses are 1½" diameter . . . . . each 32/-

— 84 G the same, black polish with fine lettering, each 40/-

Stereoscope

No. 83 with achromatic lenses costs . . . . . . 2/8 extra

— 84 and 85 with achromatic lenses costs . . . . 4/4 extra

84

Trade Mark.

Superior Revolving Stereoscopes.

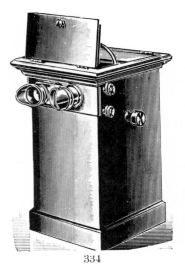

332   333   334

Revolving Stereoscopes for the uninterrupted viewing of a **larger number** of opaque or transparent stereoscopic views.

Extremely strong and handsome design.

With 2 screwed oculars, very strong turning mechanism, glass reflector and ground glass.	The same quality as 332 **but with rack and pinion focussing lenses.**	The same quality as 332 **but with rack and pinion focussing lenses, also adjustable to width between pupils of eyes.**
Dark mahogany, highly polished	**Dark mahogany,** highly polished	**Dark mahogany,** highly polished
to 25 50 views	for 50 views	for 50 views
No. **332/25** **332/50**	No. **333/50**	No. **334/50**
each **34/-** **40/-**	each **53/6**	each **67/-**

All the revolving stereoscopes can be supplied with **reflecting mirror** as shown in fig. 333 for 8/- each extra.

If fitted with **achromatic lenses,** the above instruments cost **3/4** each extra.

Stereoscopic Views

a very large selection.

No. **355/13**   Photographic Views, well executed, original photographs of all countries, also general views, size 3¹/₂″ × 7″ dozen **2/10**
—   **355/14**   Photographic Views, well executed, like 355/13 but **mounted on fine card,** size 3¹/₂″ × 7″ . . . . . . — **4/-**
—   **355/15**   Stereoscopic Views, handsomely executed mounted on fine card, only landscapes and monuments, size 3¹/₂″ × 7″ . . . . — **4/-**
—   **356/1**   Transparent Stereoscopic Views, coloured, mounted on card, a large selection, size 3¹/₂″ × 7″ . . . . — **4/6**
—   **355/12**   New Photographic Stereoscopic Views, natural history, finest execution. **Original views of interesting groups of animals in the Zoological Gardens,** size 3¹/₂″ × 7″ . . . . Set of 10 pieces **4/-**
(The views No. 355/12 are sold only in complete sets.)

Small Stereoscope for Positive Glass Views.

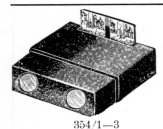

354/1—3

No. **354/1**   with 6 pictures (3 strips of double views 3¹/₈″ × ³/₄″) . . . . dozen **10/-**
—   **354/1 B**   Extra views for above in sets of 6 strips = 12 views . . . . . dozen sets **10/-**
—   **354/2**   with 6 views 2¹/₂″ × 1¹/₈″ . . . . dozen **20/-**
—   **354/2 B**   Extra views for above (30 sets stocked) . . . . set of 12 views **1/6**
—   **354/3**   for views 1³/₄″ × 4¹/₈″, without views . . . . each **1/10**
—   **354/3 B**   Views to suit above (20 sets stocked) . . . . set of 6 views **1/10**

Trade   Mark.

Reading Glasses.

Cheap quality, in nickel frame, with polished black handle.

No. **710**/38	45	51	57	63	70	77
diam. $1^1/_2$	$1^3/_4$	2	$2^1/_4$	$2^1/_2$	$2^3/_4$	3"
dozen **2/10**	**3/8**	**4/4**	**5/4**	**6/8**	**8/6**	**10/10**

710, 726

Reading Glasses.

Better quality, in brass frame with polished black handle.

No. **726**/35	51	63	77
diam. $1^1/_2$	2	$2^1/_2$	3"
dozen **7/8**	**10 6**	**16/-**	**24/-**

728

Best quality Reading Glasses.
Very strong

with carefully worked lenses giving extremely clear definition. The frames of these reading glasses are of polished German silver and are so constructed that they hold the lenses firmly together, extremely serviceable quality.

No. **728**/38	51	63	77
diam. $1^1/_2$	2	$2^1/_2$	3"
dozen **9/8**	**12/-**	**19/8**	**27/-**
No. **728**/89	102	120	128
diam. $3^1/_2$	4	$4^3/_4$	5"
dozen **36/-**	**42/-**	**72/-**	**96/-**

Same quality but **oblong**

No. **727**/1	3	4
diam. $3" \times 1^1/_2"$	$3^1/_2" \times 2"$	$4" \times 2^1/_2"$
dozen **24/-**	**30/-**	**41/-**

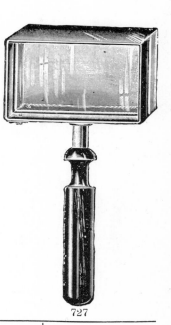

727

748 K and 749 K

Magnifying glasses
with metal handle

No. **748**/1	2	3
diameter 1"	$1^1/_8"$	$1^1/_2"$
dozen **3/8**	**4/6**	**5/4**

Sewn on card.
No. **748 K** with 4 lenses of each size
No. 748/1, 2 and 3, card **4/10**

729

Reading glasses

with **folding** handle, very strong quality.

No. **729**/25	1"	diameter, dozen	8/6
— **729**/30	$1^1/_8"$	—	9/8
— **729**/35	$1^1/_4"$	—	11/-
— **729**/40	$1^1/_2"$	—	12/-
— **729**/45	$1^3/_4"$	—	13/6
— **729**/50	2"	—	17/6

753

Tripod-magnifier

with adjusting screw, solid brass, with 2 clear lenses.

No. **753/1 M**
$1^1/_4"$ diam. each **2/-**

No. **753/2 M**
$1^1/_2"$ diam. each **2/8**

755

Linen tester

with $^3/_8"$ lens and □ hole, $^3/_8" \times ^3/_8"$, brass

No. **755**/1 doz. **12/-**

Magnifying glasses
with nickelled brass frames and sharp lenses

No. **749**/1	2	3
diameter 1"	$1^1/_8"$	$1^1/_2"$
dozen **4/6**	**4/10**	**6/-**

Sewn on card.
No. **749 K** with 4 lenses of each size No. 749/1, 2 and 3, card **5/8**

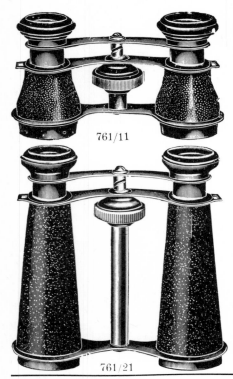

761/11

761/21

Cheap Opera Glasses

for children,

of good quality.

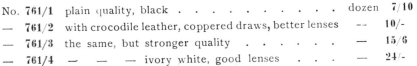

No. 761/1 plain quality, black . . . . dozen 7/10
— 761/2 with crocodile leather, coppered draws, better lenses — 10/-
— 761/3 the same, but stronger quality . . . . . . — 15/6
— 761/4 — — — ivory white, good lenses . . . — 24/-
— 761/11 **Ladies glasses,**
    black, good lenses
          dozen 20/-
— 761/12 the same but with handle
          dozen 24/-
— 761/21 **Field glasses,**
    black, light quality
          dozen 10/-
— 761/22 the same but better quality,
    good lenses . dozen 15/6

761/12

761/1

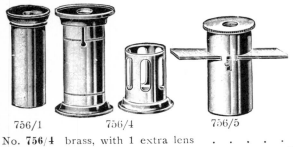

756/1   756/4   756/5

No. **756/4** brass, with 1 extra lens . . . . dozen 11/6
— **756/5** — — 3 object supports, strong quality . . . . . — 11/-

Microscopes.

Pocket microscope

plain quality.

No. **756/1** brass . . . dozen 2/6
— **756/2** — rather larger — 3/8
— **756/3** — larger still — 4/4

Universal pocket microscope.

— **757** in handsome calico covered wood case with partitions and fastener, microscope of brass with sharp definition lenses, 3 slides, 2 object supports and 1 for fluids, each 3/6

757

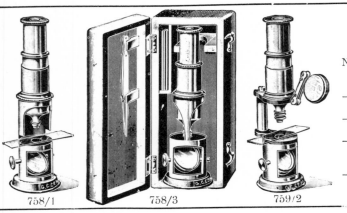

758/1   758/3   759/2

High class microscopes

very strong quality, in polished wood case.

No. **758/1** **microscope,** brass, cylindrical stand, slide tube focussing, 1 eyepiece and 1 objective lens, magnifies **40 diameters,** with forceps, 1 slide and 2 object supports . each 8/4
— **758/2** the same, but with 2 objectives, one to screw on the other, magnifies **40 and 60 diameters** . . . each 9/-
— **758/3** the same, with 3 objectives, one to screw on another, magnifies **40, 60 and 90 diameters** . . . each 11/-
— **759/1** **microscope** as above, but with **lighting lens** with double ball joint for standing on all sides, with 3 objectives, magnifying **40, 60 and 90 diameters** . . . . each 13/-
— **759/2** the same but **pillar form,** also with **light condensing lens,** with 3 objectives, magnifying **30, 50 and 80 diameters** each 17/-

---

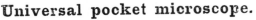

760/1

760/1

Microscope slides

(permanent) carefully and properly prepared, well got up on the regular glass slides. Object of all kinds as blood, bones, insects, tissue etc. of man, dog, cat, rabbit, also sections of wood, yarn, starch, various sorts of meal, vegetables, articles of diet, also pure and adulterated foods (100 different slides).

No. **760/1** to suit small microscopes assorted in dozens set 2/-
— **760/2** — — better — size 3"×1" — — — 9/8

No. **760/11** to suit cheap magnifying glasses in dozens set 2/-
— **760/12** — — better — — — — — 4/-

Trade Mark.

Best quality Magnifying Glasses
in horn frame.

770   771   772   772 S   772 E

Botanical magnifiers, all horn mounts, with sharp clear lenses, most substantial quality.

	Size	12	18	20	24	30	35	40	45	50	
		$\frac{1}{2}$	$\frac{11}{16}$	$\frac{3}{4}$	1	$1\frac{1}{4}$	$1\frac{1}{2}$	$1\frac{3}{4}$	$1\frac{13}{16}$	2 "	diam. of lenses.
No. 770		6/8	9/-	11/-	12/-	16/-	24/-	30/-	38/-	44/-	doz.
— 771		9/-	13/6	16/-	18/-	23/-	33/6	45/-	57/-	63/-	—
— 772		13/6	18/-	22/-	24/-	30/-	42/-	60/-	76/-		

In buffalo horn cases

No. **770 E** Horn frame, with **real tortoise shell case**, with hole, single $\frac{3}{4}$" diam . . doz. 21/-

No. **771 E** the same with hole and shade, double, $\frac{3}{4}$" diam. doz. 30/-

No. **772 E** the same with hole and shade, triple, $\frac{3}{4}$" diam. doz. 39/-

No. **772 S** **Fine naturalists magnifier**, horn mounted with English frame and hole, consisting of 3 lenses $\frac{1}{2}$", $\frac{11}{16}$" and $\frac{3}{4}$" diam. of $1\frac{1}{2}$" and $1\frac{3}{4}$" focus . . . . doz. 36/-

---

Best quality Cheese Magnifiers
in horn frame.

769/1

		Size	15	18	20	24	30	35	40	45	50	
			$\frac{1}{2}$	$\frac{11}{16}$	$\frac{3}{4}$	1	$1\frac{1}{4}$	$1\frac{1}{2}$	$1\frac{3}{4}$	$1\frac{13}{16}$	2 "	diam. of lenses
single	No. 769/1		6/-	8/-	9/6	12/-	14/-	22/6	28/6	33/6	41/-	doz.
double	— 769/2		9/-	11/6	14/6	17/-	20/-	30/-	46/-	48/-	58/-	—
triple	— 769/3		12/-	16/-	19/6	22/-	27/-	34/-	—	—	—	—

Shaving Mirrors in handsome polished wood frames.

779
with turned
wood handle

776

776
with plain
nickelled handle

Best quality, with **1 convex** (magnifying)
and **1 plain glass**.

with turned wood handle

No. 779/3$\frac{1}{2}$	4	4$\frac{1}{2}$	5	5$\frac{1}{2}$	6	6$\frac{1}{2}$	7	
4$\frac{1}{2}$	5	5$\frac{1}{2}$	6	6$\frac{1}{2}$	7	7$\frac{1}{2}$	8 "	diam. of frame
each 2/6	3/-	4/-	5/-	6/6	7/6	9/-	**11/-**	

with plain nickelled handle

No. 776/3$\frac{1}{2}$	4	4$\frac{1}{2}$	5	5$\frac{1}{2}$	6	6$\frac{1}{2}$	7	
4$\frac{1}{2}$	5	5$\frac{1}{2}$	6	6$\frac{1}{2}$	7	7$\frac{1}{2}$	8"	diam. of frame
each 3/-	4/-	5/-	6/-	7/6	9/-	11/-	12/-	

778

777 hanging

777 standing

Shaving Mirrors in superior nickelled frames with folding
handle (highly nickelled) for standing or hanging.

No. 778/1	2	3	4	
5	5$\frac{1}{2}$	6	7 "	diameter
each 8/-	9/-	10/-	14/-	

Shaving Mirrors in superior nickelled frames on highly nickelled stands with base
with lengthening rod, adjustable for any height. (In the base is
an opening so that the mirror can be hung up). **Strongest and best quality.**

No. 777/1	2	3	4	
5	5$\frac{1}{2}$	6	7 "	diameter
each 10/-	11/-	12/-	17/-	

Kaleidoscopes.

Simple quality of decorated tin with coloured glasses.

1440/10—12

1440/22—26

1440/27

1440/28

No. **1440/10** without turning head, 5" long, 1¹/₈" diam., doz. **1/6**

— **1440/11** with turning head, 6¹/₂" long, 1¹/₂" diam., doz. **3/6**

— **1440/12** the same, 9" long, 2¹/₄" diam. . . . doz. **6/-**

Handsome Kaleidoscopes, strong quality, with excellent colour effects with turning mechanism, body of prettily covered card with nickelled fittings.

No. **1440/22** with fine filling, with ornamental glass, 5" long, 1³/₄" diam. . . . . doz. **11/-**
— **1440/23** — — — and child scenes (photos), 5" long, 2¹/₂" diam. . . . . — **18/-**
— **1440/24** — — — with ornamental glass, 5" long, 2¹/₂" diam. . . . . — **18/-**
— **1440/25** — — — and child scenes (photos), 8" long, 2¹/₂" diam. . . . . — **24/-**
— **1440/26** — — — with ornamental glass, 8" long, 2¹/₂" diam. . . . . — **24/-**
— **1440/27** with superior filling, with ornamental glass on polished wood base, 2¹/₂" diam., 8" long, 10" high, each **4/-**
— **1440/28** Body of finely decorated tin, with nickelled fittings on polished wood base, 3" diam., 10" long, 13" high, with superfine filling . . . . each **8/6**

Pocket-Telescope
"ARGUS"
(patented)

Remarkable power! will focus to any distance. Strong quality with good lenses, in pocket case, with full instructions

No. **79/3** with 1 eyepiece . . . . dozen **6/-**

Tourists'
Best quality Telescopes

with planoconvex eyepieces, leather covered body, **with 3 brass draws.** High class object glasses with achromatic lenses.

No. **1403/1**	3	5	7	9		
Objective glass	1"	1¹/₈"	1³/₁₆"	1¹/₄"	1¹/₂" diam.	without
Magnifies	10	12	13	15	20 times	sunshade
Length	1¹/₂"	1³/₄"	1³/₄"	1³/₄"	2¹/₂"	
each	**11/-**	**12/-**	**14/-**	**15/6**	**22/-**	
No. **1403 S/1**	3	5	7	9		with
each	**12/-**	**13/6**	**16/-**	**18/-**	**25/-**	sunshade

Trade Mark.

Optical Lenses.

Magnifying glasses biconvex form, correctly ground, with smooth edges and long focus.

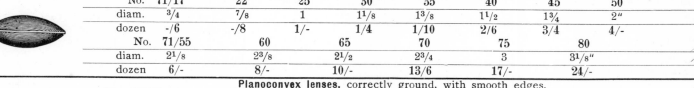

No.	70/25	30	35	40	45	50	55	60
diam.	1	$1\frac{1}{8}$	$1\frac{3}{8}$	$1\frac{1}{2}$	$1\frac{3}{4}$	2	$2\frac{1}{8}$	$2\frac{3}{8}''$
dozen	-/10	1/-	1/4	1/8	2/-	2/6	3/-	4/8
No.	70/65	70	75	85	102	112	130	150
diam.	$2\frac{1}{2}$	$2\frac{3}{4}$	3	$3\frac{1}{4}$	4	$4\frac{1}{2}$	$5\frac{1}{8}$	$6''$
dozen	6/-	7/-	8/-	11/-	20/-	32/-	48/-	72/-

Biconvex lenses, correctly ground, with smooth edges and short focus (magnifying lenses).

No.	71/17	22	25	30	35	40	45	50
diam.	$\frac{3}{4}$	$\frac{7}{8}$	1	$1\frac{1}{8}$	$1\frac{3}{8}$	$1\frac{1}{2}$	$1\frac{3}{4}$	$2''$
dozen	-/6	-/8	1/-	1/4	1/10	2/6	3/4	4/-
No.	71/55	60	65	70	75	80		
diam.	$2\frac{1}{8}$	$2\frac{3}{8}$	$2\frac{1}{2}$	$2\frac{3}{4}$	3	$3\frac{1}{8}''$		
dozen	6/-	8/-	10/-	13/6	17/-	24/-		

Planoconvex lenses, correctly ground, with smooth edges.

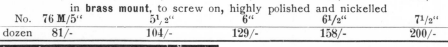

No.	72/25	30	35	40	45	50	60
diam.	1	$1\frac{1}{8}$	$1\frac{3}{8}$	$1\frac{1}{2}$	$1\frac{3}{4}$	2	$2\frac{3}{8}''$
dozen	1/4	1/8	2/6	3/-	3/8	4/10	9/8
No.	72/65	70	75	80	85	90	
diam.	$2\frac{1}{2}$	$2\frac{3}{4}$	3	$3\frac{1}{8}$	$3\frac{1}{4}$	$3\frac{1}{2}''$	
dozen	12/-	16/-	21/6	30/-	40/-	53/-	

Biconcave lenses, correctly ground with smooth edges.

No.	73/25	30	35	40	50
diam.	1	$1\frac{1}{8}$	$1\frac{3}{8}$	$1\frac{1}{2}$	$2''$
dozen	2/-	2/4	3/2	3/10	5/4

No. 75 **Prisms**
$1\frac{3}{4}'' \times \frac{3}{4}''$. dozen 5/4

Panorama Lenses

double convex form, correctly ground with smooth edges, **without mounting.**

No.	76/5''	$5\frac{1}{2}''$	6''	$6\frac{1}{2}''$	7''	$7\frac{1}{2}''$	8''	$8\frac{1}{2}''$	9''	10''
diam.	$5\frac{1}{2}$	6	$6\frac{1}{2}$	7	$7\frac{1}{2}$	8	$8\frac{1}{2}$	9	$9\frac{1}{2}$	11''
dozen	51/-	68/-	87/-	110/-	120/-	140/-	160/-	168/-	180/-	216/-

the above panorama lense in **wood mount** to let in

No.	76 H/5''		$5\frac{1}{2}''$		6''		$6\frac{1}{2}''$		$7\frac{1}{2}''$
dozen	69/-		88/-		111/-		139/-		172/-

in **brass mount,** to screw on, highly polished and nickelled

No.	76 M/5''		$5\frac{1}{2}''$		6''		$6\frac{1}{2}''$		$7\frac{1}{2}''$
dozen	81/-		104/-		129/-		158/-		200/-

76 H and M

20 D	10 D	10 D	8 D	6 D	5 D	2 D	2 D	0.25 D

Complete set of lenses

in handsome covered box,
containing 9 different lenses, $1\frac{1}{2}''$ diam.

No. **70 S** . . . . box **4/6**

Stereoscope glasses

ground prismatic, correct curvature.

No.	74/000	00	0	1	2
	$1'' \times 1''$	$1\frac{1}{4}'' \times 1\frac{1}{4}''$	$1\frac{3}{4}'' \times 1\frac{3}{8}''$	$1\frac{1}{2}'' \times 1\frac{1}{2}''$	$1\frac{3}{4}'' \times 1\frac{3}{4}''$
dozen pairs	3/4	3/8	4/10	6/-	8/-

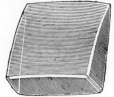

Round **stereoscope lenses**
with strong edge

No.	72 S/33	41	48	54
diam.	$1\frac{1}{4}$	$1\frac{1}{2}$	2	$2\frac{1}{8}''$
dozen	4/4	6/6	13/-	17/-

Round **achromatic stereoscope lenses,**
best workmanship

No.	72 SA/33	41	48	54
diam.	$1\frac{1}{4}$	$1\frac{1}{2}$	2	$2\frac{1}{8}''$
pair	2/8	3/8	4/6	7/6

No. **72 SO/48 Objective mounting,** well rivetted brass, for $1\frac{1}{2}''$ stereoscope lenses, with arrangement to prevent meddlers unscrewing the lenses . . . pair **5/4**

851 S/102 Cl

851 S Cl

840 BCl

TALKING MACHINES
Disc Machines and Phonographs.

858/1—2 Cl

846—847 Cl

859/1—2 Cl

858/11—12 Cl

859/3—5 Cl

859/3—5 PCl

Stereo blocks specially adapted for insertion in advertisements etc. are only supplied against invoice with fixed charges.

No.	851 S/102 Cl	851 S Cl	840 BCl	858/1—2 Cl	846—847 Cl	859/1—2 Cl	858/11—12 Cl	859/3—5 Cl	859/3—5 PCl
each	-/10	-/10	-/10	1/-	1/6	1/4	1/2	1/4	1/4

Disc Talking Machines
covered by several patents.

858/1—2

858/11—12

An experience gained and tested by many years of manufacture, as well as the peculiar design of our machines, the essential features of which are covered by several patents and registrations also the accurate solidly built mechanism with **steel driving gear,** have combined to produce a machine giving a pure clear and very loud reproduction yet at the same time sweet sounding and free from buzzing etc. The table, which is likewise of original design possesses an adhesion preventing all slipping of the record.

No. 858/1 **Disc machine,** tone arm and horn knee in one piece, highly nickelled, **regulator** (patented) which regulates the pressure of the sound box according to condition of the record, well controlled motor for records up to 10″ in diameter, on plain polished wood case $10^1/2 \times 10^1/2$″ (imitation mahogany), complete with good sound box, for **grammophone records,** without horn, each machine in cardboard box, each **20/6**

12″ flower horn for above, well japanned . . . . . — **2/-**

Machine complete 22/6

— 858/1P the same machine but with attachment for using the same soundbox with both kinds of impressions:
Disc records with **grammophone impressions**
— — — phonograph — (Edison, Pathé) each **24/6**

No. 858/2 **Disc machine** on **larger,** highly polished wood case 12 × 12″ with **stronger** mechanism for playing records up to 12″ diameter, for discs with **grammophone impressions,** without horn, each piece packed in cardboard box . . . . each **24/-**
12″ flower horn for above . . . . — **2/-**

Machine complete 26/-

— 858/2P **the same machine,** but with attachment for playing with the same sound box both kinds of records:
Discs with **grammophone impressions**
— — phonograph — (Edison, Pathé) . . each **28/-**

No. 858/11 **Disc machine,** quality same as 858/1 **but on highly finished case** with **brass corners** etc. and cast iron support, for discs with **grammophone impressions,** without horn, in cardboard box . . . . each **22/-**
12″ flower horn for above . . . . — **2/-**

Machine complete 24/-

— 858/11P ʻthe same machine but with attachment for playing with the same sound box both:
Discs with **grammophone impressions**
— — **phonograph** — (Edison, Pathé) . . each **26/-**

No. 858/12 **Disc machine,** quality as 858/2 **but on highly finished case** with **brass corners** etc. and cast iron support, for records with **grammophone impressions,** without horn, packed in handsome cardboard box, each **25/-**
12″ flower horn for above . . . . — **2/-**

Machine complete 27/-

— 858/12P **the same machine** but with attachment for playing with same sound box:
Discs with **grammophone impressions**
— — **phonograph** — (Edison, Pathé) . . each **29/-**

Cardboard boxes for 1 horn, 12″ diameter . . . . . . each -/**10**
— — — 2—3 horns, 12″ — . . . . — **1/-**

For needles and sapphires for above machines see page 235.

Trade Mark.

Highly finished Disc Machines.

No. 859/1 Disc machine with highly nickelled tone arm in one piece from the sound box to the horn knee (patented etc.), by which all buzzing is completely stopped. With specially designed bearing and support for the tone arm, allowing a free movement in all directions, with first class regulated motor with **steel drive** for playing records up to 12″ diam., with speed scale, mounted on a very highly polished wood case 11 1/2 × 11 1/2 ″, complete, with good sound box for records with **grammophone impressions,** packed in strong cardboard box, without horn

	each **28/-**
14″ flower horn for above	— **4/6**
machine complete 32/6	

Cardboard box for 1 horn of 14″ diam	each	**1/4**
— — — 2—3 — 14″ — . . . . —		**1/8**

No. 859/1P the same machine but with attachment for playing both kinds of records with the same sound box discs with **grammophone impressions**

— — **phonograph** —

(Edison, Pathé) each **35/-**

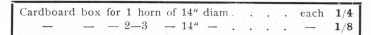

859/1—2

No. 859/2 Disc machine with highly nickelled tone arm in one piece from the sound box to the horn knee (patented), by which all buzzing is completely stopped. With specially designed bearing and support for the tone arm, allowing a free movement in all directions, with first class regulated motor with steel drive for playing records up to 12″ in diam., with speed scale mounted on a **highly polished massive (real) walnut or mahogany case,** also fitted with fine screwed sound box "Invincible" also turning attachment in the tone arm for the sound box, so that in changing needles the box will point upwards, for records with **grammophone impressions**

complete, without horn, packed in cardboard box	each	**35/-**
15 1/2 ″ flower horn for above	—	**5/-**
machine complete 40/-		

No. 859/2P the same machine, but with attachment for playing both kinds of records with the same sound box discs with **grammophone impressions**

— — **phonograph** — (Edison, Pathé) each **42/6**

Cardboard boxes for 1 flower horn 15 1/2 ″ diam . each		**1/4**
— — — 2—3 flower horns 15 1/2 ″ diam. —		**1/8**

☞ The fine concert sound box 861/84 B **"Invincible"** can also be supplied with the machines No. 858/1 and 2, 859/1; the price is **2/4** extra.

☞ The machines 859/1 and 2 can also be supplied with **larger horns** namely

instead of 14″ diam. one 15 1/2 ″ diam.	**extra**	**-/6**
15 1/2 ″ — — 16 1/2 ″ —	—	**1/-**
16 1/2 ″ — — 20 1/2 ″ —	—	**2/-**

For needles and sapphires, see page 235.

Trade  Mark.

Highly finished Disc Machines

with a finely nickelled tone arm in one piece from the sound box to the horn knee (patented), by which all buzzing is completely stopped. With specially designed bearing and support for tone arm allowing a free movement in all directions, with first class regulated motor with steel drive for playing records up to 12" diam., with speed scale with fine screwed sound box **"Invincible"** also turning attachment in tone arm so that when changing the needle, the needle holder points upwards, case of **well finished indian hard wood with brass fittings;** for records with **grammophone impressions,** each machine packed in cardboard box.

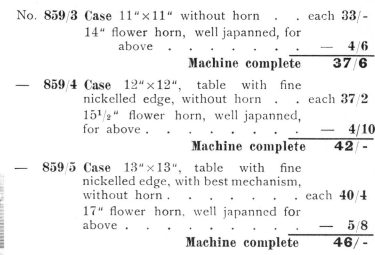

No. **859/3** Case 11"×11" without horn . . each **33/-**
14" flower horn, well japanned, for
above . . . . — **4/6**
Machine complete   37/6

— **859/4** Case 12"×12", table with fine
nickelled edge, without horn . . each **37/2**
15½" flower horn, well japanned,
for above . . . . — **4/10**
Machine complete   42/-

— **859/5** Case 13"×13", table with fine
nickelled edge, with best mechanism,
without horn . . . . each **40/4**
17" flower horn, well japanned for
above . . . . — **5/8**
Machine complete   46/-

859/3—5

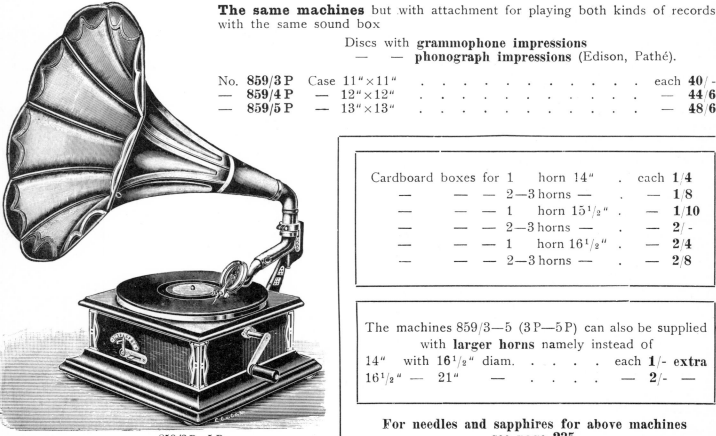

The same machines but with attachment for playing both kinds of records with the same sound box

Discs with **grammophone impressions**
— — **phonograph impressions** (Edison, Pathé).

No. **859/3 P**	Case 11"×11"	. . . . each	**40/-**
— **859/4 P**	— 12"×12"	. . . .	**44/6**
— **859/5 P**	— 13"×13"	. . . .	**48/6**

Cardboard boxes for 1	horn 14"	. each	**1/4**
— — — 2—3 horns —	. —	**1/8**
— — — 1	horn 15½" .	—	**1/10**
— — — 2—3 horns —	. —	**2/-**
— — — 1	horn 16½" .	—	**2/4**
— — — 2—3 horns —	. —	**2/8**

The machines 859/3—5 (3 P—5 P) can also be supplied with **larger horns** namely instead of
14" with 16½" diam. . . . . each **1/-** extra
16½" — 21" — . . . . — **2/-** —

For needles and sapphires for above machines see page 235.

859/3 P—5 P

Disc Machines

with sounding horn built into the case with excellent reproduction.

We have been building these so called **hornless** or **trumpetless** machines (though a horn or trumpet is built into case) for the last twelve months, we have not listed them until we obtained a **faultless, loud** and **sweetly pure** reproduction without considerably raising the cost of production. The quality and the performance of the instruments are in proportion to the price. All the mechanism is of **most substantial** make and is **well regulated, runs silently** and is provided with **steel driving gear.**

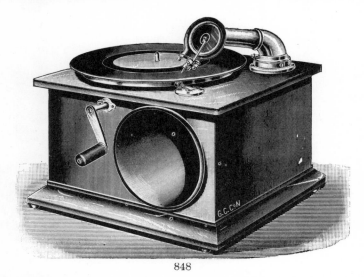

848

No. 848 Disc machine

with highly nickelled removable **tone arm,** with patent ball bearing, with steel driving gear fitted to strong motor, to play records to 10″ diam., 8³/₄″ table covered with felt, on a plain and dark japanned wood case, 8″ high, 13″ long, 13″ wide resp. 11″✕11″, with **good sound box, brake to table, speed control,** with **fine japanned metal horn** built into base, **only suitable** for records with **grammophone impressions,** complete with packing, each **32/-**

No. **848 P**   the same but **only** for **phonograph impressed** records (Edison, Pathé) . . . . . each **32/-**
— **861/132** separate tone arm — — — — — — . . . . . . — **3/-**

845

No. 845 Disc machine

with large, well polished wood case of imitation dark mahogany or rosewood, 7¹/₂″ high, 16″✕12″ resp. 14″✕11″, with strong mechanism fitted with steel driving gear, to play records to 12″ diam., 10″ table covered with felt, with the excellent screwed sound box **"Invincible",** well nickelled, **removable** tone arm with patent ball bearing, **only** for records with **grammophone impressions. Bracke attachment to table and speed regulator,** with **wood horn built in case** and sound door.
Complete with packing each **40/-**

No. **845 P**   the same, **only** for records with **phonograph impressions** (Edison, Pathé) . . . . each **40/-**
— **861/132** separate tone arm for **phonograph impressions** . . . . — **3/-**

For needles and sapphires and still better sound boxes to suit above machines, see page 236.

Trade Mark.

Disc Machines
with resounding wood horn built in case.

846

846

No. **846**   **Disc machine** in highly polished wood case, $9\frac{1}{2}$" high resp. 8", 16"$\times13\frac{1}{2}$" resp 14"$\times11$", with **sound door** and **removable lid**, strong, well regulated mechanism with steel driving gear for playing records up to 12" diam., 10" diam. table with **brake attachment** and **speed regulator,** with revolving indicator, finely nickelled **removable tone arm** with ball bearing joint (patent), **only for** records with **grammophone impressions** with „Regina" sound box of remarkably pure reproduction even in the most difficult places. Complete with packing . . . . each **52/-**

— **846 P** the same but only for **phonograph impressed records** (Edison, Pathé) . . . . — **52/-**

— **861/132** separate **tone arm** for machine 846 to permit playing also phonograph impressed records — **3/-**

847

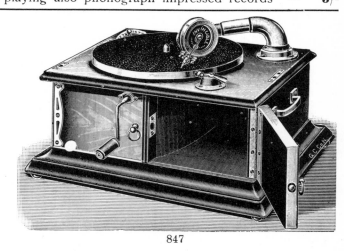

847

No. **847**   **Disc machine** of best quality, extraordinary exact workmanship. Wood case or cabinet 9" resp. $7\frac{1}{2}$" high, 17"$\times14$" resp. 14"$\times11$", of genuine walnut or mahogany, best polishing with **brass fittings, removable lid** with **lock fastening**, with strong handles for carrying machine, with sound door, strong, well regulated mechanism, with steel driving gear to play records up to 12" diam., 10" diam. table with **brake attachment** and **speed regulator**, with revolving indicator, fine nickelled, **removable tone arm**, with **attachment for turning up the sound box**, patent ball bearing joint, **only for** records with **grammophone impressions** with "Imperator" **sound box** (patented), which plays even in the high notes a wonderfully clear and pure reproduction. Complete with packing . . . . each **74/-**

— **847 P** the same but **only for phonograph impressed** records (Edison, Pathé) . . . . . . — **74/-**

— **861/132** separate **tone arm** for machine 847 to play also phonograph impressed records . . . — **3/-**

For needles and sapphires for above machines see pages 235.

Trade Mark.

Sound Boxes

for disc machines, mounted complete, with Pa. mica diaphragm and extra hard needle screw. The tube piece behind the sound box has the **standard** outside diam. of ³/₄".

Every sound box is carefully tested.

861/84A   861/84B   861/100   861/101

No. **861/84 A**	Cast metal case, black oxydized finish, with double spring lever holder	each	**2/10**
— **861/84 B**	"Invincible sound box" nickelled brass case, lever with double spring support . .	—	**5/-**
— **861/100**	"Regina" sound box (patented) in nickelled brass case with back plate screwed on, **four fold spring** lever support back plate elastic by reason of the 3 screws with springs and **rubber washer**, magnificently pure reproduction even in the highest and most delicate tones	—	**6/-**
— **861/101**	"Imperator" sound box (patented) designed like the "Regina" but with a **ball bearing** on the tube piece enabling the sound box to follow **all movements** of the grammophone or phonograph needle without strain in consequence of which this sound box obtains its wonderfully **clear pure reproduction** and can be justly described as **the best** on the market	—	**8/-**

Spare parts of sound boxes.

No. 861/86a	Piece of rubber tube, 6" long, ¹/₃₂" hole	dozen	**1/6**
— 861/86b	— — — 6" — ¹/₁₆" —	—	**1/-**
— 861/87a	Rubber ring, ³/₄" diam.	—	**-/6**
— 861/87b	— — ¹³/₁₆"	—	**-/10**
— 861/88a	Mica diaphragm Pa. 2" diam.	each	**-/6**
— 861/88b	— — Pa.Pa. 2" —	—	**-/7**
— 861/91	Needle screw, hardened steel	dozen	**1/4**
— 861/97	Screws for lever support	100 pieces	**3/6**
— 861/98	Spiral springs for back of No. 861/100 and 101	dozen	**-/10**
— 861/99	Screws for back of sound box	100 pieces	**3/6**
— 861/134a	Spiral springs for back of sound box 861/100 and 101	dozen	**-/6**
— 861/134b	Nuts for same	—	**1/-**
— 861/134c	Caps —	—	**-/2**
— 861/134d	Rubber insulation rings for the tube piece of sound boxes 861/100 and 101	—	**-/2**

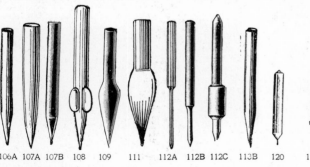

106A 107A 107B   108   109   111   112A 112B 112C   113B   120   115

Needles for grammophone records.

Only first class manufacture of best steel listed.

Loud playing needles (200 in packet).

No. 861/106 A	in envelope	1000 pieces		**1/6**
— 861/107 A	in tin box	—	—	**3/-**
— 861/107 B	— —	—	—	**3/4**
— 861/108	— —	—	—	**4/4**
— 861/109	**Concert needles** in tin box . . .	—	—	**7/4**
— 861/111	**Double tone** needles plays loud or soft tone according to position .	—	—	**2/10**
— 861/112 A	**Parlour needles,** for playing **softly**, in tin box	—	—	**10/-**

No. 861/112B	Parlour needles, **loud** playing, in tin box	1000 pieces	**10/-**
— 861/112C	— — **strong tone** — — —		**12/-**
— 861/113A	softly playing needles in envelope		**1/8**
— 861/113B	— — — tin box		**3/-**
— 861/115	**Lasting needles,** plays about 20 records		**13/4**
— 861/120	**Sapphire points** in nickel case for **Phonograph impressed** records (for all our "P" machines) can be used about 150 times without being changed.	each	**-/8**

861/1

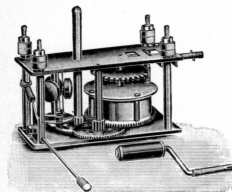

861/1 C

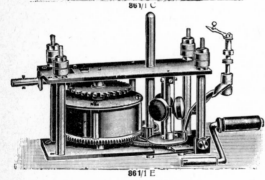

861/1 E

Accessories for Disc Machines.

Best quality mechanism with steel driving pinions.

The time of running given, is based on a speed of 85 turns in a minute and while record is playing, not while motor is running free.

No. 861/1	4 minute motor, complete with winding key, brake lever, and speed regulator to suit machines No. 858/1, 1 P, 11 and 11 P . .	each	8/-
— 861/1 A	do., 5 minute motor for machines 858/2, 12, 859/1, 2 . .	—	9/4
— 861/1 P	— 6 — — — — 858/2. 2P, 12, 12 P, 859/1, 1 P, 2, 2 P, 3, 3 P, 4, 4 P, 5 and 5 P	—	10/-
— 861/1 C	4 minute motor, with winding key, and speed regulator, for machines 848, 848 P	—	7/8
— 861/1 D	5 minute motor with winding key, and speed regulator, for machines 845, 845 P	—	9/-
— 861/1 E	6 minute motor with winding key and speed regulator, for machines 846, 846 P, 847, 847 P	—	11/-
— 861/2	Winding keys, dull nickelled, plain quality for 861/1 . .	—	-/6
— 861/2 N	ditto., highly nickelled, better quality for 861/1 A, 1 P . .	—	-/8
— 861/2 D	— for No. 861/1 C to E	—	1/-
— 861/3 a	regulating rod with handle for No. 858/1, 1 P, 11, 11 P .	—	-/2
— 861/3 b	do., for No. 858/2, 2 P, 12, 12 P	—	-/2
— 861/3 c	do., without handle for all No. 859	—	-/2
— 861/3	regulating lever for all No. 858, 859	—	-/4
— 861/5	complete regulator for No. 858/1, 1 P, 11, 11 P . . .	—	1/4
— 861/5a	do., for all No. 858/2, 12, 859/1, 2, 3, 4, 5	—	1/8
— 861/6	regulator spindle for No. 858/1, 1 P, 11, 11 P . . .	—	-/6
— 861/6a	do., for No. 858/2, 12 and all No. 859	—	-/6
— 861/7a	screws for No. 858/1, 1 P, 11, 11 P	dozen	-/10
— 861/7b	washers for all motors above	each	-/2
— 861/7 c	flat springs — — —	dozen	-/6
— 861/8	hexagon nuts for screws, brake lever or spring case 100	pieces	2/-
— 861/9	regulator springs	dozen	-/2
— 861/10a	screws for above springs 100	pieces	2/6
— 861/10b	do., regulator block	—	2/6
— 861/10c	washers for regulator screws	gross	-/6
— 861/11	regulator balls	dozen	1/-
— 861/12	— — — screws 100	pieces	2/6
— 861/13a	gear wheel with table spindle	each	-/4
— 861/13b	table gear wheel with shaft and pinion	—	-/10
— 861/14a	intermediate gear wheel only	—	-/4

No. 861/14b	the above with shaft and pinion	—	-/10
— 861/14P	do., only for P machines .	—	-/10
— 861/15	spring pa. for 858/1, 1 P, 11, 11 P, 848, 848 P .	—	1/6
— 861/16	do., for 858/2, 858/12, 859/1, 859/2, 845, 845 P	—	1/8
— 861/18	do., for 858/2 P, 12 P, 859/1 P, 2 P, 3, 4, 5, 846, 846 P, 847, 847 P . . .	—	2/8
— 861/17a	spring pins for 861/1, 1 A, 1 P	dozen	2/4
— 861/17b	do., for 861/1 C, 1 D, 1 E	—	2/4
— 861/19	spring wheel with bolt, cover, and spring pin for No. 861/1	each	1/8
— 861/19 c	do., for 861/1 c	—	1/8
— 861/20	— — 861/1 A	—	2/-
— 861/20D	— — 861/1 D	—	2/-
— 861/20P	— — 861/1 P	—	2/4
— 861/20E	— — 861/1 E	—	2/4
— 861/21	like No. 861/19 but with spring	—	3/4
— 861/22	do., No. 20	—	4/-
— 861/22P	— — 20P	—	5/2
— 861/23	winding wheel with hub and pin	—	-/4
— 861/24	do., with spindle and pin .	—	1/-
— 861/24a	do., alone	dozen	4/4

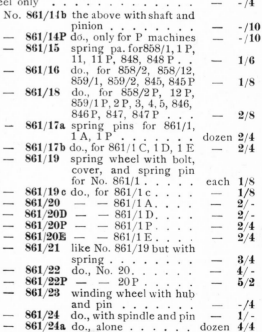

Trade Mark.

Accessories for Disc Talking Machines (continued).

No.	861/25	Winding gear with shaft and pin for No. 861/1, 1 A, 1 C, 1 D . . . . each	1/-
—	861/25 P	ditto for No. 861/1 P, 1 E . . . . . . —	1/-
—	861/26	Winding spring (helical spring) . . . dozen	1/-
—	861/27	Regulating lever spring . . . . . . —	1/-
—	861/28	Brake lever for No. 858/1, 11 . . . . —	1/4
—	861/28 a	— — — — 858/2, 12, 859/1, 2, 3, 4, 5 . . . . —	1/4
—	861/29	Hexagon nuts for plate bolts . . . 100 pieces	2/-
—	861/30 a	Under plate with 4 bolts for No. 861/1, 1 c . . . . each	-/10
—	861/30 b	ditto for No. 861/1 A, 1 D . . . . —	1/-
—	861/30 c	— — — 861/1 P, 1 E . . . . —	1/-
—	861/31 a	Upper plate for No. 861/1, 1 c . . . —	-/6
—	861/31 b	— — — — 861/1 A, 1 D . . . —	-/6
—	861/31 c	— — — — 861/1 P, 1 E . . . —	-/6
—	861/31	ditto with winding gear, shaft, pin and spring for No. 861/1 . . . . . . —	1/4
—	861/32	Screws for regulating lever . . 100 pieces	3/4
—	861/33	— — brake lever with nuts and washers . . . . 100 —	5/6
—	861/34	Pivot (steel plate) . . . . dozen	-/8
—	861/35	Screws for same . . . . . . 100 pieces	5/8
—	861/36	Steel ring for table shaft with screw each	-/2
—	861/37	Wood screws for fixing motor . . . . dozen	-/2
—	861/38	Small rubber under washer for motor —	1/-
—	861/39	Screws for fastening wood bottom . . —	-/4
—	861/40 a	Rubber feet for case . . . . —	1/6
—	861/40 b	— nails feet for case . . . . —	-/8
—	861/41	Wood screws for No. 861/40 a . . . . —	-/2

Table (flywheel) with rubber pieces cemented in the spokes (patented)

No.	861/42	8" diameter, black japanned . . . . each	3/-
—	861/44	10" — — — . . . . —	3/4
—	861/45	10" — polished and nickelled —	4/10
—	861/43	Separate rubbers for No. 861/42 . . . dozen	-/4
—	861/46	— — — 861/44 and 45 —	-/6
—	861/47	Rosette for table shaft . . . . . . each	-/2
—	861/48	Brake lever shield . . . . —	-/2
—	861/49	Regulating ocale . . . . —	-/2
—	861/50	Pointer for above . . . . —	-/2
—	861/51	Screws for same . . . . dozen	-/8

Table covered with felt with screw.

No.	861/52	9" diameter . . . . each	3/-
—	861/53 a	10" — . . . . —	3/4
—	861/53 b	10" — higly polished and nickelled —	4/10
—	861/54	Screws for No. 861/52 and 53 . . . dozen	-/4
—	861/55 a	Felt disc for No. 861/52 = 9" diameter —	2/6
—	861/55 b	— — — 861/53 = 10" —	2/10
—	861/56	Bent wire horn support for No. 858/1 each	-/2
—	861/57	— — — — 858/2 —	-/2
—	861/58	Socket for same . . . . —	-/2
—	861/59	Screws — — . . . . . . 100 pieces	2/-
—	861/60 a	Fork — — . . . . each	-/4
—	861/61	Hinge pin . . . . dozen	-/8
—	861/62	Hexagon nuts for 858/1 and 1P, 100 pieces	1/4
—	861/63	Regulating rod — 858/3 — 2P . . dozen	1/-
—	861/64	Screws for above with nuts . . . . —	-/8
—	861/65 a	Spring for same . . . . —	-/4
—	861/66	Lock nuts . . . . —	-/8
—	861/67	Bottom washer . . . . . 100 pieces	-/4
—	861/68	Sound tube for No. 858/1, 2, 11, 12 . each D. R.-P.	3/-
—	861/69	ditto, for No. 858/1 P, 2 P, 11 P, 12 P . — D. R.-P.	2/6
—	861/70	ditto, for grammophone impressions for No. 861/69 and 76 . . . . —	2/6
—	861/71	ditto, for phonograph impressions for No. 861/69 and 76 . . . . —	2/4

861/68   861/69   861/70   861/71

861/72   861/74—75   861/76

No.	861/72	Lengthening tube for No. 861/69 . . . each	1/-
—	861/73	Screws for No. 861/70, 71 and 72 . . dozen	1/8
—	861/74	Tone arm for No. 859/1, 3, 4, 5 (D. R.-P.) each	4/-
—	861/75	ditto, for No. 859/2, 3, 4, 5 (D. R.-P.) —	4/8
—	861/76	ditto, — — 859/1, 2, 3, 4, 5 in order to be able to use No. 861/70 and 71 —	2/10

861/77 and 78

No.	861/77	Horn support with tension screw and spindle screw for all No. 859 machines, well japanned . . . —	5/4
—	861/78	The same, finest polished and nickelled . . . . —	7/4
—	861/79	Screws for fixing the horn support . . . —	-/4
No.	861/80/5	Spindle . . . . —	-/2
—	861/80/7	Spiral spring } for No. 861/77 and 78 dozen	-/2
—	861/80/8	Screw . . . . —	1/6
—	861/81	Binding screw } . . . . . . —	1/-

861/83   861/82 a, b

No.	861/82 a	Horn support for No. 858/11 and 11P each	2/-
—	861/82 b	— — — — 858/12 — 12 P —	2/-
—	861/83	Table brake . . . . —	1/-
—	861/104	Top tube piece for machines No. 859 —	2/-
—	861/105	Knee piece for flower horns No. 860/108 —	1/6

861/130   861/131

Tone arms for machines 845-848.

861/132   861/133

No.	861/130 a	Tone arm for grammophone impression for No. 848 . . . . each	3/4
—	861/130 b	Tone arm for grammophone impression for No. 845 to 847 . . . . —	5/-
—	861/131	The same but with arrangement to turn sound box (D. R.-P.) . . . . . . —	7/6
—	861/132	Tone arm for phonograph impressions —	3/-
—	861/133	Bottom socket piece (D. R.-G.-M.) for No. 861/130—133 . . . . —	2/4
—	861/134 a	Spiral springs for No. 861/100 and 101 dozen	-/6
—	861/134 b	Nuts for same . . . . —	1/-
—	861/134 c	Caps . . . . —	-/2
—	861/134 d	Rubber insulation rings for the tube piece of sound boxes No. 861/100, 101 dozen	-/2

Phonographs.

Our phonographs are of surprising resonance and the reproduction of a good record is clear and distinct. They compare favourably with the most expensive machines and in spite of their low price are by no means worthless toys. Our machines are very strong and neatly finished, they are carefully tested as to perfect working before being packed.

Our phonographs have obtained among our customers quite a marked popularity on account of their substantial make and beautiful reproduction.

850 S

851 S

851 S/102

No. **850 S**

Puck Phonograph

For playing the small cylinders on the market (about 4" long and 2" diam.), with **prima motor, regulator, stop lever** (patented) **adjusting and levelling screw, reproduction sound box nickelled horn** on black japanned ornamental stand. Each machine packed in cardboard box without horn . . each **5/8**

Puck Phonograph

For playing the small cylinders on the market (about 4" long and 2" diam.), with **prima motor, regulator, stop lever** (patented), **adjusting and levelling screw, band drive, excellently performing soundbox nickelled horn** with patent support, which not only prevents the needle jumping out of the groove but also avoids the too rapid wearing out of the record.

Each machine packed in cardboard box (without horn)

No. **851 S** with black japanned ornamental cast stand, each **6/-**

— **851 G** with fine **gilt** stand . . . . — **6/6**

— **851 N** the same but with **highly nickelled** cast stand — **7/8**

The same phonographs fitted with **aluminium horn** instead of the nickeiled horn, cost

with	9"	10½"	12"	**aluminium horn**
each	-/8	1/-	2/-	**extra**

The same phonographs fitted with handsomely japanned **flower horn** instead of the nickelled horn

with	9½"	10½"	**flower horn**
each	-/4	-/6	**extra**

☞ When ordering the machines with aluminium or flower horns, it must be definitely stated which is wanted

Trade ⚙ Mark.

Inter-Phonograph

same quality and with the same fittings as No. 851, but with higher stand and **two mandrels** so that either the **small cylinder records** (about 4″ long, 2″ diameter) or the **intermediate size cylinder records** (about 4″ long, 3″ diameter) can be played.

No. **852S** with **black japanned** cast stand
each 8/-

This machine can also be supplied with an aluminium or handsome flower horn, instead of the ordinary nickelled horn. The price is then exactly the same as in the case of No. 851 machines page 238.

852 with 12″ aluminium horn

Puck Phonograph
for recording and reproducing

will play all the **small** size records in the trade (**4″** long, 2″ diameter) with **prima motor, regulator, stop lever** (patented), **levelling and adjusting screw, belt tension adjustment, excellently performing reproducing sound box, recording diaphragm** by which **recitations** and **songs** can be **recorded** on **plain cylinders, nickelled horn,** with patent support, having a spring tension, preventing any jumping of the diaphragm from the record and also the too rapid wearing of the record. Each machine packed in cardboard box (without the horn).

No. **853S** with **black japanned** cast stand . . . each **12/-**
— **853N** the above but with stand, **handsomely nickelled,** each **14/-**

853 with 10¹/₂″ aluminium horn

Phonograph "Nymphe"
on a handsome cast stand in the form of a Nymphe

for reproducing the **small size** cylinder records in the trade (about 4″ long, 2″ diameter) with **prima motor, regulator, stop lever** (patented), **adjusting and levelling screw, belt tension adjustment, excellently performing reproducing sound box, nickelled horn** with patent support having a spring tension preventing the diaphragm jumping off the record and also preventing the too rapid wearing away of the latter. Each machine packed in cardboard box (without the horn).

No. **856S** with **black japanned** cast "Nymphe" . each **6/-**
— **856G** — handsomely gilt — — . — **6/6**

These machines can also be supplied with aluminium or handsome flower horns instead of the usual nickelled horn, the prices are then the same as in the case of machines No. 851, page 238.

856

856/2 with 12" aluminium horn

Inter Phonograph "Nymphe"

same quality and with the same fittings as 856, but with higher stand and **two mandrels** so that either the **small cylinder records** (about 4" long, 2" diam.), or the **intermediate size cylinder records** (about 4" long, 3" diam.), can be played.

No. **856/2 S** with black japanned cast stand . . . each 8/-

This machine can be supplied with aluminium or handsome flower horns, instead of the ordinary nickelled horn, the prices are then the same as in the case of the machine No. 851 page 238.

New Cabinet Phonographs
very strong and handsome models.

843 B

844 N with 10½" flower horn

For reproducing the **small size cylinder records** (about 4" long, 2" diam.) in the trade, with **prima motor, nickelled regulator, stop lever** (patented), **adjusting and levelling screw, belt tension adjustment, excellently performing reproduction sound box, nickelled horn** with patent support, having a spring tension preventing the diaphragm jumping off the record and also preventing the too rapid wearing away of the latter. Mounted on polished wood cabinet.

No. **843 B** with coloured cast stand . . . . each **8/6**
— **844 N** — nickelled — — . . . . — **9/4**

These machines can be supplied with aluminium or handsome flower horns instead of the ordinary nickelled horn. The prices are then the same as in the case of machines No. 851, page 238.

Trade Mark.

Handsome Cabinet Phonographs
very strong and handsome quality.

For reproducing the **small size cylinder records** (about 4" long, 2" diam.), in the trade, with **prima motor, nickelled regulator, stop lever** (patented), **adjusting and levelling screw, belt tension adjustment, excellently performing reproduction sound box** with patent support, having a spring tension preventing the diaphragm jumping off the record and also preventing the too rapid wearing away of the latter, mounted on highly polished wood cabinet with cover.

840 B and 840 N with 10¹/₂" aluminium horn

No. **840 B** on highly **japanned** iron bedplate, bird pattern . . . . each **10/6**
— **840 N** — — **nickelled** — — — — . . . . — **11/4**
These machines can also be supplied with aluminium or handsome flower horns. The prices are then the same as in the case of machines No. 851 page 238.

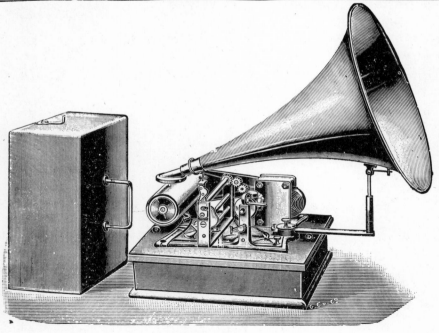

Handsome
Cabinet Phonographs
for **recording** and **reproducing**
very strong and handsome quality.

Fittings same as No. 840, but also with **recording sound box** with **spindle guide** by means of which **songs** and **words** can be recorded on **plain cylinders** with **aluminium horn** (10¹/₂" diam.), with patent support

No. **842 B/26** on **highly japanned** iron bedplate, bird pattern, each **19/6**

— **842 N/26** on **highly nickelled** iron bedplate, bird pattern, each **20/6**

The above phonographs can also be supplied with **well japanned** and **handsomely designed** flower horn (10¹/₂" diameter)

No. **842 B/102** . . . . each **19/-**
— **842 N/102** . . . . — **20/-**

Trade Mark.

16*

Separate Horns

to suit preceding
Phonographs.

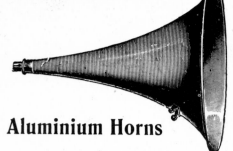

Nickel zinc Horns

Aluminium Horns

Flower Horns
handsomely japanned and
beautifully made

No. 860/60 7½" diameter . . . . each 1/2	No. **860/61** 9" diameter . . each **1/8**	No. 860/106 9½" diameter . . each **1/6**
	— **860/62** 10½" — . . — **2/2**	— 860/102 10½" — . . — **1/8**
	— **860/63** 12" — . . — **3/2**	

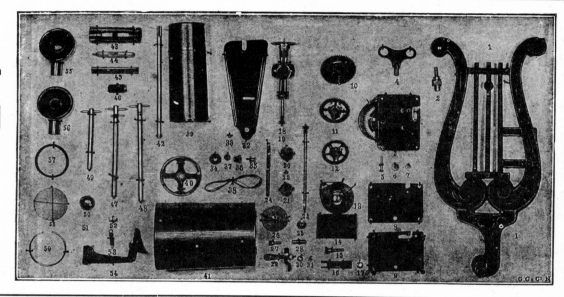

Spare parts for Puck-, Jnter- and Cabinet- Phonographs.

No. 860/1 S	Lyra stand, japanned black . . . . each	1/6
— —/1 B	— — coloured . . . . . —	1/10
— —/1 N	— — nickelled . . . . —	2/6
— —/1 IS	— black for Inter . . . —	1/8
— —/1 IB	— — coloured for Inter . . —	2/-
— —/1 IN	— — nickelled — . . —	2/8
— —/1 C	Nymphe stand japanned black . . . —	1/6
— —/1 D	— — coloured . . . —	1/10
— —/1 IC	— — black for Inter . . —	1/8
— —/1 ID	— — coloured for Inter . . —	2/-
— —/2	Foot screw . . . . —	-/1
— —/3	Motor . . . . —	1/8
— —/4	— winding key . . . . dozen	1/8
— —/5	— fixing screws . . . . —	-/4
— —/6	Washers for above . . . . —	-/2
— —/7	Motor fixing nuts . . . . —	-/3
— —/8	— front plate . . . each	-/2
— —/9	— back with bolts . . . —	-/4
— —/10	Cylinder wheel with ratchet . . . —	-/4
— —/11	Middle wheel with pinion . . . —	-/3
— —/12	Train wheel . . . . . . —	-/3
— —/13	Spring for motor . . . . —	-/6
— —/14	Cover plate . . . . . dozen	-/3
— —/15	Regulating screw . . . . —	-/4
— —/16	Brake spring . . . . . —	-/4
— —/17	Washers for above . . . . gross	-/8
— —/18	Regulator, dull complete . . . each	-/8
— —/19	— nickelled complete . . —	1/4
— —/20	Balls for above, plain . . . dozen	-/10
— —/21	— nickelled . . . . —	1/6
— —/22	Screws for regulator balls . . . —	-/2
— —/22 a	Washers for above . . . . gross	-/6
— —/23	Regulator spindle with pinion and driving grooved pulley each	-/4
— —/24	Regulator spring . . . . gross	1/8
— —/25	Hexagon block for regulator . . . dozen	1/-
— —/25 a	Screws for same . . . . —	-/2

No. 860/26	Brake disc with guide . . . . . each	-/2
— —/27	Screws for 860/16, 29, 42 . . . . dozen	-/4
— —/28	Pivot for 860/23 . . . . . —	-/4
— —/29	Stop lever . . . . —	-/6
— —/30	Washers for above . . . . . gross	-/6
— —/31	Spring for 860/29 . . . . . —	-/10
— —/32 S	Protecting plate, black . . . . dozen	-/6
— —/32 N	— — nickelled . . . —	-/8
— —/33 N	Screws for above nickelled . . . —	-/8
— —/34 G	Belt tension adjustment, black . . . —	1/8
— —/34 GN	— — nickelled . . —	2/2
— —/37	Washers for 860/34 . . . . gross	-/6
— —/38	Driving belt . . . . . 100 yards	-/4
— —/39	Puck mandrel . . . . . each	-/4
— —/40	Inter — . . . . . —	2/-
— —/42	Shaft for mandrel . . . . . dozen	-/8
— —/46 a	Plate bearing for 860/47a . . . —	-/4
— —/46 b	— — 860/47 b . . . —	1/-
— —/46 c	— — 860/47a, b and c . . —	1/-
— —/47 a	Horn support for 850 . . . . —	-/10
— —/47 b	— — 860/60 . . . . —	1/2
— —/49 a	— — 860/61 and 62 . . . —	1/2
— —/49 b	— — 860/63 . . . . —	1/2
— —/49 c	— — 860/102 and 106 . . . —	1/2
— —/50	Case with glass rod . . . . . —	-/8
— —/51	Glass rod . . . . —	-/4
— —/55	Sound box complete . . . . . each	-/6
— —/55 c	**Concert sound box** . . . . . —	-/10
— —/56	Metal part for above (diaphragm plate) . . . —	-/2
— —/57	Rubber rings for 860/55 . . . . dozen	-/4
— —/58 a	Mica diaphragms for 860/55 . . . —	-/8
— —/58 c	— — 860/55c . . . —	1/-
— —/59	Wire ring for 860/55 . . . . . —	-/4
— —/64	Glass diaphragms for 860/55 . . . —	1/8
— —/67	Recording diaphragm with steel style for 853 . . . each	1/6

Trade Mark.

Index.

Trade  Mark.

Trade   Mark.

Trade  Mark.

Trade   Mark.

List of numbers and prices.

No.	per	s.	d.	page	No.	per	s.	d.	page	No.	per	s.	d.	page	No.	per	s.	d.	page
oC	each	3	—	185	6M/14	doz.	—	6	33	9K/4	doz.	1	—	29	15/00	doz.	1	6	119
ooD	—	2	4	186	-/15	—	—	8	—	-/5	—	2	6	—	-/0	—	1	8	—
oD	—	2	—	—	-/16	—	—	6	—	10/1	—	1	8	—	-/1	—	2	8	—
oF	—	3	2	185	-/17	—	—	8	—	-/2	—	2	—	—	-/2	—	4	5	—
1A	—	1	6	—	-/18	—	1	10	—	-/3	—	2	2	—	-/3	—	5	4	—
1B	—	2	—	—	-/20	—	—	6	—	-/4	—	2	6	—	16/0	each	1	10	—
1F	—	3	6	186	-/21	—	—	4	—	10K/1	—	1	—	—	-/1	—	2	—	—
1K	—	1	6	186	-/22	—	—	4	—	-/2	—	1	2	—	-/2	—	2	—	—
1KA	—	1	8	—	-/23	—	—	6	—	-/3	—	1	2	—	-/3	—	2	—	—
1L	—	1	10	—	-/24	—	—	6	—	-/4	—	1	4	—	-/4	—	1	6	—
1P	—	—	8	—	-/25	—	—	6	—	-/5	—	3	—	—	-/5	—	1	6	—
1PA	—	1	—	—	-/26	—	—	8	—	10S/1½	—	—	8	37	-/6	—	2	—	—
1PG	—	—	10	—	-/27	—	1	—	—	-/2	—	1	—	—	-/7	—	3	—	—
1T	—	1	10	—	-/28	—	1	8	—	11/1	—	—	8	—	-/8	—	3	8	—
2F	—	4	8	185	7A/8	yard	—	4	37	-/2	—	1	6	—	-/9	—	4	—	—
3F	—	6	6	—	-/10	—	—	5	—	12D/1	each	—	2	—	-/10	—	5	6	—
3L	—	4	—	186	7F/3	—	—	5	—	-/2	—	—	4	—	-/11	—	4	8	—
4F	—	11	—	185	-/4	—	—	5	—	-/3	—	—	5	—	-/12	—	7	—	—
5/1	set	—	4	119	-/5	—	—	6	—	12L/1	—	—	5	—	-/20	doz.	1	6	—
-/2	—	—	8	—	-/6	—	—	8	—	-/2	—	—	6	—	-/21	—	1	8	—
6/0	doz.	—	3	33	7V/0	—	—	1	—	-/3	—	—	8	—	-/22	—	2	2	—
-/1	—	—	4	—	-/1	—	—	1	—	-/4	—	—	10	—	-/23	—	2	6	—
-/2	—	—	4	—	-/2	—	—	2	—	12N/1	—	—	2	—	-/24	—	3	—	—
-/3	—	—	4	—	-/3	—	—	2	—	-/2	—	—	3	—	-/25	—	3	2	—
-/4	—	—	2	—	8/1	doz.	—	4	125	-/3	—	—	4	—	-/26	—	3	8	—
-/5	—	—	2	—	-/2	—	—	8	—	12V/1	—	—	6	—	-/27	—	4	2	—
-/5½	—	—	4	—	8A	—	2	—	—	-/2	—	—	8	—	-/28	—	4	6	—
-/5¾	—	—	6	—	8B	—	1	10	—	-/3	—	—	10	—	-/29	—	5	—	—
-/6	—	—	4	—	8C	—	—	6	—	-/4	—	—	10	—	-/30	—	5	6	—
-/7	—	—	5	—	8D	yard	—	8	156	-/5	—	1	—	—	-/31	—	6	6	—
6E/10	—	—	3	—	8F/2	—	—	1	—	-/10	—	2	8	—	-/32	—	7	—	—
-/11	—	—	4	—	-/3	—	—	2	—	-/11	—	3	—	—	-/33	—	7	—	—
-/12	—	—	8	—	-/5	—	—	2	—	-/12	—	3	2	—	-/34	—	8	—	—
-/13	—	—	4	—	-/8	—	—	4	—	-,15	—	2	—	—	-/35	—	12	—	—
-/14	—	—	4	—	-/11	—	—	6	—	-/16	—	2	6	—	-/36	—	20	—	—
-/15	—	—	4	—	8R/10	—	—	10	—	-/17	—	2	—	—	17/1	—	1	2	118
-/16	—	—	4	—	-/12	—	1	—	—	-/18	—	3	—	—	-/2	—	1	4	—
-/17	—	—	8	—	-/14	—	1	—	—	12VB/1	—	—	3	—	-/3	—	1	4	—
-/18	—	—	8	—	9/1	doz.	1	4	29	-/2	—	—	4	—	-/4	—	1	6	—
-/19	—	—	6	—	-/2	—	1	4	—	-/3	—	—	5	—	-/5	—	1	6	—
-/20	—	—	8	—	-/3	—	1	8	—	-/4	—	—	6	—	-/6	—	1	6	—
-/21	—	—	8	—	-/4	—	1	8	—	-/5	—	—	6	—	-/7	—	1	8	—
-/22	—	—	10	—	-/5	—	2	—	—	13/1	doz.	1	6	31	-/8	—	1	6	—
6M/10	—	—	3	—	-/6	—	3	—	—	14/1	—	—	10	30	-/10	—	—	4	—
-/11	—	—	6	—	9K/1	—	—	8	—	-/2	—	1	—	—	-/11	—	—	6	—
-/12	—	—	4	—	-/2	—	—	10	—	-/3	—	1	2	—	-/12	—	—	4	—
-/13	—	—	4	—	-/3	—	1	—	—	-/4	—	1	6	—	-/13	—	—	6	—

Trade  Mark.

Dp. Pr.

No.	per	Price s.	d.	page	No.	per	Price s.	d.	page	No.	per	Price s.	d.	page	No.	per	Price s.	d.	page
17/14	doz.	1	—	118	22/6N	each	2	2	30	28E/1	each	1	2	36	29/7	doz.	3	8	35
-/15	—	—	10	—	23/0	—	—	5	—	-/2	—	1	4	—	-/10	—	—	9	36
-/16	—	—	10	—	-/0N	—	—	6	—	-/3	—	1	8	—	-/11	each	—	8	35
-/17	—	3	—	—	-/1	—	—	7	—	-/4	—	1	10	—	29A/1	—	—	8	—
-/18	—	3	4	—	-/1N	—	—	8	—	-/5	—	2	4	—	-/2	—	—	10	—
-/19	—	3	10	—	-/2	—	3	8	34	-/6	—	2	8	—	-/3	—	1	—	—
-/20	—	6	—	—	-/3	—	1	1	30	-/7	—	3	—	—	-/4	—	1	2	—
-/21	—	6	10	—	-/3N	—	1	2	—	-/8	—	4	6	—	29D/1½	doz.	1	2	—
-/22	—	3	4	—	-/4	—	1	6	—	-/9	—	6	8	—	29E/1	—	1	—	—
-/30	each	—	1	—	-/4N	—	1	8	—	28F/3	—	1	2	—	-/1⅛	—	—	8	—
-/31	—	—	2	—	-/11	—	1	1	—	-/5	—	2	—	—	-/1¼	—	—	10	—
-/32	—	—	4	—	-/11N	—	1	2	—	-/7	—	3	—	—	-/1½	—	1	2	—
-/33	—	—	4	—	-/12	—	1	6	—	-/9	—	7	—	—	-/2	—	1	—	—
-/36	—	—	4	—	-/12N	—	1	8	—	-/10	—	8	8	—	-/3	—	2	6	—
-/40	doz.	1	—	119	24/0	—	—	4	—	28G/0	—	1	6	—	29F	gross	1	10	—
-/41	—	2	—	—	-/1	—	—	6	—	-/1	—	2	—	—	29G/1	doz.	2	—	—
-/42	—	2	4	—	-/1N	—	—	8	—	-/2	—	2	4	—	-/2	—	3	—	—
-/43	—	1	2	—	-/2	—	—	8	—	-/3	—	2	8	—	-/3	—	3	—	—
-/60	yard	—	4	—	-/2N	—	—	10	—	-/4	—	3	2	—	-/4	—	4	10	—
-/61	—	—	1	—	-/3	—	5	8	34	-/5	—	3	10	—	29K	—	—	10	—
-/62	—	—	2	—	-/4	—	—	10	30	-/6	—	4	6	—	29M/0	—	—	8	—
-/63	—	—	8	—	-/4N	—	1	—	—	-/7	—	5	2	—	-/1	—	1	8	—
-/64	—	—	10	—	25/1½	—	2	—	31	-/8	—	7	—	—	-/1½	—	7	4	—
-/65	—	2	—	—	-/2	—	2	6	—	-/9	—	10	—	—	-/2	—	9	8	—
-/70	each	—	8	101	-/2N	—	2	8	—	28L/0	doz.	1	2	—	29R/4	—	3	4	—
-/71	—	—	10	—	-/3	—	14	6	34	-/1	—	1	6	—	-S/0	100 yards	17	—	—
-/72	—	1	—	—	-/4	—	3	10	31	-/2	—	2	8	—	-S/0	℔	15	—	—
-/74	—	—	2	118	-/4N	—	4	2	—	-/3	—	1	8	—	-S/1	yard	—	4	—
-/75	—	—	4	—	-/5	—	7	—	—	-/4	—	2	6	—	-S/1	℔	11	—	—
-/75/0	—	—	3	—	-/5N	—	7	6	—	-/5	—	3	—	—	-S/2	yard	—	8	—
18/8	—	11	—	37	-/10	—	—	2	—	-/6	—	3	2	—	-S/2	℔	11	—	—
-/10	—	36	—	—	-/11	—	—	3	—	28M/1	each	—	8	—	29W	yard	1	—	—
19/0	—	1	6	26	25G/1½	doz.	—	5	—	-/2	—	—	8	—	-/1	—	—	4	—
-/1	—	2	—	—	-/2	—	—	6	—	28S/1	—	—	8	—	30/1	each	—	10	28
-/2	—	2	6	—	-/3	—	—	6	—	-/2	—	1	2	—	-/2	—	1	2	—
-/3	—	3	8	—	-/4	—	1	—	—	-/3	—	1	4	—	-/3	—	1	4	—
-/3½	—	5	—	—	-/10	yard	—	4	—	-/4	—	1	8	—	-/4	—	1	6	—
-/4	—	10	8	27	-/11	—	—	5	—	28SE/1	—	1	8	—	-/5	—	1	8	—
-/5	—	19	—	—	-/12	—	—	7	—	-/2	—	2	—	—	-/6	—	2	—	—
-/6	—	7	8	—	-/13	—	—	10	—	-/3	—	2	4	—	-/10	—	—	10	29
-/7	—	11	8	—	25H/2	each	2	6	—	-/4	—	2	10	—	-/11	—	1	—	—
-/20	doz.	3	8	26	-/2N	—	2	10	—	28SG/1	—	2	10	—	-/12	—	1	2	—
-/21	—	6	—	—	-/4	—	4	—	—	-/2	—	3	8	—	-/13	—	1	4	—
-/22	—	8	6	—	-/4N	—	4	6	—	-/3	—	3	—	—	-/14	—	1	6	—
-/23	—	10	10	—	26/0	—	—	3	32	-/4	—	4	—	—	-/15	—	2	—	—
19V	each	—	10	—	-/0N	—	—	3	—	28T/0	doz.	3	10	—	30HL/10	—	1	—	—
19V/5	—	3	—	27	-/1	—	—	4	—	-/1	—	4	6	—	-/11	—	1	6	—
20FM	doz.	—	2	30	-/1N	—	—	4	—	-/2	—	5	6	—	-/12	—	1	8	—
-FS	—	—	3	—	-/2	—	—	4	—	-/3	—	6	8	—	-/13	—	2	—	—
-M	—	—	4	—	-/2N	—	—	5	—	-/4	—	7	10	—	-/14	—	2	4	—
21/1	each	1	—	37	-/3	—	—	5	—	-/5	—	9	8	—	-/15	—	2	8	—
-/2	—	1	4	—	-/3N	—	—	6	—	28U/0	—	2	—	—	30HR/10	—	1	—	—
-/3	—	1	8	—	27/0	—	—	3	33	-/1	—	2	8	—	-/11	—	1	6	—
-/4	—	3	—	—	-/1½	—	—	10	—	-/2	—	3	—	—	-/12	—	1	8	—
-/5	—	4	—	—	-/2½	—	1	—	—	-/3	—	4	2	—	-/13	—	2	—	—
-/6	—	5	—	—	-/3½	—	2	6	—	-/4	—	4	10	—	-/14	—	2	4	—
-/10	—	—	6	—	-/4	—	9	6	34	-/5	—	6	—	—	-/15	—	2	8	—
-/11	—	—	10	—	-/5	—	2	—	33	2SV/1	each	1	—	—	31A/00	doz.	—	4	118
-/12	—	1	—	—	-/6	—	2	4	—	-/2	—	1	—	—	-/0	—	—	10	—
-/13	—	1	2	—	-/10	—	—	3	—	28Z/1	—	—	8	—	-/1	—	1	—	—
-/14	—	1	6	—	-/11	—	—	4	—	-/2	—	—	9	—	-/2	—	1	4	—
-/15	—	1	8	—	-/12	—	—	5	—	28ZE/1	—	1	8	—	31B/1	—	1	10	—
-/16	—	2	8	—	28D/0	—	—	5	36	-/2	—	1	10	—	-/2	—	1	—	—
-/17	—	11	—	—	-/1	—	—	6	—	28ZG/1	—	2	4	—	-/3	—	1	2	—
22/0½	—	—	5	30	-/2	—	—	8	—	-/2	—	2	6	—	31BL/35	—	1	8	—
-/1	—	—	6	—	-/3	—	—	10	—	29	ball	1	4	35	-/48	—	2	6	—
-/3	—	—	8	—	-/4	—	1	—	—	29/0	doz.	—	4	—	-/54	—	3	—	—
-/3N	—	—	10	—	-/5	—	1	2	—	-/0½	—	—	6	—	31BS/1	—	1	—	—
-/4	—	7	4	34	-/6	—	1	4	—	-/1	—	—	8	—	-/1½	—	—	10	—
-/5	—	1	4	30	-/7	—	1	10	—	-/1¼	—	1	—	—	-/2	—	1	—	—
-/5N	—	1	6	—	-/8	—	3	—	—	-/1½	—	1	4	—	-/2½	—	1	6	—
-/6	—	—	2	—	28E/0	—	1	—	—	-/2	—	1	6	—	-/3	—	1	8	—
										-/3	—	2	—	—	-/3½	—	1	8	—

Trade Mark.

No.	per	s.	d.	page	No.	per	s.	d.	page	No.	per	s.	d.	page	No.	per	s.	d.	page
31BS/4	doz.	2	—	118	37/0/2	each	5	4	28	46/00	each	—	10	30	56/8	each	7	10	30
-/5	—	1	2	—	-/0/3	—	5	8	—	-/00N	—	1	—	—	-/11	—	—	8	—
31E/26	—	4	10	—	-/0/4	—	6	—	—	-/0	—	—	10	—	-/12	—	—	8	—
-/29	—	5	—	—	-/0/5	—	6	6	—	-/0N	—	1	—	—	-/13	—	—	10	—
-/32	—	5	6	—	-/0/6	—	13	—	—	-/1	—	1	—	—	-/14	—	—	10	—
-/38	—	6	8	—	37/1	—	4	6	—	-/1N	—	1	2	—	-/15	—	1	—	—
-/52	—	7	2	—	-/2	—	5	6	—	-/2	—	1	8	—	57	—	14	—	34
-/58	—	8	—	—	-/3	—	6	8	—	-/2N	—	2	—	—	-/00	—	3	2	33
31EL/48	each	—	2	—	-/4	—	7	6	—	47/1	—	—	4	35	-/0	—	4	—	—
-/54	—	—	3	—	-/5	—	8	6	—	-/2	—	—	2	—	-/1	—	5	—	—
-/67	—	—	4	—	-/6	—	15	—	—	-/3	—	—	5	—	-/2	—	6	6	—
31EL/0/48	—	—	8	—	-/11	—	1	10	—	-/10	doz.	1	—	—	-/3	—	4	—	—
- -/54	—	—	8	—	-/12	—	2	—	—	-/11	—	2	—	—	-/4	—	4	—	—
- -/67	—	—	10	—	-/13	—	2	4	—	-/12	—	3	—	—	-/4½	—	4	—	—
31F/26	doz.	1	6	—	-/14	—	2	6	—	47A/1	—	—	10	—	-/5	—	5	6	54
-/29	—	1	8	—	-/15	—	2	8	—	-/2	—	1	—	—	-/6	—	4	—	—
-/32	—	2	6	—	37L/20	—	2	6	29	-/3	—	1	2	—	-/7	—	4	6	—
-/38	—	2	8	—	-/21	—	4	—	—	47B/1	each	—	2	—	58/0	doz.	1	4	186
-/52	—	3	2	—	-/22	—	4	6	—	-/2	—	—	2	—	-/1	—	1	6	—
-/58	—	3	8	—	-/23	—	5	—	—	47C	doz.	2	6	—	-/1½	—	2	6	—
31H/38	—	2	8	—	37R/20	—	2	6	—	47D	—	1	2	—	-/2	—	2	6	—
-/52	—	3	2	—	-/21	—	4	—	—	47E/1	each	—	2	—	-/3	—	2	6	—
-/58	—	3	8	—	-/22	—	4	6	—	-/2	—	—	3	—	-/4	—	1	8	—
31M/27	each	—	6	—	-/23	—	5	—	—	-/3	—	—	4	—	-/5	—	3	—	—
-/34	—	—	8	—	38/7	—	29	—	—	-/4	—	—	5	—	-/6	—	4	10	—
-/36	—	—	10	—	-/8	—	35	—	—	-/5	—	—	6	—	-/28	—	1	6	119
-/53	—	1	—	—	40/2	—	5	8	34	-/6	—	—	8	—	-/30	—	2	—	—
-/64	—	1	6	—	-/3	—	1	—	32	-/7	—	1	—	—	-/40	—	3	—	—
-/70	—	1	8	—	-/3N	—	1	2	—	-/8	—	—	10	—	-/45	—	4	10	—
-/79	—	2	—	—	-/L/3	—	1	6	—	47F/1	—	—	4	—	-/50	—	5	4	—
-/110	—	3	6	—	-/L/3N	—	1	8	—	-/2	—	—	6	—	-/60	—	6	—	—
31N/27	—	—	8	—	-/4	—	3	8	—	-/3	—	—	7	—	58A/1	each	—	10	—
-/34	—	—	10	—	-/4N	—	4	—	—	-/4	—	—	8	—	-/2	—	—	10	—
-/36	—	1	—	—	-/5	—	4	4	—	-/5	—	1	—	—	-/3	—	1	—	—
-/53	—	1	—	—	-/5N	—	5	—	—	-/6	—	1	6	—	-/4	—	1	—	—
-/64	—	1	8	—	-/6	—	5	2	—	-/7	—	2	4	—	58/17K	doz.	—	8	—
-/70	—	2	—	—	-/6N	—	5	10	—	-/8	—	2	8	—	58L/13	gross	3	—	—
-/79	—	2	4	—	-/7	—	1	8	—	47N/4	—	—	6	—	-/16	—	4	4	—
-/110	—	4	—	—	-/7N	—	1	10	—	-/5	—	1	4	—	-/18	—	5	4	—
31P/27	—	—	2	—	-/8	—	1	10	—	-/6	—	1	10	—	-/20	—	6	—	—
-/34	—	—	4	—	-/8N	—	2	—	—	48/1	—	—	4	36	-/23	—	7	—	—
-/36	—	—	5	—	41/2	yard	—	8	—	-/5	—	1	—	—	-/24	—	7	—	—
-/53	—	—	6	—	-/2,5	—	—	9	—	-/9	—	—	2	—	-/26	—	8	—	—
-/64	—	1	—	—	-/2,8	—	—	10	—	-/15	—	3	—	37	-/27	—	9	4	—
-/70	—	1	4	—	-/3	—	1	—	—	-/20	—	1	6	—	58S/1	each	—	4	—
-/79	—	1	6	—	-/3,5	—	1	—	—	50/39	—	1	4	31	-/2	—	—	4	—
-/110	—	2	6	—	-/4	—	1	2	—	-/54	—	1	4	—	-/3	—	—	6	—
31T/38	doz.	7	2	—	-/5	—	1	6	—	-/59	—	1	4	—	59/1	doz.	—	10	186
-/52	—	8	—	—	-/6	—	1	8	—	50G/39	doz.	1	—	—	-/2	—	1	4	—
-/58	—	8	4	—	41N/2	—	—	9	—	-/54	—	1	2	—	-/3	gross	4	—	119
32	each	—	5	30	-/2,5	—	—	10	—	-/59	—	1	2	—	-/4	—	4	6	—
32N	—	—	6	—	-/2,8	—	1	—	—	50H	each	—	8	—	-/4A	—	4	10	—
32/1	—	—	5	—	-/3	—	1	2	—	50K/39	—	—	6	—	-/6	—	7	4	—
-/1N	—	—	6	—	-/3,5	—	1	3	—	-/54	—	—	6	—	-/6L	—	6	—	—
33C	—	8	6	32	-/4	—	1	6	—	-/59	—	—	6	—	-/10	doz.	1	8	—
34/1M	—	—	2	—	-/5	—	1	8	—	50 KV	—	—	2	—	-/11	—	2	—	—
-/1N	—	—	2	—	-/6	—	1	10	—	52/1M	doz.	1	8	32	60/1	each	—	6	156
-/2M	—	—	2	—	42/2	each	—	8	34	-/1N	—	1	10	—	-/2	—	—	7	—
-/2N	—	—	3	—	-/3	doz.	—	4	32	-/2M	—	2	10	—	-/3	—	—	8	—
-/10	—	—	4	—	-/3N	—	—	5	—	-/2N	—	3	2	—	-/4	—	—	9	—
-/10N	—	—	5	—	-/4	—	—	6	—	55/1	—	1	—	30	-/5	—	—	10	—
-/20	—	7	6	34	-/4N	—	—	8	—	-/2	—	1	2	—	-/6	—	1	—	—
-/23M	—	2	—	32	-/5	—	—	9	—	-/3	—	2	4	—	-/7	—	1	4	—
-/23N	—	2	4	—	-/5N	—	—	10	—	-/4	—	2	10	—	-/10	doz.	1	8	—
-/50	—	3	8	34	42V/1	gross	1	—	—	-/5	—	3	8	—	-/11	—	—	8	—
35/1	—	3	6	—	-/2	—	1	—	—	-/6	—	3	10	—	-/12	—	—	10	—
-/2	—	1	6	—	-/3	doz.	—	3	—	56/1	each	1	8	—	-/13	—	1	—	—
-/3	—	1	10	—	-/4	—	—	5	—	-/2	—	1	10	—	-/14	—	1	—	—
36/1	—	1	6	28	-/5	—	—	4	—	-/3	—	2	—	—	61/1	—	—	6	—
-/2	—	1	10	—	-/5½	—	—	4	—	-/4	—	2	4	—	-/2	—	—	8	—
-/3	—	2	—	—	-/6	—	—	8	—	-/5	—	2	6	—	-/3	—	—	8	—
-/4	—	2	6	—	44/7	each	3	6	30	-/6	—	3	4	—	-/4	—	1	10	—
37/0/1	—	4	10	—	-/8	—	4	6	—	-/7	—	6	—	—	-/5	—	2	6	—

Trade ✦ Mark.

No.	per	s.	d.	page	No.	per	s.	d.	page	No.	per	s.	d.	page	No.	per	s.	d.	page
61/6	each	6	10	156	72/30	doz.	1	8	227	80HR/54	doz.	3	8	97	81WD/54	each	7	—	96
62/1	—	2	4	—	-/35	—	2	6	—	-/67	—	4	4	—	-/67	—	8	—	—
-/2	—	2	6	—	-/40	—	3	—	—	80K/35	each	2	—	—	81WK/35	—	9	—	—
-/3	—	3	—	—	-/45	—	3	8	—	-/48	—	2	8	—	-/48	—	10	—	—
-/4	—	7	—	—	-/50	—	4	10	—	-/54	—	3	10	—	-/54	—	12	—	—
63/0	doz.	—	8	31	-/60	—	9	8	—	-/67	—	4	6	—	-/67	—	14	—	—
-/0N	—	—	10	—	-/65	—	12	—	—	80R/35	doz.	4	4	—	81WS/35	pair	4	8	95
-/1	—	1	2	—	-/70	—	16	—	—	-/48	—	4	10	—	-/48	—	5	10	—
-/1N	—	1	6	—	-/75	—	21	—	—	-/54	—	6	—	—	-/54	—	6	6	—
-/2	—	1	6	—	-/80	—	30	—	—	-/67	—	7	4	—	-/67	—	7	8	—
-/2N	—	2	—	—	-/85	—	40	—	—	80W/35	pair	5	8	—	81WT/35	—	5	—	—
-/3	—	3	8	—	-/90	—	53	—	—	-/48	—	7	—	—	-/48	—	6	—	—
-/3N	—	4	10	—	72C/103	each	3	—	156	-/54	—	8	—	—	-/54	—	8	—	—
-/4	each	—	6	—	-/115	—	3	8	—	-/67	—	9	8	—	-/67	—	9	—	—
-/4N	—	—	8	—	-/130	—	6	8	—	80WS/35	—	5	8	—	82/4M	each	3	6	221
-/6	—	—	8	—	-/150	—	9	—	—	-/48	—	7	—	—	-/4N	—	3	6	—
-/6N	—	—	10	—	72S/33	doz.	4	4	227	-/54	—	8	—	—	-/5M	—	4	—	—
-/7	—	1	2	—	-/41	—	6	6	—	-/67	—	9	8	—	-/5N	—	4	—	—
-/7N	—	1	4	—	-/48	—	13	—	—	81/10	doz.	—	10	119	-/5S	—	4	—	—
-/9N	doz.	1	4	—	-/54	—	17	—	—	-/11	—	1	2	—	82S	doz.	25	—	219
-/10N	each	—	2	—	72SA/33	pair	2	8	—	81A/35	each	—	10	95	83M	each	5	6	221
-/20S	—	—	5	—	-/41	—	3	8	—	-/48	—	1	—	—	83N	—	5	6	—
-/20SN	—	—	6	—	-/48	—	4	6	—	81B/35	—	—	10	—	83/3	—	12	—	—
-/20L	—	—	4	—	-/54	—	7	6	—	-/48	—	1	—	—	-/4M	—	8	10	—
-/20LN	—	—	5	—	-/103	each	9	—	156	81D/35	—	5	6	103	84	—	32	—	—
-/21N	—	—	5	—	-/115	—	13	—	—	-/48	—	9	4	—	84G	—	40	—	—
65/2	doz.	1	—	156	-/130	—	20	—	—	81G/35	doz.	3	4	94	85	—	24	—	—
-/3K	—	1	2	—	-/150	—	30	—	—	-/48	—	3	6	—	85G	—	28	—	—
-/3L	—	1	4	—	72SO/48	pair	5	4	227	-/54	—	4	6	—	86M	—	14	8	—
-/5K	—	1	4	—	73/25	doz.	2	—	—	-/67	—	5	8	—	86N	—	14	8	—
-/5L	—	1	6	—	-/30	—	2	4	—	81HG/35	—	2	6	—	87M	—	17	—	—
-/8K	—	1	6	—	-/35	—	3	2	—	-/48	—	3	—	—	87N	—	17	—	—
-/8L	—	1	8	—	-/40	—	3	10	—	-/54	—	3	6	—	87S	—	19	6	—
-/11	—	2	—	—	-/50	—	5	—	—	-/67	—	5	4	—	87SG	—	20	—	—
67/10	—	1	6	—	-/67	—	5	4	—	81HR/35	—	2	6	—	88/1	—	9	6	219
-/12	—	1	8	—	74/000	doz. pairs	3	4	—	-/48	—	3	—	—	-/1G	—	12	6	—
-/14	—	2	—	—	-/00	—	3	8	—	-/54	—	3	6	—	-/1GM	—	14	—	—
68/1	each	16	—	—	-/0	—	4	10	—	-/67	—	4	—	—	88M	—	11	6	221
-/2	—	19	—	—	-/1	—	6	—	—	81K/35	each	1	4	95	88N	—	11	6	—
-/3	—	20	—	—	-/2	—	8	—	—	-/48	—	1	6	—	89/1	doz.	14	8	218
-/6	—	18	—	—	75	doz.	5	4	—	-/54	—	2	—	—	-/1½	—	19	—	—
70/25	doz.	—	10	227	76/5	—	51	—	—	-/67	—	3	—	—	-/1¾	—	23	—	—
-/30	—	1	—	—	-/5½	—	68	—	—	81KR/35	—	1	8	—	-/2	—	26	6	—
-/35	—	1	4	—	-/6	—	87	—	—	-/48	—	1	10	—	-/2P	—	30	—	—
-/40	—	1	8	—	-/6½	—	110	—	—	-/54	—	2	—	—	-/3	—	28	6	—
-/45	—	2	—	—	-/7	—	120	—	—	-/67	—	3	—	—	-/3P	—	32	—	—
-/50	—	2	6	—	-/7½	—	140	—	—	81R/35	doz.	3	4	94	-/4	—	41	6	—
-/55	—	3	—	—	-/8	—	160	—	—	-/48	—	3	6	—	-/4P	—	45	—	—
-/60	—	4	8	—	-/8½	—	168	—	—	-/54	—	4	6	—	-/4NP	—	45	—	—
-/65	—	6	—	—	-/9	—	180	—	—	-/67	—	5	8	—	-/4S	—	50	6	—
-/70	—	7	—	—	-/10	—	216	—	—	81S/9	gross	16	—	94	-/4SP	—	54	—	—
-/75	—	8	—	—	76/5H	—	69	—	—	81UG/48	each	1	—	95	-/5P	—	30	—	—
-/85	—	11	—	—	-/5½H	—	88	—	—	-/67	—	1	6	—	-/5PF	—	32	6	—
-/102	—	20	—	—	-/6H	—	111	—	—	81UR/48	—	1	—	—	-/6	—	48	—	—
-/112	—	32	—	—	-/6½H	—	139	—	—	-/67	—	1	6	—	-/8	each	7	6	219
-/130	—	48	—	—	-/7½H	—	172	—	—	81W/35	pair	4	8	—	-/10	doz.	26	—	218
-/150	—	72	—	—	76/5M	—	81	—	—	-/48	—	5	10	—	-/10P	—	30	—	—
70S	box	4	6	—	-/5½M	—	104	—	—	-/54	—	6	6	—	-/15	—	36	—	—
71/17	doz.	—	6	—	-/6M	—	129	—	—	-/67	—	7	8	—	89S/0	—	9	8	219
-/22	—	—	8	—	-/6½M	—	158	—	—	81WA/35	each	3	—	96	-/1M	—	17	—	—
-/25	—	1	—	—	-/7½M	—	200	—	—	-/48	—	3	4	—	-/1N	—	17	—	—
-/30	—	1	4	—	78G/35	each	—	10	98	-/54	—	4	—	—	-/2M	—	22	—	—
-/35	—	1	10	—	-/48	—	1	—	—	-/67	—	4	6	—	-/2N	—	22	—	—
-/40	—	2	6	—	78K/35	—	4	—	—	81WB/35	—	9	4	—	-/2S	—	22	—	—
-/45	—	3	4	—	-/48	—	4	6	—	-/48	—	11	4	—	92M	each	11	—	220
-/50	—	4	—	—	78R/35	—	—	10	—	-/54	—	12	—	—	92N	—	12	—	—
-/55	—	6	—	—	-/48	—	1	—	—	-/67	—	14	—	—	92S	—	15	6	—
-/60	—	8	—	—	78T/35	doz.	5	4	—	81WC/35	—	5	10	—	93M	—	20	—	—
-/65	—	10	—	—	-/48	—	6	—	—	-/48	—	7	—	—	93N	—	22	—	—
-/70	—	13	6	—	78W/35	pair	7	8	—	-/54	—	8	—	—	93S	—	28	—	—
-/75	—	17	—	—	-/48	—	8	—	—	-/67	—	9	—	—	94/1	—	2	—	—
-/80	—	24	—	—	79/3	doz.	6	—	226	81WD/35	—	5	—	—	-/2	—	4	—	—
72/25	—	1	4	—	80HR/35	—	3	2	97	-/48	—	5	8	—	-/3	—	5	—	—
					-/48	—	3	6	—										

Trade Mark.

No.	per	s.	d.	page
94/4	each	8	—	220
95M	—	13	6	—
95N	—	14	6	—
95S	—	17	6	—
96M	—	24	—	—
96N	—	26	—	—
96S	—	30	—	—
97M	—	36	—	—
97N	—	38	—	—
97S	—	42	—	—
99/45	—	1	—	191
100/1½	—	3	—	1
-/2	—	3	6	—
-/3	—	4	6	—
-/4	—	6	—	—
-/5	—	7	—	—
101/1	doz.	15	6	—
-/2	—	24	—	—
-/3	—	36	—	—
-/4	—	42	—	—
104/1	each	3	4	6
105/2	—	5	4	7
-/3	—	7	—	—
-/4	—	10	6	10
-/5	—	15	6	—
-/6	—	23	—	—
-/6P	—	27	—	—
-/7	—	31	—	—
-/7P	—	35	—	—
108/00	doz.	14	6	41
-/1	—	24	—	—
-/2	—	36	—	—
-/3	each	5	8	—
111/00	doz.	3	—	38
-/1	each	5	10	55
113/1	—	6	6	—
114/3	doz.	7	10	49
-/4	—	13	—	—
-/5	—	18	—	—
115/3	each	6	4	—
116	—	35	—	18
118/1	—	7	—	126
-/2	—	8	—	—
-/3	—	11	—	—
-/5	—	5	6	—
-/5A	—	9	4	—
-/6	—	2	6	127
-/7	—	5	6	126
-/7A	—	7	2	—
-/8F	—	5	10	127
-/9F	—	15	10	—
-/13F	—	35	—	—
118F/10	doz.	2	6	126
-/11	—	2	6	—
119/0	doz.	15	6	52
-/12	—	7	10	—
-/13	—	12	—	—
-/15	—	18	—	—
-/16	—	24	—	—
-/17	—	34	—	—
-/18	—	42	—	—
120/0	each	2	—	—
-/1	—	3	—	—
122/1	—	14	8	43
-/2	—	27	6	—
124/1/35	doz.	14	6	81
-/2/35	—	14	6	—
-/3/35	—	14	6	—
125/1/35	each	2	8	—
-/2/35	—	2	8	—
-/3/35	—	2	8	—
126/1/35	doz.	14	6	—
-/2/35	—	14	6	—

No.	per	s.	d.	page
126/3/35	doz.	14	6	81
127/1/35	each	2	8	—
-/2/35	—	2	8	—
-/3/35	—	2	8	—
128/1/35	doz.	15	6	101
-/2/35	—	15	6	—
-/3/35	—	15	6	—
-/1/48	—	20	—	—
-/2/48	—	20	—	—
-/3/48	—	20	—	—
129/1/35	—	15	6	—
-/2/35	—	15	6	—
-/3/35	—	15	6	—
-/1/48	—	20	—	—
-/2/48	—	20	—	—
-/3/48	—	20	—	—
130/1/35	each	—	6	82
-/2/35	—	—	8	—
-/3/35	—	2	6	—
-/7/35	—	1	—	—
-/9/35	—	1	—	—
-/10/35	—	1	2	—
-/11/35	—	—	8	—
-/12/35	—	1	8	—
-/13/35	—	1	4	—
-/14/35	—	1	2	—
-/15/35	—	1	—	—
-/16/35	—	1	—	—
-/18/35	—	1	2	—
-/19/35	—	1	—	—
-/20/35	—	1	4	102
-/20/48	—	1	10	—
-/30/35	doz.	4	—	82
-/34/35	—	3	—	—
-/35/35	—	3	8	—
-/36/35	—	4	—	—
-/37/35	—	2	8	—
132DB/35	each	5	6	101
- DR/35	—	5	6	—
- DB/48	—	7	6	—
- DR/48	—	7	6	—
132/11/35	—	4	—	—
-/11/48	—	5	6	—
-/12/35	—	4	—	—
-/12/48	—	5	6	—
-/13/35	—	4	—	—
-/13/48	—	5	6	—
133/11/35	—	4	—	—
-/11/48	—	5	6	—
-/12/35	—	4	—	—
-/12/48	—	5	6	—
-/13/35	—	4	—	—
-/13/48	—	5	6	—
135/8/35	doz.	12	—	102
-/8/48	—	16	—	—
-/9/35	—	16	—	—
-/9/48	—	20	—	—
-/10/35	—	16	—	—
-/10/48	—	20	—	—
-/11/35	—	12	—	—
-/11/48	—	16	—	—
-/11/54	—	20	—	—
-/12/35	—	18	—	—
-/12/48	—	26	—	—
-/12/54	—	34	—	—
-/13/35	—	18	—	—
-/13/48	—	28	—	—
-/14/35	each	1	4	—
-/14/48	—	1	10	—
-/14/54	—	2	4	—
-/15/35	—	1	4	—
-/15/48	—	2	4	—
-/15/54	—	3	2	—

No.	per	s.	d.	page
135/16/35	each	2	8	102
-/16/48	—	3	4	—
-/16/54	—	4	4	—
-/17/35	—	1	4	—
-/17/48	—	1	10	—
-/17/54	—	2	4	—
-/21/35	doz.	7	4	100
-/21/48	—	12	—	—
-/22/35	—	14	6	—
-/22/48	—	24	—	—
-/22/54	each	3	10	—
-/22/67	—	8	—	—
-/23/35	—	2	6	—
-/23/48	—	4	—	—
-/23/54	—	7	2	—
-/24/35	—	5	8	—
-/24/48	—	8	6	—
-/26/35	doz.	7	4	—
-/26/48	—	12	—	—
-/27/35	—	15	6	—
-/27/48	—	26	6	—
-/27/54	each	3	10	—
-/28/35	—	2	10	—
-/28/48	—	4	6	—
-/28/54	—	7	8	—
-/29/35	—	6	—	—
-/29/48	—	9	—	—
138/31	doz.	7	10	53
-/32	—	12	—	—
-/33	—	15	6	—
-/34	—	24	—	—
-/35	—	30	—	—
-/36	—	36	—	—
-/37	—	42	—	—
-/38	—	48	—	—
-/40	each	2	—	—
-/41	—	4	—	—
-/42	—	6	—	—
141/000	doz.	15	6	120
-/00	each	2	—	—
-/0	—	2	10	—
-/0¼	—	3	6	—
-/0½	—	4	—	—
-/10	—	5	8	—
-/11	—	7	—	—
-/12	—	8	6	—
143/1	—	5	6	19
-/2	—	7	6	—
-/3	—	9	6	—
-/4	—	13	6	—
145/0	doz.	15	6	1
-/2	—	20	—	—
-/3	—	26	6	—
-/4	—	36	—	—
-/5	—	48	—	—
146/1	each	3	10	2
147/1	—	2	4	6
-/2	—	3	—	—
-/3	—	4	—	—
148/1	—	5	10	7
-/2	—	6	6	—
-/3	—	8	6	—
-/4	—	11	4	—
149/1	—	4	—	6
-/2	—	5	—	—
-/3	—	6	8	—
150/10	—	13	6	25
-/11	—	26	—	—
-/12	—	34	6	—
152/3	—	23	6	24
-/5	—	45	—	—
-/6	set	1	6	—
153/4	each	50	—	14

No.	per	d.	s.	page
162	each	20	6	120
173/00	doz.	3	6	38
-/0	each	2	6	—
-/1	—	4	4	55
174/3	—	10	—	8
179/1/0	—	2	10	48
-/2/0	doz.	36	—	47
-/3/0	—	24	—	—
-/4/0	—	20	6	—
-/7/0	—	6	6	—
-/8/0	—	4	—	—
-/9/0	—	7	—	—
-/11	—	6	—	—
-/12	—	7	10	—
-/13	—	11	—	—
-/14	each	2	10	—
-/15	—	4	—	—
180/2	—	8	6	120
-/3	—	8	6	—
-/4	—	10	10	—
189/000	doz.	24	—	44
-/00	—	36	—	—
-/1	each	4	—	—
195/1	—	5	—	51
-/2	doz.	9	—	39
-/3	—	8	6	—
-/4	—	18	—	—
-/5	—	8	6	—
-/6	—	9	—	—
-/7	—	8	6	—
-/8	—	9	—	—
-/9	—	9	6	—
-/10	—	9	—	—
-/11	—	14	6	—
-/12	—	13	—	—
-/13	—	30	—	—
-/14	—	8	6	—
-/15	—	11	—	—
-/16	—	9	6	—
-/17	—	15	—	—
-/20	—	15	—	—
-/21	each	3	4	42
-/22	—	5	4	—
196/00	doz.	4	—	38
-/0	each	4	—	—
-/1	—	4	10	56
-/2	—	22	—	—
197/00	—	3	—	49
-/0	each	2	—	—
215/00	doz.	15	6	128
-/0	each	2	—	—
-/1	—	3	—	—
-/2	—	4	6	—
-/3	—	6	—	—
-/4	—	7	6	—
-/5	—	9	—	—
-/6	—	10	6	—
244/2½	—	1	8	—
-/3	—	2	6	—
-/3½	—	3	4	—
-/4	—	4	10	—
-/4½	—	5	8	—
-/5	—	7	—	—
-/6	—	8	—	—
244B/3	—	3	6	—
-/3½	—	4	6	—
-/4	—	6	—	—
-/4½	—	7	—	—
-/5	—	8	8	—
-/6	—	10	—	—
245/4	—	7	—	129
-/4½	—	8	—	—
-/5	—	10	6	—
-/6	—	11	6	—

No.	per	s.	d.	page
245/7	each	15	—	129
-/8	—	16	—	—
245A/4	—	8	—	—
-/4½	—	9	6	—
-/5	—	12	—	—
-/6	—	13	—	—
-/7	—	17	—	—
-/8	—	18	6	—
245C/4	—	6	—	—
-/4½	—	7	—	—
-/5	—	9	8	—
-/6	—	10	8	—
-/7	—	13	8	—
-/8	—	15	—	—
290	—	7	—	132
291	—	9	—	—
292	—	11	—	—
293	—	12	8	—
294	—	16	—	—
295	—	20	—	—
300B	—	8	6	—
301B	—	11	4	—
302B	—	13	6	—
303B	—	14	6	—
304B	—	19	—	—
305B	—	24	—	—
306G/110	—	19	—	142
-/220	—	19	—	—
306W/110	—	19	—	—
-/220	—	19	—	—
307E/5	—	4	—	132
-/6	—	3	10	—
-/7	—	5	—	—
-/8	—	5	—	—
-/9	—	4	—	—
308BG/110	—	7	—	142
-/220	—	7	—	—
308BW/110	—	7	—	—
-/220	—	7	—	—
308G/110	—	11	—	—
-/220	—	11	—	—
308GL	—	—	10	—
308RG/15	—	—	10	—
-/20	—	—	10	—
-RW/15	—	—	10	—
-/20	—	—	10	—
-W/110	—	11	—	—
-/220	—	11	—	—
309BG/110	—	9	—	—
-/220	—	9	—	—
-BW/110	—	9	—	—
-/220	—	9	—	—
-G/110	—	16	—	—
-/220	—	16	—	—
-GL	—	1	4	—
-RG/15	—	1	—	—
-/20	—	1	—	—
-RW/15	—	1	—	—
-/20	—	1	—	—
-W/110	—	16	—	—
-/220	—	16	—	—
310B	—	30	—	143
-L	—	80	—	—
-R	—	3	—	—
311/6G/110	—	112	—	—
-/6G/220	—	132	—	—
-/6W/110	—	112	—	—
-/6W/220	—	132	—	—
-/10G/110	—	128	—	—
-/10G/220	—	148	—	—
-/10W/110	—	128	—	—
-/10W/220	—	148	—	—
-K	pair	—	2	—

No.	per	s.	d.	page
313B	each	12	—	143
-L	—	40	—	—
-R	—	3	—	—
315/0	—	96	—	139
-AD	—	104	—	—
-G	—	100	—	—
-HN	—	116	—	—
-L	—	136	—	—
-P	—	100	—	—
315/0/7	—	116	—	—
-AD/7	—	124	—	—
315G/7	—	120	—	—
-HN/7	—	136	—	—
-L/7	—	156	—	—
-P/7	—	120	—	—
318/0	—	120	—	—
319/0	—	200	—	—
321/2½	—	6	10	134
-/3	—	8	—	—
-/3½	—	10	—	—
-/4	—	11	8	—
-/4½	—	14	6	—
-/5	—	20	—	135
-/6	—	23	—	—
321A/2½	—	4	—	134
321B/3	—	10	—	135
-/3½	—	12	4	—
-/4	—	14	4	—
-/4½	—	17	4	—
-/5	—	23	6	—
-/6	—	27	—	—
321G	—	3	8	136
321GS	—	—	10	—
321GC	—	—	6	—
321KS/1	—	—	3	135
-KS/2	—	—	6	—
321M/2½	—	6	—	134
321N/2½	—	4	10	—
-/3	—	6	4	—
-/3½	—	8	4	—
321/3S	—	3	8	135
-/3½S	—	4	4	—
-/4S	—	4	10	—
-/4½S	—	5	6	—
-/5S	—	6	8	—
-/6S	—	7	4	—
321ST/1	—	—	2	—
-/2	—	—	4	—
322/6	—	58	—	137
-/6A/1	—	57	6	—
-/6A/2	—	60	—	—
-/6A/4	—	64	—	—
-/6G	—	57	—	—
-/6HN	—	75	—	—
-/6OB	—	53	—	—
-/6P/10	—	133	—	—
-/6P/13	—	93	—	—
-/16	—	71	—	—
-/16A/2	—	72	6	—
-/16G	—	70	6	—
-/16HN	—	88	6	—
-/66BG	—	165	—	—
-/66BW	—	185	—	—
-/610BG	—	180	—	—
-/610BW	—	200	—	—
322S	—	42	—	140
322T/1	—	1	2	—
-T/2	—	1	6	—
-T/3	—	2	—	—
325/5	—	34	—	136
-/6	—	40	—	—
326BG/6	—	192	—	138
-/10	—	208	—	—

No.	per	s.	d.	page
326BW/6	each	212	—	138
-/10	—	228	—	—
326NE	—	102	—	—
-P/10	—	160	—	—
-/13	—	120	—	—
327R	—	18	—	—
329/11CA	set	1	8	144
-/11CB	—	3	6	—
-/11SA	—	1	—	—
-/11SB	—	1	4	—
-/12SA	—	1	—	—
-/12SB	—	1	—	—
-/15C	—	3	6	—
-/20A	—	1	—	—
-/21A	—	1	4	—
-/21B	—	1	4	—
-/21C	—	1	4	—
-/21D	—	1	4	—
-/22A	—	1	8	—
-/23A	—	1	10	—
-/24A	—	2	—	—
-/25A	—	2	—	—
-/26A	—	2	4	—
-/27A	—	2	6	—
-/28A	—	2	8	—
-/29A	—	2	10	—
-/30A	—	3	—	—
-/31A	—	3	8	—
-/50	—	2	10	—
Photo-Films	yard	·/10 — 1/6		—
332/25	each	34	—	222
-/50	—	40	—	—
333/50	—	53	6	—
334/50	—	67	—	—
353/1	doz.	6	—	219
-/1½	—	7	10	—
-/2	—	4	8	—
-/2½	—	6	6	—
353B	100 pcs.	2	6	—
354/1	each	—	10	222
-/1B	set	—	10	—
-/2	each	1	8	—
-/2B	set	1	6	—
-/3	each	1	10	—
-/3B	set	1	10	—
355/12	—	4	—	—
-/13	doz.	2	10	—
-/14	—	4	—	—
-/15	—	4	—	—
356/1	—	4	6	—
387/1	each	15	—	130
-/2	—	17	6	—
-/3	—	20	—	—
-/4	—	24	6	—
-/5	—	29	—	—
-/6	—	33	—	—
388/1	—	23	—	131
-/2	—	26	6	—
-/3	—	34	—	—
-/4	—	40	6	—
-/5	—	50	6	—
-/6	—	55	—	—
388A	—	8	—	—
400/2½	gross	7	—	145
-/3	—	7	10	—
-/3½	—	12	—	—
-/4	—	16	—	—
-/4½	—	22	—	—
-/5	—	27	6	—
-/6	—	38	—	—
-/7	—	48	—	—
-/8	—	66	—	—
-/9	—	84	—	—

No.	per	s.	d.	page
400/10	gross	120	—	145
-/11	—	132	—	—
401/3	doz.	—	10	—
-/3½	—	1	—	—
-/4	—	1	4	—
-/4½	—	1	8	—
-/5	—	2	4	—
-/6	—	3	4	—
-/7	—	4	—	—
-/8	—	5	8	—
-/9	—	10	—	—
-/10	—	11	—	—
402/4	—	2	—	—
-/4½	—	3	—	—
-/5	—	3	8	—
-/6	—	4	6	—
-/7	—	5	8	—
-/8	—	7	—	—
-/9	—	9	8	—
-/10	—	13	8	—
-/11	—	15	4	—
405A/2½	—	—	8	148
-/3	—	—	10	—
-/3½	—	1	4	—
-/4	—	1	8	—
-/4½	—	2	—	—
-/5	—	2	10	—
-/6	—	3	8	—
-/7	—	4	6	—
-/8	—	6	—	—
-/9	—	8	—	—
405B/4	—	2	4	—
-/4½	—	3	4	—
-/5	—	3	8	—
-/6	—	5	—	—
-/7	—	6	—	—
-/8	—	7	8	—
-/9	—	10	—	—
408/3	slide	—	8	151
-/3½	—	—	10	—
-/4	—	1	—	—
-/4½	—	1	2	—
-/5	—	1	6	—
-/6	—	1	8	—
-/7	—	2	8	—
-/8	—	2	10	—
-/9	—	4	—	—
-/10	—	4	8	—
410S/10	each	3	8	155
-/11	—	4	6	—
410SM/10	—	5	—	—
-/11	—	5	6	—
411N/3	doz.	2	8	154
-/3½	—	3	2	—
-/4	—	3	10	—
-/4½	—	4	4	—
-/5	—	6	—	—
-/6	—	6	10	—
-/7	—	7	4	—
-/8	—	8	6	—
-/9	—	9	8	—
-/10	—	10	10	—
411S/10	each	2	—	155
-/11	—	2	6	—
413N/3	doz.	2	8	154
-/3½	—	3	2	—
-/4	—	3	10	—
-/4½	—	4	4	—
-/5	—	6	—	—
-/6	—	6	10	—
-/7	—	7	4	—
-/8	—	8	6	—
-/9	—	9	8	—

Trade **Mark.**

No.	per	s.	d.	page
413N/10	doz.	10	10	154
413S/10	each	2	10	155
-/11	—	3	4	—
415N/3	doz.	3	8	—
-/3½	—	4	2	—
-/4	—	4	8	—
-/4½	—	4	10	—
-/5	—	5	4	—
-/6	—	7	8	—
-/7	—	9	8	—
-/8	—	12	—	—
-/9	—	14	6	—
415S/10	each	3	4	—
-/11	—	4	—	—
416N/3	doz.	3	8	—
-, 3½	—	4	2	—
-/4	—	4	8	—
-/4½	—	4	10	—
-/5	—	5	4	—
-/6	—	7	8	—
-/7	—	9	8	—
-/8	—	12	—	—
-/9	—	14	6	—
-/10	—	16	10	—
416S/10	each	2	10	—
-/11	—	3	4	—
424A/6	doz.	3	8	149
-/7	—	4	6	—
-/8	—	6	—	—
-/9	—	8	—	—
-/10	—	11	—	—
424B/6	—	5	—	—
-/7	—	6	—	—
-/8	—	7	8	—
-/9	—	10	—	—
-/10	—	14	—	—
424S	set	15	—	152
425A/4	doz.	1	8	149
-/4½	—	2	—	—
-/5	—	2	10	—
-/6	—	3	8	—
-/7	—	4	6	—
-/8	—	6	—	—
-/9	—	8	—	—
-/10	—	11	—	—
425B/4	—	2	4	—
-/4½	—	3	4	—
-/5	—	3	8	—
-/6	—	5	—	—
-/7	—	6	—	—
-/8	—	7	8	—
-/9	—	10	—	—
-/10	—	14	—	—
425S	set	15	—	153
426/3	doz.	1	8	154
-/3½	—	2	—	—
-/4	—	2	4	—
-/4½	—	3	—	—
-/5	—	3	4	—
-/6	—	4	4	—
-/7	—	5	4	—
-/8	—	7	4	—
428/3	—	3	8	155
-/3½	—	4	2	—
-/4	—	4	8	—
-/4½	—	4	10	—
-/5	—	5	4	—
-/6	—	7	8	—
-/7	—	9	8	—
-/8	—	12	—	—
-/9	—	14	6	—
-/10	—	16	10	—
429A/4	—	1	8	146

No.	per	s.	d.	page
429A/4½	doz.	2	—	146
-/5	—	2	10	—
-/6	—	3	8	—
-/7	set	2	6	—
-/8	—	3	2	—
-/9	—	4	4	—
/10	—	5	8	—
429B/4	doz.	2	4	—
-/4½	—	3	4	—
-/5	—	3	8	—
-/6	—	5	—	—
-/7	set	3	4	—
-/8	—	4	—	—
-/9	—	5	6	—
-/10	—	6	8	—
430A/7	—	2	6	—
-/8	—	3	2	—
-/9	—	4	4	—
-/10	—	5	8	—
430B/7	—	3	4	—
-/8	—	4	—	—
-/9	—	5	6	—
-/10	—	6	8	—
438A/4	doz.	1	8	147
-/4½	—	2	—	—
-/5	—	2	10	—
-/6	—	3	8	—
-/7	—	4	6	—
-/8	—	6	—	—
-/9	—	8	—	—
-/10	—	11	—	—
438B/4	—	2	4	—
-/4½	—	3	4	—
-/5	—	3	8	—
-/6	—	5	—	—
-/7	—	6	—	—
-/8	—	7	8	—
-/9	—	10	—	—
-/10	—	14	—	—
438S	set	15	—	151
439A/4	doz.	1	8	148
-/4½	—	2	—	—
-/5	—	2	10	—
-/6	—	3	8	—
-/7	—	4	6	—
-/8	—	6	—	—
-/9	—	8	—	—
-/10	—	11	—	—
439B/4	—	2	4	—
-/4½	—	3	4	—
-/5	—	3	8	—
-/6	—	5	—	—
-/7	—	6	—	—
-/8	—	7	8	—
-/9	—	10	—	—
-/10	—	14	—	—
439S	set	15	—	152
440A/5	doz.	2	10	150
-/6	—	3	8	—
-/7	—	4	6	—
-/8	—	6	—	—
-/9	—	8	—	—
-/10	—	11	—	—
440B/5	—	3	8	—
-/6	—	5	—	—
-/7	—	6	—	—
-/8	—	7	8	—
-/9	—	10	—	—
-/10	—	14	—	—
440S	set	15	—	152
443/5	—	5	8	150
-/6	—	7	8	—
-/8	—	10	—	—

No.	per	s.	d.	page
443/9	set	12	—	150
444/4	—	3	8	—
-/5	—	5	8	—
-/6	—	6	4	—
444S/8½	—	9	8	151
447A/4	—	1	6	147
-/4½	—	1	8	—
-/5	—	2	4	—
-/6	—	2	10	—
-/7	—	3	6	—
-/8	—	7	8	—
-/9	—	8	—	—
-/10	—	9	—	—
447B/4	—	1	8	—
-/4½	—	2	4	—
-/5	—	3	—	—
-/6	—	3	8	—
-/7	—	4	6	—
-/8	—	8	10	—
-/9	—	9	8	—
-/10	—	10	10	—
447CA/4	—	—	8	146
-/4½	—	—	10	—
-/5	—	1	2	—
-/6	—	1	6	—
-/7	—	1	8	—
-/8	—	3	8	—
-/9	—	4	—	—
-/10	—	4	6	—
447CB/4	—	1	—	—
-/4½	—	1	4	—
-/5	—	1	8	—
-/6	—	1	10	—
-/7	—	2	4	—
-/8	—	4	4	—
-/9	—	5	—	—
-/10	—	5	6	—
447CS/6	—	2	8	153
-/7	—	3	—	—
-/8	—	5	8	—
-/8½	—	6	6	—
-/9	—	7	—	—
-/10	—	7	8	—
447S/5	—	4	—	—
-/6	—	5	—	—
-/7	—	6	—	—
-/8	—	8	10	—
-/8½	—	12	6	—
-/9	—	13	8	—
-/10	—	14	8	—
448	doz.	4	—	154
449A/3	—	—	10	146
-/3½	—	1	4	—
-/4	—	1	8	—
-/4½	—	2	—	—
-/5	—	2	10	—
-/6	—	3	8	—
-/7	—	4	6	—
-/8	—	6	—	—
-/9	—	8	—	—
449B/4	—	2	4	—
-/4½	—	3	4	—
-/5	—	3	8	—
-/6	—	5	—	—
-/7	—	6	—	—
-/8	—	7	8	—
-/9	—	10	—	—
450A/3	—	—	10	149
-/3½	—	1	4	—
-/4	—	1	8	—
-/4½	—	2	—	—
-/5	—	2	10	—
-/6	—	3	8	—

No.	per	s.	d.	page
450A/7	doz.	4	6	149
-/8	—	6	—	—
-/9	—	8	—	—
450B/4	—	2	4	—
-/4½	—	3	4	—
-/5	—	3	8	—
-/6	—	5	—	—
-/7	—	6	—	—
-/8	—	7	8	—
-/9	—	10	—	—
451A/4	—	1	8	147
-/4½	—	2	—	—
-/5	—	2	10	—
-/6	—	3	8	—
-/7	—	4	6	—
-/8	—	6	—	—
451B/4	—	2	4	—
-/4½	—	3	4	—
-/5	—	3	8	—
-/6	—	5	—	—
-/7	—	6	—	—
-/8	—	7	8	—
452	each	1	6	132
453	—	2	10	—
455/2	—	4	6	141
-/2D	—	6	10	—
-/3	yard	2	—	—
-/4	each	8	6	—
-/5	—	14	6	—
-/6	—	2	—	—
-/7	—	4	—	—
-/12	—	6	4	—
-/14	—	10	10	—
456A/3	doz.	—	10	148
-/3½	—	1	4	—
-/4	—	1	8	—
-/4½	—	2	—	—
-/5	—	2	10	—
-/6	—	3	8	—
-/7	—	4	6	—
-/8	—	6	—	—
-/9	—	8	—	—
456B/4	—	2	4	—
-/4½	—	3	4	—
-/5	—	3	8	—
-/6	—	5	—	—
-/7	—	6	—	—
-/8	—	7	8	—
-/9	—	10	—	—
460A/10	—	7	—	150
-/11	—	9	—	—
460B/10	—	9	—	—
-/11	—	11	—	—
466/5	each	78	—	140
-/5A/1	—	80	—	—
-/5A/2	—	82	4	—
-/5A/4	—	86	4	—
-/5G	—	80	—	—
-/5HN	—	98	—	—
-/5P/10	—	156	—	—
-/5P/13	—	116	—	—
466S	—	3	4	—
478/0	—	54	—	132
479/0	—	84	—	—
500/35	—	3	—	58
501/35	—	4	—	—
-/48	—	6	10	—
502/35	—	9	6	—
-/48	—	11	8	—
503/35	—	13	—	—
-/48	—	17	—	—
504/35	—	15	—	59
-/48	—	19	—	—

Trade Mark.

No.	per	Price s.	d.	page	No.	per	Price s.	d.	page	No.	per	Price s.	d.	page	No.	per	Price s.	d.	page
504/67	each	46	—	59	614/3	each	1	8	53	634W	each	1	6	42	647/84	each	2	—	113
505/35	—	18	—	—	-/7	—	1	10	54	634WE	—	2	—	—	-/85	—	1	—	115
-/48	—	23	—	—	-/8	—	3	6	—	634T	set	1	10	51	-/86	doz.	15	6	—
506/48	—	31	6	—	-/9	—	6	10	—	636/0	each	1	8	38	-/100	doz.	15	6	—
507/67	—	170	—	61	-/10	—	14	8	—	642/1	—	11	—	8	-/101	each	2	—	116
508/48	—	37	6	60	-/11	—	4	10	—	-/2	—	15	6	—	-/102	—	2	10	—
-/54	—	41	—	—	-/12	—	3	—	—	-/3	—	48	—	—	-/103	—	4	6	—
509/35	—	33	—	—	-/14	—	7	—	—	-/3P	—	51	6	—	-/104	—	5	8	—
-/48	—	100	—	—	615/00	doz.	4	10	38	-/5P	—	80	—	—	-/119	—	1	8	114
510/48	—	150	—	61	-/1	each	1	8	—	645/1	—	2	6	213	-/120	—	2	4	—
-/67	—	200	—	—	-/2	—	2	6	—	-/2	—	3	4	—	-/121	—	2	6	—
511/35	—	8	—	58	-/3	—	6	6	56	-/4	—	4	—	—	-/122	doz.	7	10	107
513/48	—	150	—	61	-/4	—	26	6	—	-/4F	—	4	—	127	-/123	—	13	—	—
-/67	—	200	—	—	616/1	—	4	10	55	646/1	—	33	—	53	-/124	—	15	6	—
515/35	—	21	—	62	-/2	—	4	—	—	-/2	—	40	—	—	-/125	—	22	—	—
-/48	—	31	6	—	-/3	—	37	—	—	647/1/35	each	2	—	83	-/126	each	4	8	104
516/35	—	22	—	—	621/2	—	15	—	120	-/1/48	—	2	—	—	-/127	—	8	—	105
-/48	—	33	6	—	-/3	—	30	—	—	-/3/35	—	5	—	103	-/128	—	9	8	—
517/35	—	29	—	63	622/3	—	33	—	—	-/10A	doz.	7	10	112	-/129	—	16	—	—
-/48	—	37	—	—	-/4	—	44	—	—	-/10C	—	15	6	—	-/130	—	3	6	—
518/35	—	29	—	—	-/5	—	59	—	—	-/10D	each	1	10	—	-/131	—	5	6	104
-/48	—	37	—	—	624/1	doz.	14	—	6	-/10F	—	2	10	—	-/132	—	13	6	105
519/35	—	29	—	—	625/1	each	4	6	55	-/13	doz.	4	4	115	-/135	—	4	—	104
-/48	—	37	—	—	626/3	—	1	10	40	-/14B	each	1	—	114	-/136	—	6	8	—
525/35	—	36	—	62	-/4	—	2	4	—	-/15E	doz.	15	6	112	-/140	doz.	15	6	115
-/48	—	50	—	—	-/5	—	3	—	—	-/16E	—	11	—	—	-/200	—	22	—	116
526/35	—	37	—	—	-/13	—	3	—	—	-/20E	each	3	—	—	-/201	each	2	4	—
-/48	—	52	—	—	-/14	—	4	—	—	-/21	—	5	—	104	-/202	—	3	2	—
527/35	—	40	—	64	-/15	—	5	—	—	-/26	—	2	6	112	-/203	—	5	2	—
-/48	—	60	—	—	-/20	—	7	—	—	-/29a	—	2	10	107	-/204	—	6	6	—
528/35	—	40	—	—	-/21	—	8	6	—	-/29b	—	5	8	—	649/0	—	1	8	38
-/48	—	60	—	—	-/22	—	7	6	41	-/29c	—	4	6	—	651/00	—	1	10	—
529/35	—	40	—	—	630/0	—	1	8	38	-/30a	—	8	6	108	-/12	doz.	15	6	41
-/48	—	60	—	—	-/1	—	12	—	56	-/30b	—	13	—	—	657/3/0	—	9	6	42
540/35AE	—	4	8	65	-/1B	—	—	8	—	-/30c	—	5	—	—	-/18	each	3	—	—
-/35BE	—	6	4	—	631/2A	—	2	—	45	-/31	—	4	6	107	-/36	—	5	—	—
541/35BE	—	7	6	—	-/2B	doz.	15	6	—	-/32	—	2	10	104	658/1	—	2	6	50
554/35B	—	20	8	67	-/4	each	7	—	51	-/34	—	8	—	105	-/1M	—	3	—	—
-/48B	—	27	6	—	-/5	—	9	6	—	-/36	—	2	—	107	-/2	—	6	—	—
555/35B	—	25	6	—	-/6	—	12	—	—	-/42	—	2	6	112	-/3	—	14	6	—
-/48B	—	34	6	—	-/10	doz.	7	10	44	-/47a	—	—	10	114	-/4	—	19	—	—
556/48B	—	43	8	—	-/11	—	14	6	—	-/47b	doz.	15	6	—	-/5	—	33	—	—
-/48C	—	47	—	—	-/12	—	19	—	—	-/47c	each	1	—	—	669/7	—	360	—	17
-/48D	—	50	—	—	-/13	—	24	—	—	-/47d	—	1	2	—	671/1	—	13	—	2
-/48E	—	56	—	—	-/15	—	9	6	—	-/47E	—	—	4	—	-/1P	—	16	—	—
561/35BE	—	10	—	65	-/16	—	19	—	—	-/47EO	doz.	3	4	99	-/2	—	17	—	—
-/48BE	—	16	—	—	-/17	—	24	—	—	-/48a	each	2	10	114	-/2P	—	20	—	—
563/35B	—	18	6	66	-/18	each	4	10	47	-/48b	—	4	—	—	-/3	—	22	—	—
-/35C	—	21	—	—	-/18½	—	3	—	—	-/48c	—	4	6	—	-/3P	—	25	—	—
-/48B	—	25	4	—	-/21	doz.	7	10	44	-/50	—	7	6	113	672/1	—	33	—	4
-/48C	—	29	—	—	-/22A	—	7	—	49	-/51	—	11	—	—	-/2	—	42	—	—
565/35B	—	34	—	68	-/22B	—	12	—	—	-/54	—	4	10	106	-/3	—	50	—	—
-/48B	—	43	—	—	-/22C	—	15	6	—	-/55	—	—	6	—	-/4	—	60	—	—
566/48B	—	52	—	—	-/23	—	24	—	44	-/56	—	17	—	—	-/5	—	72	—	—
571/35BE	—	8	—	65	-/24	—	13	—	—	-/57	—	25	—	—	675/3/0	—	6	—	49
572/35AE	—	13	6	66	-/25	each	1	10	—	-/58	—	1	6	99	677/6	—	110	—	5
-/35BE	—	17	—	—	-/26	—	2	6	—	-/59	—	2	6	—	-/7	—	170	—	—
-/48AE	—	20	—	—	-/27	—	2	—	45	-/60	doz.	15	6	115	-/8	—	220	—	—
573/35B	—	20	6	67	-/28	—	3	—	—	-/60A	—	7	10	—	-/10	—	9	6	3
-/48B	—	28	6	—	-/31	—	2	10	—	-/60B	—	15	6	116	-/11	—	13	—	—
574/35B	—	22	8	—	-/32	—	3	8	—	-/61	each	7	—	99	-/11P	—	16	—	—
-/48B	—	30	8	—	-/33	—	4	8	48	-/62	—	9	8	—	-/12	—	17	—	—
583/35B	—	21	—	69	-/34	—	2	4	—	-/63	—	8	—	—	-/12P	—	20	—	—
-/48B	—	28	—	—	-/35	—	1	—	—	-/65	—	11	—	—	-/12A	—	23	—	—
584/35B	—	23	—	—	-/36	—	2	10	—	-/70	doz.	7	10	113	-/12AP	—	26	—	—
-/48B	—	30	—	—	-/37	—	3	6	—	-/71	—	7	10	115	-/13	—	31	6	—
585/35B	—	26	—	—	-/38	—	6	6	—	-/72	each	3	—	113	-/13P	—	35	—	—
-/48B	—	34	—	—	633/1	doz.	15	6	43	-/73	—	4	—	—	-/14P	—	46	—	—
586/48B	—	42	6	—	-/2	each	3	—	—	-/74	doz.	7	10	112	-/15P	—	59	—	—
601/1	doz.	6	—	1	-/4	—	2	10	—	-/75	each	2	10	115	682/000	doz.	7	10	42
-/2	—	7	10	—	-/5	—	4	—	—	-/77	—	6	6	116	-/00	—	12	—	—
614/1	each	3	8	53	634/1	—	11	—	51	-/81A	—	4	—	106	-/2	—	15	6	—
-/2	—	2	10	—	634D	—	2	6	42	-/83	doz.	15	6	113					

Trade  Mark.

No.	per	s.	d.	page	No	per	s.	d.	page	No.	per	s.	d.	page	No.	per	s.	d.	page
686/1	each	18	—	19	696/13	each	33	—	9	713/21	each	2	—	121	731/14	each	8	6	121
-/2	—	24	—	—	-/13P	—	36	—	—	-/22	—	2	10	—	-/15	—	11	6	—
-/2½	—	40	—	22	-/14P	—	50	—	—	-/23	—	4	—	—	-/16	—	14	—	—
/3	—	32	—	19	-/15P	—	64	—	—	-/24	—	5	8	—	-/17	—	17	—	—
-/5G	—	77	—	22	697/1½	doz.	14	6	47	-/25	—	8	6	—	737/0	doz.	15	6	124
-/5S	—	77	—	—	-/4	—	28	—	49	-/26	—	10	—	—	-/0¾	each	2	—	—
686B/1	—	3	4	19	-/11	—	9	6	48	-/27	—	11	6	—	-/1	—	2	10	—
-/2	—	3	6	—	-/14	—	15	6	45	-/28	—	14	—	—	-/1½	—	4	—	—
687/1	—	20	—	—	-/14½	each	2	—	—	-/29	—	17	—	—	-/2	—	5	8	—
-/2	—	27	—	—	-/15	—	2	10	—	-/30	—	21	—	—	-/2½	—	7	—	—
-/3	—	36	—	—	-/16	doz.	15	6	44	-/31	—	25	4	—	-/3	—	8	—	—
687/4	—	63	—	23	-/17	doz.	30	—	44	-/32	—	28	—	—	-/4	—	11	—	—
-/5	—	85	—	—	-/19	—	15	6	45	-/33	—	32	—	—	-/5	—	14	—	124
687B	—	2	10	19	-/20	each	2	—	—	-/34	—	36	—	122	-/5½	—	14	—	125
687/4G	—	3	4	23	-/21	—	2	10	—	-/35	—	46	—	—	-/10	doz.	15	6	123
-/5G	—	3	8	—	-/25	—	2	10	—	-/36	—	52	—	—	-/10¾	each	2	—	—
688/1½	—	5	—	2	-/26	—	1	10	48	-/37	—	64	—	—	-/11	—	2	10	—
-/2	—	6	—	—	-/27	—	3	—	46	-/38	—	76	—	—	-/11½	—	4	—	—
-/2½	—	7	—	—	-/28a	—	1	10	48	717A	doz.	6	—	215	-/12	—	5	8	—
-/3	—	8	—	—	-/28b	—	2	10	—	-/1R	—	6	—	—	-/13A	—	7	—	—
-/4	—	10	—	—	-/28c	—	6	6	—	-/1U	—	7	6	—	-/13	—	8	6	124
-/5	—	12	—	—	-/28d	—	4	—	—	718/00	—	15	6	125	-/14	—	11	6	—
689/1	—	6	—	7	-/30a	—	1	—	47	-/0	each	2	—	—	-/15	—	14	—	—
-/2	—	7	8	—	-/32	doz.	4	—	46	-/1	—	3	—	—	-/16	—	17	—	—
-/3	—	9	—	—	-/33	—	6	6	—	-/2	—	4	6	—	-/17	—	21	—	—
-/4	—	12	—	—	-/34	—	6	—	—	-/3	—	6	—	—	-/18	—	28	—	—
690/11	—	17	—	3	-/35	—	11	—	—	721/20	doz.	15	6	122	739/4	—	2	6	213
-/11P	—	20	—	—	-/36	—	17	—	—	-/21	each	2	—	—	-/7	—	2	4	—
-/12	—	23	—	—	-/37	—	24	—	—	-/22	—	2	10	—	-/8	—	5	4	—
-/12P	—	26	—	—	-/38	—	24	—	—	-/23	—	4	—	—	740F/4	doz.	2	4	—
-/13	—	33	8	—	-/40	—	15	6	46	-/24	—	5	8	—	-/5	—	3	4	—
-/13P	—	36	10	—	-/41	—	20	6	—	-/25	—	8	6	—	-/6	each	—	10	—
-/14P	—	50	—	—	-/42	each	2	10	—	-/26	—	10	—	123	741/2	—	6	6	127
-/15P	—	63	—	—	-/43	—	5	6	—	-/27	—	11	6	—	-/3A	—	4	10	212
691/1	—	15	—	9	698/16	doz.	15	6	41	-/28	—	17	—	—	-/3R	—	4	10	—
-/1P	—	18	—	—	-/17	—	15	6	—	-/29	—	21	—	—	-/3RC	—	10	—	—
-/2	—	21	—	—	-/31	—	10	—	42	-/30	—	24	—	—	-/3AC	—	10	—	—
-/2P	—	24	—	—	-/32	—	21	—	—	-/31	—	27	—	—	741F	box	4	6	213
-/3	—	29	6	—	699/1	—	15	6	47	-/32	—	30	—	—	-/1	doz.	2	4	—
-/3P	—	33	—	—	-/2	—	24	—	—	-/33	—	36	—	—	-/2	—	3	4	—
-/4P	—	44	—	—	-/3	—	34	—	—	-/34	—	46	—	—	-/3	each	—	10	—
-/5P	—	56	—	—	-/4	—	14	6	45	-/35	—	60	—	—	-/L	—	—	3	—
-/21	—	51	—	11	702/10	—	6	—	215	-/36	—	76	—	—	748/1	doz.	3	8	223
-/23	—	70	—	12	-/11R	—	5	8	—	724/1	doz.	15	6	125	-/2	—	4	6	—
-/25	—	140	—	13	-/11U	—	7	2	—	-/2	each	2	—	—	-/3	—	5	4	—
-/21MC	—	1	—	14	704/1R	—	6	—	—	-/3	—	2	10	—	-/K	card	4	10	—
-/21S	—	6	—	—	-/1U	—	7	6	—	-/4	—	4	—	—	749/1	doz.	4	6	—
-/23MC	—	1	6	—	705/1R	—	5	4	—	-/5	—	5	8	—	-/2	—	4	10	—
-/23S	—	7	6	—	-/1U	—	6	10	—	726/35	doz.	7	8	223	-/3	—	6	—	—
-/25MC	—	1	10	—	706/1R	—	5	8	—	-/51	—	10	6	—	749K	card	5	8	—
-/25S	—	11	—	—	-/1U	—	7	2	—	-/63	—	16	—	—	753/1M	each	2	—	—
692/1	—	30	—	18	-/2R	—	8	4	—	-/77	—	24	—	—	-/2M	—	2	8	—
-/3P	—	72	—	—	-/2U	—	10	—	—	727/1	—	24	—	—	755/1	doz.	12	—	—
694/1	—	5	6	20	-/5R	—	6	4	—	-/3	—	30	—	—	756/1	—	2	6	224
-/1T	—	7	6	—	-/5U	—	8	—	—	-/4	—	41	—	—	-/2	—	3	8	—
-/2	—	13	—	—	-/7R	—	6	—	—	728/38	—	9	8	—	-/3	—	4	4	—
-/2T	—	15	6	—	-/7U	—	7	4	—	-/51	—	12	—	—	-/4	—	11	6	—
-/3	—	20	—	—	-/9	each	1	4	—	-/63	—	19	8	—	-/5	—	11	—	—
-/21	—	9	—	21	-/11R	—	1	8	—	-/77	—	27	—	—	757	each	3	6	—
-/21T	—	11	—	—	-/11U	—	2	—	—	-/89	—	36	—	—	758/1	—	8	4	—
-/22	—	19	—	—	-/12R	—	1	10	—	-/102	—	42	—	—	-/2	—	9	—	—
-/22T	—	21	6	—	-/12U	—	2	2	—	-/120	—	72	—	—	-/3	—	11	—	—
-/23	—	29	—	—	-/13R	—	3	4	—	-/128	—	96	—	—	759/1	—	13	—	—
694G/2	—	2	—	20	-/13U	—	3	8	—	729/25	—	8	6	—	-/2	—	17	—	—
-/3	—	2	—	—	707/1	doz.	15	6	213	-/30	—	9	8	—	760/1	set	2	—	—
-/22	—	2	6	21	710/38	—	2	10	223	-/35	—	11	—	—	-/2	—	9	8	—
-/23	—	2	6	—	-/45	—	3	8	—	-/40	—	12	—	—	-/11	—	2	—	—
696/6	—	150	—	15	-/51	—	4	4	—	-/45	—	13	6	—	-/12	—	4	—	—
-/7	—	300	—	16	-/57	—	5	4	—	-/50	—	17	6	—	-/21	—	2	—	154
-/11	—	16	—	9	-/63	—	6	8	—	731/10	each	2	—	121	-/22	—	4	—	—
-/11P	—	19	—	—	-/70	—	8	6	—	-/11	—	2	10	—	-/23	—	4	—	—
-/12	—	23	—	—	-/77	—	10	10	121	-/12	—	4	—	—	761/1	doz.	7	10	224
-/12P	—	26	—	—	713/20	—	15	6	—	-/13	—	5	8	—	-/2	—	10	—	—

Trade Mark.

No.	per	s.	d.	page
761/3	doz.	15	6	224
-/4	—	24	—	—
-/11	—	20	—	—
-/12	—	24	—	—
-/21	—	10	—	—
-/22	—	15	6	—
769/1/15	—	6	—	225
-/1/18	—	8	—	—
-/1/20	—	9	6	—
-/1/24	—	12	—	—
-/1/30	—	14	—	—
-/1/35	—	22	6	—
-/1/40	—	28	6	—
-/1/45	—	33	6	—
-/1/50	—	41	—	—
-/2/15	—	9	—	—
-/2/18	—	11	6	—
-/2/20	—	14	6	—
-/2/24	—	17	—	—
-/2/30	—	20	—	—
-/2/35	—	30	—	—
-/2/40	—	46	—	—
-/2/45	—	48	—	—
-/2/50	—	58	—	—
-/3/15	—	12	—	—
-/3/18	—	16	—	—
-/3/20	—	19	6	—
-/3/24	—	22	—	—
-/3/30	—	27	—	—
-/3/35	—	34	—	—
770/12	—	6	8	—
-/18	—	9	—	—
-/20	—	11	—	—
-/24	—	12	—	—
-/30	—	16	—	—
-/35	—	24	—	—
-/40	—	30	—	—
-/45	—	38	—	—
-/50	—	44	—	—
770E	—	21	—	—
771/12	—	9	—	—
-/18	—	13	6	—
-/20	—	16	—	—
-/24	—	18	—	—
-/30	—	23	—	—
-/35	—	33	6	—
-/40	—	45	—	—
-/45	—	57	—	—
-/50	—	63	—	—
771E	—	30	—	—
772/12	—	13	6	—
-/18	—	18	—	—
-/20	—	22	—	—
-/24	—	24	—	—
-/30	—	30	—	—
-/35	—	42	—	—
-/40	—	60	—	—
-/45	—	76	—	—
-/50	—	81	—	—
772E	—	39	—	—
772S	—	36	—	—
773/1	doz.	7	10	217
-/2	—	14	—	—
-/2½	—	20	—	42
-/3	—	24	—	217
-/3½	—	30	—	42
-/4	—	32	—	217
-/4½	—	42	—	42
-/5	—	48	—	217
-/5½	—	56	—	42
773/1B	set	—	2	217
-/2B	—	—	6	42
-/3B	—	—	8	—

No.	per	s.	d.	page
773/4B	set	1	—	42
-/5B	—	1	4	—
776/3½	each	3	—	225
-/4	—	4	—	—
-/4½	—	5	—	—
-/5	—	6	—	—
-/5½	—	7	6	—
-/6	—	9	—	—
-/6½	—	11	—	—
-/7	—	12	—	—
777/1	—	10	—	—
-/2	—	11	—	—
-/3	—	12	—	—
-/4	—	17	—	—
778/1	—	8	—	—
-/2	—	9	—	—
-/3	—	10	—	—
-/4	—	14	—	—
779/3½	—	2	6	—
-/4	—	3	—	—
-/4½	—	4	—	—
-/5	—	5	—	—
-/5½	—	6	6	—
-/6	—	7	6	—
-/6½	—	9	—	—
-/7	—	11	—	—
805/3	—	4	6	77
-/4	—	4	—	—
806/1	—	5	6	75
-/2	—	7	—	—
807/1	—	11	—	—
-/2	—	12	—	—
-/3	—	14	—	—
-/4	—	15	6	—
-/5	—	18	—	—
-/35	—	7	—	80
808/1	—	13	—	76
-/2	—	14	6	—
-/3	—	16	—	—
-/4	—	18	—	—
-/5	—	20	—	—
-/35	—	9	—	80
-/T	—	1	8	—
819/35	—	3	6	—
-/T	—	—	6	—
821/48	—	11	—	—
-/T	—	1	—	—
822/1	—	8	—	75
-/2	—	9	—	—
-/3	—	10	—	—
-/4	—	9	8	—
-/5	—	11	—	—
-/35	—	5	—	80
-/T	—	—	8	—
829/1	—	8	—	76
-/2	—	9	6	—
-/3	—	12	6	—
-/48	—	4	—	80
-/T	—	1	—	—
830/1	—	4	—	74
-/2	—	4	8	—
-/3	—	6	—	—
-/4	—	6	6	—
-/5	—	7	6	—
-/35	—	2	—	80
-/T	—	—	6	—
831/0	—	2	10	74
-/2	—	3	8	—
-/4	—	4	6	—
-/6	—	4	6	—
-/8	—	5	4	—
-/9	—	5	4	—
-/10	—	7	—	—

No.	per	s.	d.	page
831/35	doz.	15	6	80
-/T	each	—	6	—
833/1	—	5	—	75
-/2	—	6	—	—
-/3	—	7	—	—
-/4	—	8	—	—
-/5	—	9	—	—
-/35	—	3	4	80
-/T	—	—	8	—
834/2	—	8	—	78
-/4	—	11	—	—
-/6	—	13	—	—
-/7	—	10	6	—
-/8	—	16	—	79
-/9	—	5	—	77
837/00	—	5	6	—
-/0	—	10	6	—
-/3	—	22	—	78
-/4	—	20	—	79
840B	—	10	6	241
-/22	—	11	2	—
-/26	—	11	6	—
-/30	—	12	6	—
-/102	—	11	—	—
-/106	—	10	10	—
840BCL	—	—	10	229
840N	—	11	4	241
-/22	—	12	—	—
-/26	—	12	4	—
-/30	—	13	4	—
-/102	—	11	10	—
-/106	—	11	8	—
842B/26	—	19	6	—
-/102	—	19	—	—
842N/26	—	20	6	—
-/102	—	20	—	—
843B	—	8	6	240
-/22	—	9	2	—
-/26	—	9	6	—
-/30	—	10	6	—
-/102	—	9	—	—
-/106	—	8	10	—
844N	—	9	4	—
-/22	—	10	—	—
-/26	—	10	4	—
-/30	—	11	4	—
-/102	—	9	10	—
-/106	—	9	8	—
845	—	40	—	233
845P	—	40	—	—
846	—	52	—	234
846P	—	52	—	—
846-847CL	—	1	6	229
847	—	74	—	234
847P	—	74	—	—
848	—	32	—	233
848P	—	32	—	—
850S	—	5	8	238
851G	—	6	6	—
-/22	—	7	2	—
-/26	—	7	6	—
-/30	—	8	6	—
-/102	—	7	—	—
-/106	—	6	10	—
851N	—	7	8	—
-/22	—	8	4	—
-/26	—	8	8	—
-/30	—	9	8	—
-/102	—	8	2	—
-/106	—	8	—	—
851S	—	6	—	—
-/22	—	6	8	—
-/26	—	7	—	—

No.	per	s.	d.	page
851S/30	each	8	—	238
-/102	—	6	6	—
-/106	—	6	4	—
851SCL	—	—	10	229
-/102CL	—	—	10	—
852S	—	8	—	239
-/22	—	8	8	—
-/26	—	9	—	—
-/30	—	10	—	—
-/102	—	8	6	—
-/106	—	8	4	—
853S	—	12	—	—
853N	—	14	—	—
856G	—	6	6	—
-/22	—	7	2	—
-/26	—	7	6	—
-/30	—	8	6	—
-/102	—	7	—	—
-/106	—	6	10	—
856S	—	6	—	—
-/22	—	6	8	—
-/26	—	7	—	—
-/30	—	8	—	—
-/102	—	6	6	—
-/106	—	6	4	—
856/2S	—	8	—	240
-/22	—	8	8	—
-/26	—	9	—	—
-/30	—	10	—	—
-/102	—	8	6	—
-/106	—	8	4	—
858/1	—	22	6	230
-/1P	—	24	6	—
-/2	—	26	—	—
-/2P	—	28	—	—
-/11	—	24	—	—
-/11P	—	26	—	—
-/12	—	27	—	—
-/12P	—	29	—	—
858/1—2CL	—	1	—	229
858/11-12CL	—	1	2	—
859/1	—	32	6	231
-/1P	—	35	—	—
-/2	—	40	—	—
-/2P	—	42	6	—
-/3	—	37	6	232
-/3P	—	40	—	—
-/4	—	42	—	—
-/4P	—	44	6	—
-/5	—	46	—	—
-/5P	—	48	6	—
859/1-2CL	—	1	4	229
-/3-5CL	—	1	4	—
-/3-5PCL	—	1	4	—
860/1S	—	1	6	242
-/1B	—	1	10	—
-/1N	—	2	6	—
-/1IS	—	1	8	—
-/1IB	—	2	—	—
-/1IN	—	2	8	—
-/1C	—	1	6	—
-/1D	—	1	10	—
-/1JC	—	1	8	—
-/1JD	—	2	—	—
-/2	—	1	8	—
-/3	—	1	8	—
-/4	doz.	1	8	—
-/5	—	—	4	—
-/6	—	—	2	—
-/7	—	—	3	—
-/8	each	—	2	—
-/9	—	—	4	—
-/10	—	—	4	—

Trade Mark.

No.	per	s.	d.	page
860/11	each	—	3	242
-/12	—	.	3	—
-/13	—	—	6	—
-/14	doz.	—	3	—
-/15	—	—	4	—
-/16	—	—	4	—
-/17	gross	—	8	—
-/18	each	—	8	—
-/19	—	1	4	—
-/20	doz.	—	10	—
-/21	—	1	6	—
-/22	—	—	2	—
-/22a	gross	—	6	—
-/23	each	—	4	—
-/24	gross	1	8	—
-/25	doz.	1	—	—
-/25a	—	—	2	—
-/26	each	—	2	—
-/27	doz.	—	4	—
-/28	—	—	4	—
-/29	—	—	6	—
-/30	gross	—	6	—
-/31	—	—	10	—
-/32S	doz.	—	6	—
-/32N	—	—	8	—
-/33N	—	—	3	—
-/34G	—	1	8	—
-/34GN	—	2	2	—
-/37	gross	—	6	—
-/38	100 yards	—	4	—
-/39	each	—	4	—
-/40	—	2	—	—
-/42	doz.	—	8	—
-/46a	—	—	4	—
-/46b	—	1	—	—
-/46c	—	1	—	—
-/47a	—	—	10	—
-/47b	—	1	—	—
-/49a	—	1	2	—
-/49b	—	1	2	—
-/49c	—	1	2	—
-/50	—	—	8	—
-/51	—	—	4	—
-/55	each	—	6	—
-/55c	—	—	10	—
-/56	—	—	2	—
-/57	doz.	—	4	—
-/58a	—	—	8	—
-/58c	—	1	—	—
-/59	—	—	4	—
-/60	each	1	2	—
-/61	—	1	8	—
-/62	—	2	2	—
-/63	—	3	2	—
-/64	doz.	1	8	—
-/67	each	1	6	—
-/102	—	1	8	—
-/106	—	1	6	—
861/1	—	8	—	236
-/1A	—	9	4	—
-/1C	—	7	8	—
-/1D	—	9	—	—
-/1E	—	11	—	—
-/1P	—	10	—	—
-/2	—	—	6	—
-/2D	—	1	—	—
-/2N	—	—	8	—
-/3	—	—	4	—
-/3a	—	—	2	—
-/3b	—	—	2	—
-/3c	—	—	2	—
-/5	—	1	4	—
-/5a	—	1	8	—

No.	per	s.	d.	page
861/6	each	—	6	236
-/6a	—	—	6	—
-/7a	doz.	—	10	—
-/7b	each	—	2	—
-/7c	doz.	—	6	—
-/8	100pcs.	2	—	—
-/9	doz.	—	2	—
-/10a	100pcs.	2	6	—
-/10b	—	2	6	—
-/10c	gross	—	6	—
-/11	doz.	1	—	—
-/12	100pcs	2	6	—
-/13a	each	—	4	—
-/13b	—	—	10	—
-/14a	—	—	4	—
-/14b	—	—	10	—
-/14P	—	—	10	—
-/15	—	1	6	—
-/16	—	1	8	—
-/17a	doz.	2	4	—
-/17b	—	2	4	—
-/18	each	2	8	—
-/19	—	1	8	—
-/19c	—	1	8	—
-/20	—	2	—	—
-/20D	—	2	—	—
-/20E	—	2	4	—
-/20P	—	2	4	—
-/21	—	3	4	—
-/22	—	4	—	—
-/22P	—	5	2	—
-/23	—	—	4	—
-/24	—	1	—	—
-/24a	doz.	4	4	—
-/25	each	1	—	237
-/25P	—	1	—	—
-/26	doz.	1	—	—
-/27	—	1	—	—
-/28	—	1	4	—
-/28a	—	1	4	—
-/29	100pcs.	2	—	—
-/30a	each	—	10	—
-/30b	—	1	—	—
-/30c	—	1	—	—
-/31a	—	—	6	—
-/31b	—	—	6	—
-/31c	—	—	6	—
-/31	—	1	4	—
-/32	100pcs.	3	4	—
-/33	—	5	6	—
-/34	doz.	—	8	—
-/35	100pcs.	5	—	—
-/36	each	—	2	—
-/37	doz.	—	2	—
-/38	—	1	—	—
-/39	—	—	4	—
-/40a	—	1	—	—
-/40b	—	—	8	—
-/41	—	—	2	—
-/42	each	3	—	—
-/43	doz.	—	4	—
-/44	—	3	4	—
-/45	—	4	10	—
-/46	—	—	6	—
-/47	each	—	2	—
-/48	—	—	2	—
-/49	—	—	2	—
-/50	—	—	2	—
-/51	doz.	—	8	—
-/52	each	3	—	—
-/53a	—	3	4	—
-/53b	—	4	10	—
-/54	doz.	—	4	—

No.	per	s.	d.	page
861/55a	doz.	2	6	237
-/55b	—	2	10	—
-/56	each	—	2	—
-/57	—	—	2	—
-/58	—	—	2	—
-/59	100pcs.	2	—	—
-/60a	each	—	4	—
-/61	doz.	—	8	—
-/62	100pcs.	1	4	—
-/63	doz.	1	—	—
-/64	—	—	8	—
-/65a	—	—	4	—
-/66	—	—	8	—
-/67	100pcs.	—	4	—
-/68	each	3	—	—
-/69	—	2	6	—
-/70	—	2	6	—
-/71	—	2	4	—
-/72	—	1	—	—
-/73	doz.	1	8	—
-/74	each	4	—	—
-/75	—	4	8	—
-/76	—	2	10	—
-/77	—	5	4	—
-/78	—	7	4	—
-/79	—	—	4	—
-/80/5	—	—	2	—
-/80/7	doz.	—	2	—
-/80/8	—	1	6	—
-/81	—	1	—	—
-/82a	each	2	—	—
-/82b	—	2	—	—
-/83	—	1	—	—
-/84a	—	2	10	235
-/84b	—	5	—	—
-/86a	doz.	1	6	—
-/86b	—	1	—	—
-/87a	—	—	6	—
-/87b	—	—	10	—
-/88a	each	—	6	—
-/88b	—	—	7	—
-/91	doz.	1	4	—
-/97	100pcs.	3	6	—
-/98	doz.	—	10	—
-/99	100pcs.	3	6	—
-/100	each	6	—	—
-/101	—	8	—	—
-/104	—	2	—	237
-/105	—	1	6	—
-/106A	1000 pcs.	1	6	235
-/107A	—	3	—	—
-/107B	—	3	4	—
-/108	—	4	4	—
-/109	—	7	4	—
-/111	—	2	10	—
-/112A	—	10	—	—
-/112B	—	10	—	—
-/112C	—	12	—	—
-/113A	—	1	8	—
-/113B	—	3	—	—
-/115	—	13	4	—
-/120	each	—	8	—
-/130a	—	3	4	237
-/130b	—	5	—	—
-/131	—	7	6	—
-/132	—	3	—	233
-/133	—	2	4	237
-/134a	doz.	—	6	—
-/134b	—	1	—	—
-/134c	—	—	2	—
-/134d	—	—	2	—
871/3	—	15	6	72
872/3	—	15	6	—

No.	per	s.	d.	page
873/3	doz.	15	6	72
881/0	each	2	6	—
-/2	—	3	4	—
-/5	—	4	8	—
-/6	—	4	6	—
-/8	—	5	10	—
-/10	—	7	—	—
881/35	doz.	17	—	81
-/T	—	4	—	—
881P	—	6	—	—
881V	—	6	—	—
882/0	each	2	6	72
-/2	—	3	4	—
-/5	—	4	8	—
-/6	—	4	6	—
-/8	—	5	10	—
-/10	—	7	—	—
882/35	doz.	17	—	81
-/T	—	4	—	—
882P	—	6	—	—
882V	—	6	—	—
883/0	each	2	6	73
-/2	—	3	4	—
-/5	—	4	8	—
-/6	—	4	6	—
-/8	—	5	10	—
-/10	—	7	—	—
883/35	doz.	17	—	81
-/T	—	4	—	—
883P	—	6	—	—
883V	—	6	—	—
898/1	each	4	8	73
-/2	—	5	8	—
-/3	—	7	—	—
898/35	doz.	24	—	81
898/T	—	4	—	—
898P/1	—	9	—	—
-/2	—	9	—	—
-/3	—	9	—	—
898V/1	—	9	—	—
-/2	—	9	—	—
-/3	—	9	—	—
905/3	—	4	—	214
-/4	—	4	6	—
-/5	—	5	6	—
-/6	—	6	8	—
-/7	—	8	6	—
-/8	—	9	8	—
-/11	—	13	—	—
-/18	—	20	—	—
906/3	—	6	—	—
-/4	—	7	4	—
-/5	—	9	8	—
-/6	—	12	—	—
-/7	—	14	—	—
-/9	—	18	—	—
-/10	—	20	—	—
-/12	—	24	—	—
909/2	—	3	8	—
-/3	—	5	8	—
-/4	—	7	10	—
-/5	—	9	—	—
-/6	—	11	—	—
-/7	—	13	—	—
-/8	—	15	—	—
-/9	—	17	—	—
-/10	—	19	—	—
910/2	—	3	8	—
-/3	—	5	8	—
-/4	—	7	10	—
-/5	—	9	—	—
-/6	—	11	—	—
-/7	—	13	—	—

Trade  Mark.

No.	per	s.	d.	page	No.	per	s.	d.	page	No.	per	s.	d.	page	No.	per	s.	d.	page
910/8	doz.	15	—	214	969/48	each	30	—	85	998/48	each	36	—	86	1019M/20	each	2	10	198
-/9	—	17	—	—	970/35	—	21	6	103	999/35	—	28	—	—	1019P	—	3	—	199
-/10	—	19	—	—	-/48	—	30	6	—	-/48	—	36	—	—	1019R/4	—	10	6	—
915/2	—	8	8	—	-/3/35	—	13	4	—	1001/1	—	1	10	160	1019T	—	4	—	—
-/3	—	12	—	—	-/3/48	—	24	—	—	1002	—	5	4	162	1020	—	4	6	160
-/4	—	13	8	—	-/4/35	—	6	10	—	1004/1	—	7	—	160	1022/00	—	6	8	197
-/5	—	15	8	—	-/4/48	—	9	8	—	-/2	—	11	—	—	-/0	—	7	4	—
-/6	—	19	4	—	971/000	—	2	—	106	-/3	—	16	—	—	-/1	—	8	8	—
-/7	—	21	8	—	-/00	—	3	—	—	1010/1	—	13	8	161	-/2	—	12	—	—
-/8	—	24	—	—	-/0	—	6	—	—	1011	—	3	8	160	-/3	—	18	—	—
-/9	—	27	—	—	-/1	—	20	—	—	1012/0	—	23	—	197	-/3½	—	22	—	—
-/10	—	30	—	—	973/35	—	4	—	108	1013/1	—	9	8	161	-/4	—	27	—	—
918	each	3	—	79	-/48	—	5	8	—	-/2	—	15	—	—	-/5	—	36	—	—
918/10	—	8	—	73	974/10	—	—	10	—	-/3	—	20	6	—	-/5½	—	48	—	—
937G/28	doz.	1	8	83	-/11	—	2	—	—	-H/2	—	20	—	163	-/6	—	57	—	—
-R/28	—	1	8	—	975/5	—	6	—	109	-H/3	—	28	—	—	-/7	—	79	—	—
938G/28	—	2	—	94	-/8	—	6	10	—	1014/1	—	9	—	161	-/8	—	102	—	—
-/35	—	2	—	—	-/25	—	8	—	—	-/3	—	18	—	—	-/9	—	120	—	—
938R/28	—	2	—	—	-/28	—	11	6	—	-H/3	—	24	—	163	-/10	—	156	—	—
-/35	—	2	—	—	975B/35	—	4	—	—	1015/1	—	12	—	161	-/11	—	172	—	—
938/4/35R	—	2	—	83	-/48	—	4	6	—	-/2	—	18	—	—	-/12	—	196	—	—
939/35BG	—	4	6	—	975C/35	—	2	—	—	-/3	—	23	—	—	-/13	—	250	—	—
-/48BG	—	7	2	—	-/48	—	2	—	—	-H/2	—	25	—	163	-/14	—	320	—	—
-/35G	—	2	—	—	976/35	doz.	12	—	112	-H/3	—	28	—	—	-/16	—	430	—	—
-/48G	—	3	8	—	-/48	—	15	6	—	1019/1	—	2	—	199	1022A/00	—	8	10	—
-HG/35	—	1	6	—	977/35	each	1	4	—	-/2	—	2	8	—	-/0	—	9	6	—
-HG/48	—	2	—	—	-/48	—	1	8	—	-/3	—	3	4	—	-/1	—	10	10	—
-HR/35	—	1	6	—	-/54	—	1	10	—	-/4	—	7	6	—	-/2	—	14	6	—
-HR/48	—	2	—	—	979/00	—	1	8	110	-/10	—	4	—	—	-/3	—	21	4	—
-/6/35K	each	1	4	—	-/0	—	4	—	—	-/15	—	3	6	—	-/3½	—	25	4	—
-/8/35K	—	1	4	—	-/1	—	7	6	—	-/18	—	2	8	—	-/4	—	30	4	—
-/6/48K	—	1	10	—	-/2	—	1	—	—	-/19G	—	2	10	—	-/5	—	39	4	—
-/8/48K	—	1	10	—	-/3	doz.	15	6	—	-/19H	—	4	—	—	-/5½	—	52	—	—
-/6/35R	doz.	2	—	—	-/4	each	2	10	—	-/20	—	2	10	—	-/6	—	63	6	—
-/8/35R	—	2	—	—	-/5	—	5	—	—	-/21	—	3	6	—	-/7	—	90	—	—
-/6/48R	—	3	8	—	-/6	—	2	10	—	1019A/8	doz.	7	4	198	-/8	—	113	—	—
-/8/48R	—	3	8	—	980/0	—	6	6	—	-/10	—	8	6	—	-/9	—	131	—	—
-VG/35	—	1	4	—	-/1	—	9	—	—	-/12	—	10	10	—	-/10	—	167	—	—
-VG/48	—	1	10	—	-/2	—	14	6	—	-/16	—	13	4	—	-/11	—	183	—	—
-VR/35	—	1	4	—	-/5	—	2	—	111	-/20	—	16	10	—	-/12	—	207	—	—
-VR/48	—	1	10	—	-/6	—	4	—	—	1019AF/12	each	1	6	199	-/13	—	262	—	—
-/6/35W	pair	2	6	—	-/7	—	5	8	—	-/16	—	2	—	—	-/14	—	332	—	—
-/8/35W	—	4	—	—	-/10	—	5	8	—	-/20	—	2	6	—	-/16	—	442	—	—
-/6/48W	—	5	—	—	-/11	—	7	6	—	1019C/8	doz.	8	6	198	1022D/1	—	12	—	—
-/8/48W	—	5	—	—	-/15	—	10	6	—	-/10	—	9	8	—	1022DA/3	—	23	—	—
957/1/35	each	3	8	84	981/00	—	2	—	109	-/12	—	13	4	—	1025	—	5	8	162
-/2/35	—	4	—	—	-/0	—	3	10	—	-/16	—	15	8	—	1025P	—	—	8	—
957P/1	—	3	10	—	-/1	—	6	6	—	-/20	—	18	—	—	1026/2	—	50	—	206
-/2	—	4	6	—	982/.0E	dz. blocks	4	10	117	1019CF/12	each	2	—	199	-/3	—	10	—	205
958/35B	—	19	4	90	-/21E	gross	1	4	—	-/16	—	2	—	—	-/4	—	19	6	—
-/48B	—	29	—	—	983/1	box	1	—	—	-/20	—	3	6	—	-/5	—	1	6	—
961/35	—	9	—	84	-/2	—	1	10	—	1019D/12	—	1	—	198	-/8	—	39	—	—
-Tender	—	—	10	—	-/3	—	3	—	—	-/16	—	1	4	—	1026P	doz.	2	—	—
961/48	—	12	—	—	-/4	—	5	—	—	-/20	—	1	6	—	1026D	10 yards	—	10	—
-Tender	—	1	6	—	-/6	doz.	1	—	—	1019G/12	—	—	10	—	1031B/3	—	—	6	186
962/35	—	10	6	—	-/7	—	2	6	—	-/16	—	1	4	—	-/4	—	—	6	—
-Tender	—	—	10	—	-/8	box	1	8	—	-/20	—	1	6	—	-/5	—	—	8	—
962/48	—	16	—	—	-/9	—	2	—	—	1019H/12	—	1	—	—	-/5	℔	5	—	—
-Tender	—	1	6	—	-/10	doz.	—	8	175	-/16	—	1	4	—	-/6	10 yards	—	10	—
963/35	—	16	—	87	-/20	box	2	4	117	-/20	—	1	8	—	-/6	℔	4	10	—
-Tender	—	2	6	—	-/21	—	2	8	—	1019J/12	—	1	—	—	-/8	10 yards	1	—	—
963/48	—	20	—	—	987/35	each	18	—	85	-/16	—	1	4	—	-/8	℔	4	6	—
-Tender	—	3	4	—	-/48	—	24	—	—	-/20	—	1	8	—	-/10	10 yards	1	4	—
965/35	—	44	—	—	988/35	—	18	—	—	1019K/1	set	6	—	—	-/10	℔	3	10	—
-/48	—	55	—	—	-/48	—	24	—	—	-/2	—	7	8	—	1031DL	yard	—	10	—
-/54	—	68	—	—	989/35	—	18	—	—	-/3	—	8	10	—	1031J	—	—	4	—
966/35	—	8	—	84	-/48	—	24	—	—	-/5	—	9	6	—	1031S/1	25 yards	—	8	—
967/35	—	9	8	—	991/35B	—	15	6	88	-/9	—	11	8	—	-/2	—	—	10	—
968/35	—	17	—	—	-/48B	—	22	—	—	1019L/12	each	1	8	—	-/3	10 yards	—	6	—
-Tender	—	—	10	—	992/35B	—	17	4	—	-/16	—	2	4	—	-/4	—	—	8	—
968/48	—	22	—	—	997/35	—	28	—	86	-/20	—	2	10	—	-/5	—	—	10	—
-Tender	—	1	6	—	-/48	—	36	—	—	1019M/12	—	1	8	—	-/5	℔	9	9	—
969/35	—	16	—	85	998/35	—	28	—	—	-/16	—	2	4	—	-/8	10 yards	1	6	—

Trade Mark.

Table 1

No.	per	s.	d.	page
1031 S/8	℔	8	5	186
1033/00	each	2	6	198
-/0	—	4	—	—
-/1	—	14	—	—
-/3	—	2	--	—
1034	—	20	—	—
1035/1	bottle	—	8	185
-/2	—	1	10	—
1035 P	℔	1	4	—
-P/50	box	—	4	—
-P/100	—	—	6	—
1036/1	each	9	—	175
-/1 H	—	10	6	—
-/1 HV	—	15	—	—
-/1 V	—	11	6	—
-/3	—	1	8	92
-/4	—	1	8	—
-/5	—	1	8	—
-/6	—	7	—	—
-/11	—	15	—	170
-/11 H	—	16	4	—
-/11 V	—	17	6	—
-/12	—	18	—	—
-/12 H	—	19	6	—
-/12 V	—	18	4	—
-/13	—	22	—	—
-/13 H	—	23	6	—
-/13 V	—	24	4	—
-/62	—	17	—	92
-/64	—	9	8	—
1037/000	—	—	2	186
-/00	—	—	4	—
-/0	—	—	8	—
-/1	—	—	6	—
-/2	—	—	8	—
-/3	—	—	10	—
-/3½	—	—	10	—
-/3½ H	—	1	4	—
-/4	—	1	—	—
-/4½	—	1	—	—
-/4½ H	—	1	4	—
-/5	—	1	6	—
-/6	doz.	—	3	—
-/6½	—	—	4	—
-/7	—	—	6	—
-/8	each	3	—	—
-/9	doz.	1	4	—
-/10	each	—	10	—
-/11	doz.	2	6	—
-/12	—	—	4	—
1038/1	each	4	—	187
-/2	—	5	6	—
-/2½	—	6	6	—
-/3	—	8	6	—
-/4½	—	12	10	—
-/6	—	20	—	—
-/7	—	30	—	—
-/9	—	42	—	—
-/20	—	6	10	—
-/21	—	10	10	—
-/23	—	16	—	—
-/26	—	32	—	—
-/30	—	9	8	—
-/31	—	14	—	—
-/33	—	19	—	—
1039/2a	each	3	8	202
-/3	—	—	2	—
-/3 H	doz.	—	4	—
-/4	each	—	2	—
-/5	—	—	6	—
-/6	—	—	6	—
-/7	—	2	6	—

Table 2

No.	per	s.	d.	page
1039/7c	each	1	6	202
-/8a	—	3	—	—
-/8b	—	7	—	—
-/10a	—	1	10	—
-/10b	—	3	4	—
-/10c	—	5	4	—
-/16	—	10	10	—
-/20	—	2	—	—
-/22	—	9	—	—
-/24	—	7	—	—
-/27	—	—	6	—
-/28	—	—	10	—
-/29	—	3	—	—
-/30	—	6	—	—
-/32a	doz.	2	—	—
-/32b	—	3	—	—
-/32c	—	4	4	—
-/32d	—	6	8	—
-/33a	—	4	10	—
-/33b	—	8	—	—
-/34	—	4	—	—
-/35a	gross	8	—	—
-/35b	—	9	3	—
-/35c	—	14	6	—
-/35d	—	19	4	—
-/42	each	2	6	—
1040/1	—	4	—	175
1040 K/35	—	3	—	176
-K/48	—	3	6	—
-R/35	doz.	6	—	—
-R/48	—	7	4	—
-RP/35	—	8	6	—
-RP/48	—	9	6	—
-W/35	pair	7	4	—
-W/48	—	8	6	—
1041/4a	each	3	—	191
-/4b	—	6	—	—
-/5	—	4	—	—
-/6a	—	2	4	—
-/6b	—	—	6	—
-/6c	pack	—	6	—
-/10	each	19	—	189
-/11	—	5	—	—
-/12	—	30	—	—
-/13	yard	1	6	—
-/14	each	2	4	190
-/15	—	3	8	—
1042G/35	doz.	4	10	176
-G/48	—	6	—	—
-K/35	each	3	—	—
-K/48	—	3	6	—
-R/35	doz.	4	10	—
-R/48	—	6	—	—
-RP/35	—	7	4	—
-RP/48	—	8	6	—
-UG/48	each	1	2	—
-UR/48	—	1	2	—
-W/35	pair	7	4	—
-W/48	—	8	6	—
1044/7	each	42	—	203
-/8	—	35	—	204
-/9A	—	15	--	200
-/9B	—	28	—	—
-/9C	—	29	—	201
-/9D	—	54	—	—
-/9E	—	64	—	—
-/9ES	—	69	—	—
-/10A	—	41	—	—
-/10B	—	64	—	—
-/11	—	57	—	203
1045/1	—	—	8	193
-/2	—	—	10	—

Table 3

No.	per	s.	d.	page
1045/3	each	1	—	193
-/4	—	—	10	—
-/5	—	1	4	—
-/6	—	—	10	—
-/7	—	—	10	—
-/21	—	—	10	—
-/21M	—	1	—	—
-/22	—	—	10	—
-/23	—	1	4	—
-/24	—	1	—	—
-/50	100pcs.	3	8	—
1047/2	each	9	8	185
1049/2	—	9	8	—
-/3	—	14	6	—
-/4	—	19	6	—
1050/0	—	--	8	194
-/0L	—	1	6	—
-/1	—	2	4	—
-/1L	—	3	4	—
-/2	—	3	2	—
-/2L	—	5	2	—
-/3	—	3	4	—
-/3L	—	7	—	—
-/4	—	5	—	—
-/4L	—	9	—	—
1051/1	—	—	10	195
-/1L	—	1	6	—
-/2A	—	1	4	—
-/2AL	—	2	—	—
-/2B	—	1	6	—
-/2BL	—	2	4	—
-/3A	—	2	—	—
-/3AL	—	2	6	—
-/3B	—	2	6	—
-/3BL	—	3	2	—
-/4	doz.	3	8	—
-/4L	each	1	—	—
-/5	doz.	6	—	—
-/5L	each	2	—	—
-/6	—	1	2	—
-/6L	—	2	—	—
-/7	—	2	4	—
-/7L	—	3	—	—
-/7 H	—	3	—	—
-/7 HL	—	3	8	—
-/8	—	2	—	—
-/8L	—	2	10	—
-/10	—	1	—	194
-/10L	—	1	10	—
-/11	—	1	6	99
-/12	doz.	3	8	—
-/13	—	4	6	179
-/15	each	1	4	194
-/15L	—	2	—	—
-/17	—	3	4	195
-/17L	—	4	—	—
-/32	—	—	4	188
-/35	—	1	6	—
-/36	—	—	8	—
-/37	—	1	—	—
-/40	—	—	6	193
-/40 H	—	1	2	—
-/41	—	—	4	—
-/43	—	—	4	—
-/44	—	—	6	—
-/45	—	—	8	—
-/50	—	—	8	188
-/52	—	2	8	177
-/54A	each	—	10	—
-/54B	—	—	4	—
-/54L	10 pcs.	—	1	—
-/55	each	1	—	—
-/55B	—	--	10	—

Table 4

No.	per	s.	d.	page
1051/59	doz.	—	6	193
-/60	each	—	2	—
-/61	--	—	4	—
-/62	—	—	6	—
-/63	—	—	4	—
-/65	—	—	6	—
-/66	--	1	6	—
-/67	—	—	6	—
-/68	—	1	2	—
-/70	—	—	10	177
-/71	—	1	4	—
-/72	--	2	8	—
-/80	—	—	6	193
-/81	—	—	6	—
1052/00	—	2	6	196
-/0	—	3	6	—
-/1	—	4	—	--
-/2	—	5	4	—
-/3	—	7	—	—
1053/1	—	26	—	200
-/2	—	35	—	—
-/3	—	52	—	—
-/4	—	90	—	—
-/5	—	140	—	—
-/6	—	190	—	—
-/7	—	270	—	—
1055	--	21	—	204
1059/0	—	27	—	161
-G	—	66	—	163
-K/0	—	29	—	161
-/KG	—	68	—	163
1060/1	—	8	—	194
-/2	—	11	6	—
-/3	—	6	—	—
1061/1	10 pcs.	—	6	—
1062	each	13	—	196
1062E	pair	3	8	—
1066/25	each	65	—	189
1067/6	—	23	—	—
-/10	—	33	—	—
1068/2	—	11	—	190
-/4	—	22	—	—
-/6	—	56	—	189
-/10	—	70	—	—
-/11	—	8	—	190
-/12	—	12	6	—
-/14	—	4	—	—
-/15	—	8	—	—
-/17	—	14	—	—
-/25	—	98	—	189
1070/1	—	6	10	188
-/2	—	6	10	—
-/3	—	9	6	—
-/4	—	40	—	—
-/5	—	45	—	—
-/6	—	45	—	—
-/7	—	45	—	—
-/8	—	10	6	—
-/9	—	11	4	—
-/10	—	1	8	—
-/11	—	1	8	—
1074/5	—	3	6	164
-/6	—	2	8	—
-/7	—	4	4	—
-/8	--	4	4	—
-/9	—	3	4	—
1075/5	—	3	6	—
-/6	—	4	2	—
-/7	—	4	10	—
-/8	—	4	6	—

Trade Mark.

No.	per	s.	d.	page	No.	per	s.	d.	page	No.	per	s.	d.	page	No.	per	s.	d.	page
1075/9	each	4	—	164	1088/22H	each	18	8	169	1091/21H	each	19	—	181	1092RP/35	each	1	2	178
1076/5	—	3	6	—	-/22HV	—	23	4	—	-/21HV	—	23	8	—	-RP/48	—	1	6	—
-/6	—	3	2	—	-/22V	—	19	6	—	-/21V	—	20	—	—	-W/35	pair	8	8	—
-/7	—	4	10	—	-/31	—	16	8	—	-/22	—	23	—	—	-W/48	—	11	—	—
-/8	—	4	6	—	-/31H	—	18	—	—	-/22H	—	24	8	—	1093/4	each	33	—	170
-/9	—	4	—	—	-/31HV	—	22	8	—	-/22HV	—	30	8	—	-/4B	—	56	—	—
1077/0	—	4	6	160	-/31V	—	18	10	—	-/22V	—	27	—	—	1094/5	—	8	—	179
1078/0	—	5	6	—	-/32	—	19	6	—	-/51	—	17	—	174	-/5A	—	7	2	—
1079/0	—	5	4	—	-/32H	—	21	—	—	-/51H	—	20	—	—	-/5AV	—	8	10	—
-F	—	—	6	—	-/32HV	—	25	6	—	-/51HV	—	24	6	—	-/5V	—	9	8	—
1080/2	—	40	—	183	-/32V	—	22	—	—	-/51V	—	19	6	—	1096	—	15	—	166
-/2H	—	53	—	—	-/60	—	9	—	92	-/52	—	22	6	—	-H	—	16	10	—
1081	—	13	—	—	1089DG/35	doz.	—	4	184	-/52H	—	25	6	—	-HV	—	19	6	—
1083/1	—	10	6	196	-DG/48	—	—	6	—	-/52HV	—	31	6	—	-V	—	16	4	—
-/2	—	11	4	—	-DR/35	—	—	4	—	-/52V	—	26	6	—	1096/2	—	25	6	—
-/3	—	3	6	—	-DR/48	—	—	6	—	-/71	—	19	—	184	-H/2	—	26	—	—
1084/3½	—	1	6	206	-G/35	—	7	4	—	-/71H	—	20	6	—	-HV/2	—	28	6	—
-/4½	—	2	—	—	-G/48	—	8	6	—	-/71HV	—	24	6	—	-V/2	—	26	6	—
-/7	—	4	—	—	-K/35	each	2	10	—	-/71V	—	21	6	—	1096/3	—	29	—	167
1085/1	—	2	—	191	-K/48	—	3	6	—	-/72	—	24	8	—	-H/3	—	30	8	—
-/2	—	3	4	—	-M/35	—	—	4	—	-/72H	—	26	—	—	-HV/3	—	33	4	—
-/3	—	3	6	—	-M/48	—	—	6	—	-/72HV	—	31	8	—	-V/3	—	30	—	—
-/4	—	3	2	—	-MK/35	—	—	6	—	-/72V	—	28	8	—	1097	—	22	—	166
-/5	—	3	4	—	-MK/48	—	—	8	—	-/81	—	17	6	181	-H	—	28	—	—
-/6	—	2	10	—	-MP/35	—	—	6	—	-/81H	—	19	—	—	-HV	—	30	8	—
-/7	—	5	6	—	-MP/48	—	—	8	—	-/81HV	—	23	8	—	-V	—	23	4	—
-/8	—	6	—	—	-MW/35	—	—	4	—	-/81V	—	20	—	—	1097/2	—	36	6	—
-/9	—	6	—	—	-MW/48	—	—	6	—	-/82	—	23	—	—	-H/2	—	41	6	—
-/10	—	4	—	—	-/R/35	doz.	7	4	—	-/82H	—	24	8	—	-HV/2	—	44	—	—
-/11	—	3	6	—	-/R/48	—	8	6	—	-/82HV	—	30	8	—	-V/2	—	38	—	—
-/12	—	9	6	—	-/W/35	pair	6	—	—	-/82V	—	27	—	—	1097/3	—	40	—	167
-/13	—	2	10	—	-/W/48	—	8	—	—	-/91	—	19	—	183	-H/3	—	46	—	—
-/14/1	doz.	1	4	—	1090/1	each	4	10	175	-/91H	—	20	6	—	-HV/3	—	48	8	—
-/14/2	—	1	6	—	-/1A	—	6	—	172	-/91HV	—	24	6	—	-V/3	—	41	4	—
-/14/5	—	2	2	—	-/1B	—	8	8	—	-/91V	—	21	6	—	1099	—	42	—	174
-/15/1	—	7	4	—	-/3	—	1	10	93	-/92	—	24	8	—	1099H	—	45	—	—
-/15/2	—	8	6	—	-/10	—	5	6	—	-/92H	—	26	—	—	1100	—	4	—	165
-/15/5	—	9	8	—	-/11	—	8	—	173	-/92HV	—	31	8	—	1100B	—	4	8	—
1086/1	each	7	4	207	-/12	—	11	—	—	-/92V	—	28	8	—	1100G/28	doz.	3	—	176
-/2	—	6	—	—	-/20	—	8	6	93	-/100	—	9	6	93	-R/28	—	3	6	—
-/3	—	14	6	—	-/21	—	9	—	180	-/101	—	14	10	—	1100S/8½	gross	10	—	94
-/4	—	8	—	—	-/22	—	12	6	—	1092/1	—	22	—	171	1101	each	6	—	165
-/5	—	11	6	—	-/30	—	11	—	93	-/1H	—	27	6	—	1101G/35	doz.	3	6	176
-/6	—	12	6	—	-/71	—	10	8	182	-/1HV	—	34	6	—	-R/35	—	3	8	—
-/7	—	2	4	—	-/72	—	14	—	—	-/1V	—	25	6	—	1102	each	8	—	165
-/8	—	3	4	206	-/100	—	7	6	93	-/2	—	6	6	—	1107/3	—	—	10	77
-/9	—	40	—	207	-/101	—	11	—	—	-/2HV	—	8	8	—	-/11	—	3	8	172
-/10	—	34	—	—	1091/1	—	10	6	175	-/2V	—	8	—	—	-/12	—	5	—	—
-/11	—	—	2	—	-/1H	—	12	—	—	-/3	—	6	6	—	-/61	—	2	—	77
-/12	—	2	6	—	-/1HV	—	16	8	—	-/3HV	—	8	8	—	-/62	—	3	—	—
-/13	—	1	—	—	-/1V	—	12	10	—	-/3V	—	8	—	—	1110	—	17	—	162
1087/1	—	39	—	208	-/3	—	3	4	—	-/5	—	11	4	179	1111	—	20	—	—
-/2	—	152	—	—	-/3HV	—	5	8	—	-/5A	—	10	—	—	1112	—	21	6	177
-/3	—	148	—	—	-/3V	—	4	10	—	-/5AV	—	11	8	—	1157/35	—	3	10	165
1088/2	—	8	—	175	-/3¼	—	2	6	93	-/5V	—	12	10	—	-/11	—	9	—	—
-/2H	—	9	8	—	-/5	—	10	10	175	-/10	—	31	6	171	-/12	—	12	—	—
-/2HV	—	14	—	—	-/5H	—	13	8	—	-/11	—	38	—	—	1403/1	—	11	—	226
-/2V	—	10	6	—	-/5HV	—	18	4	—	-/12	—	45	—	—	-/3	—	12	—	—
-/3	—	11	—	—	-/5V	—	13	6	—	1092H/10	—	36	6	—	-/5	—	14	—	—
-/3H	—	12	6	—	-/10	—	7	—	93	-/11	—	43	6	—	-/7	—	15	6	—
-/3HV	—	17	—	—	-/11	—	15	8	173	-/12	—	50	—	—	-/9	—	22	—	—
-/3V	—	13	4	—	-/11H	—	17	—	—	1092HV/10	—	44	—	—	1403S/1	—	12	—	—
-/6½	—	3	6	92	-/11HV	—	22	—	—	-/11	—	53	—	—	-/3	—	13	6	—
-/10	—	7	6	—	-/11V	—	18	—	—	-/12	—	62	—	—	-/5	—	16	—	—
-/11	—	13	—	—	-/12	—	21	—	—	1092V/10	—	34	6	—	-/7	—	18	—	—
-/12	—	16	6	—	-/12H	—	22	6	—	-/11	—	42	6	—	-/9	—	25	—	—
-/21	—	13	—	169	-/12HV	—	29	—	—	-/12	—	51	—	—	1440/10	doz.	1	6	226
-/21H	—	14	6	—	-/12V	—	25	—	—	1092G/35	—	1	—	178	-/11	—	3	6	—
-/21HV	—	19	—	—	-/20	—	11	—	93	-G/48	—	1	2	—	-/12	—	6	—	—
-/21V	—	15	4	—	-/21	—	17	6	181	-K/35	—	4	6	—	-/22	—	11	—	—
-/22	—	17	4	—						-K/48	—	5	8	—	-/23	—	18	—	—
										-R/35	—	1	—	—					
										-R/48	—	1	2	—					

Trade Mark.

No.	per	Price s.	d.	page
1440/24	doz.	18	—	226
-/25	—	24	—	—
-/26	—	24	—	—
-/27	each	4	—	—
-/28	—	8	6	—
1505/3/35B	—	27	6	68
-/3/48B	—	36	8	—
1506/3/48B	—	46	—	—
1509/35B	—	52	—	70
-/48B	—	130	—	—
1511/35B	—	13	—	66
-/35C	—	17	—	—
-/2/35	—	15	—	—
1513/4	—	54	—	168
-/4B	—	77	—	—
-/4H	—	52	—	—
-/4HB	—	75	—	—
-/6	—	40	—	87
1514/4	—	90	—	168
-/4B	—	122	—	—
-/4H	—	90	—	—
-/4HB	—	122	—	—
-/4HWB	—	128	—	—
-/4HW	—	96	—	—
-/6	—	70	—	87
1515/35B	—	40	—	70
-/48B	—	58	—	—
1516/35B	—	41	—	—
-/48B	—	60	—	—
1517/35B	—	45	—	69
-/48B	—	56	—	—
1518/35B	—	45	—	—
-/48B	—	56	—	—
1519/35B	—	45	—	—
-/48B	—	56	—	—
1525/35B	—	55	—	70
-/48B	—	76	—	—
1526/35B	—	56	—	—
-/48B	—	78	—	—
1527/35B	—	56	—	69
-/48B	—	83	—	—
1528/35B	—	56	—	—
-/48B	—	83	—	—
1529/35B	—	56	—	—
-/48B	—	83	—	—
1601/35A	—	11	—	65
-/48A	—	14	6	—

No.	per	Price s.	d.	page
1603/4	each	35	—	167
1701/2	—	2	—	72
-/3	—	2	6	—
-/35	—	1	—	80
-T	—	—	4	—
1702/2	—	2	—	72
-/3	—	2	6	—
-/35	—	1	—	80
-/T	—	—	4	—
1703/2	—	2	—	72
-/3	—	2	6	—
-/35	—	1	—	80
-/T	—	—	4	—
1711/1	—	7	—	74
-/2	—	8	6	—
-/3	—	10	—	—
-/35	—	4	6	81
-/T	—	1	2	—
1712/1	—	7	—	74
-/2	—	8	6	—
-/3	—	10	—	—
-/35	—	4	6	81
-/T	—	1	2	—
1713/1	—	7	—	74
-/2	—	8	6	—
-/3	—	10	—	—
-/35	—	4	6	81
-/T	—	1	2	—
1721/1	—	14	—	74
-/2	—	16	—	—
-/3	—	20	—	—
-/35	—	9	—	81
-/T	—	1	4	—
1722/1	—	14	—	74
-/2	—	16	—	—
-/3	—	20	—	—
-/35	—	9	—	81
-/T	—	1	4	—
1723/1	—	14	—	74
-/2	—	16	—	—
-/3	—	20	—	—
-/35	—	9	—	81
-/T	—	1	4	—
1819/1/35B	—	7	4	76
-/2/35B	—	10	8	—
1821/1/48B	—	20	—	89
-/1/48C	—	25	—	—

No.	per	Price s.	d.	page
1821/1/48D	each	28	—	89
-/1/48E	—	34	—	—
-/2/48B	—	23	4	—
-/2/48C	—	28	—	—
-/2/48D	—	31	4	—
-/2/48E	—	37	4	—
1957/1/35B	—	8	—	88
-/2/35B	—	11	—	—
1961/2/35B	—	17	6	89
-/2/48B	—	25	—	—
-/2/54B	—	34	8	—
-/3/35B	—	19	6	90
-/3/48B	—	28	—	—
1962/2/35B	—	21	6	—
-/3/48B	—	32	—	—
1966/1/35B	—	9	4	88
-/2/35B	—	16	—	—
1967/1/35B	—	10	10	—
-/2/35B	—	17	8	—
1968/1/35B	—	26	—	—
-/1/48B	—	34	—	—
-/2/35B	—	27	6	90
-/2/48B	—	37	—	—
-/3/35B	—	28	—	—
-/3/48B	—	38	—	—
1975/5	—	6	—	177
-/8	—	7	—	—
-/28	—	12	—	—
1987/35B	—	27	—	91
-/48B	—	36	—	—
1988/35B	—	27	—	—
-/48B	—	36	—	—
1989/35B	...	27	—	—
-/48B	—	36	—	—
1997/35B	—	45	—	—
-/48B	—	60	—	—
1998/35B	—	45	—	—
-/48B	—	60	—	—
1999/35B	—	45	—	—
-/48B	—	60	—	—
3358/10	doz.	7	10	210
-/11	—	9	—	—
-/12	—	12	—	—
-/21	each	6	—	211
-/23	—	4	10	—
-/28	doz.	13	—	210
-/29	—	15	6	—

No.	per	Price s.	d.	page
3358/31	doz.	15	6	210
-/33	—	21	—	—
-/34	—	34	—	—
-/35	—	42	—	—
-/36	—	48	—	—
-/37	each	5	—	211
-/38	—	5	8	—
-/39	—	7	—	—
-/40	—	9	—	—
-/41	—	7	4	212
-/42	—	13	—	211
-/43	—	18	—	—
-/44	—	20	—	212
3759	doz.	5	6	216
-/1	—	7	10	—
-/2	—	14	—	—
-/3	—	26	—	—
-/4	—	42	—	—
-/5	—	62	—	—
3760/1	—	26	—	—
-/2	—	36	—	—
-/3	—	48	—	—
-/4	—	62	—	—
-/5	—	84	—	—
-/10½	—	11	—	—
-/10	—	13	—	—
-/11	—	14	—	—
-/12	—	15	6	—
-/13	—	21	—	—
-/14	—	24	—	—
-/15	—	33	—	—
-/16	—	42	—	—
3776	—	6	—	217
-/1	—	7	10	—
-/2	—	14	—	—
-/3	—	21	—	—
-/4	—	15	6	—
-/5	—	24	—	—
-/6	—	33	—	—
3777/1	—	14	—	—
-/2	—	15	6	—
-/3	—	24	—	—
-/4	—	36	—	—
-/5	—	48	—	—

Glass jars, zincs and carbons for batteries.

To suit battery	0 F	1 A	1 B	1047	1049	1 F	2 F	3 F	4 F	
Price of carbon	-/8		-/6		-/10	-/4	-/6	-/10	1/2	each
— zinc	-/6		-/10		1/-	-/4	-/6	-/10	1/2	—
— glass jar	-/6	-/2	-/6		-/8	-/6	-/10	1/4	2/-	—

Zinc plates and carbon jars.
0c

Carbon	-/10 each
Zinc	each -/4

Fabrik   Marke.

Supplement

1905 — ENGLISH EDITION
1914 — GERMAN EDITION

In addition to reproducing the complete 1911 catalogue in its original form, we have taken the opportunity to add to the relatively sparse information hitherto available on the products of Carette by compiling a supplement made up of edited extracts from the above catalogues. Together with the full catalogue the supplement constitutes an almost definitive guide to the range of Carette material (with the exception of the special products for Bassett-Lowke mentioned earlier and others indicated in the notes below) during the firm's most inventive years, 1905-1914, which were also the years of its greatest expansion.

The following notes may be of interest:

1.   A striking omission in the 1914 range is the absence of motor cars or aeroplanes, which were certainly represented in the 1911 catalogue.

2.   The large maroon-enamelled Carette limousine (42 cm long) illustrated on the cover is not mentioned in either the 1911 or 1914 catalogues, although other cars produced in that series are listed and illustrated (see pages 210 to 212). It is thought that these cars may have been supplied to specific stores as special orders and were not generally available to the wholesale trade.

3.   The very distinctive, white, high-tonneau Carette motor car illustrated at the rear of the cavalcade on the cover, was thought to have been produced around 1907-8. Although stationary engines, trains and boats tended to be represented by fairly stable ranges, toy motor-cars rapidly became the subject of immediate fashion, and manufacturers responded accordingly from year to year.

4.   In order to avoid duplication, the paddle steamer illustrated at the foot of page 91 of the 1905 catalogue has been taken from page 87, where it originally appeared, and substituted in place of a boat called the "Sleipner" which was still available and is illustrated in the 1911 catalogue (page 125). Likewise, on page 161,

(1905) the engraving of the 1⅕″ gauge train set has been added so as to illustrate the rather odd range of rail gauges for which there seemed to be little commercial *raison d'être*.

5.   The trains illustrated on pages 161 & 164 are virtually identical to those marketed by the smaller German firm of Johann And. Issmayer. It can only be assumed that these items were carried as purely wholesale items by Carette, as indeed was the case with several less well documented items in these catalogues.

6.   All known variations of the beautiful 'Vauclain' locomotive are illustrated and they appear on pages 60 & 87 and page 54 in the 1905 supplement.

For further specific information concerning the history and products of Carette & Co., the following books are recommended:

i.   'CLOCKWORK STEAM AND ELECTRIC' (Gustav Reder), particularly page 206 which has a very well researched short history of the company and its leading personalities.

ii.   'A CENTURY OF MODEL TRAINS' (Allen Levy), especially pages 22, 23, 24, 25, 26, 32, 33, 34, 35, 38, 43, 56, 58, 59, 61, 63, 67, 69, 71, 73, 74, 86, 100, 130, 133.

iii.   'MODEL RAILWAYS 1838/1939' (Hamilton Ellis), pages 37, 49, 50 and plates vii and ix.

iv.   'DIE ANDEREN NURNBERGER' BAND 1 (Carlernst Baecker and Dieter Haas), pages 237 to 292.

v.   'BASSETT-LOWKE RAILWAYS' (Allen Levy), pages 50 (lower left and right), 53 (top right), 57 (bottom left), 58 (top right), 67 (bottom right), 71 (top right), 72 (right), 73, 74 (left), 76 (right), 78, 79 (left), 80 (right), 81, 82, 83 (left), 86, 87, 88, 89, 90 (left), 95 (excluding Sir Sam Fay), 104 (bottom left, Northampton made 040 from Carette tooling).

Highly finished Motor-Cars.

739/1 N

739/2 N

Motor-cars

with very solid clockwork, superior finish, highly
japanned, with rubber tyres.

For straight and circular running.

No. 739/1 N
Motor delivery van

with 1 figure and 6 barrels

8¹/₂ in. long . . . . each **2/—**

No. 739/2 N   the same

with 1 figure and 8 barrels

9 in. long . . . . each **2/10**

No. **739 F**   **Figures** to 739/1 N and 2 N

dozen **1/10**

740/1 N—3 N

Motor-car

fine execution, wheels with rubber tyres, strong
clockwork, **with 4 passengers**.

No.	740/1 N	7¹/₂ in. long	. . .	each	**2/3**
„	740/2 N	10¹/₂ in. long	. . .	„	**3/9**
„	740/3 N	13 in. long	. . .	„	**5/9**
No.	740 F/1	Figures to 740/1	. .	dozen	**2/5**
„	740 F/2	„ „ 740/2	. .	„	**4/3**
„	740 F/3	„ „ 740/3	. .	„	**4 10**

685/4

No. 685/4

Steam-Motor-car

highly japanned, best construction, with
rubber tyres.

For straight and circular running, with 4 figures
10 in. long, 6²/₅ in. high 4³/₅ in. long

each **12/—**

No. **685 F**   **Figures** to 685/4

dozen **4/10**

Trade Mark.

Working Models
(continued).

No. 676/1 Clown

4½ in. high . . . . . . dozen **3/9**

No. 676/2 Round-about

7 in. high . . . . . . dozen **4/10**

No. 676/3 Round-about with Balloon

9 in. high . . . . . . dozen **6/—**

676/1   676/2   676/3

138/2   138/5

New Swings, well japanned, **very original**

No.										dozen
138/1	with 3	Figures	7	in.	high	. . . .	dozen	**5/5**
„ **138/2**	„ 4	„	9	„	„	. . . .	„	**7/6**
„ **138/3**	„ 6	„	9½	„	„	. . . .	„	**12/—**
„ **138/4**	„ 6	„	10	„	„	. . . .	„	**15/6**
„ **138/5**	„ 6	„	13¼	„	„	. . . .	„	**21/—**

No. 138/5/0 Round-about

tin japanned, plain execution, 7½ in high, 4½ in. diameter . . . . dozen **5/3**

No. 138/4/0 same better quality

9¼ in. high, 5½ in. diameter   dozen **7/6**

138/5/0   138/4/0

Working Models (continued).

697/5   697/6

Round about

nicely finished.

No. **697/5**

10¼ in. high, 7 in. diam., dozen **11/5**

No. **697/6**

14 in. high, 6 in. wide . each **1/8**

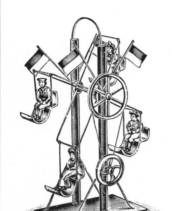
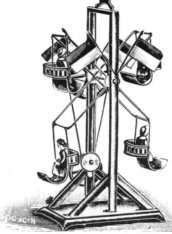

119/6/0   119/3/0

No. **119/7/0**

Russian Swings

plain execution, with
3 figures, 10 in. high . dozen **9/—**

No. **119/6/0** the same
with 4 figures, 12 in. high, dozen **12/—**

No. **119/3/0**

the same with 4 figures better quality
13½ in. high . . . dozen **18/—**

No. **120/3/0**

the same with 6 figures, superior
execution, 16 in. high . each **2/9**

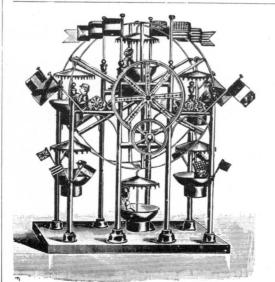

659/0

No. **659/0**

Russian Swing

elegant equipment, nicely japanned

12 in high, 9 in. long, 8 in. wide

each **5/9**

Highly finished clockwork locomotives.

Fast train-Locomotive

of **newest and most perfect construction** (exact taken from an original model), superior execution and very highly japanned.

With very solid, **extra strong clockwork, new patented regulator, brake (registered)** and **reversing gear for running forward and backward.**

No. 965/35	**35 mm gauge**	17	in. long (incl. tender) Locomotive with tender	.	each	**22/—**
„ 965/48	**48 mm gauge**	22	„ „ „ „ „	„ „ „	.	„	**31/6**
„ 965/54	**54 mm gauge**	24¹/₂	„ „ „ „ „	„ „ „	.	„	**38/—**
„ 965/35 C	the same as 965/35 **with cow catcher**		„	„ „	„ „ „	.	„	**22/—**
„ 965/48 C	„ „ „ 965/48		„	„ „	„ „ „	.	„	**31/6**
„ 965/54 C	„ „ „ 965/54		„	„ „	„ „ „	.	„	**38/—**

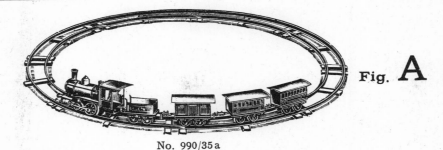

Fig. **A**

No. 990/35 a

No. **990/35 a**

Train with very strong clockwork, **35 mm gauge**

consisting of :

Locomotive with tender (No. **960/35, page 52**), 2 passenger cars and 1 luggage van, 6 curved rails (circle), length of train 28 in., length of rails 5 feet 8 in., in an elegant box . . . . each **6/6**

The locomotive and cars of the train 990/35 a can be delivered in the colours of
1) **London and North Western Railway,** 2) **Great Northern Railway,** 3) **Midland Railway.**
When ordering these please put **L** for **L & NWR, G** for **GNR, M** for **MR** to the number of the train. The extra cost for painting in these colours is for the train . . . . each **—/7**

Pullman Cars (luggage and post van).

No. 135/7/35	**35 mm gauge,** 5 in. long, 3 in. high	each	**1/—**
„ 135/7/48	**48 mm gauge,** 6¾ in. long, 4½ in. high	each	**1/8**
„ 135/7/54	**54 mm gauge,** 7½ in. long, 5 in. high	each	**2/—**
„ 135/7/67	**67 mm gauge,** 9½ in. long, 6¼ in. high	each	**4/—**

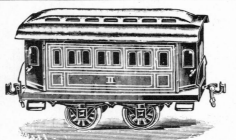

Pullman Cars (Passenger Cars).

No. 135/2/35	**35 mm gauge,** 5 in. long, 3 in. high	each	**1/—**
„ 135/2/48	**48 mm gauge,** 6¾ in. long, 4½ in. high	each	**1/8**
„ 135/2/54	**54 mm gauge,** 7½ in. long, 5 in. high	each	**2/—**
„ 135/2/67	**67 mm gauge,** 9½ in. long, 6¼ in. high,	each	**4/—**

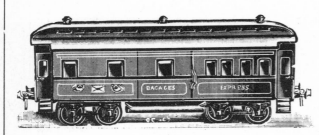

Pullman Cars (post and luggage van).
Highly japanned, with 8 bogie wheels.

No. 135/5/35	**35 mm gauge,** 9 in. long, 3½ in. high	each	**4/5**
„ 135/5/48	**48 mm gauge,** 12½ in. long, 5 in. high	each	**6/3**
„ 135/5/54	**54 mm gauge,** 14 in. long, 6 in. high	each	**8/—**
„ 135/5/67	**67 mm gauge,** 16½ in. long, 7 in. high	each	**11/—**

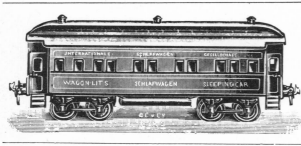

Pullman Cars (Sleeping Cars).

No. 135/4/35	**35 mm gauge,** 9 in. long, 3½ in. high	each	**4/5**
„ 135/4/48	**48 mm gauge,** 12½ in. long, 5 in. high	each	**6/3**
„ 135/4/54	**54 mm gauge.** 14 in. long, 6 in. high	each	**8/—**
„ 135/4/67	**67 mm gauge,** 16½ in. long, 7 in. high	each	**11/—**

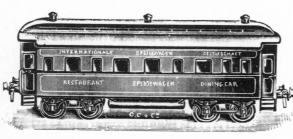

Pullman Cars (Dining Cars).

No. 135/3/35	**35 mm gauge,** 9 in. long, 3½ in. high	each	**4/5**
„ 135/3/48	**48 mm gauge,** 12½ in. long, 5 in. high	each	**6/3**
„ 135/3/54	**54 mm gauge,** 14 in. long, 6 in. high	each	**8/—**
„ 135/3/67	**67 mm gauge,** 16½ in. long, 7 in. high	each	**11/—**

All cars above can be delivered in the colours of 1) **London and North Western Railway,** 2) **Great Northern Railway,** 3) **Midland Railway.**

When ordering these please put **L** for **L & NWR, G** for **GNR, M** for **MR** to the number of the car.
The extra cost for painting in these colours is for the cars:

135/7 and 2/35 . . . . . each —/1	135/5/3 and 4/35 . . . . . each —/7
135/7 „ 2/48 . . . . . „ —/2	135/5/3 „ 4/48 . . . . . „ —/9
135/7 „ 2/54 . . . . . „ —/3	135/5/3 „ 4/54 . . . . . „ 1/—
135/7 „ 2/67 . . . . . „ —/5	135/5/3 „ 4/67 . . . . . „ 1/6

Trade Mark.

Screw Steamers

higly japanned, with solid clockwork.

712/3   712/6

No. 712/1	Ocean steamer	8³/₄ in. long						each	1/—
„ 712/2	„	„ 10	„ „					„	1/4
„ 712/3	„	„ 10¹/₂	„ „					„	1/9
„ 712/4	„	„ 10¹/₂	„ „	splendidly finished				„	2/—
„ 712/5	„	„ 11¹/₄	„ „	„	„			„	2/9
„ 712/6	„	„ 11¹/₂	„ „	„	„			„	3/5

Screw Ships of best construction

very fine japanned with substantial clockwork.

713/0¹/₂

Passenger boats

No. 713/0	5¹/₂ in. long					dozen	7/6
„ 713/0¹/₂	6 „ „					each	1/—
„ 713/1	6¹/₂ „ „					„	1/4
„ 713/2	7¹/₂ „ „					„	1/9
„ 713/3	9 „ „					„	2/—

713/4, 5 and 5a

No. 713/4

10¹/₂ in. long . . . . each 2/9

No. 713/5

13 in. long . . . . each 4/—

No. 713/5 a

13¹/₂ in. long . . . . . . each 4/7

713/6

No. 713/6

16 in. long

each 5/3

Screw Ships

higly japanned, with very
strong clockwork.

Passenger boat

No. **713/7** 16 in. long, very
splendid execution . each **6/6**

No. **713/8** **Passenger boat**, highly finished, fine execution, with officers bridge,
windlass, rigging and rudder, 16 in. long . . . . each **8/—**
" **713/9** the same, 23½ in. long . . . . " **11/—**

No. **713/10** **Screw Ship**, highly finished and fitted, 23½ in. long . . . . . each **13/6**
" **713/10 a** better finished, 23½ in. long . . . . " **19/—**
" **713/11** best made, 25½ in. long . . . . " **26/—**
" **713/12** " " 29½ " " . . . . " **32/—**

Trade Mark.

Screw Ships

well japanned, with very solid clockwork.

721/3

Man of War Boats

No.	721/000	5¾	in. long	. .		dozen	7/6
„	721/00	7	„	„	. .	each	1/—
„	721/0½	8	„	„	. .	„	1/4
„	721/1	9	„	„	. .	„	2/—
„	721/2	11	„	„	. .	„	2/9
„	721/3	12	„	„	. .	„	3/4
„	721/3 a	12¾	„	„	. .	„	4/—
„	721/4	13	„	„	. .	„	4/6
„	721/5	16	„	„	. .	„	5/10
„	721/6	18	„	„	. .	„	8/—
„	721/7	19½	„	„	. .	„	9/—
„	721/7 a	21¾	„	„	. .	„	10/2
„	721/8	24	„	„	. .	„	13/—

Man of War Boat

highly finished, well japanned, with extra strong clockwork.

721/9

No.	721/8 a	24	in. long	. . . .	each	15/6
„	721/8 b	25½	„	„	„	19/—
„	721/9	25½	„	„ better finished	„	26/—
„	721/10	29½	„	„ „ „	„	32/—

Paddle Wheel Steamer.

No. 164/1

21¾ in. long

each 13/8

737/5½

Trade Mark.

1905

Screw Ship

higly japanned with very solid clockwork

730/2

No. **730/2** „**Diving Submarine Boat**." Working by a very solid clockwork, diving and swimming, 13 in long . . . . each **3/10**

732

Sailing-boats, with substantial clockwork

No.				
No. **732/00**	6 in. long	. . .	dozen	**7/6**
„ **732/0**	8 „ „	. . .	each	**1/—**
„ **732/1**	8³/₄ „	. . . .	„	**1/4**
„ **732/2**	10 „ „	. . .	„	**2/—**
„ **732/3**	12 „ „	. . .	„	**2/9**
„ **732/4**	14³/₄ „	. . .	„	**4/—**
„ **732/5**	18¹/₅ „	. . .	„	**5/5**

719

Auto-boats, with very solid clockwork

No.				
No. **719/0**	5¹/₂ in. long	. . . . .	dozen	**7/6**
„ **719/1**	6¹/₂ „ „	. . . . .	„	**12/—**
„ **719/2**	7³/₄ „ „	. . . .	„	**16/—**
„ **719/3**	8³/₄ „ „	. . . .	„	**20/5**
„ **719/4**	10¹/₂ „ „	. . . .	„	**27/—**
„ **719/5**	12¹/₂ „ „	. . . .	„	**36/—**

722

Spy-boats, with very solid clockwork

No.				
No. **722/0**	5¹/₂ in. long	. . . . .	dozen	**7/6**
„ **722/1**	6¹/₂ „	. . . .	„	**12/—**
„ **722/2**	7³/₄ „	. . . .	„	**16/—**
„ **722/3**	8³/₄ „	. . . .	„	**20/5**
„ **722/4**	10¹/₂ „	. . . .	„	**27/**

Trade Mark.

Screw Ships

highly japanned, with very substantial clockwork.

735/3

Fire-engine Boat

This boat shows exactly all movements of large fire engine boats.

No. 735/1	9 in. long	. .	each	2/—
„ 735/2	11½ „ „	. . .	„	2/10
„ 735/3	13 „ „	. . .	„	3/10
„ 735/4	16½ „ „	. . .	„	5/5

731

Paddle-wheel boat

nicely japanned, very strong clockwork

Passenger boats

No. 731/00	6 in. long	. .	dozen	7/6
„ 731/0	8 „ „	. .	each	1/4
„ 731/1	9 „ „	. .	„	2/—
„ 731/2	10½ „ „	. .	„	2/9
„ 731/3	13 „ „	. .	„	4/—
„ 731/4	16 „ „	. .	„	5/5

738

Rowing boat

well japanned, very solid clockwork.
Rower with movable arms, exact working.

No. 738/1	9⅕ in. long	. . . .	each	2/—
„ 738/2	10½ „ „	. . . . .	„	2/9

983/0

No. **983/0 Marins**, well japanned in a nice card, consisting of 25 men officers,

dozen sets **7/3**

Trade  Mark.

1905

Powerful Electric Tramway
with overhead cable

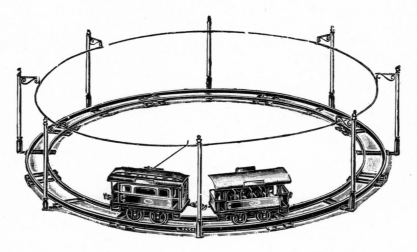

Same execution as No. 1042 but conducting by overhead cable, not through the rails. For driving there can be made use of bottle or bichromate batteries as well as of accumulators such as indicated at tramway No. 1042.

No. **1046/8** consisting of **electric motor car** and circle of rails (8 curved) . . each **10/—**

„ **1046/9** consisting of **electric motor car, one opened car,** 8 curved and 4 straight rails . . . . „ **14/6**

„ **1046/10** same, but including **two bichromate carbon batteries** with powder „ **18/—**

„ **1046/11** same, but with **two large size bottle batteries** and two bottles of bichromate powder . . . . „ **20/6**

„ **1046/12** consisting of **electric motor car,** opened car, oval circle, **accumulator** for **5 hours working** . . , ... „ **22/3**

„ **1046R** **Curved** rails to suit above, with standard and conducting wire . . „ **—/8**

„ **1046G** **Straight** „ „ „ „ „ „ „ „ „ „ . . „ **—/8**

Motor cars for above trams to be put into motion by continuous current

No. **1046/65** for **continuous current of 65 Volts** . . . . each **6/6**

„ **1046/110** „ „ „ „ 110 „ . . . . „ **7/—**

„ **1046/220** „ „ „ „ 220 „ . . . . „ **8/—**

By using a continuous current for driving above motor cars
(No. 1046/65—220) it is necessary to insert into the circuit our Universal Rheostat
No. 1074 (see page 122 of this list).

Bottle and bichromate batteries as well as accumulators
look at page 126/127 of this list.

Railways with Clockwork (without rails)

each in a nice cardboard box.

No. 920 length of cars 3½ in.

No. 920/3	4	6	7	10
consisting of Locomotive, tender and 1	2	4	5	8 cars
9½	12½	19	22½	32 in. length of train
dozen 6/—	7/3	9/6	10/6	13/6

N. 915 length of cars 4 in., each train in a cardboard box

No. 915/2	3	4	5	6	7	8	9	10
consisting of Locomotive, tender and	1	2	3	4	5	6	7	8 cars
6½	10	15	18	22	25½	27½	33	39 in. length of train
dozen 4/4	6/—	6/9	7/6	9/6	10/6	12/—	13/6	15/—

No. 917 length of cars 6½ in., each train in a fine cardboard box

No. 917/3	4
consisting of Locomotive, tender and 1	2 cars
14	21 in. length of train
dozen 13/6	16/3

No. 922 American Train

length of cars 7⅛ in.

No. 922/3	4
consisting of Locomotive tender and 1	2 cars
14½	21¾ in length of train
dozen 10/—	12/—

1905

New Railways with clockwork and rails

1 in. gauge

No. 800/1 consisting of **Locomotive, passenger car,** 5 round rails (circle), length of train $8^2/_5$ in. . dozen **8/—**

„ 800/2 consisting of **Locomotive, tender, passenger car,** 5 round rails (circle), length of train $12^4/_5$ in. dozen **10/3**

No. 800/3 consisting of **Locomotive, tender, 2 passenger cars,** 5 round rails (circle), length of train $16^4/_5$ in. . . . . dozen **12/—**

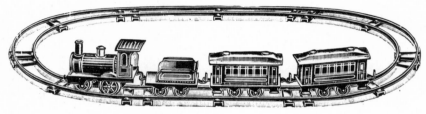

801/2

$1^3/_{16}$ in. gauge

consisting of **Locomotive, tender** and:

No. 801/0 = **1 passenger car,** 4 round rails (circle), length of train $14^1/_2$ in. . each **1/4**

„ 801/2 = **2 passenger cars,** 4 round rails (circle), length of train $19^1/_2$ in. . „ **1/8**

„ 801/4 = **3 passenger cars,** 4 round rails (circle), length of train 25 in. . . „ **2/—**

„ 801/6 = **1 passenger car,** 6 round and 4 half straight rails, small crossing **∞**, length of train $14^1/_2$ in. . . . . „ **2/3**

„ 801/7 = **1 passenger car,** 8 round and 8 half straight rails and 2 small crossings **∞**, length of train $14^1/_2$ in. . . . . „ **3/—**

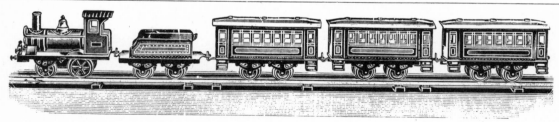

929/3

Railways with large cars

$1^4/_5$ in. gauge

consisting of **Locomotive, tender** and:

No. 929/1 **1 passenger car,** 6 round rails (circle), length of train 21 in. . . . . each **3/—**

„ 929/2 **2 passenger cars,** 6 round and 2 straight rails, length of train 29 in. . „ **3/4**

„ 929/3 **3 passenger cars,** 6 round and 2 straight rails, length of train 36 in. . „ **3/11**

„ 929/4 **2 passenger cars,** 10 round rails and **crossing,** length of train 29 in. . „ **3/11**

„ 929/5 **2 passenger cars,** 7 round rails and **1 pair of switches,** length of train 29 in. . . . . „ **4/5**

Trade Mark.

Novelty!
Double Track Railway
Novelty!

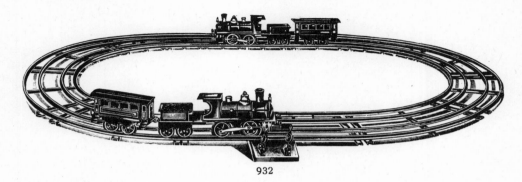

932

No. **932** **Double Track Railway** consisting of **2 clockwork Locomotives, 2 tenders, 2 passenger cars**, each train 16 in. long; 2 tracks both combined with 16 round rails, 4 straight rails and **2 brakes** allowing the child to move or to stop at will either both trains at the same time or each one alone or one after the other etc., in the opposite or same direction, packed in a show box . . . . each **9/9**

New!
Clearing Railway
New!

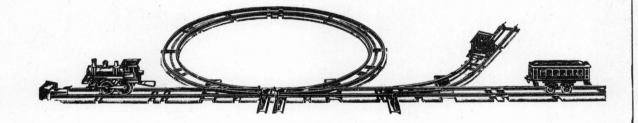

942

No. **942** **Clearing Railway**. The clockwork Locomotive fetch by itself first the tender, second the car and runs at will the circle or straight on, backward and forward, consisting of the complete train of 16 in. length, 4 rounds, 3 straight, 3 Stop Rails, 3 switches, packed in a show box . . . . . each **5/8**

New!   # Very attractive.   **New!**

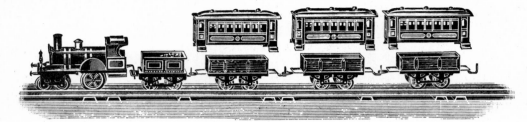

Express Trains with decomposable cars.

The cars are constructed to be dismounted and can be used as well as passenger cars as truck vans.

$1^3/_{16}$ in. gauge

consisting of **Locomotive, tender** and:

No. 803/1 **1 decomposable car,** 6 round rails (circle), length of train 16 in. each **2/—**

„ 803/2 **2 decomposable cars,** 6 „ „ „ „ „ „ 21 „ „ **2/6**

„ 803/3 **3 decomposable cars,** 10 „ and 2 straight rails „ „ „ 26¹/₂ „ „ **3/5**

„ 803/4 **2 decomposable cars,** 10 „ rails and **crossing ∞**, length of train 21 in. . . . . „ **3/6**

„ 803/5 **2 decomposable cars,** 10 round rails and **1 pair of switches**, length of train 21 in. . . . . „ **3/9**

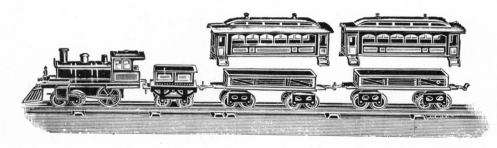

Express Corridor Trains

with decomposable cars.

The cars are constructed to be dismounted and can be used as well as passenger cars as truck vans.

$1^3/_{16}$ in. gauge

consisting of **Locomotive, tender** and:

No. 804/1 **1 decomposable pullman car,** 6 round rails (circle), length of train 18 in. each **3/3**

„ 804/2 **2 decomposable pullman cars,** 10 round and 2 straight rails, length of train 26¹/₂ in. . . . . „ **4/3**

Trade. Mark.

Hochfeine Modell-Dampfmaschinen

in technisch vollendeter Ausführung

mit feststehendem, doppeltwirkendem auf Bock montiertem Cylinder, Schieber-Steuerung mit Rollapparat, mit Kugelandrückvorrichtung, Wasserstandsanzeiger mit Schutzgehäuse, Dampfpfeife,

mit stehendem, stahlblau oxydiertem Messingkessel, vernickelten Armaturen.

Kessel und Cylinder sind auf fein poliertem Holzfundament aufgeschraubt.

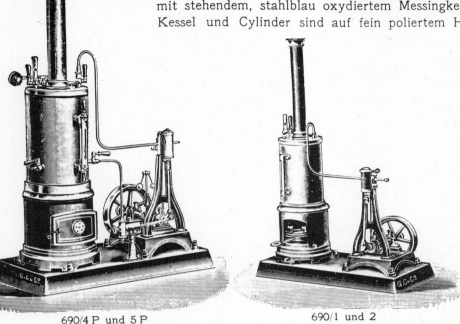

No. **690/1** 32 cm hoch, 24½ cm lang, 10½ cm breit, mit Sicherheitsventil . . . . St. M. **19.50**

— **690/1 P** dieselbe, jedoch mit Kesselspeisepumpe . . . . . St. M. **23.—**

— **690/2** 36 cm hoch, 26 cm lang, 11½ cm breit . . . . St. M. **25.—**

— **690/2 P** dieselbe, jedoch mit Kesselspeisepumpe . . . . . St. M. **28.50**

— **690/3** 39½ cm hoch, 28 cm lang, 13½ cm breit, mit Gewichtssicherheitsventil, Dampfabstellhahn, Regulator und Feuertüre St. M. **33.50**

— **690/3 P** dieselbe, jedoch mit Kesselspeisepumpe . . . . St. M. **37.—**

— **690/4 P** 44 cm hoch, 30 cm lang, 15 cm breit, wie No. 690/3 P, jedoch mit Probierhahn, Wasserstandsanzeiger mit Hähnen St. M. **46.—**

— **690/5 P** 49½ cm hoch, 32½ cm lang, 16 cm breit, Ausführung wie No. 690/4 P . . . . St. M. **54.—**

690/4 P und 5 P   690/1 und 2

Dampfkrane in sehr solider Ausführung.

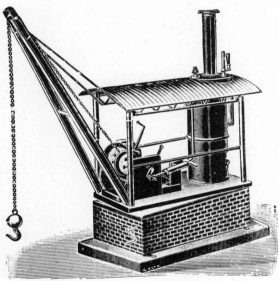

606/4

606/3

No. **606/4** **Dampfkran** mit stahlblau oxydiertem Messing-Dampfkessel und oscillierendem Cylinder, Wasserstandsglas, Sicherheitsventil, Dampfpfeife. Der Dampfkessel ist auf einen mittels Handkurbel drehbaren Sockel montiert. Der Dampfkessel ist mit einem zum Auf- und Abziehen von Lasten verwendbaren Kran verbunden, der nach Belieben ausgeschaltet werden kann, damit die Maschine auch zum Betrieb von anderen Modellen benützt werden kann.
Auf fein lackierten Sockel in Backstein-Imitation montiert und auf fein poliertem Brett aufgeschraubt. 35½ cm lang, 14 cm breit, 33 cm hoch . . . . Stück M. **13.60**

No. **606/3** **Fahrbarer Dampfkran,** bestehend aus einer Dampfmaschine mit stahlblau oxydiertem Messingkessel mit oscillierendem Cylinder, Wasserstandsglas, Sicherheitsventil, Dampfpfeife. Der außer dem Dampfkessel auf den Sockel angebrachte Kran kann durch beliebiges Verstellen der Hebel 1, 2, 3 und 4 Lasten selbsttätig auf- und abheben. Der Kran ist nach jeder Richtung hin drehbar und fährt auf den beigegebenen 1,50 m langen, geraden, auf Holzschwellen montierten Schienensträngen vor- oder rückwärts. Der Kran kann jederzeit ausgeschaltet werden, damit die Maschine auch zum Betrieb von anderen Modellen benützt werden kann.
Sehr interessantes, unterhaltendes, solid gebautes Modell. 43½ cm lang, 13 cm breit, 33 cm hoch . Stück M. **18.—**

No. **606 G/100** **Gerade Schienen** hierzu, separat, auf Holzschwellen montiert, 38 cm lang, 10 cm Spurweite . . . . . Stück M. **—.50**

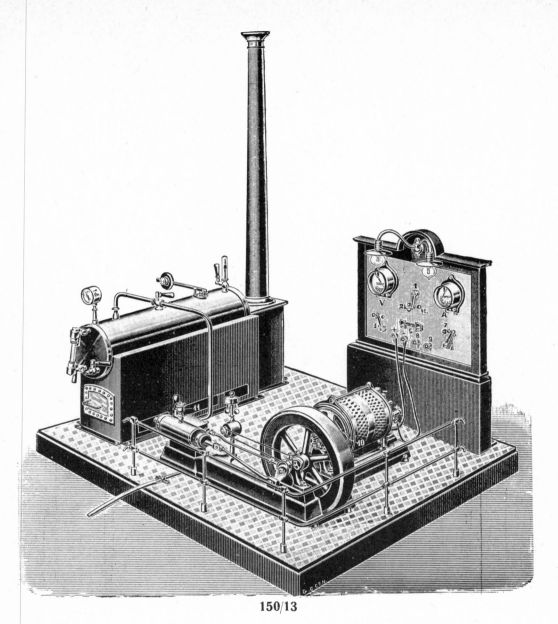

150/13

Grosse elektrische Lichtanlage

bestehend aus einem **starken,** liegenden **Messing-Dampfkessel** mit Gewichtsventil, Wasserstand, Durchlaßhahn, **Manometer,** Ablaßhahn, Dampfpfeife, Spirituslampe, **mit starkem, feststehendem, doppeltwirkendem,** äußerst **kräftigem Dampfzylinder** mit Schiebersteuerung, Ölvorrichtung, Regulator, starkem Schwungrad, Schnurlauf **mit Zahnradantrieb;** letzterer kann durch Losschrauben oder Verstellen entweder den Dynamo-Generator oder, **wenn** dieser ausgeschaltet, irgend welche andere Betriebsmodelle treiben.   Der Gleichstrom-Dynamo-Generator **ist auf Sockel** montiert, Leistung ca. 7 Volt, 0,5 Ampère.   Der Dynamo ist mit einem Schaltbrett, worauf ein **2 armiges Wandstativ** mit 2 Glühlampen von ca. 3½ Volt, 0,2 Ampère, 1 Voltmesser, 1 Milliampèremeter, 1 Schalt-**hebel** für die 2 Lampen, 1 Umschalter für event. weiter anzuschließende 2 Lampen, 1 Umschalter, 1 Sicherung **und 2 Klemmen** für Fernlichtleitung montiert sind, verbunden.   Die ganze Anlage ist auf ein starkes Fundament mit Fliesenbelag und Schutzgeländer montiert.

43 cm lang, 40 cm breit, 56 cm hoch . . . . Stück M. **140.—**

Fabrik-  Marke

Betriebsmodelle (Fortsetzung).
Solide Ausführung und feine Lackierung.

698/31

No. **698/31 Paukenschläger**, 12 cm lang, 13 cm hoch, ¼ Dutzend-Packung . . Stück M. —.80

Spiel-Dosen

als Betriebsmodelle, in polychromen Orgelkasten, 13 cm hoch, 11 cm lang,

No. **657/3/0** mit 8 Stimmen
¼ Dutzend-Packung St. M. —.90

No. **657/18** mit feinem Schweizerwerk, 18 Stimmen, St. M. **3.30**

— **657/36** mit feinem Schweizerwerk, 36 Stimmen, St. M. **5.40**

657/3/0

195/21 und 22

Orgler

No. **195/21** Spieldose No. 657/18 mit plastischer Figur . . . St. M. **3.80**
— **195/22** Spieldose No. 657/36 mit plastischer Figur . . . St. M. **6.—**

No. **682/000 Clowns am Reck**, 15 cm hoch, 11½ cm lang . . . St. M. —.80

— **682/2** größer, 27 cm hoch, 21 cm lang
St. M. **1.50**

— **682/10 Turner am Barren**, 14½ cm lg., 8 cm breit, 14 cm hoch, St. M. -.90
¼ Dutzend-Packung

— **682/11** dieselben größer, 23 cm lang, 10 cm breit, 17 cm hoch, St. M. **1.70**

682/10 und 11

682/2

Zootropen

aus russischem Schwarzblech, mit Schnurscheibe versehen, als Betriebsmodelle.

Zur Veranschaulichung von lebendigen Bildern, mit 12 Bildern.

No.	**773/2½**	**3½**	**4½**	**5½**	
Durchm.	13	16	18	24	cm
Stück M.	**1.50**	**2.—**	**2.80**	**4.—**	

Extrabilder hierzu in 2 weiteren Serien

No.	**773/2 B**	**3 B**	**4 B**	**5 B**	
zu	773/2½	3½	4½	5½	passend
Serie à 12 Bilder M.	—.30	—.50	—.70	**1.10**	

773/2½

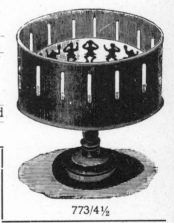

773/4½

Sehr originelles und
wirkungsvolles Betriebsmodell!

Achterbahn

No. **698/1** Während der eine Wagen selbständig herunterfährt, wird der andere hinaufgezogen; dieses Modell eignet sich für Motor- als auch für Handbetrieb. — Sehr solide Ausführung, tadellos funktionierend, 51 cm lang, 31 cm breit, 33 cm hoch, Stück M. **11.50**.

Feine Betriebsmodelle (Fortsetzung).

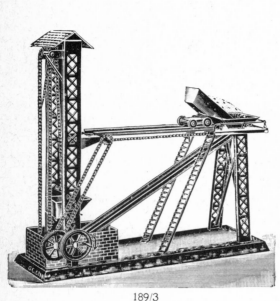

189/3

189/4

No. **189/3 Förderwerk,** in sehr solider Ausführung und hochfeiner Lackierung, sehr unterhaltendes Modell. Der Aufzugskübel zieht das Material vom Gefäß herauf, leert es in den auf Schienen fahrbaren Kippwagen, der es wiederum in den Empfangsraum transportiert, von wo es von selbst in das ursprüngliche Gefäß gelangt, 40 cm lang, 12 cm breit, 37 cm hoch . . . . Stück M. **9.—**

— **189/4 Großes Förderwerk mit Bagger** in äußerst solider Ausführung und feinster Lackierung. Nachdem das Förderwerk das Material in die Höhe gebracht hat, rollt der Kippwagen selbsttätig zur Empfangsstelle des Materials, wird dort gefüllt und läuft dann selbsttätig zurück, um das Material in die bereitgestellten Eisenbahntransportwagen (Kippwagen) abzugeben. 43 cm lang, 11½ cm breit, 31½ cm hoch, ohne Kippwagen und ohne Schienen . . . . Stück M. **7.50**

Hierzu passende Eisenbahn-Kippwagen siehe Seite 108.
Hierzu passende Schienen siehe Seite 96—101.

189/5

No. **189/5 Hütten-Förderwerk,** äußerst solid ausgeführtes und interessantes Modell, in feinster Lackierung, ladet und entladet **automatisch** die Transportkübel. 49 cm lang, 14½ cm breit, 41½ cm hoch. . . Stück M. **15.—**

Fabrik- Marke

1914

Feine solide Uhrwerk - Expreß - Lokomotiven

Spurweite 35 mm.

1801/35T

1802/35T

No. 1801/35 Lokomotive mit solidem und kräftigem Uhrwerk, mit **automatischer Vor- und Rückwärtssteuerung,** sowie Bremse, moderne Konstruktion, Windschneider am Kessel, 17½ cm lang . . . . Stück M. **5.—**

— **1801/T Tender** hierzu, 11 cm lang . . . . —.60

— **1804/35** Lokomotive in Ausführung wie 1802/35, jedoch kann die **Umsteuerung nur mit der Hand erfolgen,** also nicht automatisch, 20 cm lang, ... Stück M. **5.80**

— **1804 T** Tender hierzu, 13 cm lang . . . . — —.70

No. 1802/35 Lokomotive mit sehr solidem und kräftigem Uhrwerk, mit **automatischer Vor- und Rückwärtssteuerung,** sowie Bremse, moderne Konstruktion, Windschneider am Kessel, 20 cm lang, Stück M. **6.70**

— **1802 T Tender** hierzu, 13 cm lang . . . . . . — —.70

1803/35T

No. 1803/35 Lokomotive mit äußerst solidem und kräftigem Uhrwerk, mit **automatischer Vor- und Rückwärtssteuerung,** sowie Bremse, moderne Konstruktion, Windschneider am Kessel, 22 cm lang . Stück M. **8.20**

— **1803 T** Tender hierzu, 22 cm lang . . . . . — — -.80

No. 1939UG/35 Automatische Umschalteschiene zu obigen Lokomotiven passend, dient gleichzeitig auch als Bremsschiene . . . . Stück M. —.50

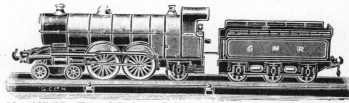

No. 928/35 Expreß-Lokomotive, 4 achsig, mit solidem Uhrwerk für Vor- und Rückwärtsfahrt, mit Bremse, feine Polychromlackierung, mit 3 achsigem Tender, 43 cm lang . . . . Stück M. **8.—**

No. 927/35 Expreß-Lokomotive, 5 achsig, mit starkem Uhrwerk für Vor- und Rückwärtsfahrt mit Bremse, feine Polychromlackierung, mit 3 achsigem Tender, 43 cm lang . . . . Stück M. **8.60**

Zu den Lokomotiven 928/35 und 927/35 können nur Schienen mit **großen** Kurven verwendet werden.

No. 943 D/35 Expreß-Lokomotive mit äußerst solidem, kräftigem Uhrwerk, 4 achsig, mit **automatischer Vor- und Rückwärtssteuerung** sowie Bremse, moderne Konstruktion, dreiachsiger Tender, 40 cm lang, Stück M. **14.50**

No. 944 D/35 Expreß-Lokomotive mit äußerst solidem, kräftigem Uhrwerk, 4 achsig, mit **automatischer Vor- und Rückwärtssteuerung** sowie Bremse, moderne Konstruktion, mit **Windschneider** am Kessel, 3 achsigem Tender, 40 cm lang . . . . Stück M. **16.—**

No. 81 BA/35 Automatische Umschalteschiene zu Lokomotiven 943 u. 944 passend, dient gleichzeitig auch als Bremsschiene, St. M. —.70

Feine Tenderlokomotive mit Uhrwerk
den neuesten Modellen des Großbetriebes nachgebaut.

In hocheleganter Ausführung und feinster Lackierung.

No. 969/35 35 mm Spurweite, mit Bremsvorrichtung und Vorrichtung zum Vor- und Rückwärtsfahren, 23½ cm lang . . . . Stück M. **16.—**

Einzelne Wagen und Schienen zu obigen Lokomotiven siehe Seite 96—108

Schnellzugs-Gepäckwagen

hochfein ausgeführt und fein lackiert.

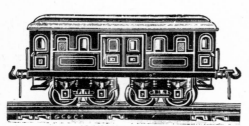

135/28/35—48

135/29/35—48

No. **135/28/35** **D-Express-Gepäckwagen**, 4 achsig mit Türen zum Öffnen und beweglicher Schiebetüre, 20 cm lang, 8 cm hoch, **Spurweite 35 mm** . . Stück M **3.10**

— **135/28/48** derselbe, für **Spurweite 48 mm**, 27 cm lang, 11 ½ cm hoch . . . . Stück M. **4.90**

No. **135/29/35** **L-Express-Gepäckwagen**, 4 achsig, mit Türen zum Öffnen und beweglicher Schiebetüre, 25 cm lang, 10 cm hoch, **Spurweite 35 mm**. Stück M. **6.50**

— **135/29/48** derselbe, für **Spurweite 48 mm**, 29 cm lang, 12 cm hoch . . . . Stück M. **10.—**

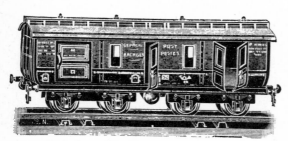

133/20/35

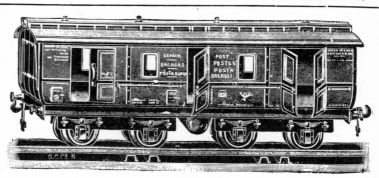

133/20/48

No. **133/20/35 Moderner vierachsiger Schnellzugs-Gepäckwagen** mit Türen zum Öffnen und beweglicher Schiebe- türe, 27 cm lang, 10 cm hoch, **Spurweite 35 mm**, **in sortierten Farben** . . . . . Stück M. **4.40**

No. **133/20/48** derselbe, für **Spurweite 48 mm**, 34 cm lang, 13 cm hoch, **in sortierten Farben**, St. M. **6.40**

Einzelne Güterwagen zu Eisenbahnen.

Billige Ausführung.
(¼ Dtz. Packung)

35 mm Spurweite.

35 mm Spurweite.

No. **130/37/35 Holzwagen,** 12 ½ cm lang, Stück M. —.**26**

No. **130/34/35 Kohlenwagen,** 12 ½ cm lang, Stück M. —.**32**

No. **130/35/35 Petroleumwagen** 12 ½ cm lang, Stück M. —.**36**

No. **130/36/35 Kippwagen,** 12 ½ cm lang, Stück M. —.**40**

Bessere Ausführung.
Stückpackung

No. **130/11/35 Langholzwagen,** 12 cm lang, 6 cm hoch, **35 mm Spurweite,** Stück M. —.**70**

No. **130/9/35 Kohlenwagen** mit Bremser- häuschen, 14 cm lang, 8 ½ cm hoch, **35 mm Spurweite** . . . . Stück M. —.**80**

No. **130/18/35 Bretterwagen**, 15 cm lang, 7 cm hoch, **35 mm Spurweite,** Stück M. —.**90**

Fabrik- Marke

Feinste Polychromlackierung.   **Solideste Ausführung.**   **Sehr solide Verpackung.**

2943 D/48 B

No. **2943 D/48 B** bestehend aus: Expreß-Lokomotive mit äußerst solidem, kräftigem Uhrwerk, 4 achsig mit **automatischer Vor- und Rück-wärtssteuerung,** sowie Bremse, moderne Konstruktion, 3 achsigem Tender = No. 943 D/48, je einem großen vierachsigen Personen- und Gepäckwagen mit Türen zum Öffnen, Zuglänge 119 cm, großes Schienenoval = 8 runde, 5 gerade Schienen sowie 1 gerade Umsteuerschiene, die auch als Bremsschiene zu benützen ist . . . . Stück M. **40.—**

2944 D/48 B

No. **2944 D/48 B** bestehend aus: Expreß-Lokomotive mit äußerst solidem, kräftigem Uhrwerk, 4 achsig, mit **automatischer Vor- und Rück-wärtssteuerung,** sowie Bremse, moderne Konstruktion, mit Windschneider am Kessel, 3 achsigem Tender = No. 944D/48, je einem großen 4 achsigen L-Personenwagen und Gepäckwagen mit Türen zum Öffnen, Zuglänge 111 cm, großes Schienen-oval = 8 runde, 5 gerade Schienen, sowie 1 gerade Umsteuerschiene, die auch als Bremsschiene zu benützen ist, Stück M. **50.—**

Solide Ausführung. Feine Polychromlackierung.

	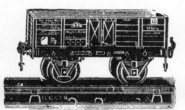	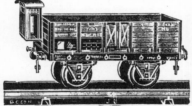	
134/86/81/35—48	134/96/91/35—48	134/86 H/81 H/35—48	134/96 H/91 H/35—48

No. **134/86/35 Kohlenwagen,** deutsche Aufschriften, **35 mm Spurw.,** 15 cm lang, 6 cm hoch, **grau** . . . . . St. M. **—.80**

No. **134/86/48** do., **48 mm Spurweite,** 19 cm lang, 8 cm hoch, Stück M. **1.20**

Obige Wagen in **brauner Farbe** No. **134/81/35—48** zu gleichen Preisen.

No. **134/96/35 Kohlenwagen,** internationale Aufschriften,35mm Spurweite, 15 cm lang, 6 cm hoch, **grau** . . . . Stück M. **—.80**

No. **134/96/48** do., **48 mm Spur-weite,** 19 cm lang, 8 cm hoch, Stück M. **1.20**

Obige Wagen in **brauner Farbe** No. **134/91/35—48** zu gleichen Preisen.

No. **134/86 H/35 Kohlenwagen** mit Bremserhäuschen, **deutsche Aufschriften, 35 mm Spurweite,** 15 cm lang, 8 cm hoch, **grau,** Stück M. **1.—**

No. **134/86 H/48** do., **48 mm Spurweite,** 19 cm lang, 10 cm hoch . . . . Stück M. **1.40**

Obige Wagen in **brauner Farbe** No. **134/81 H/35—48** zu gleichen Preisen.

No. **134/96 H/35 Kohlenwagen** mit Bremserhäuschen, **internat. Aufschriften, 35 mm Spurweite,** 15 cm lang, 8 cm hoch, **grau,** Stück M. **1.—**

No. **134/96 H/48** do., **48 mm Spurweite,** 19 cm lang, 10 cm hoch . . . . Stück M. **1.40**

Obige Wagen in **brauner Farbe** No. **134/91 H/35—48** zu gleichen Preisen.

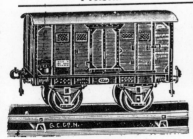	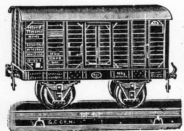	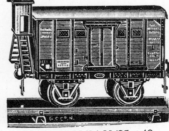	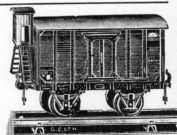
134/80/84/35—48	134/90/94/35—48	134/80 H/84 H/35—48	134/90 H/94 H/35—48

No. **134/84/35 Güterwagen,** deutsche Aufschriften, **35 mm Spurweite,** 15 cm lang, 8½ cm hoch, **grau** . . Stück M. **1.—**

No. **134/84/48** do., **48 mm Spurweite,** 19 cm lang, 11 cm hoch, Stück M. **1.30**

Obige Wagen in **brauner Farbe** No. **134/80/35—48** zu gleichen Preisen.

No. **134/94/35 Güterwagen,** inter-nationale Aufschriften, **35 mm Spurweite,** 15 cm lang, 8½ cm hoch, **grau** . . Stück M. **1.—**

No. **134/94/48** do., **48 mm Spurweite,** 19 cm lang, 11 cm hoch, Stück M. **1.30**

Obige Wagen in **brauner Farbe** No. **134/90/35—48** zu gleichen Preisen.

No. **134/84 H/35 Güterwagen,** mit Brem-serhäuschen, **35 mm Spurweite,** 15 cm lang, 10 cm hoch, **grau,** Stück M. **1.20**

No. **134/84 H/48** do., **48 mm Spurweite,** 19 cm lang, 13 cm hoch . . . . Stück M. **1.50**

Obige Wagen in **brauner Farbe** No. **134/80 H/35—48** zu gleichen Preisen.

No. **134/94 H/35 Güterwagen,** internationale Aufschriften, mit Bremserhäuschen, **35 mm Spurweite,** 15 cm lang, 10 cm hoch, **grau** . . . . Stück M. **1.20**

No. **134/94 H/48** do., **48 mm Spurweite,** 19 cm lang, 13 cm hoch . . . . Stück M. **1.50**

Obige Wagen in **brauner Farbe** No. **134/90 H/35—48** zu gleichen Preisen.

Einzelne Güterwagen zu Eisenbahnen.

Solide Ausführung, feine Lackierung.

134/85/35—48

No. **134/85/35 Bierwagen** mit **deutschen Aufschriften**, 15 cm lang, 8½ cm hoch, **Spurweite 35 mm** . . . Stück M. **1.—**
No. **134/85/48** derselbe, für **Spurweite 48 mm**, 19 cm lang, 11 cm hoch,
Stück M. **1.30**

135/13/35—48

No. **135/13/35 Petroleumwagen**, 35 mm Spurweite, 14 cm lang, 7½ cm hoch
Stück M. **1.70**
No. **135/13/48** derselbe, 48 mm Spurweite, 19 cm lang, 9 cm hoch, Stück M. **2.60**

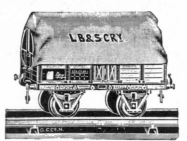

134/86 P/81 P/35—48

No. **134/86 P/35 Planwagen** mit **deutschen Aufschriften**, grau, 15 cm lang, 9 cm hoch, **Spurweite 35 mm** . . . Stück M. **1.20**
No. **134/86 P/48** derselbe, für **Spurweite 48 mm**, 19 cm lang, 12 cm hoch, St. M. **1.50**
No. **134/81 P/35** in **brauner Farbe**, Spurweite 35 mm . . . . . Stück M. **1.20**
No. **134/81 P/48** derselbe, Spurweite 48 mm Stück M. **1.50**
No. **134/96 P/35** mit **internationalen Aufschriften**, Spurweite 35 mm, grau, Stück M. **1.20**
No. **134/96 P/48** derselbe, Spurweite 48 mm Stück M. **1.50**
No. **134/91 P/35** mit **internationalen Aufschriften**, Spurweite 35 mm, braune Farbe, Stück M. **1.20**
No. **134/91 P/48** derselbe, Spurweite 48 mm Stück M. **1.50**

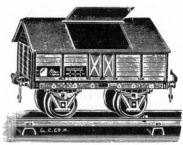

134/86 K/81 K/35—48

No. **134/86 K/35 Kalkwagen** mit **deutschen Aufschriften**, grau, 15 cm lang, 9 cm hoch, **Spurweite 35 mm** . . . Stück M. **1.20**
No. **134/86 K/48** derselbe, **Spurweite 48 mm** 19 cm lang, 12 cm hoch, Stück M. **1.50**
No. **134/81 K/35** do., in **brauner Farbe**, Spurweite 35 mm . . . Stück M. **1.20**
No. **134/81 K/48** do., in **brauner Farbe**, Spurweite 48 mm . . . Stück M. **1.50**
No. **134/96 K/35** mit **internationalen Aufschriften**, grauer Farbe, Spurweite 35 mm, Stück M. **1.20**
No. **134/96 K/48** derselbe, Spurweite 48 mm Stück M. **1.50**
No. **134/91 K/35** mit **internationalen Aufschriften**, braune Farbe, Spurweite 35 mm, Stück M. **1.20**
No. **134/91 K/48** derselbe, Spurweite 48 mm Stück M. **1.50**

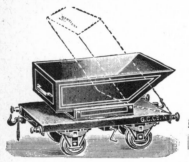

135/19/35—48

No. **135/19/35 Kippwagen**, **Spurweite 35 mm**, mit drehbarer Kippvorrichtung, 16 cm lang, 7 cm hoch . . . Stück M. **1.20**
No. **135/19/48** derselbe, **Spurweite 48 mm**, 20 cm lang, 9 cm hoch . . . Stück M. **1.70**

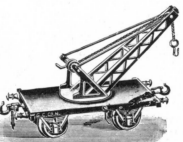

135/16/35—48

No. **135/16/35 Kranwagen**, **Spurweite 35 mm**, mit Winde zum Heben und Senken der Last, 16 cm lang, 7½ cm hoch, Stück M. **1.40**
No. **135/16/48** derselbe, **Spurweite 48 mm**, 25 cm lang, 14 cm hoch . . . . Stück M. **2.20**

130/20/35—48

No. **130/20/35 Gaswagen**, 14 cm lang, 7 cm hoch, **Spurweite 35 mm** Stück M. **1.50**
No. **130/20/48** derselbe, **Spurweite 48 mm**, 20 cm lang, 10 cm hoch . . . . Stück M. **2.—**

135/12/35—48

No. **135/12/35 Kippwagen**, **35 mm Spurweite**, 14 cm lang, 8 cm hoch . . . St. M. **1.60**
No. **135/12/48** derselbe **48 mm Spurweite**, 19 cm lang, 10 cm hoch . . . . Stück M. **2.40**

135/11/35—48

No. **135/11/35 Langholzwagen**, 14 cm lang, 9 cm hoch, **Spurweite 35 mm** . . . . Stück M. **1.—**
No. **135/11/48** derselbe, 19 cm lang, 10 cm hoch, **Spurweite 48 mm** . . . . Stück M. **1.40**

135/11 H/35—48

No. **135/11 H/35 Doppelter Langholzwagen** mit Hölzer, 28 cm lang, 9 cm hoch, **Spurweite 35 mm** . . . Stück M. **2.20**
No. **135/11 H/48** derselbe, 38 cm lang, 10 cm hoch, **Spurweite 48 mm** . . . . .
Stück M. **2.90**

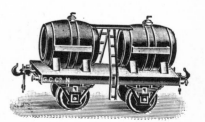

135/18/35—48

No. **135/18/35 Weintransportwagen**, 16 cm lang, 7½ cm hoch, **Spurweite 35 mm**, St. M. **2.20**
No. **135/18/48** derselbe, 20 cm lang, 10½ cm hoch, **Spurweite 48 mm** . . . . Stück M. **2.70**

Uhrwerkschiffe mit soliden Werken
in feiner Ausführung und eleganter Lackierung.

732/21

732/23

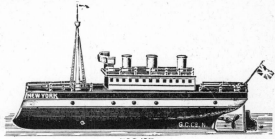
732/27

Vergnügungsdampfer

mit sehr starkem Uhrwerk, hochfein lackiert, mit Doppeldeck und Salon, Masten mit Mastkorb, naturgetreu nachgebildetem Takelwerk, großen Kaminen, Rettungsbooten, fein ausgeführten Ankern mit Ankerwinde, Kommandobrücke und Steuerrad.

Unsere Modelle sind den neuesten Typen naturgetreu nachgebildet.

										Stück Mk.	
No. **732/20**	in einfacher Ausführung, mit 2 Kaminen 18 cm lang										**1.30**
— **732/21**	— —	—	—	1 Mast, 2 Kaminen, Kommandobrücke, 20 cm lang						— —	**1.50**
— **732/22**	— —	—	—	1 — 2 —	—	Schutzgeländer, 22 cm lang				— —	**1.80**
— **732/23**	— —	—	—	1 — 2 —	—	— 24 — —				— —	**2.—**

732/29

		Stück Mk.	
No. **732/24**	Mastkorb mit Takelwerk, Schutzgeländer, Kommandobrücke, 26 cm lang		**3.—**
— **732/25**	dasselbe, 28 cm lang	— —	**3.60**
— **732/26**	mit 3 Kaminen, 30 cm lang	— —	**4.50**
— **732/27**	dasselbe, 32 cm lang	— —	**6.—**
— **732/28**	Doppeldeck mit Galerie, 36 cm lang	— —	**8.50**
— **732/29**	dasselbe, jedoch mit 2 Masten, sowie Anker, 40 cm lang	— —	**11.—**
— **732/30**	dasselbe, jedoch Anker mit Ankerwinde, 2 Rettungsboote, 42 cm lang	— —	**14.—**

732/32

		Stück Mk.	
No. **732/31**	mit 3 Kaminen, Doppeldeck mit Galerie, Kommandobrücke, 2 Masten mit Mastkorb und Takelwerk, 2 Anker mit Ankerwinde, 2 Rettungsbooten, 46 cm lang		**18.—**
— **732/32**	dasselbe, jedoch mit 3 großen Kaminen, Steuerhaus, sowie 4 Rettungsbooten, 52 cm lang	— —	**25.50**

Unsere Schiffe werden mit Aufschriften der bekanntesten Oceandampfer der Gegenwart geliefert.

1914

Ozeandampfer
mit sehr solidem Uhrwerk in hochfeiner Lackierung

mit Doppeldeck und Salon, Masten mit naturgetreu nachgebildetem Takelwerk, großen Kaminen, Rettungsbooten, Kommandobrücke, Steuerrad, Steuerhaus, **mit Aufschriften der bekanntesten Ozeandampfer der Gegenwart.**

Von Größe 734/21 ab mit Doppelschraube.

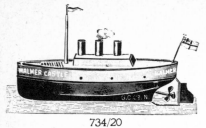

734/20

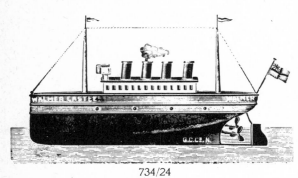

734/24

No. **734/20** einfache Ausführung, mit 3 Kaminen, 1 Mast, 18 cm lang . . . . Stück M.	**1.50**
— **734/21** einfache Ausführung, mit 3 Kaminen, 2 Masten, 19 cm lang . . . . — —	**2.—**
— **734/22** mit 3 Kaminen, 2 Masten mit Takelwerk, 23 cm lang . . . . — —	**3.—**
— **734/23** dasselbe, mit 4 Kaminen und Kommandobrücke, 25 cm lang . . . . — —	**3.60**
— **734/24** dasselbe, 27 cm lang . . . . — —	**4.50**
— **734/25** — mit 4 großen Kaminen, 31 cm lang . . — —	**6.—**
— **734/26** — 38 cm lang . . . . — —	**9.—**

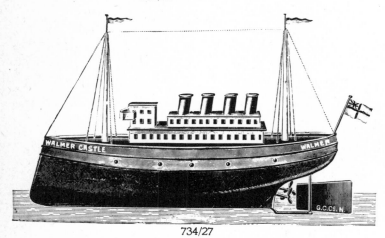

734/27

No. **734/27** **Doppelschraubendampfer** mit 4 großen Kaminen, Doppeldeck und Salon, Steuerhaus, 2 großen Masten mit naturgetreu nachgebildetem Takelwerk, Kommandobrücke, 43 cm lang . . . . . St. M.	**12.—**
— **734/28** dasselbe, mit Steuerrad, 45 cm lang — —	**15.—**
— **734/29** — 47 cm lang . . . . — —	**19.—**
— **734/30** — 51 — — . . . . . . — —	**24.—**
— **734/31** — 55 — — . . . . . . — —	**34.—**

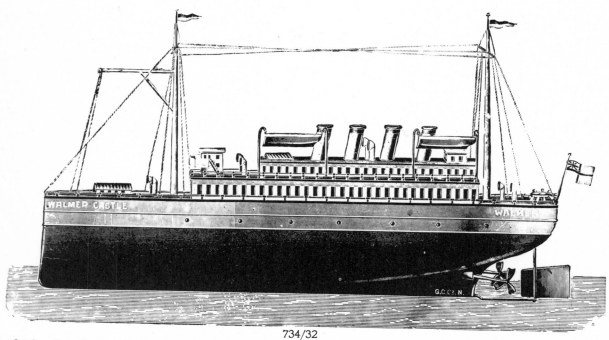

734/32

No. **734/32** **Großer Doppelschraubendampfer** mit Doppeldeck und Salon, 2 Masten mit naturgetreu nachgebildetem Takelwerk, 4 großen Kaminen, 4 Rettungsbooten, Steuerhaus, Steuerrad etc., 61 cm lang . . . . . . Stück Mk. **50.—**

Uhrwerkschiffe mit soliden Werken in hochfeiner Lackierung.

Personendampfer.
Mit sehr solidem Uhrwerk, fein lackiert.

733/20

733/22

No. 733/20	einfache Ausführung, mit 2 Kaminen, 1 Mast, 20 cm lang	Stück M.	1.50
— 733/21	— — — 2 — 1 — mit Schutzgeländer, 25 cm lang	— —	2.—
— 733/22	— — — 2 — 1 — Kommandobrücke, 31 cm lang . . .	— —	3.—

725/20   725/22   725/24

Vergnügungs=Yachten.
Mit sehr solidem Uhrwerk, geschmackvoll lackiert, mit Salon, Steuermann etc.

No. 725/20	einfache Ausführung, mit Steuermann, 20 cm lang	Stück M.	1.50
— 725/21	mit Steuerrad und Mast, 23 cm lang	— —	2.—
— 725/22	mit Steuermann am Steuer, 1 Mast, langes Verdeck, 25 cm lang . . .	— —	3.—
— 725/23	— — — — 1 — — 28 — —	— —	4.50
— 725/24	— — — — 1 — — 30 — —	— —	6.—

Flußboote.
Mit solidem Uhrwerk, hochfein lackiert, mit Promenadedeck, von Größe 736/21 ab mit Doppelschraube versehen.

736/20

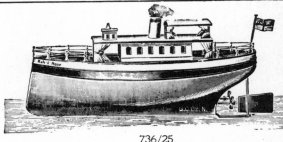

736/25

No. 736/20	18 cm lang	Stück M.	1.50
— 736/21	19 — —	— —	2.—
— 736/22	23 — —	— —	3.60
— 736/23	25 — —	— —	4.50
— 736/24	27 — —	— —	6.—
— 736/25	31 — —		

736/27

No. 736/26	mit 2 großen Kaminen, Verdeck mit Galerie, Steuerhaus, Promenadedeck, 38 cm lang	Stück M.	9.—
— 736/27	dasselbe, 43 cm lang . . .	— —	12.—
— 736/28	— 45 — — . . .	— —	15.—

Kriegsschiffe mit sehr solidem Uhrwerk in feiner Lackierung.
===== Neueste Type. =====

Feine Ausführung und Lackierung, mit Schnellfeuerkanonen in starker Panzerung, Masten mit Mastkörben, mit Luftfahrzeugen etc.
Von Größe 714/2 ab mit Doppelschraube.

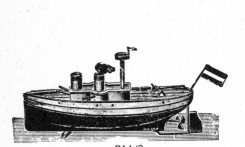

714/3   714/7

No. 714/1	einfache Ausführung, mit 2 Kaminen, 2 Kanonen, 18 cm lang	Stück M.	1.50
— 714/2	— — — 2 — 1 Mast, 4 Kanonen, 20 cm lang	— —	2.—
— 714/3	— — — 2 — 1 — mit Takelwerk, 6 Kanonen, 22 cm lang	— —	3.—
— 714/4	— — — 2 — 1 — 1 Luftschiff, 6 Kanonen, 25 cm lang	— —	3.60
— 714/5	dasselbe, jedoch 28 cm lang	— —	4.50
— 714/6	mit 2 Kaminen, 2 Masten mit Mastkorb und Takelwerk, Kommandobrücke, 6 Kanonen, 2 Luftschiffe, 32 cm lang	— —	6.—
— 714/7	dasselbe, größer, 39 cm lang	— —	9.—
— 714/8	dasselbe, noch größer, 44 cm lang	— —	12.—

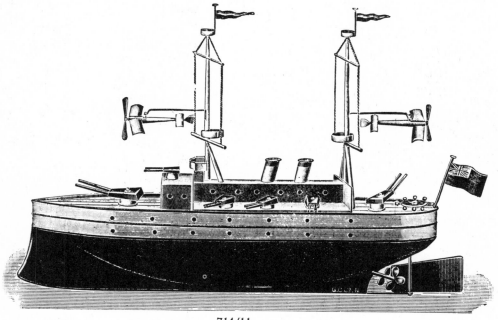

714/11

Große Kriegsschiffe.

No. 714/9	mit 2 großen Kaminen, 2 hohen Masten mit Mastkorb und Takelwerk, Kommandobrücke, Steuerrad, 18 Kanonen, 2 Luftschiffe, 49 cm lang	Stück M.	18.50
— 714/10	dasselbe, größer, 53 cm lang	— —	24.—
— 714/11	dasselbe, noch größer, 60 cm lang	— —	32.—

700/2

Schiffs-Figuren.

No. 700/1	14 originelle Schiffs-Figuren in halbmassiver Ausführung	Karton M.	—.90
— 700/2	20 — — — — — —	— —	1.40

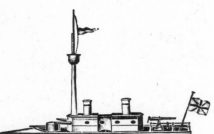

730/22

Kriegsschiffe (Panzerschiffe) mit solidem Uhrwerk

in hochfeiner Lackierung, mit gepanzertem Geschützraum, Schnellfeuerkanonen, Kaminen und Signalmasten, Panzertürmen, Rettungsbooten, Ankern und Ankerwinde, Steuer etc.

Unsere Schiffe werden mit Aufschriften der bekanntesten Kriegsschiffe der Gegenwart geliefert.

=== Modernste Konstruktion. ===

No. **730/20** einfache Ausführung, mit Kamin, 1 Kanone, 17 cm lg., (½ Dt zd.-Packg.)
Stück M. —.90

— **730/21** — — — 1 — 18 — — — 1.30
— **730/22** mit 2 Kaminen, 1 Kanone, 20 cm lang . . . . . . — — 1.50
— **730/23** — 2 — 3 — 22 — — — — — 1.80
— **730/24** — 2 — 2 — Verdeck mit Galerie,
23 cm lang, ... — — 2.—
— **730/25** mit 2 Kaminen, 5 Kanonen, Verdeck mit Galerie, Mast
mit Mastkorb, 26 cm lang. . . . . — — 3.—
— **730/26** dasselbe, 28 cm lang . . . . — — 3.60
— **730/27** — 29 — — — — — — 4.50
— **730/28** — mit Kommandobrücke, 32 cm lang . . . . — — 6.—

730/25

Grosse Kriegsschiffe.

No. **730/29** mit 2 großen Kaminen, Verdeck mit
fein vergoldeter Galerie, 8 Kanonen,
gepanzerte Geschützräume, Signal-
mast mit Mastkorb, Kommando-
brücke, Steuerrad, 36 cm lang. . Stück M. 8.50
— **730/30** dasselbe, mit 2 Masten, Anker und
Ankerwinde, 39 cm lang . . . . — — 11.—
— **730/31** dasselbe, mit 2 Ankern mit Ankerwinde, 42 cm lang . . . . — — 14.—
— **730/32** dasselbe, mit 2 großen Kaminen,
2 Signalmasten mit naturgetreu
nachgebildetem Takelwerk, 47 cm
lang . . . . — — 18.—
— **730/33** dasselbe, jedoch mit 2 Rettungsbooten, 10 Kanonen, 51 cm lang. — — 24.—

730/30

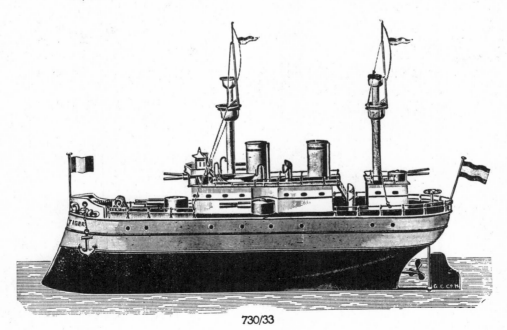

730/33

Fabrik- Marke

Torpedoboote modernster Konstruktion, mit sehr solidem Uhrwerk,

naturgetreu lackiert, Schnellfeuerkanonen, Scheinwerfer, Torpedorohr, Kommandobrücke, Mast mit Takelwerk, große Kamine, mit Doppelschraube versehen von Größe 738/21 ab.

738/20

738/25

No.				
No. 738/20	18 cm lang	. . . .	Stück M.	1.50
— 738/21	19 — —	. . . .	— —	2.—
— 738/22	23 — —	. . . .	— —	3.—
— 738/23	25 — —	. . . .	— —	3.60
— 738/24	27 — —	. . . .	— —	4.50
— 738/25	31 — —	. . . .	— —	6.—

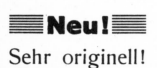 Neu!

Sehr originell!

 Neu!

Sehr originell!

Spritzboote (Feuerlöschboote) mit solidem Uhrwerk, in hochfeiner Lackierung
saugen das Wasser in die Höhe und entsenden es durch das angebrachte Spritzrohr.

No.			
No. 735/1	mit 1 Kamin, Steuermann, 1 Spritzrohr, 25 cm lang	Stück M.	4.50
— 735/2	dasselbe, mit 1 großen Kamin, 28 cm lang	— —	6.—
— 735/3	dasselbe, mit 2 großen Kaminen, 1 Mast, Steuerhaus, Steuermann, 1 Spritzrohr, 30 cm lang	— —	8.—
— 735/4	dasselbe, mit 2 Spritzrohren, 35 cm lang	— —	10.—

Sehr originell!

Sehr originell!

Unterseeboote mit sehr solidem Uhrwerk, feiner Lackierung, bis zur Luftkammer unter Wasser schwimmend.

No.			
No. 718/00	20 cm lang	Stück M.	1.50
— 718/0	23 — —	— —	2.—
— 718/1	25 — —	— —	3.—
— 718/2	29 — —	— —	4.50
— 718/3	33 — —	— —	6.—

Fabrik- ⚙ Marke

715/21

Schleppdampfer
mit solidem Uhrwerk in hochfeiner Lackierung.

No. **715/20**	mit 1 Schleppkahn,	17 cm lang	. .	Stück M.	**1.50**
— **715/21**	— 1 —	20	— —	. .	—	**2.—**
— **715/22**	— 1 —	23	— —	. .	—	**3.—**
— **715/23**	— 1 —	27	— —	. .	—	**3.60**
— **715/24**	— 1 —	30	— —	. .	—	**4.50**
— **715/25**	— 2 —	35	— —	mit		
	2 Rettungsbooten	. . . . . .	—	**6.—**

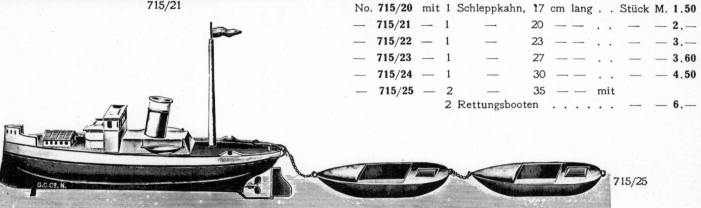

715/25

Große Schleppdampfer

mit großem Kamin, Steuerhaus mit Steuermann, mit 2 Schleppkähnen, 2 Rettungsbooten etc.

No. **715/26** 40 cm lang, Stück M. **9.—**
— **715/27** mit 2 Masten und Anker, 46 cm lang, Stück M. **12.—**

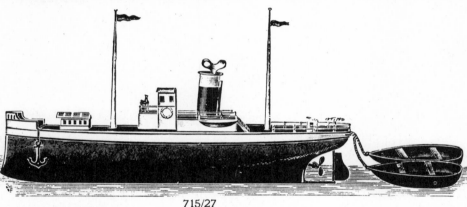

715/27

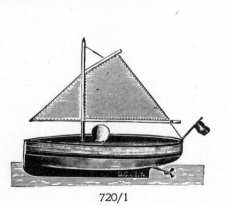

720/1

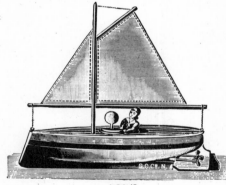

720/3

Segelboote
mit solidem Uhrwerk in feiner Ausführung und Lackierung.

No. **720/0**	einfache Ausführung, 17 cm lang	. . . .	Stück M.	**1.20**
— **720/1**	bessere Ausführung, 17 cm lang	. . . .	—	**1.50**
— **720/2**	dasselbe, 19 cm lang	. . . . . .	—	**2.—**
— **720/3**	mit Steuermann, 23 cm lang	. . . . . .	—	**3.—**
— **720/4**	— — 25 — —		—	**3.60**

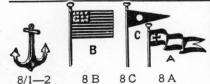

8/1—2   8 B   8 C   8 A

Schiffsanker

No. **8/1** Guß, 2½ cm hoch,
Dutzend M. **—.24**
— **8/2** Guß, 5 cm hoch,
Stück M. **—.05**

Flaggen

feine Ausführung, in verschiedenen Nationalitäten,
No. **8 A** Flagge, 9 cm lang . Stück M. **—.16**
— **8 B** Flagge, 7 — — . . — **—.14**
— **8 C** Wimpel, 6 — — . . — **—.04**

Laufwerke für Fahrzeuge

komplett montiert, sehr solide Ausführung, mit Messingzahnrädern, Regulator, Bremse mit Abstell- und Auslösehebel, massiven Spurkranzrädern samt Gestänge, Schlüssel.

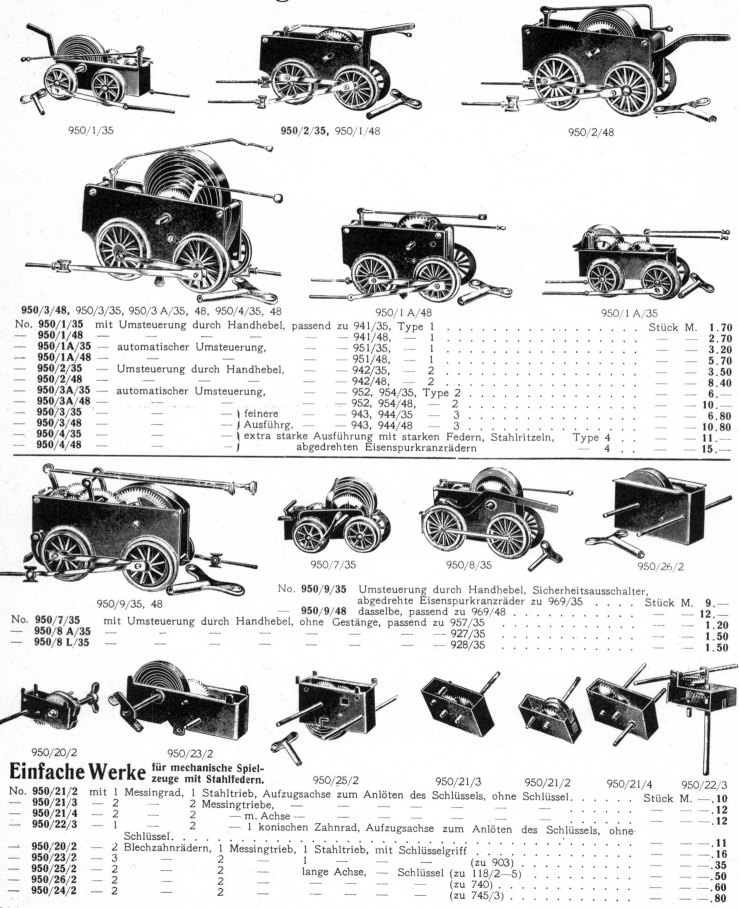

950/1/35   950/2/35, 950/1/48   950/2/48

950/3/48, 950/3/35, 950/3 A/35, 48, 950/4/35, 48   950/1 A/48   950/1 A/35

No.				Stück M.	
950/1/35	mit Umsteuerung durch Handhebel, passend zu	941/35, Type 1	. . . .	Stück M.	1.70
— **950/1/48**	—	— 941/48, — 1		—	2.70
— **950/1A/35**	— automatischer Umsteuerung,	— 951/35, — 1		—	3.20
— **950/1A/48**	—	— 951/48, — 1		—	5.70
— **950/2/35**	— Umsteuerung durch Handhebel,	— 942/35, — 2		—	3.50
— **950/2/48**	—	— 942/48, — 2		—	8.40
— **950/3A/35**	— automatischer Umsteuerung,	— 952, 954/35, Type 2		—	6.—
— **950/3A/48**	—	— 952, 954/48, — 2		—	10.—
— **950/3/35**	— — } feinere	— 943, 944/35 — 3		—	6.80
— **950/3/48**	— — } Ausführg.	— 943, 944/48 — 3		—	10.80
— **950/4/35**	— — } extra starke Ausführung mit starken Federn, Stahlritzeln,	Type 4	. .	—	11.—
— **950/4/48**	— — } abgedrehten Eisenspurkranzrädern	— 4	. .	—	15.—

950/7/35   950/8/35   950/26/2

950/9/35, 48

No.			Stück M.	
950/9/35	Umsteuerung durch Handhebel, Sicherheitsausschalter, abgedrehte Eisenspurkranzräder zu 969/35	. . . .	Stück M.	9.—
— **950/9/48**	dasselbe, passend zu 969/48	. . . .	—	12.—
No. **950/7/35**	mit Umsteuerung durch Handhebel, ohne Gestänge, passend zu 957/35	. . . .	—	1.20
— **950/8 A/35**	— — — — — — — — 927/35	. . . .	—	1.50
— **950/8 L/35**	— — — — — — — — 928/35	. . . .	—	1.50

950/20/2   950/23/2   950/25/2   950/21/3   950/21/2   950/21/4   950/22/3

Einfache Werke für mechanische Spielzeuge mit Stahlfedern.

No.			Stück M.	
950/21/2	mit 1 Messingrad, 1 Stahltrieb, Aufzugsachse zum Anlöten des Schlüssels, ohne Schlüssel	. . . . .	Stück M.	—.10
— **950/21/3**	— 2 — 2 Messingtriebe,		—	.12
— **950/21/4**	— 2 — 2 — m. Achse —		—	.12
— **950/22/3**	— 1 — 2 — 1 konischen Zahnrad, Aufzugsachse zum Anlöten des Schlüssels, ohne Schlüssel.	. . . .	—	.11
— **950/20/2**	— 2 Blechzahnrädern, 1 Messingtrieb, 1 Stahltrieb, mit Schlüsselgriff		—	.16
— **950/23/2**	— 3 — 2 — 1 (zu 903)	. . . .	—	.35
— **950/25/2**	— 2 — 2 — lange Achse, — Schlüssel (zu 118/2—5)	. . . .	—	.50
— **950/26/2**	— 2 — 2 — (zu 740)	. . . .	—	.60
— **950/24/2**	— 2 — 2 — (zu 745/3)	. . . .	—	.80